PIMLICO

99

# CHURCHILL ON THE HOME FRONT 1900-1955

Paul Addison is the Head of Modern History at the University of Edinburgh and a Fellow of All Souls College, Oxford. Among his earlier books are *The Road to 1945* – described in the *Times Literary Supplement* as 'a landmark in the writing of contemporary history' – and *Now the War is Over,* a social history of post-war Britain which he adapted into a highly acclaimed BBC television series.

# CHURCHILL ON THE HOME FRONT 1900–1955

PAUL ADDISON

**PIMLICO**

*To Rosy, Michael and James*

PIMLICO

20 Vauxhall Bridge Road, London SW1V 2SA

London Melbourne Sydney Auckland Johannesburg
and agencies throughout the world

First published by Jonathan Cape Ltd 1992
Pimlico edition, with a new preface, 1993
Reprinted 1995

Printed and bound in Great Britain by
Mackays of Chatham PLC, Chatham, Kent

ISBN 0-7126-5826-2

# Contents

# Illustrations

# *Preface to the Pimlico Edition*

Nearly half a century after the end of the Second World War, historians are still trying to come to terms with Winston Churchill. The winter of 1992–3 saw the publication of five new books about him, of which this was one, and a blazing row in the media ignited by the suggestion that Churchill ought to have negotiated a compromise peace with Hitler.[1] But why do historians continue to write about Churchill when so much has been written already? Why this insatiable desire to re-interpret and re-assess?

The appearance of this book in paperback gives me the opportunity to add some reflections on this topic. The root of the matter is familiar enough. The Second World War made Churchill into a national hero and created around him an emotional field of force that affected a whole generation. And although the warmth and gratitude were inspired by his war leadership alone, they cast a certain glow over the whole of his life and career. Episodes that had once been harshly judged were viewed in a mellow and forgiving light. But in the making of national heroes there is always a large element of myth involved and there comes a time, inevitably, when the historians seek to disentangle the myth from the reality.

The task is all the more compelling for historians because Churchill himself was a historian – up to a point. Of the peacetime events of his times he wrote little or nothing. But he wrote a six-volume history of the Second World War with himself as the central character, the sequel to a similar

[1] In order of publication the other four books were: Keith Robbins, *Churchill*; Michael Kettle, *Russia and the Allies 1917–1920: Vol III: Churchill and the Archangel Fiasco*; John Charmley, *Churchill: The End of Glory*; and Robert Blake and W. R. Louis (eds), *Churchill: A Major New Assessment of his Life in Peace and War*. It was Mr Alan Clark, reviewing Dr Charmley's book in *The Times*, who claimed that Churchill ought to have made peace with Hitler.

mammoth work on World War One. Apart from making money, his purpose
was to lay claim to a place in history as a prophetic statesman and genius of
grand strategy. Buttressed with a wealth of documentary evidence, the
architecture of his books was imposing. But they were no more free of special
pleading and self-deception than the memoirs of any other politician.

The reappraisal of the Churchill myth began as long ago as 1957, with
publication of the first volume of the diaries of Lord Alanbrooke, edited by
Arthur Bryant. Ever since then historians have been revising the Churchillian version of Gallipoli, appeasement, and the military and diplomatic
conduct of the Second World War. Over such episodes as Dakar, Greece,
the fall of Singapore, the strategic bombing offensive, the Italian campaign
and the planning of the Second Front, his military judgement has repeatedly
been called into question.

When I first began historical research in the mid-1960s, my own two
mentors on the subject were A.J.P Taylor, my research supervisor, and the
military historian Basil Liddell Hart, who was not only generous with his
time but eager to impress his views on younger historians. They convinced
me that Churchill was, to say the least, fallible in his military judgement, a
view that most subsequent writing has endorsed. Liddell Hart, who had
been a strong supporter during the war of a compromise peace with
Germany, also had a more radical criticism of Churchill. In his concentration on the exclusive objective of smashing Germany, he argued, Churchill
had lost sight, until it was too late, of the long-term danger from Soviet
Russia. The war could and should have been conducted in such a way as to
separate the German people from their rulers and bring about an early
peace. On this point, however, I found Alan Taylor more persuasive: he
maintained with great force that in the Second World War there were 'no
good Germans'.

These debates continue. The conclusion I reached was that although
Churchill was never the strategic genius of the Second World War, he was a
great political leader: the impresario of the Grand Alliance, the principal
driving force in wartime government, and the charismatic orator who lifted
and sustained popular morale. This view owed much to a growing interest on
my part in the politics of the home front during the Second World War. In
the course of writing a book on the subject I was impressed by the fact that
inside Churchill the generalissimo was an *alter ego*: a parliamentary democrat
with more than forty years of political experience behind him.

But who was this other Churchill? In the Second World War his oratory
was shot through with a vision of Britain that was archaic and romantic. But
in his youth he had been a radical, frequenting the company of Lloyd
George, H.G. Wells and Bernard Shaw. Where, then, had his radicalism

come from, and what had become of it? It was curiosity of this kind that led me to explore, in this book, the whole of his career in party politics and home affairs.

Though they have long ceased to believe in the wartime myth of Churchill, historians are still haunted by it, if only because it lives on in popular memory. But for Churchill in home affairs no clear bench-mark was visible. The official biography told parts of the story at great length, but always in the form of a chronicle that left a sizeable gap between the evidence presented and the claims that were made on Churchill's behalf. In general it seemed to me that Churchill's stock as a domestic politician was low. In some cases this was because people had no clear conception of this aspect of his career: in others because his part in particular episodes, like the General Strike of 1926, was remembered with hostility.

My first priority was to describe Churchill's activities as accurately as possible and I began the book with no preconceived idea of stating a case for or against him. But as I wrote I found that the pendulum was swinging in his favour. This was partly because I discovered more to like and admire in his political personality then most of his contemporaries did. I was much indebted to Mr Robert Rhodes James's analysis of the reasons why he inspired so much mistrust, and attracted so few supporters, before the Second World War.[2] But Mr Rhodes James tended to see Churchill through the eyes of his parliamentary critics, whose judgements, I felt, needed to be taken with a sizeable pinch of salt. Their comments often seemed to me to reflect the personal jealousies and limited horizons of the Palace of Westminster. Tadpole and Taper were doubtless scandalised by Churchill's changes of party and frequent disloyalty to the party line, but there was no need for historians to adopt the same scale of values. We ought, I felt, to be more critical of the party system and more appreciative of mavericks like Churchill who claimed to stand for a 'nation beyond party'.

But the principal aim of the book was to challenge the view that Churchill was only of interest or importance in the military and diplomatic history of Britain. I set out to show that he had much to do with the transformations of government and politics that took place during his lifetime.

Writing in 1950, Churchill looked back over the changes he had witnessed since the turn of the century:

During this first half of the terrible twentieth century all values and proportions have changed to a degree that would make the picture of British society, as it now manifests itself, very strange and startling to

[2] Robert Rhodes James, *Churchill: A Study in Failure* (1969).

those who had their heyday in the Victorian era. Though we have declined as a world power, we have immensely broadened the foundations of our national life. We have accomplished a social and political revolution, greater than France underwent at the end of the eighteenth century, without shedding a drop of blood in fraternal strife.[3]

In writing of a 'revolution' Churchill was exaggerating: and the part he had once played in Irish affairs ought to have reminded him that not all the changes had been free of bloodshed. But there is no doubt that great transformations did occur in the course of his lifetime. The aristocratic governing class into which he had been born gradually lost its political ascendancy. The limited, all-male franchise of 1900 gave way to universal suffrage, the Liberal party collapsed, and the two-party system of Tory and Liberal was replaced by a two-party system of Tory and Labour. The rise of the Labour party, meanwhile, was accompanied by the growth of the trade union movement and the propagation of socialist ideas. The state, too, was transformed, from the 'night-watchman' state of 1900, to the administrative colossus of the mid-twentieth century. When Churchill first entered Parliament in 1900, the combined expenditure of local and central government amounted to 14.4% of the Gross National Product; by the time he retired in 1955, it accounted for 36.6%.

Whether Churchill's part in all these developments was wise or foolish is a matter for debate. But it was certainly extensive, and he was no less consequential a figure than Lloyd George, Neville Chamberlain, Attlee, Bevin or Morrison. Like them he dealt with a wide range of social, economic and constitutional problems from which a line of descent can be traced to the politics of the late twentieth century. We tend to associate Churchill with a realm of imperial and military grandeur that is over and done with: but he was also one of the ancestors of modern Britain.

A polemical historian of the kind who blames contemporary problems on the follies of the past could easily frame an indictment in which much of the responsibility for the backwardness of modern Britain was pinned on Churchill. Nor would this be entirely mistaken. During the Second World War Churchill was so obsessed with the conduct of military operations that he completely neglected such long-term problems of the future as industry and education. The very idea that he might have taken a serious interest in the future of the coal industry, for example, seems far-fetched and the same is true of the lethargic peacetime administration of 1951–5. Besides, it might be added, the Churchill myth, with its aristocratic allure and nostalgia for

[3] Winston S. Churchill, *Lord Randolph Churchill* (1950 edition), p.12.

great power illusions, was plainly counter-productive in post-war Britain. Alas the problem with this kind of analysis is that it seeks to lay the responsibility for some deep-seated historical problem at the door of a single individual. With the partial exception of the Labour governments of 1945–51, the failure to modernise industry and education was characteristic of every British administration in the first half of the twentieth century. Churchill, no doubt, was more out of touch with industrial problems than most. But few politicians of his era subscribed wholeheartedly to the goals of modernisation and national efficiency.

The British political system was ill-adapted to the requirements of economic development. But it was far more successful, during Churchill's lifetime, in the achievement of two other goals: social welfare, and the preservation of liberty. Almost all British politicians, from the left wing of the Labour party to the right wing of the Conservatives, recognised that welfare and liberty had both to be pursued, and some kind of balance struck between them. But their prescriptions varied from democratic socialism at one end of the spectrum, to predominantly free market solutions at the other. One of the interesting things about Churchill is that he was so often involved in the process of altering the balance between individualism and collectivism, and thought so much about it. Perhaps, too, we ought now to revise the view that by the 1940s this was an area in which he was completely incompetent and out of touch. The Labour victory of 1945 looked very decisive at the time, and seemed to set the pattern for the future. But did it? The lasting achievement of the Attlee governments was the construction of a welfare state. But the quest for a socialist economy proved elusive and the return to power of the Churchill government in 1951 can now be seen as a more significant moment in the restoration of a liberal economy than historians used to think.

Churchill did not found a political tradition and has no heirs (except, in the literal sense, his grandson Winston Churchill MP) in politics today. Nor are the policies he prescribed for his own time of much relevance now: here or there an argument may survive but the context has changed too much. Like Churchill, therefore, this book carries with it no message – except, perhaps, a very indirect one. Some people still think of Churchill as a man of narrow, diehard views and almost mindless belligerence – and there was certainly a streak of all this in him at times. In this book, however, he comes to epitomise a very different quality: versatility. Untrammelled by narrow nationalism, ideology or social bigotry, he always had the capacity to adapt, to renew himself, and to spring some fresh surprise upon his audience. Such was the true Churchill behind the bulldog image of the Second World War.

# Introduction

Winston Churchill will always be remembered as the great war leader of 1940 to 1945. But Churchill in his time played many parts, and some are better understood than others. The subject of this book is a theme that has often sparked controversy, but never been explored in full, or assessed as a whole: his domestic policies. This is a study of Churchill in party politics and home affairs from 1900, when he was first elected to Parliament, to 1955, when the curtain fell at the end of his peacetime premiership.

The range and diversity of Churchill's career at home is often overlooked. He was first elected to the House of Commons, in 1900, as a Tory. But in 1904 he crossed the floor to join the Liberals in the defence of free trade, and began to attack his former party with extraordinary impudence and wit. In the struggle between the Liberal Government and the House of Lords, he was second only to Lloyd George as the leader of popular radicalism, and much reviled by Conservatives as a traitor to his class. He was prominent also in social reform. At the Board of Trade he introduced minimum wages and the first proposals for unemployment insurance. At the Home Office, too, he was a reforming minister, but another side of his work proved more contentious: the repression of industrial disorder.

This phase of his politics drew to a close with his appointment to the Admiralty in October 1911. His energies were diverted into the sphere of defence and shortly afterwards his career was engulfed, and almost destroyed, by the Great War. But after 1918 Churchill reappeared on the domestic scene. By this time, it seemed, his radicalism had vanished, and he stood forth as the leader of an anti-Bolshevik and anti-socialist crusade. In 1924 he returned to the Conservative party and resumed his ministerial career in home affairs. As Chancellor of the Exchequer in the Baldwin Government he restored Britain to the Gold Standard and played a prominent part in the defeat of the General Strike.

In the 1930s Churchill abandoned domestic issues and campaigned against the National Government over India, rearmament, and foreign policy. But social and economic questions returned to haunt him during the Second World War. As the head of a coalition government – and leader of the Conservative party in succession to Neville Chamberlain – he presided over a rapidly changing scene in which politics were swinging to the left and the Beveridge Report pushed social reform to the top of the agenda. Churchill claimed to be working on his own 'Four Year Plan' for post-war Britain. But with the landslide victory of the Labour party in the general election of 1945 the task of social reconstruction fell to Attlee and his colleagues. This was not quite the end of the story. When he returned to office in 1951 his Government faced a problem that was critical to the future of Conservatism: how far to accept, and how far to reverse, the work of the Labour Government.

The headlines do little justice to the breadth of Churchill's interests. He seldom, indeed, confined himself to a narrow discussion of the issues. He was a politician who loved to discourse on the general principles of politics and the relevance of the past to the present. The constant repetition of his war speeches has obscured the fact that in earlier times he often spoke reflectively of the social structure of Britain, the foundations of its prosperity, and aspirations of its people.

In one sense the aim of this book is simply to reconstruct a theme. But it is also an exploration of two closely related problems in the interpretation of Churchill: a biographical problem about the nature of his personality, and a historical problem about the nature of his place in our past.

Since Churchill's death there has been much talk of the need to strip away the mythology which accumulated around him. But this is more easily said than done. Churchill in his time was much loved, but also much hated. Vivid conceptions of him as a hero and saviour of his country were matched by no less compelling images of him as a danger to the nation. It is by no means obvious where the boundaries between myth and reality lie. The historians and biographers of today are no doubt more detached, and bring to bear fresh evidence and insights. But they still have to navigate around the archetypal images of Churchill created in his lifetime.

Even at the worst of times Churchill usually had some admirers. But it is fair to say that up to 1940 he was generally distrusted by politicians of all parties. The Conservatives, embittered early on by his defection to the Liberals, regarded him as a cad: a shameless adventurer whose pretensions to statesmanship were laughable. As David Lindsay, a Conservative whip, wrote in 1910: 'That Churchill is without conscience or scruple, without a glimmer of the comities of public reserve and deference, we all know, and all, even his closest friends, admit.'[1] But Liberals, too, had their doubts, and in the course of time a critique of Churchill developed that was generally accepted by politicians of all parties. Churchill, it was granted, possessed great drive, a fertile brain, and an eloquent tongue. There was also a mischievous schoolboy quality about him which some people found endearing. But there were two fatal flaws in his personality.

Firstly, he was a shallow opportunist who lacked stability and purpose. Devoid of loyalty to party, class, region, or religious denomination, he treated every question as a personal one in a career of absolute self-absorption. His rhetoric was brilliant but superficial, the performance of an actor-politician who lived for applause and played to the gallery. Secondly, he lacked judgment. His mind, though powerful, was rash and impulsive. Like a Rolls-Royce car with faulty steering, he was destined to plunge with all his passengers into some great chasm of disaster. Hence, it was alleged, the culminating folly of Gallipoli. 'The ghosts of Gallipoli', wrote Victor Wallace Germains in 1931, 'will always rise up to damn him anew in times of national emergency . . . What sensible man is going to place confidence in Mr Churchill in any situation which needs cool-headedness, moderation, or tact?'[2]

On the Left, this reading of Churchill was much coloured and modified by the belief that his instincts were deeply reactionary. His radical past was dismissed as a transient phase and it was taken for granted that he was profoundly ignorant of economic and social problems. The quintessential Churchill was identified as an aristocratic adventurer, militarist, and class warrior. He was accused of sending troops to shoot down striking miners at Tonypandy, and of equally rash behaviour in the General Strike. His anti-Bolshevik tirades led some to suppose that he was rehearsing the role of a British Mussolini.

Churchill, needless to say, regarded such views as malicious and distorted. With his inner detachment from party orthodoxies, he saw himself as a parliamentary democrat of consistent, moderate and far-sighted opinions. Once a radical, but now a Tory, he likened himself to Edmund Burke, who had welcomed the revolution in the American colonies, but condemned the revolution in France:

No one can read the Burke of Liberty and the Burke of Authority without feeling that here was the same man pursuing the same ends, seeking the same ideals of society and Government, and defending them from assaults, now from one extreme, now from the other.[3]

Churchill very much resented the charge that he stood for nothing in British politics. 'People often mock at me', he wrote in 1935, 'for having changed parties and labels. They say with truth that I have been a Tory, Liberal, Coalitionist, Constitutionalist, and finally Tory again . . . My own feeling is that I have been more truly consistent than almost any other well-known public man. I have seen political parties change their positions on the greatest questions with bewildering rapidity on Protection, on Irish Home Rule, and on many important secondary issues. But I have always been a Tory Democrat and a Free Trader, as I was when I first stood for Oldham more than thirty years ago.'[4]

In 1940 Churchill turned the tables on his critics. He was transformed into a national hero and many of those who had previously disparaged him began to revise their opinions. But how far did this revolution in his reputation go? Since 1940 Churchill has been almost universally acknowledged as a great war leader. To that extent at least he succeeded in imposing his own vision of history upon events. But the rest of his career in British politics, and his qualities as a domestic statesman, are matters on which opinions vary greatly.

Many, no doubt, would agree with the verdict of Michael Foot, who wrote that Churchill

> . . . never had the foggiest notion of how the British people lived, how they earned their bread, how society functioned, how it was being transformed before his eyes by forces he never even dimly discerned . . . He could be warm, humane, liberal, magnanimous. But the warmth rarely embraced the people except in his rhetoric, and the humanity could subside into tears and sentimentality.[5]

But some historians take a very different view. Churchill's official biographer, Martin Gilbert, maintains that he was animated throughout his life by a vigorous concern for the improvement of social conditions:

> Both in his Liberal and Conservative years, Churchill was a radical: a believer in the need for the State to take an active part, both by legislation and finance, in ensuring minimum standards of life, labour and social well-being for its citizens.[6]

In a review of his record as a peacetime Prime Minister, Anthony Seldon credits Churchill with a deep fund of social wisdom, and a benign political philosophy:

> He understood the supreme need to stress the liberty of the individual, though in a moral and compassionate context lacking from the arguments of latter-day advocates of free enterprise.[7]

At the heart of differing perceptions of Churchill lies the question of the relationship between his rhetoric and his politics. Even his critics conceded that in Parliament, or on the public platform, he was an orator of exceptional power. But the case against Churchill has always been that the rhetoric was mainly for show: a magnificent façade of sham statesmanship concealing the manoeuvres and mistakes of a faulty politician. Admirers of Churchill, on the other hand, tend to regard his oratory as an authentic register of his policies and opinions, and the more rhetorical passages as an expression of a romantic world view that was integral to his personality.

As Leader of the Opposition after 1945 Churchill promised that the Conservative party would 'set the people free'. But what significance ought to be attached to this kind of phrase? Was it a mere rhetorical flourish, or an expression of deeper political intent? The problem recurs throughout his career and there is more at issue here than the nature of his personality. There is the wider question of sorting out, in the domestic sphere, his role in British history. Was he, in the final analysis, a kind of glittering parasite on the surface of society? Or was he a more creative figure who shaped, for better or for worse, the government and politics of his times?

# Prologue

## 1874–1900

Winston Leonard Spencer Churchill was born at Blenheim Palace on 30 November 1874. He was the son of Lord Randolph Churchill, a Tory MP and younger son of the seventh Duke of Marlborough, and Jennie Jerome, daughter of the financier Leonard Jerome, of New York City. Through his father he was also the descendant of John Churchill, first Duke of Marlborough, the outstanding general and British commander-in-chief in the War of Spanish Succession.

The early life of Winston Churchill was deeply marked by the brief and extraordinary career of his father, whose rapid rise and even more rapid fall all occurred during his son's schooldays. Lord Randolph first entered Parliament in 1874 as a somnolent MP for the family borough of Woodstock. In 1876, following a society scandal in which Lord Randolph's elder brother quarrelled with the Prince of Wales, Disraeli sent the Churchills into exile in Dublin, where the duke was appointed Viceroy. By the time they returned, in 1880, Lord Randolph had woken up to become a forceful and ambitious politician with a considerable knowledge of Irish affairs. He made his reputation in Opposition under the Gladstone Government of 1880–1885, but his swingeing attacks on the Government were a tactical device for displacing the leader of the Conservative Party in the House of Commons, Sir Stafford Northcote. This was the aim of the 'Fourth Party', a parliamentary ginger group consisting of Lord Randolph, John Gorst and Sir Henry Drummond-Wolff, with the occasional assistance of Arthur Balfour.

While the 'Fourth Party' was active at Westminster, Lord Randolph was turning himself into a crowd-pulling platform orator. The Conservative party at this period was more strongly based in the countryside than in the towns and cities, where organisation was weak and the potential for popular Toryism had yet to be exploited. Lord Randolph seized the opportunity of identifying himself with the cause of 'Tory Democracy' – the mobilisation of the latent Toryism of the towns. As he said in a famous speech in Birmingham, in April 1884, his advice to the Conservative Party could be summed up in a phrase: 'Trust the people.'

In recognising the potential of Tory Democracy, Lord Randolph displayed a sharp insight into the future of Conservatism. But he was a supremely tactical politician in whose career it was difficult to see anything beyond the calculation of short-term personal advantage. At various times, he defined Tory Democracy in so many different ways as to empty the notion of all significance in terms of policy. To begin with he equated it with Protectionism, but as Chancellor of the Exchequer he reverted to Free Trade. Sometimes the appeal was addressed to the working classes, and sometimes to the middle classes. Sometimes he was a collectivist, supporting a state housing programme and the introduction of a statutory eight-hour day in the coal mines. At other times, he was all for *laissez-faire*. As Lord Randolph himself once remarked, Tory Democracy was 'mainly opportunism'.

Between June 1885 and July 1886 there occurred a reversal in the fortunes of the parties. An era of Liberal dominance ended when the party split over Gladstone's decision to support Irish Home Rule, and a period of Conservative rule began under the third Marquess of Salisbury. Lord Randolph had played a brilliant and unscrupulous part in manipulating the Irish question for the benefit of the Conservative Party. In 1886 he played the 'Orange Card' when he travelled to Belfast and whipped up Protestant fervour with a ringing declaration in favour of rebellion: 'Ulster will fight, and Ulster will be right.' For this and other services he was rewarded, in July 1886, by his appointment as Chancellor of the Exchequer and Leader of the House.

Lord Randolph was clearly marked out as the next Conservative Prime Minister, but he was too frantic and unstable to wait. In a clear bid for effective control of the government he began to outline his own comprehensive programme of domestic and foreign policy. In the House of Commons, the Conservatives depended upon the support of the 78 Liberal Unionist MPs, led by Joseph Chamberlain, who had broken away from Gladstone over Home Rule. Since Churchill's aim was to form a coalition with Chamberlain against Salisbury, the programme he proposed was strongly tinged with radicalism. But his plan of campaign came unstuck, quite unexpectedly, over his budget proposals.

As the centrepiece of his first budget, he planned a major reduction in the income tax, which then stood at eightpence in the pound. But how was the shortfall in revenue to be made up? At first Lord Randolph proposed a duty on imported foods, but his Treasury officials, high priests of the doctrine of Free Trade, quickly dissuaded him. Like many a Chancellor before and since, Lord Randolph decided to press for reductions in the service estimates, much to the dismay of the First Lord of the Admiralty and the Secretary of State for War. Assuming that he was indispensable, he decided to force the issue. On 20 December 1886 he wrote to Salisbury to announce his resignation over the service estimates, coupling the question with that of foreign policy. Salisbury called his bluff and replied accepting his resignation. Two days later, Lord Randolph despatched a second letter, evidently intended for public consumption, in which he tried to broaden the grounds of his resignation. There was much talk of the Government collapsing but Chamberlain, who could probably have brought Salisbury down, did nothing. George Goschen, a leading Liberal Unionist, accepted office as Chancellor. The crisis was over and Lord Randolph had suffered a great reverse, entirely of his own making.

These events cast a long shadow over the schooldays of Winston Churchill. At the time of Lord Randolph's fall from office he was twelve – old enough to be a fierce partisan of his father, but much too young to grasp the political realities. In April 1888 he entered Harrow, but as his head-master reported a year later, he was still 'very much a child'. Churchill grew up very slowly. Throughout a prolonged adolescence he was the naive disciple of a failing politician who declined to take much notice of his son, or rebuked him sternly for idleness and misbehaviour. Convinced that he was too dim and slovenly for a career in civilian life, Lord Randolph put him into the Army Class at Harrow, where he again dis-appointed his father by twice failing the Sandhurst entrance examination.

If Winston Churchill was thwarted and depressed by the relationship with his father, he was also fired by it. He looked forward to winning his father's respect and confidence, and assisting him in the reconquest of power: 'I thought of Austen Chamberlain who was allowed to fight at his father's side, and Herbert Gladstone who had helped the Grand Old Man to cut down oak trees and went everywhere with him, and I dreamed of the days to come when Tory Democracy would dismiss the "Old Gang" with one hand and defeat the radicals with the other.'[1] Churchill's relationship with his father finished on a tantalising note. At the very point his deepest wishes were about to be fulfilled (or so it seemed), suddenly the story ended.

In September 1893, having finally passed his examinations, Churchill arrived at Sandhurst as a cavalry cadet. His father began to take him up and introduce him to the leading personalities of the political world. 'Had he lived another four or five years', Churchill was to write in his autobiography, 'he could not have done without me. But there were no four or five years!'[2]

After a prolonged illness Lord Randolph Churchill died on 24 January 1895. A few days after the funeral, Winston Churchill passed out of Sandhurst and took up his commission with the Fourth Hussars at Aldershot. In some ways Churchill was now free: free of his father's control, free to enjoy the London Season, free to pursue his own career. But in other respects he was tied: tied by the memory of Lord Randolph, and tied by the Army.

Churchill's ambition was to follow his father into politics. But there was something more: an emotional drive to reverse the defeat of 1886, and obtain for his father a posthumous victory. Ironically, however, Lord Randolph had sidetracked his son by putting him into the Army. How, then, was he to escape from the Army and make his way to the House of Commons?

From January 1895 to May 1899 Churchill was a subaltern of the Fourth Hussars, and sailed with them to India when they were posted to Bangalore in the autumn of 1896. Churchill enjoyed soldiering but his plan was to enter politics and his methods were carefully calculated. He decided that wherever a war was in progress he would obtain leave from his regiment and travel to the battlefront as a war correspondent. If the war happened to be a British war, somewhere on the frontiers of the Empire, so much the better. At the same time as reporting it, he could take part in the fighting, win medals, and obtain a reputation for bravery. Finally, his war reporting could be revised and published as a book. As none of this could be accomplished without much pulling of strings, Churchill decided to exploit Lord Randolph's political network to the full, while his mother was pressed into service as a leading society hostess whispering a word or two into the appropriate ear.

Seldom, if ever, has an ambitious young man carried out such a stupendous programme of self-advertisement as Churchill between 1895 and 1900. In 1895 he travelled to Cuba and reported on the war of independence against Spain. In 1897 he took part in Sir Bindon Blood's expeditionary force against the Pathans on the north-west frontier of India, and wrote up his despatches as his first book, *The Story of the Malakand Field Force*. In 1898 he travelled to Egypt to report the reconquest of the Soudan, and fought in the decisive battle of Omdurman. His two volume history, *The River War*, published in 1899, was a major work. In the intervals of inactivity he wrote a novel,

*Savrola*, an entertaining melodrama of revolution in a Ruritanian state, with a lively narrative, wooden characters, and revealing reflections of his ideas.

Churchill's brief military career was marked by one major intellectual event. He began to study history and philosophy and lost his boyhood faith. Winwood Reade's *Martyrdom of Man*, a nineteenth-century atheist classic, destroyed his belief in Christianity, a conclusion confirmed by Gibbon's *Decline and Fall of the Roman Empire*. For orthodox religion, Churchill substituted a secular belief in historical progress, with a strong emphasis on the civilising mission of Britain and the British Empire. This was accompanied by a mystical faith, alternating with cynicism and depression, in the workings of Providence. He was inclined to believe that Providence had intervened on a number of occasions to save his life, and that he was being protected in order to fulfil his destiny – whatever that might be.

Destiny, however, was only to be accomplished by self-help. As he remarked in a letter to Lady Randolph, in January 1898: 'It is a pushing age and we must shove with the best.'[3] On his return to England after the battle of Omdurman, Churchill was much sought after for dinner parties and speeches. He was becoming famous, and infamous too in the opinion of those who could not bear the blazing egotism he radiated on all occasions.

Through Conservative Central Office, Churchill obtained an introduction to the Conservative party in Oldham. Oldham was a double-member constituency with two Conservative MPs, one of whom, James Oswald, was due to retire at the next general election. The other, Robert Ascroft, wanted to secure the nomination of Churchill as his running-mate. But the sudden death of Ascroft precipitated a by-election, upon which Oswald decided to retire immediately. There were two vacancies and the Oldham Conservatives decided to adopt Churchill in harness with a trade unionist, James Mawdsley, the general secretary of the Amalgamated Society of Operative Cotton Spinners.

Here was a wondrous advertisement for Tory Democracy: the palace and the cottage united in the persons of a young nobleman and an elderly working man. But Tory Democracy stubbornly failed to come to life. Churchill and Mawdsley did not speak the same language. Mawdsley, the only Tory trade union official, was not exactly a dedicated member of the party. His argument was that, on balance, trade unionists would get more out of the Conservatives than out of the Liberals. Churchill, on the other hand, produced many a fine phrase about Tory Democracy, but was unable or unwilling to give substance to the slogan. 'I am a Tory

Democrat,' he announced. 'I regard the improvement of the condition of the British people as the main end of modern government.' This was brave talk, but Churchill trailed off into clouds of evasion: 'I shall therefore promote to the best of my ability all legislation which, without impairing that tremendous energy of production on which the wealth of the nation and the good of the people depend, may yet raise the standard of comfort and happiness in English homes.' On social policy, Churchill confined himself to supporting the government. He commended the Workmen's Compensation Act, recently passed, and spoke warmly in favour of the principle of old age pensions, which the government had promised to deal with in the current Parliament. When asked whether he would support the payment of MPs – a measure Lord Randolph had advocated – he would say only that if there were a great demand for it in the country, he would be guided by the opinion of his constituents.[4]

From the beginning of the contest, religious issues were more important than social policy. This was not surprising, for religion was still the essential dividing line between the Tories and the Liberals. But the intense denominational rivalry between Anglicans and Nonconformists was baffling to Churchill, who could not see what the fuss was all about. The Government had recently introduced a Clerical Tithes Bill, the effect of which was to subsidise the Church of England from local rates. This provoked much hostility from the Nonconformists, some of whom might otherwise have voted Conservative. Churchill decided to sell the pass and abandon the Government line, prompting Balfour to remark: 'I thought he was a young man of promise, but it appears he is a young man of promises.'

When the voters of Oldham went to the polls, both seats were lost to the Liberal candidates: Alfred Emmott, the owner of a local cotton-spinning firm, and the shipping magnate, Walter Runciman. As the Conservatives had recently lost other by-elections, it was unlikely that they would have held Oldham with different contenders. But Churchill was inclined to take the result personally and wrote a crestfallen letter to Balfour, apologising for his change of front over the Clerical Tithes Bill. Ruefully he concluded: 'Altogether I return with less admiration for democracy than when I went.'[5]

Churchill might never have returned to Oldham to contest the seat but for the war in South Africa, which broke out in October 1899. Though he had by now left the Army, Churchill hastened to the scene as a war correspondent and, by a stroke of good fortune, was captured by the Boers shortly after his arrival, and confined with other British prisoners of war in the State Model Schools in Pretoria. In the second week of December

1899 – the 'Black Week' – the British expeditionary force to South Africa suffered three major defeats. But at that very moment Churchill contrived to escape from prison and, after lying for a few days at the bottom of a mine, was smuggled out on a freight train carrying bales of wool to Lourenço Marques. On 23 December he reappeared in Durban to find himself greeted by flags, bands, and wildly enthusiastic crowds.

Churchill was the first popular hero of the South Africa war, anticipating Roberts and Baden-Powell. As he recalled in *My Early Life*:

> The British nation was smarting under a series of reverses such as are so often necessary to evoke the exercise of its strength, and the news of my outwitting the Boers was received with enormous and no doubt disproportionate satisfaction.[6]

Having obtained a temporary commission as a lieutenant with the South African Light Horse, Churchill returned to the front, and accompanied Buller's army in the advance on Ladysmith. In a vivid despatch Churchill described how he accompanied the relief column into the town: in fact he had missed the event, and arrived some hours later.[7]

Wherever the scene of the action moved, Churchill followed. Abandoning his temporary commission, he attached himself as a war correspondent to the headquarters of the new Commander-in-Chief, Lord Roberts, who was concentrating his forces for an advance into the heart of the Boer Republics. Churchill accompanied a column of 16,000 men commanded by his close friend Sir Ian Hamilton, advancing in parallel with the main army. Travelling across the veld in style, he was accompanied by his cousin 'Sunny', the ninth Duke of Marlborough, Hamilton's ADC, and a waggon-load of delicacies from Fortnums.

Johannesburg fell on 31 May and on 5 June Churchill entered Pretoria to greet the British prisoners in the State Model Schools. It was now widely, though mistakenly, assumed that the war was over and Churchill, having achieved all that he could want and more in South Africa, sailed for home on 4 July. On his return to Oldham later that month, he was saluted by flags and drums and cheered through the streets by 10,000 people.

In September Lord Salisbury decided to dissolve Parliament and hold a general election. Strictly speaking, no election was necessary. The government had a majority of 120, and there was no constitutional requirement for another general election before 1902: the Septennial Act, which laid down a maximum life of seven years for a Parliament, was still in force. But victory in South Africa was too good an opportunity to miss when the Opposition were at sixes and sevens.

The Unionists were united by the war, but the Liberals, under the leadership of Sir Henry Campbell-Bannerman, were split three ways between opponents of the war on the left, Liberal Imperialists on the right, and a Centre majority who grudgingly accepted the war but criticised the Government as too harsh and uncompromising in its treatment of the Boers. On the Unionist side, the Colonial Secretary, Joseph Chamberlain, was the hero of the hour, epitomising the spirit of aggressive imperialism. It was Chamberlain who had pressed most strongly for a general election, and he who proclaimed that a vote for the Liberals was a vote for the Boers – the campaign theme on which the election was fought.

In Oldham Churchill concentrated on the single issue of the war. The rhetoric of Tory Democracy was laid aside, and would in any case have been difficult to sustain now that there was no longer a Tory labour candidate. Mawdsley had withdrawn from the fray (though he was not, as stated in *My Early Life*, dead), and Churchill's running mate was a stockbroker, Charles Crisp. The two Liberal candidates, Alfred Emmott and Walter Runciman, were supporters of the war, and Churchill avoided personal attacks on them. The contest, he said, was between 'the genuine turtle soup of Tory Imperialism and the mock turtle soup of Liberal Imperialism.' The Liberal party in general he characterised as 'a squabbling, disorganised rabble', and of course he played the patriotic card: 'When the troops come home you should be able to say to them – you have won your battle in South Africa and we have won our battle at home.'[8]

At the turn of the century general elections were still spread over a period of weeks, and the general election of 1900 ran from 28 September to 24 October. Oldham was one of the first constituencies to declare a result, on 1 October. In a double member constituency, every elector had two votes, and could split them between parties. Over and above his party vote, Churchill obtained a small personal vote which enabled him to push one of the Liberal candidates, Runciman, into third place. The result was as follows:

| | |
|---|---|
| A. Emmott (Lib) | 12,947 |
| W.S. Churchill (Con) | 12,931 |
| W. Runciman (Lib) | 12,709 |
| C.B. Crisp (Con) | 12,522 |

Churchill's victory was a great boost to Conservative morale and for the remaining three weeks of the campaign he was much in demand as a platform orator and feted by Balfour and Chamberlain. The Unionists won a decisive victory, but in the circumstances a less overwhelming one than might have been expected. In 1895 the Unionists had enjoyed a majority of 152. In 1900 the majority was 128. Churchill sensed that even now the political tide might be turning, or about to turn. On 8 September, in a letter to Sir Alfred Milner, the British High Commissioner in South Africa, Churchill predicted a reaction against imperialism: 'There is an amount of pent up feeling, liberalism, sentimentality, chivalry – I do not mind what it is called – which is very remarkable. The ordinary safety valves of public expression and free speech are screwed down. Some day there will be an explosion . . . ' To his father's old friend Lord Rosebery, he wrote: 'I think this election, fought by the Liberals as a soldiers' battle, without plan or leaders or enthusiasm, has shown so far the strength, not the weakness, of Liberalism in the country.'9

# I

# *Peace, Retrenchment and Reform*

## 1900–6

When Churchill first took his seat in the House of Commons, in February 1901, the one subject on which he could speak with authority was war. His maiden speech, delivered on 18 February 1901, was a review of the South African war, and he followed it up with a campaign on the question of Army reform. But Churchill soon developed a second line of expertise, this time in finance and fiscal policy. Preaching the cause of economy in public expenditure, he called for reductions in military spending and a return to the Gladstonian values of 'peace, retrenchment and reform'.

For one so young, Churchill cut a quaintly old-fashioned figure in the Conservative Party. The rhetoric of mid-Victorian liberalism was falling out of fashion as the party swung towards an expansive and expensive imperialism. In 1903 the Colonial Secretary, Joseph Chamberlain, decided that the time had come to abandon free trade and bury once and for all the political economy of the Victorians. His campaign for imperial preference and tariff reform swept through the Unionist ranks with all the force of a crusade. But it also split the party. Churchill was a prominent member of the Free Trade minority, fighting hard in the rearguard action against protectionism.

Once it was clear that Chamberlain was winning the battle for control of the party, Churchill decided to abandon the Tories. In May 1904 he crossed the floor of the House and took his place on the Liberal benches, beside David Lloyd George. Now that he was a Liberal, Churchill had of course to speak the language of Liberalism, and to revise some of his opinions. But the continuities were more significant. On free trade Churchill was obviously consistent: it was the Conservatives who had changed their minds. Demands for economy, and the reduction of military expenditure, were music to Liberal ears, and Churchill played them up for all they were worth. Generally speaking, he sounded like an old-fashioned Liberal. Of social reform, in the twentieth-century sense, he said little or nothing. He carried into the Liberal party the *laissez-faire* outlook he had acquired as a Tory.

As an absolute beginner of tender years, Churchill of necessity fashioned his early career from the politics of his elders and betters. Lord Salisbury, who was Prime Minister until 1902, was an aged and remote figure with whom Churchill had no opportunity to establish a rapport. His nephew and successor, Arthur Balfour, mistrusted Churchill as he had once mistrusted Churchill's father. Joseph Chamberlain, a genuine admirer of Lord Randolph, had the career of his own son, Austen, to consider, and made no particular attempt to cultivate Winston. Had any of these three taken Churchill up, his career would no doubt have followed a different course. But as none of them did, Churchill turned back to the legacy of Lord Randolph.

Though Lord Randolph was dead, he was still very much alive in his son's thoughts as a guide and inspiration. But there were also surviving friends of Lord Randolph to whom Churchill could turn. Among them were Sir Michael Hicks Beach, the Earl of Rosebery and John Morley, all of whom gave him support and encouragement. Somewhat naively, Churchill looked up to them as men of immense wisdom and repute – though at the same time he was manipulating them in his own interests.

One outstanding characteristic of the youthful Churchill was a disarming candour about his motives. In private he spoke freely of his restless ambition, and delighted in explaining the tricks and stratagems of the politician's trade. In the opinion of some of his contemporaries, he was simply a young man on the make. It is a judgment which still has some validity, but omits a feature of his politics remarked upon by A.J.P. Taylor: 'The mainspring of Churchill's Radicalism was generosity: a dislike of Tariff Reform as selfish, and a warm-hearted desire to benefit the poor and oppressed.'[1]

\* \* \*

The war in South Africa lasted longer, and cost more, than had been expected. In his budget of March 1900 the Chancellor of the Exchequer, Sir Michael Hicks Beach, was obliged to raise income tax from eightpence to one shilling in the pound: 5p in today's money.

In 1900 the tax system worked on simple principles. Income tax and customs and excise duties were the major sources of revenue. The income tax, levied on salaries and profits, was paid by the middle classes. At the top of the social scale a wealthy bachelor, with annual earnings of £10,000, still retained after the payment of his income tax £9,518. At the other end of the social scale, manual workers were virtually untouched by direct taxation. Their earnings fell below the threshold of £160 per annum at which the tax began. They did, however, pay indirect taxes: customs and excise duties were levied on tea, beer, wines and spirits. Sound free trade principles prevailed: there was no element of protection for British producers, or preference for colonial goods. In 1900, Hicks Beach increased indirect taxes too: the tea duty, for instance, went up from fourpence to sixpence per pound, and the beer duty was up by a shilling a barrel.[2]

The budget was well received as a necessary measure of war finance. But the war dragged on, and the cost mounted. In April 1901 Hicks Beach produced a second war budget with another round of increases: income tax rose to 1s.2d. in the pound and fresh duties were levied on sugar and coal exports. This time the budget was more controversial, with a wave of protest against the new coal duty. More significant was the long-term issue which Hicks Beach raised in his budget speech. Over the past twenty-five years, he pointed out, the growth of expenditure had tended to outstrip revenue. Plans for social betterment, or increased expenditure on the armed forces, had proved to be popular and the House of Commons had repeatedly voted in favour of them.

Hicks Beach therefore sounded a warning. It must not be assumed that when the war was over taxes would be reduced to their pre-war level: 'I am afraid that the real difficulty before us is not so much the cost of the war in South Africa and China as the increase of what may be called our ordinary expenditure.' Expenditure was outstripping revenue and it was therefore necessary 'to put our financial system on a broader basis.'[3]

While Hicks Beach was lamenting the growth of expenditure, Churchill was shaping his own strategy, which grew out of his position on the South African war. His maiden speech, on 18 February 1901, was a forthright defence of the government's conduct of the South African war. But although he believed firmly in the necessity of a clear-cut military decision in South Africa, Churchill was severely critical in private of the conduct and ethics of the war. In a letter to Milner on 17 March he wrote of

this miserable war, unfortunate and ill-omened in its beginning, inglorious in its course, cruel and hideous in its conclusion ... I have hated these latter stages with their barbarous features – questionable

even according to the bloody precedents of 1870, certainly most hor-
rible. I look forward to the day when we can take the Boers by the
hand and say as Grant did at Appomatox: "Go back and plough your
fields." Personally I am still absolutely determined to strip them of their
independence, but cannot face the idea of their being economically and
socially ruined too . . . They must be helped to rebuild their farms; the
gold mines must do that. What more fitting function for the wealth of
South African soil (better build farms in South Africa than palaces in
Park Lane!). Their widows and orphans and crippled soldiers must be
our care and once and for all there must be an end to those ugly stories
of bad faith and military dishonour which ten months' experience in the
field has convinced me are mainly founded on misunderstanding.[4]

Churchill was not anti-war, but he opposed the prevailing spirit of
vengeful militarism as ignorant and short-sighted. 'I thought we should
end the war by force and generosity', he wrote in his autobiography, 'and
then make haste to return to the paths of peace, retrenchment and reform.'[5]
One consequence of the war, and the disasters which befell Buller's
expeditionary force, was the raising of the question of Army reform.
There was an almost universal demand among Unionists for the creation
of a larger standing army in peacetime. On 8 March 1901 St John
Brodrick, the Secretary for War, announced in the House a sweeping programme of Army Reform. He proposed to organise the regulars, the militia,
and the volunteers, into a single army divided into six army corps, each
with its own regional headquarters and commander-in-chief. In time of
war, three of the corps would form a fully trained expeditionary force for
service overseas while the other three would form an army of home
defence in embryo. Overall, the size of the standing army would be
increased by 50 per cent, and the cost was estimated at £30 million
per annum. A few days later, in a note scribbled in the House of Commons
to Sir William Harcourt, the veteran Liberal politician, Churchill wrote:
'I hate and abominate all this expenditure on military armament.'[6]
Churchill, of course, had a hereditary pretext for opposing the demands of
the War Office – this was the issue on which Lord Randolph had resigned.
The Liberal party opposed Brodrick's reforms, and so did Churchill. In
a debate on 13 May 1901, he launched a frontal attack in which criticisms
on strategic grounds were coupled with the cause of economy. Quite apart
from the cost of the war, Churchill pointed out, the Army estimates had
risen from £17,000,000 in 1894 to £29,800,000 in 1901. This growth in
expenditure Churchill attributed to the defeat of Lord Randolph in 1886:
'the Chancellor of the Exchequer went down for ever, and with him, as

it now seems, there also fell the cause of retrenchment and economy . . . '
Quoting from the second of Lord Randolph's resignation letters, Churchill
repeated his father's warning that increased military expenditure encouraged an aggressive foreign policy and the risk of entanglement in a
European war. 'Wise words', he continued, 'stand the test of time, and I
am very glad the House has allowed me, after an interval of fifteen years,
to lift again the tattered flag of retrenchment and economy.'[7]

Brodrick's Army, Churchill maintained, would be too large for peacetime purposes, and too small for home defence in the event of a European
war. The Navy was Britain's shield against invasion, and a continental war
would require the mass mobilisation of manpower: 'Democracy is more
vindictive than Cabinets. The wars of peoples will be more terrible than
those of kings.'[8]

Writing for the *Daily Mail* on 17 June, Churchill expounded the case
against increased public expenditure: that it would impair Britain's competitive position as a trading nation: 'Trade is vital. All taxation is a drag
on trade. Long before the comfort of the people would be touched their
competing power would be diminished. Therefore, the amount of money
we can safely raise annually by taxation is limited. It may be a vast sum,
we may not yet have reached the end, but there are limits to it.'[9]

When the motion in favour of Brodrick's proposals was put to the
House, Churchill was the only Conservative to vote against it. But his
speech was a landmark in the making of his reputation. There was much
praise from Liberal quarters, and the radical journalist, H.W. Massingham,
expressed the hope that Churchill would one day become Prime Minister
– and Liberal Prime Minister at that.[10]

Churchill's campaign had important implications within the Unionist
ranks. His line as a back-bench MP was converging with that of Hicks
Beach and the Treasury, as they fought against rising expenditure. An
elder statesman of the Conservative party, Beach had sat in Disraeli's
Cabinet, and had at one stage been a close ally of Lord Randolph –
though not so close as to prejudice his own career. In September 1901 he
submitted to the Prime Minister, Lord Salisbury, a memorandum warning
that the long-term trend towards increased public expenditure could not
be sustained without resort to Protectionism. As a free trader, Beach was
strongly opposed to this. It was 'absolutely essential', he wrote, that a check
should be placed on the continued increase of ordinary expenditure.[11] By
this time, Churchill was in touch with Hicks Beach and concerting tactics
with him. The Chancellor's drive for economy was unpopular with many
of his colleagues, and Churchill was knowingly playing on tensions within
the Cabinet. At Churchill's invitation, Beach spoke at Oldham in October

and reiterated the need for economy when the war was over.[12] Behind the scenes, Churchill was likewise receiving assistance from the Permanent Secretary to the Treasury, Sir Francis Mowatt. Mowatt had served Lord Randolph at the Treasury, and beguiled Churchill with tales of his father's conversion from the heresies of fair trade to strict Gladstonian principles. As Churchill recalled thirty years later, Mowatt 'put me in touch with some younger officials, afterwards themselves eminent, with whom it was very helpful to talk – not secrets, for these were never divulged, but published facts set in their true proportion and proper emphasis.'[13]

While colluding with Beach, a somewhat dour personality, Churchill had another guiding star of more glamorous and erratic nature. This was Archibald Primrose, fifth Earl of Rosebery, and Liberal Prime Minister from 1894–5. Since resigning the leadership of his party in 1896, Rosebery had lived in a state of partial retirement from politics. But as a Liberal Imperialist, he deplored the party's commitment to Irish Home Rule and supported the South African war. It was widely expected that he would one day stage a triumphant return as the agent of some great transformation in British politics: a new model Liberal party, or, perhaps, a new coalition of Liberals and Conservatives. The Unionist Government was itself a coalition of Conservatives and Liberal Unionists. Might not another coalition be formed, from the same House of Commons, but under different leaders? Might not Rosebery be the man to lead it?

By July 1901 Churchill was one of a small group of young and mischievous Conservative MPs whose aim was to embarrass the government and thereby press their claims to advancement. They were sometimes known as the 'Hughligans', or 'Hooligans' after Lord Hugh Cecil, the informal leader of the group. Cecil, the youngest son of Lord Salisbury, was Churchill's closest friend in the House of Commons. Apart from the fact that both were youthful aristocrats of great intelligence, who delighted in parliamentary games, their association illustrated the attraction of opposites. Cecil was a devout Anglican for whom politics were an extension of religion. The maintenance of the Church of England was, for him, a supreme obligation overriding all other considerations. But Churchill had no religion except for Destiny and Providence, the gods of egotism. Nevertheless, they were inseparable. The other Hooligans were Henry Percy, heir to the Duke of Northumberland, Arthur Stanley, a younger son of the Earl of Derby, and Ian Malcolm, the only non-aristocrat. The Hooligans were strongly reminiscent of the Fourth Party, and like the Fourth Party they enjoyed cross-party politics, concerting tactics with the Opposition against the Government front-bench. In particular they enjoyed the encouragement and hospitality of Rosebery.

In June 1901 the Liberal leader, Sir Henry Campbell-Bannerman, made a famous speech in which he condemned the Government for carrying on the war in South Africa by 'methods of barbarism'. By seeming to attack the war, Campbell-Bannerman awoke the wrath of Asquith, Grey, and other Liberal imperialists, who called upon Rosebery to reassert his leadership of the pro-war element in the party. After a long and pregnant pause, which aroused great expectations, Rosebery delivered a major speech at Chesterfield on 15 December. Rosebery positioned himself firmly in the middle ground of politics. On the one hand he defended the military conduct of the war, including the system of concentration camps. On the other he criticised its political management and called for the opening of peace negotiations. Turning to the Liberal party, he argued that it must 'clean the slate': free itself from the Irish and the policy of Home Rule, and abandon the 'fly-blown phylacteries of obsolete policies'. Rosebery urged his party to adopt instead a programme of 'national efficiency'.[14]

After Chesterfield, Rosebery was showered with congratulations by imperialists of all kinds. Churchill wrote:

> I did not believe I could read six columns of any speech ever made without much disagreement; but – although you do not mention finance – I see eye to eye with you at almost every stage and at almost every point.
>
> Whether my agreement can take a concrete form must depend on future events; but I wish most sincerely I could review the political situation without having to consider the claims and influences of party and party machinery.[15]

Churchill was remarkably open in the support he gave to Rosebery. He began the New Year of 1902 with a speech in which he declared that Rosebery 'possesses the three requirements which an English Prime Minister must have. He must have a great position in Parliament; he must have popularity in the country; and he must have rank and prestige in the great circle of European diplomacy.'[16]

Churchill was in full agreement with Rosebery on South Africa, to which most of the Chesterfield speech was devoted. But what of 'national efficiency'? The phrase requires some explanation. The indifferent performance of Britain in the South African war had impressed on a number of people in all parties the idea that something was fundamentally wrong with British institutions. They maintained that Britain was a poorly organised and inefficient society, run by amateurs, and bedevilled by the trivialities of party politics. Britain, they believed, was unfit to compete in the Darwinian contest between states, and would sink into decline unless the system was reformed. The solution was to increase the power of the state at the expense of Parliament and party politics. The idea attracted a range of politicians and publicists including the Fabian socialists, Beatrice and Sidney Webb; Chamberlain, Milner, and the latter's young disciple L.S. Amery. Their ideas focused on the development of human resources for national and imperial ends, as Martin Pugh explains:

> Apprehension about British decline stimulated a variety of remedies including the improvement of secondary education, particularly technical and scientific, to enable Britain to compete with Germany. On the military side the critics fastened upon the crippling role of the Treasury, the lamentable amateurism of army officers and the inadequate training of their men. Military training for civilians was commended for both its physical and moral advantages. Also typical of National Efficiency advocates was the bold application of state power in the field of social welfare, for Bismarckian rather than humanitarian reasons: a healthy population was a more efficient workforce and more stable politically.[17]

In spite of his praise for Chesterfield, Churchill displayed very little interest in the idea of 'national efficiency'. He did not believe that Britain was a great power in decline, or in peril from the competition of other nations. He did not share the Germanophobia of some observers, or the belief that Anglo-German rivalry was bound to lead to war. Confident in the Royal Navy and the Pax Britannica, he inclined towards isolationism. Nor did Churchill favour a Bismarckian programme of state intervention, for that would defeat the drive for economy and his elementary faith in *laissez-faire*. On the very day he wrote to Rosebery to congratulate him on the Chesterfield speech, he was writing to his friend and fellow back-bench Unionist MP, Edgar Vincent, urging the formation of a Conservative party finance committee, to press for economy. The nucleus of the committee was to consist of the Hooligans, and each of them was to bring in three or four friends. 'I have been promised some support *privately*', he wrote a few days later, 'in moving for an Inquiry into the increase in Expenditure . . . '[18]

Rosebery laid great stress on the fact that Britain was educationally backward by comparison with Germany, and argued that educational reform was essential if the British were to catch up with the technical and scientific standards of the Germans. But Churchill took little interest in the problems of education. In March 1902 Balfour introduced the most important legislation on the subject since the Forster Act of 1870. The

Victorian board schools were to be abolished, elementary and secondary education transferred to the county and borough authorities, and the voluntary schools – mostly Anglican, but some Roman Catholic – funded out of the rates. Quite apart from its importance in strictly educational terms, the bill revived the religious antagonisms between Anglicanism and dissent. The Liberals opposed it vehemently in the House of Commons, and when it reached the statute book, at the end of 1902, the more fervent Nonconformists launched a campaign of civil disobedience through the refusal to pay rates. But Churchill never spoke on the bill during its passage through the House, nor, it seems, did he mention it in speeches in the country until January 1903, when he disposed of it in a few brief and ambivalent remarks dealing solely with the religious issues at stake. If, he argued, those who had opposed the act so bitterly were sincere in their objections they would 'give it a fair trial and then, if it fails, their opposition will be vindicated and their view will be proved right.' If they were to obstruct it and plunge the system into chaos, the controversy would never be settled: 'I believe that the Bill will prove a measure patiently, minutely and comprehensively adapted to the various needs and divergent wishes of many sorts and conditions of men.'[19]

\*

Apart from Army reform, Churchill's major theme in 1902 was finance. In his budget on 14 April Beach once more increased taxes, but the budget surprise was the introduction of a small duty on imported flour and wheat. This was hotly opposed by the Liberals, who denounced it as a tax on the people's food. But it was welcomed by protectionists. As they realised, Beach himself was a free trader and had introduced the duty for revenue purposes only. But if a subsequent Chancellor should decide to remit the corn duty in favour of colonial imports, the principle of imperial preference would be established.

Churchill took the opportunity of proclaiming his own views on finance. Speaking in the debate on the day of the budget he supported the corn duty, but the main feature of his speech was a broadside against increasing expenditure, with a demand for more effective Cabinet control. In the background, the Treasury party was again at work. Churchill had been briefed by Sir Edward Hamilton, the Joint Permanent Secretary to the Treasury, and one of Lord Randolph's advisers in 1886. In a letter of congratulation after the speech, Hamilton wrote: 'Please remember that the doors of the Treasury are always open to you. I shall be delighted at all times to render you any assistance, for your father's sake as well as your own.'[20]

An apt pupil, Churchill was now the master of the Treasury view on the social and political implications of increasing public expenditure. If expenditure continued to grow, he predicted, it would have to be financed by one of two methods, each of which was undesirable. The first of these dangers was protectionism, a danger he elaborated in his speech of 14 April. Taking a long view of the history of taxation, Churchill observed that since the franchise had been extended in the nineteenth century, there had been a steady trend towards the reduction of the tax burden on 'the masses'. As a proportion of government revenue, direct taxation (which fell mainly on the middle classes) had risen by 1900 to 52 per cent of the revenue, while indirect taxes (which fell mainly on the working classes) had fallen to 48 per cent. Churchill anticipated that if expenditure continued to increase, and the tax basis were broadened, this would mean 'serious taxation of bread and meat and other necessities of the food of the people.' Protectionism would be introduced and 'party bitterness would be aroused such as the present generation could furnish no parallel for except in the brief period of 1885-6.' Summing up at the end of his speech, Churchill was reported as saying: 'We had reached the extreme limit of practical and prudent peacetime taxation, and unless effective means were taken to curb and control the growing expenditure of the country, we would be confronted with important social, economic and political problems, which might be most dangerous to the country and the Empire, and very damaging to many causes which the Conservative Party held near and dear to their hearts.'[21]

Shortly after this, Churchill's anticipations were strikingly confirmed. On 24 April Joseph Chamberlain was the guest at one of the dinners given by the Hooligans. At the end of the dinner, Chamberlain paused as he was leaving and said: 'You young gentlemen have entertained me royally, and in return I will give you a priceless secret. Tariffs! There are the politics of the future, and of the near future. Study them closely and make yourselves masters of them, and you will not regret your hospitality to me.'[22] As Colonial Secretary, Chamberlain played host at the colonial conference which met in London between 30 June and 11 August. The conference unanimously passed a resolution urging Britain to adopt imperial preference: the question of tariffs was once more in the air.

The second danger identified by Churchill was that increasing public expenditure would lead to 'socialist' taxation: a policy of soaking the rich that would cripple a capitalist society. Churchill's biographers have noted that early in 1901 he read, on the recommendation of the Liberal politician John Morley, Seebohm Rowntree's statistical survey of poverty in York. The extent of primary poverty was undoubtedly a revelation to Churchill, who regarded it as a blot on the record of an allegedly civilised society. But it would be mistaken to imply that Rowntree's book impressed on Churchill the necessity of social reform.

When Churchill spoke again in the debates on the finance bill, on 12 May, he directly addressed the problem of poverty, and the Liberal party's claim that the Conservatives were indifferent to it. Here was a bold statement of the case for fiscal conservatism:

I would have hon Members to understand that a vivid realisation of the sufferings of the poor is not the monopoly of the Party opposite. We also possess this realisation . . . The only chance the struggling millions of whom we read in Mr Rowntree's book, and whom we see in our own constituencies, ever have of enjoying the bounties of nature and science, lies not in any socialistic system of taxation, not in any charitable enterprise, or charitable immunity from taxation, but, solely and simply, in an effective and scientific commercial development. I apprehend very grievously that there will one day come a Government in England which will put upon its programme a great Navy and a great Army; £20,000,000 for old age pensions and the housing of the poor; £25,000,000 for an elaborate system of education . . . and that the money will be raised, not equally over the whole country, but by the taxation of one particular class, a very small minority who . . . will not be able to resist it at the polls. If, in the face of the growing expenditure of this country, when the Government is confronted with demands from all quarters, we are so to arrange taxation that the great majority of the electorate will, as it were, be divorced from all real responsibility . . . we shall find ourselves in a most ruinous and paralysed condition. If ever, in this country, the incidence of taxation falls so as to make this country not a good country for capital, so as to displace it from its position as the clearing house and business centre of the world, then, indeed, the whole vast structure of our credit and authority will come clattering down, and the only choice we shall be able to offer the manufacturing multitude in England will be to emigrate or starve.[23]

Churchill accompanied his speeches on finance with an important initiative. In the House of Commons on 24 April, Churchill asked Balfour, the Leader of the House, whether the government would agree to the appointment of a Select Committee 'to consider and report whether National Expenditure can be diminished without injury to the public service, and whether the money voted cannot be apportioned to better advantage than at present.' Balfour twice rejected Churchill's proposal and an exchange of letters followed in *The Times*. Balfour still refused to concede the point, but set up instead a committee of inquiry into the problem, with Churchill as a member. When the committee began work on 15 July, Churchill was an assiduous attender, and subsequently wrote a long memorandum proposing that a parliamentary estimates committee be created, to review in retrospect the merits of the government's spending programme. Needless to say, no Cabinet was likely to create a body permanently dedicated to questioning and criticising its judgments, and nothing came of Churchill's idea.[24]

It is a fair inference that Churchill's financial initiatives were a bid for office. But when, on 11 July 1902, Balfour succeeded Salisbury, there was no place for Churchill. Churchill, for his part, had no reason to give wholehearted support to Balfour. He continued to entertain hopes of Beach and Rosebery and to speculate on the possibility of a new coalition. Beach, however, was no longer a member of the Government, having taken the opportunity of Lord Salisbury's departure to resign. To Balfour, who pressed him to remain at the Exchequer, he spoke of a deep and growing divergence of view between himself and the Cabinet.[25]

Churchill had good reason to believe that the question of tariffs was about to burst on the political scene. The implications for party politics were not in the least obscure. The Government and its Unionist supporters would be split, while the Liberals would take up the defence of free trade. Churchill thought this might conceivably be the opportunity he had been waiting for. Writing to Rosebery on 10 October 1902, he confided:

If by an 'evolutionary process' we could create a wing of the Tory party wh would either infuse vigour into the parent body or join a central coalition, *my plan* would become most important as an incident in or possibly as a herald of the movement. But the risk & peril of it would be very great, & it would carry consequences to me wh I cannot foresee: & only the conviction that you are upholding the flag for which my father fought so long and disastrously would nerve me to the plunge. The Government of the Middle – the party wh shall be free at once from the sordid selfishness and callousness of Toryism on the one hand, and the blind appetites of the Radical masses on the other – may be an ideal wh we perhaps shall never attain, wh could in any case only be possessed for a short time, but which is nevertheless worth working for; & I for my part, see no reason to despair of that 'good state.'

But I should like to bring you & Beach together. There lies the chance of a central coalition. 'Tory-Liberal' is a much better name than 'Tory Democrat' or 'Liberal Imperialist': & certainly neither paradoxical nor unprecedented. The one real difficulty I have to encounter is the suspicion that I am moved by mere restless ambition: & if some issue – such as Tariff – were to arise – that difficulty would disappear . . . [26]

Anticipating the event, Churchill decided to mark out his position in advance, delivering a powerful defence of free trade at Oldham on 23 October. Taking the high ground, he led off with the warning that tariffs would bring about unwelcome constitutional change. If the tariff question were raised, every trade in the country would agitate for protection and every MP would go to the House pledged to protect this or that industry. Alongside the legitimate pressures, corruption would develop and 'the lobbies of the House of Commons would be crowded with touts and concession-hunters . . . Rivers of money would flow into the war chest of the ministers who were prepared to protect certain great, important, well organised and progressive trades. We would grow millionaires throughout the country just as we grew hothouse flowers.' No doubt the reference to Chamberlain, who was famous for growing orchids, was not lost on the audience.

One of the main arguments in favour of tariffs was that foreign countries subsidised their producers, which led to unfair competition and the 'dumping' of cut-price goods in the British market, to the ruin of British manufacturers. Churchill argued that while the free entry of imports did lead to the decline of some industries, it in turn stimulated the creation of new and more advanced industries, which more than compensated for declining trades: 'Let them look at the case of Coventry, which, once upon a time, made silk. The silk trade of Coventry was ruined by the bounties of foreign powers, and Coventry flourishes today much more on bicycles than it ever did on silk, and would thrive perhaps much more in the future on motor-cars than it is thriving on bicycles now.'[27]

In adopting a free trade position, Churchill had one slight embarrassment to overcome. Lord Randolph had spoken in favour of protection at Oldham in 1881. In his own speech Churchill conceded that his father had once inclined towards tariffs, but insisted that he was afterwards 'a moderate Free Trader'. In the summer of 1902 he had begun work on the life of his father, and he clearly intended to argue that while Lord Randolph had at one time experimented with the idea of fair trade, he abandoned it after 1886. He was disconcerted to receive a letter from Lawrence Tipper, a Birmingham manufacturer, which challenged this version of events:

The late Lord Randolph Churchill was undoubtedly a Fair Trader at heart right up to the end. In the Committee Room of the Birmingham Town Hall, after one of his great meetings . . . his Lordship said "Within these walls I am a Fair Trader, outside I don't know anything about Fair Trade. When the Masses shout for Fair Trade then I shall be willing to take up and champion the cause.

If this was true, it was too inconvenient for Churchill to admit. He replied at once in a cutting letter of one sentence: 'The remarkable account which you give of your treatment of the confidences of the late Lord Randolph Churchill does not encourage me to embark upon a personal correspondence with you.'[28]

When Parliament reassembled after the summer recess, in October 1902, the House of Commons resounded with debate over the religious implications of the Education Act. Churchill said nothing, but departed in December for a cruise up the Nile on board a steamer chartered by Sir Ernest Cassel. Cassel, an international banker and friend of Lord Randolph's, was the Churchill family's financial adviser. At Cairo, the party was joined by Hicks Beach and his family. Besides giving Churchill much useful information for his father's biography, Beach talked current politics. Writing home to Lady Randolph, Churchill reported that he found himself in agreement with Beach 'on almost everything political' and saw many openings for co-operation with him.[29]

A disagreeable surprise awaited the Government when Parliament resumed in February 1903. A group of about 25 Unionist back-benchers mounted a root-and-branch attack on Brodrick's Army reforms and threatened to block the passage of the annual Army estimates. The moving spirit in the campaign was Churchill, who had been preparing it since the autumn. The new group, a much expanded version of the 'Hughligans', included his cousins Ivor and Freddie Guest, Sir John Dickson-Poynder, Sir Ernest Beckett, and Major J.E. Seeley, a young officer with whom Churchill had made friends in South Africa. The grey eminence behind the scenes, or so rumour had it, was Lord Rosebery. In April Churchill had to issue a public denial of the charge that the movement was intended to oust Balfour and instal a Rosebery Government.[30]

The agitation over Army reform might bring down Brodrick – as it eventually did – but it was unlikely to overthrow Balfour. Churchill's hopes of a fundamental upheaval depended upon the tariff issue. In April 1902 Beach had reintroduced a registration duty on corn. That autumn the Cabinet discussed whether or not to remit the duty in favour of colonial wheat, while retaining it on foreign imports. This was the policy for which Chamberlain pressed as Colonial Secretary. At first the decision seemed to go in Chamberlain's favour. But after his departure on a tour of South Africa, the Chancellor of the Exchequer, Charles Ritchie, swung the Cabinet in favour of repealing the duty. Chamberlain was outmanoeuvred, and Ritchie announced the abolition of the duty in his budget on 23 April 1903.

Chamberlain struck back. In a speech at Birmingham, on 15 May, he electrified the political world by proclaiming his conversion to a comprehensive scheme of imperial preference, the aim of which would be to consolidate and unite the Empire. With this he coupled a proposal for retaliation against nations which practised 'unfair competition'. Overnight, all other issues were eclipsed. Churchill seized the opportunity for which he had been waiting. Though he was to return from time to time to the question of Army reform, he leapt into the fray over the tariff controversy. On 21 May he wrote to the editor of the *Spectator*, St Loe Strachey, proposing the formation of a league to resist Chamberlain. 'Without organisation we are bound first to be silenced and secondly to be destroyed', Churchill warned. The same day, in a speech at Hoxton, he urged the Conservative party not to disregard 'the very urgent needs of our immense working class population and the real sources of our national wealth'. In a letter to Balfour on 25 May he served notice that he would be forced to reconsider his position if the Conservative party adopted tariffs. On 28 May he and Hugh Cecil attacked Chamberlain's proposals in the House of Commons.[31]

*

Before the narrative sweeps us off downstream, it may be helpful to pause for a moment and reflect on the scene. Chamberlain's Tariff Reform campaign was based on a pessimistic analysis of the state of the nation. Manufacturing industry, the protectionists argued, was gradually being destroyed by foreign competition, with grim social consequences in the shape of growing unemployment and poverty. Foreign manufacturers enjoyed the advantage of tariffs to protect them in the home market, but the British market was open to all. Chamberlain believed that Britain, like its competitors, must pursue a course of economic nationalism. In the British Empire there existed a vast potential market for the home producer, so the Empire should be converted into a single trading area, barricaded against the foreigner. Besides, this was the age of competitive imperialism. The Empire was in danger, and something must be done to unify and strengthen it, if it were not to decline and fall like the Roman Empire.

The Free Trade cause rested on optimism. The great export trades, Free Traders pointed out, were doing well, and so long as this was true it was in Britain's interests to retain a policy of free imports. Free imports were cheap imports, which kept down industrial costs and above all guaranteed the British consumer the boon of inexpensive food. Any scheme of imperial preference would entail – as Chamberlain admitted in the House of Commons on 21 May – duties on foodstuffs. Hence the people would pay, and the class issue was raised. Of necessity, the working classes spent a very high proportion of their incomes on foodstuffs, and they would be hardest hit. Alternatively wages would have to be increased, and hence the costs of production. As for the Empire, it was not in danger and there was far too much militaristic scaremongering. Free trade tended to make for peaceful relations with foreign countries: tariffs were a form of economic warfare and were likely to exacerbate military and imperial rivalries.

Free Traders conceded that it was sometimes permissible to introduce a duty on imports in order to raise revenue. The corn duty and the sugar duty, which helped to finance the war in South Africa, were cases in point, and Churchill had supported them. Some Free Traders also admitted the case for 'retaliation', or 'fair trade' as it was often called. This rested on the argument that foreign governments were subsidising their producers, 'dumping' produce in the British market, and thereby ruining British industries. The strategy was to retaliate with the aim of forcing other countries to reduce their tariff barriers. In theory, fair trade led back to free trade. Some Free Traders, including Churchill, had no objection in principle to the selective use of tariffs for retaliation, though they suspected that retaliation would open the door to more general protection. Churchill, therefore, was never an extreme Free Trader.

Nevertheless he opposed imperial preference on the fundamental grounds that free trade was the best means of stimulating the competition whereby efficiency and prosperity were increased. But in his speech to the House on 28 May he also predicted, accurately as events turned out, that Chamberlain would be unable to draw the line at imperial preference. Imperial preference would turn into a manufacturers' ramp. Taxes on foodstuffs, Churchill maintained, would result in higher costs to manufacturers, and manufacturers would reply by demanding protection for themselves:

The old Conservative Party, with its religious convictions and constitutional principles, will disappear, and a new Party will arise like perhaps the Republican Party of the United States of America – rich, materialist and secular – whose opinions will turn on tariffs, and who will cause the lobbies to be crowded with the touts of protected industries.[32]

Within weeks of Chamberlain's declaration, the Unionists began to polarise and split into rival factions. Divisions within the Cabinet were concealed for the time being by the artifice of Balfour, who temporised and announced that the government would conduct an 'inquiry' into the question. By this device he postponed the issue for the time being and, as far as possible, prevented its discussion in the House of Commons. The proposed 'inquiry' was largely fictitious: an agreement by members of the Cabinet to keep their mouths shut while they thought what to do next. But on the back-benches, and in the constituencies, an overt struggle developed.

On 1 July a meeting of 53 Tory Free Trade MPs, including Churchill, decided to organise a Unionist Free Food League, and a fortnight later Hicks Beach was appointed as chairman. On 21 July a group of Tariff Reformers responded by announcing the formation of the Tariff Reform League. Though Chamberlain's own lips were sealed, the Tariff Reform League began an energetic campaign of propaganda in Unionist constituency organisations. Churchill was a leading light, along with Hugh Cecil, among the Free Food MPs and protested loudly against the blanket imposed by Balfour on parliamentary debate.

Our view of Churchill at this point is conditioned by hindsight. We know that the movement touched off by Chamberlain carried all before it among the Unionists, and that Balfour was unable or unwilling to stop it. We know that the Free Trade Unionists, including Churchill, were overwhelmed and defeated. We know that Churchill himself crossed the floor to join the Liberals in May 1904. But in May 1903 the future was obscure. Neither of the two main factions within the party could be sure which way things would go, or what Balfour intended.

The Unionist Free Traders had two important leaders in the Cabinet: Charles Ritchie, the Chancellor of the Exchequer, and Spencer Compton, the eighth Duke of Devonshire. On the back-benches they were led by Beach and Goschen, two former Chancellors of the Exchequer. The Hooligans represented the younger generation of talent and included, in Cecil and Churchill, the rising stars of Toryism. The pillars of public life – the Treasury, the City, and most economists – were all for free trade, and so, predominantly, were the great exporting industries of coal, cotton and shipbuilding. At this early stage of the controversy the press was on balance favourable to the free trade cause, and Alfred Harmsworth, the owner of the *Daily Mail*, was busy denouncing 'Stomach Taxes' in its pages. A free trade victory over Chamberlain appeared to be a distinct possibility.

The Unionist Free Traders were a distinguished group. But they were outnumbered, on the back-benches, by the supporters of Tariff Reform, and they had no organisation outside Westminster. Chamberlain, on the other hand, had always been a master of extra-parliamentary politics. The Tariff Reform League, with generous funding from industry and an efficient propaganda organisation, formed numerous branches in the constituencies. Bowled over with enthusiasm for Chamberlain's programme, the rank and file of the party became impatient with MPs who refused to fall into line, and Churchill's own Oldham constituency association began to turn against him.

Had Churchill been in a position to dictate events, Balfour's head would have rolled, or a major realignment of parties taken place. But in his junior capacity he could do little more than act as go-between in a struggle carried on by his elders and betters. From the beginning, the Unionist Free Traders were on the defensive. This did not suit Churchill, whose instinct was to attack. Whereas many of the 'Free Fooders' were content to mount a campaign of resistance for the purpose of stiffening Balfour against Chamberlain, Churchill would have liked to create a new parliamentary combination to overthrow Balfour. 'I think this is the time for a Central Government', wrote Churchill to Harmsworth on 26 August, 'and if Lord R. lets the opportunity pass, it may never return. Why don't you have a talk with him?'[33]

Unfortunately for Churchill, the leaders to whom he looked for decisive action failed to provide it. He was forced to watch from the sidelines as the Unionist Free Traders were driven steadily into retreat. In September Balfour, who had been maturing his plans over the summer, decided to take action and reimpose his authority over the party. In a masterly sequence of moves he contrived to shed from his Cabinet the most fervent of the leaders on both sides of the question. Ritchie, the Chancellor of the Exchequer, was banished for his dogmatism in refusing to budge from undiluted free trade, and a few days later Chamberlain himself resigned. But Chamberlain departed on more favourable terms. In an extraordinary bargain with the Prime Minister, he won the right to go out and campaign for a much more advanced programme than Balfour was as yet willing to endorse. By way of setting the seal on his peace treaty with Chamberlain, Balfour appointed his son Austen Chancellor of the Exchequer in place of Ritchie.

Meanwhile Balfour had succeeded in devising a compromise position which he unveiled in a speech to the annual Unionist conference at Sheffield on 1 October. Balfour declared that he was against food taxes (thus appearing to rule out imperial preference), and against protection, but in favour of retaliation. A few days later Chamberlain inaugurated his Tariff Reform campaign at Glasgow with a thoroughgoing programme of measures. He proposed import duties on foreign corn, flour and meat (excluding bacon), a preference in favour of colonial wine, and a duty not exceeding 10 per cent on all foreign manufactures. To compensate for increasing food taxes in one direction, Chamberlain planned to reduce the domestic duties on tea, sugar, cocoa and coffee.

In principle, Churchill could find no objection to the case made out by Balfour for selective retaliation. But he argued, with good reason, that this was only the thin end of the protectionist wedge. He pointed out that in the September reshuffle the balance of power had swung further towards Chamberlain, and that Balfour was not to be trusted. In an open letter to his constituents, published on 12 October, Churchill wrote:

> Observe the signs of the weather. Mr Balfour and Mr Chamberlain reciprocate endearments. The Prime Minister has never a good word for free trade, and never uses a phrase to discourage protection. The free-trade ministers are ejected from the Cabinet. Their places are filled by some of the most rabid protectionists in the Cabinet. Mr Austen Chamberlain, the echo and exponent of his father, is sent to guard the public purse ... Mr Gerald Balfour tells us with much candour that although food taxes are not the present official policy of the Government, if Mr Chamberlain's policy proves popular they are likely to become so.[34]

Churchill still hoped for an alternative government. But his hopes depended upon three men, all of whom proved to be a disappointment. The Duke of Devonshire, for all his weight, came out of the crisis in a very wobbly condition. At first Balfour persuaded him to remain in office while his Free Trade allies were sacrificed. But they in turn persuaded him that he owed it to them to resign, which he did on 6 October. Henceforth the Duke superseded Beach as the acknowledged leader of the Unionist Free Traders, and Churchill turned to him for instructions. In December the Duke went so far as to urge all Unionist Free Traders to vote against Protectionist candidates. But he made no bid for the premiership.

Churchill had hoped that Harmsworth and the *Daily Mail* would help to pave the way for an alternative government. But to Churchill's dismay, Harmsworth's antipathy towards food taxes was overcome by his enthusiasm for the protection of manufacturing industry, and he came out in favour of Chamberlain. There remained Rosebery. 'You alone can stem the tide', wrote Churchill with growing desperation on 9 October. 'I hope you will make some conjunction with the duke, so that at Sheffield you may be able to say that you join with him in fighting for Free Trade & would if necessary serve under him.'[35]

But it was a forlorn hope that Rosebery would take decisive action and Churchill began seriously to contemplate a change of party. On 16 October he wrote to Morley appealing for assistance for the Unionist Free Traders from the Liberals: 'I hope you will try to help some of us. *I* do not mean to go back under any circumstances ... ' On 24 October Churchill poured out his feelings in a letter intended for Hugh Cecil, but never sent: 'I am an English Liberal. I hate the Tory party, their men, their words & their methods ... It is therefore my intention that before Parliament meets my separation from the Tory party and the government shall be complete and irrevocable; & during the next session I propose to act consistently with the Liberal party.'[36]

In December, Churchill was authorised by the Duke to open up negotiations on behalf of the Unionist Free Traders with two leading Liberals: Asquith, and the Liberal Chief Whip, Herbert Gladstone. The aim was to arrange Liberal support for Unionists standing as Free Trade candidates. Many of them were under attack from their constituency parties, who threatened not to readopt them. This was true in Oldham, where the party was in a state of open rebellion against Churchill. In late November he was physically debarred from entering a Tory working men's club in the constituency, and retaliated by addressing the crowd outside from the box-seat of his carriage, bareheaded in a downpour of rain.

On 23 December the General Purposes Committee of the Oldham Conservative Association unanimously passed a resolution of no confidence in him.[37] In the hope that some kind of alliance could be struck with the Liberals, the Duke authorised Unionist Free Traders to campaign on behalf of opposition candidates against Protectionists at by-elections. Churchill himself sent a message of support to the Liberal candidate at the Ludlow by-election in December. His plan was to organise, under the aegis of the Duke, an electoral alliance with the Liberals whereby some 50 Unionist Free Traders would secede from the party, just as the Liberal Unionists had seceded from Liberalism in 1886. In his by-election letter he called on Free Traders in all parties to 'form one common line of battle against a common foe.'[38]

Churchill's vision of a large-scale secession was doomed to disappointment. The Liberals, though prepared to make exceptions here and there, were reluctant to stand down their own candidates in order to rescue

Unionists in distress. On the other side, many of the Unionist Free Traders were Conservatives first, and Free Traders second. They differed from the Liberals much more than from their own party. It was inconceivable, for instance, that Hugh Cecil, whose Anglicanism was the mainspring of his politics, could join a party of dissenters who were threatening to undermine Church of England schools. Similarly Hicks Beach, who decided in 1904 to retire from politics altogether, explained to Churchill that he was first and foremost a Tory and would have to remain one. Among the handful of Unionist Free Traders who did change sides were, however, Churchill's friend J.E. Seeley, and his cousin Ivor Guest. Churchill negotiated with Gladstone on their behalf, successfully recommending Guest for Cardiff and Seeley for the Isle of Wight.[39]

At the end of 1903, Churchill was deep in discussion with Lloyd George about his future as a Liberal, and corresponding with another leading radical, Charles Trevelyan, on the same topic.[40] When the new session of Parliament opened in February, Churchill began to vote consistently with the Liberals, and the Unionist Whip was withdrawn. It only remained for Churchill, by negotiation with Gladstone, to find a suitable constituency. A number of Liberal associations were keen to adopt him as their candidate, including Manchester North-West and Sheffield Central. Churchill chose Manchester. 'I think this is much better than Sheffield', he wrote to Morley. 'I don't see how my arguments about smaller armaments could go down in a city which lives by instruments of war. On the other, what could be better than to unfurl the flag of Free Trade & Economy (they must hang together) in the constituency of the Free Trade Hall.'[41] As the centre of the cotton industry, which inclined heavily towards free trade, the north-west was particularly vulnerable to a Liberal onslaught. With several Tory seats at risk, Churchill was in many ways ideally qualified to lead the battle for Lancashire. On 29 April he formally announced his candidacy as the Free Trade candidate for Manchester North-West.[42]

Technically, Churchill was a Free Trade candidate and not a Liberal. But he behaved as a Liberal and was treated as one for all practical purposes. On 13 May he appeared for the first time on a Liberal platform, introduced by Morley at the annual meeting of the National Liberal Federation in Manchester. In the words of the *Liberal Magazine*, 'the old Reservist made no secret of his pride and satisfaction in the performance of the Young Recruit.'[43] On 31 May Churchill entered the chamber of the House and took his seat beside Lloyd George on the Liberal benches.

*

Churchill's change of party was accomplished with exceptional dexterity. Though he was determined by October 1903 to leave the Conservative party, he made it appear as though the Conservatives were driving him out. Similarly he claimed that while the Conservatives had abandoned their principles, his were still the same. But why did Churchill change parties?

The force of his personal ambition should never be underestimated. But neither should the clarity of his convictions. Unlike Lord Randolph, who was intuitive and impulsive to excess, the young Winston Churchill possessed intellect and self-control. The fiscal and financial views he developed between 1901 and 1903 were narrow, but coherent and logical, and clearly signalled his position on free trade. When the issue arose he knew where he stood. Almost all his friends and mentors – Cecil, Hicks-Beach, Hamilton, Mowatt, Morley and Rosebery – were in the Free Trade camp.

Our picture of young Winston as a simple man of action owes more to his exploits in the Soudan or South Africa than to his parliamentary career. Churchill worked as hard at his speeches and articles as Beatrice and Sidney Webb at their social research. Seldom if ever did he take a holiday from politics. 'He gave himself to work', wrote the journalist J.B. Atkins, who knew him at this period. 'When he was not busy with politics he was reading or writing. He did not lead the life of other young men in London. He may have visited political clubs, but I never saw him at an ordinary social club. I never met him walking in Pall Mall or Hyde Park, where sooner or later one used to meet most friends. I never met him at a dinner party that had not some public or private purpose.'[44]

In later life Churchill recalled that when the Free Trade question arose, he turned to the classic authorities on the subject. He read John Stuart Mill and the French economist, Claude Frederic Bastiat, and re-read Adam Smith's *Wealth of Nations* (first encountered at Bangalore). 'I then inquired where the Protectionist case was set out. No one could tell me. Apart from the masses of polemic literature now being flung out by the Tariff Reform League, there was no book of the slightest authority which expounded the doctrines of Protection.'[45] While Churchill was reading up on the subject, he was also being briefed on the case for free trade by Sir Francis Mowatt, the Permanent Secretary to the Treasury, who 'armed me with facts and arguments of a general character and equipped me with a knowledge of economics, very necessary to a young man who, at twenty-eight, is called upon to take a prominent part in a national controversy.'[46]

Churchill's writings and speeches were full of knockabout humour at the expense of Balfour and Chamberlain. But they were also lucid and logical expositions of political economy. This is not to say that his economic ideas alone account for his change of party, which plainly owed much to thwarted ambition. But they gave him the confidence to act in the knowledge that his ambitionss were no longer naked, but decently clothed in a cause he could believe in.

Naturally enough, there were many Conservatives who regarded Churchill as unscrupulous and unprincipled. While they underestimated his attachment to free trade, they were right about his egotism and consequent lack of party political identity. There was no secure religious basis to his career. He was rooted neither in the Anglicanism of the party he was leaving, nor in the dissent of the party he was joining. Nor did he regard party, and party government, with innate respect: witness his intrigues for a 'government of the middle'. It was obvious too that he delighted in the political game for its own sake. At his first encounter with Beatrice Webb, in July 1903, he talked exclusively of his electioneering plans in Oldham. 'I dare say he has a better side', she noted, 'which the ordinary cheap cynicism of his position and career covers up to a casual dinner acquaintance.'[47]

Whatever Churchill's motives, his change of party was no isolated act, but the reflection of a wider movement. The pendulum was swinging or, as John Vincent puts it: 'The balance of prejudice, of restiveness, of talent, was tilting towards "democracy" – that vague word summarising the mixture of irresponsible politics and economic spoliation which Conservatives had always feared in their picture of the future.'[48] Chamberlain's campaign for Tariff Reform generated an almost fanatical enthusiasm within the Conservative Party. But generally speaking it was an electoral liability. The wealth of the City of London and of much of British industry was still vested in free trade. It was a millionaires' cause: but also, or so the Liberals maintained, the cause of the poor. Food taxes, they claimed, would put up the price of bread while free trade would keep it down. The argument worked. By the spring of 1904 the writing was on the wall for the Unionist Government. By-elections told a steady tale of disaster in the making and the Unionist majority in the House was shaken by disunity and rebellion.

For the first time since 1880, the Liberals held the initiative and were on the attack. It appeared to be only a matter of time before the Government fell: but the skill and determination of Balfour ensured that it was quite a long time. The Unionists were to continue in office until December 1905.

\*

Churchill discovered that he was more isolated as a Liberal than he had been as a Conservative. He was no longer the member of a group like the Hooligans or the Unionist Free Traders, and his personal friends were few. Of these, the most significant was John Morley.

In 1904, when Churchill was 30, Morley was 66. An agnostic who had never found an adequate substitute for the Anglicanism of his boyhood, he already had a long career behind him as a journalist and politician. He was the biographer of Cobden and Gladstone, and like them was also a firm opponent of state intervention in the economy. A fine orator and conversationalist, Morley was an indecisive politician, and there was general agreement among his friends that his nature was markedly 'feminine': Rosebery described him as 'a perfect lady' and Campbell-Bannerman as 'that old maidish Priscilla'. He was much attracted to the qualities he did not himself possess and was a great admirer of men of power and action.[49] Churchill, with his energy, decision, and glamorous military record, appealed greatly to him. To Churchill, Morley was attractive as a friend and admirer of his father, and frequent guest at his mother's dinner-parties. Morley, no doubt, flattered and encouraged him. After a dinner-party at Morley's in December 1901 Churchill reported to Lady Randolph that 'everybody was most kind and caressing, particularly the host, who like so many of these Liberals commands my affection at once.'[50] In April 1902, when Morley led a Liberal attack on the Government over the case of the pro-Boer journalist Cartwright, detained in South Africa against his will by the military authorities, Churchill supported him. Morley gave Churchill paternal guidance in his passage from the Conservative to the Liberal party and – this is a guess – it was he who taught Churchill the language of high-minded Liberalism. Apart from Morley, none of the Liberal leaders gave Churchill any particular welcome or encouragement. Campbell-Bannerman, Asquith, Grey, Haldane and Fowler held aloof. Nor did Churchill find a circle of back-bench MPs with whom to co-operate. 'I am at this moment entirely isolated in politics – having no sort of connection with any group of politicians,' he wrote to J. Moore Bayley in October 1904.[51]

Churchill's most significant friend on the Liberal back-benches was David Lloyd George. On the day Churchill crossed the floor of the House, he took his seat beside the Welshman. Already famous as a radical, pro-Boer, and scourge of the landlord class, Lloyd George had yet to enter the charmed circle of the Liberal leadership. Eleven years older than Churchill, with a decade of parliamentary experience behind him, Lloyd George was a century older in guile and worldly wisdom. Quite how close was the understanding between them at this stage is difficult to say, but Lloyd George's hand can be traced. In the autumn of 1904, for example, he arranged for Churchill a number of speaking engagements in north Wales. They shared a platform at Carnarvon, in Lloyd George's own constituency. Repaying flattery with flattery, Churchill described Lloyd George in his speech as 'the best fighting general in the Liberal ranks.'[52]

Though Churchill had few close associates in the Liberal party, he was famous as a free trade orator and much in demand as the party battle proceeded. By November 1904 nearly two hundred constituencies had asked him to speak.[53] As a Conservative, Churchill had sometimes engaged in party political abuse of the Liberals, but in a tone of gentle mockery. At other times he had spoken of Liberals and Liberalism with a respect verging on outright admiration. Now that he was on the Liberal side, there was a marked shift of tone. Churchill was stridently and unremittingly partisan, ridiculing the Conservatives as a base and corrupting force in national life. Whether he was influenced by the platform style of Lloyd George, or simply felt that he had to prove himself as a Liberal, it is hard to judge. Either way, there were overtones of class conflict in the indictment of his former party. In his first speech to the National Liberal Federation, in May 1904, he predicted the character of a future Conservative Government:

We know perfectly well what to expect – a party of great vested interests, banded together in a formidable confederation; corruption at home, aggression to cover it up abroad; the trickery of tariff juggles, the tyranny of a party machine; sentiment by the bucketful; patriotism by the imperial pint; the open hand at the public exchequer, the open door at the public-house; dear food for the million, cheap labour for the millionaire.[54]

At Glasgow in November 1904 he accused the government of increasing subservience towards the interests of capitalism. Many people, he said, were frightened by the Independent Labour party, but there was much more to fear from the Independent Capitalist Party:

Nothing is esteemed except money, nothing accounted except a banking account. Quality, education, civic distinction, public virtue, are valued less and less. We have in London an important section of people who go about preaching the gospel of Mammon advocating the 10 per cent commandments – who raise each day the inspiring prayer "Give cash in our time, O Lord."[55]

In other passages of oratory, Churchill painted glowing word-pictures of the spirit and purpose of Liberalism. Though he could not speak for the Nonconformist conscience, and did not try to do so, he was closely attuned to modern, secular Liberalism, with its faith in economic and social progress. But while he articulated the spirit of Liberalism as Morley understood it, he was careful in the composition of his speeches to distinguish general inspiration from specific pledges. His primary electoral purpose was to rally Lancashire to the cause of Free Trade and, of course, to wrest North-West Manchester from the Conservatives. He was reluctant to encumber himself with all the bag and baggage of Liberalism and, behind the mask of rhetoric, remained a politician of singularly independent outlook.

By the spring of 1904 the Liberal party was united in vociferous agitation against the Government over the question of 'Chinese Slavery'. Strictly speaking, this was a South African issue, but it was profitably reworked, with much assistance from Labour, into a damaging domestic campaign with a potent blend of humanitarian zeal and racial prejudice.

After the end of the South African war, the gold-mines experienced a depression. In an effort to cut labour costs, the mine-owners proposed that coolies should be imported from China. Milner, the British High Commissioner in South Africa, acquiesced, and so did the Balfour Cabinet. In order to ensure that the mine-owners recovered the cost of importing the Chinese, Milner promulgated an ordinance whereby they were brought in as indentured labour, with a legal obligation to work for a minimum period. This was not the only restriction. Theoretically, the Chinese were allowed to bring their wives, but in practice they were unaccompanied males. To prevent racial mixing, and the generation of a new breed of half-castes in South Africa, the Chinese were confined to all-male compounds, where, it was alleged, 'unnatural vice' flourished. By the end of 1904 there were already 20,000 Chinese employed, and the total rose in the following nine months to 47,000.

As the facts became known in Britain, a tremendous clamour arose from the Labour and Liberal parties and the leaders of religious nonconformity. The labour ordinance was condemned for the inhuman and immoral conditions it inflicted on the Chinese, and attacked as a form of 'slavery'. At the same time, Chinese labour was represented as unfair competition against British working men who might otherwise have found employment in the Transvaal. Why was it, asked Lloyd George that a British working man could not land in South Africa without £25 in his pocket, while 'Chinamen are pouring in in shiploads'? The British Government, he claimed, could have insisted that in the wealthier mines, British labour should be employed, while black labour worked the less profitable levels.[56] Liberal and Labour propagandists linked the issue with the wider question of Tory attitudes towards labour. In March 1904 the Conservative Chief Whip wrote in his diary: ' . . . we have suffered enormously from the Yellow Labour agitation, and a dissolution of Parliament at this juncture would mean absolute annihilation.'[57]

As a politician who could speak with some authority on South Africa, Churchill might have been expected to join in the hue and cry. But apart from a few brief and evasive references to the subject, he was eloquently silent for nearly eighteen months. Not until 6 October 1905, with a general election looming, did he suddenly announce to a Liberal audience in Manchester that he had changed his mind. 'I feel that this question of Chinese labour must be the great moral issue at the next election'.[58] Yet Churchill disavowed the word 'slavery' and his language on the subject was decidedly restrained.

It is not certain why Churchill kept his distance from the agitation, but his South African experience may hold the key. His priority in 1901–2 was a generous settlement to reconcile the Boers by financing the rebuilding of their farms out of the profits of the mines. If this was still his priority in 1904–5, he would have been reluctant to deny the mine-owners the labour they were asking for. It is quite likely that he was influenced by his father's old friend Sir Abe Bailey, the South African mining magnate and politician. In January 1905 Bailey wrote to say that the experiment in Chinese labour was working well. The Chinese were prosperous and contented, and their quarters filled with trinkets, clocks and chamber pots, the latter freely adapted as crockery for eating purposes.[59]

Churchill concentrated his fire on free trade. Mindful always of his mission to mobilise Lancashire, where cotton and shipbuilding were the dominant industries, he emphasised the benefits they obtained from free trade, and the damage they would suffer from tariff wars. As integral parts of the free trade conception, he continued to champion economy in public expenditure, reductions in armaments, and hostility to 'militarism'. He never forgot the correlation, in Liberal thinking, between free trade economics and the civilising mission of free trade in the promotion of peace and international co-operation. Churchill's speeches were a masterly blend of analysis and entertainment, and clearly written on the assumption that he was addressing popular audiences who were highly intelligent and informed. In the war of words against Chamberlain and the Tariff Reform League, Asquith alone outshone him.

*

Beyond free trade Churchill was reluctant to venture. But he was always alert to the electoral currents of Lancashire, and more particularly within his prospective constituency of Manchester North-West. There were at least two occasions when constituency pressures prompted him to declare himself in the House on major issues. Firstly there was the question of the legal position of trade unions. Under the Taff Vale Judgment of 1900 the House of Lords had ruled that a trade union which took part in a strike was liable to prosecution by the employer for damages. The judgment appeared to take away the practical foundation of the right to strike. One of the first objectives of the Labour party – founded in 1900 as the Labour Representation Committee – was to obtain a revision of the judgment. To this end, a bill was introduced into the House in 1903. Churchill, who was still at this point on the Unionist side, was persuaded to support it by a correspondence with the Secretary of the Oldham Trades Council, J.R. Clynes. He was one of 17 Unionists who voted in favour of the bill, which was defeated.[60] In April 1904, while he was still completing the arrangements for his nomination in Manchester North-West, a second bill was introduced. Churchill was advised by the Free Trade League in Manchester that if he could 'satisfy our Labour friends on the point they will be your enthusiastic supporters'.[61]

Churchill responded by speaking in the debate on the second reading on 22 April and promised to vote in favour of the bill. Without referring directly to his father, he claimed to be acting in the tradition of Disraeli and Tory Democracy. But he never finished the speech: having run out of his notes he forgot what he had intended to say, dried up, and sat down with his head in his hands – fearing, perhaps, the first symptoms of the disease that had killed his father. His anxieties were groundless however and he rapidly recovered his spirits.[62] But the drama of the episode has distracted attention from the significance of Churchill's speech. Towards the end of his life Lord Randolph had predicted the emergence of trade unionism as a major political force. Churchill recognised the truth of this and was ready to seek the trade union vote. This time the bill obtained a majority, but was not proceeded with, and the question was carried forward into the general election of 1906, with the Liberals pledged to reverse the Taff Vale Judgment.

In Manchester North-West Churchill encountered for the first time the politics of immigration. In the late nineteenth century there were virtually no legal barriers to prevent immigrants from entering Britain. Consequently, from about 1880 onwards, there was a flow of Jewish immigrants fleeing from persecution in Russia and Poland. The largest settlement, in the East End of London, produced a wave of working-class anti-Semitism. In 1892, and again in 1894, the Trades Union Congress demanded legislation to prohibit the immigration of destitute aliens, who were accused of sweating British labour, and undercutting the British working man in the labour market.

For the Unionist Government, alien immigration was a useful card to play in the battle for the working-class vote. (The 'Chinese slavery' agitation, referred to earlier on, was the Liberal and Labour riposte.) In 1902 the Government appointed a Royal Commission on the subject, which reported the following year. In March 1904 the Government introduced a bill which was intended to exclude various categories of alien: those convicted of an extraditable crime, those without means of financial support, and those 'of notoriously bad character'.[63] Churchill, who had inherited a wealthy and powerful circle of Jewish friends from his father, was above suspicion of anti-Semitism. He was also very well aware that Manchester North-West contained a substantial Jewish community strongly opposed to the bill. For all that, he approached the issue as cautiously as a cat stalking a large and dangerous rat. As Michael Cohen remarks: 'He took no part in the debates in the House during the first two readings of the Aliens Bill, which took place before he crossed the floor, though he was present.' On 30 May, the day before he crossed the floor, he set out his opposition to the bill in a letter to Nathan Laski, in terms which appeared to leave no doubt about his position: 'English working men . . . do not respond in any marked degree to the anti-Semitism which has recently darkened Continental history; and I for one believe that they will disavow an attempt to shut out the stranger from our land because he is poor or in trouble.'[64]

On 8 June 1904 Churchill spoke for the first time from the Liberal benches, to protest on procedural grounds against the Government's decision to send the bill, on the grounds that it was non-controversial, to the Grand Committee on Law. On the merits of the bill he made no comment and he was in fact in two minds about whether to mount a campaign against it. As he explained in a letter to William Royle, the chairman of the Manchester Liberal Federation:

'I have been invited by the Opponents of the Aliens Bill to take a seat on the Grand Committee on Law and take part in the opposition to that measure. Such a course would be very agreeable to me, and I daresay it would be quite possible to destroy the Bill altogether at this stage; but will you kindly inform me whether my taking a prominent part in the proceedings would be likely to re-act unfavourably in the North-West division? We cannot afford to throw away a vote, and if there is any strong feeling about Aliens displacing British Labour, it would be better to leave to others the work of killing the Bill.'[65]

Royle must have reassured him, for Churchill accepted a seat on the Committee and began to engage in a vigorous campaign of sabotage. As the Conservative Chief Whip recorded in his diary on 23 June: 'Churchill meanwhile has been acting as Leader of the Opposition on the Aliens Bill. Asquith, as an ex-minister and ex-home secretary, was disgusted to find himself ousted by the whipper snapper.'[66] Churchill was not opposed in principle to the restriction of immigration. He was in favour of restrictions on criminal aliens and other 'undesirable characters', but opposed to restrictions on the entry of the poor and destitute. Meanwhile Churchill's part in the destruction of the bill won him the deep gratitude of Manchester Jewry. His initial hesitations once overcome, he took a strong line, repeated when a second Aliens Bill was introduced in April 1905. The new bill, more carefully drafted than its predecessor, introduced a means test to distinguish the relatively poor immigrant, who was to be allowed in, from the destitute, who was to be excluded. Again there was a wave of protest from Jewish communities, but this time the bill passed and was on the statute book by the time the Liberals took office in December 1905. In the general election campaign – which, it has to be recalled, followed the change of Government – Churchill made no pledge to repeal the act. 'As regards the present Act', he told a gathering of Jews on 8 January, 'it depends upon its administration whether it is an odious act or one tempered with leniency.'[67]

The issues on which politicians are silent are, of course, as important as the issues they wish to publicise. It would be untrue to say that Churchill ignored, at this stage, the problems of poverty and unemployment. But he said very little about them. Apart from the concern he occasionally expressed for the 'forgotten millions', he maintained the generally negative attitude towards social policy which he had adopted as a Conservative.

Within the Liberal party, a division of opinion was beginning to emerge between the old Liberalism of Gladstone and the new Liberalism of social reform. The dividing-line was in fact blurred, but this is no place for a full account of the ambiguities of Liberalism. Briefly, Campbell-Bannerman and the Liberal front-bench were quite content with free trade abroad, *laissez-faire* at home, and reductions in public expenditure. But the more progressive elements in the party were calling for a positive programme. As yet the phrase 'social reform' was still a very broad one, encompassing radical as well as collectivist notions: temperance and land reform were as prominent in the minds of left-wing Liberals as old age pensions or the eight-hour day.

At the end of 1903 Charles Trevelyan, the radical heir to a distinguished Whig family, wrote to Churchill to inquire what his response would be to 'a positive programme of social reform'. Churchill replied:

Perhaps you do not realise how very short is my parliamentary experience. Those subjects which have come under my view, such as Economy, Army Administration, and Free Trade, have produced in me very strong opinions, and I find, on looking back, that these opinions harmonise one with the other and seem to belong to a definite system of thought. I confess to you that so far they are entirely negative in character. I have revolted against the extravagances of the Government; I have been amazed at the blunders of the Army policy; and Protection seems to me nothing but clever men talking rubbish for corrupt motives. I would not venture to commit myself offhand to the large constructive policy which you have sketched, still less could I speak for my friends. But I feel very strongly that if people can agree about Free Trade they can agree about a great many other things, because to speak the truth, it embodies in itself almost all the living principles of Liberalism; and I think it would be very unwise at this present juncture to try to look too far ahead . . .[68]

Churchill paid lip-service to the ideas of a positive programme, but he was deliberately vague about it. In one of his first addresses to a Liberal audience, he maintained that free trade could never be defended by a purely negative policy. 'We must produce, if we are successfully to defend Free Trade, a positive and practical policy of social reform.' The audience cheered, but Churchill continued: 'Well, what is that policy to be? I am not entitled to advise you upon that.' He referred his listeners instead to the speech they had just heard from Morley, as 'the outline, at any rate, of a considerable quantity of practical business which requires prompt and immediate settlement.'[69]

Churchill had another reason for keeping his distance from questions of social reform. Where social reform implied the intervention of the state, and expenditure on new or improved social services, it conflicted with his belief in *laissez-faire* and the reduction of public expenditure. In June 1904 the Webbs sounded out Churchill's views on collectivism. Beatrice wrote sharply in her diary: 'He has no sympathy with suffering, no intellectual curiosity, he is neither scientist nor benevolent. I tried the "national minimum" on him but he was evidently unaware of the most elementary objections to unrestricted competition, and was still in the stage of "infant-school economics".' A week later Churchill told an audience at Streatham, in Lancashire, that he proposed to put on his election posters the message: 'Vote for Churchill, Cheap Food, Peace, Retrenchment and Reform.'[70] Churchill made compassionate speeches about the plight of the slum-dweller, and the Liberal mission to protect the underdog. But as yet these were sentiments, not policies. When he was challenged during the general election campaign to explain what the Government would do about unemployment, he was patently at a loss:

> The Liberals have got some men together who might be able to do something. In Mr Asquith, Sir Edward Grey, Mr John Burns and Mr Lloyd George I see many men not only of great intellectual ability but men in close and intimate touch with the real needs of the people, and I think the Government has a right to ask the electors to give them the power and as good a chance as they so freely gave to the late Administration . . . [71]

Churchill was persistently critical of the kind of capitalism represented by Chamberlain and the Tariff Reformers. He attacked them as monopolists who would corrupt the political system at home and create an aggressive imperialism overseas. But if Churchill attacked protectionism, he never ceased to expound the virtues of liberal capitalism as the mainspring of peace and prosperity. And though he might bid for trade union or working-class votes, he was perfectly clear in his opposition to socialism. In an address to working men at Coatsbridge, in November 1904, he said:

> I am not myself what is called a Socialist, nor do I believe that the Socialist philosophy is a practical or advantageous one. I am convinced that it is necessary to maintain the individual ownership of property, and I do not believe that we will get an active productivity unless we interest every individual . . . There is a very clear and definite line of cleavage between the philosophy of Liberalism as I understand its principles and the Socialist philosophy. Socialism militates against liberty. It is most important for the British working classes that they should be able if necessary to strike – though nobody likes strikes – in order to put pressure upon their employers for a greater share of the wealth of the world or for the removal of hard and onerous conditions, but in the Socialist State no strike could be tolerated. I think we should try to improve the lot of the masses of the people through the existing structure of society . . . [72]

The alliance between the Liberal and Labour parties, though never without its frictions, was highly developed in Lancashire, and Churchill was keen to maintain it. Labour at this period was a minor party and, in effect, a pressure-group on behalf of the trade unions. Though it included socialists, it was more liberal than socialist in outlook. Moreover, as the Labour alliance was of considerable electoral value to the Liberals, Churchill had every reason to embrace Lib-Lab politics.

In marked contrast was his attitude to the Social Democratic Federation, the Marxist party which had broken away from Labour under its leader H.M. Hyndman. Hyndman, like Churchill, was active in Lancashire politics as the candidate for Blackburn. Lord Randolph had greatly enjoyed his company, but this was a connection his son was not keen to renew. The SDF were hostile to the Liberals and the Liberals hostile to the SDF. Churchill disliked, and perhaps feared, the SDF's attempts to agitate the unemployed on behalf of the 'right to work'. In December 1904 he wrote to William Royle:

I gathered from the reports in the papers that the Unemployed Meeting had not been an unqualified success. I am very glad I was not there. It is quite impossible for any responsible speaker to satisfy extremists and revolutionaries and perfectly easy for any irresponsible speaker by going one better than anyone else. Certainly I am not going to enter into competition of that character ... If you read the accounts of the Ateliers Nationaux in Paris in 1848, you will see what grave dangers may attend these sort of experiments.[73]

In the intervals between his political activities, Churchill continued work on the life of his father. Up to a point his approach was thoroughly professional: he immersed himself in the documents, supplemented them with interviews, and shaped the materials into a well-organised and powerful interpretation. But in writing an ambitious book on recent political history Churchill was advertising himself and for the sake of his career he had to make certain that the book fulfilled a number of conditions. It had to be flattering about Lord Randolph, tactful about living people, and serviceable as a myth to justify his own career. That he should have achieved all of this is a measure of his creativity and intellect, but the past had to be subordinated to the present. Churchill needed an interpretation that would serve as a bridge between his father's Toryism and his own Liberalism. In the story as it took shape in his mind, Lord Randolph began as a Tory but evolved towards Liberalism. Hence Tory Democracy was Toryism with a Liberal slant, and Lord Randolph during his final years in the wilderness was an advanced radical and social reformer. The paradox here was that Lord Randolph was inclined to Protectionism, a feature of his career which had to be minimised or explained away. In writing his father's life Churchill identified himself with a myth of Tory Democracy, while detaching himself from the reality.

Lord Randolph Churchill had opposed votes for women, and so indeed had Lady Randolph. But in March 1904, when a female suffrage bill was before the House, Winston Churchill voted in favour of it. The vote occurred at the critical point when he was negotiating for Manchester North-West, and there was probably a Manchester connection. Ever since 1867 female suffrage societies had been carrying on a constitutional campaign for the vote, and several bills had been introduced by MPs sympathetic to the cause. Though Liberals were more likely to vote in favour than Conservatives, female suffrage was never a party issue, and opinion in both parties was changing. In 1897 the House of Commons voted in favour of a female franchise bill by a substantial majority. But this was a gesture only: MPs knew that the Government would not allow the bill to proceed, and that even if they did, the House of Lords would reject it.

The women's movement had a considerable following in Lancashire, where there was strong and active support from female workers in the cotton factories. In October 1903 Mrs Emmeline Pankhurst, the widow of a radical barrister, founded in Manchester a new suffragist organisation, the Women's Social and Political Union, which was closely associated with the Independent Labour Party. Churchill's decision to support votes for women may well, therefore, have been a token of goodwill towards Manchester radicalism. But the sequel was as unwelcome as it was unexpected. The W.S.P.U. began to adopt 'militant' tactics. To begin with, these were mild enough, or at any rate mild by comparison with later activities. But at the time they were regarded in respectable society as a shocking breach of lady-like convention. The W.S.P.U. decided to disrupt public meetings by interrupting speakers and staging demonstrations in the hall. Churchill was sharing a platform with Sir Edward Grey in Manchester, on 13 October 1905, when the first of the W.S.P.U. demonstrations occurred. Annie Kenney rose to ask Churchill whether, if elected, he would do his best 'to make Women's Suffrage a Government measure?' When neither Churchill nor Grey would reply, Kenney with Christabel Pankhurst started to protest loudly. Arrested outside the hall, they were convicted of assault and imprisoned after refusal to pay a fine. Replying to a letter from Royle about Christabel Pankhurst, Churchill wrote: 'I hope the quiet and seclusion may soothe her fevered brain.'[74]

If this remark is any guide, Churchill thought the women of the W.S.P.U. were off their heads. From a practical point of view they were also a nuisance. The W.S.P.U. decided to single out Churchill's meetings for attention, sabotaging whatever message he was trying to convey. 'You should endeavour to come to some understanding with them', wrote Churchill to Royle on 28 November, 'and point out how damaging their action is to their own cause. I am certainly not going to be henpecked into a position on which my mind is not fully prepared, and if I am subjected to any further annoyance, I shall say plainly that I do not intend to vote for Female Suffrage in the next Parliament.'[75] In the New Year of 1906, in the thick of the general election campaign, Churchill was beginning to make a speech when there was uproar at the back of the hall, and Sylvia Pankhurst began to shout interruptions. Churchill invited her on to the platform, where she demanded to know whether the Liberal Government would give women the vote. In the heat of the moment Churchill lost his temper and announced that in view of the treatment he had received, 'nothing would induce me to vote for giving votes to women'. But recovering himself he withdrew this remark and while trying to express respect for Sylvia Pankhurst's 'conscientious zeal', warned that he would not be 'hen pecked'.[76] Here was public confirmation of Churchill's ambivalence on the question of votes for women.

\*

So hyperactive was Churchill that even more could be said about this early back-bench phase of his career. But it is time to bring the Parliament of 1900 to a close. On 4 December 1905 Balfour took the gamble of resigning in the hope that the Liberals would be too divided among themselves to form a stable or convincing administration. On 5 December Campbell-Bannerman took office, and a stable and convincing Liberal administration was established. In the new Government, Grey was Foreign Secretary, Asquith Chancellor of the Exchequer, and Gladstone became Home Secretary. Campbell-Bannerman offered Churchill the post of Financial Secretary to the Treasury, but Churchill persuaded the Prime Minister to make him Under-Secretary to the Colonies. In the official biography Randolph Churchill commented that 'he may have calculated that he would have little chance to shine in the House with so experienced and formidable a chief as Asquith sitting at his side. On the other hand, as Under-Secretary to the Colonies he would have as his chief Lord Elgin in the House of Lords. He thus would have the management of parliamentary business . . . '[77]

Polling in the general election took place between 12 January and

7 February. On 13 January Churchill was elected for North-West Manchester with a handsome majority over the Conservative candidate, Joynson-Hicks:

| | |
|---|---|
| Churchill (Lib) | 5,639 |
| Joynson-Hicks (Unionist) | 4,398 |
| Liberal majority | 1,241 |

As later results were declared, the extent of the Conservative defeat became apparent. The Liberals had won a landslide victory with 377 seats against the Unionist total of 157. The 53 Labour MPs and 83 Irish Home Rulers were unlikely to vote with the Unionists, but even if they did the Liberals still had a commanding overall majority. On 17 January Churchill wrote to Hugh Cecil of the Tories: 'Their crowning & irretrievable disaster, wh my father always foresaw, always laboured to avert, is now upon you. More than that. There is a potent underslide sweeping us to new chores.'[78]

# 2

## The Cause of the
## Left-Out Millions

## 1905–9

From December 1905 to April 1908 Churchill was Under-Secretary at
the Colonial Office. The lion's share of his time was devoted to such
urgent problems as the restoration of self-government in the defeated
Dutch republics, the repatriation of Chinese labour, and the pacification
of the recently acquired East African Protectorate. But he never lost sight
of home affairs. When he set off, in the autumn of 1907, for a tour of East
Africa, he took with him to read on the voyage a number of books on
socialism, 'to see what the socialist case really is.'[1]

Churchill was an unlikely candidate for conversion to socialism. But
it was during his period at the Colonial Office that he first announced
his conversion to a collectivist social policy. Liberalism, he declared in
October 1906 was 'the cause of the left-out millions'. Borrowing from the
Webbs the concept he had previously rejected he continued: 'I look forward
to the universal establishment of minimum standards of life and labour,
and their progressive elevation as the increasing energies of production
permit.'[2]

At the time of this declaration there was little sign that the Liberal
Government was experimenting with new ideas. The landslide victory
of 1906 was in the main a triumph for the old Liberalism of free trade,
religious dissent, and economy in public expenditure. Social reform, as
most Liberals understood it, was a matter of reforming the licensing laws,
or amending the Education Act to eliminate the privileges of Church of
England schools.

Yet Churchill had referred to 'a potent underslide sweeping us to
new chores'. Perhaps he was thinking of the electoral pact with Labour,
and the presence in the new House of Commons of some 29 Labour

MPs. But this was not the only reason why the questions of poverty and unemployment were coming to the fore. The Protectionists, led by Chamberlain, maintained that tariffs would protect employment and raise the money to pay for social reform. Most Liberals recognised that if they were to meet these challenges they must find something new to say to the working-class electorate. For the majority of Liberal candidates, this took the form of a pledge to support the introduction of old age pensions.

The sequel is well known. Between 1906 and 1914 the Liberals created a prototype welfare state. Old age pensions were followed by minimum wages and compulsory social insurance against sickness and unemployment. Between the financial years 1907–8 and 1913–14 the expenditure of central Government on social services more than doubled from £17 million to £38 million. (The total expenditure of central Government, meanwhile, rose from £130 million to £168 million.) It was partly in order to pay for the increased cost of social policy that Lloyd George introduced radical new taxes on wealth in the 'People's Budget' of 1909.

The Liberal welfare reforms were limited and piecemeal, but out of them was to grow the universal, comprehensive welfare state of the mid-twentieth century. Perhaps that is why they have acquired an aura of historical inevitability. There were, indeed, long-term trends in politics and social thought underlying the Liberal reforms. But the specific measures introduced before 1914 were the work of a handful of civil servants and politicians. The civil servants, however, could not act without their masters: the initiative rested with ministers. In the final analysis, the factor which tipped the scales was the conjunction in Cabinet after April 1908 of Asquith as Prime Minister, Churchill as President of the Board of Trade, and Lloyd George as Chancellor of the Exchequer. In the hands of Campbell-Bannerman, Morley, Burns, Runciman or McKenna, the late Victorian state might well have carried on with a minimum of alteration.

Churchill brought a commanding intelligence to social policy, and a genuine sympathy for the poor. But the driving force was undisguised ambition. On his African journey, in November 1907, he met the Governor of Uganda, Sir Hesketh Bell. When he learnt that Bell was 43 Churchill remarked that by the time *he* was that age – in ten years' time – he would be Prime Minister.[3] The timetable was all the more pressing because of Churchill's fear that he would die young. In the meantime, as he confided to Charles Masterman in February 1908, he believed that he was called on by Providence to do something for the poor. 'Why have I always been kept safe within a hair's breadth of death,' he asked, 'except to do something like this?'[4]

The routine careerist has no ambition except to get to the top. Churchill was a careerist whose ambition was to make history. History was, indeed, almost a religion for Churchill, and historical immortality a substitute for the Christian promise of life after death. Nor was there any contradiction in his mind between making history and the unswerving pursuit of self-advancement. Under the dispensation of an all-wise Providence, they came to the same thing in the end. When Masterman, a devout Anglican, taxed him with the enjoyment of power for its own sake, he replied with a text from Deuteronomy: ' "Thou shalt not muzzle the ox when he treadeth out the corn". That shall be my plea at the day of judgment.'5

In the Parliament of 1906 the guiding star of Churchill's ambition was Liberalism. His aim was to achieve a leading position in the Liberal Party and he studied the moods and mentalities of Liberalism like a bachelor wooing his bride-to-be. His decision to take up social reform was extremely shrewd, since it was here, if·anywhere, that the party's future lay. But although Churchill was on his best behaviour as a Liberal, there was always a certain ambivalence about his politics.

As a Liberal, he spoke the language of high-minded, moralising radicalism. He attacked protectionism, imperialism, militarism, monopolies, the drink trade, the House of Lords and, of course, that fount of all evils, the Conservative party. As a newcomer to Liberalism, who was obliged to learn what others took for granted, he became a more eloquent and articulate spokesman for the party than many who were born and bred in its traditions. But who could forget his aristocratic Tory origins, his military training and imperial adventures? The weekends at Blenheim, the friendship with F.E. Smith, the landed society in which he moved, all placed a question mark over his radicalism that was accentuated by the contrast with Lloyd George. The language of radicalism, wrote Lady Bonham-Carter, was Lloyd George's native tongue, but it was not Churchill's. He spoke it 'with a difference' and the explanation was plain enough: 'Lloyd George was saturated with class consciousness. Winston accepted class distinction without thought.'6

The ambivalence was also manifest in Churchill's rhetoric and writings. This is much clearer to historians, who pore over the texts, than it was to contemporaries who judged by the headlines. Churchill alternated between radical attacks on privilege, and a conservative vision of social reform. When speaking of the measures for which he was personally responsible at the Board of Trade, he often stressed their importance as an antidote to Socialism. Similarly, he emphasised the parallels between social reform in Britain, and the reforms introduced by Bismarck in imperial Germany.

Presented in this light, social policy had much more to do with the goal of national efficiency, than the struggle for social justice.

In retrospect we can see that Churchill's politics were compounded of a radicalism that was to prove transitory, and a paternalism that was to endure. But the distinction springs from hindsight. In the eyes of contemporaries, and perhaps of Churchill himself, his politics were indivisible: the politics of a radical adventurer whose future was unpredictable.

\* \* \*

Since it bears indirectly on his approach to social reform, a word or two needs to be said of Churchill's record at the Colonial Office. By contrast with his ministerial chief, Lord Elgin, a cautious Whig, Churchill displayed a much livelier sense of the plight of the underdog in the British Empire. The historian of Churchill and Elgin at the Colonial Office writes:

> He had a generous and sensitive, if highly paternalistic, sympathy for subject peoples, and a determination to see that justice was done to humble individuals throughout the empire. He had this sympathy to a degree which was rather rare among British administrators, and even politicians, at this time . . . He insisted on questioning the colonial office assumption that officials were always in the right when complaints were made against government by Africans or, as was more probable, by Asians. He campaigned for an earnest effort to understand the feelings of subject peoples in being ruled by alien administrators "to try to measure the weight of the burden they bear." '7

This concern was mixed with a streak of political calculation. Unlike Elgin, who graced the benches of the House of Lords, Churchill had to address an overwhelmingly Liberal House of Commons that included many vociferous critics of imperialism. He needed to convince his own side that after the long, dark years of Tory reaction, a radical dawn had broken over the Empire, and was always vigilant lest some barbarous act by settlers or officials expose the Colonial Office to attack. In February 1907, for example, he was informed that 160 members of the Kisi, a Bantu tribe in the East African Protectorate, had been killed in punitive raids. In an angry minute he wrote:

> It looks like butchery, and if the H. of C. gets hold of it, all our plans in E.A.P. will be under a cloud. Surely it cannot be necessary to go on killing these defenceless people on such an enormous scale.'8

Churchill's views on social reform were characterised by a similar blend of authentic paternalism and political self-interest.

The glimmerings of Tory Democracy apart, Churchill's interest in social policy was first awakened in 1906, by the tensions arising from the Lib-Lab electoral alliance. In July he spoke on behalf of his cousin F.E. Guest, the Liberal candidate in a by-election at Cockermouth. In a touch of historical myth-making he lined himself up as a direct descendant of the Grand Old Man of Liberalism:

> We have a maxim in the Liberal party, which was first used by the late Mr Gladstone and which was the central point in the doctrines of my father, Lord Randolph Churchill. I mean the maxim: 'Trust the People.'[9]

Alas the people were not always to be trusted. Owing to the intervention of a Labour candidate, Robert Smillie, Cockermouth fell to the Conservatives.

Smillie's intervention was a violation of the spirit of the electoral agreement between Labour and the Liberals. Churchill condemned Labour for splitting the progressive vote, and warned that the Liberals might retaliate by opposing Labour candidates.[10] But second thoughts prevailed and he decided to put, as positively as he could, the argument that it was in Labour's interests to co-operate with the Liberals. Since he was due to speak in Scotland he wrote to inform the Scottish Liberal Whip, Alexander Murray, of his intentions:

> I shall certainly have to refer to the Liberal-Labour situation at Glasgow. It is a mistake to dwell on theoretical differences, except when the object is to make a difference wh. does not really exist . . . I should therefore be inclined rather to isolate the wreckers who vilify the Liberal party and hand its seats over to the Tories, than to raise any divergences between Liberalism and Socialism. We are all collectivists for some purposes & individualists for others. But what we have to deal with is not a political philosophy, but an obscure gang of malignant wirepullers.'[11]

In his speech on 11 October Churchill maintained that Labour could only succeed in alliance with the Liberals. It was being argued, he said, that there could be no progress until the Liberal party had been destroyed by Labour. But in that event the result would be, as in Germany, the triumph of a reactionary, anti-socialist movement. In Britain, property was very widely distributed:

There are millions of people who would certainly lose by anything like a general overturn, and they are everywhere the strongest and best organised millions. And I have no hesitation in saying that any violent movement would infallibly encounter an overwhelming resistance, and that any movement which was inspired by mere class prejudice, or by a desire to gain selfish advantage, would encounter from the selfish power of the 'haves' an effective resistance which would bring it to sterility and destruction.

Pursuing his argument, Churchill tried to brush aside the philosophical differences between liberalism and socialism. In order to accomplish this he was obliged to argue that in practice the Liberals were no less a party of collectivism than Labour. But this involved him in a redefinition of liberalism and he ended up making a philosophical statement after all. There was, he maintained, no hard-and-fast line between individualism and collectivism:

No man can be a collectivist alone or an individualist alone. He must be both an individualist and a collectivist ... Collectively we have an Army and a Navy and a Civil Service; collectively we have a Post Office and a Police, and a Government; collectively we light our streets and supply ourselves with water; collectively we indulge increasingly in all the necessities of communication. But we do not make love collectively, and the ladies do not marry us collectively, and we do not eat collectively and we do not die collectively, and it is not collectively that we face the sorrows and the hopes, the winnings and the losings of this world of accident and storm. No view of society can possibly be complete which does not comprise within its scope both collective organisation and individual incentive. The whole tendency of civilisation is, however, towards the multiplication of the collective functions of society.

Having manoeuvered himself on to philosophical grounds, Churchill went on to explain the policies that would follow: the taxation of unearned increment on land, the expansion of municipal enterprise, and the adoption by the state of the role of reserve employer. 'I look forward', he declared, 'to the universal establishment of minimum standards of life and labour, and their progressive elevation as the increasing energies of production may merit.'

At this point the plan of blurring philosophical distinctions collapsed.

Having proclaimed himself a collectivist, Churchill was so eager to distinguish collectivism from socialism that he set out a robust, Darwinian defence of capitalism:

> The existing organisation of society is driven by one mainspring – competitive selection. It may be a very imperfect organisation of society, but it is all we have got between us and barbarism . . . I do not want to see impaired the vigour of competition, but we can do much to mitigate the consequences of failure. We want to draw a line below which we will not allow persons to live and labour, yet above which they may compete with all their manhood. We want to have free competition upwards; we decline to allow free competition to run downwards.[12]

Churchill had stumbled into a declaration of support for the New Liberalism, which the more advanced Liberals had been advocating since the 1890s. It is instructive to compare his views with those of Lloyd George, who spoke in Cardiff on the same day. Lloyd George warned that the Labour party would sweep Liberalism away unless the Liberals dealt with the social condition of the people and the presence of widespread poverty 'in a land glittering with wealth'. But unlike Churchill, he was steeped in the radicalism of the nineteenth century. He attributed the existence of poverty to 'drink and the vicious land system', and there was no such word as 'collectivism' in his vocabulary.[13]

For Churchill in 1906, social reform was a means of cementing Lib-Lab politics. But there was also a second means: the extension of the legal rights of the trade unions. The Liberals were pledged to replace the Taff Vale Judgment with legislation conferring greater protection on the trade unions. But how extensive was the protection to be? There was some dispute about this. Asquith and the other lawyers in the government wished trade unions to be held responsible for actions by their members. But Labour MPs rejected this and proposed outright immunity from all civil proceedings against trade unions or their agents. The Prime Minister, Campbell-Bannerman came down on the side of Labour and complete immunity was conferred by The Trade Disputes Act of 1906.[14]

Technically the act restored the legal situation which had existed before the Taff Vale Judgment of 1900. But it did so in a new industrial context in which the unions possessed greater bargaining power, and the capacity for strike action on a national scale. Churchill gave a warm welcome to the bill:

> That is a great measure. The better the trade unions were organised

the more tolerant had been their conduct, the wider had been their outlook, the more frequent has been the avoidance of violent measures; and the Bill . . . is one from which nothing need be apprehended, and which should secure the support of all who value the real interests of democracy.[15]

So impressive was Churchill's performance at the Colonial Office that by the end of 1906 Campbell-Bannerman was considering whether or not to promote him to the Cabinet as President of the Board of Education. In view of the fact that the House of Lords had just wrecked the Government's Education Bill, the appointment would have placed Churchill in the very thick of the party battle, and it was a great compliment that he should be considered for it. But Campbell-Bannerman decided against: 'he is only a Liberal of yesterday, his tomorrow being a little doubtful.'[16] Education went to Reginald McKenna. At about the same time Campbell-Bannerman made a definite offer to Churchill, inviting him to succeed Bryce at the Irish Office: another highly sensitive post. According to Sir Henry Lucy, the veteran parliamentary sketch writer, Churchill indicated that he was willing, but Campbell-Bannerman had second thoughts and withdrew the offer.[17] The new Chief Secretary for Ireland was Augustine Birrell.

Churchill spent most of 1907 immersed in colonial affairs, and rarely surfaced to express himself on domestic politics. In April he appeared at Drury Lane Theatre, on a stage representing a village green overshadowed by treetops, to give an address on the favourite Liberal theme of land reform. Extolling the Government's proposals for smallholdings, and the reform of urban rating in England, he bolstered his case with the late Victorian theory of the 'physical deterioration' of the urban working-class.[18]

A companion speech on Scottish land reform, delivered at Edinburgh in May, included a forlorn appeal to Rosebery, as a great territorial magnate and former Liberal Prime Minister, to range himself on the side of social reform: 'It is a great question for him and by his action his position in history may easily be determined.' Rosebery, however, was sulking on the cross-benches of the House of Lords, resentful of a Liberal Government which had the insolence to exist without him. In August he attacked the Government's Scottish land reforms with great contempt in the House of Lords.[19] Churchill and Rosebery remained on cordial terms, but Churchill had outgrown him. Meanwhile he was making new friends: F.E. Smith, the Conservative MP for Liverpool Walton, a buccaneering barrister and fervent Protectionist; and Sir John Fisher, the First Sea Lord and genius of naval reform.

Since there was no autumn session of Parliament in 1907, Churchill was free to travel. On a jaunt with F.E. Smith, he attended the French Army manoeuvres, a sign of the unsleeping interest in military questions which set him apart from most Liberals. In October he set off on an imperial tour from which he did not return until January. Mixing business with pleasure he descended on Malta, Cyprus and East Africa. To the dismay of the Colonial Secretary, Lord Elgin, and his Permanent Secretary, Sir Francis Hopwood, who had been looking forward to an interlude of peace and quiet, Churchill sent back long memoranda on colonial policy.

When he was not interrogating local officials, or out on safari shooting twenty-three different species of wild animal in ten days, Churchill was revolving in his mind the future of domestic politics. On 13 November Campbell-Bannerman suffered a severe heart attack: a change of Prime Minister, and a Cabinet reshuffle, were obviously on the cards. On 22 December, while travelling on the White Nile, Churchill wrote to J.A. Spender, the editor of the *Westminster Gazette*, to give him 'the fruit of my Central African reflections'. Affected, perhaps, by the socialist literature he had taken with him on his travels, he predicted a political future dominated by the class struggle:

No legislation at present in view interests the democracy. All their minds are turning more and more to the social and economic issue. This revolution is irresistible. They will not tolerate the existing system by which wealth is acquired, shared & employed. They may not be able, they may not be willing to recognise themselves unable, to devise a new system. I think them very ready to be guided & patient beyond conception. But they will set their faces like flint against the money power – heir of all other powers and tyrannies overthrown – and its obvious injustices. And this theoretical repulsion will ultimately extend to any party associated in maintaining the status quo. But further, however willing the working classes may be to remain in passive opposition merely to the existing social system, they will not continue to bear, they cannot, the awful uncertainties of their lives. Minimum standards of wages & comfort, insurance in some effective form or other against sickness, unemployment, old age, these are the questions and the only questions by which parties are going to live in the future. Woe to Liberalism, if they slip through its fingers . . . [20]

When Churchill returned to England, the political scene was unsettled. Campbell-Bannerman was staging a recovery but his prospects were uncertain. Churchill seized every opportunity to advertise his ambitions in the field of social reform. 'I am prepared to work for a minimum standard of life and living', he told an audience in Manchester on 22 January. 'This is no new idea, but it is one which is taking a prominent place in politics, and one which will be the principal concern of my political life.'[21]

Churchill was now in touch with a leading young Liberal reformer, Charles Masterman. On 12 February he astonished Masterman by pouring out to him all his hopes and plans, and his belief that he was called by providence to do something for the poor. That night Campbell-Bannerman suffered another heart attack and lay confined in his room at 10 Downing Street. There was no doubt about the succession: Asquith was universally acknowledged as the next Prime Minister.

For the moment, Campbell-Bannerman refused to admit defeat, and as the weeks passed politics remained in suspense. On 7 March an article by Churchill appeared in *The Nation*, entitled 'The Untrodden Field in Politics'. This had all the appearance of a personal manifesto. There was now, Churchill wrote, a 'concentration of many different and conflicting forces on home questions ... all the more striking in contrast with the period of foreign and colonial activity to which they have succeeded.' Meanwhile, he continued, an important change had been taking place in the 'internal conception' of the Liberal party: 'It has not abandoned in any respect its historic championship of Liberty, in all its forms under every sky; but it has become conscious of the fact that political freedom, however precious, is utterly incomplete without a measure at least of social and economic independence.' Churchill believed there was a movement in progress towards a National Minimum, but that as yet it was 'a mood rather than a policy'. Identifying the problems to be tackled, Churchill pointed to the 'evils' of an unregulated labour market characterised by unemployment, casual employment, and juvenile labour: 'Swarms of youths, snatched from school in the period of life when training should be most careful and discipline most exacting, are flung into a precocious manhood, and squander their most precious years in erratic occupations, which not only afford no career for them in after life, but sap and demoralize that character without which no career can be discovered or pursued.' Looking to the future, Churchill argued in favour of Labour Exchanges to eliminate casual employment, the 'scientific treatment' of the residuum of the unemployable, the institution of Wage Boards in 'sweated industries', the use of public works to counteract fluctuations in world trade, and the expansion of technical colleges and continuation schools 'to train our youth in the skill of the hand, as well as in arts and letters.'[22] Shortly after this Churchill dined out with the Fabian socialists, Beatrice and Sidney Webb. Beatrice recorded in her diary that: 'He had swallowed whole Sidney's scheme for boy labour and employment, had even dished it up in an article in *The Nation* the week before.'[23]

\*

Churchill's thinking owed much to the radical publicists of the New Liberalism. Manchester, a stronghold of Lib-Lab politics, was his territorial base, and C.P. Scott, the editor of the *Manchester Guardian*, a mentor who ensured that his speeches were well reported. Churchill was also in touch with the circle of advanced Liberals who gathered around H.W. Massingham, the editor of *The Nation*, and attended his weekly lunches: J.A. Hobson, J.L. Hammond, L.T. Hobhouse, Charles Masterman and others. In such quarters he picked up the language of the New Liberalism, with its conception of human nature as both individualist and collectivist.[24]

Churchill was the first major politician to articulate the ideology of the New Liberalism, but it would be wrong to suppose that he was captured by Liberal thinkers. If they were making use of him, he was making use of them. The arrangement worked well enough, but Churchill was a pragmatic politician who sought ideas wherever he could find them. There is, however, no sign that Lloyd George, who was busy at the Board of Trade with the Port of London Bill, gave Churchill inspiration at this point.

With Campbell-Bannerman still clinging to his post, Asquith began to plan a new administration. Having decided that Churchill must be promoted to the Cabinet, he summoned Churchill to see him on 12 March. They discussed three possibilities: the Colonial Office, the Admiralty, and the Local Government Board. Two days later Churchill wrote to Asquith commenting on each of the three. He was enthusiastic about the Colonial Office on the grounds that he knew the work and was well qualified to undertake it. The Admiralty, he explained, he could not discuss owing to a personal difficulty – his uncle, Lord Tweedmouth, was the First Lord. But given a choice between the Colonial Office and the Admiralty, he would choose the Colonial Office. As for the Local Government Board, there was no place in the Government 'more laborious, more anxious, more thankless, more choked with petty & even squalid detail', and he had very little training in the detail of domestic politics, or acquaintance with the Poor Law. 'Dimly across gulfs of ignorance I see the outline of a policy which I call the National Minimum Standard ... I am doubtful of my power to give it concrete expression', wrote Churchill. The Local Government Board must be the 'fountain' for all the measures intended to grapple with the evils of unemployment, but 'I am sure you will find people much better qualified than I am for service in this arena.' Churchill ended his letter with the observation that such great responsibilities would attach to the Local Government Board, that the status of minister ought to be raised to that of Secretary of State.[25]

On one reading, Churchill's letter was a rejection of the Local Government Board on the grounds that domestic matters of which he knew little were unattractive to him. As he remarked at the time to his private secretary, Edward Marsh: 'I refuse to be shut up in a soup kitchen with Mrs Beatrice Webb.'[26] As the Local Government Board was a notoriously hidebound department, imbued with the mentality of the Poor Law for which it was responsible, it was unlikely to appeal to Churchill's vaulting ambition. But a second reading suggests an alternative interpretation. Churchill was ready to accept the Local Government Board on condition that it was transformed into the power-house of social policy, and the status of its minister revised accordingly. Hence Churchill's discussion of the National Minimum and all it would comprise. In spite of his protestations Churchill did, in fact, accept the offer of the Local Government Board, expecting that pensions, labour exchanges and unemployment insurance would all fall within its scope. Only at the last minute was he switched to another department.[27]

On 3 April Campbell-Bannerman resigned. As Edward VII was unwilling to interrupt his holiday in the south of France, Asquith travelled all the way to Biarritz to receive the royal commission to form a Government and upon his return to London offered Churchill the Board of Trade, which Churchill accepted. How Churchill came to be diverted to the Board of Trade is not known, but there is a plausible explanation. The Board of Trade was the department mainly responsible for labour policy. As a springboard for the National Minimum it was much more suitable than the Local Government Board, where no change of minister was made: John Burns, a trade unionist and opponent of social reform, remained at his post.

Churchill took office as President of the Board of Trade on 12 April 1908, but was unable to begin work for a month. Constitutional practice decreed that a newly-appointed Cabinet minister should be re-elected, so a by-election had to be arranged in Manchester North-West. When Churchill lost the by-election, on 23 April, he accepted an invitation to contest Dundee, a safe Liberal seat, and fought a second campaign which resulted, on 9 May, in his return to Parliament with a comfortable majority.

The two constituencies were very different. Manchester North-West was a predominantly middle class seat which had been held by the Conservatives from 1885 to 1906. Since the beginning of 1908 the

Conservatives had won three by-election victories over the Liberals and were confident of striking a major blow for Tariff Reform in the heartland of Free Trade. The Conservative candidate, Joynson-Hicks, was known to be a reluctant Tariff Reformer, but in Manchester this was probably to his advantage. The socialist candidate, Dan Irving of the Social Democratic Federation, stood without the support of the Labour party and was peripheral to the contest.

Churchill addressed himself primarily to three sections of the constituency which he feared might go over to the Conservatives: the Unionist Free Traders, the Jews and the Irish. Social reform was relegated to a minor role. As in 1906, Free Trade took pride of place in Churchill's campaign. Receiving once more the endorsement of the Free Trade League, he went out of his way to appeal to commercial interests. Manchester, he pointed out, was the historic citadel of free trade, and a Conservative victory would be interpreted as a triumph for the Tariff Reform League. Tariff Reformers had predicted that if free trade continued, the cotton trade would be ruined: but cotton exports were at a record level. He was keen to draw attention to his work at the Colonial Office in opening up new supplies of raw cotton in Nigeria and East Africa. More generally, he tried to impress on the commercial community the fact that the Liberals had reduced national expenditure and cut income tax to ninepence for everyone with an income below £2000 a year.[28]

On social policy, Churchill was defensive. He admitted that some of the Liberal Government's measures, like the Trade Disputes Act, or the Workmen's Compensation Act, were alienating middle-class voters. In the hope of allaying such anxieties, he put the case for social reform as the key to social stability. Why was it, Churchill inquired, that life and property were more secure in England than in any other country, in spite of the fact that other countries had repressive laws which were harshly enforced?

Our security of property – I put this to the businessmen of Manchester – arises from that very class struggle which you see ceaselessly going on here in this country, and of which this election is only the incidental manifestation . . .

The Government of a State is like a pyramid, and I have told you before that the function of Liberalism is to broaden the base of the pyramid and so increase the stability of the whole. There lies the true evolution of democracy; that is the true method whereby reform is always made to step in to block the path of revolution.[29]

Churchill was again successful in the quest for Jewish votes. The failure of the Liberal Government to repeal the Aliens Act was a disappointment to Manchester Jewry, but Churchill could truthfully claim that the Government had in many ways negated the act in practice. Grievances remained: the lack of 'receiving houses' at ports of entry, where immigrants could be given temporary accommodation and the high price of the naturalisation fee. Extracting a timely concession from the Home Secretary, Gladstone, Churchill announced that receiving houses would be established, and he promised to press in Cabinet for the reduction of the naturalisation fee. As polling day approached, a correspondent complained in the *Jewish Chronicle*, there was a determined attempt 'on the part of certain members of the community to coerce Jewish voters to vote for Mr Churchill'.[30]

Towards the end of his campaign, and mindful of the significant Irish vote in the constituency, Churchill announced 'a distinct acceptance of a new and advanced position on the Irish Question'. The Liberal Government had pledged itself not to introduce Home Rule during the present Parliament. But the Liberal party in the House of Commons, including Churchill, had recently voted in favour of a motion by John Redmond, the leader of the Home Rule Party, calling for the Irish people to be given 'legislative and executive control of all purely Irish affairs'. As the Government had insisted on adding the phrase, 'subject to the supreme authority of the imperial parliament', it was not at all clear whether Irish policy had changed, but Churchill claimed that it had. When the present Parliament was over, Churchill said,

'and I say this with the full concurrence and approval of my right hon friend the Prime Minister – I am strongly of the opinion that the Liberal party should claim full authority and a free hand to deal with the problem of Irish self-government without being restricted to some measure of administration and devolution of the character of the Irish Councils Bill.'[31]

Churchill was again harassed by the suffragettes, who campaigned fiercely against him and later claimed the credit for his defeat. He himself blamed the Roman Catholic priests. Joynson-Hicks and the Conservatives argued that Liberal education policy would undermine the religious autonomy of Roman Catholic schools. The priests, apparently, retaliated by urging Catholics to vote Conservative. Churchill complained of the 'sudden and organised transference of between four and five hundred Catholic votes'.[32] If this was correct, it did indeed explain

Churchill's defeat, for he lost by a narrow margin:

| | |
|---|---:|
| W. Joynson-Hicks (Con) | 5,417 |
| W.S. Churchill (Lib) | 4,988 |
| D. Irving (SDF) | 276 |
| Conservative majority | 429 |

On free trade, education, licensing, social reform and Ireland, Churchill proclaimed the same policies in Dundee as he had in Manchester. But the rhetoric was modified to take account of a potentially dangerous challenge from the Left. Dundee was a predominantly working-class city in which the jute and linen industries were the principal employers. A double-member constituency, it had returned two Liberal MPs at every general election from 1832 to 1900. In 1906 the representation was divided, by *ad hoc* agreement, between a Liberal and a Labour MP, Alexander Wilkie, the general secretary of the Ship Constructive and Shipwrights' Association. But it was still reckoned to be a safe Liberal seat. Churchill was advised by Asquith and the Liberal Whips to accept the invitation from the Liberals of Dundee on the grounds that it was 'a life seat and cheap and easy beyond all experience'.[33]

Dundee, however, was not quite as safe as it had been. The by-election coincided with a recession in the jute trade and a lock-out at the Caledon shipyard. In his study of Churchill and Dundee, Tony Paterson writes: 'Over half the population were in dire need. All the charitable organisations in the town tried to bring some relief to the desperate poverty which festered in the damp and miserable slums. Door to door collections were organised, soup kitchens were erected, farmers from the surrounding areas provided vegetables free and the local butchers donated beef and bones.'[34] Churchill was opposed by a Labour candidate, G.H. Stewart of the Post Office Workers, campaigning for the 'right to work', while on the periphery of the contest was the independent socialist Edwin Scrymgeour, a local councillor renowned for his prohibitionism. 'I am a fanatic', Scrymgeour announced, 'and we want more of them in the House of Commons.'[35]

For Churchill the risk was that by splitting the radical vote, the two left-wing candidates would deliver the seat into the hands of the Conservative, Sir George Washington Baxter. Baxter, a jute manufacturer and local philanthropist, was a Tariff Reformer campaigning on the damage done to the jute trade by German competition. Churchill, therefore, had to address himself primarily to working-class audiences and interests.

In Dundee Churchill was obliged to admit the existence of a trade recession. He retaliated by appealing to class interest:

I say to you with all solemnity that this talk about broadening the basis of taxation which you hear on every side means one thing and one thing only – it means making the poor pay more ... I believe this Tariff Reform movement constitutes the most formidable attempt to alter social balances in these islands that we have seen since the Labourers Act in the fourteenth century or the Enclosures Act in the eighteenth century, and I call upon you, upon those of you who stand forward and speak in the name of Labour, whatever else they may do or think, to set their faces like flint against an attempt which is not only to preserve the existing social balance, and that is hard enough in all conscience, but to make it more oppressive to the weak and poor throughout our country.[36]

It was a notable feature of Churchill's electioneering style that he was extremely careful about the promises he made. The poverty and unemployment of Dundee cried out for something to be done and Churchill had high hopes that he could do it. But although he appealed to the Government's record on questions like the Trade Disputes Act, or old age pensions, he made no airy promises of improvement, and avoided specific pledges. All he would say was: 'I see a wide field for State enterprise to embark upon.'

Churchill's principal tactic was to mount an aggressive attack on socialism. In a speech at the Kinnaird Hall, on 4 May 1908, he set out to show that liberalism and socialism were conflicting philosophies:

Socialism seeks to pull down wealth; Liberalism seeks to raise up poverty ... Socialism would kill enterprise; Liberalism would rescue enterprise from the trammels of privilege and preference. Socialism assails the pre-eminence of the individual; Liberalism seeks, and shall seek more in the future, to build up a minimum standard for the mass. Socialism exalts the rule; Liberalism exalts the man. Socialism attacks capital; Liberalism attacks monopoly.

Socialism, Churchill continued, was as a creed of utopian illusions, 'a monstrous and imbecile conception which can find no real foothold in the brains and hearts of sensible people.' Having stigmatised the Labour and socialist candidates as extremists, Churchill went on to argue that all moderate Labour men were Liberals at heart:

Labour in Britain is not Socialism. It is quite true that the Socialistic element has imposed a complexion on Labour, rather against its will, and has been largely supported in its actions by funds almost entirely supplied by Trade Unions. But Trade Unions are not Socialistic. They are the antithesis of Socialism. They are undoubtedly individualistic organisations, more in the character of the old Guilds, than they are in that of the smooth and bloodless uniformity of the masses.[37]

There was a much larger Irish vote in Dundee than in Manchester North-West, and local Liberals feared the defection of Irish voters to the Labour candidate, a supporter of Home Rule. The priests, meanwhile, were instructing their congregation to vote Conservative, as in Manchester. For Churchill this was a delicate problem. The Cabinet had no enthusiasm for Home Rule, and if he went too far towards promising it, Asquith would be forced to contradict him. The most that Churchill could do was to emphasise the Irish question, and to address a meeting of the United Irish League. The League, fortunately for him, was solidly pro-Liberal. Its Scottish Secretary, O'Donnell Derrick, urged Irish voters to 'make the sign of the cross opposite the name of Winston Churchill'. They seem to have done so.[38]

When the votes were counted on polling day, 9 May, Churchill was fearful of defeat. Scrymgeour's agent saw him 'standing alone in a corner twisting little rubber bands around his fingers, and as each one broke he threw it away. He was obviously in a very agitated condition.'[39] But Churchill was returned with a clear majority:

| | |
|---|---|
| W.S. Churchill (Lib) | 7,079 |
| Sir G. Baxter (Con) | 4,370 |
| G.H. Stewart (Lab) | 4,014 |
| E. Scrymgeour (Prohib) | 655 |
| Liberal majority | 2,709 |

Secure at last, Churchill took his place in Asquith's Cabinet. Shortly after this a development occurred that was to shape his career for some years to come. Churchill entered into a political alliance with the Chancellor of the Exchequer, David Lloyd George. Since their first encounter, on the occasion of Churchill's maiden speech, there had been many signs of mutual admiration. But the relationship had been intermittent and they played quite separate roles in the Government of Campbell-Bannerman. In the Asquith Cabinet their interests converged for the first time.

From very different backgrounds, Lloyd George and Churchill had both arrived at a position on the radical wing of the Liberal party. Lloyd George had preached the radicalism of dissent while Churchill was exploring the frontiers of social democracy. But Lloyd George was broadening his horizons. As Chancellor of the Exchequer he was keen to finance the social policies with which Churchill was experimenting at the Board of Trade. Both aimed to capture for Liberalism the fertile territory of social reform which must otherwise be occupied by the Labour or Conservative parties. Both wanted to increase expenditure on social policy – at the cost of economies elsewhere.

In the spring of 1908, a struggle broke out within the Cabinet over the Army estimates. R.B. Haldane, the Secretary for War, had been carrying through a series of Army reforms which included the introduction of a General Staff, and the creation, for purposes of home defence, of the Territorial Army. For service overseas Haldane planned an expeditionary force consisting of one cavalry and six infantry divisions.

When Asquith took office, he was under pressure to reduce military expenditure, and appointed a committee consisting of Lloyd George, Churchill and Harcourt, to review the War Office estimates. Lloyd George pressed hard for economies – and so did Churchill. Churchill maintained that Haldane's proposed Army was too big. The forces intended for home defence were 'at least double' the number required to deter an invader. The expeditionary force of 166,000 men was, he claimed, stronger by 42,000 than the force proposed by Brodrick in 1901, 'which was criticised and opposed by practically the whole of the present Cabinet ... No other nation has ever made so dangerous and provocative a provision as a force of 166,000 expressly ready at a month's notice to cross the seas and effect a descent upon the territory of any Power.' Churchill rounded off his critique with nine proposals for the reduction of expenditure, amounting in all to an alternative scheme of Army reform.[40]

Haldane retaliated by pointing out the many demands which the British Army might have to face at any one moment: a war with Russia over Afghanistan might coincide with a war against Germany on the Continent. Churchill replied: 'These nightmares should leave the advocates of economy undismayed. It is submitted that skilful diplomacy and wise administration should be able to prevent in the future, as in the past, such a formidable and sinister conjunction of dangers. But if diplomacy and administration should unhappily fail, it is obvious that our existing Army, whether doubled or halved, will be equally incompetent to cope with them.'[41] This extremely aggressive behaviour convinced Haldane that Churchill was trying to get rid of him, but Viscount Esher observed: 'This may be so. My idea is that Winston wanted to push to the front of the Cabinet. He thinks himself Napoleon.'[42]

The Cabinet was split, but Asquith shielded Haldane from attack and the argument died down – only to break out again over the naval estimates. Reports that Germany was expanding its naval programme led to an agitation in favour of building more dreadnoughts for the Royal Navy. By the end of July the Cabinet was again divided, with Lloyd George and Churchill insisting that four dreadnoughts would be sufficient for the current year, the First Lord of the Admiralty, McKenna, pressing for six, and the big Navy lobby outside the House calling for eight. The Financial Secretary to the Treasury, Charles Hobhouse, confided to his diary: 'Winston Churchill's introduction into the cabinet has been followed by the disappearance of that harmony which its members all tell me has been its marked feature. He and Lloyd George have embarked on a crusade against expenditure and are fighting Asquith, Grey and Haldane.'[43]

Churchill made his opposition to the arms race public. In a speech to Welsh miners in Swansea on 14 August he attacked the alarmists who predicted that a war between Britain and Germany was inevitable. There was, he maintained, 'no collision of primary interests – big, important interests' – between Britain and Germany, and there was nothing to fight about in spite of 'snapping and snarling' in the press and the London Clubs.[44] It was no coincidence that at that moment Lloyd George was visiting Germany and emphasising the need for an understanding between the two countries. But if Churchill was acting in concert with Lloyd George, the Welshman was the dominant partner. At the end of the month they were together at Llangollen as guests of the Bishop of St Asaph. One day when they were out walking Churchill suddenly exclaimed: 'You are much stronger than I: I have noticed that you go about things quietly and calmly, you do not excite yourself, but what you wish happens as you desire it: I am too excitable, I tear about and make too much noise.'[45]

*

During the summer recess, Churchill's thoughts turned briefly away from politics to private life. At a dinner party in March 1908 he had been introduced, for a second time, to the beautiful Clementine Hozier. Like Churchill himself, she was the child of an unhappy marriage. Her mother and father had parted, in great bitterness, when Clementine was only six. Estranged from her father, who died in 1907, Clementine was unsure of herself with the opposite sex and had twice broken off engagements. In

Churchill, perhaps, she found a suitor whose gaucherie and sincerity were reassuring. For Churchill it was imperative to avoid a wife who resembled his wanton and predatory mother. In Clementine he found a woman whose beauty was mingled with earnest opinions, a puritan reserve, and a readiness to follow and support him in his career.

On 11 August Churchill plucked up the courage to propose – in the Temple of Diana at Blenheim Palace – and was accepted. 'The girl literally hasn't half a penny', wrote Lady Selborne to her husband, 'so it may be regarded as a genuine love match.'[46] Winston and Clementine were married at St Margaret's, Westminster, on 12 September, with the Bishop of St Asaph officiating and Hugh Cecil as best man. According to Lloyd George, who was among the witnesses signing the register, Churchill began talking politics in the vestry.[47] After a brief honeymoon, he settled down again to the work of the Board of Trade, which had occupied him only intermittently since his appointment.

At intervals in the wooing of Clementine, Churchill was also wooing the miners – a romance that was to prove short-lived. The coal industry at this period was a colossus which employed some 900,000 men, and the mining communities of Scotland, the north of England, and south Wales, were bastions of Liberalism. Since many of the mine-owners were also Liberals, the coal industry appeared to exemplify the harmony of capital and labour upon which Liberalism was founded. Industrial relations, though sometimes fraught, were usually settled without recourse to lock-outs or strikes.

One of the long-standing demands of the miners' unions was the statutory limitation of the working day to eight hours, a measure Lord Randolph had supported in the twilight of his career. This was not so much a class demand by the miners against the colliery owners, as a plan for a producers' cartel to restrict the output of coal and put up the price to the consumer – or so its opponents maintained. Nevertheless it was pressure from the miners' unions which prompted the Asquith Government to consider the question in the spring of 1908.

The Eight Hours Bill was the work of the Home Secretary, Herbert Gladstone. Of his Cabinet colleagues, Churchill alone spoke up in favour of the bill,[48] and he championed it again on the floor of the House at the end of the debate on the second reading. Taking issue with the bill's opponents, he predicted that improvements in efficiency would offset the effects of reduced working hours, and that any fall in output would be 'temporary and transient' in character. In any case, he continued, the main argument in favour of legislation was social rather than economic:

The general march of industrial democracy is not towards inadequate hours of work but towards sufficient hours of leisure. That is the movement among the working people all over the country. They are not content that their lives should remain mere alternatives between the bed and the factory. They demand time to look about them, time to see their homes by daylight, to see their children, time to think and read and cultivate their gardens – time, in short, to live.

Churchill followed up his speech with addresses to gatherings of Scottish and Welsh miners. At a miners' gala in the Rhondda Valley, he coupled the Eight Hours Act with the cause of temperance and received, according to the Rhondda District minutes, 'thrice-prolonged applause'.[49]

The regulation of the coal mines was the responsibility of Gladstone and the Home Office. At the Board of Trade Churchill was primarily concerned with the workings of the labour market, and especially with the problem of unemployment. This had been a recurrent issue in politics ever since the 1880s. In theory the Poor Law prevented the unemployed from starving, but it was under fierce attack for its inadequacies and a Royal Commission on the Poor Law had been appointed in 1905. While the Liberal Government awaited its findings, a downturn in the trade cycle produced a sense of political urgency. As unemployment rose, the Liberals came under pressure from both Left and Right. While the Labour party campaigned for the 'right to work', Tariff Reformers revived the campaign for protectionism. The Liberals stood in need of an alternative way forward.

The Board of Trade was an excellent point of departure. The Permanent Secretary, Hubert Llewellyn Smith, was an outstanding civil servant. A Quaker, with a double first in Maths from Balliol, Llewellyn Smith had been influenced by the collectivist teachings of Jowett and T.H. Green, and taken part in the University settlement movement among the poor of the East End of London. Entering the civil service, he joined the Board of Trade and created in 1894 the Commercial, Labour and Statistical Department, which had the task of collecting statistics on wages and unemployment, and served as Whitehall's databank on the labour market. Under Llewellyn Smith's supervision, the Labour Department conducted a series of investigations into the causes of unemployment and the possible remedies. An outstanding administrator, he rose quickly to the top and was Permanent Secretary by the age of 43. Never a socialist, he was a social reformer who believed in a judicious balance between self-help and collectivism. In the words of Roger Davidson, Churchill found in him 'one of the ablest guides in Whitehall, with an unrivalled experience of the administrative terrain to be encountered.'[50] Llewellyn Smith himself was ably assisted by the head of the Labour Department, Arthur Wilson Fox, another firm believer in 'grandmotherly control by the State'.[51]

In the background, the problem of unemployment was under discussion by a Royal Commission on the Poor Law. Much attention was paid to the example of imperial Germany, where compulsory social insurance covered twelve million workers against sickness, disablement, and old age – but not unemployment. Germany also had a network of labour exchanges through which industrialists could notify unemployed workers of vacancies. Organised or subsidised by the municipal authorities, the German labour exchanges enjoyed the confidence both of the employers and the trade unions. In Britain there were voluntary trade union schemes of social insurance, and some private labour exchanges: but there was no comprehensive state system. Among those calling for the reform of the labour market in Britain was William Beveridge, a social reformer and journalist on the *Morning Post*. A tour of Germany in September 1907 confirmed his belief in labour exchanges and converted him to the principle of social insurance. That autumn he prepared research papers on these topics for the Board of Trade.[52] On 6 April, a few days before Churchill's appointment to the Board of Trade, a number of its officials gave evidence to the Royal Commission 'in favour of a voluntary system of labour exchanges combined with experimental schemes of compulsory unemployment insurance'.[53] Churchill was not ready to take action until July 1908, when he summoned a meeting at the Board of Trade attended by Llewellyn Smith, Wilson Fox, Sidney Webb and Beveridge. He announced that he proposed to adopt a scheme of voluntary labour exchanges, invited Beveridge to frame the proposals, and appointed him as a full-time official.[54] In July he circulated to several Cabinet ministers a memorandum under his own name, but mainly written by Beveridge, setting out the case for labour exchanges. Inside the Board of Trade, Llewellyn Smith was less enthusiastic, warning Churchill that 'the problem bristles with all kinds of difficulties'.[55]

Since Churchill relied so much on the advice of his officials, it may be imagined that he was no more than a mouthpiece or puppet of the civil service. But without him his officials would have been powerless. Churchill was a political entrepreneur who arrived at the Board of Trade with a prior commitment to reform. It was Churchill who decided to act in advance of the report of the Royal Commission on the Poor Law; Churchill who gave instructions for proposals to be drawn up, discussed, and submitted to the Cabinet; and Churchill who bore the responsibility for persuading the Cabinet and the House of Commons to accept them. In the shaping of policy he also made his mark. When labour exchanges were under discussion, Beveridge proposed two alternative types of scheme: one run by local authorities and the other by central government. It was Churchill who decided on a single organisation under the direction of Whitehall. He also insisted that they should be staffed by social reformers, trade unionists and others directly appointed by the Board of Trade, instead of by civil servants.[56] This bold extension of ministerial patronage was later reversed.

At this point Lloyd George lent an impetus to policy-making. On his visit to Germany in August 1908 he was deeply impressed by the German scheme of health insurance and decided that he too would enter the field of legislation. When Churchill went to stay with him at Llangollen they discussed the social programme and agreed to divide it between them: Churchill was to carry on with preparations for unemployment insurance, while health insurance was to be the responsibility of Lloyd George.[57]

At the Board of Trade, Beveridge and Llewellyn Smith set to work on a comprehensive scheme linking labour exchanges with unemployment insurance. In memoranda circulated to the Cabinet in December Churchill put forward the outline of a draft bill, of which Part I would deal with unemployment insurance and Part II with labour exchanges. Churchill explained how the two projects were connected:

> The establishment of Labour Exchanges is necessary for the efficient working of the insurance scheme; for all foreign experiments have shown that a fund for insurance against unemployment needs to be protected against unnecessary or fraudulent claims by the power of notifying situations to men in receipt of benefit so soon as any situations become vacant. The insurance scheme, on the other hand, will be a lever of the most valuable kind to bring the Exchanges into successful operation; for the employers, interested in reducing friction in the passage of workmen from job to job, and in not drawing fresh men into a trade while any man already insured in it is standing idle, will turn naturally to the use of a Labour Exchange.[58]

At the end of 1908, after more discussions with Lloyd George, Churchill agreed to revise his legislative strategy. Social insurance, he explained to Asquith, would have to be presented as a whole, so unemployment insurance must be postponed until the completion of Lloyd George's plans for insurance against sickness. This left Churchill to press on, for the time being, with the introduction of labour exchanges, but his vision of social policy extended far beyond the measures for which the Board of Trade was responsible. As he wrote to Asquith on 29 December:

There is a tremendous policy in Social Organisation. The need is urgent & the moment ripe. Germany with a harder climate and far less accumulated wealth has managed to establish tolerable basic conditions for her people. She is organised not only for war, but for peace. We are organised for nothing except party politics. The Minister who will apply to this country the successful experiences of Germany in social organisation may or may not be supported at the polls, but he will at least have a memorial which time will not deface of his administration.

Churchill went on to propose a series of measures which, he believed, the House of Lords would not dare oppose:

1. Labour Exchanges & Unemployed Insurance
2. National Infirmity Insurance etc;
3. Special Expansive State Industries – Afforestation – Roads:
4. Modernised Poor Law i.e. classification:
5. Railway amalgamation with State Control and guarantee
6. Education compulsory till 17 . . .

I say – thrust a big slice of Bismarckianism over the whole underside of our industrial system, & await the consequences whatever they may be with a good conscience.[59]

Churchill's letter gives some idea of the significance he attached to welfare reforms. They were to be constructive bipartisan measures which the House of Lords could not reject on party grounds. The question of whether or not the Government would obtain an electoral advantage was secondary. The primary purpose was to strengthen the state by organising society more efficiently.

Churchill was right to point out that many aspects of social policy were consensual, or intended to be. The Board of Trade itself maintained close contact with both unions and employers and could not afford to alienate either. Churchill, Beveridge and Llewellyn Smith were all conscious of the need to win the consent of both sides of industry. Each side feared that labour exchanges would tip the scales of the class war against them. Trade unions were fearful that labour exchanges would be used to break strikes, by supplying employers with 'blackleg' labour. Employers feared that labour exchanges would become centres of industrial discontent, encouraging workers to become more independent of their employers.

Churchill's method of overcoming this problem was to persuade each side that it would obtain the advantage. On 17–18 June, in conferences with representatives of the TUC, and the engineering and shipbuilding unions, he encouraged them to think of labour exchanges as recruiting points for trade unions and agreed to amend the bill to protect trade union principles: no worker was to suffer disqualification or prejudice at the hands of the labour exchange for refusing a vacancy created by a trade dispute, or for refusing work at rates lower than those prevailing in the trade or district. These concessions did not, of course, prevent a labour exchange from supplying labour to an employer engaged in an industrial dispute.

On 18 August Churchill met representatives of the engineering and shipbuilding employers. As José Harris writes:

> Churchill's answers to the employers were directly contrary to those he had given to the unions a month earlier. He denied that exchanges would enable unionists to bring pressure to bear on unorganised workmen, because strict and impartial discipline would be maintained among workmen waiting for a job. Moreover he pointed out that 'if anybody had said a year ago that the trade unions would have agreed to a government labour exchange sending 500 or 1,000 men to an employer whose men were out on strike ... [nobody] would have believed it at all.'[60]

There was also controversy over unemployment insurance. Over the winter of 1908–9 Beveridge and Llewellyn Smith continued to work on the subject and Churchill submitted a draft bill to the Cabinet on 17 April. As Churchill explained in an accompanying memorandum, the bill proposed to cover 2,250,000 workers in trades with a high level of seasonal and cyclical unemployment – one third of all workers in industrial occupations. Employers and workmen were each to contribute twopence a week for every worker insured and the state one and a third of a penny. Benefits were to be paid for 15 weeks only at a cost to the state not exceeding £1,000,000 per year for the first five years.[61]

When the scheme was put to the Cabinet on 26 April there was much opposition, as Churchill wrote to his wife, 'from that old ruffian Burns and that little goose Runciman'. Apparently they feared that compulsory insurance would erode self-help and lead to the abuse of the scheme.[62] A Cabinet Committee, set up to review the proposals, devoted much time to possible abuses of the system by 'malingerers', and Beveridge, as his biographer explains, 'spent the next few months closing loopholes and inventing safeguards against bogus claimants, extravagant trade unionists, the unemployable and the wilfully unemployed'.[63] In particular Beveridge proposed to disqualify from benefit workers dismissed for drunkenness and dishonesty, and workers who discharged themselves.

Churchill argued strongly against these proposals in a memorandum of 6 June 1909. He too wanted to incorporate strict safeguards against malingering into the scheme. But he preferred impersonal principles of deterrence to subjective moral judgments:

> The spirit of the Insurance Scheme is not to weaken the impulse of self-preservation, but to strengthen it by affording the means of struggle; and the fear of running through benefits, of passing out of the area of the Insurance Scheme altogether, must be constantly operative. If the same man is repeatedly unemployed, that is itself proof of demerit, and the rules of the Insurance Scheme should be so framed that men repeatedly unemployed pass out of its area and cease to enjoy its benefits . . .
>
> I do not feel we are entitled to refuse benefit to a qualified man who loses his judgment through drunkenness. He has paid his contributions; he has insured himself against the fact of unemployment, and I think it arguable that his foresight should be rewarded irrespective of the cause of his dismissal, whether he lost his situation through his own habits of intemperance or through his employer's habits of intemperance. I do not like mixing up moralities and mathematics . . . Suppose a man has a row with his employer, perhaps a person only one step higher than himself socially, or that there is ill-temper on both sides, hot words pass, the employer swears at the man, or the man at the employer, the man is dismissed and the employer refuses a discharge note and answers all inquiries in an unfavourable manner, is the Insurance Office going to accept the employer's version of what has occurred? Is the Insurance Officer going to try the case as between the two?[64]

Clearly Churchill feared that moral criteria for disqualification would be open to abuse by employers, and give rise to a mass of vexatious disputes. He was reinforced in this view by the belief that the employer's contribution of 2d. a week per employee would be deducted from wages. This meant, wrote Churchill, that in practice the workman would subscribe 4d.: 'I believe that the whole system will prove to be nothing more or less than wage-spreading.' In view of this fact, it was obviously 'contrary to sense and justice' to deprive the workman of the benefits for which he had paid. But Churchill lost the argument. Beveridge was able to show that trade union rule books incorporated similar safeguards against undeserving claimants of union benefits.

Safeguards against 'improper' claimants were incorporated in the draft bill.[65]

In the main, Churchill's Board of Trade reforms transcended party politics. When he announced his proposals for labour exchanges and unemployment insurance to the House of Commons, on 19 May 1909, they were welcomed from all sides. From the Opposition front-bench, F.E. Smith declared his support and assured Churchill that he need expect no significant opposition from the Conservative party. The decision of the Conservatives to treat Churchill's proposals as non-partisan was all the more striking in view of the fact that by this time fierce party warfare had broken out over Lloyd George's budget. For the Labour party, Arthur Henderson welcomed the proposals as a first instalment of Labour's campaign for the Right to Work. The only reservation he expressed was one of regret that the Government did not propose a more extensive scheme of unemployment insurance. When Churchill replied that the Government would take powers to extend the scheme, should it prove a success, Henderson was effusive in his response. Later on there was to be some opposition from trade unionists to unemployment insurance, but Churchill responded to this by inviting the unions to further consultations.[66]

As Churchill explained, a bill for labour exchanges was to be introduced in the current session, while unemployment insurance was to be held over until 1910, in order to dovetail with Lloyd George's scheme for health insurance. The Labour Exchanges Bill was passed by both Houses without serious debate, and the first eighty labour exchanges were opened on 31 January 1910.

Churchill's third major initiative at the Board of Trade was the statutory regulation of wages in the 'sweated trades'. In the East End of London there were a multitude of tailoring and dressmaking workshops in which the employees, mainly women, received excruciatingly low rates of pay. A minority of the employees were drawn from Jewish immigrant families: hence the anti-alien agitation of the 1890s (to which reference has already been made). Conditions in these trades were of especial concern to the rising generation of women social reformers associated with the trade unions and the Labour party. One of the first investigations was carried out by the Women's Industrial Council, which in 1898 proposed state intervention in the form of licensing. But the Australian state of Victoria had introduced a more direct form of control: Wages Boards with the power to enforce statutory minimum wages. From 1900 onwards Sir Charles Dilke introduced an annual private member's bill to create British Wage Boards, and in 1906 the *Daily Mail* mounted an exhibition to illustrate the appalling conditions in the sweated trades. The House of Commons was favourably disposed. Where the protection of female workers was concerned, it was generally thought that overriding moral principles were involved, and few MPs were prepared to endorse unrestricted market forces. Tariff Reformers welcomed the measure as a type of protectionism, reducing the alleged danger of competition from immigrant workers. On 21 February 1908, when a Wage Boards Bill was debated in the House, 'it was clear that its principle was approved by the entire House without distinction of party or class'.[67]

The regulation of factories and workshops was the responsibility of the Home Office. But the Home Secretary, Herbert Gladstone, announced that the Government could not accept the principle of a minimum wage, and that the Home Office would be unable to take on the extra administrative burden. In the summer of 1908 however, a parliamentary select committee published a report favourable to wage boards, and Churchill took over the responsibility of preparing a bill. The drafting of the bill was mainly the work of Sir George Askwith, whom Churchill had appointed to succeed Wilson Fox as controller-general of the Labour Department, with some assistance from Beveridge. Churchill circulated a preliminary memorandum to his Cabinet colleagues in January 1909, and a draft bill on 27 March. When the bill was introduced into the House of Commons on 28 April, Churchill was delighted by the response, writing to Clementine: 'The Trade Boards Bill has been beautifully received & will be passed without a division. A. Balfour & Alfred Lyttelton were most friendly to it, & all opposition has faded away.'[68]

As with unemployment insurance, the Trade Boards Act was strictly limited in the number of trades it covered, and modest in the benefits it was likely to confer. It covered four trades: ready-made tailoring, paper box making, machine lace-making, and chain-making. There was provision under the act for its extension to other trades, but for the moment some 200,000 employees were covered, of whom 140,000 were women. For each trade there was a central Board consisting of equal numbers of employers' and workers' representatives, with additional appointees of the Board of Trade.

In circulating the final draft of the bill to his colleagues, Churchill again sought to draw a clear line between the principle of the national minimum, and socialism:

These methods of regulating wages by law are only defensible as exceptional measures to deal with diseased or parasitic trades. A gulf must be fixed between trades subject to such control and ordinary economic industry. A clear definition of sweated trades must comprise (a) wages *exceptionally* low, and (b) conditions prejudicial to physical and social welfare.

Churchill also emphasised that boards would have to fix wages at competitive rates which kept workers in employment.

To screw up the home wages without a proportionate movement of factory wages might only improve the home worker into extinction. All rates in any trade must be co-ordinated to hold the balance between one district and another.[69]

Labour exchanges, unemployment insurance, and wage boards, were all devices for the long-term regulation of the labour market. But the Board of Trade also taught Churchill about the problems of cyclical unemployment resulting from fluctuations in trade. On 17 August 1908 Churchill circulated to the Cabinet a memorandum on the state of employment and trade in the first six months of the year. Owing to a recession in international trade, manufacturing exports were in decline and the level of unemployment, as measured by trade union returns, was 8.2 per cent in June 1908 as compared with 3.7 per cent in June 1906, and 3.6 per cent in June 1907. In a covering note Churchill warned that 'taking the figures of unemployment in conjunction with the shrinkage in wages and comparatively high level of food prices, it is evident that a period of unusual severity for the working classes has begun, and that conditions may become more stringent in the course of the winter.'[70]

Churchill decided that something must be done to prevent the hardships in prospect. One of his ideas was that the Admiralty should expedite the shipbuilding programme and place orders for ships on Tyneside and the Clyde, where levels of unemployment were high. Lloyd George tried the proposal on the First Lord of the Admiralty, Reginald McKenna, but without success. Churchill intervened. While honeymooning in Baveno in September 1908, he wrote to McKenna warning of the consequences of inaction: 'The distress on the Tyne and on the Clyde cannot fail to be exceptionally acute during the whole of the coming winter and will produce a grave unrest among the artisan classes greatly to the prejudice of all the most essential interests of the Government.' McKenna replied that he was indeed mindful of the situation and that the Admiralty was doing its best to place contracts as early as possible. A formal Cabinet decision to accelerate the shipbuilding programme was taken on 20 October.[71]

Churchill now developed a more comprehensive idea of contra-cyclical public works. As he explained to an audience at Dundee, on 9 October 1908:

There ought to be in permanent existence certain recognized industries of a useful, but uncompetitive character, like, we will say, afforestation, managed by public departments, and capable of being expanded or contracted according to the needs of the labour market, just as easily as you can pull out the stops or work the pedals of an organ.[72]

Churchill hoped that his officials would turn the idea into a workable scheme, but Llewellyn Smith proceeded at a cautious pace. Shortly before the budget, in April 1909, Churchill inquired what progress was being made, as he hoped to announce the plan in conjunction with the bill for labour exchanges. Llewellyn Smith replied that it would be desirable first of all to reach a conclusion about changes in the administrative structure of the Board of Trade, made necessary by coming legislation.[73] If this was an attempt to divert Churchill from the project, it did not succeed. In June he wrote a long letter to Lloyd George reproducing the idea in the most bold and imaginative terms.

Since the appointment of a Cabinet Committee on unemployment the previous October, various plans had been put forward for public works to counteract unemployment. But Churchill complained to Lloyd George that they were not yet properly 'clamped together'. Churchill's own conceptions rested on military analogies. The functions of the Board of Trade in employment policy resembled those of the Intelligence Department in the Army, which did not govern policy or command the troops, but studied war, accumulated and sifted information, and prepared plans. The Board should therefore supply the rest of Whitehall with forecasts and plans. But there should also be an executive body charged with the co-ordination of policy across the whole range of public and municipal works:

We should reproduce for the defence of this country against poverty and unemployment, the sort of machinery that we have in existence in the Committee of Imperial Defence to protect us against foreign aggression. There should be formed a Committee of National Organisation (call it what you will) analagous in many respects to the Committee of Imperial Defence. The Chancellor of the Exchequer should *ex officio* preside over the new Committee, just as the Prime Minister presides over the old; and the Presidents of the Board of Trade and Local Government Board should be *ex officio*. Members of the one just as the War Office and Admiralty Chiefs are members of the other.[74]

Little came of Churchill's brainwave. The Liberal Government never did develop the comprehensive policy and machinery he envisaged, though Lloyd George was to announce, in the 1909 budget, the creation of a development commission with the vaguely defined purpose of investing in afforestation and other national resources. But this same budget opened a new chapter of political history. At the Board of Trade, Churchill continued with his legislative programme. But it was thrust into the shadows now by the controversy over Lloyd George's plans for the taxation of wealth. In social policy Lloyd George had followed where Churchill led. In fiscal policy it was Lloyd George who led and Churchill who followed – for a time.

# 3
## The Peers Versus
## the People

### 1909–11

The Lloyd George budget of 1909 marked the beginning of a period of intense party warfare. The Conservative party employed its majority in the House of Lords to reject the budget, thus producing a constitutional deadlock between the Upper and Lower Houses. In 1910 two general elections were fought on the issue, but neither resolved it. The Conservatives failed to win, and the Liberals proceeded to introduce legislation to reduce the powers of the Upper House. But it remained to be seen whether the Upper House would consent to the reduction of its own powers. The crisis persisted until August 1911, when the House of Lords voted in favour of the Parliament Bill. But one crisis foreshadowed another. Now that the power of the House of Lords was reduced, the door was open for the introduction of Irish Home Rule, a still more deeply divisive constitutional issue.

In the course of these events, a reorientation occurred in Churchill's politics. Churchill at this period was a politician living simultaneously on two different levels. At one level he was a leading strategist in party politics. At a second level he was a departmental minister as President of the Board of Trade and, after February 1910, Home Secretary. On both levels there were clear shifts in his position between 1909 and 1911. There was a shift to the right in his attitude both to party politics, and labour and social questions. Doubtless there were connections between these two developments, though it is by no means easy to say what they were. The present chapter is concerned with the party political dimension: the labour and social questions are postponed to the following chapter on Churchill as Home Secretary.

As to the calculations that were passing through Churchill's mind, the documents provide some clues. The most important is to be found in Churchill's changing perceptions of Germany. Up to 1909 he had no expectation of a war in Europe. There was, he told a Liberal rally in the July of that year, no real antagonism between Britain and Germany: 'Don't allow yourselves, I implore you, to be led away by those foolish guides who try to make out that there is a great and fundamental collision between those two peoples. They have nothing whatever to fight about, and nowhere whatever to fight in . . . '[1] But in November 1909 he circulated to the Cabinet a report, prepared on his instructions at the Board of Trade, on the finance of the German naval programme. Churchill concluded that imperial Germany was fast approaching an internal crisis, and he posed the question: 'Will the tension be relieved by moderation or snapped by calculated violence?' As Churchill later wrote in *The World Crisis*, this was the first time he recorded a 'sinister impression' of German intentions. When the Agadir crisis arose in July 1911, Churchill and Lloyd George abandoned the radical wing of the Cabinet and joined the Liberal Imperialists – Asquith, Grey and Haldane – in a firm stand against the Kaiser. With his mind captivated by preparations for war, domestic issues began to recede in importance: 'Liberal politics, the People's Budget, Free Trade, Peace, Retrenchment and Reform – all the war cries of our election struggles began to seem unreal in the presence of this new preoccupation.'[2] Churchill's changing attitude towards party politics was also inspired by the constitutional problems arising out of the House of Lords crisis and Irish Home Rule. In particular he did not wish to see British politics subordinated to Irish questions. His object was to restore the authority of the British parties over their Irish allies and here again he seemed to be anticipating the politics of national unity.

\* \* \*

The budget of 1909 was intended to solve a political and a financial problem. The political problem was the use of the House of Lords by the Conservative party to veto Liberal legislation. The question arose again in November 1908 when the House of Lords rejected the Licensing Bill. The Liberals were furious but divided over tactics. Some favoured a direct attack through legislation to restrict the Lords' veto. Others favoured the use of financial legislation to restore the Government's authority. It was an established constitutional convention that money bills could not be amended by the House of Lords. In theory they could be rejected, but this would be a very drastic step and in the case of the budget such a step was almost unthinkable. When the Lords rejected the Licensing Bill Churchill was furious and looked to the budget as the obvious counter-measure. Sitting next to Lucy Masterman at dinner on 26 November he 'stabbed at his bread, would hardly speak ... "We shall send them up such a Budget in June as shall terrify them, they have started the class war, they had better be careful." '3 Liberals made no secret of their thinking and there was some talk among the Conservatives of a House of Lords veto. But it was hard to believe such an extreme course would be adopted. On 26 December Churchill wrote to Asquith to say that he had learnt that Lansdowne, the Conservative leader in the House of Lords, 'utterly scouts the suggestion that the Lords will reject the Budget Bill.'4

The Government's financial policy was also running into difficulties. In 1905 the Liberals had taken office as the party of economy and had succeeded at first in reducing expenditure and taxation. But in the course of 1908 the balance tilted back towards rising expenditure. The principal factors at work were a reduction in revenue due to the trade recession, the higher than expected cost of non-contributory old age pensions, and the burden of increased naval expenditure resulting from the arms race with Germany. In preparing his budget for 1909 Lloyd George faced a deficit for 1909–10 of £16½ millions.

Lloyd George decided to frame a radical budget in harmony with the New Liberalism of social reform. His strategy was to meet the deficit through increased direct taxation of the wealthiest classes, or, as we might say, to 'soak the rich'. The two principal devices were to be a more steeply graduated scale of income tax, and the introduction of land taxes. The proposals in their final form were announced by Lloyd George in his budget speech on 29 April. The standard rates of income tax were to remain where Asquith had left them in the budget of 1907. But income tax was to go up from 1s. to 1s.2d. in the pound on unearned income and incomes of more than £3000 p.a. A new supertax, of an additional 6d. in the pound, was to be levied on incomes exceeding £5000 p.a., in which case all income above £3000 p.a. was taxable. There were three new taxes on land: a tax of 20 per cent on the 'unearned increment' of land on sale or inheritance; a tax of a halfpenny per pound on the value of undeveloped land; and a 10 per cent tax on the increased value of a lease which terminated. In addition Lloyd George proposed to increase death duties by one-third, raise taxes on liquor licences and spirits, and levy new taxes on motor cars and petrol.

The making of the budget was a turbulent affair, with pandemonium at the Treasury and acrimony in Cabinet. The disturbed atmosphere was partly due to Lloyd George's erratic and intuitive method of policy-making, which appalled some of his colleagues. As Hobhouse, the Financial Secretary to the Treasury, recorded on 12 April: 'George has demanded the preparation by Depts. and Draftsmen of successive schemes of Licences, land taxation, and death duties each more impossible than the other, and every week the Cabinet has thrown out scheme after scheme ... Neither he nor the Cabinet have had time to consider details of clauses, and it was only owing to my searching scrutiny of some of his land tax proposals ... that the Govt. failed to adopt *sub silentio* an absolutely unworkable scheme.'[5]

In later years, Lloyd George liked to recall that several of his Cabinet colleagues had resisted his proposals as too extreme. Granted the tensions within Liberalism between wealth and radicalism, such arguments were always liable to break out. But Lloyd George was not the most reliable source of oral history, and the supporting evidence is thin.

What of Churchill? The budget touched and threatened the class interests of the aristocracy from which he sprang. His friends and relations would be adversely affected. But there is no documentary evidence that he opposed the radical thrust of the budget. The Cabinet, of course, kept no minutes, and Churchill wrote no letters or memoranda on the central issues. But there is a context to bear in mind. Since the previous autumn Lloyd George and Churchill had been working hand in glove with a carefully negotiated division of labour between them. As we have seen, Churchill had been muttering in private about a class war budget in retaliation against the House of Lords, and it is very likely that he and Lloyd George had agreed in advance on the general character of the budget. There was always a touch of rivalry between the two, but in the spring of 1909 all the indications were that the alliance was in good working order. Three weeks before the budget Churchill was in touch with Lloyd George over the timing and presentation of the proposals for unemployment insurance. Reading between the lines we can see that Churchill wanted to get the credit by making the announcement first, and was much put out when Lloyd George proposed to include it in the budget.[6] As a reforming and spending minister, Churchill depended on the goodwill of the Chancellor of the Exchequer. He was most unlikely to risk the future of his plans by falling out with Lloyd George. On the contrary, Churchill had every reason to support the main principles of the budget.

But his cousin, Ivor Guest, was horrified. On 4 May he wrote to protest against the harshness of the new rates of death duty as they affected his family estate. Guest complained that as the estate was settled, could not be broken up, and had a paper value far in excess of its market value, the various taxes proposed were 'onerous, capricious, and often assessed on non-existent wealth'. Churchill took up the point with

Lloyd George and proposed that landowners should be given the option of paying death duties in land. This would presumably be done by legislation to free landowners from the rules of settlement, for Churchill envisaged that as a consequence the great estates would be broken up and some of the land transferred to the ownership of the state 'for the purposes of smallholdings, village gardens, and public purposes generally'. The fact that land could be used for the payment of death duties would also serve to protect the landlord against the overvaluation of his property.[7]

These were radical proposals. The Government would actively assist the break-up of landed estates and the growth of state-owned land. But Lloyd George was reluctant to give Churchill credit for his radicalism. The day after Churchill wrote Lloyd George was motoring down to Brighton with Charles and Lucy Masterman when the conversation turned to the budget. Lloyd George spoke 'with some contempt on the idea that Winston Churchill was the author of the Budget. "Winston", he said, "is opposed to pretty nearly every item in the Budget except the 'Brat', and that was because he was expecting soon to be a father himself." '[8] This was probably malice on Lloyd George's part. Although Churchill was the first cousin of the Duke of Marlborough, he had no great attachment to the cause of the landed estate. Travelling through western Germany in September 1909 he was impressed by the prosperity of agriculture and manufacturing, and the absence of park walls and country seats. As he wrote to Clementine: 'All this picture makes one feel what a dreadful blight & burden our poor people have to put up with – with the parks and palaces of country families almost touching one another & smothering the villages and industry.'[9]

The budget proposals alienated Liberal financiers in the City of London, and were denounced by the ever more futile Rosebery as 'inquisitorial, tyrannical and Socialistic'. The Conservatives, meanwhile, declared war on the budget and campaigned against it both inside and outside the House of Commons. Now, they believed, was the moment to strike down Free Trade finance. They attacked it as a threat to property and capitalism – the thin end of the socialist wedge. From his sickbed in Birmingham, the crippled Joseph Chamberlain urged on the forces of Tariff Reform, and called for the House of Lords to reject the budget. A Budget Protest League was formed under Conservative auspices, and the Liberal party replied with the Budget League, of which Churchill was appointed President.

The budget, and the constitutional issues arising from it, dominated British politics from May to December 1909. There is no need to follow Churchill every step of the way, or to examine all the arguments he employed. But some features of the budget campaign deserve to be highlighted.

Churchill frequently emphasised the moderation of the budget proposals. Distinguishing between the wealthier classes, the middle classes and the working classes, he acknowledged that the budget would place a greater burden on the wealthy. But he replied forcefully to Conservative allegations that landlords and capitalists were about to be ruined by socialist measures, and business confidence destroyed. He pointed out that while the capital wealth of Britain had been increasing rapidly in recent years as had income from profits and salaries, wages had risen much more slowly. The choice was between wealth and wages, and in view of the accumulation of wealth over the previous ten years, it was reasonable to ask for a contribution from the wealthy. But in the budget the working classes were also to make a contribution, through higher duties on whisky and tobacco which accounted for almost half of the increase in revenue:

> While the working classes have borne the extra taxation upon their tobacco and whisky in manly silence, rage and fury is poured upon the Government by the owners of this ever-increasing fund of wealth, and we are denounced as Socialists, as Jacobins, as Anarchists and Communists, and all the rest of the half understood vocabulary of irritated ignorance.[10]

Besides, Churchill asserted, the taxes on wealth were modest and would be unlikely to affect the standards or amenities of the rich: 'Be sure of this – after the taxes which this budget imposes are in force our island will still be the best place in the world for rich people to dwell in . . . '[11] As for the middle classes, Churchill said little of them, except to remark once or twice that they were not substantially affected by the budget. Churchill employed the phrase 'middle classes' loosely and there are problems of definition here. But the historian of the People's Budget, Bruce K. Murray, endorses the judgment. The budget, he writes, was carefully designed 'to avoid directly antagonising the bulk of the middle classes'. There were to be no large new tax demands upon small traders, white-collar workers or the majority of professionals.[12]

While this may have been the intention of the budget, the Conservatives did their best to rattle middle-class voters by painting the budget as an assault on property. In response, Churchill resorted repeatedly to two lines of defence. First was the Whig thesis about the security of property, to which he had already given an airing at the Manchester by-election of 1908. Churchill now reworked the argument with a moral flourish. As he told a gathering of Scottish Liberals in October 1909:

The security of property depends upon its wide diffusion among great numbers and all classes of the population, and it becomes more secure year by year because it is gradually being more widely distributed ... I speak of the immediate security of property, but the security of property over long periods of time requires another condition. It must be supported by the moral convictions of the people and if those moral convictions of the nation are to be retained there must be a constant and successful effort to reconcile the processes by which property is acquired with ideas of justice, of usefulness, and of general benefit.[13]

Churchill was arguing that a measure of social justice was in the long-term interests of property and privilege. This was a far cry, of course, from radical conceptions of social and economic equality.

The second line of defence was to strike a patriotic and imperial note with the rhetoric of national efficiency:

We have had over here lately Colonial editors from all the colonies of the British Empire ... Is it not impressive to find that they are all agreed – coming as they did from Australia or Canada or South Africa – that the greatest danger to the British Empire and to the British people was not to be found among the enormous fleets and armies of the European Continent or in the solemn problems of Hindustan? It is not in the Yellow Peril or the Black Peril, or any danger in the wide circuit of colonial and foreign affairs. It is here in our midst, close at home, close at hand, in the vast growing cities of England and Scotland, and in the dwindling and cramped villages of our denuded countryside. It is there you will find the seeds of Imperial ruin and national decay.[14]

A master of precision when he wished to be, Churchill loved to create such atmospheric impressions. A decaying society, an imperial race in decline – here were right-wing anxieties, skilfully interwoven with the radical rhetoric of social justice.

Churchill was at his most rigorous and logical in expounding the fiscal principles on which the budget rested. Lloyd George had grasped intuitively the ideas of J.A. Hobson and the New Liberalism, and incorporated them in his budget proposals. But as Peter Clarke points out, it was Churchill who 'voiced the intellectuals' concerns most effectively, and this because he had evidently taken the trouble to understand their arguments'. The Conservatives alleged that the budget was anti-capitalist. Churchill replied that it was intended to discriminate between the profits of enterprise and investment, and the profits accruing to inheritance or the passive ownership of land. The land taxes, in particular, were designed to appropriate a share of the unearned increment of the urban landlord: agricultural land was exempt as long as it remained in agricultural use. The Liberals were restating their traditional claim to represent the 'industrious classes' against the idle rich. As Churchill explained to a party rally in Leicester in September 1909, the state was now adopting a new attitude towards wealth:

> We do not only ask today: "How much have you got?" We also ask: "How did you get it?" Did you earn it by yourself, or has it just been left to you by others? Was it gained by processes which are in themselves beneficial to the community in general, or was it gained by processes which have done no good to anyone, only harm? Was it gained by the enterprise and capacity necessary to found a business, or merely by bleeding and squeezing the owner and founder of the business? Was it gained by supplying the capital which industry needs, or by denying, except at an extortionate price, the land which industry requires?

When a collection of Churchill's speeches entitled *Liberalism and the Social Problem* was published in November 1909, they were applauded by J.A. Hobson as 'the clearest, the most eloquent, and the most convincing exposition' of the New Liberalism.[15]

One of the major differences between the Old and the New Liberalism was, of course, the purpose to which revenue was put. Churchill explained that the budget was an integral part of a 'far-reaching plan of social organisation designed to give a greater measure of security to all classes, but particularly to the labouring classes'. Much of the litany was familiar by now: unemployment insurance, labour exchanges, old age pensions, and so on. But Churchill also gave considerable prominence to the Development Bill which, he believed, would further his plan for the use of public works to counteract unemployment. The bill empowered the Government to set up a fund for economic development to spend on afforestation, roads, harbours and other public works. In the Leicester speech Churchill said:

> I should like to draw your attention to a very important clause in that bill, which says that the prosecution of these works shall be regulated as far as possible by the conditions of the labour market, so that in every bad year of unemployment they can be expanded so as to increase the demand for labour at times of exceptional slackness and correct and counterbalance the cruel fluctuations of the labour market.[16]

The summer and autumn of 1909 were a very tense period in party politics. There was no summer recess: day by day the budget made its way through the House of Commons against a background murmur of diehards exhorting the Lords to reject it. On 16 July Lord Lansdowne, the Leader of the Conservatives in the Upper House, delphically pronounced that Conservative peers 'would not swallow the Finance Bill whole without mincing'. Speaking at Edinburgh the next day Churchill declared that the Government would accept no changes to the Finance Bill after it had completed its passage through the House of Commons. But then he overreached himself by threatening a dissolution of Parliament if the Lords attempted to amend the bill.[17]

A brief but incandescent row followed. Churchill had spoken as though the Cabinet had already decided its policy, and the royal prerogative were in the Government's pocket, but he had consulted neither Asquith nor King Edward VII. Fire and brimstone descended on Churchill's head from Buckingham Palace and 10 Downing Street. At the Cabinet, Churchill protested that he had been misunderstood. But as Asquith reported to the King: 'The Prime Minister, with the general assent of his colleagues, pointed out that unauthorised statements on matters of high policy made by an individual minister without previous consultation, and purporting to speak on behalf of the Government, are quite indefensible and altogether inconsistent with Cabinet responsibility and ministerial cohesion.'[18]

Asquith preferred to treat the rejection of the budget by the Lords as unthinkable: a constitutional outrage so great that the peers would never dare to commit it. Nor, at first, did most leading politicians expect it to happen. But it was obvious from their speeches in the summer of 1909 that Lloyd George and Churchill were determined to inflict a humiliating defeat on the Lords and hence on the Conservative party and Tariff Reform. On 30 July Lloyd George raised the stakes in a speech at Limehouse in which he attacked dukes and landlords to such good effect that Edwardian plutocracy was deeply offended. Edward VII complained that Lloyd George's language was 'calculated to set class against class and to inflame the passions of the working and lower orders against people who happened to be owners of property.'[19] On the Conservative side, attitudes hardened. The Tariff Reformers looked forward to the opportunity of forcing a general election, while Lloyd George and Churchill, confident that the budget was popular and the right ground on which to fight, looked forward to a showdown. On 4 November the third reading of the Finance Bill was carried in the House of Commons. On 30 November the Bill was rejected in the House of Lords by 350 votes to 75.

The House of Commons was prorogued and a general election campaign began.

In spite of the constitutional conflict, the underlying struggle in the general election would be between Free Trade and Tariff Reform, as in 1906. Churchill's tactics reflected this. In November he refreshed himself on the subject by examining the arguments put forward in John Stuart Mill's *Principles of Political Economy*. Taking the example of the imposition of import duties on German linen, Mill had noted several disadvantages but argued that in theory the foreigner would pay. Churchill took issue with Mill in a memorandum sent for comment to the Commercial and Labour Department of the Board of Trade: 'The fault in the argument appears to me to consist in tracing with great precision all the consequences which follow a rise in the price of German exports in the English market, and omitting to trace the similar consequences which would follow upon a rise in the price of British exports in the German market.' In Churchill's opinion, Mill had missed the point: the one major disadvantage resulting from an import duty would be a reduction in the volume of Anglo-German trade. Churchill, however, was not advancing dogmatic opinions. He wanted his advisers to criticise his critique of Mill, in order to discover where the truth of the matter lay.

The episode helps illuminate the working of Churchill's mind. Churchill had a powerful intellect which he could apply to economic arguments. But in the final reckoning he was not sure of himself, and relied on the experts to correct and guide him. To Churchill, arguments were the ammunition of electoral warfare, and he proposed to equip himself with the most effective firepower. John Stuart Mill might be a famous name, but as an arsenal of rusty weapons he was of no use to a fighting politician. Churchill did, however, quote Mill in Manchester in support of the taxation of unearned increment on property.[20]

Mill's use of linen to illustrate his case was of some relevance to Churchill. Linen and jute were the principal industries of Dundee. But more to the point, the textile trades were at the core of the Free Trade interest. Churchill still retained his links with Lancashire and the cotton trade. In preparation for a ten-day 'pilgrimage' around Lancashire, he made sure that he was fully briefed by his officials. In a memorandum to the Commercial Department of the Board of Trade, on 18 November, he listed the towns in which he was due to speak and continued:

Please let me have a note on the trade and labour conditions in each of these towns, the special industries, their state at the present time,

new industries or mills recently started, and any other matter which
may strike you as likely to be useful to me.

2. Prepare me some statistics dealing with the British and German
cotton industries, showing their respective size, exports to protected
and neutral markets, growth by value, by bulk and by spindles etc.

3. Let me have a short note on the trade of Lancashire as a whole.

4. Compare the trade activity of Lancashire, exports, imports, etc.,
per head of the population with the trade activity of great protected
countries.

5. If an average of 10 per cent were imposed on imports of foreign
manufacturers mention what articles or categories of articles would be
included in schedules which are used in the cotton industry. To what
extent are flour and leather used?[21]

According to the myth of British constitutional history, civil servants were
strictly neutral in matters of party politics. But just as Treasury officials
had briefed Churchill against Tariff Reform in 1903, so now the officials
of the Board of Trade were happy to brief him for the same purpose in
1909.

Churchill's Lancashire tour of December 1909 was a triumphant revival
of 1905–6, but with a difference. Free trade was the underlying issue, but a
subordinate one, eclipsed by the politics, however theatrical and contrived,
of class conflict: the budget and the struggle between the Government and
the House of Lords. Churchill dealt belligerently with the peers, exploiting
to the full the democratic theme of the conflict between an elected House
of Commons and an Upper House consisting (except for bishops and law
lords) of hereditary legislators.

When he challenged the Conservatives to justify the character and
composition of the Lords, a reply was attempted by Lord Curzon,
who asserted the superior wisdom of hereditary legislators, and quoted
the maxim of Renan: 'All civilisation has been the work of aristocracies.'
Churchill tore this to shreds. Christianity, he pointed out, had originated
among the poor. As for the arts, 'what great picture was ever painted by
a duke?' Science and mechanical invention had developed outside the
charmed circle of the aristocracy. Many great generals had become peers,
but few peers had become great generals. Curzon had remarked on the fact
that so many Prime Ministers and holders of other important offices had
belonged to the House of Lords rather than the House of Commons. 'I
can quite believe that', Churchill replied. 'It only shows the undue political

authority which has been engrossed all these years by a small, limited, and unrepresentative political class.'[22] Churchill's language was usually dignified but in the middle of an election campaign he could sling mud with the best of them. In a speech at Glasgow on 10 January 1910 he described the Upper House as 'filled with doddering peers, cute financial magnates, clever wire pullers, big brewers with bulbous noses. All the enemies of progress are there – weaklings, sleek, smug, comfortable, self-important people.'[23]

Following his tour of Lancashire, Churchill spoke in many parts of Britain. In Dundee his appearances were fleeting, but when polling day arrived on 22 January he and his running mate, Alexander Wilkie, were returned by predictable and substantial majorities:

| | |
|---|---|
| Winston S Churchill (Lib) | 10,747 |
| A. Wilkie (Lab) | 10,365 |
| Seymour Lloyd (Con) | 4,552 |
| Glass (Lib Unionist) | 4,339 |
| Edwin Scrymgeour (Prohib) | 1,512 |

In Dundee, Churchill had increased his majority. In Lancashire, where he had campaigned so vigorously, the Liberals won several seats from the Conservatives. But these results reflected the growing appeal of the Liberals to the industrial working-class. Elsewhere, and especially in the south of England, the Liberals were vulnerable as middle-class voters returned to the Conservatives. The Conservatives, in fact, made a sweeping gain of 116 seats, increasing their representation in the House to 273. The Liberals, with only 275 seats, lost their overall majority. For their continuation in office they depended upon the support of 41 Labour MPs, and 71 Irish Nationalists, but it was far from certain that the Irish would sustain the Government. As practised by Lloyd George and Churchill, the politics of social reform may have done more to diminish than to increase support for the Liberal party.

\*

In the weeks following the general election of 1910, the Liberal Government almost collapsed. The Liberals depended for their majority upon two other parties: the Irish Nationalists and Labour. The Labour party threatened to withdraw its support unless the Government introduced legislation to reverse the Osborne Judgment of 1909, which made the trade union political levy illegal. But this was bluff. Labour could not do without the Liberals. The Irish, at a pinch, could.

The alliance between the Liberals and the Irish Nationalists was a purely tactical one, and quite implausible in some ways. 'It is one of the supreme ironies of modern British history,' writes Professor Gilbert, 'that the normal allies of the Irish Nationalist party were not the Conservatives, with whom they agreed upon clerical education, licensing, occupier land purchases, local government reform, and even tariffs, but rather the Liberals, the party of secular education, temperance, and Parnell-murdering nonconformity.'[24] In Ireland, the liquor and licence duties proposed in the 1909 budget had made the Liberals more unpopular than ever.

As long as the House of Lords retained its power to veto legislation, Irish Home Rule was impossible. John Redmond and his party were therefore determined that if the Government failed to act against the House of Lords, they would bring it down. In a menacing speech on 11 February Redmond served notice that unless the Liberals introduced a bill to abolish the Lords' veto, the Irish would vote against the budget.

When the Cabinet reassembled in February, ministers did not know whether or not the Government would survive, and an early general election was expected. Nor could they agree how to proceed over the House of Lords. It was generally accepted that whatever solution was adopted, the Upper House must lose its power of veto over money bills. Beyond this, there were two principal alternatives. The first, known as the 'suspensory veto', was to retain the existing hereditary composition of the House of Lords but replace the veto with a more limited power of delaying legislation, in effect for a period of up to three years. This had been proposed by Campbell-Bannerman in 1907, adopted as a resolution by the House of Commons, and reiterated as Liberal policy ever since. The principal Conservative objection to the veto was that it would create a single chamber legislature, thus unbalancing a balanced constitution. But Campbell-Bannerman had taken this into account by proposing that the duration of Parliament should be reduced from seven years to five. This would give the House of Commons less opportunity of overriding the Lords.

A handful of Labour and Liberal MPs favoured the outright abolition of the Lords, but most politicians recognised that some assembly was needed to limit and revise the House of Commons. The constructive alternative was to reform the composition of the Upper House, and there was an obvious radical case for abolishing hereditary legislators and replacing them by a more representative body. But as Halevy explains, there were two possible drawbacks to this approach. 'On the one hand it was a difficult problem which it would take time to settle, and the previous November had made it clear that a settlement of the relations between the two Houses could not be delayed. And on the other hand there was a danger that such reform by making the constitution of the House of Lords less of an anachronism might strengthen its position in face of the Commons.'[25]

Churchill's first reaction was to press, in company with Grey, Haldane, McKenna, Runciman and Crewe, for a reformed second chamber. As he saw it, the main considerations were tactical and electoral: 'There is only one question: How to bring the party into a general election against the House of Lords on the best possible grounds.' Churchill favoured concessions to the Irish over the budget, followed by a bill to establish 'an elective second chamber based upon the Parliamentary suffrage'. When the Lords rejected this, the Government would dissolve and hold a general election on the principle of the abolition of hereditary legislators.[26]

Churchill followed up this advice to his colleagues with proposals for the reconstitution of the Upper House. Personally, he wrote, he would not be frightened of a single chamber system.

> The stability of this country does not depend upon its form of Government, but upon the general balance of the nation, the diversity of interests, the ever-widening diffusion of property, and the intelligence and strong character of the British people. The masses of wage-earners have only to vote once or twice with some approach to solidarity to do anything they like with our Parliamentary machinery.

But Churchill went on to admit the merits of the case for a second chamber, to revise legislation from a non-party, 'or at least from a differently constituted party point of view, and to interpose the potent safeguard of delay. I recognize also its soothing effect upon large classes, who fear that their special interests may be ill-treated by the House of Commons.' A few sentences later Churchill went on to express a less elevated view. 'When we speak of a reformed Second Chamber, what we mean is a Second Chamber which will enable us to pass Home Rule, Welsh Disestablishment, Plural Voting and other Party bills. What the Conservatives mean is a Chamber which will enable them more effectually to resist these measures.'

Churchill – who did not claim originality for his plan – envisaged an Upper House of 150 members: 100 elected by 'very large constituencies', who would co-opt, in strict proportion to party strengths another 50 members. Elections were to be held every eight years, while the House of Commons was to adopt the quinquennial system, with elections every five years. All candidates were to be selected from a panel of those automatically qualified by a period of public service in the House of Commons, local government, or some other area of public life. To lend the new House an imperial dimension, there were to be two non-voting representatives of each of the Dominions. The second chamber would possess a suspensory veto on all legislation up to the third year.[27]

Electoral systems are seldom neutral in their effect upon the parties. Churchill's proposal would have abolished the built-in Tory majority in the Upper House and created a party political assembly elected at eight year intervals. The plan would also have entailed the creation of 50 double-member constituencies, with the intention, it may be guessed, of enabling the Liberal and Labour parties to extend the kind of electoral arrangement which worked so well in Dundee. Whether or not this followed, there would now be the fruitful possibility of a Liberal Upper House delaying the legislation of a Conservative House of Commons.

When Parliament met on 21 February Liberal morale suffered two swift hammer blows. The majority of Liberals, whether in the House or the constituencies, were strongly in favour of the Campbell-Bannerman proposals for a suspensory veto. They were dismayed when the King's Speech indicated that the Cabinet were undecided between the veto and reform of the second chamber. But worse was to come. No matter what the House of Commons proposed, the Conservatives in the House of Lords were certain to argue that there was no electoral mandate for it. They would reject any bill touching the powers or composition of the Upper House. In the final analysis, the only means by which the Government could overcome the opposition of the Lords was by creating, or threatening to create, enough new peers to swamp the Tory majority. Some 520 new peers would have to be created. But this in turn could only be accomplished with the consent of the King, Edward VII. During the election campaign Asquith had strongly implied, without actually saying so, that he had in his pocket a promise from the King to create the necessary number of peers. On 21 February he was forced to admit to the House that he had never received such an assurance. The whole truth would have been even more devastating: the King had written to him stipulating that he would be unwilling to create more peers until after a second general election.

The Liberal party, and Asquith's Cabinet colleagues, were dismayed. On the afternoon of 25 February the Cabinet reached the brink of resignation but were dissuaded by Lloyd George and Churchill – or so Lloyd George claimed that evening.[28] The Government staggered on. Churchill was advised, in no uncertain terms, that Lancashire Liberals would not accept a policy of House of Lords reform. 'People simply won't listen to it', wrote C.P. Scott. 'The fighting spirit of the party is still strong, but if they are not strongly led & speedily it will evaporate and we may whistle for our North of England majorities.' 'At present', wrote William Royle, '*everyone* is dead set against any reform of the House of Lords.'[29] So extensive was party discontent that in the circumstances there was nothing for it but to stage a retreat. Churchill and the other ministers who favoured a reformed second chamber agreed to go ahead at once with the Campbell-Bannerman formula, and a Cabinet committee was formed to draft veto resolutions to put before the House. On the long-term question, ministers agreed to differ for the time being. Churchill refused to let the matter drop. In a speech at the Free Trade Hall, Manchester, on 19 March, he supported the abolition of the veto but attempted to rally the Liberal party in favour of reform of the second chamber. 'A system whereby important and peculiar political privileges are to be transmitted from father to son, generation after generation, to the remote end of time, are to be enjoyed and exercised irrespective of the merits, the intelligence, or the character of the descendants, and utterly regardless of the wishes of their fellow subjects, is in my judgment not a system which can be left untouched in any scheme of democratic policy.' Entire passages of the speech were taken, with hardly a word altered, from his Cabinet memorandum of 14 February. Reiterating the view that he personally would not be afraid of a single chamber system, he threw in a quotation from Lord Randolph: 'I have never feared the British democracy. Give me a fair arrangement of the constituencies and one part of the United Kingdom will correct and balance the other.'[30]

Shortly after this, Churchill was forced to abandon House of Lords reform. The Cabinet committee on the subject recommended the policy of the veto and the dissident ministers were overruled by the full Cabinet. The only concession towards them was an agreement that the preamble to the Parliament Bill should declare the Government's commitment to undertake fundamental reform 'hereafter'. The 'hereafter' was never to be.

On 30 March Asquith invited the House of Commons to accept three resolutions representing the Government's policy. The first declared that the House of Lords should have no right to reject or amend a Money Bill; the second that the House of Lords should not be able to reject a bill more than twice in one session; and the third – a counterweight which increased the importance of the delaying power – that the duration of Parliament should be restricted to five years. Churchill, in a speech on behalf of the resolutions, warned that if the Liberal party were denied the power to govern, 'those who are grouped now under the standard of party will reform themselves in those evil days under the standards of class. The class line must become, if the party system is shattered, the line of demarcation.'[31]

The resolutions were passed with the support of the Irish Nationalists, and Asquith went on to promise that in the event of the rejection of the resolutions by the Lords, the Government would seek guarantees from the King in advance of a general election. This was enough to satisfy Redmond and the Irish. They voted in favour of the resolutions, and in a critical vote on 18 April, in favour of the 1909 budget, including the whisky duty. The Government had survived the immediate crisis, but it was clear that another clash with the Lords, followed by another general election, were on the cards.

On Friday 6 May King Edward VII died. Such was the mystique of monarchy that against a backcloth of official mourning, party politics appeared suddenly to be quite unseemly. The editor of *The Observer*, J.L. Garvin, seized the opportunity of flying a favourite kite. In his weekend editorial he called for a constitutional conference between the parties, to resolve the deadlock over the House of Lords. There ought to be, he argued, 'a Truce of God' in order to spare the new King, George V, from involvement in party politics. Garvin was a strong Conservative and Tariff Reformer, but he was not acting from narrow party motives. In another editorial, the following Sunday, he argued that constitutional reform would open the way to an agreed programme of social reform, to be carried by a Liberal Cabinet with the full consent of the Conservatives. Behind this plan lay the hope of converting the Liberal Cabinet to imperial preference. Joseph Chamberlain, from his sickbed in Birmingham, was persuaded to give his blessing to Garvin's initiative.[32] In close touch with Garvin, and full sympathy with his strategy, was another disciple of Joseph Chamberlain, F.S. Oliver, a leader writer for *The Times*.

Attention focused on the proposal for a conference to resolve the deadlock over the House of Lords. There was something in this for both parties. For the Conservatives there was the chance of reopening the question of the House of Lords, and settling it on terms more favourable to themselves. For the Liberals there was the opportunity of wriggling off a painful hook. They suspected that the new king was a not-too-simple Tory who would drag his feet over the question of 'constitutional guarantees'. If he did so, an early general election could be nothing but disastrous. The Liberals would have to go to the country on the issue of the House of Lords, but without a commitment from the King to create peers. To cut a long story short, the party leaders agreed to a series of private constitutional conferences, and between 17 June and 29 July, when the summer recess intervened, thirteen meetings took place. There were four representatives from each party: Balfour, Chamberlain, Lansdowne and Cawdor for the Conservatives, and Asquith, Lloyd George, Birrell and Crewe for the Liberals. The negotiations, which quickly resolved themselves into a debate over the powers the House of Lords would possess in relation to a bill for Irish Home Rule, were a delicate exercise, conducted and prolonged on both sides for tactical purposes.

Churchill was outside the proceedings but optimistic about the outcome. In conversation with his father's old friend, Wilfred Scawen Blunt, on 31 July, he confided that he expected the Liberals to remain in office for five years:

> The general election will be held in March, & he hopes to get an agreement for Home Rule between the two parties & a sort of agreement about the House of Lords which will enable the two parties to take turns of office without any revolutionary change.[33]

When the summer recess arrived on 2 August there was still no sign of agreement between the parties. The apple of discord was Irish Home Rule, though ostensibly the discussion was about the powers of the House of Lords to deal with constitutional legislation.

Churchill set off for a Mediterranean cruise on board a yacht belonging to his old friend Baron De Forest. Known as 'Tuty', the Baron was the adopted, illegitimate son of the Austrian Jewish banker, Baron Hirsch. The friendship was hereditary, for Hirsch had been one of Lord Randolph's companions, and Churchill had known 'Tuty', who was five years younger, since boyhood. In the general election of January 1910, Churchill had spoken on his behalf at Southport, where De Forest had stood, unsuccessfully, as the Liberal candidate. Churchill, it should be added, loved the company of raffish adventurers like 'Tuty'. In plutocratic, cosmopolitan circles he found a release from the gentlemanly monotony of English culture.

While Churchill was cruising the Mediterranean, Lloyd George was thinking out an audacious proposal for a Grand Coalition Government. In a memorandum of 17 August, he criticised the party system for playing into the hands of the extremists on both sides, with pernicious consequences for the settlement of difficult and complex problems of government. Lloyd George argued that a coalition, free of such influences, would be able to carry out an extensive social programme on the basis of compromise. The Conservatives would be asked to endorse the Liberal domestic programme, including Lloyd George's national insurance scheme, in return for somewhat vaguely defined concessions on tariffs, compulsory military training, and imperial policy. The plan was a genuine invitation to the Conservatives to negotiate a deal, and was therefore secret. There was no element of public posturing, and nothing was revealed until many years later. From Lloyd George's point of view, there was much to be said for the idea. As a radical pragmatist who liked to get things done, he was genuinely frustrated by the constitutional crisis and keen to get it out of the way. But this could only be done by outmanoeuvring the Irish. As long as they were in a position to play off one party against the other, Irish Home Rule would block the path of constructive social action. A coalition would free the Liberals of dependence on Redmond and his party, and enable the Cabinet to impose an Irish policy. As for his own personal ambitions, Lloyd George kept his calculations entirely to himself. But if a scheme so startling and revolutionary were to succeed, Lloyd George might well expect the premiership as a reward for his services.

The first to be taken into Lloyd George's confidence was his principal ally Churchill, who returned from holiday at the end of September. Inviting Churchill and his wife to stay at Criccieth, Lloyd George explained that he wanted to talk over Government strategy: 'I am perfectly certain that our more important associates have no plan of operations in their minds. This aimlessness, if persevered in, means utter disaster . . . I think it is just the time when we ought to be thinking out our next step (a) if Conference succeeds, (b) if it fails. I have some ideas, and I think they are winning ones; in fact, I have two alternative sets of ideas.'[34]

Lloyd George put his ideas to Churchill on the golf-course – or so he was later to tell Lord Riddell:

> I said to Winston, 'I have two alternatives to propose – the first to form a coalition, settle the outstanding questions, including Home Rule, and govern the country on middle lines which will be acceptable to both parties but providing measures of moderate social reform. The other, to formulate and carry through an advanced land and social policy.' Mrs Winston, who was there, said, 'I am for the second.' Winston replied, 'I am for the first.' L.G. said to me, 'I shall never forget the incident. We were playing golf at Criccieth. Winston forgot all about the game and he has never forgotten our conversation.'[35]

Churchill was captivated by the idea of coalition, and poured out his enthusiasm to Charles Masterman, who was horrified by the thought of a moral surrender to Conservatism. 'Winston keeps on discussing it with Charlie', wrote Lucy Masterman on 12 October, 'and meets all Charlie's objections with "Oh, you are in one of your soup kitchen moods!" He got more and more passionate in favour of it, praising government by aristocracy and revealing the aboriginal and unchangeable Tory in him.'[36]

In his enthusiasm for a coalition, Churchill did not propose to abandon social reform. On the contrary, he intended that he and Lloyd George should carry their alliance into a coalition and, as he wrote, 'impart a progressive character to policy'.[37] But what did Lloyd George mean by a more radical alternative, and why was Churchill opposed to it? Presumably Lloyd George intended to go beyond the People's Budget with a more radical programme of land reform. Churchill, on the other hand, wished to draw the line. He was now Home Secretary, an office traditionally ranked as of equal importance with the Treasury. He was more independent of Lloyd George than he had been at the Board of Trade. He could hint now at the possibility of a parting of the ways.

In October the constitutional conference was resumed, providing Lloyd George with the appropriate background against which to advance his plan. The memorandum was shown to F.E. Smith, Balfour and a handful of other leading politicians from both sides of the House, including Asquith. On the Liberal side, Lloyd George and Churchill were strongly supported by Grey and Crewe, though Asquith was understandably tepid. Balfour was ready to explore the possibilities, or claimed that he was, and Lloyd George was ready to make substantial concessions, or promised that he would. In a supplementary memorandum of 20 October he proposed immediate colonial preference for goods currently paying duties, and an investigation into the tariff system. In place of Irish Home Rule, Lloyd George suggested a federal scheme of Home Rule All Round.[38]

In the end, the party leaders could not agree. Balfour was not in a position to concede Home Rule, even when it was presented as part of a scheme of all-round devolution for the United Kingdom. The coalition discussions collapsed, and the party truce ended with the last of the constitutional conferences early in November.

*

The collapse of the constitutional conference was swiftly followed by the second general election of 1910. On 16 November the King secretly conceded to Asquith a pledge that if the Liberals were returned to power, he would consent to the mass creation of peers if asked. The Liberals were now in a position to appeal to the electorate on the issue of the House of Lords, and were optimistic that they would gain seats. Parliament was dissolved on 28 November and the constituencies went to the polls between 3 and 19 December.

As Home Secretary, Churchill was entering a stormy phase of his career, embroiled with Labour over the Tonypandy riots and with the suffragettes over the conduct of the Metropolitan Police on 'Black Friday'. From these events the general election offered a welcome if temporary relief.

Renewing his links with Lancashire, Churchill began his campaign with a speech at the Manchester Free Trade Hall, in his former constituency. In Manchester North-West, which had reverted to the Liberals at the previous general election, the new Conservative candidate was Andrew Bonar Law. Bonar Law challenged Churchill to abandon Dundee and fight him for his old seat, with a gentleman's agreement that the loser was to remain out of the House for the whole of the next Parliament. Fortunately for Bonar Law, who failed to win the seat, Churchill did not take up this bogus challenge.[39]

After Manchester, Churchill raced around the country to speak in Bradford, Lambeth, Colchester (where the candidate was his old friend Sir Edgar Vincent), Grimsby, Chester, Southwark, Swindon, Dartford, Poole (in support of F.E. Guest) and the Isle of Wight (in support of J.E. Seeley). Only three days of electioneering were allowed for Dundee, which Churchill had begun to take almost for granted as a safe seat.

There is no need to run all through Churchill's campaign speeches, which for the most part covered the familiar ground of the House of Lords and Free Trade. One novel element in the campaign was the proposal, floated by J.L. Garvin in *The Observer*, for a referendum on the question of tariffs. The referendum was a constitutional device which had never been employed in Britain. The Conservatives seized upon it as a means of unburdening themselves of the incubus of Tariff Reform. With the party deeply divided over food taxes, which many Conservatives regarded as an electoral liability, the referendum was a stratagem for reuniting the party and eliminating the issue from the general election campaign. On 29 November, Balfour himself announced that a Conservative Government would submit its tariff proposals to a referendum if the Liberals agreed to do likewise with Irish Home Rule.[40]

Churchill's first reaction was to admit that there were 'some questions for which a referendum might be an appropriate solution.' He instanced female suffrage, and (with a note of party menace), the taxation of property. But it would be 'very unfair on minorities like the Welsh or like the Irish or like the Scots' if they were brushed aside by the abstention or indifference of the majority of the United Kingdom. 'I do not believe that a system of Referendum would conduce to the good government of our country if it came into general adoption ... we believe in democracy acting through representative institutions.' When

Balfour adopted the referendum, Churchill welcomed the proposal to submit Tariff Reform to the electorate: 'I do not care how it is killed so long as it is killed.' But he was sharply critical of the referendum on principle: 'We think it a bad and vicious system for a country to adopt.'[41]

In the general election of December 1910 the Conservatives were on the defensive. Churchill pilloried them for losing faith in tariff reform, and as ever singled out Balfour for special attention. Speaking in Sheffield, in the hall in which Balfour had unveiled his compromise on tariffs in 1903, Churchill revelled in the Opposition's disarray:

> What a ridiculous and pitiful spectacle is the rout of a great political party! General Scuttle is in command, frantic appeals for quarter and mercy rend the air, the white flag is hung out over the Tory clubs, over many noble residences and many a public house. Arms, colours, baggage and ammunition are all scattered behind a long line of flight. England has never witnessed such a spectacle since the days of Naseby and Marston Moor. And in the complex confusion at the head of the rout what do we discern? In the very forefront of the retreat gleams the white feather of their leader, the leader who, as I heard him say in this very building some seven years ago, 'means to lead'. The leader who means to lead the flight. Mr Balfour, like Charley's Aunt, is still running.[42]

There was a faint warning to Churchill in the result of the election at Dundee. He and his running mate Alexander Wilkie, the Labour candidate, were re-elected, but with a diminished majority. Henry Pelling points out that while there was a 1 per cent swing against the Liberals in Scotland, the swing against Churchill and Wilkie was 7 per cent. Voting was as follows:

| | |
|---|---|
| W.S. Churchill (Lib) | 9,230 |
| Alexander Wilkie (Lab) | 8,957 |
| Sir George Baxter (Con) | 5,685 |
| J.S. Lloyd (Con) | 4,914 |
| Edwin Scrymgeour (Prohib) | 1,825 |

Nationally, too, the election results were an anti-climax. There was very little change from January. The Liberals and the Conservatives both obtained 272 seats, the Irish Nationalists 84 and Labour 42. Nevertheless, the Liberals had turned a corner. The constitutional issue was now settled: by hook or by crook the Parliament Bill would go through, and the House of Lords' veto would be curbed. Henceforth the Liberals would enjoy much greater freedom to ensure the passage of party legislation. After that, the principal cloud on the horizon was Ireland, for the Liberals were still dependent upon the Irish Nationalists, and a Home Rule Bill would have to be introduced.

On 3 January Churchill wrote to congratulate Asquith on his leadership during the campaign, and to offer his advice on future strategy. Churchill was still pursuing the line of co-operation between the parties which had been canvassed since the death of Edward VII. He was ready to conciliate the Conservatives by modifying the 1909 budget, and hopeful – another intriguing twist – of agreement on naval rearmament. Firstly, Churchill argued, the Government must establish authority by passing the Parliament Bill, and the Liberals must not shrink from the creation of 500 peers if necessary. But the time would then be ripe for a new approach:

> After the Veto has been restricted, I hope we may be able to pursue *une politique d'apaisement*. I trust that some of the disappointment of defeat may be mitigated by a liberal grant of Honours (following the precedent of the last Coronation) to prominent members of the Opposition. Privy Councillorships for Bonar Law & FE: the Order of Merit for Joe [Chamberlain]; a proportion of Tory Peers and Baronets; something for the Tory Press. If you cd find a little place for Neil [Primrose] it wd please Rosebery in spite of himself.
> Then on policy. We shd offer to confer with the Conservatives not only on the reform of the Lords but on Ireland. On the Poor Law, Boy Labour & Insurance there is already common ground. I should like to come to an understanding with Balfour about the Navy, if necessary letting him & Cawdor have full access to all Admiralty information ... The sharp edge might be taken off the Licence duties where they are really cutting too deep. Death duties ought not to fall on landed estates more than once in 25 years. We ought to pursue a national & not a sectional policy: & to try to make our prolonged tenure of power as agreeable as possible to the other half of our fellow countrymen.[43]

If the politics of appeasement were to succeed, the Irish question had somehow to be defused. But how? In January 1911, Asquith set up a Cabinet committee on Home Rule under the chairmanship of Lord Loreburn. The other members were Birrell (the Irish Secretary), Churchill, Lloyd George, Grey, Haldane and Samuel. With the exception of Birrell, members of the committee were strongly impressed by the case for 'Home Rule All Round', Joseph Chamberlain's formula of 1886.

England, Ireland, Scotland and Wales would all have separate Parliaments with devolved powers, but subordinate to an Imperial Parliament at Westminster. One of the advantages claimed for this scheme was that it contained Irish separatism by locking the Irish into the United Kingdom on the same terms as the English, the Scots and the Welsh. For this reason it was likely to be more attractive to Unionists, some of whom, like Joseph Chamberlain's son Austen, were known to favour Home Rule All Round. Federalism would also dispose of the glaring anomaly in Gladstonian Home Rule: the double standard whereby the Irish would continue to be represented at Westminster, with the right to vote on the domestic affairs of Britain, while domestic affairs in Ireland were devolved to an all-Irish assembly.[44]

Churchill was strongly in favour of a federal solution, but he did not believe that a scheme of four devolved assemblies would work. As he wrote in a paper for the committee on 24 February: 'It seems to me absolutely impossible that an English Parliament, and still more an English Executive, could exist side by side with an Imperial Parliament.' Since imperial affairs could not in practice be separated from English party politics, a collision between the Parliaments would result whenever the two assemblies were controlled by different parties.

To overcome this difficulty Churchill ingeniously proposed, in a second paper on 1 March, that the United Kingdom should be divided into ten areas, 'having regard to geographical, racial, and historical considerations'. For each area, a local administration and elected assembly would be created, and women would have the right to vote and serve in all these bodies. Churchill envisaged that major responsibilities would be devolved, including education, licensing, land, housing, police, agriculture and the poor law.[45] Lloyd George proposed a much more limited scheme of Irish Home Rule accompanied by English, Welsh and Scots grand committees of the Westminster Parliament.

Churchill's plan was radical. If adopted, it would have turned the United Kingdom into a federal state with some resemblance to the United States, Canada or Australia. But it was too imaginative and enlightened a plan to match the political realities. The Irish Nationalists were adamantly opposed to a federal solution, and so was the Irish Secretary. Birrell fought hard in Cabinet for the old Gladstonian formula, and gradually won round his colleagues. First the Churchill plan was dropped, then the Lloyd George plan.[46] Like the Titanic, the Cabinet steamed ahead in a fog of ignorance, until suddenly the great iceberg of Protestant Ulster loomed up ahead.

*

Meanwhile the House of Lords crisis was carried to a conclusion. The Parliament Bill was introduced by Asquith on 21 February and Churchill wound up the debate with a powerful speech the following day. Reflecting on the workings of parliamentary democracy, Churchill commented on the Conservative proposal to introduce the referendum as a means of resolving deadlocks between the two Houses. The referendum, he warned, was a dangerous instrument for Conservatives to adopt. There was deliberate irony in his endorsement of the use of referenda for particular purposes: 'I think there is a large class of measures dealing with the redress of great inequalities of property in this country, particularly of property in land, on which a Referendum might very effectively be used.' As Churchill explained in a report on parliamentary proceedings to the King: 'The Conservatives seem vy doubtful about the Referendum, & Mr Churchill tried to show them some of its perils from the point of view of property. It would be a dangerous thing to put a measure of a confiscatory character to the direct vote of millions of people, the vast majority of whom have only what they earn each week by constant toil.' In the House, Churchill rounded out his argument with a general condemnation of referenda as a continuous element in government. The stable foundations of parliament would be replaced by 'a tossing sea of frenzied electioneering', and parliamentary institutions would give place to 'the worst forms of Jacobinism, Caesarism, and Anarchy . . . '[47]

Churchill made frequent contributions to the debates on the Parliament Bill at the committee stage. On 15 May, when the bill completed its third reading in the House, F.E. Smith moved the rejection of the bill in a remarkably conciliatory speech in which he observed that in spite of the conflict over the House of Lords, 'a larger area of politics has been withdrawn from the party spirit than at any time in recent memory.'[48] In a response which may well have been preconcerted with his friend on the Opposition benches, Churchill wound up for the Government by conjuring up the new spirit of accommodation foreshadowed in his letter to Asquith. He anticipated that once the bill was passed, the two parties would be in a position to meet as equals and settle the problem of the composition of a reformed second chamber. At the close of the speech he opened up a broader perspective:

Here we are in full collision, in fierce and furious debate, upon a tremendous constitutional change. And yet, side by side with this question . . . it is true to say that there is a greater degree of agreement between parties in the House of Commons on many large aspects of public policy than has existed before in living memory. We do

not underrate the facts brought out by the hon. and learned member
for the Walton division [Mr F.E. Smith]. The leader of the Opposition
joins the Prime Minister at the Guildhall in the cause of peace. Large
numbers of Liberal and Conservative members join together in an
interesting constructive sphere of Colonial policy. In the great field
of social matters hon. Members below the Gangway find, from the
front Opposition bench, support on a question like that of the relief
of destitution . . .

The passage of the Parliament Bill marks a new era in our politics
– an era not of strife but of settlement. The time has surely come
when the country should clear off its arrears. The time has surely
come when the outworn controversies of the Victorian period should
be honourably settled and cleared out of the way; and when the House
of Commons, freed from the tyranny of congested business, freed also
from the tyranny of a partisan Veto, may turn with all its strength to
those problems of social, national and Imperial organisation on which
the welfare and future of our country depend.[49]

When a governing party appeals for consensus, and a steady devotion to
the national interest, its opponents are unlikely to be deceived. There is
no more blatant party manoeuvre than a solemn, patriotic appeal to the
Opposition to lay aside party differences. But in the case of Churchill's
speech, the context must be recalled: the constitutional conferences and
coalition proposals of 1910 were fresh in his mind. Lloyd George, with
whom Churchill was still working in close harmony, was bidding for the
support of the Conservatives on national insurance, with the assistance of
Garvin at *The Observer*.[54] As we have seen, Churchill was also prepared
for substantial concessions over policy. Perhaps he envisaged that a period
of party co-operation would lead on ultimately to a more broadly-based
Cabinet including Balfour and F.E. Smith.

On 18 May, three days after the speech which has just been quoted,
the inaugural dinner of the 'Other Club' took place, of which Churchill
and F.E. Smith were the joint founders. The Other Club was bipartisan,
with 12 Liberal and 12 Conservative MPs among the initial 41 members.
As proof that the club was no coalition conspiracy, the Liberal and Conservative Chief Whips were enrolled, as were both of the King's private
secretaries. But the Club did illustrate the fact that, behind the scenes of
parliamentary warfare, many Liberal and Tory politicians were *habitués* of
London Society, where a more detached and sophisticated view of party
politics prevailed than in the provinces. Churchill and F.E. Smith knew
the extent to which party politics were contrived, and they were familiar

with the private understandings which often lay behind public debate.[51] When they both emphasised in the House of Commons the extent of agreement between the parties, they were deliberately minimising the Home Rule issue, which in other circumstances they might have chosen to inflame, and were, perhaps, playing for an Irish settlement as a prelude to a Cabinet which would include them both. In June, and in spite of protests from Balfour, F.E. Smith received the Privy Councillorship which Churchill had urged Asquith to bestow upon him.

Churchill's hopes of an era of party co-operation were soon to be dashed. Excluded from office since 1905, the Conservatives were seething with frustration. Undercurrents of almost violent antagonism to the Liberals were threatening the leadership of Balfour. On 23 May the Parliament Bill was introduced into the House of Lords, where Lansdowne, the party leader, pursued a policy of amending the bill rather than rejecting it. Where this policy would lead was uncertain. But in June a Tory squire, Lord Willoughby de Broke, began a 'no surrender' movement in favour of rejecting the bill outright, and was joined by Lord Halsbury, a former Lord Chancellor. The revolt of the 'Diehards' or 'Ditchers' as they were called, spread to the House of Commons. On 24 July Asquith was howled down in an outbreak of parliamentary hooliganism in which the ringleaders were Lord Hugh Cecil and F.E. Smith – the latter converted suddenly from a moderate into a militant by the prospect of overthrowing Balfour. 'Our behaviour was inexcusable', wrote the Conservative Chief Whip in his diary.[52]

Directed as much against Balfour's leadership as against the Government, the Diehard movement gathered force. Balfour and Lansdowne were placed in an almost intolerable dilemma when they were informed that George V had agreed in principle to the mass creation of peers, which would destroy the Tory character of the Upper House. Under the provisions of the Parliament Bill, the House of Lords still retained the power to delay legislation for two years, and it would have been an act of folly for the Conservative party to cast this advantage away. Disaster was narrowly averted by Curzon, who organised a number of Conservative peers to vote in favour of the bill, or abstain, as the lesser of two evils. On 10 August 1911 the bill was passed by a majority of 131 to 114.

Defeated over the House of Lords, the Diehards joined with other frustrated elements in the party to oust Balfour from the leadership. In November, Balfour resigned and was succeeded by Andrew Bonar Law. Law did the only thing which could be done in the circumstances. Placing himself at the head of the rebellious elements in the party, he led the party towards extremism. Though he was never quite as extreme as he sounded, his style of leadership ruled out the era of compromise and settlement envisaged by Churchill. Though they were cast as enemies on the parliamentary stage, Balfour and Asquith were great friends in the wings, and Balfour in practice was a considerate Leader of the Opposition. Bonar Law, however, had nothing in common with the Prime Minister. In February 1912, as he and Asquith walked in procession after the King's Speech, he remarked: 'I am afraid I shall have to show myself very vicious, Mr Asquith, this session. I hope you will understand.' As for Churchill, Balfour had been amused by him, but Law regarded him with 'profound mistrust'.[53]

# 4

## *Two Faces of a Home Secretary*

## 1910–11

In home affairs, no phase of Churchill's life was more crowded with activity than the years 1910 and 1911. Already a leading strategist in the party struggle, his domestic responsibilities were multiplied when Asquith promoted him to the Home Office in February 1910. Churchill was Home Secretary for a period of less than two years. But he was stimulated by the diversity of the problems within his new departmental empire, and the blaze of publicity which attended the more controversial of them. His ambition was to get things done and to leave behind a number of legislative memorials for posterity to admire.

Churchill still saw himself as a humane and radical statesman, pursuing the course he had marked out at the Board of Trade. 'I am one of those', he said in January 1910, 'who believe that the world is going to get better and better.'[1] Much of his work at the Home Office bore witness to the sincerity of this conviction. His ambitious programme of penal reform, though never completed, marked the pinnacle of his achievement in social policy. But Churchill's desire to go down in history as a great reforming Home Secretary was overtaken, in the end, by events which turned his political personality around to reveal the other side of paternalism: the maintenance of paternal authority.

The Home Secretary was the minister responsible for the preservation of law and order. By chance, Churchill's period at the Home Office coincided with a major outbreak of industrial unrest, accompanied by riots and the risk of violent conflict between trade unionists and strike-breaking workers. In the circumstances, any Home Secretary would have taken firm action to quell disorder. Nor was Churchill the melodramatic villain of left-wing tradition, sending in the troops to shoot the strikers. But unlike many politicians, he never shrank from conflict when he believed that an issue had to be resolved. When the duties of a Home Secretary pushed him into the front line against militant labour, he responded with fervour and a determination to prevent a general strike. By the time Churchill left the Home Office it was no longer certain whether he regarded the Conservatives, or the rising Labour movement, as the principal enemy. He embodied, to a remarkable extent, both the reforming and the conservative potential of the last Liberal Government.

\* \* \*

Churchill's claims to promotion were strengthened by a sparkling performance in the general election campaign of January 1910. In February 1910 Asquith decided to offer him the most difficult and delicate of assignments: the Irish Office. But Churchill feared that his career would run into a cul-de-sac, and refused. 'There are many circumstances connected with it', he wrote, 'which repel me. Except for the express purpose of preparing & passing a Home Rule Bill I do not wish to become responsible for Irish administration.'[2]

Churchill sought the Admiralty or the Home Office, where there was a vacancy caused by the appointment of Herbert Gladstone as Governor-General of South Africa. Asquith decided to make him the Home Secretary. For Churchill, who was still only thirty-five, this was promotion indeed. The Home Office ranked with the Foreign Office and the Treasury as one of the three great offices of state next to the premiership. Like the Board of Trade, it was an expanding department whose responsibilities had increased with the growth of central government.

The Home Office was, in fact, a hybrid organisation. Since the Victorian period it had become increasingly involved in the regulation of social conditions. It was responsible for the enforcement of the laws governing working conditions in factories, mines and shops, and the administration of the Workmen's Compensation Act. But it still retained its original character as a ministry of internal security.

In spite of its overall responsibility for the maintenance of law and order, the Home Office had limited powers over the police. The Metropolitan police were directly under the Home Secretary's control, but the police outside London were independently organised, with a minimum of Home Office supervision, by the borough and county authorities. In the event of a breakdown of law and order, policing outside London was a local responsibility. But if the police were unable to maintain order, and the magistrates requested military assistance, it was the Home Secretary's duty to decide whether or not to authorise the despatch of troops. The Home Office also exercised a miscellany of powers in the general sphere of repression and control. Churchill was the minister responsible for the activities of the Special Branch of the Metropolitan Police, the restrictions imposed on immigration under the Aliens Act of 1905, and the regulation of explosives and firearms.

On the judicial side, the Home Secretary had important powers in the administration of criminal justice, including the right to exercise the royal prerogative of mercy by pardoning an offender or reducing the sentence imposed by the court. In every case of murder, it was the duty of the Home Secretary to decide whether the death sentence should be carried out.

Through the Prisons Commission, a division of the Home Office created in 1877, the Home Secretary was responsible for the control of prisons and the rules governing prison discipline. By the time Churchill arrived at the Home Office, a series of major reforms had been carried out under the enlightened regime of Evelyn Ruggles-Brise, the chairman of the Prison Commission since 1895, and Herbert Gladstone, who had been Home Secretary since 1905. A less imaginative politician than Churchill might well have concluded that penal reform had run its course, and a period of consolidation was needed. This was probably the view of Churchill's two senior officials: the Permanent Secretary, Sir Edward Troup, and of Ruggles-Brise himself. Churchill, however, decided that much more needed to be done. His first action was to improve the conditions of imprisoned suffragettes, a matter of which more will be said later. His intention was to carry through a sweeping revision of penal policy along three main lines of advance: the improvement of prison conditions, the exclusion of petty offenders from gaol, and the reform of sentencing policy.

The previous autumn Churchill had discussed prison conditions with his father's old friend, Wilfred Scawen Blunt. An eccentric Tory rebel who supported Home Rule for Ireland, Blunt had once served a two-month sentence in Galway and Kilmainham gaols, with hard labour, after conviction under the Irish Crimes Act. When he described his experiences to Churchill the latter replied: 'I am dead against the present system, and if I am ever at the Home Office I will make a clean sweep of it.' One of his first actions as Home Secretary was to telegraph Blunt requesting a copy of a memorandum by him on prison reform. He also confided to a young admirer, Violet Asquith, his plans for the introduction of lectures, libraries and entertainments for prisoners.[3]

Among those who lobbied Churchill in favour of prison reform was the novelist and playwright John Galsworthy, who was campaigning strongly against the practice of 'separate confinement', whereby prisoners began their sentences with a period of up to nine months' isolation in a cell. Galsworthy preferred to describe this as 'solitary confinement' – a phrase which stuck. He had already persuaded Gladstone to reduce the period to a standard three months for all prisoners, a change that was due to come into force on 1 April 1910. He now wrote to Churchill urging him to strike 'a crushing blow' at the system.

Churchill was ready to listen. Accompanied by Ruggles-Brise he attended, on 21 February 1910, the opening night of Galsworthy's play *Justice*, which portrayed the alleged horrors of the system. Ruggles-Brise, who thought the play unfair, fought back with competing arguments. Churchill was, perhaps, unwilling to ride roughshod over a senior official with long experience of prison reform. Declaring that he was impressed by the importance of 'making the first period of prison life a severe disciplinary course', he compromised. In May 1910 he announced that separate confinement would be reduced to one month for the majority of offenders, and three months for recidivists.[4]

After this Churchill displayed less interest in the reform of prison rules. He believed firmly in discipline and punishment and gave no support to the campaign to abolish the flogging of prisoners. On a private member's bill to end flogging he wrote a single word of instruction for his officials: 'Block'.[5] He turned instead to his other priorities: the exclusion of petty offenders from gaol, and the reform of sentencing policy.

To understand exactly what Churchill was trying to achieve, some background is necessary. In late Victorian Britain 'crime' was almost by definition an offence committed by the poor. White collar and commercial crime were rare, or at any rate rarely the subject of prosecution. The great majority of offenders were drawn from the ranks of labourers, paupers, vagrants and the unemployed, and were prosecuted for petty theft, habitual drunkenness, or other street offences. The children of the poor were also frequent offenders, and often sent to prison. Sentencing policy varied greatly, but a short prison term was normal for minor offences, and magistrates sometimes inflicted sentences of great severity on recidivists – seven years for stealing a hen, or ten for stealing a garden fork.[6]

By the late nineteenth century it was common ground among penal reformers that too many people were being sent to prison who were capable of 'moral reformation'. It was also recognised that sentencing policy was arbitrary and often excessive. By the time Churchill arrived at the Home Office, much had been accomplished by Ruggles-Brise and Gladstone. The borstal system had been established as an alternative to prison for young offenders. Children under fourteen had been excluded from prison under the Children Act of 1908. A Court of Criminal Appeal had been created for the express purpose of reviewing the sentences passed by magistrates and judges.

Churchill was not content. He brought to the Home Office the strong sense of natural justice, and sympathy for the underdog, of which he had already given proof at the Colonial Office and the Board of Trade. Yet it would be wrong to suppose that he nurtured a tender sympathy for criminals. Rather he believed that under the penal system as it stood, the punishment for petty criminals and youthful offenders was often disproportionate to the crime.

In a speech to the House on 20 July Churchill set out one of the most important aims of his penal policy: 'The first real principle which should guide anyone trying to establish a good system of prisons would be to prevent as many people as possible getting there at all.' Ninety thousand people, Churchill told the House, had been sent to prison in 1909 for the non-payment of fines. Many of them would have been able to pay had they been allowed more time to do so, and he foreshadowed legislation to give them a longer period of grace in which to pay. The next important category consisted of young offenders between the ages of sixteen and twenty-one. 'There is a disaster in sending any lad of that age to gaol,' Churchill declared, and he went on to point out that a social injustice was involved:

It is an evil which falls only on the sons of the working classes. The sons of other classes may commit many of the same kinds of offences and in boisterous and exuberant moments, whether at Oxford or anywhere else, may do things for which the working classes are committed to prison, although injury may not be inflicted on anyone. In my opinion no boy should go to prison unless he is incorrigible or committed some serious offence . . . I hope the House will not be startled at the proposal I am going to make. I see no reason why we should not introduce some form of defaulters' drill – I do not mean military drill, for that would be dishonouring the profession of arms, but I think there are systems which might be extremely salutary which at the same time would be extremely disagreeable.[7]

Churchill had already elaborated his idea for 'defaulters' drill' in discussion with Home Office officials. In a minute of 8 July he wrote:

Rowdyism, gambling, stone-throwing etc., ought not to be punished with imprisonment or with fines which increasingly lead to imprisonment. On the other hand, these offences cannot go uncorrected. Magistrates should have the power to order in lieu of fine or imprisonment up to 28 days defaulters' drill. This drill should consist of physical extension motions, Swedish gymnastics with or without dumb-bells. Unless other arrangements can be made it should be held at the Police Station. The boys should not be exhausted, but the training should be severe, and rigorous discipline preserved.[8]

Since Churchill proposed that penal drill be carried out in police stations, the Home Office decided to sound out the opinion of the Police Constables. Of the six who were invited to comment, all gave a general welcome to the idea except for the Chief Constable of the West Riding of Yorkshire, who warned of the danger of confusing policing with punishment. Instead, he maintained, boys should receive compulsory schooling or instructive employment such as market-gardening. A second round of inquiries, addressed to the Chief Constables of all major towns in England and Wales, produced another round of favourable responses, but again there was a dissenting voice. The Chief Constable of Birmingham pointed out that the working-class boys with whom the police had to deal in Birmingham were already so underfed and physically deficient that any form of physical drill 'would probably be a very severe punishment'. For good measure he added:

I am opposed to any form of punishment which is not improving to the individual in some respect. The old form of defaulters' drill in the army and in prisons, i.e. "pack drill" – marching up and down in heavy marching order – or carrying a shot from one side of the yard to another, is no good to any person and breaks a man's spirit.[9]

Encouraged by the positive response of the majority of Police Constables, Churchill pressed on with his plan. It was included, with all his other proposals for penal reform, in a Cabinet paper of 25 October entitled 'The Abatement of Imprisonment'. Churchill explained to his colleagues that his first major objective was to reduce the number of petty offenders who were sent to prison. He therefore proposed three lines of advance of which the first, the treatment of young offenders, included the idea of penal drill. The second line of advance would be to abolish imprisonment for debt. This led him to raise once more the question of the class bias of the law:

The law at present is open to the grave reproach of partiality between rich and poor. Only workpeople are sent to prison for not paying their debts ... A thoroughly vicious system of credit, based on no proper security, is spreading among the working classes throughout the country. Its consequences are injurious both to thrift and honesty. Touts and tallymen go round with ever greater frequency and press cheap jewellery, musical instruments, and many other non-necessary articles upon the workman, and still more the workman's wife in his absence. The weekly payments, enforceable by imprisonment, are a source of endless vexation and worry to the household, and often cause fierce quarrels; not infrequently the workman is taken from his work to prison (under our man-made laws!) for his wife's debts, and often his family is kept by the parish while the State is revenging by imprisonment the injury of a private creditor.

Churchill proposed thirdly to reduce the number of people imprisoned for non-payment of fines by extending the time allowed for payment. He also hoped to do away altogether with terms of imprisonment of under one month. Out of a total of 205,000 committals in 1909, he noted, 61 per cent were for periods of a fortnight or less. To exclude them from gaol he proposed that all sentences of under one month should be suspended.

He rounded off his memorandum with an extraordinary passage in which he linked prison reform to social policy in general. Churchill envisaged that all the deviants and misfits of society should be classified into categories, and placed in appropriate institutions:

Classification is the essence of penology. We have already been led to create a number of specialist institutions: Parkhurst, Broadmoor, Aylesbury, Borstal, are instances which occur. We have already embarked upon, or are moving forward towards, many other specialised establishments; homes for inebriates, and for inebriate prostitutes, institutions for the criminal weak-minded, detention prisons for recidivist convicts, disciplinary training establishments for juvenile adults, labour colonies like Merxplatz for loafers and vagrants – all are coming *disconnectedly* into view. It would be far better not to make more exceptions from the dead-level of the general prison system. I should propose to survey them as a whole, and organise them (gradually, of course), into one complete series of carefully graded specialist institutions conveniently distributed throughout the country, and adapted to the suitable treatment of every variety of human weakness and misdemeanour.

Concluding that the Courts were too numerous and too ill-informed to operate a scientific system of imprisonment, Churchill proposed that a Home Office Board of Classification should be set up to 'consider the case of all offenders after their being sentenced, and distribute them to receive their appropriate treatment throughout the different penal corrective and curative institutions of the prison system.'[10] Here again we glimpse the fervour which lay behind Churchill's Edwardian reforms: a faith in the centralising, scientific state, and a vision of national efficiency that ranged far beyond the more limited, piecemeal measures we associate with his name.

In Cabinet the proposal for penal drill was hotly opposed by the President of the Board of Education, Walter Runciman. 'I would observe', he wrote, 'that it is advocated by many Chief Constables. Their advice is coloured to some extent by their military or semi-military training, and military influences in the past have seldom led to any intelligent developments in the prison system.'[11] Runciman had no need to spell out for his colleagues the message that Churchill too had a military mentality that was somewhat at odds with liberalism.

In spite of Runciman the proposal for penal drill was referred to a Home Office committee charged with drafting a bill for the 'abatement of imprisonment'. By December 1910 Churchill was hard at work on the draft.[12] But in 1911 the bill was crowded out of the parliamentary timetable by House of Lords reform, and faded from view. In 1914 Churchill's successor at the Home Office, Reginald McKenna, introduced a Criminal Justice Amendment Bill. But the only one of Churchill's proposals to be included was the extension of the period of grace for payment of fines, and even that was diluted by allowing magistrates the discretion of insisting on early payment.[13]

One lesser achievement deserves to be recorded. Churchill hoped that something could be done to reduce the problem of recidivism if more was done for prisoners after their release from gaol. Under existing arrangements, the welfare of discharged prisoners was in the hands of a multitude of voluntary societies who distributed charity and worked to rehabilitate the offender. The police were also involved. Where convicts were granted a remission of sentence for good conduct, they were released on a licence which obliged them to report regularly to the police. In concert with Ruggles-Brise, Churchill proposed a radical reorganisation. The prisoners' aid societies were to be co-ordinated into a single body and, with the help of Treasury funds, converted into a semi-official agency in which the Home Office was strongly represented. The stigma of police supervision was to be done away with entirely, except for 'refractory' cases.[14]

When Churchill first arrived at the Home Office he was advised by his predecessor, Herbert Gladstone, to pay special attention to the supervision of sentencing, and override his officials if necessary:

> The office presents, as a rule, the traditional view of treatment, which in most cases is quite right. But they cannot bring to bear the outside, impartial view of human nature and human society which necessarily belongs to the Home Secretary. It very often happens that examination of the sordid affairs of rather discreditable and useless people involves a great deal of time. But you will find that if you give this generously you will be repaid by being able to lift up not a few miserable creatures out of trouble and disgrace.[15]

No advice could have been more congenial to Churchill, who quickly signalled his resolve to curb judicial excesses.

On 11 April a twelve-year-old boy, Charles Bulbeck, was convicted by the Haywards Heath bench of stealing a piece of cod valued at fivepence. The chairman of the bench ordered him to be birched and detained at a reformatory for seven years. The following day Churchill sent a telegraph asking for the birching to be suspended. He was too late to prevent this but in response to questions in the House on 14 April he announced that he had ordered the boy to be discharged and returned to his parents. The case, and Churchill's dramatic intervention, received extensive coverage in the press.[16]

What most perturbed Churchill was the new system of 'preventive detention' which had been introduced in the 1908 Prevention of Crimes Act. The aim was to discriminate against habitual offenders by enabling the courts to sentence them to a term of imprisonment of between five and ten years, over and above the punishment awarded for the most recent offence. Churchill feared that preventive detention would lead 'to a reversion to the ferocious sentences of the last generation'. As Radzinowicz and Hood explain in their magisterial history of penal policy:

> He was appalled to find that repetition was the criterion for imposing preventive detention, irrespective of the gravity of the offences committed. The information he called for showed long lists of offenders sentenced for such trivialities as stealing a pair of boots, or two shillings, or four dishes, or handkerchieves, or fowls or slates or whatever. Churchill's strictures on the judges, his battle against the Director of Public Prosecutions and against his own Home Office advisers make fascinating reading.[17]

On a visit to Dartmoor in the autumn of 1910 Churchill and Lloyd George met a prisoner called David Davies who was known, from his tending of the prison sheep, as the 'Dartmoor Shepherd'. Davies was an old hand: an incorrigible petty offender who had been sentenced ten times since his first conviction – before Churchill was born – in 1870. But Churchill and Lloyd George were outraged to discover that he had been sentenced, the previous year, to three years' penal servitude and ten years' preventive detention for stealing two shillings from a church offertory. Churchill remitted most of his sentence and he was released, in a blaze of publicity, at the end of 1910. The Shepherd, alas, quickly relapsed into his old way of life, and when he was arrested for housebreaking in April 1911, Churchill was exposed to the mockery of the Opposition. But he was unshaken in his determination to restrict the use of preventive detention, and proposed to his officials a formula that would have ruled it out in 85 per cent of cases. When his officials protested, Churchill threatened to abolish preventive detention by amending the law. As a compromise, a circular was issued to the courts stressing that preventive detention should be reserved for 'the worst class of professional criminals'. Whether Churchill's intervention was the decisive factor is hard to say. But from 1911 the use of preventive detention began to decline, and it faded away altogether after the First World War.[18]

Churchill would have liked to lay down a uniform scale of penalties to be applied by the judges. But he had no constitutional right to do so. What he did possess was the power to set an example to the courts. He was, therefore, extremely active in the revision of sentences. Unlike previous Home Secretaries he did not wait for pleas of mercy, but searched through the criminal calendars seeking for cases of injustice.[19] The accession of King George V in May 1910 was marked, on Churchill's advice, by a partial remission of sentences for 11,000 prisoners. Nor was he content to study the problems on paper alone. In October 1910 he visited Pentonville prison and according to Masterman was much impressed by 'the attractiveness of the little boys that were in prison there. There was almost nothing of the criminal type about them at all.' On leaving Pentonville, he ordered that the sentences of all the boys he had interviewed should be reduced.[20]

It was the Home Secretary's duty to decide whether convicted murderers should live or die and Churchill made it a rule to examine every case thoroughly. In the decade 1900–1909 40 per cent of murderers were reprieved, but Churchill reprieved 49 per cent, or twenty-one out of the forty-three cases which came before him. He was, however, a convinced supporter of the death penalty and regarded it, in a sense, as merciful. As he remarked in a letter to the Foreign Secretary, Sir Edward Grey: 'To most men – including all the best – a life sentence is worse than a death sentence . . . '[21]

*

If Churchill never completed his agenda in penal policy, the same was true of his efforts in another sphere of reform. He inherited from his predecessor the draft of a bill to regulate the hours and conditions of shop assistants. But as Gladstone warned, the subject was 'undoubtedly a difficult one, and will necessitate a great deal of trouble'.[22]

Churchill introduced the Shops Bill into the House of Commons on 4 June. Summarising its provisions for the benefit of King George V, he explained:

> It seeks to limit the hours of shop assistants to 60 hours a week exclusive of meals; to prevent their being employed after 8 o'clock (except in special trades and circumstances) on more than three nights in the week; to secure a universal half holiday & some lesser things. There are about a million shop assistants & half a million shopkeepers, of the shopkeepers nine tenths serve their own little shops themselves, & only one tenth employ assistants. No restriction is placed by the Bill on the little shops who in fact get a certain advantageous preference thereby . . . [23]

The bill also proposed to arrest and reverse the practice of Sunday trading, which had been growing in recent years, and restrict it to specific trades and districts.

From a party political point of view, the Shops Bill seemed at first to be a clever piece of work. Shop assistants represented a poor and ill-organised section of the working classes. Since the 1880s philanthropists and social workers, and the National Union of Shop Assistants, had campaigned for a reduction in working hours and improvements in conditions. In this respect the Shops Bill reflected the New Liberalism of social reform, with a close family resemblance to Churchill's minimum wage legislation. At the same time, by an ingenious twist, the bill was intended to favour the rank and file of the Old Liberalism: the small, self-employed shopkeepers.

Liberal politicians were uneasily aware that in favouring the working-class, they were in danger of alienating the small tradesmen to whom the party owed so much of its support. The Shops Bill clearly favoured the self-employed shopkeeper or street trader against the retail chain stores. No limit was placed on the working hours or closing times of the self-employed shopkeeper or his family. But employers of labour would have to accept a 60-hour week with compulsory closing at eight o'clock. The self-employed would therefore be in a position to undercut them. As large families with five or six children were still common in the Edwardian period, the unrestricted family business posed a considerable threat to the larger retailers. The Sunday trading provisions compounded the difficulty. Churchill proposed exemptions for Jews and street-traders, and here too the Government was declaring that some were more equal than others in the market place.

With hindsight, it is obvious that the employers were unlikely to stand back and allow the Government to undermine their competitive position. But it was far from obvious at the time. Neither Gladstone nor Churchill anticipated the extent of the resistance. Churchill, indeed, told the House on 4 July that he regarded the Bill 'not only as a non-party bill, but as a non-controversial measure'.[24]

The sequel is described in Michael Winstanley's history of shopkeeping before 1914. The Home Office was besieged by deputations of tradesmen, complaining that the bill would place the self-employed in a privileged position and was therefore 'unfair' to the rest of the trading community. Churchill was repeatedly urged to impose early closing on all shops, a proposal he was bound to reject: a revolt of small shopkeepers would be very damaging electorally. Alternatively, he was urged to recognise members of a shopkeeper's family as employees for purposes of the bill. As one retailer put it: 'A man could work a vast business round the corner or next door with three or four sons or daughters . . . and he could oppose the man who is employing labour.' Initially, Churchill rejected the argument, but as the pressure grew he prepared to retreat, and offered to redefine 'family' as husband, wife and one other member, with all others to be classed as assistants.[25]

The Shops Bill revealed Churchill's talent for improvisation and flexibility. Writing to Asquith in December 1910 he was still optimistic about the outcome:

I am quite sure I can count upon a great deal of help from the younger and more advanced Tories in taking this measure through. I spent a lot of time before the election in receiving some thirty deputations of the different interests affected, and as you will see from the copy of the Bill enclosed, I have cut the original model (which I inherited) to ribbons and practically remade it. I have every reason to believe that the opposition of numerous interests affected will have been enormously diminished by the changes, and I should propose to go on with the process of conference and deputation to conciliate all parties during the whole progress of the measure.[26]

Reintroducing the bill on 31 March 1911, Churchill told the House that the Government was sticking firmly to three main points: a 60-hour week, a guaranteed half-day off, and a reasonable time for meals. On Sunday trading there were puzzling questions still to be resolved, but Churchill reaffirmed the Government's resolve to stop this 'growing evil'.[27] The Home Office, however, continued to receive angry deputations of tradesmen and the bill was subjected to continuous assault and amendment in the committee stage. Churchill's efforts to exempt Jewish tradesmen from the restrictions on Sunday trading were resented by some non-Jewish traders. But in Manchester Churchill's Jewish allies were far from satisfied. On 29 June Nathan Laski wrote to Churchill begging him to receive a deputation: 'I make this appeal to you with confidence, because I can claim strenuous service to the Liberal party for over thirty years, and this is the first time I have made a request to a Liberal Minister on a matter which touches so closely our religious susceptibilities.' Laski wanted Churchill to include in the bill scheduled areas of Manchester, Leeds and Liverpool, where Jewish Sunday trading would be permitted. Churchill replied that specific areas could not be scheduled, since the boundaries would have to be determined by local inquiries.[28]

In committee, the bill disintegrated. When Churchill moved to the Admiralty in October 1911, he carried with him the bedraggled remains. As he admitted to the House on 30 November: 'There is no doubt whatever that it has become necessary, if legislation is to go forward at all on the subject, to drop the greater part of the bill.'[29] A week later Churchill introduced it in its final form. The most important provision, the 60-hour week, had been eliminated, and the bill now contained no statutory limitation of working hours. The Sunday trading provisions had also disappeared. There remained only the weekly half-holiday and reasonable intervals for meals. Such was the Shop Act of 1912, a testimony to the power of organised tradesmen in the House of Commons: they were, no doubt, important contributors to Liberal and Conservative party funds. The small shopkeepers, though numerous, were politically mute, while the National Union of Shop Assistants had little of the bargaining power of the industrial unions. Hence the Shops Bill ended in defeat for Churchill and the Liberalism of working-class welfare.

*

The Shops Act, however neutered, was a straightforward example of legislation to improve social conditions. But running through Edwardian social reform was a repressive strand of concern for the control of dangerous or anti-social minorities. The Webbs, for example, and their protégé William Beveridge, believed that vagrants should be detained in penal colonies. So too did Churchill, who explored the question thoroughly and was eager for legislation. 'As for tramps and wastrels,' he explained to King George V, 'there ought to be proper Labour Colonies where they could be sent for considerable periods and made to realise their duty to the State ... It must not however be forgotten that there are idlers and wastrels at both ends of the social scale.' The King, a dutiful character who was trying to throw off the louche atmosphere of his father's court, was deeply offended by Churchill's reference to the idle rich, and protested to Asquith against Churchill's 'socialistic' principles.[30] But he had a point: the regulation of society by the state was increasing, and Churchill was proposing to extend it further. In the event, his Unemployment Bill of 1911 failed for lack of parliamentary time, and labour colonies were never established.

As Home Secretary Churchill was also much interested in the possibility of sterilising the 'unfit'. Like most educated people of the time, he was much impressed by the theory of eugenics. Eugenics was based on the belief that heredity was far more important than environment in determining the physical and mental qualities of the population, and the eugenics movement enjoyed a considerable vogue between the turn of the century and the First World War.[31]

According to the eugenists, Britain was threatened by the 'degeneration of the race'. The 'unfit', who were concentrated among the poor, were reproducing themselves more rapidly than the 'fit' who were to be found mainly among the middle classes. The remedy, they argued, was for Governments to practise positive eugenics through tax incentives to the middle classes to have more children, and negative eugenics through measures to prevent the procreation of the unfit.

In 1904 the Balfour Government appointed a Royal Commission to inquire into the 'feeble-minded'. When the commission reported in 1908 it recommended that certain categories of the mentally inadequate should be compulsorily detained in institutions. As the Home Office was the department responsible for mental institutions, the proposal went to Herbert Gladstone, who deferred a decision, leaving the matter to be taken up by Churchill.

Shortly after Churchill's appointment as Home Secretary he received a pamphlet extolling the practice of the 'sterilisation of degenerates' in the state of Indiana, where it was provided for by state law. In May 1910 he

sent a minute to the Permanent Secretary, Sir Edward Troup, asking him
to examine the idea: 'I am drawn to this in spite of many Party misgivings
... Of course it is bound to come some day.' The pamphlet was forwarded
to Horatio Donkin, Medical Adviser to the Prison Commission, whose
verdict was scathing. 'The real fact is', he wrote, 'that no one hardly who
tries to propagate doctrine or stimulate action in the matter of sterilization
has informed his or herself of the elementary grammar of Heredity ... '
Having visited mental institutions in the United States, Donkin continued,
he had gathered that all the instructed and sensible doctors regarded the
propaganda for sterilisation as 'the outcome of an arrogation of scientific
knowledge by persons who had no claim to it'. In case there was any
remaining doubt about his views, Donkin characterised the pamphlet as
'a monument of ignorance and hopeless mental confusion'.[32]

There matters rested for the moment. On 15 July, Asquith and Churchill
received a deputation on mental welfare which included Montague
Crackanthorpe, the President of the Eugenics Society. Crackanthorpe
made a renewed plea for the segregation of the feeble-minded, and
pointed out that in the United States some states had laws forbidding
marriage between the mentally retarded. Churchill cautiously replied that
there were 'immense difficulties' surrounding the question, and that some
might think that it belonged 'more to the politics of the future'. But if anything could be done to segregate the 130,000 feeble-minded people 'so
that their curse dies with them', future generations would be grateful.[33]

Behind the scenes, and in spite of the outright opposition of Donkin,
Churchill was still pursuing the idea of sterilisation. At the end of July
Troup tried his best to dissuade him. In the present state of feeling, Troup
argued, it was 'useless to attempt anything. I don't think any Committee,
Departmental or Parliamentary, wd have courage to report in favour of
the proposal whatever the opinions of the individual members might be.'
But Churchill pressed on. In September he wrote a memorandum to his
officials explaining why he was so attracted to the idea of sterilisation.

I think there must be a considerable class among the feeble-
minded who might be allowed to live outside special institutions
if only one could be sure that they did not continue to multiply
in the next generation the evils from which we suffer so greatly in
our own. I am surprised that Dr Donkin, with his great experience,
should throw doubts upon the enormous influence of heredity in the
transmission of defects physical, mental and moral. A very large
proportion of criminals are abnormal only in the weakness of their
faculty of self-control. Surely that weakness is definitely traceable

in a great number of cases to parentage. I cannot agree with him that "virtue and vice, honesty and dishonesty" are "concrete virtues acquired by the individual". On the contrary it is natural to men, in contradistinction to animals, to be virtuous and to be honest, to have that restraining power to repress the baser promptings of their lower nature, and virtue and honesty are the rule and not the exception in the human species. A minority exhibit a failure to control the primary animal promptings, and a still smaller minority again use their intelligence from a definitely immoral standpoint. It is that middle class, whose human intelligence is so far defective as to deprive them of the average restraining power, that we should seek by sterilisation of the unfit to prevent.

This question must be considered in its proper place in relation to the treatment of the mentally defective. For my part I think it is cruel to shut up numbers of people in institutions, to them at any rate little better than prisons, for their whole lives, if by a simple surgical operation they could be permitted to live freely in the world without causing much inconvenience to others. I certainly do not look forward to that millennium for which some scientists appear to hanker when the majority of the human race will be permanently confined within the walls of state-maintained institutions, attended by numerous doctors, and guarded by legions of warders.[34]

It is rare to discover in the archives the reflections of a politician on the nature of man. Churchill's belief in the innate virtue of the great majority of human beings was part and parcel of an optimism he often expressed before the First World War. In his view, sterilisation was a libertarian measure intended to free unfortunate individuals from incarceration. But let us turn over the coin. Churchill's optimism was tempered, it seems, by a fear of national decline which he had never expressed before. In December 1910 he wrote to Asquith:

I am convinced that the multiplication of the Feeble-Minded, which is proceeding now at an artificial rate, unchecked by any of the old restraints of nature, and actually fostered by civilised conditions, is a very terrible danger to the race. The number of children in feeble-minded families is calculated at 7.4; whereas in normal families it is but 4.2 ... Runciman [President of the Board of Education] tells me that he has now got 12,000 feeble-minded and defective children in the Special Schools; many others are in residential homes. These are all segregated and kept under control until the age of

16. At 16 the parents claim them in the hope of making some profit out of their earnings. The girls come out by the thousand at 16, are the mothers of imbeciles at 17, and thereafter with surprising regularity frequent our workhouse lying-in wards year by year. The males contribute an ever broadening streak to the insane or half insane crime which darkens the life of our towns and fills the convict prisons.

As Churchill explained to Asquith, he was certain that one day the 'acquiescence' of the feeble-minded in a sterilising operation would enable a large number of them to regain their liberty. In the meantime he proposed a stopgap measure for the segregation of children.[35] No more was heard of this and if a bill was drafted it never saw the light of day. But the momentum in favour of legislation continued after Churchill's departure from the Home Office. In 1912 the Government introduced a bill for the detention of various categories of the feeble-minded, but withdrew it after opposition from libertarian back-benchers. In 1913 the bill was reintroduced with amendments to disarm the critics, and passed into law as the Mental Deficiency Act. By this time the power to prevent the procreation of the unfit had been whittled away to exclude all but the pauper mothers of illegitimate children. There was no mention of sterilisation.

Churchill's intentions were benign, but he was blundering into sensitive areas of civil liberty. The same can be said of his policy towards aliens, a problem which briefly returned to haunt him. Churchill had led the Liberal opposition to the Aliens Bill of 1904, and opposed the Aliens Act of 1905. In the Manchester by-election of 1908 he had claimed, with some justification, that the Liberal Government had 'practically smashed' the act and rendered its worst aspects 'nugatory'. He also promised that the Government would make further concessions by establishing receiving houses and reducing the naturalisation fee. The first of these promises was carried out by Gladstone in 1909, but the second was overlooked.[36]

As Home Secretary, Churchill began to view the aliens question in a new light. This was partly due to a dawning consciousness of the possibility of war. Hitherto, Churchill had publicly and privately discounted talk of the German threat as alarmist. But now his perceptions were changing and by October 1910 he was talking to W.S. Blunt of 'the coming war with Germany'.[37] When viewed in this new perspective aliens, or at any rate German aliens, could be seen as potentially dangerous.

In his history of the British secret service, Christopher Andrew tells how Churchill expanded the operations of the home department of the

Secret Service Bureau headed by Vernon Kell:

> Churchill served as first chairman of the Aliens Subcommittee of
> the CID, founded in March 1910, and approved the preparation by
> Kell of a secret register of aliens from probable enemy powers (chiefly
> Germany) based on information supplied by local police forces ... In
> the following year Churchill added a major weapon to Kell's armoury
> by greatly simplifying the interception of suspects' correspondence.
> Hitherto Home Secretaries had signed individual warrants for every
> letter opened. Churchill introduced the practice of signing 'general
> warrants authorising the examination of all the correspondence of
> particular people upon a list to which additions were continually to be
> made.

The evidence compiled by Kell convinced the authorities, quite errone-
ously, that the Germans had an extensive espionage network in Britain.[38]

If some aliens were suspected of espionage, others were suspected of
anarchist or revolutionary tendencies. In December 1910, three policemen were murdered when they interrupted a raid on a jeweller's shop
in Houndsditch by a gang of anarchists from the Baltic states. The leader
of the gang, supposedly, was the mysterious figure 'Peter the Painter'. In
the New Year of 1911 the gang were discovered holed up and armed
at a house in Sidney Street, in the East End. When they opened fire on
the police, the police requested the assistance of troops. Overcome with
excitement, Churchill dashed to the scene in time to witness the house
catch fire and burn down with the gang inside it.

Churchill attended out of sheer impulsiveness and could not help interfering. He instructed the fire brigade to let the house burn down. His
prominence in the episode made him all the more vulnerable to attack.
The murder of the three policemen had triggered another round of
anti-alien agitation, with Gladstone and Churchill under attack from
*The Times* and sections of the Conservative party for allowing virtually
uncontrolled immigration. The Jewish population of the East End were
vilified for their alleged association with crime. When Churchill arrived on
the scene at Sidney Street he was greeted with cries of 'Oo let 'em in?'
At the Palace Theatre Biograph, where an early newsreel of the incident
was shown, Churchill's appearance was greeted with boos and shouts of
'shoot him'.[39] A Conservative MP, Edward Goulding, proposed to introduce a bill tightening up immigration procedures and extending police
powers over aliens already resident.

Churchill decided that something had to be done to appease the anti-alien campaign. On 19 January he circulated a draft bill to the Cabinet in which he proposed that aliens convicted of offences should be liable to expulsion by the Home Secretary unless the court recommended otherwise. In addition, aliens would not be allowed to possess firearms without a licence from the police, and aliens who were suspected of criminal intentions and could not find sureties for their behaviour were to be liable to expulsion. As Churchill explained to the Cabinet, 'two naughty principles' were involved: firstly, a deliberate differentiation between the alien and the British subject, and secondly, the deportation of an alien before an offence had been committed. Churchill introduced the Bill under the Ten Minute rule on 18 April 1911, expressing the wish that it should be considered jointly in committee with Goulding's private member's bill. But there, unexpectedly, the story ended. The sensation of Sidney Street was fading, and anti-alien fever in decline. Both bills were allowed to lapse on the pretext that no parliamentary time was available.[40]

*

Churchill's policies as Home Secretary were seldom original. He picked up ideas that were 'in the air', or acted on the findings of official inquiries. The proposals he put to the Cabinet had been thoroughly discussed beforehand with his officials. But Churchill was very different in style and personality from the McKennas and the Runcimans, the prudent men of business who formed the backbone of the Liberal Government. Unlike them he suffered from a hyperactive imagination and a histrionic urge. He was captivated by ideas and longed to dramatise them on the democratic stage. The result was a tension between Churchill and his officials. It was not only that Churchill sought bold initiatives: he sought a theme or programme in which a number of different proposals were combined. His style of thinking was both aggressive and strategic and may well have originated in his military career. His officials, meanwhile, were obliged to examine each proposal separately, and apply to it the test of administrative viability. As Troup himself put it: 'Once a week or oftener Mr Churchill came to the office bringing with him some adventurous or impossible projects; but after half an hour's discussion something was evolved which was still adventurous but not impossible.' Troup, however, had spent thirty years at the Home Office before Churchill appeared on the scene: sheer force of habit must have conditioned his response. Harold Butler, a junior civil servant in 1910, wrote later of Churchill's prison reforms: 'The old hands in the department were rather dismayed by the temerity with which he challenged principles and practices which had remained sacrosanct for many years.'[41]

Biographers of Churchill have often remarked on his tendency to concentrate on a single campaign at a time: Economy in 1901, Free Trade in 1904, Social Reform in 1908, and so on. But the Home Office interrupted the pattern. Almost every week Churchill had to juggle with a diversity of departmental problems. Over and above these were the many alarms of a strangely troubled period in which the rage of the suffragettes coincided with the 'great industrial unrest' of 1910–14.

In the politics of Edwardian Britain, the suffrage question was always of marginal significance. The supporters of votes for women had neither the industrial nor the political bargaining power of labour. The Pankhursts and their followers were easily written off as a fanatical minority, unrepresentative of the great majority of women. But the suffrage issue was nevertheless a cause of much vexation to the Government. Ministers were heckled and harassed by unruly women who repeatedly challenged them to justify their position. A further embarrassment was the division of opinion within the Cabinet. Some ministers, including Grey, Haldane, Lloyd George and Churchill, were on record as favouring votes for women, while others, including Samuel, McKenna, and Asquith himself, were known to be hostile.

One frustrating aspect of the situation for the suffragists was the fact that a majority of MPs were sympathetic in principle. In February 1908 a private member's bill proposing a limited measure of female enfranchisement was passed on second reading by a majority of 179, with 218 Liberals voting in favour and only 53 against. The stumbling-block was the Cabinet, which refused to provide parliamentary facilities for the passage of a suffrage bill. The National Union of Women's Suffrage Societies, led by Mrs Fawcett, was prepared to tolerate the delay and continue along the constitutional path. But the Women's Social and Political Union, led by Mrs Pankhurst, was increasingly impatient. A window-breaking campaign in June 1909 signalled a new and more militant phase. The women convicted chose to go to prison rather than pay a fine, and announced that unless they were treated as political prisoners, they would refuse to obey prison rules. As a further protest, they went on hunger-strike.

Hunger-strikes now became a standard tactic. The initial response of the Home Office was to release the hunger-strikers. But in September 1909 the policy of forcible feeding was introduced. On the authority of Gladstone, a woman could now be pinned down by prison wardresses, while medical officers forced a tube through one of her nostrils to a depth of twenty inches, and milk was injected. Among those who protested loudly against forcible feeding were the journalist H.N. Brailsford, and the founding father of the Labour party, Keir Hardie. Liberals, for the most part, accepted it as a necessary response to the histrionics of obstreperous and irrational women. In October 1909 Churchill told a meeting of the Women's Freedom League at Dundee that militant tactics were counter-productive: 'Your cause has marched backwards.' His temper was not improved when he was attacked at Bristol railway station by Miss Theresa Garnett, who flourished a dog whip and cried out: 'Take that in the name of the insulted women of England.' Churchill averted the blow by grabbing the whip and putting it in his pocket.[42]

In January 1910, while Gladstone was still Home Secretary, the prison conditions of suffragettes were highlighted by the courageous actions of Lady Constance Lytton, an active supporter of the Pankhursts whose brother Victor was the second Earl of Lytton. In response to allegations that forcible feeding posed a risk to the lives of women who were in poor health, Gladstone declared that it was never undertaken without prior medical examination. Lady Constance, who was suffering from a weak heart, decided to put this to the test. Disguising herself as a poor seamstress under the name of Jane Warton, she got herself arrested for a breach of the peace in Liverpool, and was sentenced to fourteen days' imprisonment at Walton Gaol. After four days on hunger-strike, during which she refused a medical examination, she was forcibly fed by a doctor who knelt on her knees to insert the tube, while prison wardresses held her down. After this, the doctor slapped her on the face, as though to show contempt. 'The horror of it was more than I can describe,' Lady Constance wrote. But after a few more days of forcible feeding her identity was discovered and the Home Office ordered her immediate release.

Her brother at once began a campaign for a full inquiry by the Home Office. Gladstone, however, denied allegations of mistreatment and refused an inquiry. Churchill's first action at the Home Office was to review the case. On 11 February he informed his officials that he did not intend to carry out an inquiry, and issued an instruction that in future forcible feeding was to commence within 48 hours of the start of a hunger-strike. Requesting them to draft a reply to Lytton, he wrote: 'Endeavour to couch it throughout in a manner which will safeguard our position while showing consideration to Lord Lytton.'[43]

Churchill knew the Lyttons well. He had once been engaged to Lytton's wife, Pamela, a misalliance that had given way to a close but platonic friendship. Victor Lytton, a Unionist Free Trader, was a friend and former ally. Churchill, nevertheless, stuck firmly by his decision to regard the case as closed. In a robust minute to his officials on 28 February he wrote:

I do not attach much importance to Lady Constance Lytton's charges, many of which are trivial and others imaginary. The business of forcibly feeding an unruly and hysterical woman must in any case be disagreeable in its details; and must furnish to a mind prepared to seek material for an attack on prison administration, a certain amount of highly coloured, or colourable material.

In Churchill's view, the one point of real substance in the case had been the failure to detect Lady Constance's heart problem. Gladstone had stated that forcible feeding was never undertaken without prior medical examination, but in this case the rule had been broken:

Pray let it be understood in future that before forcible feeding is resorted to, in every case, a written and formal certificate must be given by the medical officer, showing that he has thoroughly examined the prisoner and that he considers that no harm can result from the process.

Churchill now instructed that forcible feeding of hunger-strikers should begin after 24 hours.[44]

Churchill's decision to refuse an inquiry into the treatment of Lady Lytton was an early indication that he intended to protect his officials by screening the Home Office from critical scrutiny. If the allegations were indeed so trivial, an inquiry would surely have vindicated the Home Office. Lytton, however, made no complaint of Churchill's conduct. Churchill, for his part, hoped to reduce the tension by relaxing the rules under which suffragette prisoners were held.

On 31 January Mrs Pankhurst had declared a truce with the Government: militant tactics would be called off until further notice in the hope that conciliation and compromise would prevail. Churchill seized the opportunity. On 28 February he wrote to his Permanent Secretary, Sir Edward Troup, proposing the creation of a category of offender never previously recognised in Britain: the political prisoner. Political prisoners would be granted privileges denied to common criminals: 'I am not sufficiently acquainted with the details of prison administration to develop this idea with any thoroughness', he continued, 'but it seems to me that food might be obtained from outside on payment, that the prisoner should wear his [sic] own clothes, that no compulsory work should be executed, that no cutting of hair or any unnecessary interference with usual habits should be practised.'

On 4 March Troup reported that both he and Ruggles-Brise were opposed to the idea of a separate category of political prisoner: 'If political motive is admitted in extenuation of a minor offence, it is difficult to resist the application of the same principle to graver offences, and even to political murders which are, from the public standpoint, the worst of all murders.' However, Troup advised, the result Churchill wanted could be achieved by other means. Ruggles-Brise had devised a formula to cover prisoners 'who are persons of good antecedents, and who have been convicted of offences which do not involve dishonesty, cruelty, indecency, or serious violence'.[45]

As Churchill now discovered, Ruggles-Brise had already drawn up, in concert with Troup and Gladstone, detailed proposals which coincided with Churchill's opinions. But Gladstone had never reached the point of decision. Churchill announced the change of policy to the House of Commons on 15 March. Subject to the approval of the Home Secretary, the Prison Commissioner was to allow concessions 'in respect of the wearing of prison clothing, bathing, hair-cutting, cleaning of cells, employment, exercise, books, and otherwise'. Churchill's announcement received a good press, but Gladstone was extremely angry, complaining to Churchill that he was claiming the credit for measures devised by his predecessor. Churchill sent him copies of the relevant Home Office minutes to prove that he had acted independently.[46]

By his timely concessions over prison discipline, Churchill bolstered the uneasy truce between the W.S.P.U. and the Government. Indeed it now seemed that Churchill was prepared to go one step further by lending his support to a bill, sponsored by Lytton and Brailsford, to enfranchise female householders.

The enfranchisement of women was a complex issue. Generally speaking suffragists argued that women should be given the vote on the same terms as men. But the franchise in Britain was still restricted to householders. If the vote were to be given to women on the same terms as men, the logical outcome was that women householders only should be enfranchised. But this would mean granting the vote to a small minority of unmarried women. The alternative was to adopt some formula that would enable a substantial number of married women to vote.

The suffragists were in difficulty. As long as the male franchise was restricted, there was no simple or logical basis on which they could proceed. Whatever the formula proposed, it would be open to attack on the grounds that it enfranchised an arbitrary and unrepresentative section of the female population. The Liberals, meanwhile, faced a party political dilemma. The majority of Liberals favoured votes for women as a matter of principle. But they feared that a household franchise would confer the

1   The Radical Twins: Churchill and Lloyd George about 1909.

2　The New Liberal: promoted to the Cabinet as President of the Board of Trade, Churchill speaks at the Manchester North-West by-election of April 1908, where he was defeated.

3　Target for the Suffragettes: Churchill is interrupted at the Dundee by-election of May 1908 by Miss Moloney, whom he later described as 'a peculiarly virulent Scotch virago, armed with a large dinner-bell'.

4-5   On and off duty: Winston and Clementine Churchill on a visit (left) to one of the newly opened Labour Exchanges in February 1910 and (right) holidaying at Sandwich in July 1914.

6   Unlikely Anglican: appointed as an ecclesiastical commissioner of the Church of England, Churchill leaves Buckingham Palace after a convocation of clergy.

7   The 'Battle of Stepney': Churchill keeps abreast of developments at 100 Sidney Street, the scene in January 1911 of a pitched battle between two anarchists, a horde of armed policemen, and a platoon of Scots Guards.

8   First Lord of the Admiralty: Churchill inspects boys of the training ship *Mercury*, 1912.

vote on propertied women who would reinforce the Tory party at the polls. The long-term solution, no doubt, was universal suffrage, but this was sure to be rejected by the House of Lords, and could not be enacted until their lordships' powers were reduced.

The truce declared by the Pankhursts was intended to provide the Liberal Government with a breathing-space in which to reconsider the franchise issue. The hope was that, with the support of some Cabinet ministers, facilities would be granted to a private member's bill. To this end Lytton and Brailsford established, in the spring of 1910, a conciliation committee to work for the passage of a non-party measure.

Brailsford wrote to Churchill asking him to endorse the general aim of the committee, and enclosing the draft of a bill to give the vote to women on the basis of a household franchise. Brailsford explained that he was only seeking Churchill's endorsement of the general principle of a non-party measure. 'The formula is vague & not at all compromising to you. It does not commit you either to the municipal basis, or to procedure by private bill.' Churchill gave his blessing to the formula, while carefully reserving his position on the detail. As he wrote to Brailsford on 19 April: 'I do not wish to be committed at the present juncture to any special form or basis in or upon which the franchise is to be granted to women.'

On 6 June Lytton called on Churchill at the Home Office and presented him with a revised version of the draft bill. Churchill told Lytton that there was no chance of any bill on the subject being carried through the House in the current session: the Government could not spare the parliamentary time necessary for the passage of legislation. This was a great blow to Lytton, but Churchill went on to say – perhaps to soothe him – that he was favourably impressed by the proposals and the effects they would have on the electoral system. Churchill then sent the draft bill to the Liberal Whips for comment. Fearing the consequences for the Liberal vote, they objected strongly. Three days later Churchill wrote to Lytton confirming that it would be impossible to pass it in the current session, and adding: 'I am also told that the Bill itself is open to many objections on the score of being partial and undemocratic.'

Although Churchill had made it very plain that in his view the bill could not pass before the dissolution of Parliament, neither Lytton nor Brailsford had any reason to think that he was opposed to it. On 2 July Churchill discussed the bill at some length with Brailsford, and explained that he had some doubts about the details. Churchill mentioned in particular the possibility of 'faggot voting' – the granting by wealthy men of property to their wives and daughters in order to enfranchise them. Brailsford assured

Churchill that the Committee had already prepared an amendment that would meet this objection.[47]

The bill was introduced into the House on 11 July. At this point, according to Lucy Masterman's account, Churchill was intending to vote in favour. But Charles Masterman reminded him that Lloyd George was opposed, and began to put the arguments against.

Winston began to see the opportunity for a speech on these lines, and as he paced up and down the room, began to roll off long phrases. By the end of the morning he was convinced that he had always been hostile to the Bill and that he had already thought of all these points himself . . . Charlie thinks that his *mind* had up till then been in favour of the suffrage but that his *instinct* was always against it. He snatched at Charlie's arguments against this particular Bill as a wild animal snatches at its food.[48]

On 12 July Churchill delivered a speech to the House of Commons denouncing the bill root and branch. He began with a lukewarm declaration of support for female suffrage. There was, he declared, a proportion of women in all classes who were capable of exercising the vote for their own and the public good. But the grievance was 'greatly exaggerated' and the great mass of women did not want the vote. The bill was 'anti-democratic' because it would give an entirely unfair representation to property, and lead to the multiplication of faggot votes by wealthy husbands or fathers: the Conservatives would obtain a great electoral advantage. The bill denied the vote to wives and mothers, but how could this be justified? A prostitute might qualify, but if she married she would lose her entitlement to vote, and only regain it through divorce. Rounding off a bitter and angry speech, Churchill announced that he would vote against the bill.[49] Asquith and Lloyd George also spoke against, but the bill was carried on second reading by 299 votes to 189. The Government, however, refused to budge. No facilities for the passage of the bill were granted, and it lapsed with the dissolution of Parliament in November.

Brailsford and Lytton were incandescent with rage. 'I beg to inform you', wrote Brailsford to Churchill, 'that in discussing your conduct in today's debate, I shall be obliged to describe it as treacherous.' Lytton attacked Churchill in speeches at suffrage meetings, and entered into an acrimonious correspondence. Instead of addressing Churchill as 'Dear Winston' he now wrote: 'Sir'.[50]

Brailsford and Lytton both alleged that Churchill had reneged on a promise to support the bill. This was an exaggeration, but Churchill had certainly raised their hopes with expressions of interest and sympathy. Besides, his attack was so vehement as to call into question his support for the basic principle of votes for women. Was he opposed to the bill simply because it would benefit the Conservative party? Or did the speech betray an underlying antipathy to female enfranchisement? Whatever the explanation, Churchill realised that he had mishandled his friends. 'I do greatly regret', he wrote to Edward Marsh on 26 September, 'not having warned him [Lytton] and Brailsford in advance.'[51]

Despite the failure of the Conciliation Bill, the W.S.P.U. continued to hope for a change of mind by the Cabinet. From July to November the 'truce' was maintained, and the campaign pursued by peaceful methods. Churchill, however, was apprehensive. In October 1910 two male suffragists, Victor Duval and George Jacobs, approached Lloyd George to remonstrate with him. Churchill fired off a minute to Troup instructing him to demand from Sir Edward Henry, the Commissioner of the Metropolitan Police, 'an explanation of the circumstances in which the Chancellor of the Exchequer was assaulted last night by a gang of male suffragists. I cannot understand how it was that proper protection was not accorded to him ... ' Troup and Henry sought to calm Churchill by pointing out that although Duval had insulted Lloyd George, and seized hold of his coat, there had been no gang and no assault. Churchill minuted:

> The fact remains that an assassination with a knife could easily have taken place ... It wd. be important if it could be shown that these ruffians are not genuine adherents or misguided enthusiasts for the cause of women's suffrage, but hired persons ... The organisation of gangs of paid ruffians to make personal attacks on ministers ought to be treated with the extreme rigour of the law.

Here again Churchill was mistaken. Inquiries revealed no evidence that either man was a paid agitator. They were genuine supporters of the cause.[52]

On 12 November Sir Edward Grey confirmed the Government's refusal to allow parliamentary time for the Conciliation Bill, and the W.S.P.U. announced that a militant demonstration would take place at the opening of Parliament.[53] When Parliament reassembled on 18 November a deputation of three hundred women set out for the House of Commons. As on previous occasions, they tried to break through police cordons. In the past this had led to scuffles with the police, but this time the police adopted more aggressive tactics: 'Reluctant to make arrests, the police used a variety of means to force the women back: women were kicked, their arms were twisted, their noses were punched, their breasts were gripped, and knees thrust between their legs. After six hours of struggle, 115 women and four men had been arrested.'[54] These events, with their disturbing overtones of mass sexual assault, were to pass into the folk memory of the women's movement as 'Black Friday'.

Churchill, who recognised at once that something discreditable had occurred, intervened to order the release of most of the women arrested. Four days later there was a second battle with the police when two hundred women invaded Downing Street with the aim of forcing their way into Asquith's presence. Stones were thrown and windows broken. Asquith had to be rescued and rushed away in a taxi, while the Irish Secretary, Augustine Birrell, got caught up in a mêlée of angry women, and dislocated his knee trying to escape. The police fought back hard and 185 arrests were made. Once more there was evidence of police brutality, and once more Churchill intervened to withdraw charges against most of those arrested. The suffragettes bracketed the 'Battle of Downing Street' with 'Black Friday' in their case against the Government.

The leaders of the W.S.P.U. alleged that on Black Friday the police had acted on the direct instructions of Churchill in order to terrorise and humiliate the women. With the assistance of Dr Jessie Murray, H.N. Brailsford compiled a dossier of 135 eye-witness accounts, nearly all of which bore out the charge of 'unnecessary violence' on the part of the police. Published on 23 February 1911, their report pointed the finger of suspicion at Churchill: 'We cannot resist the conclusion that the police as a whole were under the impression that their duty was not merely to frustrate the attempts of the women to reach the House, but also to terrorise them in the process.'[55]

Black Friday was not, in fact, a Churchillian atrocity. Churchill had tried to prevent the situation but had acted too late or, perhaps, been misunderstood. The nub of the matter was the reluctance of the police to make arrests in the early stages of the demonstration. In a minute to the Commissioner of Metropolitan Police on 22 November Churchill sought to put his own action in a favourable light:

My instructions were clear. The women were to be arrested as soon as any defiance of the law was committed by them. They were not to be allowed to exhaust themselves in struggling for hours with the Police. Prompt arrest is essential. I regret that through misunderstanding they [sic] were not carried out. The order is explicit for the future. All suffragettes who defy the police are to be arrested. Prosecution can be considered afterwards.

In a tactful reply, Henry placed a different construction on events:

> I have explained that by the express direction of Mr Gladstone when
> S. of S. & after much experience of Suffragette agitation, instructions
> were given me that arrests were not to be made unless absolutely
> unavoidable, as the police were being adversely criticised for arresting
> them too promptly. When Mr Churchill made it quite clear to me that
> he desired arrests to be effected as soon as possible, I informed him
> that it was too late for me to instruct the men on this occasion, they
> were already out on the streets. Mr Churchill will remember that, at
> first, he decreed that arrests, if possible, should be altogether avoided.[56]

To sum up, it appears that prior to Black Friday Churchill had
upheld Gladstone's policy of avoiding arrests if possible. Hence the
prolonged confrontation between the women and the police. On the
day itself he changed his mind, by which time his verbal instructions
to Henry were too late to affect the course of events. But there had
been many previous encounters between the police and the suffragettes
without such ugly consequences. Why the extra degree of physical force on
this occasion?

As Andrew Rosen has pointed out, the police called out to guard
the House of Commons were normally constables from 'A' division, who
were accustomed to ritualised encounters with the women. But on Black
Friday police with no previous experience of suffragette demonstrations
were drafted in from the East End of London: 'They were, moreover,
used to dealing with poor and ill-educated people who were seldom able
to make police brutality a *cause célèbre* ... That the police found in the
youthful femininity of their assailants an invitation to licence, does not
seem, all in all, surprising.' As one of the women, Mrs Georgina Solomon,
observed in a letter of protest to the Home Office: 'The methods applied to
us were those used by the police to conquer the pugilistic antagonist, to fell
the burglar, to maim the hooligan, or to reduce to inanity the semi-barbaric
and dangerous rough.'[57]

Churchill and his officials were determined that no blame should fall
on the Home Office or the police. They denied that any deliberate police
brutality had occurred, shielded the police from inquiry, and absolved
themselves of all responsibility for error. Within days of Black Friday,
evidence of police excesses began to pour into the Home Office. Telling
photographs and eye-witness accounts appeared in the press. In a letter
to *The Daily Telegraph* on 23 November the Vice-President of the Royal
College of Surgeons, C. Mansell-Moulin gave a graphic description of

assaults by the police. But Sir Edward Troup was unimpressed by such allegations:

> As regards the conduct of the police on Friday, the violence & persistence of some of the women made a certain degree of roughness unavoidable. But judging by what I saw myself, and what I have been told by other persons, I am certain that speaking generally they behaved with extraordinary forbearance and good humour. If it is true that women were "thrown down and struck" by the Police it is open to them to take proceedings – they have means in abundance – but of course it is not true.[58]

The Home Office defence was to argue that allegations of police misconduct were nothing but a propaganda exercise and would not stand up to investigation in court. But it would have been no easy matter for witnesses to recall and identify the actions of individual policemen. Another method of uncovering the truth would have been to institute, as Brailsford and others demanded, an impartial inquiry. But Churchill refused this.

Brailsford and the W.S.P.U. imagined that an inquiry would bring to light some special instruction by Churchill. But Churchill was on firm ground when he denied to the House that any such instruction had been issued. The W.S.P.U. did not believe him. 'I say orders were given', wrote Emmeline Pankhurst in 1914, and the accusation was to follow him for years to come.[59] By a curious coincidence, Black Friday took place only ten days after another episode shortly to be described – the Tonypandy riots, and the despatch by Churchill of troops and police to the Rhondda Valley. November 1910 was the moment at which Churchill's reputation as a militarist, cracking down on popular protest with physical force, crystallised both for Labour and the suffragettes.

In the general election of December 1910 votes for women was a minor issue. But Asquith held out an olive branch by pledging that in the next Parliament the Government would grant facilities for the passage of a bill 'so framed as to admit of free amendment'. Churchill, in reply to women's deputations in Dundee, held to the position he had taken up over the Conciliation Bill: support for the principle of female enfranchisement, coupled with a refusal to commit himself to any particular bill.[60]

In January 1911 a fragile truce was restored between the Government and the W.S.P.U. In February Sir George Kemp announced that he would introduce, as a private member's bill, a revised version of the Conciliation Bill. To comply with Asquith's pledge, the bill was framed to allow free amendment. In its revised form, based on a simple household qualification, the bill obtained a second reading on 5 May and passed by 255 votes to 88. But Asquith had promised only to assist a bill at some time during the current Parliament, and not necessarily during the present session. On 29 May Lloyd George announced that no time could be found at present: a week would be set aside in the next session.

But it was Lloyd George who finally torpedoed the Conciliation Bill. Writing to the Chief Whip, the Master of Elibank, on 5 September, he warned that the bill would add 'hundreds of thousands of votes' to the Tories:

> We have never really faced the situation manfully and courageously. I think the Liberal Party ought to make up its mind as a whole that it will either have an extended franchise which would put working men's wives on the Register as well as spinsters and widows, or that it will have no female franchise at all.[61]

By this date the Parliament Act was on the statute book and the door was open to wider franchise reform. Lloyd George persuaded the Cabinet to change course. On 7 November 1911 Asquith announced that in the next session, the Government would introduce a bill providing for manhood suffrage. It would be so drafted as to allow an amendment for the inclusion of women. Churchill, who was by now First Lord of the Admiralty, was deeply alarmed. Since 1904 he had always claimed to support votes for women. Now there was an imminent proposal that all women over the age of 21 would be enfranchised. Here then was the moment of truth – to which the sequel will appear in due course.

*

Reviewing the political scene in November 1910 Beatrice Webb observed:

> The big thing that has happened in the past two years is that Lloyd George and Winston Churchill have practically taken the *limelight*, not merely from their own colleagues, but from the Labour Party. They stand out as the most advanced politicians. And, if we get a Liberal majority and payment of members, we shall have any number of young Fabians rushing for Parliament, fully equipped for the fray – better than the Labour men – and enrolling themselves behind these two radical leaders.[62]

Beatrice Webb was writing at a time when Churchill was preparing another great offensive against the Conservative party and the House of Lords. Though many doubted his sincerity, it was clear at least what role he was playing. He was the radical champion of the 'progressive alliance' between the Liberals and Labour.

In that alliance it was still the Liberals who set the pace and outshone the small, trade union pressure group known as the Labour party. Labour was, indeed, almost a satellite of Liberalism. The majority of Labour MPs owed their seats to an electoral pact with the Liberals. No less critical was the dependence of Labour on the Liberals in respect of trade union law. In the Osborne Judgment of 1909 the House of Lords had ruled that it was unlawful for a trade union to devote money to political objects. Hence the Labour party was no longer entitled to receive money from trade union funds. Labour, of course, appealed to the Liberals to reverse the judgment by amending the law.

In the two general elections of 1910, the Lib-Lab electoral pact was in good working order. From the Liberal point of view there was much to be said for keeping it in repair. There was no reason to suspect that Labour were about to break free and challenge the Liberals as a party of government. But without the support of Labour and the Irish Home Rule party the Liberals would be unable to govern. Unlikely as it was that Labour would rebel, it was in the Government's interest to ensure continuing Labour support.

Churchill had been a practitioner of Lib-Lab politics since 1904. He was pro-labour in the sense that he stood for a non-socialist, non-militant labour movement, under Liberal patronage. His social and economic policies, and support for trade union rights, all fitted into the pattern. Nor did he neglect patronage in the literal sense. At the Board of Trade he had grasped the importance of incorporating the trade unions into the administration of labour exchanges. At the Home Office he created two new posts of Labour Adviser, and 30 new inspectorates of mines and quarries, to which trade unionists were appointed.[63]

At about the same time the Lib-Lab alliance began to come under severe strain on the industrial front. Between 1910 and 1914 there occurred a series of major strikes in the coal mines and the docks, and the first national strike on the railways. A multitude of smaller disputes blew up at the same time. The primary cause was economic: a decline in the purchasing power of wages, coinciding with a tightening of the labour market. Workers had both a grievance and the bargaining power with which to enforce their demands.

The wave of industrial unrest owed little to the permanent officials of trade unions, who were swept along by the militancy of the rank and file. Strikes often began as spontaneous local disputes which spread outwards and upwards until the whole of a union was involved. Sometimes workers were trying to establish a union branch for the first time, or to overcome a refusal by the employer to recognise a union for negotiating purposes. Trade unionism flourished and union membership rose from 2,477,000 in 1910 to 4,135,000 in 1914. But the motive force was pressure from below: by implication the leadership of the Labour movement – the Parliamentary Labour Party, and the Parliamentary Committee of the TUC – was under attack.

The opportunity was seized by a small band of industrial militants propagating the revolutionary doctrine of syndicalism. The syndicalist gospel, which had originated in France, dismissed as futile the constitutional methods of the Labour party and the TUC. Parliament, according to the syndicalists, was a sham intended to delude and exploit the working-class. They preached the overthrow of capitalism by means of a general strike in which workers seized control of the industries in which they were employed.

The syndicalists are often said to have counted for little in the world of labour. The strike wave, it is argued, would have occurred without them. The trade unions were largely impervious to syndicalist doctrine, and carried on in their usual pragmatic and sectional fashion. Yet the presence of the syndicalists did alter the situation in at least two significant respects. Firstly perceptions of industrial unrest were coloured by the knowledge that a revolutionary minority was at work. Secondly, the idea of the general strike began to permeate the trade union world. Few believed in the general strike as a means to social revolution. But many regarded it as a means by which industrial demands could be enforced on the Government and the community. For it was true, as the syndicalists claimed, that should the trade unions ever combine for a common purpose, they now had the power to inflict severe damage on the economy.

Churchill was deeply disturbed by militant industrial unrest and reacted strongly against it. He became, to this extent, anti-labour. But like most parliamentary politicians he was careful to distinguish between the 'militants' and the 'moderates' of the labour movement. It would be wrong to suppose that he turned against the working-class, the Labour party, or the trade unions, as a whole. But he did begin to fear the influence of subversive and revolutionary elements.

The first major strike occurred in the coalfields. Churchill himself had been instrumental in sealing the unwritten contract between the miners and the Liberal party through his support for the Eight Hours

Act of 1908. In 1909, the Miners Federation of Great Britain decided to affiliate to the Labour party, and the union's representatives in the House of Commons became Labour MPs. But this in itself made very little difference to the Lib-Lab alliance at Westminster. Active co-operation with the Liberals continued.

In the coalfields the alliance began to unravel as a direct consequence of the Eight Hours Act, which came into force in July 1909. The miners intended to follow up their success in limiting hours by negotiating minimum wage agreements. The employers aimed to compensate for loss of output by economising on wages. Late in 1910 a dispute erupted in south Wales and by 1 November strike action affected all the collieries belonging to the Cambrian Combine in the Rhondda Valley.[64]

On 7 November, as miners toured the pits expelling officials and closing down machinery, violent clashes occurred between police and strikers outside the Glamorgan colliery at Llwynypia, a quarter of a mile from Tonypandy. Fearing that the police would be overpowered, the Chief Constable of Glamorgan requisitioned two companies of infantry and two hundred cavalry from the military authorities, informing the Home Office of his action the next morning. Meanwhile advance warning of the troop movements reached William Abraham, Lib-Lab MP for the Rhondda, president of the South Wales Miners' Federation, and better known as 'Mabon'. Mabon appeared at the Home Office on the morning of 6 November to plead with Churchill to withhold the troops.[65] After a conference with Haldane, the Secretary for War, Churchill wired the Chief Constable to inform him that metropolitan police were to be substituted for soldiers. The cavalry were to go no further than Cardiff while the infantry were to halt at Swindon. To the men on strike Churchill sent a personal message that was read out to them at a mass meeting on the afternoon of 8 November:

> Their best friends here are greatly distressed at the trouble which has broken out and will do their best to help them get fair treatment. Askwith, Board of Trade, wishes to see Mr. Watts Morgan with six or eight local representatives at Board of Trade, 2 o'clock tomorrow. But rioting must cease at once so that the enquiry shall not be prejudicial and to prevent the credit of the Rhondda Valley being impaired.[66]

But rioting did not cease. With the metropolitan police still on their way from London, fighting broke out again outside the Glamorgan colliery and spread to the main square of Tonypandy. One man, Samuel Rays, received a fatal injury to the skull. Later in the evening rioters rampaged through Tonypandy looting or damaging some sixty-three shops. With ominous news filtering through from the Rhondda, Churchill had already lifted his ban on troop movements, which did not, therefore, outlive the day on which it was promulgated. On the following day General Nevile Macready, whom Churchill had appointed to command the troops in the valley, reported that a detachment of Lancashire fusiliers was on duty at Llwynypia.

The Tonypandy affair was to give rise, in later years, to conflicting legends. Among the south Wales miners, folk-memory asserted that Churchill had sent in the troops to crush the strike, with consequent bloodshed and loss of life. As late as 1950 the allegation surfaced in a general election campaign, and Churchill was forced to defend himself. But in so doing he fostered the alternative legend that order had been restored by policemen wielding nothing more lethal than rolled-up umbrellas. In the second volume of the official biography of Churchill, Randolph Churchill asserted that his father had intervened to prevent the despatch of troops to the area. Readers were left to assume that no troops ever reached the Rhondda.[67]

Strange to say, the principal facts of the matter have been on record all along in Hansard, and the pages of an official report published in 1911. In recent years the distortions have been stripped away and the scope for controversy narrowed. Churchill's initial reaction was that of a Liberal Home Secretary on his best behaviour with a general election in the offing. He was eager to avoid the use of troops and hopeful that Lib-Lab politics would prevail over industrial strife. His message to the miners was a plain intimation that peaceful conduct would be rewarded by sympathetic arbitration. When riots continued, and troops were sent, Churchill made strenuous efforts to avoid direct confrontation between troops and people. Macready reported:

> In accordance with the verbal instructions of the Home Secretary, the general line of policy pursued throughout the strike was that in no case should soldiers come in direct contact with rioters unless and until action had been taken by the police. In the event of the police being overpowered ... the military force would come into play, but even then each body of military should be accompanied by at any rate a small body of police to emphasise the fact that the armed forces act merely as the support of the civil power.[68]

By preventing bloodshed, Churchill also prevented a debacle for Liberalism. In spite of Tonypandy, some life remained in the old Lib-Lab relationship and 'Mabon' was returned as MP for the Rhondda. But as labour historians record, Tonypandy marked a turning-point in the coalfields. The older trade union leaders were under attack from a new generation of militants inspired by Noah Ablett, the leader of the south Wales syndicalists. Mabon's vote in the general election of December 1910 was down by more than three thousand, a loss of nearly a quarter of the support he had won in January. Though he remained President of the South Wales Miners' Federation, the Cambrian dispute destroyed his influence in the union. Churchill's restraint, therefore, availed him little. The soldiers did not kill anybody, but they remained in the Rhondda until October 1911 and as David Smith observes, their presence 'ensured that the miners' demands would be utterly rejected'.[69] Nor were the metropolitan police, a body of English intruders, likely to be regarded as neutral. In the House of Commons Keir Hardie quoted several allegations of police brutality, and on a number of occasions demanded that Churchill institute an inquiry. Indeed the conduct of the metropolitan and other police imported from outside the district quickly superseded the question of the use of troops as the major source of embarrassment to Churchill, who refused an inquiry into the subject.[70]

There is one hint in the sources that Churchill feared a sinister undercurrent to the strike. He warned the Cabinet that 'bombs, detonators, fuses, pick-axe heads and revolvers were being secreted'.[71] But in the aftermath of Tonypandy, he did his best to sustain Lib-Lab politics in the coalfields. Pit accidents were still frequent and the year 1910 had produced the largest death toll ever recorded in the industry. Churchill's response was to bring forward new legislation to improve safety regulations and reduce the number of fatal accidents. The proposals contained in his Coal Mines Bill derived mainly from the report of a Royal Commission, with some additions by the Mines Department of the Home Office. Churchill supplied the political drive, and, no less important, obtained the necessary finance by appealing to Lloyd George:

> The feeling among the miners' leaders is thoroughly friendly to the Government, and very hopeful that effective action is going to be taken to stop this awful waste of human life ... I am certain that a really bold and sweeping policy would be immensely popular throughout the country and that the expense would not be judged in any quarter.[72]

The Coal Mines Act of 1911 was a valuable measure which took its place in a long line of legislation on safety in the pits. But it could not bridge the gulf that was opening up between the Government and the miners, and Churchill was to express great hostility to them in the coal strike of 1912.

One other aspect of the Tonypandy affair claims our attention. Traditionally, the maintenance of law and order had been a local responsibility. In her study of the policing of industrial disputes, Jane Morgan shows that Tonypandy marked the beginning of a shift towards greater control by the Home Office. Churchill's appointment of General Macready to command both troops and police was an extraordinary constitutional innovation. For the duration of the crisis the authority of the local magistrates was superseded: 'Industrial disorder of this kind was seen for the first time as a national emergency, one that required a co-ordinated response, civil and military, from the state.'

There was an illuminating sequel. The Glamorgan police authority, a Labour-controlled body, refused to foot the bill for the services of the metropolitan police. The local authority, they pointed out, had sent in a requisition for troops, but had never requested police from London. In March 1911 Churchill retaliated by introducing a bill to make local authorities liable for the expenses incurred whenever the Government sent in troops, or police from outside the district. Here was another sweeping change in prospect: 'By this measure, which was to apply retrospectively to the police alone from 1 November 1910, Churchill would be allowed to dispatch police, or military, or naval forces around the country in times of crisis, without their being requested by the local authorities – who would, nevertheless, have to pay the cost.' This rather cheeky bill received no support and had to be dropped, leaving the Home Office to pick up the bill for the expenses of the metropolitan police.[73]

\*

Labour questions were seldom as dramatic as Tonypandy. There was still, for example, the problem of the legal status of trade unions to consider. In October 1910 the Cabinet began to discuss the consequences of the Osborne Judgment. Loreburn, Samuel, Runciman, Buxton and Pease were in favour of reverting to the situation as it stood before the Osborne Judgment: trade unions would recover the power to make a compulsory levy on their members for political purposes. They were opposed by Asquith, Crewe, McKenna, Burns and Churchill, who took the view that 'to compel a man to subscribe to his political opponent & give him no option but to starve was unsupportable'. As no agreement could be reached, the question was held over for examination by the law officers, and the discussion resumed, in the shadow of Tonypandy, on 22

November. Loreburn, Samuel, Buxton and Pease declared themselves in favour of 'majority rule' with a conscience clause. This would enable a trade union to establish a political fund if a majority of the members voted in favour, while allowing objectors to opt out. Grey and Morley stood out for contributions on a purely voluntary basis. Churchill and Haldane 'took an extreme anti-Trade Union view supported by Burns'.[74]

If Churchill did indeed express extreme views, they were overruled. As Asquith reported to the King, the Cabinet decided on a policy that was broadly favourable to the unions:

(1) Payment of Members, & of official expenses
(2) Restoration by legislation to the Trade Unions of the power ... of providing a fund for Parliamentary and municipal expenditure & representation
But by way of safeguard
(3) The power not to be exercised until it has been "effectively ascertained" (by secret ballot, or some other mode of procedure) that it is the wish of the members of the Union and
(4) In no case is a member to be compelled to contribute to the fund, or to suffer any disability for refusing to contribute
(5) The fund to be kept separate from the general funds of the Union.[75]

Churchill was a member of the Cabinet Committee which prepared the first draft of the Trade Union Bill, and it was he who introduced it into the House of Commons on 30 May 1911. Whatever the opinions he had expressed in Cabinet, he now rested the Government's case squarely on the proposition that it was 'quite impossible' to prevent trade unions from entering politics: 'The sphere of industrial and political activity is often indistinguishable, always overlaps, and representation in Parliament is absolutely necessary to trade unions . . . ' While placing a strong emphasis on the right of trade unionists to opt out of the political levy on conscientious grounds, he went on to express the warmest approval of trade unions in general:

I consider that every workman is well advised to join a trade union. I cannot conceive how any man standing undefended against the powers that be in this world could be so foolish, if he can possibly spare the money from the maintenance of his family, not to associate himself with an organisation to protect the rights and interests of labour . . . [76]

The Trade Union Bill of 1911 had to be halted in its tracks while the juggernaut of the Parliament Bill rolled by, but in 1913 it was reintroduced in substantially the same form, and this time enacted.

Did Churchill foresee that a measure which guaranteed the funding of the Labour party might have consequences fatal to Liberalism? It is unlikely that he did. The Asquith Government was moving confidently ahead with an ambitious programme of social reform. On 4 May 1911 Lloyd George placed before the House of Commons his new health insurance plan – Part 1 of the National Insurance Bill. On 25 May Churchill spoke in support of Part 2, the unemployment insurance scheme which he had pioneered at the Board of Trade. 'There is no proposal in the field of politics which I care more about,' Churchill declared. 'There is exhilaration in the study of insurance questions because there is a sense of elaborating new and increased powers which have been devoted to the service of mankind ... we bring in the magic of averages to the aid of the million.'[77]

In the spring of 1911 the dispute in the south Wales coalfield was still rumbling on, but it was no longer a focus of political attention. In June, however, a second wave of industrial action began with a national seamen's strike in the ports. This rapidly spread to the dockers and in August, the railway workers joined in. The Government was suddenly faced by the possibility of an almost complete standstill in the import and distribution of food supplies. The local authorities, prompted by the port and shipping employers, appealed to the Government to provide troops or extra police for the protection of strike-breaking workers. In June, Churchill authorised the despatch of extra police to Hull. In July, responding to an appeal from the Lord Mayor of Manchester, he moved a detachment of the Royal Scots Greys to Salford. In south Wales troops were sent to Cardiff, Newport, and Pontypridd. When riots broke out again at Tonypandy, they were suppressed, the Chief Constable of Cardiff reported, by the dispositions of the Somerset Light Infantry, in conjunction with the police.[78]

In the policing of the dispute Churchill strove to ensure the impartial enforcement of the law as between workman and employer. On 4 August he settled, in consultation with Troup, the following guidelines for the use of the Metropolitan police in the London dock strike:

> Owners have a right to load or unload cargoes by voluntary labour imported if necessary, and the Police Authorities will secure them the exercise of that right. The Police Authorities must, however, be the judges in each particular case as to the time, manner and circumstances in which any importation of outside labour or other step likely to lead to disturbance will be taken ...

Strikers have a right, under the Trade Disputes Act, 1906, to picket for the purpose of peacefully persuading labourers from working during the course of the dispute. These rights must be respected. In exercise of these rights the Police Authorities will allow the strikers to place pickets in convenient positions provided that the pickets confine themselves to peaceful persuasion, are not in numbers sufficient to intimidate, and do not cause an obstruction to the traffic ... [79]

During the first week of August a general strike of transport workers in Liverpool precipitated riots on a scale approaching that of a local civil war. Acting once more on the request of the local authority, by 14 August Churchill had given orders to bring the strength of forces in the city up to a complete brigade of infantry and two regiments of cavalry. The following day one man was shot dead by troops when a crowd attempted to prevent the movement of a prison van escorted by soldiers. As a further precautionary measure, Churchill arranged with the Admiralty for the cruiser *Antrim* to be despatched to the Mersey to assist in the protection of the docks.[80]

Churchill recognised that industrial discontent was grounded in legitimate grievances. He urged an inquiry by a committee representing the employers, unions and the Government, to investigate the causes of unrest and propose remedies. At the same time, he argued that events were coming to a head and that decisive issues would soon have to be confronted:

Serious crises have been in recent years, and very often lately, surmounted only by a narrow margin of safety and now specially a new force has arisen in trades unionism, whereby the power of the old leaders has proved quite ineffective, and the sympathetic strike on a wide scale is prominent. Shipping, coal, railways, dockers etc. etc. are all uniting and breaking out at once. The 'general strike' policy is a factor which must be dealt with.

While control can probably be maintained, even in a dozen or more simultaneous Tonypandys or Manchesters, control would be more difficult if the railways went, and adequate control must mean great uncertainty, destruction of property, and probably loss of life.[81]

The first moment of truth occurred early in August when the London docks were brought to a standstill. Pressure built up on Churchill from various quarters to send in the troops to unload the ships and convoy food through the city. On 11 August he informed the King that 25,000 soldiers were being held in readiness outside the capital.[82] But whether from innate caution, or because he was influenced by the pleas of Ben Tillett, Churchill decided to allow time for mediation by G.R. Askwith, the chief industrial conciliator at the Board of Trade. The dispute was finally settled by a meeting at the Home Office on 18 August and Tillett subsequently recorded his gratitude to the Home Secretary: 'He refused to listen to the clamour of class hatred, he saved the country from a national transport stoppage becoming a riot and incipient revolution.'[83] But Churchill himself drew a different conclusion. Writing to the King he claimed that the Government's intention to use very large bodies of troops had exercised a potent influence on the men's decision: 'They knew they had reached the psychological moment to make their bargain, & that to go on was to risk all that they had within their grasp.'[84]

During the national railway strike of 18–19 August, Churchill again employed the army in a display of force calculated to make the strikers back down. In preparation for the strike, troops were marched into London and thirty-two other towns in England and Wales.[85] Previously the use of troops had been governed by two principles: firstly they were only provided at the request of the local authority concerned, and secondly it was understood that such requests were only to be made after a breakdown of order had occurred. But on the eve of the strike Churchill swept these conventions aside and suspended the Army Regulation which required a requisition from a civil authority.[86] The purpose of the troops, apart from the protection of the rail network from sabotage, was to enable the companies to continue as best they could with non-union labour. This led directly to the incident at Llanelli on the second day of the dispute. A train driven by blackleg labour was halted by strikers, and soldiers of the Worcestershire regiment intervened to clear the tracks. After the reading of the Riot Act, troops fired into the crowd killing two men.[87]

Churchill appears to have had the support of Asquith and most of the Cabinet. Lord Crewe recorded that the Prime Minister and his colleagues were 'full of fight against these dangerous elements'; Lloyd George was out of step in his more conciliatory approach.[88] After a summer of discontent the unprecedented challenge of a simultaneous national stoppage by all four railway unions convinced respectable opinion that the world was about to be turned upside down. The conjunction of the crisis at home with persistent tension abroad in the aftermath of the Agadir incident contributed to a spasm of acute insecurity. *The Times* commented on 16 August: 'These trade unionists in their crazy fanaticism or diseased vanity are prepared to starve the whole population, including of course their own families and all the ranks of "Labour" to ruin the country and leave it defenceless to the world.'[89]

Churchill's own apprehensions were connected, apparently, with fear of subversion in Germany. No doubt his chairmanship of the Aliens Committee of the CID had something to do with this. He was also informed by Guy Granet, the general manager of the Midland Railways, of allegations that labour leaders were receiving payments from a German agent called Bebel. On 18 August the clerk of the Privy Council, Sir Almeric Fitzroy, noted in his diary: 'Winston Churchill is said to be convinced that the whole trouble is fomented by German gold, and claims to have proof of it, which others regard as midsummer madness.'[90]

In the event, the rail strike was rapidly ended by the intervention of Lloyd George. But Churchill's role was a focus of controversy. Conservatives applauded him for taking decisive action. But there were loud protests from the Labour party and left-wing Liberals, who accused him of imposing the army on local authorities against their will, and introducing troops into peaceful and law-abiding districts. Former allies, like W.H. Massingham of *The Nation*, and C.P. Scott of the *Manchester Guardian*, turned against him. Keir Hardie went further by accusing Asquith and Churchill of deliberately sending soldiers to shoot and kill strikers, an allegation repeated in his pamphlet entitled *Killing No Murder*.[91]

We have it on the authority of Lucy Masterman that when Lloyd George settled the rail strike, Churchill immediately telephoned him to say that he was sorry to hear of it: ' "It would have been better to have gone on and given these men a good thrashing." '[92] The reforms Churchill had pursued at the Board of Trade and the Home Office were paternal in spirit and intended to enhance the authority of the state. When sections of the working-class began to challenge the state's authority, Churchill adopted a belligerent posture: the spirit of insubordination must be broken. By the end of the long, hot summer of 1911 his identity as a radical reformer had been fatally compromised in the eyes of radicals and socialists.

Churchill stoutly defended himself. In a handwritten letter to William Royle, the organiser of the Liberal party in Manchester, he argued:

The progress of a democratic country is bound up with the maintenance of order. The working classes would be almost the only sufferers from an outbreak of riot & a general strike if it cd be effective would fall upon them & their families with its fullest severity. At the same time the wages now paid are too low and the rise in the cost of living (due mainly to the increased gold supply) makes it absolutely necessary that they shd. be raised. I have never heard of the British people complaining (as they now do) without a good & just cause.

I believe the Government is now strong enough to secure an improvement in social conditions without failing in its primary duties.[93]

# 5
## *Undertones of War*

## 1911–18

In July 1911, while Churchill was still at the Home Office, there occurred a fateful turning-point in his career. On 1 July it was announced that the German gunboat *Panther* was on its way to the port of Agadir in Morocco. Ostensibly this was a demonstration against the growing influence of France in Morocco, but whether Morocco was the real issue, or a way of testing the strength of the Anglo-French *entente*, or a pretext for war, no one in London could tell. For several weeks during July and August, the months in which industrial strife was at its most intense, war with Germany appeared imminent.

Lloyd George and Churchill, who had previously been regarded as pacifically inclined radicals in foreign policy, declared themselves in favour of resisting Germany. Lloyd George signalled his change of position in the Mansion House speech of 21 July. Churchill gave no public indication of his views, but to him the crisis was of even greater significance. Stimulated by the prospect of hostilities, he plunged for the first time into the study of the naval and military role of Britain in a European war. On the initiative of Asquith, he was invited to a secret meeting of the Committee of Imperial Defence on 23 August, which reviewed the war plans of the Army and the Navy. The meeting exposed the inadequacy of the Admiralty and the need for an overhaul of the machinery of naval planning.

The Admiralty was technically a Cabinet post inferior to the Home Office. But it was extremely glamorous, carrying with it a romantic association with the Royal Navy, the uniform of First Lord of the Admiralty, and cruises aboard the Admiralty yacht *Enchantress*. Haldane, the Secretary for War, had a high opinion of himself and pressed Asquith to send him to the Admiralty to sort out the confusion exposed by Agadir. But Churchill had an even higher opinion of himself, and pressed Asquith still harder. Asquith gave in, decreeing that Churchill and McKenna, the existing First Lord, should change places. McKenna was profoundly reluctant but had to accept Asquith's bidding. Churchill, for his part, could hardly wait to dismiss his first Admiral. He took office on 21 October 1911. On 28 November he announced to the House of Commons that three of the four Sea Lords had been replaced.

Churchill had long been interested in naval and military questions. But he had never before connected them with the glittering opportunities of fame and adventure which had recently presented themselves. Agadir transported him into a new world of deliciously exciting possibilities. His state of mind was very like that of his fictional contemporary Mr Toad, after his first encounter with a motor-car: 'They found him in a sort of trance, a happy smile on his face, his eyes still fixed on the dusty wake of their destroyer. At intervals he was still heard to murmur: "Poop-poop!" '[1]

It is almost true to say that from the Agadir crisis of 1911 to the Armistice of 1918, Churchill was interested in nothing but war, preparations for war, and the conduct of naval and military operations. Inevitably, a study of Churchill in home affairs must diverge sharply from biography at this point, accelerating past some of the most spectacular and controversial episodes of his career. But the domestic undertones must not be overlooked. There were times when peacetime issues, like Ireland or votes for women, demanded his attention. There was also a strong thread of continuity between the social and the military phases of Churchill's career. Churchill appreciated the importance of the home front in wartime, and he tended to apply to it the collectivising mentality he had acquired in social and economic affairs.

\* \* \*

The Agadir crisis served as a reminder of the fact that one of Britain's potential weaknesses in time of war was its dependence on imported food and raw materials. If the supply of imports were cut off, the population would starve and the economy collapse. One of the risks which had to be taken into account was the possibility that in time of war the cost of insurance for shipping would rise to the point at which shipowners would cease trading, and imports would come to a stop. Mindful of this danger, a Royal Commission had recommended in 1905 that the Government should introduce a scheme of state insurance against war risks.

The question became a significant issue in the conflict between supporters and opponents of state intervention. Between 1905 and 1910 the issue was the subject of a desultory debate in Whitehall, with the Board of

Trade and the Admiralty in favour of the proposal, and the Treasury successfully opposing it. There the matter rested until the summer of 1911, when the Government experienced simultaneous shocks at home and abroad. Transport strikes temporarily paralysed the import and distribution of food, and revealed the alarmingly low level of food stocks in the major cities. This at the very moment when a war with Germany appeared to be imminent. 'By the middle of September', writes David French, 'both crises had passed their peak but they had left behind them at least one positive legacy. They had awoken the Home Secretary, Winston Churchill, to the possibility that a similar crisis could occur on the outbreak of war.'[2]

In a letter to Asquith, Churchill warned that a future Home Secretary 'might have to maintain order without the military assistance which is available in ordinary circumstances; and nothing would more inevitably lead to riots and disturbances than a shortage of the food supplies, or even a considerable rise in the price of necessaries due to mere panic.' The solution, Churchill believed, was a state scheme to cover war risks to shipping. He was converted to the idea by Sir Frederick Bolton, an insurance broker and shipowner whose previous efforts to convince the Government had failed. On 13 September Churchill forwarded Bolton's proposals to McKenna, the First Lord of the Admiralty, who had already studied the problem and was plainly unimpressed. Within forty-eight hours of taking over from McKenna at the Admiralty, Churchill took the matter up with Asquith and pressed for the appointment of a subcommittee of the Committee of Imperial Defence to review the question.[3]

Asquith responded by appointing a subcommittee under the chairmanship of Churchill himself. The committee set to work in December 1911, but Churchill encountered strong resistance from the Permanent Secretary to the Treasury, Robert Chalmers, and Walter Runciman, who was present in his capacity as a shipowner. They believed that in war as in peace the laws of supply and demand would hold good, or, as French puts it 'that higher freight rates and food prices would combine to encourage shipowners to send their vessels to sea regardless of the danger.' In order to break the deadlock Churchill turned to Llewellyn Smith, his former guide and mentor at the Board of Trade, and invited him to produce a new version of the scheme.[4]

When the new scheme was put to the Committee of Imperial Defence in February 1913, Churchill did his best to instil a sence of urgency into pitched the argument high. German commerce raiders, he predicted, might well succeed in deterring shipowners from trading. The consequent rise in food prices would produce popular discontent on such a scale that the Government might be forced to conclude an early peace on disastrous terms. But he was again blocked by Chalmers and Runciman, with the assistance now of McKenna. Runciman and McKenna argued that Churchill was exaggerating the danger from German commerce raiders, and that the scheme as drafted would lay the Treasury open to fraud by unscrupulous shipowners. Owing to the indecision of Asquith, the matter was to remain in suspense until the very last days of peace. Then, on 31 July 1914, the shipowners began to clamour for action. Opposition to the measure disappeared and on 3 August a bill embodying Llewellyn Smith's scheme was introduced into the House of Commons, and swiftly passed into law.[5] It cannot be a coincidence that Churchill and Llewellyn Smith, who had collaborated on state insurance against unemployment, should have been the authors of state insurance against war risks to shipping. The collectivist reforms of the pre-war Liberal Government in social policy were an unconscious preparation for the role the state would play in wartime.

*

The broader picture of Churchill's activities as First Lord of the Admiralty is well known. As Arthur Marder has written, his frequent visits to the fleet and the dockyards 'earned him little popularity'. Tales were circulated of his arrogance towards officers on board ship, while at the Admiralty he offended his advisers by trying to force his opinions upon them.[6] Churchill was an abrasive, but authentic innovator. He created a naval war staff responsible for operational planning. With the enthusiastic support of Sir John Fisher, he laid down the construction programme for a new Fast Division of battleships, the 'Queen Elizabeth' class, equipped with 15-inch guns and fuelled by oil instead of coal. There was an element of Liberalism in his policies, or at least in their presentation. On two occasions he proposed to name a battleship *Oliver Cromwell*, but was overruled by King George V. More substantially, he tried to operate the Napoleonic principle of the career open to talent by increasing the opportunities for promotion of seamen and petty officers. There was also one direct link with his previous involvement in social policy: his reform of conditions on the Lower Deck.

As Churchill explained to the Cabinet in October 1912, there had been no increase in the rate of pay for Ordinary and Able Seamen since 1857. Their diet had improved, and there were more specialist ratings to which they might rise, but the fact remained that the sailor's basic pay had declined markedly by comparison with the wages of soldiers, policemen, railwaymen, dockers and others. And as Churchill pointed out, the Navy could not be insulated from the industrial unrest of the period:

> ... there is a deep and widespread sense of injustice and discontent
> throughout all ranks and ratings of the Navy. This discontent and the
> grievances which produce it are fanned and advertised in Parliament
> and the press. It is rendered more dangerous by every successful
> strike for higher wages which takes place on shore. It is rendered
> more legitimate by the social legislation upon which Parliament is
> engaged, and by measures like the Minimum Wage Bill which secure
> to the coal-miner rates of wages which, though spoken of in terms of
> biting contempt by the miners, are nearly double what the sailor can
> hope to obtain ... The reports of the German agents dwell continually
> upon the discontent of the sailors with their conditions of pay, and there
> is no doubt that German opinion on this point is as well founded as it is
> widespread. We have had great mutinies in the past in the British Navy,
> and we ought not to continue to bear the responsibility of refusing all
> redress to grievances so obvious and so harsh.[7]

Encouraged by Fisher, in 1912 Churchill introduced a number of
reforms including the abolition of some humiliating forms of punishment
and the introduction of a more generous system of leave.[8] But pay was
the key issue. Churchill proposed that after three years' service, weekly
pay should be increased by fourpence to two shillings, at a cost to the
Treasury (including a small sum for officers' pay) of £552,000 a year.
To his dismay, the Estimates Committee of the Cabinet cut the sum
on 1 November to £336,000. There was to be no pay increase until six
years' service had been completed. In vain Churchill appealed to the full
Cabinet, circulating for their information a 'loyal appeal' or 'Naval Magna
Carta' drawn up by representatives of the Lower Deck. (This remarkable
document contained a long list of demands including the right to wear
plain clothes when on leave, the issue of free kit, and the provision by
the Admiralty of naval sanatoria for the victims of tuberculosis contracted
while in service.) On 27 November the Cabinet rejected his plea for the
restoration of the more generous rate of pay originally proposed, at which,
so Hobhouse recorded, he 'stormed, sulked, interrupted'.[9] Unlike the
miners, the seamen had no votes and no constituencies.

At the Board of Trade, Churchill had called for the nationalisation
of the railways. At the Admiralty, he nationalised the Anglo-Persian Oil
Company. There was, of course, no ideological motive. This was a rare
case, as Marian Jack has shown, of a company persuading a Government
to take it over. The Anglo-Persian Oil Company was threatened by

competition from Shell and eager to obtain the position of monopoly supplier to the Admiralty. Though Shell was based in London, and a majority of its directors were British, the shareholding was 60 per cent Dutch. This enabled Anglo-Persian to impress on the Foreign Office and the Admiralty the idea that Shell was essentially a foreign concern, and therefore unreliable from the point of view of national security. It was also alleged that Shell, which had ambitions to take over Anglo-Persian, was seeking to create a world monopoly. The Foreign Office, the Admiralty, and Churchill himself, were all taken in by company propaganda.[10]

So far as Churchill and the Admiralty were concerned, the primary requirement was a secure and continuous supply of oil to meet the needs of the new fast division of oil-fired ships. Accordingly Churchill appointed, in 1912, a Royal Commission on Fuel Oil, under the chairmanship of Fisher, to report on the supply and use of oil for naval purposes. Churchill himself was a reluctant nationaliser. His first inclination, like that of his advisers, was to negotiate a twenty-year supply contract. In December 1912, when the company itself proposed a government stake in the ownership, Churchill rejected the idea. He was converted, as Dr. Jack informs us, by the recommendations of the Royal Commission and War Staff. Churchill announced the new policy to the House of Commons on 17 July 1913:

Our ultimate policy is that the Admiralty should become the independent owner and producer of its own supplies of liquid fuel, first, by building up an oil reserve in this country sufficient to make us safe in war and able to override price fluctuations in peace; secondly, by acquiring the power to deal in crude oils as they come cheaply on to the market ... The third aspect of the ultimate policy is that we must become the owners, or at any rate the controllers at the source of at least a proportion of the supply of natural oil which we require.[11]

In August 1914 the Government purchased a controlling share in The Anglo-Persian Oil Company. Strictly speaking, this was an unnecessary measure. Even if the company had been taken over by Shell, oil contracts would have been secure, and no Shell monopoly would have resulted. But in the long run ownership did bring an advantage in terms of price. After the First World War, the British Government obtained cheaper oil than it would have done on the open market.[12]

A further consequence of Churchill's study of defence problems was a change in his attitude towards conscription. Since the manpower requirements of the Royal Navy were small and easily met, this was not an issue directly affecting the Admiralty. But potentially it was of immense significance for the recruitment and training of the Army, and hence for war preparations in general.

On the Continent, the conscription of young men for a period of military service was the norm. In Britain it was the great unthinkable. Ever since 1660, wars had been fought by volunteer armies, and freedom from conscription had come to be regarded as one of the hallmarks of English liberty. But towards the end of the South African war, a ripple of dissent appeared. A National Service League was founded to promote the ideal of compulsory military training in peacetime. This was a modest plan, involving short periods of annual instruction under canvas, and quite distinct from conscription into the Army. But it was widely regarded as a step towards outright conscription, and correspondingly unpopular. In 1905 the Presidency of the League was taken over by Field-Marshall Lord Roberts on his retirement as Commander-in-Chief, but the lustre of his name made little difference. Compulsory national service was a hobby-horse for retired military men and obscure Tory back-benchers.

Gradually, however, Anglo-German rivalry, and the tuning up of patriotic feeling by right-wing publicists, began to lend a certain respectability to the campaign. Haldane's new Territorial Army opened up a fertile field for propaganda. The Territorials were a force raised for the purpose of defending the homeland against invasion: so, it could be argued, every male citizen had an obligation to defend hearth and home by training for the Territorials. In July 1909, a bill for the compulsory territorial training of all men between the ages of eighteen and thirty was introduced into the House of Lords with the support of Roberts and the National Service League, and obtained 103 votes.

After the Agadir crisis of 1911, the question was again 'in the air', though most party politicians were still reluctant to touch it – the Liberals from principle, the Conservatives, perhaps, from fear of the electoral consequences. In the New Year of 1912 Roberts pressed Churchill strongly to take up the question of a national service, arguing that Agadir had exposed the fact that the Army, both regular and territorial, was unprepared for war. Churchill replied: 'I was when I first went into Parlt strongly opposed to the principle of compulsory service. I am disposed somewhat differently now towards it. As to the right of the State & the duty of the citizen there can be no doubt. But I am far from certain that it is necessary or that it would be convenient.'[13]

The fact that Roberts should approach Churchill is illuminating in itself. The word was out that Churchill was a changed man: no longer the economist and pro-German, but a big navy man strong for national defence. The impression was reinforced by Churchill's clear and firm response, in the opening months of 1912, to the proposed new German naval law. In February 1912 the Government embarked on negotiations with Germany to end the naval arms race, and Lord Haldane was despatched to Berlin in search of an agreement. Churchill supported the negotiations, but only on condition that Britain retained a clear-cut margin of naval supremacy. Speaking in Glasgow on 9 February 1912 he warned that while the Fleet was a vital necessity to the British Empire, the German Navy was from some points of view 'more in the nature of a luxury'. When he presented the naval estimates to the House, on 18 March, he swept away the cobwebs of evasion and proclaimed for the first time the goal of a 60 per cent superiority in capital ships over Germany alone. His speech won high praise from the Conservative press – though Conservative politicians continued to mistrust him profoundly, a fact of which he was probably oblivious. To Churchill, yesterday's politics were battles to be recalled in a mellow and magnanimous spirit. But the wounded and the defeated were slow to forgive.

In March 1913 eleven Conservative MPs and one Liberal sponsored a private member's bill to introduce compulsory training for the Territorial Army. Churchill, who was deep in the study of plans for the defence of Britain in the event of an attempted German invasion, was greatly excited. In private he was all in favour of the bill and tempted to declare himself in public. The unexpurgated version of the Riddell diaries reveals the way his mind was working:

> He outlined to me his views on national service and other matters. He said that he felt he must make an early declaration on the subject and proposed to say that while the Navy was thoroughly efficient and while there was no cause for immediate alarm, he could not see his way to oppose a scheme of national service . . .
> Winston then proceeded to put forward a proposal for a national party. He said, "The time will soon be ripe for a joinder of the two parties. A national party could secure great aims. The Conservative section in exchange for a system of national service could agree to a minimum wage for agricultural labourers and other trades, and to a reform of the land system. Our national life requires more organisation and more discipline. There is a body of sensible men in both parties who are tired of the existing state of things. In both parties there are fools at one end and crackpots at the other, but the great body in the middle is sound and wise.[14]

On 10 April, when the Cabinet debated the Government's response to the bill, Churchill, Lloyd George and Haldane declared their support for compulsory training, while McKenna, Runciman, Hobhouse and Harcourt were opposed.[15] The Government decided not to support the bill and Churchill not to declare himself. None the less the episode is worth recording for the vivid glimpse it affords of Churchill rehearsing, behind the scenes of party rhetoric, the politics of national unity.

\*

Churchill was not wholly absorbed in defence. Under Asquith, there was genuine Cabinet government. The whole range of policy was discussed in Cabinet and ministers communicated freely with one another on matters outside their own particular departmental responsibilities. The First Lord of the Admiralty aired his views on many topics, and of these one of the most important for the future of British politics was the reform of the franchise.

Asquith had announced in November 1911 that the Government proposed to introduce a bill providing for manhood suffrage. Rightly or wrongly, Liberal party agents in the constituencies were convinced that franchise reform would benefit the party at the next general election. To this extent, the bill was a straight party issue between the Liberals and the Conservatives. But Asquith had also announced that the bill would be so drafted as to allow for an amendment to include votes for women. The problem was that votes for women was still a controversial issue within the Liberal party.

The Women's Social and Political Union believed that Asquith's promise was a trick intended to postpone votes for women indefinitely. But Churchill feared the opposite: that female enfranchisement was about to become a reality. Churchill had opposed the Conciliation Bill in 1910 on the grounds that it was undemocratic and advantageous to the Conservative party. He was now confronted with the prospect of an amendment that was democratic and (arguably) advantageous to the Liberal party. Given that his previously stated objections had now been met, would he declare himself in favour of a women's suffrage amendment? The answer was in the negative. In December 1911 Churchill wrote to Asquith, Grey, Lloyd George, and the Liberal Chief Whip, Elibank, to express vehement opposition. The enfranchisement of eight million women, he warned Elibank, could never be accomplished without a general election. The opposition of the King and the House of Lords, together with the unpopularity of votes for women, would force a dissolution of Parliament. Moreover the Government and the party would split as the Conservatives had split over free trade in 1903: 'What a ridiculous tragedy it would be if this strong Government and party which has made its mark on history were to go down on Petticoat politics!' Churchill's solution was to promise two referenda: 'first to the women, to know whether they want it: and then to the men to know whether they will give it. I am quite willing to abide by the result.'[16] No doubt he would have been, for in all probability the male electorate would have voted in favour of the continued exclusion of women. How the women would have voted is impossible to judge.

Churchill still claimed to be a suffragist, as the editor of the *Manchester Guardian*, C.P. Scott, discovered when lunching with him in January 1912. Churchill explained that he would admit to the franchise 'the women who really want and need it – graduates, doctors, poor law Guardians and members of town councils – by categories, as many as could be devised perhaps 100,000 in all.' The origins of this idea can be traced back to a scheme prepared for Churchill by Sir Edward Troup at the Home Office in July 1910.[17] As more than seven million men already had the vote under the existing franchise, and a further extension was in prospect, Churchill's scheme would have reduced the female vote to a drop in the ocean – which was, of course, the intention. As he remarked to Lord Riddell in March 1912: 'The truth is we already have enough ignorant voters and don't want any more.'[18]

Churchill's opposition was unavailing. The franchise bill was duly introduced, and passed its second reading on 12 July 1912. Grey, the Foreign Secretary, put down an amendment in favour of including women on the same terms as men. There the matter rested until the third and final reading of the bill, which was due to begin on 24 January 1913. When the Cabinet reviewed the bill in the New Year, Churchill expressed some reservations about the extent of male suffrage. The qualifying period of residence was to be reduced from twelve to six months. Churchill, together with Grey, Samuel, Buxton and Hobhouse, wanted to put up the qualifying age from twenty-one to twenty-three or twenty-five. When Asquith said that it was too late to alter the bill, Churchill got very excited and demanded that the Whips be taken off and a free vote taken when the bill came to a division.[19]

Churchill was also disturbed by the prospect that large numbers of soldiers would obtain the vote for the first time. Under the existing franchise, soldiers in married quarters were entitled to the vote, but not soldiers in barracks. Under the terms of the bill, a barracks was to be counted as a residence, and Churchill estimated that the number of soldiers on the register would increase from about 10,250 to about 75,000. In a Cabinet memorandum of 8 January he warned:

No one can possibly doubt that the extension of the vote to 75,000 men dwelling together in large masses under military discipline will produce the immediate development of a class campaign for the improvement of the soldiers' conditions. We shall have, in fact, a tremendous trade union made, voting as a trade union, and able to force their will on any point they care about sufficiently by the use of lethal weapons.'[20]

Shortly after this, Churchill was relieved of all his anxieties about franchise reform by an unexpected twist in the parliamentary plot. On 23 January, Bonar Law asked for a ruling from the Speaker of the House on whether the amendments in favour of female suffrage were in order. The Speaker ruled that as the amendments would substantially alter the bill, they could not be accepted, and another bill would have to be introduced if votes for women were to be included. On 27 January the Cabinet decided that it could not break its promise to the suffragists by proceeding with a measure of male franchise alone. Once more the issue was postponed.

Both moderate and militant feminists were outraged. The National Union of Women's Suffrage Societies broke with the Liberal party and allied itself with Labour. The Pankhursts and their followers, convinced that the Speaker's ruling was a Government conspiracy, turned to more extreme tactics. Pictures were defaced, telephone wires cut, buildings set on fire, and bombs exploded in empty churches. The suffragettes stopped just short of murder, but their extreme behaviour played into the hands of the opponents of women's suffrage. In Parliament, opinion swung sharply against votes for women, and Churchill could breathe again in the knowledge that the threat had receded over the horizon.

There was also, in Churchill's view, a class threat posed by militants among the industrial workers. In December 1911 Churchill's own constituency of Dundee witnessed a strike of dockers and carters which closed the jute factories and threw 30,000 textile workers out of employment. Three hundred men from the first battalion of the Black Watch were drafted into the city.[21] In the New Year of 1912 a general strike broke out in Glasgow. Over dinner at the Other Club, in February 1912, Churchill remarked that what had most impressed him on his recent visit to Scotland was 'the unfriendly and disaffected attitude of the working classes. He said they evidently mean trouble.'[22]

There was indeed more trouble ahead. The Miners Federation of Great Britain was determined to enforce on the employers a national minimum wage of five shillings a week for men, and two shillings a week for boys. The Cabinet faced the prospect of the first ever national coal strike. The possibilities of economic disruption, social disorder, and political collapse in the coalfields were so alarming that on 20 February the Cabinet decided to intervene. But the miners refused to accept the Government's compromise proposals. On 1 March some 850,000 miners went out on strike. Another 1,300,000 workers were thrown out of work as a consequence.

Churchill's reaction must have owed something to the fact that the ships of the Royal Navy were still mainly dependent upon coal. There was no immediate shortage of stocks, but Churchill undoubtedly had the long-term danger in mind. Only the previous September, he had been urging McKenna, his predecessor at the Admiralty, to build up coal stocks in preparation for a future general strike.[23]

On 1 March Churchill made a tolerant and sympathetic reference to the strike in a speech at a London dinner. But his words should also be read as a veiled warning to the miners to behave themselves and settle the dispute quickly:

The miners are a great community. They have great responsibilities entrusted to them. They have a great part in our national life. We owe them much, and they owe us much. They are flesh of our flesh and bone of our bone. Of course they are trying like everyone else in this restless age to better themselves, but I have yet to learn that the miners of this country would pursue a course, with their eyes open, which they believed would involve deep and lasting injury, or bring suffering on the great mass of their poorer fellow-countrymen.'[24]

Such exhortations reflected the fact that the Cabinet were in a weak position. During the first two weeks of March Asquith and other ministers tried in vain to persuade the miners' leaders to modify their demands. The miners, for their part, were convinced that the Government would be forced to come down on their side, and coerce the owners into a settlement. Sure enough Asquith announced, at a conference of miners and mine owners on 15 March that the Government would introduce statutory minimum wages, to be determined by local boards. No figures were to be specified in the legislation.

Grey, Buxton and Lloyd George were parties to this decision, but Asquith had acted without consulting the Cabinet. Next morning – a Saturday – an emergency meeting of the Cabinet was summoned, and a very full account of the discussion was recorded by the Chief Whip, J.A. Pease, in his diary. Morley spoke strongly against the principle of fixing wages by statute. Lloyd George was strongly in favour and spoke of nationalising the mines if the arrangements were not accepted by the owners. Grey too supported legislation on the grounds that the alternative was 'chaos, riots, bloodshed, national loss, disaster and misery'. Churchill, however, was against the proposals. As the author himself of minimum wage legislation, he was not opposed to the principle of state interference, but he believed the Government must resist attempts to coerce it. As Pease recorded, he

> took great exception to the proposals and said that he could not accept legislation, it was a surrender to menace, it gave the victory to the men when they were in the wrong, & at the very moment when they were breaking up all over the kingdom & quarrelling among themselves, & many ready to go back to work & end the strike.

Evidently, Pease continued, Churchill and Lloyd George had differed before entering the Cabinet: 'their eyes & teeth were flashing.'[25]

The bill was introduced into the House of Commons on 19 March. The miners, however, demanded that the five shilling and two shilling minimum wage rates be written into the bill. In the Cabinet, the only minister to support the miners' demand was Lloyd George. He was overruled, and the decision went in favour of the majority of the Cabinet who preferred the middle position of carrying on with the bill as it stood. Churchill, however, took up a position at the opposite end of the spectrum from Lloyd George. 'Churchill', wrote Pease on 21 March, 'was for forcing men with soldiers, & advocated a strong course to induce men to come back to work by Gov protection & higher pay guaranteed. We all listened to such twaddle with impatience . . . '[26]

The Minimum Wages Act was passed on 29 March, and shortly afterwards a miners' ballot produced a majority in favour of a return to work. The crisis was over, but others were anticipated, and Lloyd George was put in charge of a Cabinet committee on industrial unrest. Churchill was not a member, and rumour had it that he and Lloyd George were now out of step. 'The alliance between LG and Winston has broken up,' Masterman told Riddell at the end of April. 'They are still as friendly as ever, but are not concerting joint plans of action as formerly.'[27]

This was true. On some issues Churchill and Lloyd George were still allies. But on others they disagreed openly in Cabinet. The diaries of Riddell and Lucy Masterman reveal that Lloyd George lost no opportunity to convey the impression that Churchill's growing conservatism was the cause of the rift. In July 1912, for instance, he told Riddell of his belief that in recent weeks Churchill had been thinking of 'going over to the other side'.[28] But there is no evidence to support this allegation and it would be unwise to take Lloyd George's opinions at face value. Lloyd George valued Churchill as a subordinate but feared him as an equal.

In social policy Churchill had accepted a subordinate role. But in naval affairs he was entirely independent, and making a reputation on his own account. There was, besides, a perennial conflict between the Admiralty's demands for expenditure and the Treasury's determination to balance the books.

It was true that Churchill was wobbling towards the Right on various issues, and coalition-minded from time to time. But Lloyd George's own position was ambivalent. In 1910 he had secretly proposed to compromise Liberal policies in a coalition with the Conservatives. Though posing as the leader of left-wing Liberalism in the country, he was a pragmatist in Cabinet. On such key issues as the exclusion of Protestant Ulster from Irish Home Rule, or compulsory national service, he was in step with Churchill and out of step with radical opinion. Like Churchill, he was in close touch with F.E. Smith, and unlike him enjoyed tolerably good relations with Bonar Law. The greater distance between Churchill and Lloyd George may have owed something to differences of opinion, but it was mainly due to an underlying tension between two rival leaders.

\*

In social policy, Churchill and Lloyd George were no longer close, but there was no rift between them. Churchill was proud to claim that he was one of the originators of social insurance. Speaking of the National Insurance Bill in October 1911 he told his Dundee constituents: 'There is no proposal in the whole field of politics which I care more about than this insurance scheme.'[29] But the electorate were less enthusiastic. To the dismay of Liberal party managers, the proposals for compulsory health insurance, which covered more than fifteen million workers and their employers, proved unpopular. Nor was this surprising. Compulsory insurance contributions might entitle people to benefits at some future date, but they closely resembled a poll tax on the entire working-class. Employers, too, were liable to protest against the imposition of a compulsory levy on profits. The National Insurance Bill eventually reached the statute book in December 1911, but there were still question-marks over its future.

There was much excitable talk of a campaign of civil disobedience to wreck the scheme, but this particular threat failed to materialise. When the first contributions fell due, in July 1912, all but a handful of diehard libertarians complied with the law. There remained only the problem of overcoming the resistance of the medical profession. January 1913 was fixed as the date at which the health insurance scheme was to come fully into operation with the payment of the first benefits. But the British Medical Association was holding out for higher capitation fees, and a reduction in the number of workers covered by the scheme. As this was merely a dispute about doctors' pay, Lloyd George was confident that he would be able to strike a deal, and the Government had little to worry about. Speaking at Dundee in September 1912 Churchill celebrated health insurance as an accomplished fact, extolling Lloyd George as 'a man of genius, a man of courage, armed with power, a man sprung from the people'. Of the act itself he spoke as though it marked the beginning of a new epoch in history:

> We are an insured nation. Whatever may happen to the Government or to individual Ministers, be it bad or be it good, whatever the ebb and flow of party politics may be, this tremendous step – as great as anything which Bismarck ever did for the social life of Germany – has been taken. It can never be retraced and you and your children and your children's children, every household in the country, every class in the State will pay the contributions and draw the benefits and be influenced and affected by this legislation every week of their lives.[30]

After a timely concession by Lloyd George on capitation fees, the BMA's opposition began to collapse, and health insurance came into operation, as planned, on 15 January 1913. So, too, did unemployment insurance covering about two and a quarter million men – thus finally bringing into existence the scheme initiated by Churchill at the Board of Trade.

National insurance was a controversial issue throughout 1912, but Lloyd George was already looking ahead to the next phase of social politics. In July 1912, he set up, with the permission of Asquith, an unofficial Land Inquiry Committee. The object of the committee was to prepare a programme of land reform on which the Liberals could fight the next general election. Churchill agreed to lend his support and brief himself on the subject. With a staff of seventy researchers the Committee began a remarkably thorough investigation of such problems as 'landlord-tenant relations, agricultural rents and wages, town land values and rating, land development, rural depopulation, exploitation of natural resources, and special land conditions in Scotland and Wales.'[31]

The Land Committee had barely begun its work when Lloyd George was threatened by scandal. He and two other ministers – the Attorney

General, Rufus Isaacs, and the Chief Whip, Alexander Murray – were accused of speculating in the shares of the Marconi Company on the basis of privileged information acquired as members of the Government. All three had purchased shares in the American Marconi Company, shortly after the acceptance by the Government of a tender from the British Marconi Company to build a chain of wireless stations throughout the British Empire. The managing director of British Marconi, Godfrey Isaacs, was the brother of Sir Rufus Isaacs. Around these facts, discreditable in themselves, many libellous inventions were embroidered in right-wing periodicals. Since the Isaacs were Jews, as was the Postmaster General, Sir Herbert Samuel (who in fact knew nothing of his colleagues' financial speculations), there was plenty of scope for anti-semitic propaganda. More generally, the Marconi affair was held up by the Government's enemies as a revelation of the corrupt, plutocratic core of Liberalism. In October 1912 the Government was obliged to agree to the appointment of a Select Committee of the House to investigate the allegations.

Churchill was untouched by the scandal and, had he so wished, could simply have distanced himself from Lloyd George with many hypocritical expressions of sympathy. But as Randolph Churchill points out in the official biography of his father, Churchill intervened powerfully to shield Lloyd George from attack. He persuaded two Tory barristers, Carson and F.E. Smith, to appear in a libel action on behalf of Isaacs and Samuel; lobbied Northcliffe to play down the affair on the grounds that Lloyd George was blameless; and appeared himself before the Select Committee to mount a pugnacious counter-attack against the 'scandalmongers'.[32] The report of the Select Committee, published in June 1913, cleared all the accused of charges of corruption or improper conduct. It was, of course, a whitewash. But if Lloyd George had escaped, it was partly at least through the efforts of Churchill. The Marconi affair put Lloyd George in Churchill's debt. Perhaps, indeed, this was the intention: Masterman and Riddell were convinced that Churchill and Northcliffe were trying to 'rope L.G. into the National Service party'. Northcliffe himself remarked: 'This business will draw L.G.'s teeth. He cannot attack the rich as he has done in the past.'[33]

With the Marconi affair out of the way, Lloyd George began to prepare a land reform campaign for the autumn of 1913. In a speech at Bedford, on 11 October, he foreshadowed a programme to improve the housing and wages of agricultural labourers, and increase security of tenure for farmers. Churchill, who had agreed to assist in the campaign, followed up with the announcement in Manchester on 18 October of a pledge to introduce a minimum wage for agricultural workers.

Since Churchill had legislated for minimum wages in the sweated trades, it was of course appropriate that he should announce the extension of the principle to agricultural workers. As he was careful to point out, there were parallels between the lot of the unorganised worker in the town and in the countryside. 'It has hitherto been found impossible to form and maintain any effective union of agricultural labourers. They are weak, they are scattered, they are poverty-stricken, they are intimidated, they are held by the social and agrarian system in a grip which keeps them bound and tied at every point in absolute dependence.' Churchill did not go into details, or commit the government to the machinery of the Trade Boards Act. But he did promise 'minimum standards of wages for agricultural labourers through the resolute intervention of the State'.[34]

There was more to this pronouncement than met the eye. Land reform was not very popular with Lloyd George's Cabinet colleagues, and he badly needed Churchill's support. As he confided to Riddell, he therefore decided to strike a deal with Churchill:

I have made a bargain with Winston. He has agreed to support my land policy with which he is not in sympathy and I have agreed to give him more money for the Navy. You may call this a bribe, but I have nothing to gain personally. I am only endeavouring to carry out my scheme of social reform, which I believe is for the good of the people. I am not at all sure that the bargain will meet with the approval of some of our party. Indeed I already see signs that it will not.[35]

Churchill's plea on behalf of the agricultural labourer was actually a bid for increased naval expenditure.

The bid almost failed. A widespread revolt against Churchill swept through the Liberal party in the winter of 1913–14. Pacifists, economists and social reformers joined forces to attack the First Lord of the Admiralty for profligate spending and the acceleration of the arms race. In the opening weeks of the New Year a Cabinet cabal, led by Simon, Samuel and Runciman, attempted to force Churchill's resignation by demanding humiliating cuts in the naval estimates. Lloyd George, wavering between loyalty to Churchill, and the need to maintain his reputation as a radical, joined briefly in the hue and cry but in the end relented, and found a compromise which gave Churchill most of what he had wanted in the first place.

At the root of Liberal discontent was the perception that Churchill was increasingly unreliable from a party point of view. The naval estimates crisis coincided with a split in the Cabinet over Ulster. Here too Churchill was at odds with average Liberal opinion. Liberals tended to be intolerant of the claims of Carson and the Ulster Unionists for separate treatment. They underestimated both the solidarity of Protestant Ulster and the military challenge posed by the Ulster Volunteer Force. Churchill and Lloyd George, who appreciated both these factors, favoured the exclusion of the predominantly Protestant counties of Ulster from Irish Home Rule. But of the two, it was Churchill who publicised his sympathy for Ulster, and dined out with Tory politicians to discuss the possibilities of a compromise solution. To Liberals it appeared that Churchill was already halfway across the causeway of treachery.

Churchill was active in the politics of the Irish question from October 1913 to the outbreak of war in August 1914. A detailed narrative of his Irish activities would take us too far afield for present purposes, but one simple question is worth asking. *Why* was Churchill so involved?

By the autumn of 1913 it appeared certain that Home Rule would be enacted by July 1914. The House of Lords had rejected the bill twice but could not, under the provisions of the Parliament Act, reject it for a third time. On both sides of the House of Commons, the party leaders were playing games with the Irish question. But these were games with loaded pistols. Bonar Law and the Conservatives were championing the right of Ulster to resist Home Rule by force if necessary. This was no idle threat. By the beginning of 1914 the Ulster Volunteer Force, which was openly drilling and training in defiance of the state, and equipped with imported weapons, numbered some 80,000 men. The Asquith government, though exceedingly reluctant to meet force with force, had the constitutional power to order the Army and the Navy to suppress a rebellion.

The party leaders on both sides assumed that at some point short of civil war the party game would be called off and a settlement reached. This probably explains Churchill's desire for a leading role. An Irish settlement would remove at a stroke the main source of antagonism between the two parties, and open the way to a coalition. Churchill's quest for an Irish settlement was probably a means to an end: the creation of a national government. This was, indeed, the construction Churchill himself placed on events when he came to write about them after the war: 'I hoped for a settlement with the Conservative Party not only upon the Home Rule Bill with Ulster excluded, but also on other topics which ever since 1909 [sic] had been common ground between some of those who were disputing so angrily.'[36]

Churchill had excellent contacts on the Conservative side in F.E. Smith and Austen Chamberlain. To that extent, he was well placed to prepare the ground for a cross-party compromise. The Cabinet, meanwhile, was beginning to move in the direction Churchill wanted. On 9 March 1914 Asquith proposed for the first time a concession to Ulster: each county was to have the right to opt out for a period of six years. Carson at once rejected the idea, demanding indefinite exclusion. But now at least the Government had a position from which it could negotiate, and this in itself was a great advance.

It was at this point that Churchill's hopes of arranging a settlement were dashed. The Cabinet decided that having made a concession to Ulster, the Government was now in a position to assert its authority. Ministers were also alarmed by police reports warning that the Ulster Volunteers might be about to seize barracks and arms depots. Was a coup intended? The Cabinet did not know, but it was decided to take precautionary measures. A special committee on Ulster, of which Churchill was a member, was set up to co-ordinate military and naval movements. But the chairman, Lord Crewe, fell ill, and Churchill dominated the proceedings. These were extremely hasty and muddled. The Commander-in-Chief of British troops in Ireland, General Paget, was given confusing verbal instructions. On the one hand he was instructed to take purely precautionary measures by moving troops to barracks and arms depots. On the other, Churchill and Seely, the Secretary for War, spoke of hypothetical operations against the Ulster Volunteers, leaving Paget with the impression that he was to prepare for the coercion of Ulster.

The Government's preparations were exposed and discredited by the Curragh Incident of 20 March, when a number of cavalry officers, informed that major operations against the Ulster Volunteers were in the offing, declared that they would rather be dismissed than take part in active military operations against Ulster. The Conservatives were convinced that a plot to smash the resistance of Ulster by armed force had been thwarted by patriotic army officers. These allegations were far-fetched, but it only takes a smattering of plausible evidence to validate a myth.

A month of uproar ensued. The Tories, infuriated by Churchill's apparent change of front over Ulster, and suspecting that he was the mastermind in the 'conspiracy' against Ulster, heaped scorn and abuse on his head. Nor was he to be forgiven for many years to come. Just as the Labour party remembered Tonypandy, and the suffragettes Black Friday, so Conservatives recalled the infamous part Churchill was alleged to have played in the attempted 'pogrom' against Ulster. Right across the spectrum of British politics, Churchill was associated with the excessive use of force in peacetime.

There is no definite proof that Churchill intended to bring about a military showdown in Ulster – but he may have done. It was characteristic that he should alternate, as in his dealings with labour, between the redress of grievances, and the imposition of order by force if necessary. 'Churchill', writes Pat Jalland, 'could be the strongest ministerial advocate of Ulster exclusion, but also the keenest to use firm methods to control the illegal preparations of the Ulstermen ... '37 Whatever the truth about his intentions, Churchill had thrown away the one important card he possessed in the politics of the Irish question: his reputation as the friend of Ulster. But he was never easily discouraged, and there was one more card up his sleeve. Even if it turned out to be the Joker, he was determined to play it.

In 1911 Churchill had taken up the idea of United Kingdom devolution: a federal structure for the British Isles, with regional parliaments exercising powers devolved by the Imperial Parliament at Westminster. Speaking at Dundee, in September 1912, he envisaged that once Home Rule was established in Ireland, self-government along the same lines would be extended to Scotland and Wales. But as he pointed out, a workable federal system would also require the division of England into regions, and this was a more difficult enterprise. Some regions, like Yorkshire, Lancashire, or Greater London were geographically distinct, but elsewhere regional boundaries were harder to define. But Churchill argued that it could be done and he added: 'I have no hesitation in saying, after some years' experience in the public affairs of this country, that larger units of local government would be an advantage from every point of view.'38 This was no idle reflection. At the Board of Trade and again at the Home Office Churchill had been impressed by the chaotic multiplicity of minor local authorities. One of the attractions of a federal system, from Churchill's point of view, was that it might help to reconcile the Conservatives to Irish Home Rule. It also seemed to offer a solution to the problem of Ulster. In the Spring of 1914 Churchill and F.E. Smith helped to draft a House of Commons appeal for the six counties of Ulster to be excluded until United Kingdom devolution was established. The thinking behind this was that the anxieties of Ulster would be relieved if Ireland were locked into a federal framework: a questionable assumption. 78 Liberals and 56 Conservatives signed the appeal, but it was too rational a scheme for the frenzied party atmosphere of 1914.39

At the end of July 1914 there was still no agreement between the leaders of the four parties to the Ulster dispute: the Ulster Unionists, the Irish Nationalists, the Liberals and the Conservatives. The Asquith Government stood on the brink of an Irish disaster. But on 23 July the Austrian ultimatum to Serbia set in motion a train of events culminating in war. On 29 July the Cabinet decided to inform Germany that she could not count on British neutrality, and France that she could not count on British intervention. For a few days the Cabinet was divided between a 'war' party, consisting of Asquith, Grey, Haldane, Churchill and Birrell, and a 'peace' party consisting of Lloyd George, Harcourt, Morley, Pease and Samuel.

Churchill pleaded with Lloyd George to come over to his side: 'All the rest of our lives we shall be opposed. I am deeply attached to you & have followed your instinct and guidance for nearly ten years.' Like almost everyone at this point, Churchill expected the war to be short and inexpensive. He promised Lloyd George that he would continue to support social reform, if Lloyd George would support the war: 'Together we can carry a wide social policy – *on the conference basis* your idea – wh you taught me. The naval war will be cheap – not more than 25 millions a year.'[40]

Churchill's reference to 'the conference basis' harked back to Lloyd George's coalition project of 1910, and forward to the coalition which he now hoped to see arising from the crisis. In the belief that the Liberals might split, and several Cabinet ministers resign, Churchill sounded out the Conservatives about the possibilities for coalition. On 31 July the message was carried to Bonar Law and the other Conservative leaders by F.E. Smith, another eager coalitionist. The Conservatives agreed to support the Government in the event of war, but refused to have anything to do with Churchill's proposal. In Bonar Law's judgment it was premature, and savoured too much of intrigue.[41] In retrospect it seems extraordinary that Churchill possessed so little insight into Bonar Law's personality. Bonar Law was a solid, straightforward, Ulster puritan, incapable of trusting such a flighty and flamboyant creature.

On 3 August German armies invaded France and Belgium. The 'peace party' in the Cabinet disintegrated, and Lloyd George fell in behind Asquith and Grey. On 4 August, war was declared against Germany.

*

The decision for war in August 1914 was taken in almost complete ignorance of the consequences. The politicians were wholly unaware of the fact that a total war of tragic proportions, lasting more than four years, and costing the lives of some 772,000 British and Irish servicemen, lay ahead.[42] Whitehall had been preparing for a short and inexpensive war in which the major British contribution was the blockade of Germany by the Royal Navy.

The only minister to anticipate mass mobilisation was the new Secretary of State for War, Lord Kitchener, appointed on 5 August. At one of his first Cabinet meetings, Kitchener startled his colleagues by announcing that he intended to base his calculations on a war lasting three years. Nor would sea-power alone determine the outcome. There would be great land battles in which Britain must bear a part proportionate to the magnitude of its power: hence armies of millions must be put into the field. The rest of the Cabinet, impressed as they were by the Kitchener mystique, were unconvinced. Grey noted that Kitchener's prediction 'seemed to most of us unlikely, if not incredible'. On 8 August, Churchill instructed the Admiralty to plan for a war lasting nine months – an instruction he did not revise until May 1915.[43]

For a Liberal Government, it was a factor of the greatest importance that Kitchener proposed to raise his new armies through voluntary enlistment. So high was his reputation, that criticism of his judgment was almost unthinkable. As long as Kitchener supported the voluntary principle, the Liberals had little reason to fear a Tory attack over conscription. Yet this did not prevent Churchill from trying to raise the conscription issue at a Cabinet meeting on 25 August. Ministers were alarmed by the continuing advance of the Germans towards the Channel ports, and Churchill appears to have argued that conscription would be the best way to reinforce the British Expeditionary Force. But this argument, voiced at a moment when volunteers were flocking to enlist, fell flat. As J.A. Pease noted, the rest of the Cabinet thought that conscription was irrelevant:

> Churchill harangued [sic] us for half an hour on the necessity of compulsory service. Pointing out the importance of young unmarried men going to the front rather than the Territorial, a married man who had trained with limited obligation, & now his patriotism was being exploited by being pressed into going abroad & almost compelled to agree to do so, whilst others were loafing & cheering & doing nothing for their country etc. etc. etc. We all sat and listened, much bored. The PM took it with impatience – the matter he said was not urgent.[44]

In peacetime, when politicians considered 'the people', they thought of them first and foremost as voters. In wartime, they had to think of them as human resources to be mobilised for the armed forces and the production of munitions. At the Admiralty, Churchill had no recruitment problem on his hands, but he was concerned about the war economy. The Navy was not, as it appeared to be, an independent floating world, but a seaborne outpost of industry, dependent on coal, steel and engineering. At the outbreak of war Churchill was relieved to discover that the syndicalist threat to the Admiralty's coal supplies had faded. The miners, he wrote, 'having apparently satisfied themselves of the justice of the war . . . will cut all the coal we need.'[45]

Industrial peace was shortlived. As tens of thousands of men abandoned their civilian occupations to enlist in Kitchener's new armies, industry began to suffer dislocation. By the end of September 750,000 men had enlisted: recruitment was to continue at an average rate of 125,000 a month up to June 1915. Among the recruits were many skilled workers from the engineering trades essential to war production. As the Government placed more and more orders for military equipment, the shortage of skilled workers became a major bottleneck in the war effort. Employers bid frantically against one another for labour, and wages rose: but the increases were far outstripped by the rise in the cost of living. By February 1915, food prices were 22 per cent higher than in July 1914, while the cost of housing and coal had also risen sharply. The Labour party, a greater force in wartime than in peace, began a campaign against profiteering and called for state intervention to hold down prices and profits.

On 15 February 1915 engineering workers on Clydeside went on strike for an extra tuppence an hour, led by a committee of shop stewards known as the Central Labour Witholding Committee. At a Cabinet meeting on 24 February both Churchill and Lloyd George denounced the strikers and, to the dismay of their colleagues, called for drastic measures to prevent such strikes in future. In one of his love letters to Venetia Stanley, Asquith wrote of the 'turbid torrent of diffuse & shambling unreason . . . which was poured forth on the subject of strikes & compulsory labour & martial law, by Winston and Lloyd George at the Cabinet yesterday.'[46] Fortunately for the Government, the Clyde workers eventually agreed to refer the dispute to the Production Committee. This was a body of three officials, under the chairmanship of the Chief Industrial Commissioner, Sir George Askwith, which had recently been set up with the aim of co-ordinating the supply programmes of the Admiralty and the War Office. The Production Committee also served as a tribunal for arbitration, and settled the dispute by awarding a penny an hour as a war bonus.

For the Asquith Government, the problem ran very much deeper than a single dispute on the Clyde. If Kitchener's new armies were to be equipped with munitions, skilled workers would have to be diverted from inessential work to war production, and the restrictive practices built up by the unions in peacetime set aside in the interests of mass production. But how was all this to be achieved? Was the accent to be placed on the conciliation of workers, or were they to be subject, like soldiers, to compulsion?

Lloyd George took the lead with radical proposals for the control of labour by the state. It is interesting to see that he was supported by Churchill: the old alliance between them was still in working order. Lloyd George favoured a number of drastic amendments to the Defence of the Realm Act. By 26 February he was ready with a draft bill for the prohibition of strikes and lock-outs, the introduction of compulsory arbitration, and powers to prevent the movement of workers from essential to inessential work. Churchill, meanwhile, formulated his own opinions in a Cabinet paper of 3 March.

So far as labour policy was concerned, Churchill endorsed Lloyd George's draft bill. But his paper was mainly concerned with the question of profiteering, and the extent to which the state should intervene to reduce it. As Churchill saw it, a distinction had to be drawn between transport on the one hand, and manufacturing industry on the other. The basis of the distinction, not quite explicitly stated, was that the railways and shipping lines were simply charging the state for services which they provided, with the same rolling stock and vessels, in peacetime. As they were enjoying windfall returns on fixed assets, Churchill argued that they should be placed under state control for the duration of the war. The armaments firms, on the other hand, were investing risk capital in the production of new weapons and supplies, and making prodigious efforts to adapt themselves to the emergency. All this activity was dependent upon Government contracts and the profit motive: take these away and the arms firms would become discontented, and war production 'paralysed'. Socialists might argue for the nationalisation of the arms firms, but if this were to occur, the state would pay out in compensation what it would otherwise have paid in profits, which would be a bad bargain, or officials would try to supplant management and there would follow 'a complete collapse of the existing system of supply.'

As for the cause of strikes, Churchill acknowledged that 'class envy and anti-war spirit' led a small section of workers to complain against the profit system, but in his opinion workmen did not care very much whether they were working for private employers or the State: 'What they care for is good wages and good conditions of labour'. Nothing therefore was to be gained by 'pandering to socialistic ideas'. Churchill's own solution envisaged a combination of rewards and penalties, supposedly for employers as well as workmen. Under the provisions of Lloyd George's bill, he argued, employers would receive legitimate profits, but wages would receive a double boost: firstly through the redistribution of excess profits in the form of higher wages, and secondly by state bonuses for workers who kept good time.[47]

Churchill's opposition to socialism was unabated. But he resembled the other architects of pre-war social reform – Lloyd George, Beveridge, and Llewellyn Smith – in seeking greater powers for the state over the war economy. Generally speaking, such views were unwelcome to the other members of the Asquith Cabinet. While they were by no means committed to doctrinaire *laissez-faire*, they were cautious men of business who preferred to advance step by step. When the Cabinet again discussed the matter on 4 March, Lloyd George and Churchill were overruled in favour of a less controversial bill imposing on employers the onus of restricting inessential work, and conferring on the Government powers to take over factories and workshops essential for the war effort. On 7 March Asquith told his wife Margot that Lloyd George, Kitchener and Churchill had suggested imprisoning men who would not work in wartime. This caused Margot to observe in her diary: 'Winston is a Tory and knows nothing of the British workman. He looks upon him as a mere machine to whom high wages make all the difference.'[48] It would have been more accurate to say that Churchill was a Liberal in his recognition of working-class grievances, and a Tory in his desire for order and compulsion.

Lloyd George decided to change tack and see what he could obtain through a more conciliatory approach to labour. Accordingly he began a round of negotiations with the trade unions (17–19 March), which culminated in the 'Treasury Agreement'. This was a voluntary agreement between the unions and the state. The Government undertook to restrain excess profits by agreement with the arms manufacturers, while the unions agreed to the relaxation of restrictive practices and the abandonment of strikes in favour of arbitration.

In Lloyd George's opinion there was one other major obstacle to war production: drink. Admiralty and War Office officials were convinced that the excessive consumption of alcohol was a major cause of delays in munitions and transport centres. The shipping employers were equally vocal in blaming the drink problem for the late completion of Government contracts. In a speech at Bangor on 28 February, Lloyd George advertised the issue: 'Drink is doing more damage in the war than all the German submarines put together.' The press, ever servile in the quest for easy scapegoats, took up the anti-drink campaign, and King George V announced on Easter Monday that he was taking the pledge for the duration of the war.

Lloyd George, of course, had an axe to grind: he had long been associated with the temperance cause. He was tempted to come out in favour of prohibition, or the very different alternative of state purchase of the liquor trade. Churchill, who believed in alcohol as a matter of principle, was sceptical of the claim that drink was a major problem. When his own officials sent Lloyd George a paper about the evil effects of drink in the shipyards, Churchill contradicted them. As he wrote to Lloyd George on 7 April:

> I do not feel that I cd myself accept responsibility for this document. I have no doubt the facts are accurate, but I do not feel convinced that they represent the general labour situation. Naval officers & officials are prone to dwell on the weaknesses they notice in working men, & this is also true of employers ... I fear that if your energies are dissipated in a great prohibition campaign, the comparatively small practical measures which wd. deal with the local evils, and the misbehaviour of minorities in particular places, will be overlooked. Certainly the Admiralty wd have instituted some very effective curtailment of hours & other measures against drinking in the military ports under the Defence of the Realm Act, if we had not thought it better to remit the matter to you for general treatment. I beg you to think of this. I am also hopeful about enlisting men into guilds or unions of Government workers. I think the most hopeful line is to restrict the quantities of alcohol in particular beverages. After all the French are drinking their wines, and the Germans are drinking their beer; and we have never been a drunken and inefficient nation as the Russians were.[49]

Neither of Lloyd George's extreme alternatives was adopted. Instead, in June 1915, a Central Control Board was established with powers to restrict the hours of public houses, and forbid the sale of alcoholic drinks, in military and munitions centres.

*

As a career, politics has often been likened to snakes and ladders. Ever since 1900, Churchill had shown he was sure-footed in scrambling up one ladder after another. But in 1915 he landed on a snake and suddenly descended to the bottom of the board.

The full sequence of events which preceded Churchill's downfall is brilliantly chronicled by Martin Gilbert in Volume III of the official biography. Some 447 pages are devoted to Churchill's activities between the outbreak of war and his dismissal from the Admiralty, the period in which the disastrous Gallipoli campaign was conceived and begun. Gilbert's account establishes the fact that the responsibility for Gallipoli did not rest with Churchill alone. Asquith, Kitchener, and Fisher – whom Churchill had recalled as First Sea Lord in October 1914 – were all entitled to a share of the blame, but shrewd enough to ensure that Churchill alone was the scapegoat.

But it is also true that Churchill brought misfortune upon himself. He suffered from the delusion that he possessed military genius. In social and economic affairs he was ready to be guided by Lloyd George, or restrained by his officials. But in naval and military affairs he was convinced that his judgment was superior. 'I feel I have it in me,' he confided to Riddell in April 1913, 'I can visualise great movements and combinations.'[50] No doubt he could, but he was over-excited by the possession of military authority. There were early warnings of this during the rail strike of 1911, and the Curragh episode of 1914. In October 1914 he suddenly abandoned the Admiralty to organise the defence of Antwerp, and telegraphed the Cabinet offering to take command of British forces. In his irresponsible way, Asquith was much amused, but failed to draw the conclusion that Churchill was unbalanced about war and ought to be moved from the Admiralty. In November 1914 Asquith appointed him to the new War Council, charged with the supreme direction of operations. In January 1915 the War Council, buoyed up by Churchill's confidence and enthusiasm, authorised a naval attack on the Dardanelles.

It was left to the Conservative party to remove Churchill from the conduct of the war. Most Conservatives loathed Churchill as a renegade, and were ready to seize any excuse for humiliating him. But as it happened, he afforded them good party grounds for attack. To a very great extent the Conservatives were the party of the officer class. They took the view that in civil-military relations, politicians should never override the judgment of professional soldiers and sailors. Churchill, however, tended to do so, or at least to mistake the silence of the admirals for agreement with his opinions. If only he had been more alert to the danger, he would have recognised that his First Sea Lord, Admiral Fisher, was not only a reluctant convert to the Dardanelles, but potentially mutinous, and somewhat mentally unbalanced. On 15 May, in the belief that he could oust Churchill and seize control of the war at sea, Fisher resigned.

Only the previous day *The Times* had carried a sensational report from its military correspondent, Colonel Repington, alleging that the British offensive on the western front was failing through lack of high explosive shells. Thus on two successive days major blows had fallen on the Asquith Government, and a motion of no confidence was to be expected from the Conservative Opposition. Asquith skilfully defused the crisis by inviting the Conservatives on 17 May to join a Coalition Government. The Conservatives accepted, but only on certain conditions, which included the dismissal of Haldane and the demotion of Churchill to the minor office of Chancellor of the Duchy of Lancaster. Ever since 1910 Churchill had looked forward to the creation of a Coalition Government. Now it had arrived, and all but crushed him. His only consolation was that he kept his place as a member of the War Council, now reconstituted as the Dardanelles Committee. Churchill intended to use all his remaining influence to urge the reinforcement of the Dardanelles, in the hope that victory might yet vindicate him. He was down but not entirely out.

*

The Asquith Coalition was artfully contrived to contain the Conservative party within a predominantly Liberal administration. The Conservatives obtained half the seats in the Cabinet, but the great offices remained in the hands of the Liberals. The leader of the Conservative party, Bonar Law, had to content himself with the Colonial Office. Meanwhile Grey continued as Foreign Secretary, McKenna succeeded Lloyd George at the Exchequer, and Simon replaced McKenna at the Home Office. The critical task of resolving the crisis in the supply of arms and equipment was entrusted to Lloyd George, at the head of the new Ministry of Munitions.

Lloyd George recognised that the Treasury agreement had failed. Neither the unions nor the Government had carried out their part of the bargain. There were more strikes and industrial disputes than ever, and the shortage of skilled labour was acute. Lloyd George at once began to press for new powers of industrial compulsion. Among the possibilities he considered was the extension of military discipline to workers in the shipyards and armament firms. They were even to have uniforms and the prospect of winning a medal. In a speech on 3 June, foreshadowing drastic measures, Lloyd George called for 'greater subordination in labour to the direction and control of the State'. Churchill was again closely in step with his old ally. Addressing his constituents in Dundee on 5 June he extolled the system of voluntary recruitment to the Army but drew a contrast between service overseas and 'service at home, service for home defence and to keep our fighting men abroad properly supplied and maintained'. To this end, 'our whole nation must be organized – must be socialised if you like.'[51]

Four days later Churchill circulated to the Cabinet a bill for the conscription of labour. Under its provisions, the Government would be empowered to 'direct any person to perform any duty necessary for the prosecution of the war or the safety of the State', provided only that no one be required by law to work overtime, or on more than six days a week, or for wages not in accordance with the Fair Wages resolution of the House of Commons. The penalties for disobedience would be, for the first offence, a fine not exceeding one week's wages, and for the second, imprisonment for up to a month, with or without hard labour. It was A.J. Balfour, the former leader of the Conservative party, and Churchill's successor at the Admiralty, who warned most strongly against these proposals when they were discussed in Cabinet. How, Balfour inquired, were workers to be coerced?

> This is not the way in which Englishmen can be got either to feel or to think. Everybody recognises that in the Army discipline is necessary and cowardice disgraceful. But it requires great imagination and originality to see that for an artisan to be drunk on Monday morning is as bad as for a soldier to disobey orders; or that going to a race meeting may be as bad as bolting from the trenches. If this, or anything like this, be true, we shall assuredly find that a certain proportion of our workmen refuse to obey; and they will invoke in defence of their refusal all the familiar commonplaces about the sacredness of personal liberty. If we fine or imprison them they will become martyrs; and martyrdom may engender a feeling of sullen opposition among their brother workers which will be far more disastrous to the cause of national production ... [52]

On 10 June Lloyd George outlined to the Cabinet his proposals for the imposition of quasi-military discipline on workers in Government controlled establishments. When some Conservative ministers objected that the application of compulsion in industry would be mistaken unless accompanied by military conscription, Lloyd George fell back on more limited proposals, drafted by Beveridge and Llewellyn Smith with the aim of translating the Treasury agreement into law. The resulting Munitions of War Act, of July 1915, applied to factories and workshops scheduled as essential for war production. In all these workplaces the right to strike was abolished and compulsory arbitration substituted. In order to expedite the 'dilution of labour' (the substitution of semi-skilled for skilled workers), restrictive practices were abrogated for the duration of the war; and in order to prevent skilled workers from migrating to inessential work, it was decreed that no worker could leave his employment without obtaining a 'leaving certificate'. For its part the Government undertook to restrict war profits to 20 per cent above the level of profits in 1914, and to 'use its efforts' – a vaguely phrased commitment – to restore restrictive practices after the war. The Government also took reserve powers to deal with industrial disputes outside the 'controlled establishments'. Part I of the act empowered the Government to proclaim a strike illegal in any industry.[53]

During the second half of 1915 the Conservatives stepped up the pressure for military conscription, and the Liberals began to split over the issue. The majority of Liberals from Asquith down were opposed, as were the Labour party and the Trades Union Congress, but in August 1915 a War Policy Committee of the Cabinet was appointed to inquire into the case for conscription. The chairman was Lord Crewe and the other members were Curzon, Austen Chamberlain, Selborne, Arthur Henderson, and Churchill. The sheet-anchor of the anti-conscriptionists was Kitchener, but his commitment to the voluntary principle was pragmatic. If he could be persuaded that conscription was essential, he would swing in its favour. For the moment he did not swing, but by the end of August both Churchill and Lloyd George had told the Committee of their support for conscription. Churchill went further and signed, along with the three Conservative members of the Committee, a minority report contradicting Kitchener's position.[54] There was now a prospect that unless Asquith moved towards conscription, Lloyd George and Churchill would ally with the Conservative ministers against him. Early in October the attempt was made, but Asquith successfully took refuge in Lord Derby's new recruiting scheme, and Kitchener was not yet prepared to side with the conscriptionists. So the crisis was deferred for the time being, and another ladder was kicked away from Churchill just as he was beginning to climb it.[55]

All this time the Dardanelles Committee had been split over the future of the campaign, with Churchill the most passionate member of the pro-Gallipoli faction, and Bonar Law hardening into the most determined opponent of the operation. By the beginning of November, the advocates of evacuation were gaining the upper hand, and Asquith seized the opportunity of abolishing the Dardanelles Committee, replacing it with a War Committee from which Churchill was dropped. For Churchill this was the final humiliation. On 15 November he resigned, announcing his intention to depart for active service on the western front. Shortly afterwards the Cabinet decided to evacuate all British troops from the Dardanelles. Henceforth Churchill's reputation was to be indelibly stained by the blood shed in a lost cause.

In January 1916 Churchill obtained a commission as the commander of the 6th battalion of the Royal Scots Fusiliers, with a handsome young Scots laird and Liberal, Archibald Sinclair, as his second-in-command. Captain Churchill served for a hundred days in the line near Ploegstreet, a relatively quiet sector of the western front. But the high fever of politics never left him. In April, hoping that the Government would break up over conscription, he urged Lloyd George to resign and help form 'the party of the future'.[56] The Asquith Government survived the crisis and full conscription for all males between the ages of 18 and 45 was introduced in May. But, tempted by the thought of casting himself as Leader of the Opposition, Churchill resigned his commission, returned home, and began to make speeches in the House of Commons criticising the conduct of the war.

His other main line of attack was to call for an official inquiry into the conduct of the Gallipoli operation. In the hope of turning the tide of publicity in his favour, he devoted much effort to working up his contacts in the press, and briefing them with his own version of the inside story. On 20 July the Government announced the appointment of a Select Committee on the Dardanelles, and for the rest of the year Churchill concentrated on the collection and preparation of the evidence he intended to submit.

At this time Churchill was a very isolated figure, grateful for support from the small fry of politics. In April 1916 he renewed an almost forgotten contact with Alexander McCallum Scott, the Liberal MP and journalist who had published the first biography of Churchill in 1905. McCallum Scott was still an admirer of Churchill and, having been commissioned to produce a revised version of the book, sought him out for background briefings. Churchill, of course, obliged, and showed McCallum Scott his dossier on the Dardanelles. In return, McCallum Scott, and his fellow Liberal back-bencher, Pratt, gave Churchill some helpful advice. On 18 August McCallum Scott noted in his diary:

1. Impressed upon him that the Coalition had solid support in the country.
2. His recent speeches in the House were doing him no good ... He was girding too much at the Government on side issues.
3. Let him confine himself to the great central issue, the war. Set himself to impress some definite conception of the character of the war upon the public mind.
4. E.G. on the adjournment debate let him emphasise the view that it may last a long time yet, & we ought to organise ourselves at home on the basis of a long war.[57]

Churchill was much taken by this advice and began to prepare a speech. As a left-wing Liberal, McCallum Scott was much concerned with social conditions, and drew Churchill's attention to the problem of working-class unrest, and the need for state intervention to counteract it. When Churchill spoke in the House, on 22 August, he emphasised the fact that wartime inflation was eating deeply into the working-class standard of living. Since the outbreak of war, he pointed out, the price of food had risen by 65 per cent. The labour force, he argued (though he spoke of 'the people') would not accept deprivation side by side with the 'enormous profits made by private persons'. Churchill was not referring here to the profits of the munitions manufacturers, which in theory at least were regulated by the Munitions of War Act. His attack was directed against the shipowners.

As in March 1915, Churchill distinguished between the profits accruing to the munitions industry, and the profits made from transport. Where there was 'extraordinary service in time of war' there might be a claim for extra profits. But since the shipowners were already insured by the Government, all they had to do was send their ships to sea as usual, and fix the freight charges, which had become extortionate and 'an absolute scandal'. The logical solution was to requisition the entire merchant fleet, impose reduced freight charges, and ration the distribution of food. As in the heyday of his social reforming period, Churchill drew attention to the predicament of the poorest:

The housekeeping of the rich and of the well-to-do is not materially affected by a price which would simply starve the poorest classes out of existence. The classes which are affected by the rises which have taken place and are continually taking place in the price of foodstuffs are soldiers' wives on separation allowance, the discharged wounded with their weekly allowance of 20s if married and 10s if single, the old age pensioners whose cases have been brought repeatedly before us, the professional classes, the poorer paid industrial workers and clerks ... but the case of no class compares for one moment with that of the poorest class, because there is a limit below which it is not possible, with the strictest economy in the home, however miserable, to maintain life. Therefore I say that to begin to restrict consumption, which it may be necessary to do, merely through the agency of price ... is the most cruel and unfair manner of dealing with a great national and economic problem ... A war with all its evils should at least be a great equaliser in these matters. If we are to look upon the whole nation as an army, on our men and women as an army struggling for a common purpose, then they are all entitled to their rations and to secure the necessary supplies at prices which their strenuous labour is not incapable of meeting.[58]

In November 1916 a Conservative back-bench revolt, led by Sir Edward Carson, triggered off a sequence of events which led to the resignation of

Asquith and the appointment, on 6 December 1916, of Lloyd George as Prime Minister. Churchill was known to be a strong critic of Asquith's administration. Nothing could have been more indicative of his isolation than the fact that none of the participants in the movement for change consulted him or invited him to take part in their discussions.

Lloyd George's part (whether real or imagined) in the crisis which brought him to power, was so deeply resented by Asquith and his followers that they refused to serve in the new Government. Consequently the Conservative party obtained the lion's share of appointments and became, from that moment on, the dominant party in the state. The Foreign Office, the Treasury and the Home Office all fell into the hands of Conservatives: Balfour, Bonar Law, and Cave. Though Lloyd George himself wanted to restore Churchill to office, Austen Chamberlain, Walter Long, Robert Cecil and Curzon insisted as a condition of their support that Churchill should be excluded. As yet, Lloyd George was not in a strong enough position to override them, so Churchill remained in limbo.

The report of the Dardanelles Commission in March 1917 lifted some of the blame from Churchill's shoulders and marked the first stage in his political rehabilitation. In May the sky again brightened a little when his cousin F.E. Guest was appointed Coalition Chief Whip. A powerful speech by Churchill in a secret session of the House on 10 May prompted Lloyd George to initiate moves for his return, and efforts to appoint him as the head of the new Air Board having run into resistance, Lloyd George offered him the Ministry of Munitions. The appointment was announced, without prior consultation with Bonar Law or other Conservative leaders, on 18 July. Such was the explosion of anger in the Conservative party that Bonar Law was almost forced to resign, and the Government's life trembled in the balance. In the midst of the storm, Churchill surprised the Cabinet Secretary, Maurice Hankey, by telling him that he had no idea of the depth of feeling against him until the appointment was announced. But a glimmer of the truth seemed to penetrate when he admitted that he had got 'a bit above himself' at the Admiralty.[59] The storm over Churchill quickly blew itself out, leaving him once more securely entrenched in office. This time, however, he was in a more subordinate position than at the Admiralty. The Minister of Munitions was not a member of the War Cabinet, and only attended War Cabinet meetings for items of business relevant to his department.

*

In the summer of 1917 Churchill imagined that he was about to restore himself to power as a man of the people. Shortly before his return to office, he was musing to McCallum Scott about his hero, Napoleon:

> Churchill told me the other day that he has always been much impressed by a saying of Napoleon: "I have always moved with five million people". That was one of the secrets of his [Napoleon's] power – his perception and his success in forecasting the movement of the popular mind. That is the secret of politics.

Since constitutional convention required that a newly appointed minister should submit himself for re-election, Churchill was compelled to fight a by-election in Dundee. But as McCallum Scott discovered, he relished the prospect:

> He is a new man already, full of confidence, vigour, decision. He smells the battle afar off. The "Press" gangs & cliques show to great advantage in London but he will show them who can command the big battalions among the people.

One of Churchill's first actions at the Ministry was to have his bronze statue of Napoleon placed on a table opposite his desk.[60]

At the Dundee by-election Churchill was opposed once more by Edwin Scrymgeour, who stood as a socialist, prohibitionist, and anti-war candidate. J.F. Sime, the Secretary of the Jute and Flax Workers' Union, attacked Churchill as 'one of the last men in Parliament who will do anything for the working classes.' But the majority of trade union leaders were supporters of a coalition in which the Labour party was represented, and Churchill was able to call on the help of two Lib-Lab miners' leaders, Stephen Walsh and William Brace. Walsh sent a message commending Churchill for his services to the working classes, while Brace, who was Under-Secretary at the Home Office, spoke on Churchill's behalf as a representative of the Labour party. On 29 July Churchill was comfortably returned with the full support of the Dundee Conservatives, with 7,302 votes against the 2,036 cast for Scrymgeour.[61]

Churchill was the fourth Minister of Munitions, following in the footsteps of Lloyd George, Edwin Montagu, and Christopher Addison. The munitions crisis was long past, and war industry fully mobilised. The Ministry itself, which had begun with two tables and a chair, had grown into a large bureaucracy with a headquarters staff of 12,000 officials, housed in palatial hotels.

There was less scope for dramatic change at the Ministry than in the early days of heroic improvisation, as Christopher Wrigley has remarked.[62]

But there was plenty for Churchill to do all the same. First of all he wished to change the internal structure of the Ministry. There were fifty separate departments, each reporting separately to the Minister and referring to him decisions great and small. The Minister alone was in a position to form an overview and co-ordinate policy. Churchill disliked this. He had never been in the habit of solitary decision-making, and much preferred the regular Whitehall model in which the minister was assisted by a small 'cabinet' of senior civil servants. He therefore grouped the fifty departments into ten large units, each with its own head directly responsible to the Minister. The ten heads of the departmental groups were then formed into a Munitions Council, chaired as a rule by the Minister, and charged with the overall co-ordination of policy. The idea seems to have worked out well, with the Council exercising 'a true collective responsibility'.[63] Churchill also believed that the Ministry was top-heavy with bureaucrats. On his arrival he set himself the goal of reducing the numbers of the headquarters staff by three or four thousand. But his injunctions had no effect whatever. As he complained ruefully to his heads of departments in March 1918, 'the process has proceeded in exactly the opposite direction'. By the time of the armistice, the headquarters staff had risen to a total of 25,000.[64]

The Ministry of Munitions had been created to supply the Army, and its purpose was unchanged. Through the summer and autumn of 1917 the murderous and futile battle of Passchendaele was fought to the bitter end in Flanders. Churchill's task was to furnish the British Commander-in-Chief, Sir Douglas Haig, with all the material he required for another great offensive in the spring of 1918. Though he had long been a critic of the offensive strategy on the western front, Churchill was now hopeful that the military stalemate could be broken by the mass production of the latest and most lethal weaponry, especially tanks, aircraft, and gas shells.

Churchill had to struggle for the resources he needed to fulfil the munitions programme: chiefly steel, shipping, and labour. But in the case of labour, the problem was not so much a numerical shortage of workers, as the danger of strikes, industrial disputes, and more general disaffection from the war effort. One of the most urgent tasks awaiting Churchill at the Ministry was the appeasement of discontent among the skilled workers in the shipbuilding and munitions industries.

To appreciate the position we must first go back to the spring of 1917, when various circumstances had combined to produce a wave of strikes, accompanied by a more general groundswell of grumbling and resentment. In its desperation to find more men for the western front, and at the same time to increase munitions production, the Government was determined to squeeze the engineering industry hard. Against the better judgment of Christopher Addison, the Minister of Munitions, Lloyd George and the War Cabinet proposed to comb out more engineering workers for the Army, while simultaneously extending dilution from essential war work to engineering firms engaged in private commercial production. But since 1914 there had grown up in the engineering trades a formidable shop stewards movement, bent on the defence of craft privileges, and largely superseding the authority of the officials of the Amalgamated Society of Engineers. In May 1917 the shop stewards organised an unofficial strike, lasting more than three weeks, of 200,000 workers in the engineering trades. The Government was forced to compromise, accepting restrictions on its right to recruit skilled men, and postponing the extension of dilution.

From the War Cabinet's point of view the crisis was not yet over. Ministers feared that the militancy of the skilled workers was merely the cutting edge of general working-class discontent, and that socialist agitators were preparing to exploit the situation by turning the people against the Government. Many of the activists in the shop stewards movement – which extended beyond engineering into many other trades – were members of the ILP (Independent Labour Party), or of two small revolutionary parties, the BSP (British Socialist Party) and the SLP (Socialist Revolutionary Party). Following the February revolution in Russia, and the establishment of Kerensky's Provisional Government, socialist expectations were running high throughout Europe, and it did not seem impossible that food shortages, war weariness, and other demoralising factors might precipitate a revolution in Britain.

Acting with great speed and decision, Lloyd George set up eight regional commissions to report on the causes of industrial unrest. Their reports arrived on 17 July, the day before the announcement of Churchill's appointment. The commissioners concluded that in general the most widespread sources of discontent were the soaring cost of living, and the resentment by wage-earners of profiteering; for certain regions, factors such as the shortage of housing, industrial fatigue, and the poor quality of wartime beer, were cited.[65]

Responding to the findings of the commissioners, the Government began in July 1917 to swing towards the appeasement of labour. Food subsidies were introduced, a Ministry of Reconstruction created under Addison, and social reforms promised in housing and education. In these circumstances the appointment of Churchill was something of a gamble on Lloyd George's part. Was he the right man to deal with the world of labour? Some of his old progressive allies still believed that he was. The Webbs, for instance, who thought that reconstruction required 'one big brain at the top', regarded him as the best man available.[66]

Churchill understood very well the political requirements of the hour, and pressed ahead at once with measures to conciliate the skilled worker. He had inherited from his predecessor the draft of the Munitions of War bill, the purpose of which was to extend dilution to private work. The bill, however, was strongly opposed by the Amalgamated Society of Engineers, whose members voted decisively against it in a ballot. Churchill's first reaction was to press on. At a conference of trade unionists on 1 August he appealed for their support in passing the bill. But he quickly changed his mind in response to the strength of trade union opposition. The plan to extend dilution was abandoned and Churchill put forward in its place a short bill for the appeasement of industrial unrest. Rather than risk more industrial trouble during the parliamentary recess, he rushed the bill through all its stages in a week. Introduced by Churchill on 14 August, it received the Royal Assent seven days later.[67]

According to the Commissions of Industrial Unrest, one potent source of grievance in war industry was the continuation of the leaving certificate, whereby a munitions worker could not move to another job without official permission. The Munitions of War Act simply abolished the leaving certificate – though the Minister retained the power to prevent munitions workers from quitting war industry for private work. In another demonstration of the new spirit of goodwill, Churchill decided to release the activists deported from the Clyde in 1915 for fomenting strikes. Clydeside had been relatively unaffected by the recent strikes, and it was a fair guess that no harm would come from releasing the deportees. Churchill summoned David Kirkwood, formerly chief shop steward at the Beardmore Works, who demanded to be reinstated in his old position. Shrewdly summing up Kirkwood as a reluctant rebel, Churchill arranged for him to be appointed manager of a shell factory belonging to Beardmore's, and within six weeks, owing to a new bonus scheme introduced by Kirkwood, production at the factory was the highest in Britain.[68]

Churchill's next contribution to industrial policy was a round of inflationary wage increases. This too stemmed from the need to conciliate the skilled worker. In outline, the problem Churchill faced can be stated simply enough. But in detail it was a matter of immense complexity and, given the powers at his disposal, there was no simple solution. Most skilled workers in war industry were on time-rates: they were paid according to the number of hours they worked. But these rates had been fixed through collective bargaining over many decades. In spite of wartime increases, they owed more to custom and tradition than to the circumstances of the war economy. Meanwhile, as the dilution of labour proceeded, so more and more repetition work was handed over to semi-skilled workers. The semi-skilled workers, most of whom were newcomers, were on piece-rates: they were paid according to the quantity of goods they produced. In a booming war economy, this enabled them to earn more than the skilled time-workers, a situation the latter resented all the more keenly because it was they who taught the repetition workers how to do the job. In theory, the problem could have been solved by extending the system of payment by results to the skilled time-workers. But to this the trade unions were opposed on the grounds that once the standard hourly rate were abandoned, collective bargaining would give way to a multitude of individual bargains, and piece-rates would be reduced.

As the Ministry of Munitions had very limited powers over wages, the situation was largely beyond its control. Only in state-owned munitions factories was the Ministry the employer and paymaster. Over the rest of war industry, the Ministry had effective powers over women's wages, but men's wages were in the main determined by market forces and collective bargaining.[69] Hence the skilled time-worker steadily lost ground and by the summer of 1917 the problem was acute: seven out of the eight regional commissions on industrial unrest identified the economic disadvantage of the skilled time-worker as a source of discontent. The abolition of the leaving certificate threatened to exacerbate the situation. There was no longer anything to prevent a skilled time-worker from abandoning his job, however essential it might be to the war effort, in order to obtain better paid employment in piece-work.

Churchill believed that something must be done to redress the grievance. The Munitions of War Act therefore included a clause (drafted by the poet Humbert Wolfe, a Ministry official), empowering the Minister to fix time-rates. Churchill then referred the question to a committee of employers and trade unionists under Major J.W. Hills, MP. But the employers pressed for a system of payment by results while the unions demanded a 20 per cent increase on standard rates. Churchill tried to break the deadlock by instructing the committee to drop the employers' proposal. The employers, however, insisted that payment by results was fundamental, and the only way that output could be increased. They therefore refused to sign the final recommendations of the Hills Committee, which recommended an advance of between 10 per cent and 15 per cent for skilled engineers on time-work.

Churchill pressed hard for a decision, but not without consulting the interests and the experts. He remitted the report of the Hills Committee to a committee of his own officials, who produced two alternative proposals, 'A' and 'B'. Further discussion with Major Hills, and further consultations with unions and employers, produced another alternative, 'C', which envisaged an advance of 15 per cent for 207,500 men. Churchill then put forward 'C' to an interdepartmental conference on 8 October, attended by George Barnes, the Labour party's representative in the War Cabinet, and officials from the Admiralty and the Ministry of Labour. Finally, Churchill put the proposal to the War Cabinet on 12 October.[70]

Unfortunately for Churchill, there was no Whitehall consensus to be found. He was strongly opposed by Sir Lyndon Macassey for the Admiralty and Sir David Shackleton for the Ministry of Labour. Invited to state their objections in front of the War Cabinet, they predicted that the attempt to raise the wages of a limited class of skilled workers would fail: all classes of skilled men would demand the same increase, and so would the piece-workers.[71] In point of fact this was a consequence Churchill was prepared to risk. As he had confided to L.S. Amery two days earlier, he was inclined to satisfy munitions workers 'even if it involved progressive deterioration of all their money values'.[72]

The War Cabinet accepted Churchill's view that action must be taken. The Government had pledged itself to do something for the skilled time-workers and the matter was urgent because leaving certificates were about to be abolished. Two members of the War Cabinet, Milner and Barnes, were entrusted with the final decision, and opted for a 12.5 per cent bonus for 250,000 men, to come into force immediately. To cut a long story short, the predictions of the critics were amply fulfilled. For several months a surge of wage demands pulsed through the economy as first of all other classes of skilled workers on time-rates, then the semi-skilled piece-workers, then workers outside war industry, pressed for the 12.5 per cent. There were many strikes, and the War Cabinet tried in vain to hold the line with brave declarations that enough was enough.

Churchill was reluctant at first to admit that he had made a mistake. When the menacing state of industrial relations was discussed by the War Cabinet on Christmas Eve, 1917, he argued that the perpetual agitation for wage increases

> was due very largely to the fact that the wage-earners were convinced that enormous profits were being made both by the employers and by profiteers engaged in trade and exchange. He was convinced that one of the only means of stopping these demands would be for the Government to take the whole of the excess profits instead of 80 per cent.

In his capacity as Chancellor of the Exchequer, Bonar Law replied that from his experience in raising the Excess Profits Tax from 50 per cent to 80 per cent, he feared that the proposal would meet with 'tremendous opposition from all classes of employers', and would also 'destroy all incentive to increased output'. It was, therefore, 'out of the question at present'.[73]

By the beginning of 1918 it was obvious that the 12.5 per cent bonus was turning into a fiasco. In January, Barnes, who had been one of the joint authors of the final War Cabinet decision, made a discreditable attempt to shift the blame by accusing Churchill of 'butting in' with the 12.5 per cent. This was brazen, but it was true that a mistake had been made, and that Churchill was more responsible than anyone else. On 30 January McCallum Scott wrote:

The *Morning Post* has resumed its old attacks ... His enemies in the House are sniping. His friends are doubtful. Barnes in the War Cabinet, stabs him in the back. The War Cabinet itself gives him no support & indeed seems bent on taking labour questions out of his hands.[74]

Churchill made a good scapegoat. But in his bafflement over strikes and industrial disputes, he reflected the disarray of the Lloyd George Government. Ministers did not know how to restore industrial peace. Veering erratically between coercion and conciliation, they tried to find a balance between the two and failed. In June 1918 the Government tried once more to limit the mobility of skilled workers, who were still being poached by one employer from another and often by one Government department from another. To ensure that craftsmen were retained in the most essential jobs an attempt was made to institute a system of embargoes, preventing employers from taking on more skilled labour than was deemed necessary by the Ministry of Munitions. The following month a series of strikes broke out in protest in the engineering works of Coventry, Birmingham and Manchester. Organised by the shop stewards in defiance of the national officials of the engineering unions, the strikes alarmed the union leaders almost as much as the Government. The Government's Trade Union Advisory Committee issued an appeal to the strikers to return to work. This greatly assisted Churchill who from the beginning of the dispute had urged the War Cabinet to threaten the strikers with conscription. The War Cabinet agreed, Lloyd George issued an ultimatum, and the strikers returned to work. In a draft statement for the press which was never issued, Churchill had intended to include a denunciation of subversive elements, warning that workers:

must be on their guard against certain evil and subterranean influences which are at work ... There is an under-current of Pacifism, Defeatism and Bolshevism at work which it would be affectation not to recognise and folly not to mark down.[75]

In the fourth and final year of the war there was nothing like a coherent industrial order in Britain. In spite of the creation of the Ministry of Labour in 1916, there was no department with undivided authority in industrial relations. There was no effective planning of wages, prices or manpower. Churchill, for once, had no vision of the way forward. The problems defeated him and he drew the conclusion that in wartime industrial relations were bound to be in a terrible mess. In this respect, at least, he was disillusioned by 1918 with the collectivist state. Speaking off the record to a delegation of engineering employers in October 1918, he frankly admitted the extent of the failure:

Looking round upon the field of battle in industry, I suppose you see what you see on every battlefield – chaos, wreckage, confusion and waste on every side. I do not believe myself that during the continuance of a war you will get a good solution of these labour difficulties; for what are you going to base yourselves on?

... As I have repeatedly said, a great many employers are not directly interested in keeping wages within reasonable bounds; they are far more interested in boosting up their particular product. The workmen and even the large majority who are patriotic say: "Why should we not get our share of all that is going?" and the State has not yet found itself capable or competent or strong enough to intervene with broad, clear rulings which have been obeyed. Even in Germany, with all their authority and power over the individual, they have had a good deal of industrial disorder. Here we have complete industrial disorder from that point of view.[76]

\*

The labour troubles of the Great War were mainly due to the relative decline in the income and status of the craftsmen or 'aristocrats of labour'. But their loss was others' gain. War industry had opened up opportunities for the unskilled, and especially for women. In July 1914 there were 214,000 women employed in engineering and munitions; by 1918, almost a million, of whom the vast majority were employed on Government work, their wages and conditions regulated by the Ministry of Munitions. In this way Churchill was once again brought into contact with 'the woman question'.

In November 1917 Churchill addressed the first meeting of a new advisory committee of women trade unionists at the Ministry. Unusually for him, Churchill reflected on the long-term social consequences of the war:

> We are incomparably the greatest employers of women there has ever been in the world, we are the pioneers of women's employment in the industrial and even the military field. Whatever may be the future position which women's labour will take after the war, it will be enormously influenced by the actual practice which has been followed when so much is in the making, and when so much control is vested in the organisation of the Ministry of Munitions. Therefore we are really at the head stream of history in regard to women's place in the industrial life of Britain, perhaps as far as this present century is concerned. The interests of women in industrial life must not be an incident of the Great War. Now is the time during the Great War for us to perceive, discover and proclaim the principles which should regulate, for perhaps the lifetime of a whole generation and perhaps for longer, the lines of advance on which women's industrial work should proceed.[77]

Politicians were in the habit of making flattering references to the role of women in the war effort, and the 'debt' they were owed by the 'nation'. But it would be wrong to dismiss Churchill's words as mere rhetoric. He was about to formulate a scheme of industrial reconstruction in which women workers were of central importance.

During the Great War more than a million women had joined the labour force for the first time. But what was to become of them at the end of the war? Were they to return to their traditional roles as housewives or domestic servants, or continue in full-time industrial employment? This question now had significant electoral implications. The war had removed many of the obstacles to the enfranchisement of women. By November 1917 the Representation of the People Bill, extending the vote to all men over the age of 21, and the great majority of women over the age of 30, had passed through all its stages in the House of Commons. Whatever his personal reservations, Churchill gave no sign of opposition. As a major employer of women munitions workers, he would indeed have been foolish to do so. On the positive side, he saw in the enfranchisement of women an industrial opportunity.

As Minister of Munitions he bore a direct responsibility for the planning of the transition from war to peace. On 3 November 1917, he set up within the Ministry a standing committee on demobilisation and reconstruction, attached to the Munitions Council. The committee was directed by Churchill to prepare 'a great scheme, necessarily crude and bold in its outline, of what enterprise each class of munitions production is to be turned to.' While the Ministry of Munitions was charged with planning the demobilisation of war industry, the Ministry of Reconstruction was expected to plan for the demobilisation of labour: but for obvious reasons there was no clear-cut division of responsibility between the two departments.[78]

Churchill took a lively interest in the subject. Though industrial relations had proved such an intractable problem in wartime, he looked forward to an enduring post-war settlement with labour. By the autumn of 1918 he was convinced that demobilisation presented an opportunity for a major social and industrial advance. He argued that the restrictive practices of the craft unions, which had been set aside for the duration of the war, should be permanently abandoned, leaving women and unskilled workers in possession of the ground they had gained in wartime.

In 1915 the Government had promised the craft unions that in return for their co-operation during the war, restrictive practices would be restored when the war was over. Accordingly, a bill for the restoration of pre-war practices was submitted to the War Cabinet. When the bill was first discussed on 3 October, Churchill spoke strongly against it:

> In his view, the profound changes which had taken place during the war had altered the conditions under which the Government's pledges had been given. Parliament's views of the obligations of the citizen in wartime had been changed by the Military Service Acts. It was urged that it was important, in the event of a general election, that the Bill should be introduced before the dissolution of Parliament. To that it might be replied that a large number of women were about to be enfranchised, and to restore pre-war trade union practices would mean the exclusion of many of these women from industry. The proper way to meet the claim of the trade unions was not to put an impossible Bill on the Statute Book, but to institute industrial conditions which would be far more satisfactory to the trade unions than pre-war conditions.[79]

Disagreement with Churchill was expressed by Addison, the Minister of Reconstruction, and Roberts, the Minister of Labour, who argued that the Government must fulfil its pledges.

The bill was again discussed by the War Cabinet on 16 October. Again Churchill spoke strongly against it:

> He had within the last few days met with no opposition when he had explained to bodies of workmen that it was impossible to redeem the Government's pledges. The War Cabinet was being asked to approve a Bill which was absurd and vicious. It was a Bill to entrench a number of small and close corporations in restraint of trade, and would probably meet with the resistance of the great majority of the unskilled and women workers.

Churchill urged that the Government should retain state controls for a period of two years after the war, during which an attempt would be made to come to terms with labour through a National Conference, 'at which problems of wages and conditions of production might be examined, and a charter for labour drawn up.' He was strongly supported by the Secretary of State for Air, Lord Weir, the owner of a major engineering firm on Clydeside. 'Whatever procedure was adopted,' said Weir, 'the dominating issue should be to preserve the great progress in productive methods brought about by the war.'[80]

Lloyd George had so far been absent from the proceedings, leaving Bonar Law to chair the War Cabinet. On his return, he was inclined at first to back Churchill, but retreated in the face of stern warnings from Addison, Roberts and others, who pointed to the threat from the shop stewards movement if the Government's pledges were not redeemed. The War Cabinet did adopt the idea of a National Conference to discuss the future of industry, but on restrictive practices Churchill was overruled. The post-war sequel has been described by Keith Middlemas:

> The immediate outcome of restoration ... justified Churchill's fear of a wave of strikes like 1911 and his mordant prediction that female employment would suffer as a result. Trade unions ignored the wartime expectations of most female and many unskilled workers who had taken the places of dilutees, and their understandable but ungenerous haste to restore male skilled employment on pre-war ratios set back for years the standards briefly achieved in low-paid and casual labour industries, to say nothing of the cause of equal pay, which Lloyd George and Churchill had shown some inclination to adopt.[81]

It is not surprising that Churchill wanted to turn the flank of the craft unions. They, or at any rate the shop stewards movement, had repeatedly got in the way of the production drive, and embroiled Churchill in the fiasco of the 12.5 per cent bonus. The Ministry of Munitions was dedicated to the principle of dilution, and the Director of Civil Demobilisation, Sir Stephenson Kent, was keen to impress on Churchill the lesson of war production: that 'the vaunted skill of the mechanic can be much more easily acquired than the mechanic has given the world to believe . . . '[82]

*

If Churchill did not wish to see the restoration of the status quo in industry, the same was true of his approach to party politics. But restoration would hardly have been possible in any case. Since Lloyd George's accession to the premiership in December 1916, the Liberal party had been crystallising into rival factions, one looking to Lloyd George and the other to Asquith. In the Maurice debate of 9 May 1918 the split was dramatised when Asquith led 98 Liberals into the lobby against the Government. On 17 May Churchill and other Liberal allies of Lloyd George gathered at the House of Commons to form the nucleus of a separate Liberal grouping, with Churchill's cousin F.E. Guest as Chief Whip. In July agreement was reached between the Lloyd George Liberals and the Conservatives to fight the next election on a joint programme, perpetuating the wartime Government as the Government of peacetime reconstruction.[83]

Churchill's ideal of a peacetime Coalition was at last to be realised. But the Liberal party was to be compromised, a prospect which alarmed Liberals of the true faith. In October 1918 Archibald Sinclair reported to his wife Churchill's prediction that 'the trend of development is to consolidate the Tories and Radicals in one great bourgeois party – democratic and progressive but based on the existing social order – and to leave the Labour party to fight for the New Social Order.' As Sinclair confessed, he was disturbed by the prospect and felt no enthusiasm for 'Lloyd George and Winston's Tory Democracy, founded upon a strong, egotistic, National State with permanent compulsory service, cold support of the League of Nations, and conscription for Ireland.'[84]

But the gulf between the Liberal and Tory positions had narrowed during the war. The Conservatives, though insisting on special treatment for Ulster, were no longer rigidly opposed to Irish Home Rule. The free trade issue had lost some of its force with the introduction by a Liberal Chancellor of the Exchequer, McKenna, of selective customs duties in 1915. Above all, the Coalition Government seemed to work harmoniously enough, superseding the battle cries of the Edwardian era. Inevitably, there was some horse-trading and jostling for position. Churchill was chiefly concerned to obtain a promise from Lloyd George that the War Cabinet would be ended and a peacetime Cabinet – or, in other words, a Cabinet containing Churchill – restored. On the fiscal question the Coalition Liberals were ready to bend but not break, as Henry Pelling explains: 'They decided that they could accept some infringements of Free Trade, such as fiscal arrangements to protect key industries, to provide Imperial Preference, and to prevent "dumping" of foreign goods below cost.' Churchill accepted most of this, but was inclined to grumble about 'dumping', fearing that the party balance might be tipping too much in favour of the Conservatives.[85]

A Coalition victory at the polls was inevitable. Except in Ireland, where Sinn Fein was preparing a challenge, there was no alternative Government in sight. Only the Asquithian Liberals, with 250 candidates, and the Labour party, with 388, stood outside the Lloyd George Leviathan. But the leaders of the Coalition were far from complacent. Owing to the extension of the franchise, the electorate had almost tripled in size since 1910, from 7,694,000 to 21,392,000. Within that electorate, Lloyd George and his allies sensed the presence of a working-class more numerous and powerful than ever before. The trade union movement had been expanding rapidly. The Labour party was poised for a major advance. The soldiers and the women would expect rewards for their contribution to victory. Here were the considerations which led the leaders of the coalition to stress their commitment to social reform, especially in housing. Hence Lloyd George's promise of 'a fit land for heroes to live in'.

Churchill was much in favour of the appeasement of labour. On 21 November he wrote to Lloyd George urging him to promise the taxation of war profits:

Why *should* anybody make a great fortune out of the war? While everybody has been serving the country, profiteers and contractors & shipping speculators have gained fortunes of a gigantic character. Why shd we be bound to bear the unpopularity of defending old Runciman's ill-gotten gains? I wd reclaim everything above £10,000 (to let the small fry off) in reduction of the War Debt.[86]

In fact no pledge to tax war profits was made by the Coalition leaders.

The Coalition claimed to include 'patriotic Labour', a rump of Labour politicians who stayed with the Coalition when the Labour party withdrew after the armistice. Among them was Alexander Wilkie of the shipwrights, who was once again Churchill's running-mate in Dundee. Opposing them were a Labour party candidate, James S. Brown, and the indomitable

Scrymgeour. In a bid to prove that he was still a radical reformer, Churchill pledged himself once more to the nationalisation of the railways. But John Sime, the Secretary of the Jute and Flax Workers' Union, replied: 'Jute Workers! Mr Churchill is in favour of your husbands, sons, and brothers ... being Prussianised under conscription. He has done nothing for the workers of Dundee. He uses them for his own purposes.'[87]

As the election campaign of 1918 progressed, questions of social reform were thrust into the background by cries of revenge against Germany. Churchill, who had never been a jingoist or a chauvinist, refused to declare himself in favour of hanging the Kaiser or squeezing Germany 'until the pips squeaked'. But in any case he had no need of electoral stunts. At that particular moment the Lloyd George Coalition was an overwhelming and unstoppable force. In Dundee the result of the election was as follows:

| | |
|---|---|
| W.S. Churchill (Co Lib) | 25,788 |
| A. Wilkie (Co Lab) | 24,822 |
| E. Scrymgeour (Prohib) | 10,423 |
| J.S. Brown (Lab) | 7,769 |

On 26 December 1918 Churchill wrote a long letter to Lloyd George about the composition of the new Government. The concluding flourish showed that he still attached much importance to social policy:

I hope you will endeavour to gather together all forces of strength and influence in the country & lead them along the paths of science & organisation to the rescue of the weak and the poor. That is the main conception I have of the Victory Government & from it we may draw the prosperity & stability of the Empire.[88]

# 6

# *The Impact*
# *of Labour*

## 1918–24

In the opening months of 1919 British policy-makers looked out upon a world disordered by the Great War. Germany was on the brink of chaos and the whole of Europe lay under the shadow of the Bolshevik revolution. In Egypt and India, independence movements were challenging the British Empire. In Ireland the triumph of Sinn Fein had resulted in the collapse of British authority over most of the country. Britain itself was swept by a tide of industrial unrest and the Government feared the declaration of a general strike. 'The whole world', remarked Churchill at a meeting of the War Cabinet, was 'in the melting pot.'[1]

In the aftermath of the war British politics were dominated by the search for stability both at home and abroad. Plainly, the world of August 1914 could never be wholly restored. The party system, the economy, and Britain's role in the world, had all to be adapted to take account of harsh and unwelcome realities. The burden of statesmanship fell on the Lloyd George Government of 1918 to 1922. No government composed of mere politicians could possibly have been equal to the task. Yet by trial and error the Lloyd George Government did succeed in mapping out the contours of a post-war settlement in foreign, imperial, and domestic policy. Though its record was flawed by great mistakes, it ranks nevertheless as one of the landmark administrations of the twentieth century.

In his post-war premiership, Lloyd George rose to machiavellian heights of achievement. In the diplomacy of peacemaking, the defusing of industrial unrest, and the negotiation of the Irish Treaty, he towered above his colleagues. Churchill, of course, was a subordinate whom Lloyd George was careful to cast in secondary roles. Beaverbrook described his attitude towards Churchill at this period as 'harsh and overbearing, at times almost insulting'. Churchill, for his part, reacted against Lloyd George's policies at many points.[2]

Lloyd George liked to convey the impression that Churchill was a warmonger, a spendthrift, a diehard imperialist and a Tory in all but name. But there were many sides to Churchill. As Secretary of State for War, from January 1919 to February 1921, he conformed to Lloyd George's caricature in one respect at least. His passionate campaign for the overthrow of the Bolshevik regime in Russia was a venture into the realm of the impossible, and isolated him within the Government. But in 1920 he did not hesitate to defend, against a hostile Tory House, the decision to sack General Dyer for the massacre at Amritsar. As Colonial Secretary, the office he held from February 1921 until the fall of the coalition, he showed his diplomatic talent for negotiation and compromise. He played a leading role in the settlement of the Middle East at the Cairo Conference of March 1921, and again in the negotiations which led up to the Irish Treaty of December 1921.

In home affairs Churchill was far more active than his departmental responsibilities might appear to suggest. From 1918 onwards the underlying problem in British politics was the 'impact of Labour'.[3] Ever since the Reform Act of 1867 the Liberal and Conservative parties had competed for the votes of working men. Hence Lord Randolph Churchill's cry of Tory Democracy, and the reforms which his son Winston had carried through at the Board of Trade. But up to 1914 the class issue had been contained by the party system. The two major parties were divided by other issues, like religion and free trade, which cut across class divisions.

The effect of the Great War was to blur the distinctions between the Conservative and Liberal parties. From 1916 onwards the leaders of the Conservative party worked harmoniously with Lloyd George in the conduct of the war. At the top a kind of national unity was created among a small band of ministers drawn from both major parties. When the Coalition went to the country in the general election of 1918 it was generally understood on all sides that although the Coalition Liberals were the minority partners, they had a special role to play as the left-wing of the Coalition, with a strong commitment to social reconstruction and a significant appeal to the working-class electorate. The sweeping Coalition victory in the general election of 1918 appeared to confirm that the Government was embraced by the broad mass of the people. 136 Coalition Liberal MPs were returned in alliance with 383 Tories. The Labour party, with 57 seats, and the Asquithian Liberals, with 20, were dissident fragments beside the Coalition monolith.

At first the leaders of the Coalition expected that the Labour party and the trade unions, though outside the Government, would co-operate in the politics of national unity. But this optimistic mood quickly faded in the face of industrial unrest. Ministers were not unduly worried by strikes within particular firms or industries, but they feared that industrial unrest would develop into something more dangerous: a general strike intended to challenge the authority of Parliament. This was a threat to which Churchill had responded belligerently as Home Secretary in 1911. In 1919–20 he again clashed bitterly with the labour movement, but this time the conflict was projected into a different sphere: the war of intervention against the Bolsheviks. A vivid image of Churchill as a militarist and class warrior was indelibly stamped on the collective consciousness of labour. But how far that reputation was justified remains to be seen.

From 1920 onwards the 'impact of labour' entered a new phase. The Labour party was beginning to win by-elections in 'safe' Coalition seats. It was now clear for the first time that Labour was no longer a minor party but was on course to obtain a majority of seats and to form a Government. This raised a major question of party political tactics. How was the electoral advance of Labour to be stemmed? Churchill's response was to engage in a rhetoric of negative anti-socialism, in the course of which he stigmatised Labour as 'not fit to govern', and linked the socialist danger at home with the Bolshevik peril abroad. But his position was more complex than it seemed. Though negative in public, he was conciliatory on social questions in the Cabinet room: there was something histrionic about his warnings to the nation.

One factor to remember is the extent to which Churchill needed the Labour party as an enemy for career reasons. His anti-socialist convictions were not in doubt. But his talk of the socialist peril was carefully orchestrated and it is open to doubt whether he really feared the Labour party of MacDonald, Snowden, Henderson and Thomas. Churchill had often argued for a Liberal-Conservative Coalition that would enable him and his friends to run the Government. Now such a Coalition existed Churchill was eager for it to be made permanent. But what rationale could be found for maintaining indefinitely in peacetime a Government accidentally created by war?

The electoral advance of Labour supplied an answer. The only solution to the socialist peril, Churchill maintained, was for the two wings of the Coalition to merge into a Centre or National Party. The idea of 'fusion' was no Churchillian eccentricity, but a project seriously entertained by Lloyd George, Bonar Law and many of the Coalition's supporters. Nevertheless, Churchill's call for fusion revived the suspicion that he was a rootless careerist whose ambition was simply to rejoin the Conservative party. Churchill, however, never thought in these terms. What he stood for was a genuine fusion in which the Conservatives were obliged to accept a Liberal principle to which he was far more steadfastly attached than Lloyd George: Free Trade.

In October 1922, the Coalition was overthrown by a rebellion of the Tory back-benches. Churchill was out of office and also out of Parliament after his decisive defeat by Labour in Dundee. There followed a period of many twists and turns in party politics, which Churchill managed to exploit to his own advantage. Two strokes of luck worked in his favour. Firstly, in 1923, Baldwin led the Conservatives into a general election with a pledge to introduce tariffs. This gave him the opportunity of taking his stand once more as a Free Trade Liberal, while also displaying a renewed interest in social questions. Though he was defeated as a candidate in the general election of 1923, he had set up his stall in the market-place and was ready to wheel and deal. Secondly, the Liberal party decided to put a minority Labour Government in office in 1924. This enabled Churchill to lead a secession of right-wing Liberals, opposed to Labour but committed to Free Trade, into the Tory camp. In October 1924 he was re-elected to the House of Commons as the 'Constitutionalist' candidate for Epping. In 1904 Free Trade had been Churchill's passport from the Conservative to the Liberal parties. In 1924 Free Trade again served him as a passport on the return journey, but this time 'anti-socialism' was stamped on every page. It was still Churchill's view, however, that the most effective way of opposing socialism was to improve the condition of the working classes. His ambition in 1924 was to vindicate his father's slogan of Tory Democracy.

* * *

On 10 January 1919 Lloyd George appointed Churchill Secretary of State for War and Air. By the time he arrived at the War Office a crisis was already in the making. Morale was plummeting in the Army and mutinies were starting to break out. That same month, major strikes were threatened in the coal mines and on the railways, and a general strike broke out in Glasgow. A spirit of rebellion was passing through Britain.

In November 1918 there were 1,640,000 British troops on the western front, and another 420,000 in Salonika, Palestine and Mesopotamia. Except for a few thousand regular soldiers who intended to remain in the Army, the troops were longing to return home and impatient for demobilisation. The War Cabinet, however, had adopted a demobilisation plan which aroused the anger of officers and men alike. Under the Government scheme, the demand from employers for labour was to determine the order in which men were released. As Martin Gilbert puts it: 'A soldier who had served four months, but had been offered an industrial job, could come home. A soldier who had served for four years, but had been offered no job, must remain in uniform.'[4] Announced on 7 January, the plan set in train disastrous consequences. The manifest injustice of ignoring a man's length of service produced a sharp decline in discipline and rumblings of mutiny. But there was also an organisational problem. Even though the war with Germany was over, the Government still required more than a million men for the British Armies of Occupation in Germany and Mesopotamia, and for service in India. Under the demobilisation scheme it was assumed that the numbers required would be raised from volunteers. But now the Army was melting away as men were released for civilian employment. The remainder could be held as conscripts for a period of six months after the armistice, but after that conscription was due to lapse. So unless some drastic action were taken, the Government might be left with nothing but the skeleton of an Army by May 1919.

Churchill took decisive action. Sweeping aside Sir Eric Geddes, who had been appointed as co-ordinator of demobilisation, he devised with the help of his advisers an alternative plan. All men who had enlisted before 1916 were to be released, and all men over 40. Three out of four soldiers were to be sent home and the pay of the fourth increased. But in order to provide for the Armies of Occupation, peacetime conscription was to be introduced – if only in a limited and temporary form – for the first time.[5]

Before the new scheme could be implemented there was a final protest against the old. On 30 January, 5,000 British troops in an army camp at Calais demanded to be sent home. Haig, the Commander-in-Chief, suppressed the mutiny and informed Churchill that he proposed to try the three ring-leaders by court-martial and have them shot. Churchill had no ministerial authority to prevent this, but he warned Haig to desist: 'Unless there was serious violence attended by bloodshed or actual loss of life, I do not consider that the infliction of the death penalty would be justifiable.' Haig, though much offended by Churchill's intervention, took his advice: no executions were carried out.[6]

Churchill's demobilisation plan was the work of a politician who recognised the need to conciliate the troops. The situation had been all the more dangerous in view of the potential conjunction between discontented soldiers and discontented workers. On 30 January Churchill was instructed by the War Cabinet to prepare 'a complete scheme and organisation of military forces throughout the United Kingdom to act in aid of the civil power in the event of a national strike of a revolutionary character.'[7] A few days later the Cabinet set up an Industrial Unrest Committee to co-ordinate the activities of the police, the armed forces, and local and central Government, in the event of an emergency. Though Churchill himself was not a member of the committee, the precedent he had set in the rail strike of 1911 was referred to and adopted as Government policy. On 25 March the Cabinet agreed that in the event of a large-scale strike, the military authorities would have the right to decide where and how troops could be used: no longer would a request from the local magistrate be necessary.[8]

But could the troops be relied upon? In February, Churchill authorised a War Office circular which instructed commanders to report weekly on the political sentiments of the troops. Commanding officers were asked whether troops would respond to orders to assist in preserving the public peace, whether they would assist in 'strike-breaking', and whether they would parade for service overseas, 'especially to Russia'. The findings were illuminating. It was reported that troops could be relied upon to preserve the peace and resented unofficial strikes. But they were opposed to strike-breaking and thought it would not be fair if they were asked to perform the work of 'blacklegs'. They were prepared to serve overseas – but not in Russia.[9]

It is not clear what conclusions Churchill drew from the findings of the circular. But it is clear that he was well aware of the need for a calculating sensitivity in the handling of strikes. There is little on the record to show that as Secretary for War he was a military hothead in industrial disputes, or diverged significantly from the cautious but firm approach of his colleagues. At the end of January 1919 a general stoppage of work in favour of a 40-hour week took place in Glasgow. The strike was an unofficial one, triggered by a sudden downturn of employment in the shipbuilding and engineering trades, and organised by a committee under the chairmanship of Emanuel Shinwell. On 30 January the War Cabinet met under Bonar Law to consider what action to take. Churchill called for decisive action once the Government had public opinion on its side:

> Mr Churchill said that we should not exaggerate the seriousness of this disturbance ... The disaffected were a minority, and, in his opinion, there would have to be conflict to clear the air. We should be careful to have plenty of protection before taking strong measures. By going gently at first we should get the support we wanted from the nation, and then troops could be used more effectively.

Bonar Law declared that he did not disagree with a word Churchill had said.[10]

The following day a mass meeting of 30,000 strikers in George Square, Glasgow, resulted in several baton charges by the police and the arrest of Shinwell, Gallacher, Kirkwood and others. By 1 February nineteen infantry battalions had been moved into the city and six tanks stationed near the city centre. Within a fortnight, the strike petered out.[11]

On 4 February Churchill was present at the War Cabinet to discuss the threat – never in fact to materialise – of an electricity strike in London. The minutes record Churchill's views on the use of troops:

> Mr Churchill said that he was not prepared to say that soldiers could not be obtained, but he had always tried to keep the Army out of an affair of this kind ... He could not see, however, the distinction between the war and a great civil emergency, though that emergency had not yet been reached. At a certain point he would not hesitate to use troops if it was a question of saving lives. It seemed to him that the government should face this challenge, and he had no doubt of the substantial loyalty of the mass of the nation. The threatened electrical strike was one of a series of attempts of a well-organised minority to obtain extravagant concessions. If we allowed this sort of thing to go on, the day would arrive when all authority would be discredited ... He would frame legislation to deal with the situation, and make the agitators amenable to law by fine and imprisonment.[12]

The strike was averted when the electricians were threatened with prosecution under wartime emergency powers which the Government still retained. Two months later the War Cabinet discussed the draft of a bill making it a penal offence for electricity workers to go on strike without warning. Churchill took the opportunity of defining the strategy the Government ought to pursue in industrial disputes:

> In the next few years discrimination would have to be shown, and people taught to draw the line between strikes against private employers and strikes which affected the whole community. If a stable government was not going to fight for the upholding of these principles it could have no permanent foothold.[13]

Churchill went on to spell out this doctrine in Parliament and the press. Embarrassed by the publication of the secret War Office circular in the *Daily Herald*, he defended himself in the House of Commons by seeking to draw a line between industrial and political disputes:

> To use soldiers or sailors ... to take sides with the employer in an
> ordinary trade dispute, to employ them as what are called "black legs",
> would be a monstrous invasion of the liberty of the subject, and I do say
> without hesitation that it would be a very unfair, if not an illegal, order to
> give to the soldier. But the case is different where vital services affecting
> the health, life and safety of large cities or great concentrations of people
> are concerned. Light, water, electric power, transport, the distribution
> of food, all these are indispensable ... If any of these commodities or
> facilities are suddenly cut off, the State must intervene and come to the
> rescue of the population.[14]

Churchill's attitude towards the trade unions at this period was very
similar to that of Lloyd George and other ministers. The primary concern
of the Government was the restoration of social stability and from this
point of view there was something to be said for bolstering the authority
of the trade unions. As ministers saw it, the fundamental problem was a
turbulent and unruly labour force. Trade unions were organisations with
which the Government could negotiate, and through which it might hope
to moderate the behaviour of the industrial masses. On 4 February 1919
the War Cabinet discussed a strike for union recognition by the railway
clerical workers. Churchill commented:

> Trade union organisation was very imperfect, and the more mod-
> erate its officials were, the less representative it was; but it was the
> only organisation with which the government could deal. The curse
> of trade unionism was that there was not enough of it, and it was not
> highly developed enough to make its branch secretaries fall into line
> with the head office. With a powerful trade union, peace or war could
> be made.

Bonar Law was thinking along similar lines. Trade union organisation,
he remarked, was 'the only thing between us and anarchy'.[15]

While Churchill was ready to fight if necessary, his belligerence was
coupled with a continuing belief in the value of social appeasement.
In January 1919 Riddell recorded in his diary a conversation in which
Churchill 'spoke strongly in favour of better conditions – cheap houses,
higher wages, etc. His conception of the State consists in a well-paid,
well-nurtured people, managed and controlled by a Winston or Winstons.'[16]

Churchill also expressed his views in Cabinet. In the hope of achieving industrial peace, the Government summoned employers and trade union leaders to a National Industrial Conference on 27 February. On 4 April the Conference agreed a set of recommendations which included a maximum 48-hour week and a minimum time wage. When the proposals came before the Cabinet, Churchill spoke up in favour of legislation: 'The Secretary of State for War strongly approved recognition of the principle of wage minima. In his opinion the real answer of ordered society to Bolshevism was the frank recognition of minimum standards and open access to the highest posts in industry.'[17] Though some of the recommendations were taken up by the Government, no action was taken to implement the minimum wage proposal, nor did Churchill pursue it. There was too little consensus between unions and employers for the Conference to be more than a short-lived experiment.

At the end of the war both the railways and the coal mines were under state control. Both the railwaymen and the miners were campaigning for nationalisation. Furthermore, they formed two of the unions in the Triple Alliance of miners, railwaymen and transport workers. The Triple Alliance, which had first appeared in 1914 but lapsed during the war, was dedicated to the syndicalist method of Direct Action to coerce Government and society. Its re-establishment in January 1919 greatly alarmed the Government.

It was in the Government's interest to drive a wedge between the railwaymen and the miners, and ministers were more inclined to make concessions to the railwaymen, whose leader, J.H. Thomas, was a notorious 'moderate' much seen in the company of high society. From several cordial references to him in Churchill's speeches we may infer that 'Jimmy' and 'Winston' got on well together over the brandy and cigars. During the 1918 general election Churchill and a number of other ministers had pledged themselves to the nationalisation of the railways. The Ways and Communications Bill of February 1919 actually included powers of state purchase. But in July 1919 Bonar Law, as leader of the Conservative party, declared his opposition to railway nationalisation. Churchill's protests were in vain, and the power to nationalise was dropped from the bill.[18]

As in 1912, Churchill was distinctly hostile to the miners. In February they submitted to the Government demands for a 30 per cent increase in earnings, a six-hour day, and the nationalisation of the mines. To gain time, Lloyd George persuaded the miners' executive to postpone the strike and take part in a Commission under Lord Sankey to inquire into the future organisation of the industry. But the members of the Commission split into opposing groups and presented, on 20 June, four conflicting reports. The Labour representatives, including the miners, called for nationalisation and workers' control; the mine-owners, and the industrialist Lord Gainford, were for unreconstructed private enterprise; Sir Arthur Duckham, a mining engineer, argued for a system of state regulation short of public ownership; and Sankey himself came down in favour of nationalisation.

While Lloyd George procrastinated, the miners went on strike in an attempt to force the issue. Meeting Churchill on 22 July, Riddell found both him and Clementine 'very violent' against the miners. 'Churchill said: "This is the time to beat them. There is bound to be a fight. The English propertied classes are not going to take it lying down." '[19] When the War Cabinet discussed the coal industry on 7 August, Churchill reiterated his support for the nationalisation of the railways, but opposed state ownership of the pits on the grounds that it was not a part of the Government's mandate and would be unacceptable to Parliament. Nor would he concede that the case for nationalisation had been proved on its merits. But he did not rule it out entirely:

> ... it would be wrong to meet the question of nationalisation with a direct negative, and he thought that the policy of the government lay in a compromise between the Gainford and the Duckham proposals. If some of the owners disagreed with this course it would place the government in the middle position, which it ought to occupy ... This view had been borne in upon him, although he was not opposed to nationalisation in principle.[20]

Like Churchill, the majority of ministers were opposed to nationalisation, though two Coalition Liberals, Addison and Montagu, spoke in favour.[21] The final decision was to opt for the Duckham plan. The miners, however, failed to grasp the opportunity presented to them. By rejecting Duckham they enabled the Government to postpone the question indefinitely. In 1921 the Government returned both the railways and the mines to the control of their owners.

*

In Churchill's view, a far more important issue than the future of the coal industry was the taxation of war wealth. This highly controversial subject arose out of the financial consequences of the war. In the main, the cost of the war had been met through borrowing rather than taxation, and the National Debt had increased stupendously from £706.2 million in 1913–14 to £7,481.1 million in 1919–20. So great was the burden of interest payments on the debt that by 1924, when Churchill became Chancellor of the Exchequer, almost half the annual revenue had to be devoted to the servicing of the debt.

Politicians of all three parties agreed that the National Debt must be reduced, but how? The Labour party proposed a 'capital levy', whereby all wealth above a certain level would be conscripted in a single instalment. This idea was also taken up by radical Liberals, who calculated that such a levy would raise £6,000 million and cancel out most of the National Debt. In spite of its socialist origins, the idea was seriously entertained by the Treasury, leading economists, and the Board of Inland Revenue. But the great majority of Conservatives were strongly opposed to it on the grounds that industry would be damaged, and the idea perished with the onset of the depression in the summer of 1920.

Churchill was opposed to the capital levy but he strongly supported the most widely canvassed alternative, the taxation of war wealth. Whereas a capital levy would be a tax on all personal wealth, a war wealth duty would be a tax on the amount by which personal wealth had increased between 1914 and 1918. The yield would therefore be much lower, and the contribution to paying off the National Debt a modest one. But from the political point of view, a war wealth duty would have the advantage of targeting an unpopular minority: people who had made a fortune out of the war while a quarter of a million British soldiers were losing their lives. The Labour party, though preferring a capital levy, endorsed the taxation of war wealth as a tolerable alternative.[22]

In August 1919 the Chancellor of the Exchequer, Austen Chamberlain, delivered a stern warning to his colleagues about the need to reduce public expenditure. This was the first shot in a long Treasury campaign to deflate the economy and restore a balanced budget.[23] Churchill proposed substantial cuts in the Army and Air Force budgets. In a Cabinet paper of 1 August he urged that the fighting forces be instructed to plan on the assumption that no major war would occur during the next five years. 'This', he wrote, 'would wipe out a whole series of obligations and anxieties which the military and naval authorities have at present to reckon with.' If military expenses were cut, he argued, the Cabinet would then be in a position to restrict the non-military budget and 'the process of handing out buns to the Labour Party should at any rate be sufficiently curtailed to balance the account.'[24]

Yet Churchill proposed to hand his own bun to the Labour party. In a letter to Lloyd George on 4 August he wrote:

I do not see how we can look the working classes in the face while these enormous war fortunes remain untouched ... I don't wonder there is an ugly spirit abroad when everyone can see a whole new class of millionaires who made their fortunes while 5/6ths of the industries of the country were in suspension or abeyance & every little shopkeeper who cd march was serving in the trenches. This sense of injustice rankles in every heart and is in my opinion at the root of our troubles.[25]

Under pressure from Churchill and two other Coalition Liberals, Addison and Montagu, Chamberlain asked the Board of Inland Revenue to investigate the idea. For the sequel we must jump ahead to the following year. The Board having decided that a war wealth duty was technically feasible, a Select Committee was appointed in February 1920 to draw up a detailed proposal. Treasury officials supported the idea as a contribution to deflation. Though it would only raise £500 million altogether, a drop in the ocean of the National Debt, it would cut the inflated value of war loans to their 1914 level, and thus reduce the purchasing power of consumers. But the idea encountered much opposition from the City, the Federation of British Industries, and the Conservative party. When the Cabinet discussed the Report of the Committee on 4 June 1920, the majority of ministers followed the lead of Bonar Law in rejecting the duty. 'In the end', writes Mary Short, 'it was only Churchill who stayed with the duty and he saw the rejection of it as a fatal blow to the democratic credentials of the government: his dissent was recorded in the Cabinet minutes.'[26] Churchill had argued consistently since 1918 for the taxation of war wealth, recognising both the financial and the political advantages that a bold measure would bring. In October 1921 he wrote to Lloyd George of the Coalition Government's record: 'The first and greatest mistake in my opinion was leaving the profiteers in possession of their ill-gotten war wealth. Had prompt action been taken at the beginning of 1919, several thousand millions of paper wealth could have been transferred to the State and the internal debt reduced accordingly.'[27]

*

On war wealth, Churchill's ideas were near to Labour's. But on Russia they were poles apart. This is not the place for a history of Anglo-Soviet relations, nor for the long and fascinating tale of Churchill's private war against the Soviet Union. But some background is helpful. When the Bolsheviks seized power in October 1917, they called off the war against Germany. In a frantic effort to reconstitute an eastern front, the allied powers despatched troops to various parts of Russia. When civil war broke out, the allies began to assist the anti-Bolshevik forces: the white Russian armies, and the newly-independent states which had broken away from the Russian empire. From the British point of view, the war of intervention was always a sideshow in which the Japanese, the Czechs and, of course, the Russians themselves were expected to do most of the fighting. At the end of the war with Germany there were only 14,000 British troops in Russia.

The defeat of Germany cast doubt on the need for allied intervention. But at the War Cabinet on 23 December 1918 Churchill called for large-scale military intervention by the allies. He was at once opposed by Lloyd George in a heated exchange of opinions which marked the beginning of a long rift between them.[28]

Churchill's obsession with Bolshevism was both military and ideological. On the military side his appointment as Secretary for War gave him direct responsibility for British troops in Russia, and placed him in contact with the battlefronts of the Russian civil war. With the smell of battle in his nostrils he was deeply excited, and supremely confident that victory would go to the white Russian armies under Yudenich, Kolchak and Denikin. His ambition was to be the grand strategist of allied intervention.

Churchill's Marlborough complex was coupled with a primal hatred of the Bolshevik revolution. When he spoke of the Bolsheviks, his language became extreme and his emotions overcame him. Churchill was an aristocrat and, as Lloyd George wrote, his 'ducal blood ran cold' at the fate of the Russian nobility. Beyond that, Churchill recognised that a fundamental battle of ideas had begun. He paid Lenin and Trotsky the tribute of recognising that their own conception of history was diametrically opposed to his own. In the name of the international class struggle they were bent on destroying all the forces which Churchill regarded as the mainsprings of civilisation and progress: capitalism, the liberty of the individual, the rule of law, parliamentary democracy and the British Empire.[29]

The Lloyd George Government as a whole was determined to prevent Bolshevism in Britain. But Churchill was alone in his determination to suppress Bolshevism in Russia. While his colleagues were content to contain Bolshevik Russia, Churchill wanted to overthrow the regime and impose a liberal constitution. The principal objection of Lloyd George and other ministers was not that a liberal Russia was undesirable, but that it was impossible. Britain did not possess the financial or military means to bring about a counter-revolution. The best way to liberalise the regime would be to enter into commercial relations with the Bolsheviks: a continuation of the war of intervention would only serve to strengthen the Bolsheviks' grip.

Churchill tried to present himself as merely the servant of the War Cabinet's policy on Russia. But he was rapidly identified by Labour as the most extreme anti-Bolshevik within the Government. Labour's antagonism to Churchill owed something to memories of his period as Home Secretary. But now two factors combined to kindle animosities into a blaze. Firstly, there was a widespread admiration in the Labour movement for Bolshevism as a socialist experiment. Whatever its flaws, this was a society in which there were no landlords and no capitalists. In blackguarding Russia and sending troops against it, Churchill was making war on Utopia.[30] But secondly the Labour movement was anti-war. Churchill was vilified as a man who lived and hungered for war, and was bent on militarising Britain.

On 6 March 1919 Churchill introduced his bill to prolong conscription up to April 1920 for some classes of men who were already in the Army. This, as we have seen, was necessary in order to maintain the British Armies of Occupation in Germany and the Middle East. Churchill promised that only volunteers, and no conscripts, would be sent to Russia. But on the Left there was deep suspicion of his motives. The editor of *The Nation*, H.W. Massingham, Churchill's ally in the bygone days of Edwardian radicalism, wrote to him: 'That with your gifts you should start again this crazy game of war, when for years every country will be hanging on by its eyelids to its mere existence, is more than I can understand.'[31] But it was the *Daily Herald* which singled out Churchill for attack.

The *Herald* was the newspaper of the Labour Left. Edited by George Lansbury, it featured the talents of a galaxy of writers including W.N. Ewer, H.N. Brailsford, Francis Meynell and William Mellor. With true socialist fervour, it denounced capitalism, militarism and imperialism, supported direct action by the trade unions and, of course, condemned the war of intervention against the Bolsheviks.[32] On 2 May 1919 the *Herald* opened an attack on Churchill with an article by B.N. Langdon Davies entitled 'The Churchill Danger'. This article deserves notice as the first thorough statement of the left-wing case against Churchill. He was condemned for his use of police and troops against strikers in 1910 and 1911. The responsibility for the violence of the police against the suffragettes on 'Black Friday' was laid firmly at his door. Antwerp and the Dardanelles were cited as the disastrous mistakes of a military adventurer. Since the end of the war, Churchill had prolonged conscription, sent conscripts to fight against the Bolsheviks, and at home attempted to crush the aspirations of workers by the display of armed force. In a few years, wrote Langdon Davies, it would be necessary to decide the future of the social order in Europe. 'With Churchill in command at the War Office we shall approach the decision a conscript and militarised nation, we shall have within our own borders repression and violent revolt, we shall be dispatching all over the world the armies of imperialist aggression.'[33] The *Herald* created the definitive left-wing myth of Churchill, into which later events could be slotted. Tonypandy was repeatedly referred to, and it was from this time onwards that it became the cornerstone of the myth. Much to Churchill's embarrassment, the *Herald* also obtained and published a copy of the War Office circular inquiring into the political attitudes of the troops. Churchill retaliated by attacking the *Herald* as subversive: 'The whole intention of this paper is to provoke an outbreak in the form of a mutiny or a general strike, or preferably both together, in the hope that a general smash up and overthrow of society may result.'[34]

*

Though Churchill was deeply alarmed by industrial unrest, he was not yet anxious about the challenge from the Labour party. To Churchill, party politics were still Liberal and Conservative politics. The old parties would determine the future while the Labour party was patted benevolently on the head as a moderating influence in the industrial world. It was generally assumed at the time that the Coalition would continue in being and gradually develop into a more united force. Some younger MPs were positively idealistic about the prospect of maintaining national unity, and associated it with a progressive social policy at home. A New Members Coalition Group, formed in April 1919, urged the case for 'fusion' upon the Whips. The chairman, Oscar Guest, was the brother of Freddie Guest, the Liberal Chief Whip, Churchill's cousin and crony. The Secretary, just returned from the western front, was Oswald Mosley.[35]

Churchill had shown enthusiasm for a 'government of the middle' in 1901 and again in 1910. Now his object was to convert a government of the middle into a permanent body. On 15 July, in a move prearranged with Lloyd George, Churchill spoke at a dinner arranged by the New Members Coalition Group and attended by more than 100 MPs. Churchill put the case for the fusion of the two wings of the coalition into a Centre Party. His argument was based on the proposition that party politics, which had taken Britain to the brink of civil war in Ireland in 1914, had been superseded by the war and ought not to be revived. In home affairs, Churchill adopted a moderately progressive stance and reverted to the language of Edwardian social reform:

'Take, for instance, the question of nationalisation versus public ownership, collectivism versus individualism. Some people are going about with the idea that this is going to be the great line of cleavage in British politics. I do not believe it for a moment. Every one of us is a collectivist for some things, and an individualist for others.'[36]

There was no hint in the speech of hostility to the Labour party. Indeed, F.E. Smith, who apparently arrived on the scene by accident in an alcoholic haze, rose to say that the Labour party, which might take office in the next few years, had a great future.[37]

The proposal for fusion ran into the sands. Until 1921-2 the Coalition was a remarkably united body, and as long as it was united the question of fusion did not appear urgent. Once the Coalition became disunited, coalition was no longer practicable. But over time the case for fusion changed. In the summer of 1919 the loss of two by-elections to Labour at Bothwell (29 July) and Widnes (30 August), began to put a different complexion on the situation. In December 1919 Labour defeated the Coalition Liberal candidate in the by-election at Spen Valley. Why this result should have triggered alarm is hard to say. The Liberal victory was due to the fact that the Liberal vote was split between rival Labour candidates. But suddenly the penny dropped: the Labour party was on the march.

Lloyd George took the lead in advocating fusion. 'National unity alone can save Britain, can save Europe, can save the world', he proclaimed on 7 December 1919. In the New Year, Churchill took up the cry. Asquith had called for a return to party politics but, Churchill warned at Sunderland on 3 January, the break-up of the Coalition 'could only result in pushing the Labour Party into power at a period in their development when they are quite unfitted for the responsibility of government.'[38] Read today, the speech appears dull, but at the time it flashed a reactionary signal. *The Nation* accused Churchill of talking like Castlereagh and Sidmouth after Peterloo. The Darwinian allegation that Labour was 'unfit' rankled deeply:

> This man who has made the most criminal misjudgment that has been made since the day when the Kaiser invaded Belgium, who has sent British soldiers to their death in a cause as hopeless as it was inhuman, who has added these hideous burdens to the burdens that were crushing the life out of Europe, who has kept his place solely because of the prestige of his class, has the patrician insolence to talk of the incompetence of the Labour Party.[39]

With Bonar Law and other Conservative leaders ready to acquiesce in fusion, Lloyd George concentrated on winning over the Coalition Liberals. As Kenneth Morgan explains, some of the Coalition Liberals were reluctant. The two great enthusiasts for fusion were Christopher Addison, the Minister of Health and Churchill – but for different reasons.

Addison saw in fusion a chance to press on with a bold programme of social reconstruction, and proposed that the new party should include the word 'Reform'. Churchill, however, thought the emphasis should be on the defence of the established order, and wanted to introduce the word 'Constitution' into the party's name.[40]

Churchill was to support Addison's housing programme when it was under attack. But Addison wanted the coalition to respond sympathetically to Labour, while Churchill wanted to found the Coalition on anti-Labour solidarity. Churchill seemed oblivious of the fact that in his own predominantly working-class constituency of Dundee, popular opinion was turning against him. Instead he chose to elaborate his argument that Labour was unfit to govern to a Dundee audience on 14 February. Labour, he argued, were unfit to govern for three main reasons. Firstly they were a class party, fighting a battle of class interests. Secondly, they had no useful or helpful policies. They might have been expected to have a clearly thought-out policy for the nationalisation of the mines, but they could not make up their minds whether they were syndicalists or socialists in this respect. ('A voice: "Ye dinna understand it, mon" '). Their remedy for unemployment was to reduce output. On housing, they had stuck to trade union rules and rejected dilution in the building trade, thus denying ex-soldiers the chance of employment. Thirdly, Churchill argued, socialist doctrines would shatter prosperity and cast away the British Empire. Surprisingly, perhaps, Churchill did not allege that Labour were unfit to govern because they were pro-Bolshevik or semi-communist. But his conclusion was no less inevitable: there must be a united stand against Labour.[41]

In March, Bonar Law and Lloyd George agreed that each would attempt to sell fusion to his own wing of the Coalition. But at a meeting of Liberal ministers on 16 March, a majority were against, and Churchill's pleadings were in vain. Two days later a speech by Lloyd George to Coalition Liberal MPs was a total failure when he 'banged the anti-socialist drum as crudely as Churchill and with as little effect'.[42] Meanwhile, doubts had developed on the Conservative side as well, and fusion was postponed into an indefinite future. Lloyd George had bungled it.

In August 1920 the clash between Churchill and Labour came to a head over the Councils of Action movement. In the spring, war had broken out between Russia and Poland, and with it renewed fears of a war between Britain and Russia. In May 1920 dockers at the port of London refused to load arms supplies aboard a ship, the *Jolly George*, bound for Poland. On 31 May Churchill spoke out indignantly at the Cabinet: 'The transport workers won't allow arms to go to the Poles to smash the Bolshevists nor to save the police from the Irish Bolshevists. We ought to take the transport workers by the throat.'[43]

In the first few days of August 1920, with the Red Army threatening Warsaw, armistice talks between Poland and the Soviet Union broke down and the Foreign Secretary, Curzon, warned the Russians that if they advanced any further, Britain would come to Poland's aid. On 6 August *The Times* warned that war was imminent: 'We must face it with the same unanimity and the same courage with which we faced the crisis of 1914.' Local branches of the Labour party organised anti-war demonstrations and on 9 August a joint conference of the TUC, the National Executive of the Labour Party, and the Parliamentary Labour Party, adopted Ernest Bevin's proposal for a Council of Action to organise a general strike against war. Three hundred and fifty local Councils of Action were set up throughout the country, and there were many small-scale strikes.

The crisis passed, and the fortunes of war turned against the Bolsheviks, but in 1920 Churchill was presented with irrefutable evidence of Soviet incitement of internal unrest in Britain. Two Soviet trade delegates, Kamenev and Krassin, had recently arrived for the ostensible purpose of negotiating an Anglo-Soviet trade treaty. They had smuggled in a large consignment of precious stones from the sale of which they financed the *Daily Herald* and other left-wing organisations. They were also in contact with the Council of Action. All this was brought to light when their correspondence with Moscow was intercepted by the Government Code and Cypher School.[44] The intercepts were brought to Churchill's attention by Sir Henry Wilson, the Chief of Imperial General Staff, who was beginning to suspect that Lloyd George was a traitor and might have to be removed in a coup. Churchill was convinced, as he wrote to Lloyd George, Bonar Law and Balfour, that 'a veritable plot is being hatched against England & France'. Writing to the Prime Minister on 25 August he argued for the expulsion of the Soviet trade delegates:

> Are we really going to sit still until we see the combination of the money from Moscow, the Kamenev-Krassin propaganda, the Council of Action, and something very like a general strike, all acting and reacting on one another, while at the same time our military forces are at their very weakest?[45]

Churchill's fears of internal subversion were heightened when, on 31 August, the Triple Alliance unions decided to support a miners' strike for higher pay. Urged on by Wilson and the intelligence chiefs, Sinclair and Thomson, Churchill demanded that Lloyd George take action. Lloyd

George responded by expelling Kamenev, leaving Krassin at the head of the delegation.

On 21 September Churchill put forward a strong Cabinet memorandum calling for the expulsion of the entire Soviet delegation.[46] Lloyd George, however, made light of the Bolsheviks' activities. On 18 November the Cabinet decided to accept in principle a treaty with Russia. This so upset Churchill that he was unable to speak on the rest of the agenda – but he did not resign. Strong though his convictions were, he was not willing to sacrifice his career for them. His old friend F.E. Smith, now Lord Birkenhead, warned him that if he resigned over the treaty, he would be supported by 30 Tory MPs who disagreed with him on 90 per cent of other subjects.[47] An Anglo-Soviet Trade Treaty was finally signed on 16 March 1921.

The collusion between the Soviet trade delegation and the British Left led to a hardening in Churchill's rhetoric. Though still paying lip-service to the idea of a responsible Labour leadership, he was sharpening the axe against the Labour party. In a speech of 4 November he warned: 'There is a growing feeling that a considerable section of organized Labour is trying to tyrannise over the whole public and trying to bully them into submission, not by argument, not by recognised political measures, but by brute force.' For Churchill, domestic subversion was to be understood as part of a world-wide Bolshevik conspiracy:

> The danger at the present time does not exist only, or even mainly, in these islands. What of India, Egypt, Ireland? Do you not think it possible that there is some connection between all the revolutionary and subversive elements by which we are now being assailed? . . . Why, for instance, should the Egyptian extremists give money to the *Daily Herald*? Why does Lenin send them money, too? Why does he also send money to Sinn Fein? We know that intense efforts are being made to disturb India, and that similar efforts are being made to cause a great breakdown of trade and industry at home in the hopes of creating unemployment and consequently suffering and discontent . . . In fact there is developing a world-wide conspiracy against our country, designed to deprive us of our place in the world and to rob us of the fruits of victory.[48]

By this time Churchill had reached an impasse at the War Office. His anti-Bolshevik campaign had failed, but had left him embroiled in a morass of controversy with Labour. In February 1921 Lloyd George shrewdly decided to move Churchill to the Colonial Office, with full power to conclude a settlement of the Middle East. For the time being Churchill retained his portfolio as Secretary for Air. Churchill's handling of the Cairo Conference (12–22 March 1921) was highly successful, but followed by a rending quarrel with Lloyd George. On 17 March Bonar Law was forced by ill health to resign the Conservative leadership. He was succeeded by Austen Chamberlain, who at the same time quit the Treasury to become Leader of the House. Churchill made no secret of the fact that he wanted the Treasury, but Lloyd George appointed Sir Robert Horne instead. Churchill entered one of his rebellious, trouble-making phases.[49]

At the end of March 1921 the leaders of the Triple Alliance conferred over an imminent strike in the coal industry. The railwaymen and the transport workers agreed to begin sympathetic action on 16 April. On 15 April, on the pretext that the miners should resume negotiations with the Government, the other two unions cancelled their strike. This was the occasion notorious in history as 'Black Friday', since it marked the end of the Triple Alliance. The coal dispute dragged on. Churchill, in a transparent display of personal pique, intervened at Cabinet on 24 May to attack Horne's handling of the strike. 'So far', Churchill declared, 'the unemployment dole has kept the country quiet and prevented a violent upheaval but at enormous expense to the state. It is plain we could have stopped the strike very much more cheaply in advance. There is a great feeling for the men in the country.' When Lloyd George appeared to approve the idea that the employers should fight to a finish, Churchill interjected: 'That is the worst thing I have heard.'[50]

Churchill's discontent coincided with a trough in the Government's fortunes and a growing Tory outcry against 'extravagant' public expenditure. One of the principal targets of the campaign against 'squandermania' was the Addison housing programme, and Lloyd George had attempted to appease the critics by sacking Addison from the Ministry of Health in March 1921. But he had kept him on as Minister without Portfolio on a salary of £5,000 a year. Conservative MPs regarded this as a brazen example of favouritism and extravagance. They were prepared to rebel, bringing down Lloyd George and the coalition, unless Addison was dropped. It is not entirely clear what happened next, except that Beaverbrook, Birkenhead and Churchill engaged in some kind of intrigue against Lloyd George. They may have encouraged Addison to stand firm and thereby precipitate a Tory revolt that would bring Lloyd George down. They may have envisaged that Churchill or Birkenhead would succeed as Prime Minister. In any event, Lloyd George foiled the manoeuvre by climbing down: he cut Addison's salary and promised that he would only remain Minister without Portfolio until the end of the parliamentary session.[51]

*

Churchill had his own contribution to make to the cause of economy. On 14 June he announced that military expenditure in Palestine and Mesopotamia, which had been running at an annual figure of £40 million in 1920–1, would fall to £10 million in 1922–3. The savings were largely due to the success of the Cairo conference and to Churchill's ingenious scheme for shifting the responsibility for peace-keeping in Mesopotamia from the military garrison to the much less expensive alternative of the RAF. His economies, however, cut no ice with the Labour party. The Labour candidate in Dundee, E.D. Morel, frequently condemned him for 'the costly and reckless extravagance in Mesopotamia'.[52]

While Churchill cut military spending, he was opposed to cuts in the housing programme. As we have seen, Addison had been dismissed from the Ministry of Health in April 1921. His successor, Sir Alfred Mond, determined to put a stop to the housing drive. On 30 June the Cabinet Finance Committee, chaired by Horne, discussed his proposal to scale down the housing programme from 250,000 to 176,000. This was strongly resisted by three Coalition Liberals – Addison, Montagu and Churchill. At a conference of ministers the next day, Churchill again lined up with Addison and other dissenting voices, but they were overruled by a Cabinet Committee and Addison resigned.[53]

Churchill's dissent over housing cuts may have been due to lingering resentment at Horne's appointment as Chancellor. But we must not overlook the impact of the depression on Churchill's politics. The post-war boom came to an end in the spring of 1920 and was followed by a sharp downturn in the fortunes of the great Victorian export industries: coal, cotton, shipbuilding, iron and steel. In November 1920, unemployment insurance had been extended to cover several million workers, a move which Churchill welcomed as an essential bulwark against Bolshevism. But the scheme was too late to be of help to workers who were already unemployed. And for those qualifying under the scheme, the weekly benefit was only payable for fifteen weeks. Terrified of riots by the starving unemployed, the Government introduced another six weeks of extended benefit. But by the autumn of 1921 many workers had exhausted all their entitlements.

On 7 September 1921 Lloyd George summoned his ministers to a Cabinet meeting in Inverness, where he happened to be on holiday, to discuss Ireland. This was followed by various meetings at nearby Gairloch, where Lloyd George discussed with his colleagues the problem of unemployment. At a conference after dinner on 15 September Lloyd George held forth on the importance of the exchange rate. Since 1919 the Treasury and the Bank of England had steadily pursued a policy of internal deflation, in order to increase the value of the pound against other currencies. The ultimate objective was to restore Britain to the gold standard at the pre-war parity of the pound to the dollar. Lloyd George now called this policy into question. Had the Government not carried deflation too far? Churchill, Riddell recorded, 'was emphatic in pointing out that the country was being sacrificed upon the altar of the banks.'[54]

Churchill had particular difficulties to face in Dundee, where the jute trade was severely affected by short-time working, wage reductions, and unemployment. From December 1920 onwards he had been bombarded by letters and telegrams from John Sime, the general secretary of the Jute and Flax Workers' Union, demanding action on behalf of the unemployed. In England, workers could obtain poor relief from the local authorities. But under the Scottish poor law, it was technically illegal for relief to be paid to the able-bodied poor. Early in September 1921 there were riots in Dundee when outdoor relief was withheld from the unemployed by the Parish Council. Churchill immediately took the matter up with the Cabinet but could not get the ban on outdoor relief lifted. The Scottish Office, however, issued a circular urging local authorities to relax the rules and the Dundee Parish Council resumed relief payments.

On 23 September Churchill met representatives of the Town and Parish Councils to listen to their representations. Under attack from a Labour councillor, John Reid, Churchill tried to turn the tables by attributing social distress to the disruptive effects of strikes on the economy. He repeated the tactic in a speech the following day.[55] In reality, Churchill suspected that the Government's own policy was at fault.

On 28 September he sent Lloyd George a memorandum on unemployment in which he described the 'very grievous situation' which had arisen in parts of Scotland where local authorities had reluctantly broken the law. Churchill wanted an act of indemnity to legalise what had been done and a precise definition of the circumstances in which the Government would agree to fund contributions to poor relief.

On the broader issue, Churchill complained that cuts in the housing programme would aggravate the unemployment problem in the coming winter. The Government's unemployment policies were a muddle and ought to be sorted out for political reasons: 'The problem of unemployment now before us deserves to be treated on the basis of some general principle which for good or ill we can expound and defend when we meet our constituents . . . ' While accepting that relief works must be adopted as a temporary palliative, Churchill did not regard them as a satisfactory solution to the problem, and looked to financial policy to supply the key. He again questioned the Government's policy of deflation and suggested that the time had come to reverse it: 'Should our policy remain the austere bankers' policy which it has been since the bankers got the traders in their power after the short post-war boom?'[56]

Lloyd George, in reply, accused Churchill of trying to place the blame for unemployment on his colleagues in the Cabinet Finance Committee – chaired by Horne. As for housing, Lloyd George maintained that the cuts had brought down the cost of housing and increased the pace of construction. Churchill retorted that in Dundee the municipal housing programme had been brought to a standstill and the Town Council had complained vehemently: 'I had a bad time with them.' On unemployment, Churchill said that he did not pretend to know the answer, 'though I have a feeling that if we went on hammering away for say a week or two we would get to the bottom of it and frame a definite policy.'[57]

Churchill wanted to ensure that the Coalition retained substantial working-class support. But in the months to come he was too distracted by Irish affairs to follow up his critique of domestic policy. Nor did it figure in his rhetoric. The greater priority, for Churchill, was the maintenance of the alliance between the Coalition Liberals and the Conservatives.

Since the collapse of the fusion plan, the future of the Coalition had been in doubt. But at the end of 1921 it suddenly acquired a new lease of life as a result of events in Ireland. Between 1919 and 1921 Ireland was in revolt. Lloyd George, with the energetic assistance of Churchill as Secretary for War, pursued a strategy of counter-terrorism against the IRA. Two paramilitary forces, the 'Black and Tans' and the 'Auxis' were granted a licence to carry out reprisals. Some of these 'reprisals' took the form of atrocities against innocent people which confirmed, in many quarters, his bloodstained reputation. In March 1921 the Roman Catholic bishop of Melbourne, Australia, visited Dundee and condemned Churchill as the enemy of Ireland.[58]

Then, in June 1921, the Cabinet suddenly reversed its policy and invited Sinn Fein to enter into negotiations. On the British side the most remarkable feature of the negotiations was their bipartisan character. The Irish question had divided the Conservative and Liberal parties since 1886. But in the autumn of 1921 Lloyd George and the leaders of the Conservative party agreed on the solution of partition. The six predominantly Protestant counties of Ulster were to remain a part of the United Kingdom, retaining the separate Home Rule Parliament which had been granted them in 1920. But the remaining twenty-six counties of Ireland were to be granted independence as a 'Free State' within the British

Empire. Churchill was one of the leading figures in the final stage of the negotiations, which culminated in the signature of the Irish Treaty on 6 December 1921.

The Irish Treaty did not solve the Irish question. But it was nevertheless a triumph for Coalition politics. Under the leadership of Austen Chamberlain, the Tory high command gave their full support to the Treaty. The revolt of a substantial section of the Conservative party seemed to underline the value of the Coalition as a Government of the middle way. With the encouragement of Birkenhead and Beaverbrook, Lloyd George decided to seize the opportunity of dissolving Parliament and going to the country. The attempt was thwarted in January 1922 by the chairman of the Conservative party, Sir George Younger, who leaked the story to the press. So hostile was the Conservative reaction that the election plan had to be dropped, though the party agreed to maintain the Coalition, on a trial basis, for a further year.

When Lloyd George first broached the idea of a snap general election, Churchill was hesitant. Possibly he feared the influence of Beaverbrook, who was trying to persuade Lloyd George to ditch Free Trade in favour of imperial preference – a move that would have embarrassed and undermined Churchill.[59] But Churchill was still an ardent coalitionist. Addressing a Liberal audience on 20 January 1922, he capitalised upon the Irish Treaty as the fulfilment of Gladstone's work, and an achievement that would have been impossible without the co-operation of the two historic parties. But having opened on this note of Liberal triumph, Churchill artfully proceeded to the argument that Liberals ought now to adopt a more conservative position:

here have been times – perhaps they will come again – when a great political resurgence, such as Mr Gladstone on more than one occasion invoked, is necessary to cleanse the State, to widen its bounds, to beat down obstruction, to curb privilege and authority; but this is not such a time. This is a time of great exhaustion for our country and for all the world ... Recuperation requires stability, it requires national co-operation, and not party strife.[60]

Churchill's grand design of an anti-socialist coalition assumed that the Liberals would have to abandon the radical thrust of their social policies. One small but very telling incident shows the direction in which he was moving. At the Board of Trade Churchill had instituted minimum wages in certain low paid industries, to be enforced by statutory trade boards. Since

1918 the principle had been extended to the jute factories in Churchill's own constituency. With the onset of the depression, the jute employers complained loudly to Churchill that minimum wages were pushing up their costs. At the Cabinet Home Affairs Committee on 29 May 1922, Churchill pleaded that it was essential to make drastic changes to wage regulation in the jute trade.[61]

In March 1922 Churchill issued a number of proclamations in favour of the conversion of the Coalition into a National Party. Invariably the accent was upon fear of socialism rather than expectations of social progress. As he told an audience at Northampton on 25 March: 'Conservative conviction and Liberal principles and sentiments are both exposed to the new and gathering attack of the Socialist parties, behind which crouches the shadows of Communist folly and Bolshevik crime.' Churchill was confident that his anti-socialist strategy would succeed both at the national level and in his own constituency. He fully expected that with the support of both the Liberal and Conservative Associations, he and his fellow candidate David MacDonald would hold both Dundee seats for the Coalition Liberals.[62] The spring of 1922 found Churchill hopeful of bright prospects for the Coalition. He was optimistic about the prospects for a revival in trade and a reduction in unemployment and urged the Chancellor of the Exchequer, Robert Horne, to make substantial tax cuts even if this meant violating the sacred Treasury principle of a balanced budget.[63] Horne, who was indeed under strong pressure from the business community to cut taxes, decided on a bold stroke of financial opportunism: a cut of one shilling in the pound in income tax, to be financed by suspending the sinking fund. When Horne revealed the details of the budget to his colleagues, on 22 April, Churchill was almost alone in urging the Cabinet to go for an even bigger splash: a cut of two shillings in the pound to be paid for by deferring the cost of war pensions.[64]

Churchill's grand design for an anti-socialist coalition implied a contract whereby the Liberals would abandon their more radical social policies in return for Conservative acquiescence in Free Trade. But how far were the Conservatives prepared to acquiesce? For Churchill this was a highly-charged question. Lloyd George, who liked to denigrate Churchill behind his back as a crypto-Conservative, had to admit that on Free Trade Churchill was 'almost fanatical'. Where Churchill showed his Liberal backbone Lloyd George, indeed, was almost invertebrate. Caring little for Free Trade, he was suspected of harbouring strong protectionist sympathies. In September 1919 he announced three important concessions to the Tariff Reform lobby. Tariffs were to be introduced firstly to protect industries, like the manufacture of scientific instruments, of key importance to the economy; secondly in retaliation against the 'dumping' of foreign goods in Britain below the selling price in the country of origin; and thirdly in order to protect home industry against exports from countries with severely depreciated or 'collapsed' currencies.

At first the Coalition Liberals succeeded in blocking the promised legislation. But in February 1921 a Safeguarding of Industries Bill was introduced into the House of Commons with provision for a protective duty of one-third on imports in all three categories. By August 1921 the bill was on the statute book. Much depended on the way in which the principles of the act were interpreted by the Board of Trade, under Stanley Baldwin, and it was quickly obvious that they would be given a strong protectionist twist. In February 1922 a back-bench Liberal, Wedgwood Benn, introduced a motion to repeal the act. Of the 122 Coalition Liberals, 19 voted against and 87, including Churchill, were absent or abstained. Churchill feared that the inroads into Free Trade were going too far and urged Lloyd George, without success, to carry through a fundamental review of the act: 'When we are told that we must keep out the glass eyes of certain dolls and must charge a special duty to protect us from the squeak contained in some small toy dogs, it is evident that our policy is liable to be brought into ridicule.'[65]

The protectionist lobby was not the only factor working against the Coalition. Many Conservatives had been fortified in their hostility to the Government by the Irish Treaty. They also believed that the Conservatives could defeat Labour without the assistance of Lloyd George and Churchill – both of whom were in fact extensively reviled in the world of labour. With hindsight it is apparent that the Coalition could no longer fulfil any of the great public purposes for which it had claimed to stand. The transition from war to peace had been accomplished with some success and no longer provided a *raison d'être*. As the Government's legitimacy faded, the careerism of a political clique was exposed as the one remaining driving force. Lloyd George, Birkenhead and Churchill had reached a point where they were no longer in harmony with the development of party politics, but were seeking to stifle it by intrigue. Churchill's anti-socialism was an attempt to conceal an almost bankrupt enterprise behind a cloak of dignity.

In the autumn of 1922 a crisis over foreign policy produced a last attempt to consolidate the Coalition. In 1920 the Greeks had imposed on the Turks, with the full backing of Lloyd George and the allied powers, the draconian Treaty of Sèvres. But the Treaty had been rejected by Turkish nationalists under the leadership of Kemal Pasha, who resumed the war against Turkey. In September 1922 Turkish forces advanced towards the

British garrison at Chanak, on the Asian shore of the neutral zone provided for by the Treaty of Sevres. For a few days it appeared that the garrison might be attacked or overrun. On 15 September the Cabinet decided that Britain, in concert with France and Italy, would guarantee the neutral zone together with the freedom of the Straits. On 17 September the Cabinet decided to exploit the crisis by calling a general election in the name of national unity.[66]

The crisis fizzled out unexpectedly. The French and the Italians abandoned the neutral zone, and the Dominions refused to support the British Government. In spite of this the Cabinet stood firm and on 20 September instructed the British commander at the Straits, General Harington, to defend Chanak. On 28 September an alarming report of Turkish movements led the Cabinet to instruct Harington to deliver an ultimatum to the Turks: Harington wisely procrastinated and within a few days the immediate crisis was over. But the Turks continued to advance towards Constantinople and East Thrace. Ought they to be resisted, and if necessary by war? The Cabinet began to divide between a peace party and a war party, with Lloyd George, Birkenhead, Churchill and Worthington-Evans in the war party. Gradually the peace party prevailed, and the crisis ended on 10 October when the Turks agreed to an armistice.

The decision to call a general election still stood, and it was this which led to the fall of the Coalition. At the famous Carlton Club meeting on 19 October Conservative MPs voted by 187 to 87 in favour of Tory independence. On 23 October Lloyd George resigned, and was succeeded as Prime Minister by Bonar Law.

The general election of 1922 was a confused affair. The leading ex-ministers of the Coalition were thrust into limbo. The Coalition Liberals were still severed from the independent Liberals. Lloyd George's leading Conservative allies, including Austen Chamberlain, Birkenhead and Horne, took the field as critics of Bonar Law. At Dundee the local Liberal association nominated two candidates for the two-member seat: Churchill, and D.J. MacDonald. Both of them enjoyed the support of the Conservative association. But to Churchill's anger and dismay, the local Asquithian Liberals decided to run an independent Liberal candidate, R.R. Pilkington. The Labour party nominated E.D. Morel and allowed the Prohibitionist, Edwin Scrymgeour, as the other Labour candidate in all but name. The left-wing vote, however, was also split by the presence of the Communist candidate, William Gallacher.

Churchill was recovering from an operation for appendicitis when the campaign began, and his wife Clementine stood in for him as best she could. He did not arrive in Dundee until 11 November, four days before polling, and even then he was too weak physically to stand. Of all his electoral campaigns so far, this was the feeblest. In a series of letters to his constituents from his sickbed he carped against Bonar Law's Government but was unable to discover a theme. His election address dealt miscellaneously with war debts, Chanak, and the Irish Treaty. Unemployment merited a single sentence describing it as 'the first of all the tasks which lie before the new government'.[67] The contest itself was marked by extraordinary displays of hostility to Churchill. On 13 November, while trying to speak seated on a platform in the Caird Hall, he was howled down for the first time in his career. The result was a clear-cut left-wing victory for Scrymgeour and Morel:

| | |
|---|---|
| E. Scrymgeour (Independent) | 32,578 |
| E.D. Morel (Labour) | 30,292 |
| D.J. MacDonald (Liberal) | 22,244 |
| W.S. Churchill (Liberal) | 20,466 |
| R.R. Pilkington (Ind. Liberal) | 6,681 |
| W. Gallacher (Communist) | 5,906 |

As the figures show, Churchill's support was diminished by personal unpopularity: he received 1,178 votes fewer than his Liberal running-mate, MacDonald. But even if he had been personally popular, Churchill would have been defeated. In a poor and depressed industrial constituency, the Labour tide was running too strongly for the Liberal breakwater to hold. Churchill understood this and responded with magnanimity to his defeat. 'When one thinks of the kind of lives the poorer people of Dundee have to live', he wrote to the civil servant Humbert Wolfe, 'one cannot be indignant at the way they voted'.[68]

Nationally, the election was a triumph for Bonar Law and the Conservative party. They obtained 345 seats, against 142 for the Labour party, 62 for the Coalition Liberals, and 54 for the Independent Liberals. Labour took its place in the new House as His Majesty's Opposition.

As the dust settled and the new Government played itself in, Churchill decided to lie low and wait upon events. On 2 December he left for six months' holiday in the south of France, announcing that he looked forward to a rest from politics. He recuperated from his operation and worked hard to complete his latest book, *The World Crisis*. For all he knew, the next general election might be five years hence. At best he must bide his time until a suitable by-election occurred. But under what label would he stand? He probably did not know.

Churchill remained silent for six months – the longest period of silence in a career stretching from 1900 to 1955. On 4 May 1923 he spoke at an Aldwych Club luncheon and outlined his familiar argument for combined action by the Liberal and Conservative parties to resist socialism. But otherwise he gave no hint of which way the cat would jump.[69] On 22 May Bonar Law was forced by ill health to retire and was succeeded, to general surprise, by Stanley Baldwin: Curzon had been the favourite.

*

Churchill was now detached from Lloyd George and hopeful that Baldwin would accommodate him. Shortly after Baldwin took office Churchill was asked by Horne where he stood politically and replied: 'I am what I have always been – a Tory Democrat. Force of circumstance has compelled me to serve with another party, but my views have never changed, and I should be glad to give effect to them by returning to the Conservatives.'[70] Sensing, no doubt, that a decent interval was required before he could change parties for a second time, Churchill played a waiting game. He also had to make sure of the Conservative position on Tariff Reform: he could not afford to surrender his Free Trade identity. The Protectionist L.S. Amery recorded a conversation with Churchill at the end of September 1923:

> He sounded me very anxiously about what our intentions were on the tariff issue, strongly urging us not to throw away a good position but to continue peacefully in office for the next two or three years. He told me that the Liberals were very anxious to have him back but that he was not having any ... I have no doubt that he has hesitated as to whether he should wait and rejoin us later or join the Liberals now and the tariff question will no doubt decide him.[71]

For Baldwin, the first priority was to restore party unity by restoring Lloyd George's Tory allies to the fold. He therefore raised the tariff issue in order to drive a wedge between Lloyd George on the one hand, and Chamberlain, Birkenhead and Balfour on the other. In October 1923 he declared his conversion to tariffs and called a general election. The Liberal party was forced to re-unite and Asquith went through the motions of reconciliation with Lloyd George.

This unexpected development forced Churchill into the fray. With the Free Trade cause in danger, he could not remain on the sidelines and retain his credibility. Nor could he ignore the possibility that a Liberal party reunited under Asquith might actually win the election, or at any rate form a minority government. On 11 November he issued a statement confirming his position on Free Trade, as a result of which several invitations to stand arrived from Liberal constituency associations. Four of the invitations were from seats in Manchester, where Churchill had campaigned so successfully in 1906 and 1910. On 16 November Churchill travelled to Manchester and denounced Protection in the Free Trade Hall.

Since 1919 many aspersions had been cast on the validity of Churchill's Liberalism. But on Free Trade he still carried weight in the Liberal party. In the constituencies, many Liberals hoped that as in 1906 he would contest a Tory-held seat. But now Churchill was anxious to turn Free Trade in an anti-socialist direction. He chose to accept an invitation to stand from the Liberals of West Leicester, a seat held for Labour by Pethick-Lawrence, the author of Labour's plan for a capital levy.[72] Churchill hoped at first that no Conservative candidate would oppose him and that he would be left to carry the anti-socialist banner, but in this he was disappointed. As in the Edwardian period, Churchill presented Free Trade as the middle way between the rival extremes of Protectionism and Socialism. This time the argument was illustrated by reference to Leicester's boot and shoe trade, but otherwise the message was unchanged: 'The Protectionists would tax the poor and the Socialists would pillage the rich.'[73] Churchill argued forcefully against protectionist and socialist economics, briefing himself in his attack on the capital levy with the help of a Treasury civil servant, Sir George Barstow. One sentence of a letter he wrote to Barstow illuminates in a flash his attitude towards the Labour party: 'I am sure there would be no objection on political grounds to your assisting me, as both the Government and the Liberal Party are equally fighting this principle and the Chancellor himself has denounced this measure.'[74] If the two historic parties of government were opposed to the capital levy, a civil servant was fully entitled to brief a politician against Labour, a party that was outside the system. But when voting took place on 6 December Churchill was defeated by Labour for a second time:

| Pethick-Lawrence (Labour) | 13,634 |
| Churchill (Liberal) | 9,236 |
| Instone (Conservative) | 7,696 |

If the Conservatives had won the general election and proceeded to introduce protection, Churchill would have continued to march with the Liberals and, no doubt, struck up once more his old alliance with Lloyd George. But in the new House of Commons the Conservatives, with 258 MPs, lacked a majority. The next largest party was Labour, with 191 seats, while the Liberals had 159. The Liberals, therefore, held the balance between Labour and the Conservatives. Baldwin decided that rather than resign he would meet the House of Commons and seek a vote of confidence. This placed the Liberals in a dilemma. Were they to accept the onus of turning the Conservatives out and installing a Labour Government for the first time?

In a statement on 12 December, Asquith indicated that when the new Parliament assembled the Liberals would put Labour in. Churchill took the opposite line. Writing to Asquith's daughter, Violet Bonham-Carter, he urged that the supreme object of Liberal policy must be to prevent a Labour Government, and warned that many Liberals would refuse to accept the new party line and co-operate, instead, with the Conservatives.[75] On 18 January Churchill went public in a letter to *The Times* in which he declared: 'The enthronement in office of a Socialist Government will be a serious national misfortune such as has usually befallen great States only on the morrow of defeat in war.' On 21 January the Baldwin Government was defeated by the combined votes of Labour and Liberal MPs and Ramsay MacDonald took office as the first Labour Prime Minister – receiving a private letter of congratulations from Churchill.[76]

Churchill had now broken with Asquith and positioned himself to ally with the Conservatives against Labour. A courageous stroke of opportunism carried him closer to his goal. When a by-election occurred in the Abbey division of Westminster, Churchill, with the encouragement of Rothermere and Beaverbrook, decided to stand as an Independent seeking both Conservative and Liberal support. The manoeuvre was intended to signal to the Conservatives Churchill's value as a politician who could deliver the support of discontented Liberals for whom Labour was the principal enemy. Churchill reported to Clementine that some 30 Liberal MPs and 30 candidates wished to act with the Conservatives. 'Do not let the Tories get you too cheaply', warned Clementine – a lifelong Liberal.[77]

Churchill's hopes of winning the support of the local Conservative association were dashed when they adopted Otho Nicholson, the nephew of the previous member, as their candidate. Nevertheless Churchill was tacitly encouraged by Baldwin, and a pro-Churchill breeze began to blow in some quarters of the Conservative party. Unlike his predecessor Bonar Law, who tended to be negative on social questions, Baldwin stood for a more paternalistic Conservatism in which the Labour party was to be treated with respect, and a truce declared in the class war. Churchill recognised that if he were to blend in with the age of Baldwin, the rhetoric of negative anti-socialism would no longer suffice. It was time to run social reform up the flagpole again. In an election address on 12 March he began as follows:

Although my war record is frequently referred to, I have a large number of measures of social reform to my credit. These seem to have been forgotten. My interest in social reform is very real, and it is only because I feel that I will be able to assist in remedial legislation dealing with housing, and the extension of National Insurance, so as to give real security against the common hazards of life, that I am willing to stand before you.[78]

Churchill's candidature was a gamble. A derisory vote would have eliminated him from the next round of the political game. But at the polls on 19 March he demonstrated his electoral potential by almost winning the seat. The result was:

Nicholson (Conservative)    8,187
Churchill (Independent)    8,144
Brockway (Labour)    6,156
Scott Duckers (Liberal)    291

In spite of this some Conservatives feared the price the party might have to pay for an alliance with Churchill. Neville Chamberlain, the younger son of Joseph Chamberlain, was a hereditary protectionist and social reformer. He confided to his diary the conclusions of a conversation with his friend Edward Wood, later to become Lord Halifax:

To get 30 more supporters might seem attractive but (1) it would drive a wedge under our Protection door which would make it harder to open (2) it would mean more difficulty in any rapprochement with Labour ... Winston Churchill could only handicap us in the country. In the House he would be a power but his line would be to attack the Socialists which could only drive the moderates into the arms of the extremists.'[79]

Such anxieties failed to prevent the process of mutual reconciliation between Churchill and his former party. On 7 May at Liverpool he addressed a Conservative party meeting for the first time in twenty years, though not yet as a Conservative. In the first Labour budget Philip Snowden, the Chancellor of the Exchequer, had abolished the McKenna duties of 1915. Churchill seized the opportunity of demonstrating that his commitment to Free Trade was moderate and flexible and would not prevent him from acting with the Conservatives. He condemned the repeal of the duties as 'an aggressive act of pedantry and faction'.[80]

Churchill carried over into this new phase of his career the interest in housing which had been sparked by the Addison affair of 1921 and, perhaps, by his defeat at Dundee in 1922. At the Ministry of Munitions he had come into contact for the first time with methods of mass production which involved the dilution of skilled labour. Much impressed he had opposed at the end of the war the restoration of pre-war craft restrictions. One of the leading protagonists of dilution was the Glasgow industrialist Lord Weir, the owner of a major engineering company who had served under Churchill at Munitions. In 1923 Weir unveiled a plan for houses to be mass produced in pieces and assembled by unskilled labour. His intention was to by-pass the building trade unions and recruit the labour force directly from the ranks of the unemployed. Weir pressed his plan on the politicians as the solution to both the housing and unemployment problems. Most of the politicians responded warily, but Churchill adopted the Weir plan with great enthusiasm and expounded it in the press. It was the type of bold social experiment he could imagine himself presenting to the electorate with many an oratorical flourish, and he believed that it would strongly appeal to the newly-enfranchised women voters. The purpose of the housing programme, he wrote, was not 'to satisfy the fads of social reformers, but to meet the practical requirements of the workman's wife'.[81]

Churchill's alliance with the Conservative party was finalised in July when Conservative Central Office, hitherto aloof, agreed to assist Churchill in finding a seat. In September he was adopted as the Constitutionalist candidate for Epping. Formally speaking he was not yet a Conservative, but the 'Constitutionalist' label has no Churchillian eccentricity. It was often adopted at this period in places where Liberals and Conservatives had entered into an anti-Labour pact. There was no such pact in Epping, but Churchill was trying to appeal to the Liberal vote in the constituency.

On 8 October 1924 the Labour Government fell, brought down by a Liberal motion for an inquiry into the Campbell case – the dropping by MacDonald of the prosecution of J.R. Campbell, editor of the Communist *Workers Weekly*, for publishing an article inciting troops not to obey orders.

In his campaign at Epping Churchill touched again on the need for new initiatives in housing and social insurance. But anti-socialism was the dominant theme and he played the anti-Bolshevik card for all it was worth. A few days before the election the *Daily Mail* published the notorious 'Zinoviev' letter, purporting to be a letter from Zinoviev, the President of the Comintern, to the Communist Party of Great Britain. The comrades were instructed to support the Anglo-Soviet negotiations initiated by the Labour Government, and to distribute money for the mobilisation of the working classes. The intelligence community had leaked the letter to the press with the intention of creating an electoral scare that would ensure Labour's defeat. The Russians denounced the letter as a forgery and so it may have been, but as Christopher Andrew has pointed out, its contents were an accurate reflection of Comintern policy.[82]

On election day, 29 October 1924, Churchill was returned with a majority of nearly 10,000 votes:

| | |
|---|---|
| Churchill (Constitutionalist) | 19,843 |
| Granville Sharp (Liberal) | 10,080 |
| McPhie (Labour) | 3,786 |

The Conservatives won 419 seats, giving them a majority in the House of more than 200 over Labour, with 151 seats, and the Liberals with 40. Churchill may well have concluded that the Zinoviev letter played an important part in the result. In November he wrote to the new Foreign Secretary, Austen Chamberlain, to call for the breaking off of diplomatic relations with Russia. 'When millions have been so excited on the subject during the Election', he exclaimed, 'it would be most dangerous to disappoint their reasonable expectations . . .'[83]

On 5 November Baldwin invited Churchill to become Chancellor of the Exchequer. ' "I should like to have answered, 'Will the bloody duck swim?'," Churchill recalled, "but as it was a formal and important conversation I replied, 'This fulfils my ambition, I still have my father's robes as Chancellor. I shall be proud to serve you in this splendid office.' " '[84]

# 7
# *The Return*
# *to Gold*

## 1924-25

Baldwin's victory in the general election of 1924 opened a new era in British politics. A two-party system of Conservative and Labour was now firmly established. Adrift since 1922, the Coalition Conservatives were reunited with their old party. Baldwin made Austen Chamberlain Foreign Secretary, and Birkenhead Secretary for India. The appointment of Churchill as Chancellor completed the isolation of Lloyd George and the burial of the post-war Coalition. The Liberals, who had governed the country only ten years before, were relegated to the role of third or minor party. Paradoxically, they were now of critical importance as the fulcrum of the two-party system. Nearly three million people, or 17.6 per cent of the electorate, voted Liberal in 1924. Baldwin and MacDonald saw themselves as competing for the middle ground of Liberal opinion.

Contemporaries believed they were entering a more settled and peaceful world. Since 1921 industrial militancy had been on the wane as the bargaining power of labour was sapped by unemployment. The General Strike of 1926 was to be the last great alarm, the end of a syndicalist era. On the Continent, relations between France and Germany were eased by the Locarno pact of October 1925 and peaceful prospects stretched ahead as far as the eye could see. The Soviet Union, having failed to carry the revolution beyond the frontiers of Imperial Russia, was retreating into isolation. Peace was indeed the main theme of the Baldwin Government, or such was the rhetoric: peace abroad through the 'spirit of Locarno', and peace at home through the reconciliation of the classes.

How far did Churchill, that most protean of personalities, enter into the spirit of Baldwinism? Ever since Gallipoli, Churchill had been a thwarted politician. Though Lloyd George had restored him to office he had also kept him in check, like a stern Victorian father repressing an unruly son. Baldwin was a patron of a very different kind. Though quite as ruthless as Lloyd George when the occasion demanded, he was keen to delegate and capable of long periods of inertia. In appointing Churchill to the Treasury he intended both to satisfy his ambition, and to provide generous scope for his abilities.

For Churchill the Treasury brought a fulfilment of the past and the promise of greater things to come. Here he could continue the work of his father and vindicate his memory. On his first day he took with him his father's robes as Chancellor, which had been stored in a trunk since 1886. As for the future, Chancellors of the Exchequer lived at No 11 Downing Street, next door to the Prime Minister. The Treasury was a recognised stepping-stone to the premiership. If Baldwin had fallen under the proverbial bus, most Conservatives would have wanted Neville Chamberlain to succeed him. But Churchill would have been a strong contender.

The Treasury was the most powerful department in Whitehall and the most searching test so far of Churchill's capacity in home affairs. He set out to prove that he was worthy of the responsibility. Contrary to expectations, he was loyal to Baldwin and won the support of the broad mass of Conservative MPs as a pillar of the Cabinet and first-class debater in the House. He cultivated back-bench Tories in the smoking-room and, conscious of his reputation for antagonising Labour, set out to treat the Opposition with patience and courtesy. In August 1925 Neville Chamberlain, who had been anxious at first about the impact of Churchill, wrote to Baldwin:

> Looking back over our final session I think our Chancellor has done very well, all the better because he hasn't been what he was expected to be. He hasn't dominated the Cabinet, though undoubtedly he has influenced it; he hasn't tied us to pedantic Free Trade though he is a bit sticky about safeguarding of Industries. He hasn't intrigued for the Leadership, but has been a tower of debating strength in the House of Commons. And taking him all round I don't think there can be any dispute but that he has been a source of increased influence & prestige to the government as a whole.[1]

It was a promising start, with Churchill on his best behaviour. But for all that he was something of a misfit. Though separated from Lloyd George, he still belonged in style and spirit to an age of political adventure which had come to an end in 1922. He lacked the gentlemanly restraint, and moral respectability, of the new régime. The old Churchill – noisy, pushful, and self-advertising – was waiting in the wings and ready to bound on to the stage. It was no accident that he quarrelled with his officials, antagonised Labour in the General Strike, or drove Neville Chamberlain to the brink of resignation. But a dynamic politician will always generate a field of force around him. Hostile comments, expressed in the heat of the moment, afford little insight into the interest and importance of Churchill's record at the Treasury.

There is little truth in the idea that Churchill was bored by economic affairs. The depression in British industry, and the spectre of mass unemployment, were always at the forefront of his imagination. He revelled in the parliamentary drama of the budget, and the prospect of a triumph in the House excited him almost as much as the prospect of a military victory in wartime. As his private secretary, James Grigg recalled, his minutes to his officials were peppered with military metaphors:

> We used to get great amusement from his creation of fortifications here and masses of manoeuvre there, from his mining and counter-mining and other stratagems derived from his Sandhurst days and his Napoleonic reading.[2]

Another sign of Churchill's consuming interest was his voracious appetite for work. Early in the morning he would go through the papers his private office had assembled for him, and would then dictate minutes relating to the papers in the box, or to anything else which occurred to him:

> The range of his official interests alone was extraordinary, and it might easily happen that the minutes of a single morning covered the whole region between the draft of an important State paper or ideas for the next Budget and some desired improvement in the make-up of files or the impropriety of the Office of Works supplying Czechoslovakian matches in a British Government establishment.[3]

Churchill is often thought to have been out of his depth in economic affairs, but this is a half-truth. As Peter Clarke has argued, Churchill was in a sense a very well prepared Chancellor, with a strong belief in the axioms of sound finance which he had learnt as a young man, under the tuition of Treasury officials. In his economic ideas Churchill was essentially a Gladstonian Liberal who believed in the operation of self-regulating markets. The role of government, in his view, was to maintain sound finance, and otherwise abstain from intervention.

Of course it may be said that Churchill's ideas were outmoded, but this was far from obvious at the time. His Treasury advisers, though sometimes alarmed by his methods, shared and reinforced his Gladstonian world-view. The Cambridge economist, John Maynard Keynes, attacked the Treasury line and called for a programme of public works. But Keynes had yet to invent Keynesianism: a theory to validate his policies. The Conservatives were not yet ready for protectionism, nor Labour for state socialism. So it did not seem impossible that orthodox Treasury policies would lead Britain out of the depression. With hindsight, Churchill's Chancellorship can be seen as a final, spirited attempt to revive the political economy of 1914, before it was overwhelmed in the Slump. As Churchill himself put it: 'I was the last orthodox Chancellor of the Victorian epoch.'[4]

In the final analysis Churchill was not a very successful Chancellor. The depression persisted, and the Conservatives went on to lose the general election of 1929. In defence of Churchill it has to be asked whether, in the circumstances, anyone else would have done any better. Economic problems are notoriously intractable. But Churchill was, perhaps, an agent or accomplice in the misfortunes of the British industry. It was his decision, in March 1925, to return Britain to the Gold Standard. For a Chancellor who believed in the eternal verities of sound finance, there was much to be said in favour of a return to gold. But Churchill was troubled by doubts and forebodings that were borne out in full measure by subsequent events.

\* \* \*

During his first weeks at the Treasury, Churchill began work on his budget for 1925. Most Chancellors were content to balance the books by orderly accounting. But Churchill was a political strategist in the tradition of Lord Randolph and David Lloyd George. His aim, wrote Grigg, was to make the Treasury 'an active instrument of Government social policy instead of a passive concomitant or even, as it sometimes was, an active opponent.'[5] The outstanding feature of his first budget was the manner in which he linked and balanced his proposals to form an overall design.

The centrepiece was a substantial reduction in income tax. Since income tax at this period was levied only on fees, salaries, and company profits, this was a measure for the benefit of the middle classes. To balance this, Churchill proposed a new state pension scheme for the benefit of the working classes. As he explained to Baldwin it would be difficult to give relief to the professional man, the blackcoated worker, and the employer, 'unless from the standpoint of social and political justice a relief to the direct taxpayer should be accompanied by a benefit to the mass of the public . . . The assumption by the State of the very large capital liabilities involved in the new insurance for the benefit of the mass of the people might well be taken as an equipoise in the general scheme of the Budget . . . '[6]

In the Baldwin Cabinet the leading authority on social insurance was the Minister of Health, Neville Chamberlain. But the subject was of great interest to Churchill as a link with his Liberal past. The first state pensions scheme, introduced by Asquith in 1908, entitled men and women over the age of 70 to a means-tested pension of five shillings a week. These were extremely modest benefits, but since they were funded wholly out of taxation they were viewed by the Treasury as an expensive and open-ended commitment. Shortly after this, Lloyd George discovered social insurance. Both he and Churchill concluded that additional pensions ought to be funded on the insurance principle, and built into the forthcoming scheme of health insurance. But Lloyd George's plan for widows' and orphans' pensions was killed in 1911 by the resistance of the industrial assurance companies, who feared that it would take away profitable business.[7]

By the end of the First World War there was a broad current of opinion in favour of the expansion of social insurance. Where pensions were concerned, two main possibilities were discussed: a contributory scheme for those between the ages of 65 and 70, and pensions for widows and orphans. In 1923 Bonar Law set up a committee of civil servants under Sir John Anderson to inquire into the future of pensions. The following year the committee reported to Snowden, the Labour Chancellor, in favour of extending health insurance to include old age pensions at 65, and widows' pensions with allowances for orphans and dependent children. But the Labour Government fell before any decision was taken. Meanwhile a committee of the Conservative Shadow Cabinet under Neville Chamberlain was investigating the idea of 'all-in insurance': the creation of a single insurance scheme to include pensions along with health and unemployment insurance.

On 26 November 1925 Chamberlain submitted to the Cabinet a draft bill for old age and widows' pensions, which he was planning to introduce in 1926. Later that day he met Churchill to discuss the financial basis of the scheme. Churchill and Chamberlain had never worked together before, and knew little of one another's methods. To Chamberlain's astonishment, Churchill offered to finance his proposals in return for a partnership in which Chamberlain would 'work the plan with him *keeping everything secret*'. Churchill explained that he would like to bring the legislation forward to 1925 and announce it in his first budget as a counterpoise to the reduction of income tax. 'It was curious', wrote Chamberlain, 'how all through he was thinking of personal credit & it seemed plain to me that he regretted he was not Minister of Health. He spoke of the position. "*You* are in the van. *You* can raise a monument. *You* can have a name in history" etc. . . . '8

Churchill's unspoken thought, we may guess, was that he and Chamberlain together could repeat the success of the Lloyd George-Churchill combination in the Asquith Cabinet. 'I was all for the Liberal measures of social reform in the old days,' he told the Assistant Cabinet Secretary, Thomas Jones, 'and I want to push the same sort of measures now.'9 This time, however, Churchill would supply the finance while Chamberlain devised the policies. Chamberlain, for his part, was delighted to accept the offer and agreed to advance the date of his pensions bill. On 3 December the Cabinet agreed to make it a part of the programme for 1925.10

In order to finance his budget, Churchill was obliged to search for economies. On 26 November he obtained the Cabinet's agreement to a review of the long-term plans of the armed forces, and foreshadowed an attack on naval expenditure. On public spending more generally, he urged his colleagues to 'concentrate on a few great issues in the social sphere, such as the solutions of the housing problem and an "all-in" insurance scheme, rather than fritter away our resources on a variety of services . . .'11

Early in December Churchill learnt that the Admiralty was demanding large increases in expenditure in order to counter the long-term danger from Japan. In a quick retaliatory blow he warned Baldwin that if the Admiralty's demands were met, there would be 'nothing for the taxpayer and nothing for social reform'. And for what, he asked, was the Admiralty preparing? 'A war with Japan! I do not believe there is the slightest chance of it in our lifetime.' Churchill was once again the radical peacemonger of 1908, dismissing the prophets of war in the Far East as he had once dismissed the prophets of a European war. Through January and February battle raged between the Treasury and the Admiralty until the Cabinet imposed a temporary truce. Pending a further inquiry into the naval programme, the Admiralty agreed to accept Churchill's ceiling on expenditure.12

Churchill was free now to press on with his plans for tax cuts and social insurance. Income tax was to be cut by sixpence in the pound to four shillings. But almost every Chancellor since Gladstone had aimed to reduce the income tax. More distinctive was Churchill's intention to shift part of the direct tax burden from active to passive wealth. To this end he proposed to reduce the Super Tax – a band of higher tax rates payable on incomes of over £2,500 p.a. – and increase by a proportionate amount the yield from Death Duties.

Churchill explained the thinking behind this to Sir Richard Hopkins, the Chairman of the Inland Revenue. He wished, he wrote, to give the greatest relief to

professional men, small merchants and business men – superior brain workers of every kind. Where these classes possess accumulated capital in addition to their incomes, the increase in Death Duties operating over the same area will reclaim a substantial proportion of the relief afforded by the reform of the Super Tax. The doctor, engineer and lawyer earning 3 or 4 thousand a year and with no capital will get the greatest relief; the possessor of unearned income derived from a capital estate of 2 or 3 hundred thousand pounds, the smallest relief; while the millionaire will remain substantially liable to the existing scales of high taxation . . .

The process of the creation of new wealth is beneficial to the whole community. The process of squatting on old wealth though valuable is a far less lively agent.[13]

In his budget speech on 28 April Churchill delighted the Conservatives with his announcement of sixpence off the income tax. But there was a cool response when he explained that the £10 million reduction in Super Tax was to be balanced by a £10 million increase in Death Duties. He also increased, for income-tax payers, the allowances on earned income, as distinct from 'unearned' or investment income. A married clerk on £300 p.a. found his tax bill cut by 44.5 per cent as a result of the Churchill budget. Perhaps Churchill was too eager in his first budget to reduce the level of personal taxation. *The Economist*, at any rate, complained: 'If the Chancellor really wanted to release money to put back into industry he could have used the money to better advantage by relieving companies of taxation which falls upon the sums they put into reserve, or by giving additional assistance for the relief of local rates.'[14]

As planned, Churchill also announced that Chamberlain would shortly be introducing an old age and widows' pensions bill. Though it was mainly the work of Chamberlain it owed much to Churchill, and might not have prospered without him. On the one hand it required long-term financial commitments on a scale which tended to alarm industrialists and Treasury officials. On the other hand, there was certain to be criticism from the Government benches in the House. With Churchill's support, however, the bill would be sure to advance through Whitehall and Westminster like a staff car protected by an armed convoy.

Churchill did more than lend his support to the pensions plan. He subjected it to critical scrutiny on financial, industrial and political grounds. A thick file of correspondence bears witness to the thoroughness of his inquiries. He wanted to ensure that he was committing himself to a sound, long-term scheme, and one that could successfully be defended in the House of Commons.

His method was to interrogate his officials about the potential flaws in the scheme. Some of his concerns were expressed early on in a memorandum to the Permanent Secretary, Warren Fisher. He was especially worried about the heavy and increasing liabilities the scheme would impose on the Exchequer. If the Government were 'mortgaging the future to that extent,' there must be 'powers of easement' in the scheme. Such powers were, in fact, incorporated in the final bill, which provided for employers and employees' contributions to increase at ten year intervals up to 1956.

Potential opposition to the bill had also to be assessed. What would be the attitude of the insurance companies? How great a burden would the scheme place on industry, and how far would the cost to the employers be offset by the effect of sixpence off the income tax? On this point the reply was not reassuring. At the Board of Inland Revenue Sir Richard Hopkins estimated that in the case of the coal owners they would gain £637,000 in tax cuts, and lose £1,500,000 in insurance contributions.[15]

Churchill hoped that the plan would prove acceptable to all parties in the House, but his main anxiety on this score was that the rates of contribution proposed by the Anderson Committee were too high. Sixpence a week from both employer and employed was 'a pretty stiff poll tax, having regard to their existing obligations. To what extent, for instance, would the Labour party use the argument "You are only making us stand on our own tails"?' Churchill was especially keen to elicit the opinions of Radicals like Masterman, MacNamara and above all Lloyd George: 'I would like to have the Liberals with us in a thing like this.'[16] But no such approach appears to have been made. It was most unlikely that Chamberlain, as the proud author of the bill, would allow the Liberals to interfere with it.

On 4 March a powerful employers' delegation, led by Lord Weir, lobbied Churchill to warn against the extension of social insurance. Productive industry, Weir declared, could not stand the burden of growing social expenditure, which was far higher in Britain than in other industrial countries. The psychology of the situation had also to be considered: 'Many of us believe that thrift and self-help have been a big asset in the past, and the habit of work has been a pretty big influence in building up the character of our people ... and we really believe that the incidence of these measures is beginning to impair that character.' Churchill replied in the very same language he had employed to justify social insurance in the Edwardian period:

> Personally, I feel that that system of insurance, whatever may be the effects on the self-reliance of the individual, is going to be an absolutely inseparable element in our social life and eventually must have the effect of attaching the minds of the people, although their language and mood in many cases may not seem to indicate it – it must lead to the stability and order of the general structure.[17]

Though Churchill replied so confidently, he too was concerned about the impact of the scheme on credit and industry, and sought the opinion of his Controller of Finance, Sir Otto Niemeyer. In reply Niemeyer presented both sides of the argument. Considerable financial and industrial risks were, he stressed, involved. But against them could be placed one consideration of great importance:

> It is plain that some scheme of the kind contemplated must certainly be framed in the next few years. The vital question from a financial, if not from a social, point of view, is whether the scheme should be contributory or non-contributory ... it is much more difficult to keep the scale of benefits of a non-contributory scheme within reason; people are slow to see that payment by the state in the last resort comes out of their own pockets.[18]

It was important, in other words, to pre-empt the possibility of redistributive legislation by a Labour Government.

In spite of their very different backgrounds and personalities, Chamberlain and Churchill continued to collaborate remarkably well. As a rational man of business, in harness with an aristocratic adventurer, Chamberlain sometimes found the experience trying. As he confided in a letter to his sister Hilda, on 5 April:

> Winston is a rather trying person to work with for he never sticks to anything for two minutes together and when you have had a conference in order to arrive at a final decision on doubtful points your one certainty is that the agreement arrived at will be thrown overboard a few hours afterwards ...
>
> The latest thing I am considering is that while contributions shall

begin at once, i.e. on Jan 1 1926 & widows pensions at once, old age pensions should not accrue until a year's contributions had been paid. This would relieve the Treasury from giving anything to those now over 70 but not in receipt of full pension, or to their wives until they reach the age of 70. Winston is so frightened of having a surplus in the earlier years that he is inclined to chuck money about with a liberal hand. No doubt this would be very popular at the moment but with industry in its present condition of depression I feel that we have no right to an exhibition of vicarious generosity for which the nation will get no return whatever.[19]

In his budget speech Churchill outlined the details of the bill. In the case of a male workman, he and his employer were each to contribute fourpence a week; a female worker and employer would each pay tuppence. The benefits would consist of ten shillings a week for widows, and various payments for children up to the age of 14, payable from 1 January 1926. Another ten shillings a week would be payable to old age pensioners between the ages of 65 and 70 from 1 January 1928.

In taking some of the credit for pensions reform, Churchill aligned himself with the progressive Toryism of Baldwin while emphasising the continuity of his commitment to social reform. He treated the House to a long passage with many Edwardian echoes:

It is not to the sturdy marching troops that extra rewards and indulgences are needed at the present time. It is to the stragglers, to the exhausted, to the weak, to the wounded, to the veterans, to the widow and the orphans that the ambulance of the State and the aid of the State should, as far as possible, be directed. The old *laissez-faire* or *laissez-aller* ideas of mid-Victorian radicalism have been superseded, and no one has done more to supersede them than the right. hon. Member for Caernarvon Boroughs [Lloyd George]. I am proud to have been associated with him from the very beginning of those large insurance ideas.

Lloyd George later rose to say that he was delighted that Churchill had undertaken to complete the insurance scheme they had pioneered together – though he believed that the state ought to bear a larger proportion of the costs.[20] Chamberlain himself believed that credit should be given where credit was due. As he confided to his diary:

In a sense it *is* his scheme. We were pledged to something of the kind, but I don't think we should have done it this year if he had not made it part of his budget scheme, and in my opinion he does deserve special personal credit for his initiative and his drive.[21]

The benefits under the scheme were fixed well below the level of subsistence and were no guarantee against poverty. The cost to the Government, some £4 million per year, was modest by comparison with the annual cost of war pensions: £67.3 million in 1925–6. But here was a landmark nevertheless: the first contributory scheme of state pensions, covering more than 15 million people. In conjunction with other sources of income the new benefits freed thousands of unfortunate people from dependence on the poor law. Churchill's involvement underlined his commitment to the idea of the state as the provider of a safety net. But he was also impressed by the long-term cost to the Exchequer, which the Government Actuary projected as far ahead as 1960, and anxious to keep it within manageable bounds. He was equally aware of the strong apprehensions expressed by industrialists about the effect on their costs and competitiveness. Perhaps, therefore, the act was a lesson for Churchill in the limits of social insurance: a terminus beyond which no further extension was feasible.

\*

Of one thing Churchill was certain. He had not become Chancellor of the Exchequer in order to preside over the liquidation of free trade. But in the course of his reconciliation with the Conservatives he had accepted two minor infringements of free trade doctrine: imperial preference and the 'safeguarding' of industries against unfair competition from abroad. One of his first actions at the Treasury was to proceed with another Safeguarding Bill, an occasion he turned into a parliamentary triumph. Runciman, Mond and Lloyd George all attacked him for abandoning Free Trade. Picking them off one by one, Churchill convicted them all of supporting similar measures in the past.[22]

In view of the fact that he proposed to give away so much revenue in his budget, Churchill could hardly overlook the value of minor protective duties in helping to balance the books. His Labour predecessor, Philip Snowden, had abolished the McKenna duties. First introduced in 1915 as an emergency wartime measure, they covered a curious selection of articles: clocks, films, motor-cars and musical instruments. Churchill reinstated the McKenna duties out of sheer expediency, as he explained to the House: 'To some they are a relish, to others a target, and to me a revenue. They will bring in £1,600,000 a year in the first year and nearly

£3,000,000 a year in a full year. We cannot afford to throw away revenue like that.'[23] Churchill also introduced, for revenue purposes, duties on silk and hops, and propitiated the ghost of Joseph Chamberlain by extending imperial preference on sugar, tobacco and other items in line with the proposals of the 1923 Imperial Economic Conference.

'You ask for impressions of the Budget & the Budget speech,' wrote Chamberlain to his sister Hilda on 2 May 1925. 'It was a great triumph for Winston who enjoyed himself thoroughly and treated his subject with masterly skill, relating every part to the whole, abounding in witticisms & overflowing with spirits and good humour.' On the Conservative side, he reported, the budget was regarded as 'very satisfactory on the whole' but further reflection was producing a reaction. 'Commendation of the boon to the black coated worker is general but people do not like the new death duties. The McKenna duties are a cause of much rejoicing but speaking generally industry is somewhat disgruntled over silk and over the new pensions burden.'[24]

Chamberlain said nothing of the most important decision announced in the budget, the return to the Gold Standard at the pre-war parity of $4.86 to the pound. Long foreshadowed, the decision caused little surprise or controversy and was almost universally welcomed. But three months later the economist John Maynard Keynes published his famous pamphlet attacking the decision: *The Economic Consequences of Mr Churchill*. Keynes estimated that in restoring the pre-war parity of sterling, Churchill had overvalued the pound by 10 per cent. Consequently workers in the export trades would be required to reduce their wages or face unemployment. The only alternative was a sharp deflation of the entire domestic economy through credit restriction and massive unemployment.

Generally speaking, economic historians have also regarded the decision as a mistake, and various estimates have been made of the human cost in unemployment. T.J. Hatton calculated that had the exchange rate been 10 per cent lower in 1928, unemployment would have reduced by a figure somewhere between 331,000 and 643,000. Working on the same assumption about the exchange rate, D.E. Moggridge estimated that the Government could have reduced unemployment from 10.8 per cent, the average for the year, to 4.7 per cent. 729,000 more people would have been in employment.[25] Twenty years later Churchill told his doctor, Lord Moran, that the return to gold had been the biggest blunder of his life: 'Montagu Norman had spread his blandishments before him till it was done, and had then left him severely alone.'[26]

Some authorities doubt whether the return to gold had such damaging consequences. But assuming that Keynes and the Keynesian historians are right, how did Churchill come to make such an important blunder?

At the start of the twentieth century, most of the world's trading nations adhered to the Gold Standard. Their currencies were convertible into fixed quantities of gold, which acted as the almost universal standard of value. Hence international exchange rates were fixed, and one pound could be exchanged for $4.86. Economists believed that the Gold Standard was a self-adjusting regulator of international trade. A nation with a balance of trade deficit would begin to lose its gold reserves and would therefore put up interest rates in order to promote an inflow of gold. Prices would fall, exports become more competitive, and the balance of trade would be restored. Churchill himself had expounded this view of the Gold Standard, and linked it to the workings of free trade, in the Edwardian period.[27]

During the Great War, the allied powers pegged their exchange rates at levels close to pre-war parities, and the Gold Standard remained legally intact. In practice the costs and prices of different countries diverged and Britain experienced a roaring inflation which depressed the real value of the pound against the dollar. Hence it was impossible at the end of the war to restore the pre-war exchange rate of $4.86 to the pound. In March 1919 the British authorities suspended the Gold Standard and allowed the pound to float. By February 1920 it had fallen to $3.40 to the pound.[28]

In 1918 the Treasury and the Ministry of Reconstruction appointed a Committee on Currency and Foreign Exchanges after the war, under the chairmanship of the retiring Chairman of the Bank of England, Lord Cunliffe. The committee assumed without question that the primary objective of post-war policy must be to restore the Gold Standard at the pre-war parity. But since it would be ten years before normal trade was restored there would have to be a period of transition in which strict deflationary policies reduced British price levels to those of the United States.[29]

After the war the return to gold was the primary objective of the Treasury and the Bank of England. Augmented by the depression, the deflationary policies of Austen Chamberlain began to take effect, and the pound rose again against the dollar. By the end of 1922 sterling had risen to $4.63. After a relapse in 1923 it strengthened again in 1924 and by the beginning of 1925 stood within 2.5 per cent of the pre-war parity. In March 1924 the Labour Chancellor, Philip Snowden, reaffirmed the goal of a return to gold, and later in the year the Chamberlain-Bradbury Committee, which he had appointed, recommended a return to gold when American prices rose.

By the time Churchill entered the Treasury, it looked as though a return to gold need not be long delayed. Nor could a decision be avoided. Under an act of 1920 the suspension of the Gold Standard was due to end, unless deliberately extended by further legislation, on 31 December 1925. The Governor of the Bank of England, Montagu Norman, found the Chancellor in a receptive mood. On 12 December Churchill reported to Baldwin:

> The Governor of the Bank will, I hope, have told you this weekend about the imminence of our attempt to re-establish the gold standard, in connection with which he is now going to America. It will be easy to attain the gold standard, and indeed almost impossible to avoid taking the decision, but to keep it will require a most strict policy of debt repayment and a high standard of credit. To reach it and have to abandon it would be disastrous.[30]

In January 1925 Norman consulted with the chairman of the U.S. Federal Reserve Bank, Benjamin Strong, and negotiated a credit of $500 million in order to provide a safeguard against a drain of gold reserves from London. Discussions on the procedure for the return to gold followed within the Bank. On 26 January the Chamberlain-Bradbury Committee delivered another report, this time recommending a return to gold in the near future. But the committee estimated that although the pound was now close to its pre-war level against the dollar, the restoration of parity would require a reduction of 6 per cent in British prices.

At the end of January Churchill, who had been occupied by the settlement of inter-allied war debts, decided to grasp the problem. Two of his officials, Sir John Bradbury and Niemeyer, and the Governor of the Bank, were asked to comment on a remarkable memorandum, 'Mr Churchill's Exercise', in which he raised potential objections to the return to gold. The purpose of the exercise was clearly set out. It was essential, wrote Churchill, 'that we should be prepared to answer any criticisms which may be subsequently made upon our policy'. In setting down ideas and questionings he did not wish it to be inferred that he was opposed to the Gold Standard: 'On the contrary I am ready and anxious to be convinced as far as my limited comprehension of these technical matters will permit.' Evidently Churchill was asking his officials to brief him for the parliamentary and public debate that would inevitably follow the decision.

Churchill recognised that restoration of the pre-war parity would necessitate a strict monetary policy. The most substantial point he raised was the effect such a policy would have on the merchant, the manufacturer, the workman and the consumer, whose interests 'do not by any means exactly coincide either with each other or with the financial and currency interests'. If a return to gold could only be maintained by a Bank Rate of 5–6 per cent, 'a very serious check would be administered to trade, industry and employment.'[31]

None of the participants in Churchill's exercise replied effectively to this point. They could not conceive the possibility of a divergence of interests between industry and the city. Montagu Norman asserted that cheap money was more important for 'psychological' than 'fundamental' reasons. The return to gold, he agreed, *would* require a high bank rate, and producers had no business to question this: 'In connection with a golden 1925, the merchant, manufacturer, workman &c., should be considered (but not consulted any more than about the design of battleships).' Bradbury, at least, was more reassuring: 'I should not be at all surprised if very shortly after the restoration of the free gold market a period of cheap money and easy credit becomes necessary to repel an influx of unwanted gold.'[32]

Churchill was not convinced that the case had been answered. On 21 February there appeared in *The Nation* an article by Keynes opposing the return to gold and arguing for a managed currency. Having digested the article, and Niemeyer's critique of it, Churchill wrote to Niemeyer:

> The Treasury have never, it seems to me, faced the profound significance of what Mr Keynes calls "the paradox of unemployment amidst dearth". The Governor shows himself perfectly happy in the spectacle of a Britain possessing the finest credit in the world simultaneously with a million and a quarter unemployed ... The community lacks goods, and a million and a quarter people lack work. It is certainly one of the highest functions of finance to bridge the gulf between the two. This is the only country in the world where this condition exists. The Treasury and the Bank of England policy has been the only policy consistently pursued. It is a terrible responsibility for those who have shaped it, unless they can be sure that there is no connection between the unique British phenomenon of chronic unemployment and the long, resolute consistency of a particular financial policy ...
>
> It may be of course that you will argue that the unemployment would have been much greater but for the financial policy pursued; that there is not sufficient demand internally or externally to require the services of this million and a quarter people; that there is nothing for them but to hang like a millstone round the neck of industry and on the public revenue until they become permanently demoralised. You may be right, but if so, it is one of the most sombre conclusions ever reached. On the other hand I do not pretend to see even "through a glass darkly" how the financial and credit policy of the country could

be handled so as to bridge the gap between a dearth of goods and a surplus of labour; and well I realise the danger of experiment to that end. The seas of history are full of famous wrecks. Still if I could see a way, I would far rather follow it than any other. I would rather see Finance less proud and Industry more content.[33]

Unlike 'Mr Churchill's exercise', his letter to Niemeyer was a powerful expression of personal opinion. Churchill strongly suspected that mass unemployment was the result of exchange rate policy since 1919. As we have seen, this was a view he had previously expressed in 1921. But Churchill did not have sufficient technical command of the problem to be sure that Keynes was right and his officials wrong. He knew that he was out of his depth. Niemeyer, in his rejoinder, skilfully turned the argument about unemployment on its head. The Gold Standard, he argued, was an employment policy:

> As the result of war there has been a great decrease in wealth, and there is consequently less effective demand. The only permanent remedy is to recreate the losses of war – really, not merely by manufacturing paper – and what we have to do for this purpose is (1) to stabilise our currency in relation to the main trading currencies of the world, (2) to reconstruct the broken parts of Europe and (3) to encourage thrift and the accumulation of capital for industry.[34]

The truth may be that Churchill swung between one opinion and another as now this argument, and now that, captured his mind. In a letter to a colleague at about this time Niemeyer wrote: 'Winston cannot make up his mind from day to day whether he is a gold bug or a pure inflationist.'[35] Finally Churchill decided that he would have the issue argued out in front of him. He arranged a dinner party on 17 March attended by two protagonists of the Gold Standard, Niemeyer and Bradbury, and two of its critics, Keynes and McKenna. Keynes argued that a return to the pre-war parity would produce a disparity of 10 per cent between British and United States prices, with consequent wage-cuts, strikes, and unemployment. Bradbury argued that as the pound was already close to the pre-war parity the adjustment would be small. Contractions in basic industry were likely but also desirable as resources were shifted to newer forms of enterprise. Churchill listened carefully to the pessimists' case but finally asked McKenna, as a former politician, what decision he would take from the political point of view. The gist of McKenna's reply was: 'There is no escape. You have got to go back; but it will be hell.'[36]

To sum up, it would appear that Churchill's fears of the consequences for industry and employment were overcome partly by the arguments of the Treasury and the Bank, and partly by overriding political necessity. Though Keynes, McKenna and Beaverbrook were all critics of the restoration of the Gold Standard, they were all outsiders. The insiders, the officials of the Bank and the Treasury, were unanimously in favour. On several occasions since the war British governments had pledged themselves to the restoration of the Gold Standard. The Conservatives were strongly in favour and so, for the most part, were Labour and the Liberals. Lord Randolph had fallen from office by pursuing a quarrel over the budget at the very moment when he was in a position to secure the succession to the premiership. His son was unlikely to make a similar mistake. On 20 March the final decision was taken at a meeting of Churchill, Baldwin, Austen Chamberlain, Norman, Niemeyer, and Bradbury. Churchill was to announce the restoration of the Gold Standard in his budget on 28 April, and it would come into effect the following day.[37]

Churchill took great care over the presentation of the decision to the House. In spite of the fact that he could take for granted an overwhelming body of opinion in his favour, he recognised the need to justify the decision in rational terms that would stand the test of debate and indeed of history. The budget speech itself was so overcrowded with announcements that Churchill deferred a full statement of his case until 4 May when he introduced the Gold Standard Bill, a measure to back up the restoration of gold with precautionary measures to protect the pound against speculators in the currency market.

Churchill was firstly careful to emphasise that while he had done his best to understand the arguments, he had relied on the advice of the experts. 'I do not pose as a currency expert,' he said. 'It would be very absurd if I did; no one would believe me. I present myself here, not as a currency expert, but as a Member of Parliament with some experience in dealing with experts and weighing their arguments.' The critics argued that since the end of the war the authorities had operated a managed currency with great success, so why not continue with it? To this Churchill replied that it was because the authorities had been so successful that he paid so much attention to their views: 'When the men who have managed the currency so well, according to the opponents of the present bill, tell me that they can manage the currency no longer upon this basis, and tell me that it would have been impossible to have managed it so far unless they had always had the return to the Gold Standard as a goal to steer towards . . . surely their opinion should carry great weight.'[38] Churchill explained that he had also endeavoured to think out the problem for himself and gave the House 'three great reasons – economic, social, and imperial, which convinced me that we should return without delay to an international gold standard'. First of all he argued that without the City of London, and its worldwide interests in finance and business, 'this crowded island' would not be able to support its present population. 'The great working-class population such as we have here requires, above all things . . . close and continuous contact with reality.' It was therefore vital to prevent the inflation of the currency 'whatever Government was in power', and the Gold Standard would achieve this. 'For good or for ill, it will shackle us to reality'.

Churchill's 'social' reason for the return to gold was the advantage the working-class would obtain from the stability of earnings. 'We are not a self-supporting country. We have this immense working-class population . . . These people are dependent mainly on overseas food and our industries are dependent on overseas raw materials. What is one of their principal interests? It is surely stability of prices.' The effect of inflation was that wages lagged behind prices. But when deflation occurred, wage cuts were demanded: either way, great strikes occurred in the process of adjustment.[39]

In the discussions leading up to the return to gold, the Empire had seldom figured as an anxiety. But Churchill played the imperial card to good effect. 'If we had shown ourselves incapable of taking up any position at all, the self-governing Dominions of the British Empire might have gone on to the Gold Standard by themselves, and the Mother Country alone would have been left to pursue a different policy. They would therefore all have traded with the United States on a gold basis, a condition of affairs disastrous from every point of view.' This helped Churchill to dispose of the criticism that the return to gold would benefit the United States more than Britain: 'The great free trade economist Bastiat, in a celebrated sentence, declared that all legitimate interests were in harmony, and I see no reason why what benefits the United States should not perhaps benefit us in our special needs as much or even more.'[40]

By putting the case so vigorously, Churchill put himself in an excellent position to claim the credit should all go well. But his studious avoidance of optimistic predictions, and strong emphasis on the responsibility of the experts, would afford him some protection if things went wrong.

*

Churchill's principal achievement at the Treasury was to hold the line in defence of Free Trade. In May 1925 one of the major industries, steel, applied for safeguarding. But as Churchill immediately pointed out in a letter to Baldwin, the safeguarding of steel would open the door to demands from every other major industry for protection:

> Hitherto the Safeguarding procedure has only touched articles of small consequence to the general trade of the country, and those have been of a finished or luxury class. Steel, however, is one of the fundamental basic raw materials of national industry. It affects in one way or another all the greatest trades in the country: shipbuilding, factory and house building, railways and tramways, bridges, engineering of all kinds and every form of machinery. Most of these trades are themselves hard pressed by foreign competition, and all of them are increasingly making use of cheap foreign steel. If British steel is to be protected, it will be impossible to resist a demand for a corresponding measure of protection against foreign competition to all the users of steel.

Churchill threatened to resign in the event of a protectionist duty on steel. 'It would be the signal', he wrote to Baldwin on 19 June, 'for the reopening of the old controversy in its sharpest form.' He urged Baldwin to resist an inquiry – the usual procedure when an industry applied for safeguarding – and appoint a Royal Commission to investigate the depression in the industry.[41]

At first it seemed as though the decision might go against Churchill. After Cabinet on 26 June L.S. Amery recorded:

> The safeguarding of iron and steel led to a confused discussion. Winston trying desperately to avert the drift towards the only possible conclusion. His suggestion that the application for a safeguarding committee should be definitely rejected found no favour. But it was decided to suspend matters pending an investigation by the Committee for Civil Research . . .[42]

The committee duly took evidence, in private, from manufacturers in the steel, shipbuilding and engineering industries. On 19 November Churchill argued strongly before the committee that steel would recover without protection and that the best way to encourage the industry was through amalgamations. He urged that the Government should refuse a public inquiry, and won his case. Baldwin announced the decision on 12 December.[43] After this the protectionist campaign lost momentum and Churchill was left once more in possession of the heartland of Free Trade.

While Churchill beat off the critics over steel, he was exposed to attack by the mounting crisis in the coal industry. Keynes had predicted that as a consequence of the return to gold attempts would be made to reduce wages. In the summer of 1925 events appeared to prove him correct. The Gold Standard was by no means the only cause of the coal industry's troubles, but it was certainly an aggravating factor. At the end of June 1925 the mine owners gave notice of their intention to reduce wages as from 31 July. As an alternative they invited the miners to work longer hours for existing rates of pay. The miners rejected the terms, and the Government was faced by the prospect of a long and damaging dispute in the coal trade. Baldwin responded by setting up on 11 July a committee of inquiry under a Scottish lawyer, H.P. Macmillan.[44]

Keynes now published a series of articles in the *Evening Standard*, blaming the coal crisis on the Gold Standard: 'The plight of the coal miners', he wrote, 'is the first, but not – unless we are very lucky – the last, of the economic consequences of Mr. Churchill.'[45] Keynes had, in fact, no personal quarrel with the Chancellor: his attack was directed against the Treasury officials on whose advice Churchill had acted. But Liberal and Labour politicians took up the cry that Churchill was to blame. When Lloyd George joined in Churchill protested: 'The Gold Standard is no more responsible for the condition of affairs in the coal industry than is the Gulf stream.' In reply to Keynes himself, he stigmatised the policy of devaluation as a device for subsidising exports, and cutting wages by stealth.[46]

The miners could no longer turn for assistance to the Triple Industrial Alliance, which had broken up in 1921. They turned therefore to the General Council of the TUC. Herbert Smith, the President of the Miners' Federation, obtained a promise of support from the General Council, and the union boycotted the hearings of the Macmillan Committee. Remembering, no doubt, the Sankey Commission of 1919, the miners called for the appointment of a Royal Commission. Meanwhile the Macmillan Committee, reporting on 28 July, came down broadly on the side of the miners, opposing longer hours and recommending a national minimum wage as a first charge on the industry before profits. At the same time the General Council lumbered into action with a pledge to support the miners through an embargo on movements of coal. The threat of a General Strike was vague and even the preparations for the coal embargo were confused and uncertain. But in the event the General Council was not called upon to act. At the last minute, in an unexpected turn of events, Baldwin and Churchill drew up a plan for a nine-month subsidy to the industry of £10 million. The proposal was approved by the Cabinet on the evening of the same day, 30 July, with some opposition from Salisbury, Joynson-Hicks, and Bridgeman.[47]

The Cabinet were swayed by two main considerations: firstly, fear of the economic and financial repercussions that a prolonged coal dispute would bring; and secondly, anxiety that the machinery for maintaining essential services in the event of a general strike was not yet ready.[48] On 6 August Churchill told the House of his hope that, given a breathing-space, the coal industry might resolve the conflict between the miners and the coal-owners. But he also stressed the Government's need to gain time for preparations on the propaganda front:

... if you are going to embark on a struggle of this kind, make quite sure that decisive public opinion is behind you; be quite sure that the majority of the nation understand what the quarrel is about.

Churchill placed the strongest emphasis on the factor that touched him most deeply as Chancellor: finance. A coal strike lasting thirteen weeks would, he estimated, cost sixty to seventy million pounds in lost revenue, enough to sweep away the tax concessions of the budget and postpone the scheme for widows' and orphans' pensions.[49]

Churchill continued to be deeply apprehensive about the effects of a strike. On 23 October he warned that 'all the brighter prospects will be shattered and overclouded if next spring we are exposed to a serious industrial convulsion in the coalfields or on the railways'. At the Cabinet Expenditure Committee on 18 November, he remarked that a labour crisis in the spring 'might indeed involve an increase in direct taxation and a return to War Budgeting.'[50] But in public he warned that the Cabinet would face up to a conflict if necessary: 'Do not let it be supposed that if we are sincere in our efforts to preserve peace and promote tranquillity, we are incapable of doing our duty should all such efforts fail.' Eventually, the miners would have to accept the economic realities: 'There are too many miners. The cost of production is still too high, apart from the subsidy which cannot be continued, for the present maintenance of the export trade.'[51]

The financial clouds were gathering. In the budget Churchill had rashly set himself the target of reducing overall expenditure by £10 million a year. But the coal subsidy made this impossible, and savings were hard to find. The Chancellor's campaign to reduce naval expenditure met with very limited success: in the summer of 1925 it was the admirals who won the battle of Baldwin's ear. As he scoured Whitehall for economies, Churchill's thoughts turned to the problem of unemployment benefit, which had changed out of all recognition since his days at the Board of Trade.

Since the war unemployment insurance had been extended to cover the vast majority of manual workers. But with the coming of long-term unemployment it had become thoroughly mixed up with the payment by the Exchequer of 'uncovenanted' benefit, better known as 'the dole', to workers who had used up their insurance claims. Churchill strongly favoured the outright abolition of uncovenanted benefit and its replacement by discretionary payments. This was a logical enough position for an advocate of social insurance to adopt, but he had not adopted it before. September 1925 found him warning the Minister of Labour, Steel-Maitland, that uncovenanted benefit was 'rotting the youth of the country and rupturing the mainstream of its energies.'[52]

Among those who were unimpressed by the economy drive was the industrialist Lord Weir. Some useful work was being done, he wrote to a friend, 'but once again I have to keep dinning in to the PM and Winston the fact that one cannot make a country prosperous through economies. A creative and constructive end must always be of major importance, and I believe I am having a little success in getting them to concentrate on these lines.'[53] Weir was still hopeful of persuading the Government to invest in the mass production of his prefabricated steel houses. But this was to be one of the unrealised projects of the Baldwin Government. In the draft of an unsent letter to Chamberlain, in February 1925, Churchill declared that he was ready to place a Government order for a quarter of a million emergency houses, and complained that Chamberlain was only experimenting 'on a tiny scale'. But Chamberlain was not the only obstacle. Housing was the responsibility of the local authorities, who were frightened off by the combined opposition of unions and employers in the building trades. They in turn could point to falling house prices which reduced the urgency of alternative building methods. In July 1925 Churchill authorised the construction of about 20,000 Weir houses over the next two years, but only 3000 were completed: a figure just 247,000 short of Churchill's target.[54]

In the corridors of Whitehall, meanwhile, the Chancellor's stock was falling. Grigg, his private secretary, was telling tales against him to Baldwin's confidant, Thomas Jones:

Grigg thinks that within a year Winston will have committed some irretrievable blunder which, if it does not imperil the Government, will bring Winston down. Grigg admitted going to great lengths: 'I have even intrigued with other Ministers" to try and save the Chancellor from what Grigg thinks to be mischievous courses. "He is such a poor judge of men, and lets himself be led by rogues and wrong'uns like F.E. Guest and that coterie.'[55]

In October Churchill took the chair at a meeting of the Cabinet Economy Committee and proposed various cuts in Neville Chamberlain's budget at the Ministry of Health. 'Of course they were impractical', wrote Chamberlain, 'and I had no difficulty in making hay of him.' Among those present at the meeting was the Permanent Secretary to the Treasury, and head of the civil service, Warren Fisher. As a Treasury official, Fisher owed a professional loyalty to Churchill. But he was delighted to see him discomfited and arranged to see Chamberlain at the Ministry of Health. In his diary Chamberlain recorded:

W.F. is evidently thoroughly miserable and out of sympathy with his chief whom he describes as "a lunatic", "an irresponsible child, not a grown man" and so forth. He declares that all the heads of dept. have lost heart. They never know where they are or what hare W.C. will start. In October [1924] when he came in the finances were in a thoroughly healthy condition but he was warned that everything pointed to a stand easy budget. However that did not suit him and he set to work at once to devise spectacular tax reductions & to balance them with the costly Pensions scheme which could quite well have waited another year . . . And now in the mess he had got himself into he was proposing the maddest ideas, e.g. to cut all Government servants down by 5 per cent including civil service, fighting services, postmen, police and teachers . . .

Fisher told Chamberlain that he had warned Baldwin against Churchill 'innumerable times', but the Prime Minister had done nothing. 'If you don't have him out', he warned Chamberlain, 'he will bring you down.'[56] It is interesting to speculate on Fisher's motive. As the head of the civil service, he may well have feared Churchill's threat to reduce the number of permanent officials. Whatever the cause of his intrigue, it was quickly detected by Churchill, who reacted with disdain.[57]

The outcome of Churchill's quest for cuts in Government spending was the Economy Bill, published on 11 March 1926, which budgeted for savings of £8–10 million in the next financial year. Most of the savings were to be obtained by reductions in the Treasury's contributions to health and unemployment insurance. In the case of health insurance, the effect was to prevent the provision of extra benefits under the scheme. In the case of the unemployment insurance fund, which was already heavily in debt, the effect was to perpetuate the debt. As Churchill had planned, uncovenanted benefit was withdrawn from certain classes of men and women, thus throwing them back on the poor law. The desperate search for candle-ends was best reflected by the clause in the bill which proposed to save a few pounds by reducing the number of polling days in Orkney and Shetland from two to one. The bill as a whole was given a rough ride through the House.[58]

With the coal crisis due to come to a head when the Government subsidy expired at the beginning of May, the prospects for the economy were overshadowed by uncertainty. Immersed in the preparations for his second budget, Churchill could only hope that industrial peace would prevail. He was also cheered by the belief that he had recently discovered a lucrative new source of revenue for the Treasury. A House of Commons Committee had recommended a tax on horse-race betting and a former Chancellor, Sir Robert Horne, had calculated that it would yield something like £17 million a year.

The state of the betting laws was peculiar. It was legal to bet at the race-course, or to bet on credit by wire or telegraph to a betting office. But the most common form of betting, a cash bet with a bookie's runner in the street, was illegal. The House of Commons Committee proposed that street bookmakers should be registered and set up in offices where cash bets could be placed. They would then be taxed on a percentage of their turnover. In December 1925 Churchill met a deputation which included the chairman of the Committee, Sir Henry Cantley. As always, he was anxious to arm himself against potential criticisms in the House of Commons, and asked members of the deputation how they would respond to various hypothetical objections.

> To my mind one of the most obvious objections is the creation of the street betting house near the public house or wherever it may be in the poorest streets to which people would resort in long queues for the purpose of wasting their substance in this form of excitement. What do you say about that?

Churchill also wanted to know whether there was a danger that once betting was legalised, the habit would become compulsive for many people:

> On their way to work they would read a large blackboard with a list of the horses running and so on and the odds and advertisements to say "we give the best odds" or "prompt settlement", whatever it may be, "step inside", and there is a nicely lighted, well-equipped place which they have only to go in on their way to work and leave 2s.6d. or 5s. and if they

win on their way home they can go in and collect the money ... Don't you think a very great number of people might get into the wrong habit of following the racing returns, which is an acquired habit, personally I have not been able to take a particular interest in horses, but I know perfectly well if I started following it closely my field of interest would be lighted up in this respect. I have no doubt that people get bitten by it and take to it and you find them becoming very very keen. I am afraid we might be accused, don't you think so, of having deliberately spread and multiplied the vice – I won't say vice but evil?

On these and other points Churchill received reassuring replies from members of the deputation.[59]

Seduced by the prospect of a substantial addition to the annual revenue, Churchill ignored the objections of the bookies and the warnings of Treasury officials, and announced the betting tax in his budget on 26 April 1926. Bookmakers both on and off the course were to register, and pay a levy of 5 per cent of their turnover. In its editorial column *The Sporting Life* remarked: 'It looks as if Mr Churchill will add one more to his lengthy list of political gambles, and go down in history as the man who put the Chance into Chancellor!'[60] The gamble did not succeed. When large numbers of bookmakers evaded the tax, Churchill tried to win them over by successive reductions in the rate of tax in the budgets of 1927 and 1928: to no avail.

With the exception of the betting tax, the 1926 budget was a pedestrian affair. Churchill was obliged to admit that he could not fulfil his promise to reduce Government spending by £10 million a year. Faced with a potential deficit of £7,900,000 he budgeted for a surplus of £14,100,000 with a variety of expedients. £5.5 million was to be extracted from the brewers by the simple device of reducing their period of credit for the payment of Excise Duty from three months to two. £7 million was transferred from the Road Fund, which had previously been regarded as a fund intended exclusively for expenditure on the roads.

Churchill also tinkered once more with protectionism, extending the McKenna duties, which already covered the 'pleasure' motor-car to include the 'commercial' motor-car. For this he incurred the displeasure of doctrinaire Free Traders. Though commending Churchill warmly for orthodoxy in balancing the budget, *The Economist* detected a hidden agenda: 'The design, if we are not mistaken, is to shift the burden of taxation year by year in such a way as to introduce piece by piece a wide system of Protection and to present it to the country at the next Election as a *fait accompli*.'[61]

Churchill had no such plans, and could happily ignore the criticisms of pedantic Free Traders. But he had framed his budget on the assumption that the wheels of trade and industry would continue to turn as usual in the coming year. This assumption was about to be overturned.

# 8

# *The General Strike and After*

## 1926–29

During the winter of 1925–6 contingency plans for the defeat of a general strike were drawn up by the Supply and Transport Committee of the Cabinet, under the chairmanship of the Home Secretary, Joynson-Hicks. But ministers still hoped that a strike could be avoided by the negotiation of a settlement in the coal industry. In March 1926 hopes were raised by the report of the Samuel Commission, which proposed a carefully balanced compromise.

The employers' case for wage cuts was endorsed. But on the question of hours, the report upheld the miners in their refusal to extend the seven-hour day. The report also put forward several ideas for the long-term reorganisation of the industry, including the nationalisation of mineral rights, the amalgamation of pits, enforced if necessary by the Government, and improvements in research and distribution. The commission opposed a continuation of the subsidy and recommended that wage cuts should be negotiated only after the acceptance by both sides of the reorganisation proposals. The report did not, however, state clearly whether wages should be settled at district level (as the employers demanded) or at national level (as the unions demanded).

Churchill was among the members of a Cabinet Committee set up to consider the Government's response to the Samuel Report. But he was no longer in a conciliatory frame of mind. The previous July he had come out in favour of the gradual acquisition of mineral royalties by the state. Now he opposed the idea, arguing that the reorganisation of the industry could be accomplished without this. He was joined by Lord Salisbury, who contended that one instalment of nationalisation would lead to another.[1] The Cabinet, having decided that it was best to conceal such reservations, put out a statement accepting the Samuel Report in general, and offering to assist in carrying it through if both miners and owners accepted it.

Deep in his budget preparations, Churchill took little part in the next stage of the crisis. The Samuel Report was welcome to neither side in the coal industry. The owners would have nothing to do with reorganisation, and continued to insist on longer hours. The miners welcomed reorganisation, but would have nothing to do with wage reductions. As the stalemate developed, Churchill revealed his attitudes in a letter to P.J. Grigg: 'I am quite ready for a fight with the Coal Miners. I feel quite differently about it to what I did last August.'[2]

On 23 April, with one week to go before the subsidy ended and a lock-out began, Baldwin tried a last initiative and summoned representatives of unions and employers to Downing Street. Herbert Smith for the miners declared that he was ready to see 200,000 miners put out of work by pit closures rather than accept the employers' terms on wages and hours.[3] Here was one drastic solution: but the coal-owners preferred to keep all their pits open and cut back on wages. Baldwin could have averted a general strike by compelling the owners to accept the contraction of the industry. This would have won for him the support of the TUC General Council and left the miners to decide whether to fight on alone over pay and hours of work. Baldwin, however, took as his yardstick the acceptability of a settlement to the owners, and exerted only the gentlest pressure on them. Neither Chamberlain nor Churchill dissented from this negligent approach.

The final phase of negotiations from 30 April to 3 May was conducted by four members of the General Council and three members of the Cabinet – Baldwin, the Minister of Labour, Steel-Maitland, and the Secretary for India, Lord Birkenhead. Churchill took no part except when the full Cabinet assembled. The search for an agreed formula was pursued through a series of tense meetings until the small hours of 3 May. About midnight the news came through that printers on the *Daily Mail* had refused to print an editorial entitled: 'For King and Country'. On learning this, Baldwin and the Cabinet decided to break off negotiations on the grounds that the strike had already begun.[4]

Ever since the General Strike, tradition has asserted that Churchill played the part of a dangerous extremist, driving the pacific Baldwin into a conflict that might well have ended in bloodshed but for the Prime Minister's skilful control of his fire-eating Chancellor of the Exchequer. The story that Churchill forced Baldwin to break off the negotiations was first published in the *New Statesman* a fortnight after the end of the strike. Churchill was alleged to have said that 'a little blood-

9   The Triumvirate: Lloyd George, Birkenhead and Churchill leave 10 Downing Street on their way to the House of Commons, 1922.

10   The 'Independent Anti-Socialist': Churchill canvassing in the open air market at Berwick Street, Soho, during the Abbey by-election of March 1924. He lost by 43 votes.

11  Budget Day: Churchill on the way to present his third budget in April 1927.

12  The Prince and the Politician: The Prince of Wales, later King Edward VIII, with Churchill at a game of polo.

13  The Old Firm: the Foreign Secretary, Lord Halifax, greets the Prime Minister, Neville Chamberlain, on his return from meeting Hitler at Bad Godesberg, September 1938.

14  The New Team: Churchill's War Cabinet pose for the cameras in the garden at 10 Downing Street, October 1940. They are, from left to right (standing), Arthur Greenwood, Ernest Bevin, Lord Beaverbrook, Sir Kingsley Wood and from left to right (seated), Sir John Anderson, Churchill, Clement Attlee, and Anthony Eden.

15   Portrait of a Great Man: Churchill photographed by Cecil Beaton in the Cabinet Room at 10 Downing Street, December 1940.

16   Sporting Touch: Churchill shakes hands with Denis Compton (Army and England) at the England v. Scotland match at Wembley, October 1941.

letting' would be all to the good. Three years later Ernest Bevin, the general secretary of the Transport and General Workers' Union, said that if Churchill had not entered the Cabinet Room on the evening of 2 May, there would have been no General Strike: 'The two sides were in another room getting almost to the last clauses to hand to the Prime Minister, when Mr Churchill walked in and upset the Cabinet, and we had the ultimatum.' So respectable did the story become that it passed into academic history and in the first edition of his history of trade unionism Henry Pelling wrote: 'Baldwin was at the mercy of his own intransigents, Churchill, Birkenhead, and Joynson-Hicks.'[5]

The story is plainly a myth. Throughout the events which led up to the strike, Baldwin was the unchallenged arbiter of industrial policy. It was he who set the framework for negotiations in the final week, and he who broke them off with the unanimous agreement of the Cabinet. By the afternoon of 2 May the Cabinet was reluctant to pursue the formula devised by Birkenhead who, like Churchill, was falsely identified in later accounts as a member of the 'war party'. In the evening the Home Secretary, Joynson-Hicks, received a phone call informing him of the stoppage at the *Daily Mail*. The Cabinet assumed, or wished to assume, that the printers were acting on the instructions of the General Council. 'This', wrote L.S. Amery, 'turned the scale and made it clear that the only issue that really mattered for the Government and with the public now was the issue of the General Strike.' Baldwin's right-hand man, J.C.C. Davidson, was later to write in his unpublished memoirs: 'It has often been written that the extremists forced Baldwin's hand, but nothing could be further from the truth.'[6]

If tradition is mistaken in one respect, it is nearer the mark in another. It is quite true that in some ways Churchill took an extreme line during the strike. To understand his actions we must escape for a minute from the Cabinet Room and try to envisage the situation as the British awoke on the morning of Tuesday 4 May.

In a sense the term 'general strike' is misleading, for the TUC only called out selected groups of workers in the first instance. Transport workers were in the front line: the railways stopped, the docks were silent, and there were few buses. Nor were there any newspapers, the printworkers having also been called out. The miners, of course, were already locked out of the pits. The other industries affected were steel, metals, chemicals, building, electricity, and gas. At Ecclestone Square a Strike Organisation Committee, in which Bevin was the moving spirit, directed events. Enthusiastic local strike committees, the heart of the action, organised picketing, food permits, local bulletins, demonstrations and public meetings. The Government, meanwhile, was putting into practice its emergency plans. In Whitehall the co-ordinating authority was the Supply and Transport Committee of the Cabinet, which issued instructions to the Civil Commissioners in the regions. Volunteers moved food supplies by road, and special constables were enrolled to maintain law and order.

Addressing the House on 3 May, Baldwin depicted the strike as a challenge to the constitution. As Davidson recalled:

> Baldwin took an extremely simple but very stubborn line, that the General Strike was an attempt at political revolution – the destruction of the Constitution – and the perpetrator must surrender before conversations were possible. It was in his mind – and we talked it over every day as the strike drew to a close – that there was no question of arguing, and when even Neville Chamberlain, whom everybody thought was a pretty hard and stiff person, suggested that conversations be opened with the TUC or certain members of it, Baldwin said in effect: 'They are Englishmen. They have committed a grave error. This is not a matter for compromise. They must admit that they have done wrong.'[7]

The Cabinet united behind Baldwin's refusal to compromise. But there were tactical differences over the management of the crisis. Baldwin and the majority worked on the shrewd assumption that the General Council of the TUC could be detached from the miners. They deliberately abstained from language or measures that would drive the 'moderates' of the TUC into a deeper alliance with the 'militants' of the coalfields. Churchill, however, was for piling on the pressure to break the strike. True to form, he was all for heightening the conflict once the issue was joined. Needless to say he did not intend to risk a bloody civil war. But he wanted to shake an intimidating fist at the strikers.

The difference of mentalities was brought to light on the fourth day of the strike when Thomas Jones was preparing the ground for an appeal by Baldwin intended to split the union leadership at Ecclestone Square. Jones went to Churchill to enlist his support, but as he recorded in his diary, he was overwhelmed by 'a cataract of boiling eloquence, impossible to reproduce. "We were at war. Matters had changed from Sunday morning. We were a long way from our position then. We must go through with it." '[8]

Among the curiosities of the strike was the appearance of a Government newspaper, *The British Gazette*, intended to fill the vacuum left by the closing down of the national press, and present the Government's view. Prompted by Davidson, the Newspaper Proprietors' Association offered to give all possible assistance in the production of an official daily strike bulletin. On the evening of 3 May Churchill called a meeting and it was decided to requisition the offices and plant of the *Morning Post*, whose editor H.A. Gwynne had offered to put them at the Government's disposal. There was a great flurry of activity as volunteer compositors and engineers were assembled, and arrangements made for distribution by a fleet of motor vehicles.

As might be expected of a Government newspaper, *The British Gazette* was top-heavy with controllers. Though H.A. Gwynne continued to occupy the editor's chair, he was responsible now to David Caird, a publicity officer at the War Office charged with general editorial supervision. He in turn reported to J.C.C. Davidson, the minister responsible for publicity, and submitted copy to him whenever he felt it necessary. Baldwin then decided that Churchill would be usefully employed as editor-in-chief, a position that was never formally defined. Churchill, an old hand at journalism, began to contribute leading articles and intervene in the content of the paper.[9]

With its four overlapping editors, and four small pages, *The British Gazette* was ready to encounter the rival TUC publication, *The British Worker*, edited by Hamilton Fyfe and produced at the offices of the *Daily Herald*. The *Gazette* claimed that trade unionists were moderates in the grip of extremists. The *Worker* claimed that the peacemakers in the Cabinet had fallen victim to the wild men of the Right. The *Gazette* gave prominence to reports of men going back to work while the *Worker* would not mention them. The *Worker* publicised appeals for peace from church leaders, including the Archbishop of Canterbury. At the *Gazette* Davidson tried to suppress the Archbishop's appeal but was later obliged to print it on the back page.

Churchill wanted to hot up the war of words and produced several militant editorials that were censored by Davidson, the originals of which were unfortunately destroyed by bombing during the Second World War. Davidson wanted to publish a report of the celebrated football match between policemen and strikers at Plymouth, an evocation of Baldwin's England. Churchill, who perhaps resented the impression that the police were fraternising with the enemy, wanted to keep it out. The issue went to Cabinet, where Davidson won. The general strike exposed in Churchill the lack of steady, English restraint for which he had so often been criticised in the past. According to Thomas Jones writing six days into the strike, James Grigg thought that 'Winston always has in mind the doing of things which would impress posterity, that the articles he dictates for *The British Gazette* are conceived with an eye either to his next book, or to his biographer, and that he hasn't the slightest interest in or sympathy with the common people.'[10]

\*

Churchill was just as bellicose in another sphere. At the start of the strike Baldwin appointed him to the Supply and Transport Committee, which had long been in charge of the Government's preparations. The chairman of the committee, Joynson-Hicks, played a cautious hand and succeeded in living down his reputation as 'Mussolini Minor'. But according to Davidson much argument was provoked by the interventions of Churchill and Birkenhead, who regarded the strike as 'an enemy to be destroyed'. Differences of opinion came to a head over the use of troops to convoy food supplies from the London docks: 'Winston was all for a tremendous display of force; machine guns, hidden but there, should be placed along the route; tanks should be used in addition to armoured motor cars; and so on.' Churchill was overruled, and the convoy passed off peacefully.[11]

On the morning of 7 May the Cabinet decided that troops should be kept in reserve, away from the disturbed areas, and should 'only be used in the last resort'. As an alternative to the use of the regular soldiers, a civil force was to be raised from volunteers in the Territorial Army. Churchill was put in charge of a Cabinet Committee to work out the details and report back the same day. At 9pm he read to the Cabinet his report on the formation of a Civil Constabulary Reserve, which 'met with unanimous approval'.[12]

One other instance of Churchill at his most excitable deserves notice. At the start of the strike Baldwin decided to allow the BBC, under its Director-General John Reith, a measure of autonomy. But Churchill favoured outright Government control, a view he stated emphatically at a meeting of the Supply and Transport Committee on 6 May. Once again the difference of opinion reflected Churchill's desire for an overt demonstration of authority. Baldwin preferred to conceal the influence of the Government behind the fiction that the BBC was independent. As Reith noted in his diary, the Cabinet sided with Baldwin. 'The Cabinet decision is really a negative one', he wrote. 'They want to be able to say that they did not commandeer us, but they know that they can trust us not to be really impartial.'[13]

All told, there was much truth in the left-wing notion of Churchill as the extremist of the General Strike. Yet it was convenient for Baldwin, with his carefully constructed reputation as a moderate, that Churchill should be depicted as a menace. Years later he told his biographer, G.M. Young, that the cleverest thing he had ever done was to put Churchill in charge of *The British Gazette*: 'otherwise he would have wanted to shoot someone.' After objections from Churchill, this phrase was deleted from the published version of the biography.[14]

Happily for Baldwin, Churchill's exuberant and extroverted personality lent itself readily to caricature. In 1927 H.G. Wells published his novel *Meanwhile*, in which one of the characters describes the General Strike in a series of letters to a correspondent in Italy:

> As might be expected Winston has gone clean off his head. He hasn't been so happy since he crawled on his belly and helped snipe in Sidney Street. Whatever anyone else may think, Winston believes that he is fighting a tremendous revolution and holding it down, fist and jaw. He careers about staring, inactive, gaping, crowded London, looking for barricades.[15]

On 12 May the General Council of the TUC called off the strike. To cover their abandonment of the miners, they grasped at a promise by Lord Samuel to do his best to secure a settlement along the lines of his report. No doubt they were encouraged by a conciliatory broadcast from Baldwin, in which that master of atmospherics undertook to secure a just settlement of the coal dispute. But the TUC had failed to extract any binding commitment from the Government. They had, in fact, surrendered, and with their surrender an era came to an end. The syndicalist threat of a General Strike was permanently discredited.

But the dispute in the mines continued. On the first day of the General Strike, Tom Jones had asked Baldwin and Churchill what line he should take in explaining the Government's policy to Labour politicians. Churchill replied that there were two disputes in progress: a General Strike on which the Government could not compromise, and a trade dispute in the coal industry, on which they were prepared 'to take the utmost pains to reach a settlement in a conciliatory spirit'.[16]

The Government did indeed strive for a settlement. On 14 May, Baldwin submitted new proposals to the miners and mine-owners. Wages were to be subject to compulsory arbitration by a National Wages Board under an independent chairman, and a shadowy offer was made of legislation on the amalgamation of pits. In the interim, standardised wage cuts were to be imposed, but tapered with the aid of a renewed subsidy.[17] Had the miners been able to foresee the consequences of prolonged resistance, they would have grasped these terms as the best available. They fulfilled at least two of the miners' aims: a basic, nationally agreed wage, and continued Government involvement in the industry. But fortunately for the coal-owners, who were strongly opposed to the plan, the miners missed their chance and rejected it out of hand.

Churchill was dissatisfied with this outcome. Now the strike was over he wished to resume his strategy of balancing the budget and finding a surplus for some politically attractive project. The longer the coal dispute lasted, the worse the consequences for the Exchequer. 'The coal stoppage', he wrote impatiently to Baldwin on 9 June, 'is now beginning to cut deep into our prosperity and finance. I do not feel convinced that the right course is being taken to give it the best chance of being ended.' As President of the Board of Trade, Churchill had witnessed the introduction of a statutory eight-hour day in the mines. But it had since been replaced by a seven-hour day, and the eight-hour day outlawed. In June 1926 Churchill called for legislation to reintroduce the eight-hour limit. The ordinary miner, he believed, would prefer longer hours to less pay.[18] Legislation followed. In July the seven-hour day was suspended and the owners posted up new district wage-scales. But still the miners resisted and August passed with no fresh indication of a settlement. When, however, miners in some areas began to return to work, the Miners Federation decided that it was time to save something from the wreck.

At the beginning of September the leader of the Labour party, Ramsay MacDonald, presented himself as an intermediary between the miners and the Cabinet Coal Committee, of which Churchill was a member. Baldwin, who was on holiday at Aix, was kept closely in touch. The Miners Federation announced that they were prepared to enter negotiations 'with a view to a reduction in labour costs'. Churchill seized the initiative and invited both miners and owners to a three-cornered conference on the basis of the miners' declaration. Churchill anticipated opposition from the owners, who were opposed to national wage agreements, but told Baldwin that he was prepared for the clash. Baldwin was alarmed by the possibility of a settlement imposed on the owners. His desire, he explained to Churchill, was to 'wean the Coal Industry from the Government'. The miners, he warned, would want the Government to be a party to the agreement, but such a commitment on the Government's part might 'fall on us like a load of bricks within a measurable distance of the general election.'[19]

Convinced that he had the Cabinet behind him, Churchill advanced on a collision course with the mine-owners. At a conference with the Mining Association on 6 September he raised the principal issue: 'Let me state what, in my judgment, is the issue across the table at the moment. It is, is there to be any National Agreement at all, or is the industry in future to be regulated purely by district agreements without any National Wage Negotiating Body?' In a lengthy discussion the owners stubbornly resisted national machinery and towards the end Churchill adopted a threatening tone. If the owners would not budge, he warned, 'we shall have to move forward upon our own course of action in your absence.'[20]

Churchill's threat to coerce the owners produced a hostile reaction in the Conservative party. His friend and cousin Lord Londonderry, a major coal owner, wrote him a sharp letter complaining that Churchill had 'come down on the side of Cook and Smith'. Birkenhead weighed in, inquiring why a national agreement should be imposed on the owners, when they were strong enough to obtain district agreements. Back-bench opposition was activated by the National Confederation of Employers' Associations.[21]

Churchill persisted, producing draft clauses of legislation at the Coal Committee on 16 September. But ministers were turning against him. When Churchill unfolded his scheme to the Cabinet on 24 September, L.S. Amery recorded, 'it soon became obvious that nobody liked it very much'. Churchill battled on. The Cabinet would only allow him to offer the facade of a national agreement, but he did his best to make the most of it. On 27 September, refreshed by a pint of champagne (or so Tom Jones surmised), he rose in the House to put the Government's case, and in a speech of great sparkle and wit appealed to the miners not to turn down the offer. 'In their heart of hearts', wrote Jones, 'the Cabinet hate this offer, and are dreadfully afraid it may be accepted. During this brilliant performance the PM's face was turned towards the Official Gallery, and covered with one of his hands. He looked utterly wretched . . . '[22] Baldwin must have been greatly relieved when the miners rejected the proposal.

Negotiations were at an end but for a few more weeks the dispute lingered on. Churchill feared that it would continue indefinitely. In a Cabinet paper of 2 November he argued that the miners were able to sustain themselves because of the poor law relief received by their wives and children. 'These reliefs,' he wrote, 'turned to the best advantage by communal kitchens, enable the married miner to live upon the food of his family. No wonder the struggle continues.' The owners, meanwhile, were now heavily in debt to the banks, 'and now feel that the banks must carry them to the end. Therefore the incentives to a settlement on both sides are simultaneously weakened.'

Churchill put forward for discussion a drastic plan to end the dispute by the coercion of both sides. The owners would be legally compelled to offer interim terms laid down by the Government, pending the introduction of a compulsory arbitration tribunal. As for the miners:

In any case where the men are willing to return on these conditions and the conditions are refused by the owners, the men to be considered as unemployed and eligible for full scale benefit. Where the employers open the pits on the prescribed terms and the men or any men refuse to return, all relief to their families to cease within one week of the passage of the Bill.

The Cabinet must balance the exertions and dangers of such a policy against the really frightful injuries to national wealth and character inherent in indefinite prolongation of the stoppage over very large portions of the coalfields.[23]

If anything justifies the view that Churchill was the enemy of the miners, it is this proposal to force them back to work by starving their wives and children. When the Cabinet discussed his ideas on 3 November, copies of the paper were handed round and ministers invited to return them to the Cabinet Secretary as soon as possible. The Cabinet decided there was no decision they could usefully take at the moment.[24] Churchill himself had second thoughts and realised that he had gone too far. On 11 November he wrote: 'In view of the fact that men have returned in the month and that there are many indications that this number will steadily increase we do not feel that the facts warrant our coming forth with so drastic a policy, and it is perhaps better for the country to pay a still heavier price in its general trade and prosperity than for us to be committed to such very large inroads upon the liberty of individuals . . . '[25]

*

One immediate consequence of the General Strike was a revival of Conservative demands for action to curb the trade unions. Among the questions raised was the use of trade union funds for political purposes, an issue familiar to Churchill from pre-war days. In the Osborne Judgment of 1909 the House of Lords ruled that it was illegal for a trade union to maintain a political fund. After much debate, the Asquith Government decided to restore the right to a political fund, provided that a ballot of union members revealed a majority in favour. All members would then be liable to contribute to the fund subject only to the right of individuals to 'contract out' – a right which might have to be exercised in the face of strong pressure from work-mates or trade union officials. In May 1911 Churchill defended the principle of 'contracting out' in the Commons, and discounted the danger of intimidation. There had never been a time, he argued, when 'any attempt to bully, to persecute, to harry individuals in the tolerant exercise and expression of their opinions is more severely censured and condemned . . . ' That, he declared, was the safeguard.[26]

Between 1911 and 1924 the transformation of Labour into a major party, and of Churchill into a Conservative, led him to revise his opinions. Majority opinion in the Conservative party was strongly in favour of contracting-in, which it was hoped would deal a severe blow to Labour party funds. Shortly after his return to office in 1924 Baldwin asked Churchill for his opinion. Churchill favoured contracting-in. The first principle, he wrote, must be 'to liberate working men from the unfair and humiliating position of being compelled under threat of ruin and starvation to subscribe to the propagation of political principles which they detest.' But characteristically, he argued for a balancing factor to compensate the Labour party. The aim, he wrote, must be 'not to hinder by want of funds the less wealthy classes in the nation from using to the full their constitutional rights and so being continuously assimilated into the British Parliamentary system.' Churchill therefore proposed the state funding at general elections of all candidates who obtained 'an adequate number of votes'. This, he added, 'would make men of all Parties more free from unwholesome excesses in Party Discipline.'[27]

Baldwin did not accept Churchill's advice but opted for creative inertia. When on 6 March 1925 a Conservative back-bencher, Mr Macquisten, introduced a private member's bill designed to replace contracting-out by contracting-in, Baldwin rose to make a famous speech asking the House to drop the bill in the interests of industrial harmony, and borrowing the words of the Anglican liturgy: 'Give peace in our time, O Lord.' Churchill was deeply impressed by the masterly fashion in which Baldwin had controlled the situation, and wrote to Clementine: 'A strong Conservative party with an overwhelming majority and a moderate and even progressive leadership is a combination which has never really been tested before. It might well be the fulfilment of all that Dizzy and my father aimed at in their political work.'[28]

The trade union question slumbered again until the General Strike, when the Cabinet fleetingly considered emergency legislation as a weapon in the struggle. Churchill, like the rest of the Cabinet, was enthusiastic at first, but after a weekend's reflection thought it better to avoid provocation.[29] With the defeat of the strike, there was much to be said for inaction. The trade unions were demoralised, their membership was continuing to decline due to the depression, and industrial militancy was on the wane. But Conservatives were eager to inflict some kind of punishment.

At the end of June, a Cabinet Committee under the Lord Chancellor, Lord Cave, proposed the registration of all trade unions, the compulsory submission of their rules for official scrutiny, and provision for strike ballots. Unions in the civil service would be forbidden to affiliate to the TUC and general strikes were to be illegal.[30] Churchill proposed to add to the legislation his earlier plan for the state funding of general elections. In spite of the opposition of the Minister of Labour, Steel-Maitland, the Cabinet decided to go ahead with a bill including the reform of the political levy. But they were not prepared to accept Churchill's idea of state-funded elections.[31]

The Trade Disputes Act – first published as a bill in April 1927 – made all sympathetic strike action illegal, except within the trade or industry in which a strike occurred. Contracting-out was replaced by contracting-in. Trade unions in the civil service were forbidden to affiliate to the TUC. There was no provision for compulsory strike ballots, but the definition of 'peaceful picketing' was tightened up with the aim of preventing intimidation.[32] Sixteen years earlier Churchill had argued that it was impossible to prevent trade unions from entering politics: 'The sphere of industrial and political activity is often indistinguishable, always overlaps, and representation in Parliament is absolutely essential to trade unions . . . ' But now he maintained that trade unions should 'mind their own business.' In a message of support to E.L. Spears, the Conservative candidate at the Bosworth by-election, he wrote:

> For industrial matters there are the Trade Unions; for politics there are elections, Parliament, Party clubs and Organisations of all kinds. It is very important to the good government of our country and to working class prosperity to keep these things separate and to use the right tools for each task.[33]

In fact the Trade Disputes Act did not keep the unions out of politics. Nor did the reform of the political levy deal a fatal blow to the funding of the Labour party which, indeed, was to win its greatest electoral victory in 1945 under the system of contracting-in. As for industrial relations, the effect of the act was largely symbolic. The absence of a general strike after 1926 owed nothing to the act. Nevertheless, trade union leaders deeply resented the symbolic humiliation imposed on them. Bevin's biographer, Alan Bullock, tells us that he regarded the measure as 'an act of petty vindictiveness inspired by class and party spite', and swore that he would never rest until it was repealed.[34]

*

Time and again in the 1920s issues which Churchill had dealt with in the Edwardian period reappeared on the political agenda. Among them were two constitutional problems: House of Lords reform and votes for women.

In view of the possibility that Labour would one day obtain a majority in the House of Commons, Conservatives believed that something must be done to make the Upper House more effective. In June 1925 Baldwin appointed a Cabinet Committee, of which Churchill was a member, to look into the subject. The committee recognised that if the House of Lords were to be granted more powers, its composition would have to be reformed. Any attempt to increase the authority of a purely hereditary assembly would play into the hands of the Opposition parties.

In 1910 Churchill had proposed an Upper House directly elected from a panel of public servants recruited automatically by virtue of the offices they held. They were to include peers and MPs who had served for ten years in Parliament. By 1925 his prescription was rather more conservative. Direct elections, he argued, were inimical to the idea of a Chamber of Elder Statesmen, detached from 'passing moods and vulgar errors'. He proposed an Upper House elected by the House of Commons from a panel of 1,200 notables, including all hereditary peers, MPs who had sat for twelve years or more, and the holders of various public offices. One-third of them would retire at every dissolution of Parliament, or once every four years, whichever period was the shorter. Regional groupings of MPs would each elect a quota from the panel to the Upper House.

As we have seen before, Churchill enjoyed constitution-making. His plan, though far from original, was typically ingenious. He could argue that since the composition of the Upper House would reflect, over the long run, the composition of the House of Commons, it was fair to all parties. A sequence of Labour majorities in the Commons would certainly have translated, under Churchill's plan, into a Labour majority, albeit a very staid and respectable one, in the upper House. This would not have been possible under the proposals of his old friend Birkenhead, the Secretary for India. Having sat in the upper House since 1919 Birkenhead had become a part of the furniture and recommended a minimum of change.[35] This suited Baldwin, who took advantage of the general lack of enthusiasm for House of Lords reform to bury the issue in December 1926 by postponing a decision indefinitely.

One of the ideas discussed in connection with House of Lords reform was the election of an Upper House by regional electoral colleges. Churchill seized on this idea to renew the case for devolution which he had put between 1911 and 1914:

The need for larger units of local government is deep and obvious. The two most active commercial nations, before the War, Germany and the United States, conducted their affairs by means of scores of powerful local governments, woven together in a federal system, and in the United States at least these local units are the foundation of the Senate. The attempt to transact all affairs small and great at Westminster is attended by grave inconveniences, nor can a Parliament charged with such a multiplicity of business really fulfil the functions of an Imperial or even a national assembly.

Churchill proposed the creation of sixteen local Parliaments on the scale of the London County Council but with a much larger share of the revenues than they currently possessed, and 'responsibilities and powers much beyond those which are devolved at present'. As he pointed out, devolution might also be utilised as an alternative basis for House of Lords reform. The local Parliaments, like the States of the American Union, would choose the Second Chamber from a panel of their own members plus the hereditary peerage. 'Far reaching as these projects may seem,' wrote Churchill, 'I do not believe that in achievement they would require more than the two or three years at our disposal.'[36] Churchill's proposal vanished without trace.

Reform of the Upper House was hardly a burning question. But votes for women was still a subject of agitation among the suffragists. Under the Representation of the People Act the franchise remained unequal: men got the vote at 21, and women at 30. In the general election of 1924 Baldwin promised to equalise the franchise, but the matter was far from settled, and there was much discussion in Cabinet of how and when – or, indeed, whether – to proceed. A Cabinet committee on the franchise, appointed in December 1926, was advised by Conservative Central Office that the enfranchisement of younger women would damage the party electorally. 'In the industrial areas,' warned the party chairman, J.C.C. Davidson, 'particularly in those areas where women work in the mills, it was believed that such a measure would bring on to the electoral rolls a large majority of votes for the Labour Party, by reason of their being under the influence of Trade Union officials.'[37]

Baldwin and Chamberlain both reflected on the possibility of changing the voting age to 25 for both sexes. But the qualifying age for men had been 21 for more than five hundred years – since 1405 in fact. A party which put the clock back to the era of *Henry IV Part I* was unlikely to succeed at the polls. As an alternative, Churchill recommended Lord Eustace Percy's proposal for a two-tier franchise. Men and women would obtain the vote on an occupational basis between the ages of 21 and 25, and a residential basis thereafter. As he explained to the franchise committee: 'The adoption of this proposal would involve the risk of universal suffrage at a later stage, but the proposal had the great advantage that it would satisfy all legitimate demands without any real breach of principle.'

Unable to agree, the committee referred the problem back to the Cabinet, which decided in favour of an equal franchise at the age of 21. But with the help of Birkenhead Churchill mounted a last ditch resistance. Labour, he argued, was still not ready to govern:

> In a few years the assimilative power of British institutions, the healing process of peace, the revival of world prosperity, may ease the whole position. Above all, the Labour party, amalgamating with Liberal elements, may well be steadily developing into a trustworthy though unpalatable alternative administrative instrument.[38]

He recommended once more Lord Eustace Percy's fancy franchise. But Churchill and Birkenhead lost the argument and Baldwin announced, on 13 April 1927, that a bill would shortly be introduced. The Equal Franchise Act followed in 1928.

At the time of Churchill's first election to the House, in 1900, the electorate had consisted of some 6,730,000 men. By 1929 it consisted of 28,850,000 men and women. Even in 1900 Churchill had been unfamiliar with the lives and opinions of the voting population. It seems fair to say that he knew even less of the mass electorate of the 1920s, and least of all about the suburban middle classes who populated his own constituency of Epping. But as always he was confident of his oratorical powers, and eager to address as wide a public as possible. In 1928 he tried to arrange for his budget speech to be broadcast live from the House, a proposal that was vetoed by Baldwin. In compensation the Director-General of the BBC, Sir John Reith, invited him to give a 15-minute talk from Savoy Hill – the first ever ministerial broadcast on a budget.[39]

While he argued for checks and balances to counteract universal suffrage, Churchill believed, like his father before him, that the best form of defence was attack. As he had written in 1921: 'I have always understood that from the Eighties onwards the policy of the leaders of the Tory democracy was not to put their faith in little dykes or dams devised to arrest the public will, but in vigorous political action throughout the constituencies of the country.'[40] What most distinguished Churchill from his colleagues in the Baldwin Cabinet was his quest for large electoral themes.

With the budget of 1925 Churchill's Chancellorship had got off to a flying start. But he had lost momentum since then. After the failure of his bid to settle the coal dispute in the autumn of 1926 he was a politician without a song to sing – except, of course, for the usual ballad of anti-Bolshevism.

In January 1927 Churchill paid a visit to Italy and was much impressed by Mussolini and his regime. 'If I had been an Italian,' he declared in Rome, 'I am sure I should have been whole-heartedly with you from the start to finish in your triumphant struggle against the bestial appetites and passions of Leninism. But in England we have not yet had to face this danger in the same deadly form. We have our own way of doing things.' The fascist press were delighted, and gave great prominence to Churchill's remarks. Here, for the first time, was an eminent foreign statesman placing a seal of approval on Mussolini's great experiment.[41] In fairness to Churchill it has to be said that while he was much censured by the British Left for whitewashing an authoritarian regime, there was no shortage of liberals and socialists who were prepared to perform the same service for the Soviet Union. The irony is that Churchill was taken in by the appearance of order and efficiency in Mussolini's Italy: it was a ramshackle affair.

Churchill returned home to a deteriorating financial prospect. The General Strike and the prolonged dispute in the coal industry had ruined the calculations upon which the budget of April 1926 had been based. Instead of a surplus of £14 million, Churchill now faced, at the end of the financial year 1926–7, a deficit of £36.5 million. In preparing his third budget he was determined to restore a surplus. It is, in fact, very doubtful whether Churchill ever balanced the books. It is more likely that he ran a small deficit, concealed by short-term expedients and creative accountancy. But he was anxious to demonstrate his attachment to orthodox finance by creating the appearance, at least, of a balanced budget.[42] There was no great dishonesty in this. He was determined to achieve real economies, and pressed on with cuts in the civil service and the armed forces. On the revenue side, he was always inclined to hope that trade would pick up and yield a larger income than expected.

Churchill introduced his third budget on 11 April 1927. It was patently full of expedients. Churchill announced that he would seize the remainder of the Road Fund and reduce the brewers' credit by another month. Income tax on property under Schedule A was to be payable in a single instalment in the current financial year, instead of two instalments of which the second was payable in the following year. Pottery and motor-tyres were added to the extraordinarily miscellaneous list of protected imports and *The Economist* fumed with indignation: 'Mr Churchill seems determined to maintain his record as the most consistent imposer of Protectionist duties that we have had in Britain for a hundred years.'[43]

On the Conservative side the budget was generally welcomed as an ingenious escape from the dreaded prospect of higher taxation. But the sense of relief was temporary. Churchill feared that both he and the Government had lost their way. Privately he was more and more convinced that he had been led astray over the Gold Standard, and he laid the blame on the Governor of the Bank of England, Montagu Norman. As Grigg writes: 'The events of 1925 and 1926 undoubtedly led to something very like an estrangement between the Chancellor and the Governor of the Bank of England ... Of course they met frequently – they had to – and this gave the Chancellor of the Exchequer abundant opportunities to make speeches about the evil effects of the Gold Standard – partly abusive, partly derisory and not entirely unmeant. The Governor retired more and more into his carapace, and so the necessary relations of confidence and candour ceased to exist.'[44]

Thwarted by the intractability of the situation, Churchill wrote to Niemeyer in May 1927:

> We have assumed since the war, largely under the guidance of the Bank of England, a policy of deflation, debt repayment, high taxation, large sinking funds and Gold Standard. This has raised our credit, restored our exchange and lowered the cost of living. On the other hand it has produced bad trade, hard times, an immense increase in unemployment involving costly and unwise remedial measures, attempts to reduce wages in conformity with the cost of living and so increase the competitive power, fierce labour disputes arising therefrom, with expense to the State and community measured by hundreds of millions.

Whereas, wrote Churchill, Britain had pursued deflation, Germany had undergone a disastrous inflation leading to financial collapse. But as a result of inflation, German industry was free of the burden of internal debt and the German economy was beginning to thrive:

> In ten years' time therefore if the policy which the Treasury and the Bank have with such remarkable ability and skill pursued be carried to its logical conclusion, we may well see Great Britain with a debt still heavier – nominally and in reality – with crushing taxation, bad trade, high unemployment and great discontent; and on the other hand Germany with no internal debt, with reduced Reparations, with far lighter taxation, with ever expanding trade, and the contentment which comes from a sense of returning prosperity.

Later that year Niemeyer left the Treasury to join the Bank of England. Retrospectively, Churchill judged him as harshly as Norman. As he wrote to Hopkins, in July 1928: 'The Niemeyer attitude of letting everything smash into bankruptcy and unemployment in order that reconstruction can be built up upon the ruins, is neither sound economics nor wise policy.'[45]

In spite of his withering judgment of the policies pursued since 1918, Churchill was not attracted by the Keynesian remedy of public works. As he saw it, the main problem was that the rigorous pursuit of deflation had imposed excessive burdens on industry. By depressing trade, deflation had reduced the Government's income and increased its expenditure. Industry, therefore, was overloaded with taxation and the best way to stimulate production was by cutting taxes. In the spring of 1927 he discovered a new theme which, he believed, might hold the key to a trade recovery and the revival of the Government's fortunes: the derating of industry.

*

There was no subject more complex than local government finance. The one member of the Baldwin Cabinet who thoroughly understood it was the Minister of Health, Neville Chamberlain. The long association of his family with the municipal affairs of Birmingham had prepared him for the task to which he devoted most of his time at the Ministry of Health – the reform of local government, and the recasting of the relationship between central and local authorities. He began with the Rating Act of 1925, a comprehensive reform of the rating and valuation system, which concentrated the power to levy rates in the hands of the larger local authorities. This cleared the way for the fulfilment of a greater ambition: the reform of the poor law. Chamberlain proposed to abolish the poor law guardians, transfer their powers to the county and borough councils, and institute a more centralised system of financial control, the block grant, which was intended to prevent Labour authorities from spending too much of the ratepayers' money on poor relief.

Churchill knew little of local government. But inevitably the Treasury was drawn into Chamberlain's plans. To Chamberlain's dismay, Churchill at once began to interfere. Impressed by the advantages to the Treasury of the block grant system, under which grants would be settled for a period of five years in advance, he urged Chamberlain to extend it beyond health to include education and other local services.[46]

Chamberlain and Churchill managed to compose their differences by postponing the issue. Meanwhile Churchill saw the electoral advantages of poor law reform and came out strongly in favour of legislation at a Cabinet meeting in December 1926. The Colonial Secretary, L.S. Amery, recorded in his diary: 'Winston warmly commended the whole scheme. I fear he is always ready to spend millions on domestic purposes whether to find favour or buy off opposition but hates spending thousands on imperial purposes.'[47]

Churchill at this period was cultivating the younger and more progressive Conservative MPs who wanted a more positive policy on unemployment. When Robert Boothby wrote to him in October 1926, attacking the Government for its neglect of the coal industry, and quoting in support of his argument Lord Randolph Churchill, Churchill's response was to appoint him his Parliamentary Private Secretary.[48] As he pondered the subject of local government finance Churchill recalled a casual remark by another young Conservative MP, Harold Macmillan, about the defects of the rating system.[49] At some point in the spring of 1927 Macmillan's remark about the rates suddenly fused in his mind with his general sense of political frustration, and the impending reform of the poor law.

On 6 June Churchill wrote a long and remarkable letter to Baldwin arguing that the Government was drifting into stagnation and unpopularity, and urgently required a policy to restore its fortunes. 'Each year', wrote Churchill, 'it is necessary for a modern British Government to place some large issue or measure before the country, or to be engaged in some struggle which holds the public mind.' Churchill proposed to find from the next budget a 'mass of manoeuvre' of some £30 million and devote it to 'a substantial reduction of the rates'. This, he wrote, would help every class, but especially producers, 'and no one would it help more than those very basic industries that employ the greatest mass of labour and have to use the largest quantities of real property.' Churchill envisaged that derating could be turned into 'a steamroller that would flatten out all the petty interests which have obstructed Block Grants and rating reform' and commend itself to every town, every part of the country and every class – or, as he wrote in a parallel letter to Chamberlain, 'every Constituency'.[50] Baldwin gave Churchill permission to pursue the idea and by September, following discussions inside the Treasury, it had crystallised in Churchill's mind, changing from a plan to reduce rates in general, to a scheme for the exemption of industry and agriculture.[51] Churchill hoped that his derating scheme could be interwoven with Chamberlain's Local Government Bill to form a single, sweeping measure. On 18 October 1927 he wrote to Chamberlain outlining his plans and seeking his co-operation. But Chamberlain reacted with horror. In a letter to Hilda Chamberlain he wrote: 'As usual, he looks not at the merits but at the electioneering value of any project that I put up to him and he seems to want to draw me into some new mad idea which is at present simmering in that volatile and turbulent brain of his.'[52]

As rivals for the succession to Baldwin, Churchill and Chamberlain were destined to clash, and the grounds for conflict were extensive. The whole tendency of Chamberlain was to reduce politics, in Benthamite fashion, to a question of economic and efficient administration. Churchill, on the other hand, regarded administrative problems as the raw material from which great political themes were constructed. Here was a contest, by proxy, between Birmingham Town Hall and Blenheim Palace.

Chamberlain expected the worst. At the beginning of December he warned Baldwin that Churchill was likely to provoke a Cabinet crisis. 'For some time now,' he wrote to Hilda Chamberlain,

> he has been dwelling on a plan for the next Budget, which I regard as unwise, immoral, and dangerous. It is dangerous because as usual it is only the idea he has got. He has nothing worked out but he gets so enamoured with his ideas that he won't listen to difficulties or wait until plans have been made to get over them. It's like Gallipoli again.[53]

Chamberlain underestimated Churchill. Treasury officials had been studying and preparing the derating plan for months. And as Churchill recognised, no plan could be regarded as definitive before it was discussed in Cabinet. He was quite ready to amend it in the light of criticisms or objections.

Churchill put forward his ideas in a carefully argued Cabinet paper of 12 December 1927. The strength of his case lay in the dramatic force and simplicity of the plan. A small number of major advantages were stressed, and a host of minor drawbacks passed over in silence. Churchill's main premise was the complete abolition of rates on industry and agriculture, a dramatic stroke intended to transfer the cost from the producer to the consumer, who would pay through taxes. Producers would in fact be expected to repay about a quarter of what they gained through a profits tax. But all producers would benefit and the depressed industries most of all. A petrol tax, striking at road transport, would boost the railways and the coal industry. If, in addition, the railways were included in the scheme, they would be able to reduce freight charges and hence their customers' costs. As the depressed areas tended to have the highest rates and lowest profits under the existing system, they would enjoy the greatest relief. Costs would be reduced in the exporting industries and employment protected.

The detailed arguments were linked to an overall vision of economic policy unchanged since 1903. The derating plan was intended to sustain a free trade abroad, and a liberal economy at home. Protectionism would be outflanked. Socialism would be checked by breaking the cycle of declining industry, high rates, and poverty, which created fertile breeding-grounds for 'a virulent Socialising and pauperising propaganda.'[54]

Churchill quickly realised that his plan for a profits tax was unlikely to be well received. Colleagues warned against the use which might be made of it by a future Labour Government. In a revised version of his plan, circulated to the Cabinet in January, Churchill proposed to drop the profits tax and partially restore the rates. Instead of total exemption, industry would enjoy a rate relief of 75 per cent.[55] If this was intended to mollify Chamberlain, it did not succeed. When the derating scheme was first discussed in Cabinet, on 20 January, Chamberlain was strongly critical. He warned that local authorities might suffer a permanent loss of revenue. More significantly, he spoke as a citizen of Birmingham, with its tradition of business leadership in civic affairs. Derating, he warned, would lead to the withdrawal of businessmen from participation in local government. Though Chamberlain spoke with great authority, the majority of the Cabinet were swayed by Churchill's enthusiasm, and welcomed the plan as a means of bringing relief to hard-pressed farmers and industrialists.[56] Politically, too, it was attractive as an answer to the Government's critics, and a demonstration of the Conservative will to tackle the problems of the depressed areas.

Over the next three months, Cabinet politics were enlivened by complex debates over derating in which the chief protagonists were Chamberlain and Churchill, with Baldwin and the Cabinet acting as mediators. It was a long and intricate story of which only a summary will be given here.[57] Chamberlain fought hard for the exclusion of the railways and persuaded the Cabinet to agree. But in the meantime Churchill, egged on by Harold Macmillan, had reverted to the idea of the total exclusion of industry from the rates, and almost carried the Cabinet with him. Then, a few days before the budget, Churchill decided to reopen the question of the railways. When Chamberlain opposed him, Churchill appealed to Baldwin and made a scene. Marching about the room, and shaking his fist, he launched into a tirade against Chamberlain. Baldwin, who was very good at playing Churchill and Chamberlain off against one another, decided to come down on Churchill's side. On 20 April the Cabinet reversed its previous decision and included the railways in the derating scheme.[58]

Churchill unveiled his plan in the budget on 24 April 1928. As from October 1929 agriculture was to be entirely free of rates and industry relieved by 75 per cent. The income local authorities lost through derating was to be restored to them by the Exchequer in the form of quinquennial block grants, and the Exchequer was to find the money, in part, from a new tax of fourpence a gallon on petrol. 'I am not of course suggesting', Churchill declared, 'that the present difficulties of British industry or the distresses of the wage-earning population in certain areas will be cured completely by any relief that can be afforded upon the rates . . . We boast no panacea, but we are sure that the relief of the rates upon production is the first, the most obvious, and the most urgent remedy which Parliament can apply.'[59]

The budget speech, noted L.S. Amery a few days later, 'was done with Winston's best literary skill and above all with his power of investing the business with importance . . . There is no doubt that the first impression was very favourable indeed and our party was delighted and is I think still very happy at the end of the week.' *The Economist*, for its part, hailed the budget as 'a serious attempt – perhaps the most important since the introduction of Free Trade – to adapt our financial policy to the needs of productive industry.'[60] Churchill's derating initiative did succeed in thwarting yet again the protectionist wing of the party. In July 1928 Baldwin and Churchill, acting together, suppressed a protectionist revolt of some two hundred Conservative MPs.[61] But in other respects derating failed, for various reasons, to live up to Churchill's expectations. The only members of the public directly affected were manufacturers and farmers. The Labour and Liberal parties mounted a strong opposition, claiming that derating benefited only capitalists and landlords. The scheme was savaged by the *Daily Mail*, the mouthpiece of Lord Rothermere, who was impatient for additional cuts in the income tax. Chamberlain, who bore the responsibility for implementing the scheme as part of his Local Government Bill, was privately sceptical of its value and muted in his declarations on the subject. Churchill himself tended to play down its significance as time went on. At a by-election in February 1929 he said only: 'The scheme is one which might conceivably give a fillip to British industry.'[62]

*

Churchill's hopes of seizing the initiative in economic policy were disappointed. At the same time the Government found itself under attack from an unexpected quarter. The Liberal party was experiencing a revival under the leadership of Lloyd George, who had recently supplanted Asquith. Lloyd George's strategy was to identify the party with radical ideas for the revival of agriculture and industry, and the elimination of mass unemployment. At the end of 1926 he set up what later became known as the Liberal Industrial Inquiry, with Keynes as chairman of the committee on financial and industrial organisation. The outcome was the publication in February 1928 of the Liberal 'Yellow Book', *Britain's Industrial Future*, which proposed the creation of employment through a large-scale programme of loan-financed public works. That spring the Liberals appeared to be reviving electorally as well, with two by-election victories over the Conservatives at Lancaster and St Ives.

Immersed in his derating plans, Churchill at first paid little attention to Lloyd George's challenge. But in July 1928 Keynes published in the *Evening Standard* an article entitled 'How to organise a wave of prosperity'. The Treasury, Keynes argued, had made the fundamental mistake of deflating prices in the belief that costs would automatically follow them downwards. The Bank of England ought to liberalise credit, and the Chancellor of the Exchequer 'reverse his pressure against capital expenditure'. Churchill asked his officials to comment on Keynes's article – 'the first occasion on which official scrutiny of Keynes's ideas on public investment was called for.'[63] The two officials concerned, Hawtrey and Leith-Ross, both gave adverse reports on Keynes's proposals and there the matter rested for the time being.

But in the New Year of 1929 two Conservative members of the Cabinet began to panic at the prospect of the forthcoming general election, and the assault they would face from the Opposition parties over unemployment. The Home Secretary, Joynson-Hicks, proposed a programme of loan-funded public works in the colonies and Dominions, to stimulate exports and migration, supplemented by road-building at home. The Minister of Labour, Steel-Maitland, gave a general blessing to Joynson-Hicks's ideas, but also posed in sharp terms the question of economic theory. What were the effects of capital investment by the state?

> Is it or is it not true that if capital be directed to such schemes it will not be forthcoming in the same abundance for more natural and more fruitful ordinary business? This question concerns a cardinal principle of finance and financial policy . . . And after 8 years of financial orthodoxy and 8 years of unabating unemployment, ought we not to ask for a reasoned proof, for some foundations of belief that the financial policy by which we guide our steps is right?[64]

As Peter Clarke points out, this challenge from within the Cabinet led to a crystallisation of ideas. Treasury officials had never believed that public works provided a long-term solution to unemployment. But they had never before had to explain themselves. Churchill invited two officials, Frederick Phillips and G.C. Upcott, to demonstrate the fallacies in the argument.

They in turn prepared, in collaboration with Leith-Ross, a memorandum defining for the first time, the 'Treasury view'. Essentially they argued that public works could do nothing in themselves to bring about a trade revival: £1000 raised by the Government, whether in loans or taxation, was £1000 denied to business. The only effect of state investment was to crowd out private investment. Churchill decided to circulate the memorandum as a Cabinet paper and gave it his endorsement:

> It is to be hoped that we shall not let ourselves be drawn by panic or electioneering into unsound schemes to cure unemployment, and divert national credit from the fertile channels of private enterprise to State undertakings fomented mainly for political purposes. The devastating nature of the criticism which could be applied to a policy of curing unemployment by a large loan expenditure of an unprofitable character, whether on the roads or elsewhere, would only become apparent after a Government was committed to that policy and to the promise based upon it.[65]

Baldwin, fearful no doubt of opening up the divisions within the Conservative party, managed to prevent a Cabinet discussion of the issue, and the Churchill-Treasury view triumphed by default.

On 1 March 1929 Lloyd George launched his election campaign with a speech in which he promised schemes to bring down unemployment to 'normal proportions' within a year. Shortly afterwards the Liberal party published a sixpenny pamphlet, jointly written by Keynes and Hubert Henderson, entitled *We Can Conquer Unemployment*. A loan-financed programme costing £250 million was to create 600,000 jobs within two years.[66] Long ago, in 1908–9, Lloyd George and Churchill had concerted plans for a 'national development fund' to reduce unemployment. But Churchill no longer believed that public works could solve the problem. Over lunch at Philip Sassoon's, on 6 March, he held forth on the subject to several of his colleagues: 'We should not try to compete with L.G. . . . but take our stand on sound finance. I remember in Gairloch when the unemployed figures were tremendous, we toyed with these big national schemes of artificial employment, but L.G. came down after a few days' reflection solidly against them.'[67] But Lloyd George was on the march and had to be answered: later that month the Liberals won two by-elections from the Conservatives.

The arguments of the Treasury memorandum lay to hand. Born of divisions within the Cabinet, they were now to be turned against the Opposition. Churchill decided to introduce the Treasury case against public works into his budget speech and as always he debated the problem with his advisers before deciding how to present it to the House of Commons. Churchill recognised the intellectual difficulty of putting a categorical case against public works, when the Government already undertook public works itself – housing and roads for example. As he wrote to Leith-Ross:

> You will see for yourself the delicacy of an argument which on the one hand declares that all Government borrowing simply withdraws money from ordinary enterprise, and then proceeds to boast that we have done it, and are doing it on a gigantic scale. I do not say that these arguments cannot be reconciled, and I am trying to do so; but pray, address your mind to the subject and let me have the result in the course of a few days.

Leith-Ross replied that although the sources of investment were finite, *some* public works might be more efficiently undertaken by the Government than by private enterprise: but the criteria had to be stringent. The true remedy for unemployment was for workers to accept a reduction of 10 per cent in their wages, or increase their productivity to the same extent.[68]

In his budget speech, on 15 April 1929, Churchill put the case against public works as a remedy for unemployment. But he did so with great subtlety. He was determined to emphasise that he based himself, not on the whims and fancies of Winston Churchill, but on 'the orthodox Treasury view'. According to this view, when the Government entered the money market it did so in competition with industry for finance. Hence there was an onus upon Government only to borrow where the need was paramount: for national security, for work that was necessary but would not otherwise be undertaken, or for spending that would produce a higher return than if left to private enterprise.

By these criteria, Churchill was able to justify the substantial sums which the Government already spent on capital investment. 'We ourselves', he explained, 'have certainly not followed any absolute rule ... We have set on foot and carried into effect far-reaching and carefully considered programmes of housing, roads, telephones and agricultural development.' £300 million had already been spent on capital development, with another £50 million committed for the future. But here Churchill skilfully turned the argument. Although so much had been spent, and all for necessary purposes, 'for the purpose of curing unemployment the results have certainly been disappointing. They are in fact so meagre as to lend colour to the orthodox Treasury doctrine which has steadfastly held that, whatever might be the political or social advantages, very little additional employment and no permanent additional employment can in fact and as a general rule be created by State borrowing and State expenditure.'[69]

Churchill also took the opportunity, in his budget speech, to review the past five years. He was able to show that in spite of the disruption of 1926, living standards had risen, the balance of trade improved, and the budget returned to a healthy surplus through prudent finance: 'Our greatest economy in this Parliament has been upon armaments.' On the Gold Standard, Churchill concealed his deeper misgivings. It had brought, he argued, privations as well as rewards but his hope was 'that the privations are minor and temporary and that the rewards will be major and permanent'. 'Among present discontents' it was a consolation that the City of London had regained its international pre-eminence.[70] Churchill put up an able defence of his record, but there was no great triumph to which he could point, nor could he offer a vision of any great promise for the future. His Chancellorship, like the Baldwin Government, was drawing to a close on a note of anti-climax. In the budget Churchill was able to remind his audience that derating was about to take effect. Where Lloyd George backed road-building, Churchill backed the railways, which 'have much more to give to the revival of industry'. In addition to derating, they were to benefit from the abolition of the passenger duty, on condition that the funds released were to be used for the modernisation of the railways. The boldest stroke of his final budget was to abolish the tea duty, which had existed since the reign of Elizabeth I: 'There is no other comfort which enters so largely into the budget of the cottage home, or the still humbler budgets of the old, the weak and the poor.' But the betting tax, he ruefully admitted, had proved to be a fiasco and would have to be repealed. Its failure was due to 'the volatile and elusive character of the betting population'.[71]

Churchill salvaged one small item from the ruin of the betting tax. The Jockey Club and the National Hunt Committee complained that attempts to levy the betting tax at race courses had led to a decline in attendances at race-meetings. They urged Churchill to repair the damage done to the sport by introducing into Britain the totalisator or 'tote' – a betting machine which automatically registered bets and calculated the odds. Churchill recommended the idea to the Cabinet, which agreed in November 1927 to facilitate the passage of a private member's bill legalising the tote. In the 1929 budget Churchill introduced a duty of 0.5 per cent on the proceeds of the tote.[72]

The general election took place on 30 May. The election campaign, Churchill told a women's meeting in his constituency, 'is the dullest I can remember'.[73] This was true and Churchill too had lost his sparkle. His denunciations of socialism were routine, as though he were simply going through the motions. There was more fun to be had in attacking his old friend Lloyd George, in the knowledge that he would appreciate a slanging match: 'How crude, barbarous and ignorant is a policy which would gather hundreds of thousands of unemployed together in gangs and set them to make racing tracks for Liberal profiteers to run their cars upon.' Churchill's first ever election broadcast, on 30 April, began well but the language grew tired and windy: 'We have to march forward steadfastly along the high road. It may be dusty, it may be stony, it may be dull, it is certainly uphill all the way. But to leave it is only to flounder in the quagmires of delusion and have your coat torn off you by the brambles of waste. It is a good and plainly-marked road . . . '[74]

The most revealing of Churchill's remarks during the campaign was his complaint that he was given so little time on the radio:

> Broadcasting, that wonderful new instrument that would enable vast democracies of the future to live in complete touch with the vital issues of the day, is grudged and doled out minute by minute. After 33 years' experience in Parliament and public life, I was allowed only 30 minutes to speak to 30 millions of people.[75]

Used to discoursing for an hour or two on the platform or in the House, Churchill found it hard to attune himself to a mass medium. At 54, he was still comparatively young for a Cabinet minister of the period, and five years younger than Neville Chamberlain. But his political experience went back further than that of the other Conservative leaders, who had been out of office until 1915. There was a period feel about Churchill now, and a poignant reminder of this during the campaign with the death of Lord Rosebery. That long-forgotten figure brought back memories of Lord Randolph, and youthful plots with the 'Hughligans' at Dalmeny.

In the general election, on 30 May, Churchill was returned for Epping, but his share of the vote was down sharply:

| | |
|---|---|
| W.S. Churchill (Con) | 23,972 |
| G.G. Sharp (Lib) | 19,005 |
| J.T.W. Newbold (Lab) | 6,472 |

As Henry Pelling points out, there was a 9.4 per cent swing to the Liberals at Epping, which may have owed something to the growth of new suburbs in the constituency.[76] But there was of course a general swing away from the Conservatives in the country at large. Baldwin and the Conservatives were beaten.

As the results came in, Churchill sat with a whisky and soda, totting up the returns, getting redder and redder in the face, and 'bowing his head like a bull about to charge'.[77] The Labour party obtained the largest number of seats, 288, but still lacked an overall majority. But the Liberals, with 59 seats, were content for the moment to sustain a minority Labour Government under Ramsay MacDonald. For the Conservatives, with 260 seats, there was no immediate prospect of a return to office. MacDonald, it was clear, would lead the Government along the paths of moderation for an indefinite period. In politics, it seemed, there were quiet times just around the corner.

# 9
# *Right Turn,*
# *Left Turn*

## 1929–39

Churchill was in New York, at the end of a North American tour, during the Wall Street Crash of October 1929. He was staying at the flat of Percy Rockefeller and witnessed the suicide of a ruined financier, who 'cast himself down fifteen storeys and was dashed to pieces, causing a wild commotion and the arrival of the fire brigade'. In his *History of the Second World War* Churchill recalled how the credit structure of the United States, upon which so many Americans depended for the purchase of homes, cars, and household goods, collapsed. 'Twenty thousand banks suspended payment. The means of exchange of goods and services between man and man was smitten to the ground; and the crash on Wall Street reverberated in modest and rich households alike.'[1]

The Wall Street Crash was both a symptom and a cause of the collapse in the world economy which followed. World trade fell by 1932 to one-third of its volume in 1929. In desperation the industrial nations turned inwards and attempted to revive their home market by means of increased tariff barriers. But throughout North America and Europe unemployment rose to unprecedented levels as industry and agriculture cut back their production. In Britain the world slump was superimposed upon the prolonged depression of the export industries since 1920. When the second Labour Government took office in June 1929 the total number of registered unemployed already stood at 1,164,000. In the course of 1930 a steady rise took the figure from 1,520,000 in January to 2,500,000 in December. In January 1932, 2,850,000 men and women, or 21.9 per cent of the insured population, were out of work.

The slump was a disaster for the Labour party. The Labour Government was powerless to prevent the growth of unemployment, and the soaring cost of unemployment benefit was a financial and political millstone around its neck. But the Conservative Opposition had problems of their own. The slump revived all the old controversies within the party over tariff reform and the Protectionists seized the initiative, dragging a reluctant Baldwin behind them. The campaign for Empire Free Trade placed a large question-mark over the future of Churchill.

Churchill's response was remarkable. In October 1930 he abandoned the cause of Free Trade, the one principle to which he had clung tenaciously through all the twists and turns of his career. He was opposed to Baldwin's bipartisan approach to Indian constitutional reform, and found his way to a new position on the right wing of the Conservative party. In January 1931 he resigned from the Conservative Shadow Cabinet and placed himself at the head of a rebellion against Baldwin's policy. But Churchill did not confine himself to the Indian question. As Churchill saw it, the abandonment of Britain's mission in India was one aspect of a failure of national will. He presented himself as a leader who stood for a patriotic reassertion of the national interest in every sphere – including the slump. In one of the great somersaults of his career, he turned himself into a vigorous advocate of protectionism. He even adopted the most controversial aspect of the protectionist programme, which he had regularly denounced since 1903: food taxes.

If Churchill was bidding for office, or the leadership of the Conservative party, he failed. Some observers imagined that the slump would transform British politics. Dynamic leaders would rise to the top; radical movements would form; Britain might even swing towards communism or fascism. But nothing of the kind occurred. The main effect of the slump was to entrench in office a National Government led by MacDonald and Baldwin, the two politicians who had governed the country in turn since 1923. The two great adventurers of British politics, Churchill and Lloyd George, were excluded.

The National Government was elected in November 1931 with a 'doctor's mandate' for the treatment of a sick economy. But owing to the rise of Nazi Germany the politics of economic recovery were soon displaced by the politics of defence and foreign policy. In the official biography of Churchill, Martin Gilbert has described the development, week by week, of Churchill's campaign for the expansion of the RAF, and the creation of a Grand Alliance against Hitler. But what were the implications for Churchill's position in party politics?

By severing his last remaining link with Liberalism, the collapse of Free Trade had liberated him from the politics of the Centre. In his India campaign of 1931 to 1935 he joined hands with the type of Tory who would cheerfully have seen him hanged in 1910. But in 1935 his India campaign ended in defeat, with the passage of the Government of India Bill. The politics of reaction had failed him. Meanwhile, on the question of Nazi Germany, he was discovering that many of his natural allies were Liberals, left-wing intellectuals, or trade unionists. In party political terms Churchill moved sharply to the Left in his quest for a new cross-party alliance. These manoeuvres, which in a way foreshadowed the Coalition Government of 1940 to 1945, also revived echoes of the past. Free Trade was dead, and so too was the coalition of Conservative, Liberal and Labour politicians which had once upheld it. But the nascent alliance of anti-German forces in British politics was highly reminiscent of the Free Trade movement of 1904–5, in which Churchill had played such a prominent part, and Joseph Chamberlain had gone down to defeat.

\* \* \*

The fall of the Conservative Government in June 1929 led to a period of instability in the party. The authority of Baldwin, who had twice lost a general election, had been so weakened as to invite a period of faction-fighting and a struggle for the succession. Defeat also opened up once more the debate within the party over protectionism. The debate was mainly a tactical one, for the great majority of Conservatives were inclined to protectionism but restrained by fear of the electoral consequences of a commitment to 'food taxes'. Churchill stood out as the one leading figure in the party with a deeply-rooted attachment to free trade. He was also, in his own mind at least, a contender for the party leadership.

No sooner was the general election over, than the jockeying for position began. In the new Parliament the Liberals, under the leadership of Lloyd George, held the balance between Labour and the Conservatives. Lloyd George was ready to offer the Conservatives a deal: an alliance to bring down the Labour Government, in return for the promise of electoral reform. Such a deal would inevitably frustrate once more the Tariff Reformers in the party. Churchill was all for an alliance with Lloyd George and pressed it on Baldwin. On 27 June, with Baldwin's permission, he met Lloyd George for confidential discussions and gave him to understand that the Conservatives would accept an inquiry into electoral reform. But that same day two leading Tariff Reformers, L.S. Amery and Neville Chamberlain, got together and agreed to adopt the opposite strategy of blocking an arrangement with the Liberals. On 30 June the plot thickened when Lord Beaverbrook suddenly entered the fray and proclaimed a campaign for Empire Free Trade.[2]

Intricate manoeuvres followed. In the debate on the address, on 3 July,

Churchill reached out to Lloyd George with a declaration of Conservative support for an inquiry into electoral reform. For Churchill, anti-socialism was still the trump card. The gulf between the socialist party and the rest of the country was, he insisted, 'impassable'. But the following day Neville Chamberlain made a speech to the Empire Industries Association asserting that the Conservatives were now free to revise their policies in a protectionist direction. Amery took direct issue with Churchill in a speech to the House on 9 July: 'I let go and expressed my dissent from Winston who last week did some unauthorised holding out of hands to the Liberals and talked his usual rubbish about the impassable gulf between socialism and the rest of the country. I said the real gulf was not between those who differed only in degree whether on socialism or on protection but between those who were prepared to take practical measures and those who were tied down by dead dogma.'[3]

For all the skirmishing, free trade was still secure. In the summer of 1929 it was generally expected that trade would improve and unemployment fall, with a consequent improvement in the Government's electoral prospects. When the 'Shadow Cabinet' met to concert tactics on 11 July, the impassioned pleas of Amery fell on deaf ears. Baldwin refused to budge. Austen Chamberlain, Cunliffe-Lister and others were strongly in favour of co-operation with the Liberals leading ultimately to fusion. With Neville Chamberlain giving only half-hearted support to Amery, the discussion played straight into the hands of Churchill. Amery despaired of his influence:

It is quite evident that he has been colloguing vigorously with Lloyd George since the election and is heading straight for a coalition in which no doubt everything I have ever worked for is definitely to be thrown over. Undoubtedly he has been most successful, for he has not only succeeded in strangling any real policy while we were in office but in securing our defeat and reducing most of the party in consequence to such a state of fear that he can do anything with them. I thought I never saw such a lot of rabbits as my colleagues yesterday afternoon.[4]

While these manoeuvres were in progress, Churchill was taking up his new role as Shadow Chancellor. Churchill had never previously occupied a seat on the Opposition front-bench. He was eager to impress and applied himself conscientiously to the task. In the budget debates between April and July 1930, he spoke at length on seventeen days. On 17–18 July, during a debate which turned into an all-night sitting he rose to speak on eighteen occasions.[5]

Churchill's tactics in Opposition were simple. When the Labour Government behaved like an orthodox capitalist administration, he larded them with praise for abandoning the fallacies of socialism. This was a mischievous ploy intended to play on the divisions in the parliamentary Labour party between left-wing dissidents and the front-bench. But when the Government itself veered towards the Left, or could plausibly be represented as doing so, he would open up an anti-socialist barrage and revive his favourite doctrine of the impassable gulf between socialism and the Opposition parties.

'In its first six months of office', writes Robert Skidelsky, 'the Labour Government undoubtedly made a good impression on the country.'[6] MacDonald, the Prime Minister, made successful appearances on the international scene. At home the responsibility for economic policy was divided between the Chancellor of the Exchequer, Philip Snowden, a pillar of strict Victorian finance, and the businessman's friend J.H. Thomas, the Lord Privy Seal, who was charged with special responsibility in the field of employment. With Snowden and Thomas in charge, capitalists could sleep soundly in their beds. The one sign of radicalism was the appointment as Chancellor of the Duchy of Lancester of Sir Oswald Mosley, a 32-year-old baronet of great egotism and ambition, who believed in Keynes and a new economic order. But he was too junior to affect the course of Government policy.

On unemployment, Labour began where the Conservatives had left off. In the debate on the address, on 3 July 1929, Thomas unveiled a modest programme for the reduction of unemployment: a five-year road-building programme of up to £37½ million, credit facilities of up to £25 million for public utilities, and an annual subsidy on the cost of loans for public development.[7]

Churchill complimented Thomas on his 'very moderate and sensible' proposals. The road-building programme, he pointed out, had been taken over from the previous Government. The other proposals were equally unexceptionable and there were no serious differences between the Government and the Conservative party on this score. For the little band of socialists from the Clyde he expressed ironic compassion: 'They dreamed that they were clearing a pathway along which the toiling millions were to advance towards Utopia, but they wake to find that all they have been doing was to set up a ladder by which the hon. Baronet the Member for Smethwick [Sir Oswald Mosley] could climb into place and power.' In a debate shortly afterwards on the loan guarantee scheme, Churchill went out of his way to congratulate Thomas 'on not being hampered by foolish Socialist ideas about profit-seeking being a crime, all that nonsense about rent and interest being exploitation.' But if Thomas's measures were harmless, they were also useless, and would dash the hopes that Labour had raised of a dramatic reduction in unemployment:

> The schemes of the Lord Privy Seal for curing the great problems of unemployment are absolutely visionary and futile ... He might just as well go down on to the terrace some afternoon when the tide is high, take a tea cup from one of the tables, and try to bale out the Thames ... [8]

When Parliament rose for the summer recess, Churchill set sail for Canada on the *Empress of Australia*. The trip was mainly for recreation, though Churchill was not unmindful of the part played by Canada in the debate over imperial preference – Beaverbrook, after all, was a Canadian. Among Churchill's fellow passengers was Leo Amery, with whom he discussed the tariff question freely and at great length. Amery recorded:

> He is all for trying to find some formula for his Canadian speeches like "a girdle around the Empire", but on essentials he is still where he was 25 years ago, in intellectual conviction at least, for he is no longer prepared to fight for that conviction as he was. He just repeats the old phrases of 1903 and no argument seems to make any difference on him. He can only think in phrases and close argument is really lost on him ... Towards the end of this discussion I got up to go and Winston to undress, ending in his putting on a long silk nightshirt and woolly tummy band over it. W. asked why I was smiling and I replied: "Free Trade, Mid Victorian Statesmanship and the old-fashioned nightshirt, how appropriate a combination" and left him.[9]

Churchill, who was accompanied by his son Randolph, was thrilled by the lakes and forests of Canada, the farms of the great prairies, and the oil-fields of Calgary. But when Randolph spoke snobbishly of the Calgary oil magnates as too uncultured to spend their money properly, his father rebuked him sharply: 'Cultured people are merely the glittering scum which floats on the deep river of production.' So attracted was Churchill by the broad horizons of Canada, and the lucrative prospects for development, that he wrote home to Clementine: 'I have made up my mind that if N[eville] Ch[amberlain] is made leader of the CP or anyone else of that kind, I clear out of politics & see if I cannot make you and the kittens a little more comfortable before I die.'[10]

\*

During the autumn of 1929 Churchill and Chamberlain continued along divergent paths. The morale of the party was low, Chamberlain wrote in October, but if Baldwin withdrew 'the succession would come either to Churchill or myself, and I don't know which I should dislike most!'[11] Churchill still hankered after an alliance with Lloyd George. In December Thomas Jones reported, in a letter to a friend: 'Winston is restive and would much prefer to be running in double harness with L.G. than with the cautious S.B. He told me the other day that all three parties would go into the melting pot in the next two years and come out in a different grouping.'[12] Chamberlain, on the other hand, loathed Lloyd George personally, and was separated from him politically by Free Trade. That autumn he decided that he would take the lead in advocating a policy of protection and Empire Trade. In November negotiations began between Chamberlain and Beaverbrook to establish a common front. 'Winston, of course', wrote Chamberlain in his diary, 'is dead against food taxes . . . can't see that it is impossible to deal with L.G. because he couldn't deliver the goods.'[13]

From December to March Chamberlain was absent from Britain on an east African tour. It was a convenient absence. On 10 December Beaverbrook and Rothermere launched the Empire Crusade, with 'Empire Free Trade' as their goal. The Protectionist movement had always consisted of two related themes: protection for British industry against foreign competition, and imperial preference. Beaverbrook, the main instigator of the Empire Crusade, took little interest in industrial protection. His aim was to create free trade within the empire on the basis of food taxes. The British were to allow the free import of food from the Dominions and colonies while discriminating against foreign produce. In return the Dominions were to do away with the tariffs they imposed on British manufactured goods in order to protect their own infant industries. Empire Free Trade was a quixotic, even utopian project. It was questionable whether the British public would accept comprehensive import duties on foreign food. It was improbable that the Dominions would abandon the protection of manufacturing industries. Nevertheless the Empire Crusade, like Joseph Chamberlain's Tariff Reform campaign before it, kindled a flame in the constituencies. With Baldwin's leadership under growing attack, Chamberlain was clearly in line for the succession.

Churchill faced a dilemma. Ought he to step into the breach with a heroic defence of Free Trade, or keep his head down with a view to slipping quietly away from the battlefield? The idea of binding the British economy to the Empire was as uncongenial to him as ever. But as Amery observed, he was half-hearted in his resistance. In January 1930

Beaverbrook invited him to his London home, Stornoway House, to try to talk him round. 'They talk all the time about Empire Free Trade,' recorded Harold Nicolson, who was present:

> Winston says that he has abandoned all his convictions and clings to the conviction of free trade as the only one which is left to him. But he is clearly disturbed at the effect on the country of Beaverbrook's propaganda. He feels too old to fight it.[14]

While he rejected the blandishments of Lord Beaverbrook, Churchill was disorientated and uncertain of his convictions. In this he was not alone. Even in the temples of Liberalism, the old unquestioning faith in Free Trade was beginning to crack. In the course of 1930 J.A. Hobson, E.D. Simon and J.M. Keynes all expressed their doubts.[15] Meanwhile the fortunes of the Labour Government were in decline. Attacked by the Left for abandoning socialism, they were accused by Liberals and Conservatives of irresponsible finance. Much was made of the rising cost of unemployment benefit, and the growing deficit of the Unemployment Insurance Fund. Under the rules established by the Baldwin Government all workers with a record of 30 contributions over the previous two years were permanently entitled to unemployment benefit. Others, who could meet a less exacting test of contributions to the fund, were to receive transitional benefit for the next twelve months, after which, it was supposed, trade would recover. But trade did not recover, transitional benefit had to be extended, and by the end of Churchill's term as Chancellor the Fund was in debt with a borrowing requirement of £40 million.

All claimants to unemployment benefit, covenanted or uncovenanted, had been subject since 1924 to a test whereby they must be 'genuinely seeking work'. In his search for economies, Churchill had insisted that the administration of the rule be tightened up, as a result of which 251,000 claims were disallowed in 1928–9. But the Labour party went to the country in 1929 with a commitment to abolish the 'genuinely seeking work' clause.

In the new Government the Minister of Labour was Margaret Bondfield, the first woman Cabinet minister. She acted quickly to relax the administration of the test. This was followed, in the Unemployment Insurance Bill of November 1929, by a proposal to abolish the test in its old form. Whereas hitherto a claimant for benefit might be expected to prove that he or she had gone in search of work and been unable to find it, now the test was to be readiness to accept an offer of employment from a Labour Exchange. The bill also proposed to restore the balance of the Insurance

Fund by the simple device of transferring the cost of transitional benefit to the Exchequer.[16]

In the early months of 1930 the rise in unemployment gave rise to a spate of new claims for unemployment benefit. Once more the Unemployment Fund recorded a growing deficit. Margaret Bondfield was forced to go back on her previous plan of cutting the Fund's borrowing requirement, and forced to increase it to £50 million in March and £60 million in July.[17] Sensing that the Government was drifting into a financial muddle, the Conservatives went on the attack, and Churchill was wheeled into position as big parliamentary gun. In a debate on 28 March he made much play of the Government's about-turn on the borrowing require-ment, quoting Snowden and Bondfield against themselves. Turning to the administration of benefit, he alleged 'a wholesale and scandalous relaxation in the conditions of unemployment benefit'. Under the new law, any man who had paid 30 weeks' contributions could go on drawing benefits indefinitely:

> He need never seek work again. He need never prove that he has sought work again. He cannot be asked to prove that he is genuinely seeking employment. In the never-to-be-forgotten words of the Attorney-General [Sir William Jowitt], he can sit and smoke a pipe until an offer of employment is actually brought to him.[18]

Henceforth Labour ministers were in the dock, with the Conservatives as chief prosecuting counsel. In his budget on 14 April 1930, Snowden, who needed an extra £47 million to balance the books for the coming year, put up the tax on beer, increased surtax and death duties, and raised income tax by 6d. in the pound to 4s.6d. Churchill responded the following day with a debating speech in which he took the opportunity of restating the views on taxation which he had expressed as Chancellor. He attacked the increase in the surtax increase on the grounds that it would impede the creation of wealth: 'If the great incentive to saving and reinvestment on the part of the very rich is impaired, injury will follow to the whole community ... it is this process which has been found in every country, and particularly in the United States of America, to be the most swift and powerful means of rationalising industry, of discovering and gaining and commanding markets, and thus creating new wealth and employment.'[19]

Churchill worked hard enough at his parliamentary duties, but the sparkle was gone, and he was too reliant on stock phrases and points. In May 1930 Sir Oswald Mosley resigned from the Government following the rejection by the Cabinet of his proposals for economic expansion. Mosley had three main ideas, expounded to the House of Commons in his resignation speech on 28 May: a measure of state control over banking and industry; a long-term shift, with the aid of tariffs and import controls, from exports to the home market; and various short-term measures to reduce unemployment, including a three-year road programme. Churchill's response was pedestrian. Ignoring the first two elements, he rejected public works on the grounds that both the Labour Government and its Conservative predecessor had investigated the idea and found it unsatisfactory.[20]

Churchill's lukewarm defence of financial orthodoxy reflected the fact that he was losing his faith in free trade. The doctrines of liberal economics were under attack and Churchill could no longer reconcile the principles he had learnt as a young man with the realities of the world slump. In the course of 1930 the terms of the debate within the Conservative party shifted strongly in favour of Chamberlain and the Protectionists. As industries contracted, and unemployment rose, businessmen began to plead for the introduction of a tariff shelter. The momentum was accelerated by the Empire Crusade. In February the two press lords, dissatisfied with Baldwin's equivocations, set up the United Empire party which, with the *Daily Mail*, and the *Daily Express* acting as loudspeakers, agitated in the constituencies and attacked Baldwin. The next step was to put up United Empire candidates against Conservative candidates who refused to support the campaign. Guerrilla warfare rumbled on, and Baldwin's authority seemed to come and go like the face of the Cheshire cat.

Churchill was rattled by the Empire Crusade. Turning down in March a request from Conservative Central Office to make speeches in the country he explained that 'being attacked by the Beaverbrook-Rothermere party, I have to fix a large number of small meetings to save my constituency'.[21] In 1903 Churchill had rejected Balfour's compromise formula on protection. But now he grasped eagerly at a compromise devised by Baldwin to conciliate his critics while retaining room for manoeuvre. On 4 March Baldwin announced his new policy. The Conservatives would enter the next general election with no commitment to food taxes. But the next Conservative Government would summon an imperial economic conference and if there should then emerge from it an agreement to tax imports of food, the issue would be put to the electorate at a referendum.

Churchill was delighted by the formula and made it plain that in his view Beaverbrook and Rothermere should accept it in the best interests of the party, which hinged on the necessity of winning over the Liberal vote. The effect of the campaign, he maintained, had been to drive the Liberals into the arms of Labour. The Conservatives ought to concentrate instead upon an agreed programme of electoral reform to enable the two non-socialist parties to find common ground.[22]

Heedless of Churchill, and impatient of Baldwin, the press lords pushed on. Churchill, who wanted the whole issue to go away, conceived an ingenious plan for distancing himself from the controversy. The House of Commons, he argued, was well suited to deal with the ordinary type of party question such as had occupied it before 1914. But it was inadequate for the handling of economic problems, which could only be cured 'when expert, disinterested, free, and non-party proposals are shaped by persons specially competent in industry, business and finance'.[23] There should therefore be an economic sub-Parliament of experts to debate the economy and devise a programme.

In June, Churchill elaborated the case for an Economic Parliament in his Romanes lecture at the University of Oxford. He began by setting out with great clarity the classical economic doctrines which he had learnt in his youth, and expounded once more as Chancellor of the Exchequer. These doctrines had for more than a century 'found their citadels in the Treasury and the Bank of England'. Free imports, the repayment of debt, rigorous economy, a profound distrust of state-stimulated industry or borrowing to create employment, an absolute reliance on private enterprise, these principles were 'all part of one general economic conception, amplified and expounded in all the Victorian text-books'. But whatever might be thought of these doctrines, he continued, 'we can clearly see that they do not correspond to what is going on now.' For a politician who only twelve months previously had been championing Treasury orthodoxies, this was a startling admission, and others were to follow:

The growth of public opinion, and still more of voting opinion, violently and instinctively rejects many features of this massive creed. No one, for instance, will agree that wages should be settled only by the higgling of the market. No one would agree that modern world-dislocation of industry ... should simply be met by preaching thrift and zeal to the displaced worker. Few would agree that private enterprise is the sole agency by which fruitful economic activities can be launched or conducted. An adverse conviction on all these points is general, and practice has long outstripped conviction. The climate of opinion in which we live today assigns the highest importance to minimum standards of life and labour ... It is admitted increasingly every day that the State should interfere in industry – some say by tariffs, some by credits, some say by direct control, and all by workshop regulation; and far-reaching structures of law are already in existence under several of these heads.[24]

The root problem, as Churchill saw it, was 'the strange discordance between the consuming and producing power'. Every attempt to solve the riddle so far had failed, 'from the extremes of Communism in Russia to the extremes of Capitalism in the United States'. At home the House of Commons was so dominated by the 'antagonisms of class and party', and the need for popular election cries, that it was ill-adapted to deal with economic policy. Hence the need for a Parliament of experts. He proposed that the traditional Parliament should choose 'in proportion to its party groupings a subordinate Economic Parliament of say one-fifth of its numbers', to reach its conclusions by voting.[25]

Some of Churchill's critics, detecting in his proposal shades of Mussolini's corporate state, have hinted at fascist influence. There is not much in this. Churchill was arguing for a debate side by side with Parliament, not for a system of corporate representation to replace or diminish Parliament. The idea had, indeed, an English ancestry. 'He didn't seem to be aware', wrote H.A.L. Fisher, the Warden of New College, 'that the Sidney Webbs, Alfred Milner and Arthur Henderson had all been there before him in suggesting a measure of this kind.'[26] Ramsay MacDonald had already taken a step along the road through the appointment, in January 1930, of an Economic Advisory Council which included economists, businessmen and trade unionists.

Churchill was trying to beat a dignified retreat from Free Trade by delegating economic policy to an expert consensus. The Economic Parliament would put an end to the polarised debate between free trade and protection, raising it to the plane of 'high, cold, technical, and dispassionate or disinterested decision'.[27] Behind the scenes, he continued to fume against the press lords and the Empire Crusade. 'He says it will hand over South America to the Yanks, split the Empire for ever, and shatter the Conservative party into smithereens', wrote Harold Nicolson in July.[28] Yet he could not bring himself to rebel against the march of events.

At the long-awaited Imperial Conference at the end of September the Canadian Prime Minister, R.B. Bennett, proposed a 10 per cent tariff or 10 per cent increase in tariff on all imports into the Empire – not Beaverbrook's plan of Empire Free Trade, but a halfway house he was ready to endorse. The Labour Government brushed the plan aside. Baldwin, urged along the road by Neville Chamberlain and Amery, considered with his colleagues in the Shadow Cabinet a draft statement accepting the proposal in principle as the basis of Conservative policy at the next general election. The loophole of the referendum was discarded. Churchill demurred and Baldwin wrote him a letter anticipating a break, but expressing the hope that Churchill would remain. When the statement was issued, it proved sufficiently vague for Churchill to write to Baldwin accepting it, but with an important caveat: 'I cannot consent to the protective taxation of staple foods.'[29]

Baldwin was under very great pressure. Beaverbrook and Rothermere had again taken the offensive and were running a United Empire candidate against the official Conservative in a by-election at South Paddington. On 20 October Beaverbrook demanded to know whether Baldwin would accept duties, not simply quotas, on foreign foodstuffs. In a letter to *The Times* on 22 October Baldwin asked that he be given 'a completely free hand to discuss with the Dominions all the alternative methods, including taxation on foreign foodstuffs'. Churchill was even prepared to swallow this. 'Winston has not yet given tongue on our manifesto', wrote Baldwin to Davidson the following day. 'He told Freddie Guest that he was in doubt whether to "lay an egg" or not. To which Freddie replied, "when in doubt whether to lay an egg or not, don't lay it." '[30] Here was prudent advice. On 30 October the United Empire candidate romped home to victory in South Paddington.

\*

Since the autumn of 1929 there had been rumblings of discontent in the Conservative party over Baldwin's position on India. On 31 October 1929 the Viceroy of India, Lord Irwin, issued on behalf of the Liberal Government a declaration promising that India would ultimately achieve Dominion status. Many Conservatives were deeply disturbed when Baldwin lent his approval to the Declaration in a parliamentary debate on 7 November. 'Throughout the debate', Samuel Hoare reported to the Viceroy, 'Winston was almost demented with fury . . . '[31] The Government then proposed to summon a Round Table Conference in London at which Indian representatives would enter into negotiations about constitutional reform. Baldwin supported the conference but Churchill opposed it. In September 1930 he wrote to Baldwin to warn him that 'very strong currents of feeling and even passion are moving under the stagnant surface of our affairs, and I must confess myself to care more about this business than anything else in public life.'[32]

Churchill was prepared to accept provincial self-government as recommended by the Report of the Simon Commission in June 1930. But when the Round Table Conference opened in November, the discussion moved on to the creation of an all-India federation with an all-India assembly and a measure of self-government at the centre. To this Churchill and his diehard allies were deeply opposed. At the conclusion of the conference on 19 January 1931, MacDonald announced that the Government would now work towards a federal constitution. On 26 January, Baldwin aligned himself firmly with MacDonald in the House of Commons. The following day, Churchill wrote to Baldwin resigning from the Shadow Cabinet and immediately embarked on a campaign to mobilise the Conservative party against the transfer of power in India.[33]

It is often said that Churchill devoted himself to one theme at a time, to the exclusion of all else. But in taking up India he did not forget the tariff question. The India diehards with whom he was now allied were in the main Protectionists like Sir Henry Page-Croft or John Gretton. As the India campaign accelerated, Churchill took care to advertise his conversion to protectionism and, with his customary rhetorical skill, to blend it with the imperial theme. In the budget debate of April 1931 he went out of his way to express his agreement with Neville Chamberlain on the tariff question:

> I agree with my right hon. Friend the Member for Edgbaston in what he said yesterday. The compulsive need for revenue must bring the tariff. The tariff . . . must become the agency by which the growing importance of the home market must be recognised. The institution of the tariff will afford occasion for striking those new bargains with foreign countries which are necessary and which, wisely handled, may play an important part in welding together the production and consumption of our Empire, before the present process of dispersal and disintegration has reached its fatal end.[34]

Underlying Churchill's reactions to the world slump lay a buoyant confidence in the recuperative powers of capitalism. At a lunch party at Chartwell in August 1930 he was challenged by a youthful guest who claimed that the capitalist order was breaking down. 'More mush!' Churchill retorted. 'Capitalism will right itself. What is Capitalism? It is merely the observance of contract, that's all. That's why it will survive. At present it is depressed all over the world. It is not symptomatic of failure as you suppose.'[35] Churchill's words were backed by deeds. In a remarkable footnote Martin Gilbert has compiled a list of Churchill's pre-tax literary earnings from 1929 to 1937, totalling more than £100,000. Much of this he invested in shares, starting at the bottom of the market in the depression. Early in 1930 he invested £2,969 in Marks and Spencer. During 1931 he invested heavily in the United States, purchasing £6,760 of shares in General Motors. In July 1932 he wrote to his stockbroker Horace Vickers: 'I do not think America is going to smash. On the contrary I believe that they will quite soon begin to recover.'[36] Churchill believed that the United States would serve the world as the engine of recovery. In February 1931 he drew for the House of Commons a glowing picture of his mother's country:

> It is my belief that the United States, before the great crash of October 1929, had come nearer to achieving the joint ideals of capital and labour than any community at any time. There we had the inhabitants of 20,000,000 or 25,000,000 homes making, by mass production under private enterprise, under ruthless Free Trade within a vast protected Empire, a couple of hundred standardised articles which were consumed by those very same 25,000,000 households whose members produced them. There we had capital interested in high wages and short hours for the workers, and there we had workmen vigilantly guarding the interests of the industries with which they felt themselves identified.

Churchill attributed the collapse of the American economy to an 'orgy of speculation', but predicted that it would recover, and with it a large part of the world economy.[37] Churchill was speaking in a debate on unemployment insurance in which he strongly attacked the Labour Government. He wanted to show, as he explained to Robert Boothby, 'that it is my earnest desire to help the party as much as possible'.

The India campaign was going very well and it was generally expected that Baldwin, who was under attack from all sides, would shortly resign the party leadership. Churchill was hopeful of succeeding him. On 26 February he wrote to Clementine: 'It is astonishing looking back over the past six weeks what a change has been brought in my position ... Anything may happen now if opinion has time to develop.'[38]

Churchill's action was generally interpreted at the time as a blatant personal bid for power. L.S. Amery wrote in his diary:

> I wish it had happened over the food duties and not over India. By choosing the latter as his pretext Winston is playing for the support of Rothermere and even to some extent of Max and is incidentally covering himself in his own constituency. I imagine his game is to be a lonely and formidable figure available as a possible Prime Minister in a confused situation later on.[39]

Churchill was 56 by now and time was running out. As he had confided to Clementine, the premiership was the only goal for which he remained in politics. His India campaign bore all the hallmarks of a last bid for the glittering prize. But calculation was interwoven with conviction. Amery himself was convinced that Churchill was a politician of incorrigibly old-fashioned outlook. Churchill's belief in the 'White Man's Burden' made it impossible for him to accept the notion that India might one day be governed by Indians.

On 1 March 1931 Baldwin decided to quit. But at the eleventh hour he changed his mind, fought back, denounced Beaverbrook and Rothermere, and re-established his authority. With hindsight we can see that the leadership crisis was over. Churchill's bid for power had failed, and Baldwin's recovery turned Neville Chamberlain, his principal defender, into the undisputed heir-apparent. 'Thus', wrote Charles Loch Mowat, 'was the stage set for the thirties: the clash of personalities and policies had blindly decided who was to dominate the policy and character of the British government in the tragic decade, and who was to be left out of office.'[40] Churchill did not sense the turn of the tide: buoyed up by the widespread support he was receiving over India, he marched steadily forward into a historical cul-de-sac.

As unemployment increased, the financial troubles of the Labour Government deepened. When Philip Snowden presented his second budget, in April 1931, Churchill revelled in the occasion. Snowden, who had condemned with great severity Churchill's ingenious techniques for balancing the budget, had been forced to adopt similar expedients. 'Winston sitting next to me', wrote Amery, 'could not restrain his delight and appreciation of a Budget which out-Winstoned Winston in its robbing of henroosts and resolute indifference to the future. The whole thing is of course a gamble on prosperity returning in the next few months.'[41] When Churchill spoke in the debate he poked much fun at Snowden and congratulated him on the abandonment of Socialism.

By June 1931 the Opposition parties were in full cry over the rising deficit of the Unemployment Insurance Fund, and the growing cost of transitional benefit. Churchill joined in the attack. On 18 June the Government introduced a bill to increase the borrowing rights of the Insurance Fund from £90 million to £115 million. Churchill opposed the bill. 'There has come into existence', he said, 'a new vested interest, a dole vested interest, and behind it is enforced by the dole vote.' Taking a stand once more upon his own record in social insurance he declared:

I hold most strongly that a line must be drawn without delay, clear and unmistakeable, between insurance and assistance. The insured pay for themselves: let them draw the benefits they have purchased by State organised thrift. The assisted stand in another category: they must be provided for according to their needs . . .

I repudiate the suggestions of an inhumanitarian position on this side of the House . . . All my life I have been engaged at frequent intervals, short intervals, in dealing with great schemes of insurance . . . All these great schemes, which were largely copied from Germany and which derived inspiration from that great Empire built by Bismarck, who saw and understood how a nation could be made strong and its people united . . . now constitute the characteristic social bulwark of the British working classes.[42]

Churchill did not explain what sacrifices would be required of workers who were on the dole.

By July, rumours were circulating that MacDonald and Baldwin were planning a National Government to deal with the financial crisis. On 21 July, at a meeting at Archibald Sinclair's home, Lloyd George discussed the position with Churchill and Oswald Mosley, dangling before them the prospect of a united Opposition under his leadership. Mosley, who had broken away from Labour to found his own organisation, the New Party, was tempted. But Churchill refused to be drawn. He was, no doubt, reluctant to abandon the path he had worked out for himself, and submit once more to the leadership of Lloyd George.

Shortly after this Lloyd George fell ill, while Churchill set off on holiday to the south of France. By the second week of August the Government was in a deep financial and political crisis. The pound was falling sharply on the foreign exchanges and there was an imminent risk that Britain would be forced off the Gold Standard. To prop up the pound, the Government entered into negotiations with bankers in New York for an emergency loan. The bankers insisted that the Government must not only balance the budget but cut unemployment benefit by 10 per cent. The Cabinet split and on 24 August MacDonald resigned. To the astonishment of his colleagues he announced on his return from Buckingham Palace that he had accepted an invitation from the King to form a National Government for the purpose of carrying through emergency measures, after which normal party politics would resume and a general election take place. MacDonald's colleagues were dumbfounded. All but Thomas, Snowden, and Lord Sankey refused to support a National Government, and went into opposition under the leadership of Arthur Henderson. The Conservatives under Baldwin, and the Liberals – led, in the absence of Lloyd George by Herbert Samuel – agreed to participate, and the National Government was formed on 25 August. Owing to his differences with Baldwin and MacDonald over India, Churchill was not invited to serve, nor did he expect an invitation. Deliberately detached from the crisis, he was painting at Juan-les-Pins, and keeping his thoughts to himself.

Speaking in the House of Commons on 8 September, Churchill argued that there would be no revival of British industry until a tariff were proclaimed. He urged the Government to go to the country as soon as possible with a protectionist programme, and appealed to the Liberals to co-operate.[43] It is fascinating that Churchill, who had so often chided the Conservative party for its protectionist tendencies, was now in the vanguard of the movement for tariffs, while Baldwin and his party were bogged down by their alliance with the Free Trade elements in the National Government. When Snowden introduced, on 10 September, an emergency budget to raise taxes and cut expenditure Churchill told a meeting in his constituency: 'This budget represents the last expiring convulsion of Treasury Cobdenism. I have thrown that off for ever.'[44] Forceful phrases: but Churchill was going through a bad patch. Robert Bruce Lockhart, a Beaverbrook journalist who saw much of Churchill at this period, observed in his diary: 'Winston is very weak these days – like a schoolboy trying to get into the team. He is nearly always slightly the worse for drink.'[45]

Snowden's budget failed to prevent a continued flight from sterling and on 21 September the Government abandoned the Gold Standard. Churchill's response was to urge 'a measure of protection for industry and agriculture' – an explicit endorsement of taxes on food as well as manufactured goods.[46] On 5 October the Cabinet decided to call an election. There was to be no commitment to tariffs on the part of the Government as a whole, but Conservatives would be free to put the case for protection while MacDonald appealed vaguely to the electorate for a 'doctor's mandate'. On 27 October the National Government was returned to power with a stupendous landslide victory, winning 556 seats to Labour's 52. In the Epping constituency Churchill was opposed by Comyns Carr, a Free Trade Liberal, and a self-sacrificing Labour candidate, James Ranger. The result was as follows:

| | |
|---|---|
| W.S. Churchill (Con) | 35,956 |
| A.S. Comyns Carr (Lib) | 15,670 |
| J. Ranger (Lab) | 4,713 |

In the Government reshuffle which followed Neville Chamberlain was appointed Chancellor of the Exchequer in place of Snowden, and Sir John Simon was elevated to the Foreign Office. But there was no place for Churchill or Lloyd George. Churchill explained to the House of Commons that his attitude towards the new Government would be one of 'disciminating benevolence'. But, he warned, 'if the National Government were to lead to national impotence there would be a terrible disappointment, with a terrible reckoning to follow.'[47] A long and critical speech to the House on India, on 3 December, gave warning of the line Churchill intended to take.

*

In the newly-elected National Government the Conservatives moved swiftly to introduce protectionism. This produced a Cabinet crisis in which the Liberal ministers, led by the Home Secretary Sir Herbert Samuel, threatened to resign but were persuaded to remain in office on the basis of an 'agreement to differ', which allowed them to protest against the policies of their own Government. On 4 February 1932 Neville Chamberlain introduced the Import Duties Bill which proposed a general duty of 10 per cent on almost all manufactured goods and some foodstuffs, excluding meat and wheat. Goods from within the Empire were to be exempt, pending the Imperial Economic Conference due to be held in Ottawa during the summer. The Treasury was granted authority to introduce additional duties if they were recommended by a new body, the Import Duties Advisory Committee under Sir George May. On 21 April the committee reported in favour of a substantial round of tariff increases, including a raising of the duty on manufactured goods to 20 per cent.

Like other critics of the Government Churchill ridiculed the 'agreement to differ' and the embarrassing predicament of Samuel, whose front-bench statements contradicted those of his colleagues. But on the main issue, Churchill announced that he would accept the Government's policy in its entirety. As for the warnings he had once given about the inevitable corruption of a tariff policy by vested interests, he now declared that his previous fears had been groundless: 'There has been no scramble of great interests, no log-rolling, bribery or corruption, none!'[48]

The Cabinet had now to grasp the thorny problem of imperial preference. At the Imperial Economic Conference, which opened in Ottawa on 21 July, the British Government initiated a complex round of bargaining with the Dominions. The British were prepared to grant preference to Dominion foodstuffs in return for action by the Dominions to cut the duties imposed on manufactured goods from Britain. But as the Dominions were trying to develop their own industries, they were reluctant to expose them to British competition. They nevertheless demanded that Britain introduce duties on foreign meat and wheat in order to yield an imperial preference. After prolonged and acrimonious negotiations, twelve agreements were signed. The British agreed to introduce a duty on wheat, to reduce foreign meat imports by quota, and to retain the existing preferences on imperial foodstuffs. The Dominions, instead of cutting the duties on British manufactures, agreed to impose a higher rate of duty on foreign manufactures. The Ottawa agreements were an anti-climax which disappointed the more ardent imperialists. On the other hand they were too rich for the digestion of Samuel and the other Liberal ministers, who resigned on 28 September.

Churchill, who resented the Dominion pressure for increased food taxes, privately poured contempt on what he called 'Rottowa'. But in public he was mindful of his manners and merely commented: 'There may be a good many people who do not think much of Ottawa now, but perhaps their children may think more of it, and their grandchildren more still.'[49]

Churchill occasionally criticised the Government for its lack of drive over unemployment. In February 1933 the Chancellor of the Exchequer, Neville Chamberlain, foolishly predicted that high levels of unemployment would persist for the next ten years. Churchill delivered a slashing attack on him. 'Ten years!' he exclaimed. 'I see the figure of the breadwinner, the father of the family, sitting in his chair in the cottage. Ten years!' Churchill argued that by timely measures the previous year, the Government could have created 250,000 jobs.[50]

Although Churchill favoured a stimulus to home demand, he believed this could only act as a palliative. Likewise tariffs, though useful, were no panacea. Churchill's prescription for the slump was international action to raise price levels. He first unfolded his analysis in the budget debates of September 1931, at a time when Britain still adhered to the Gold Standard. The root cause of the depression, he argued, was not the Gold Standard itself, but the shortage of gold due to its accumulation by France and the United States, who between them held two-thirds of the world's stock, and kept one-third permanently out of circulation. 'It has been dug up out of a hole in Africa', Churchill explained, 'and put down in another hole that is even more inaccessible in Europe and America.' As gold became dearer, so prices fell and credit was destroyed. Unless the supply of gold were increased, or some new medium of exchange developed, 'the continued fall in prices and the continued destruction of credit will reduce our civilisation surely, and in no very great interval of time, to a bleak and ferocious barbarism.' Churchill therefore proposed that the British Government should summon an international conference to raise the level of prices.[51] In later speeches Churchill attributed the problem to the transfer of gold to France and the United States in settlement of war debts. Churchill appears to have borrowed his thesis of the maldistribution of gold from the Swedish economist Gustav Cassel, 'whose extraordinary pregnant and suggestive statements have appeared from time to time in recent years.'[52]

Although Britain abandoned the Gold Standard in November 1931, and the pound was devalued, the other great world currency, the dollar, was still linked to gold. Churchill now hoped that the United States would abandon gold and join with Britain in an expansionist monetary policy. In December 1931 he left England to embark on a lucrative lecture tour of the United States. It was nearly terminated when, on 12 December, Churchill looked the wrong way while crossing Fifth Avenue, and was knocked down by an oncoming taxi. But he recovered and gave a series of addresses on the theme of 'The Pathway of the English-Speaking Peoples'. Specifically he proposed, in a speech at Cleveland, Ohio, that the two nations should agree to revalue commodity prices at the 1928 level. Writing to Robert Boothby from Chicago, he explained:

> I have gone the whole hog against gold. To hell with it! It has been used as a vile trap to destroy us. I would pay the rest of the American Debt in gold as long as the gold lasted, and then say – "Hence-forward, we will only pay in goods. Pray specify what goods you desire."
>
> 'Surely it has become a public necessity to get rid of Montagu Norman. No man has ever been so stultified as he has in his fourteen years' policy.[53]

Shortly after this Boothby called for Norman's resignation in a speech to the House.

Churchill hammered home his attack on the American Gold Standard in two major speeches in the House and a broadcast to the United States.[54] The election of Franklin D. Roosevelt to the Presidency in November 1932, and the opening stages of the New Deal, raised Churchill's hopes. He was delighted when, on 6 March 1933, Roosevelt suspended the Gold Standard. Shortly after this Roosevelt began a deliberate policy of raising prices. 'From that moment', writes Douglas Jay, 'prices began to rise in commodity markets, as one purchaser after another tried to get in first.

Gradually, through the summer months of 1933, the ripple spread round the world.'[55] 'I for one frankly rejoice', Churchill told the House in July 1933.[56] But one other obstacle to recovery remained. Ever since 1919 Churchill had regarded the gigantic National Debt resulting from the First World War as a burden on the economy. He now urged that Britain should follow the example of other countries in writing down the value of the debt. At a constituency meeting in August 1933 he declared:

> This cancer of unemployment is eating out the heart of the people. Here in the south – the prosperous, ancient, long-settled Conservative south – we see no serious unemployment. But that is nothing to what is happening in the north, or in the poorer working-class areas.
>
> I can only say that reform of the monetary system so as to procure a steady recovery in the value of new effort compared to old debts and fixed charges is an absolutely necessary factor in revival here at home. We should all watch with sympathy and earnest attention the heroic experiment which the President of the United States is making. If he fails it will be not only an American, but a world disaster. For myself I put far more hope in the resolute mental energy of President Roosevelt than in the venerable and chilling orthodoxy of Mr Montagu Norman.[57]

With hindsight, Churchill's campaign for Anglo-American co-operation can be seen as a rehearsal on the economic plane of his efforts to achieve an Anglo-American alliance in 1940–1. In 1933 the time was not yet ripe. Although Roosevelt took the dollar off the Gold Standard, he did not intend this as a prelude to the expansion of world trade through international currency agreements. On 12 June 1933 a World Economic Conference opened in London with an ambitious agenda for the liberalisation of world trade. But on 3 July it was torpedoed by a message from Roosevelt announcing that the United States rejected the idea of a currency agreement. Henceforth the United States pursued, like Britain and Germany, a policy of turning inward to develop the home market. Two years later Churchill was to deplore Roosevelt's action as 'a milestone on the downward march of human fortunes'.[58] But he never entirely lost faith in his own vision of Utopia: the union of the two main branches of the 'English-Speaking Peoples'. In 1937 he sent Roosevelt a sketch of 'the currency of the future': a bank note with the pound and dollar signs intertwined. Roosevelt kept it on his desk, with a lot of other bric-a-brac.[59]

Initially Churchill expressed great admiration for the New Deal. But in economic affairs he was no collectivist and soon reacted against the growing intervention of the federal government in capitalist operations. He criticised Roosevelt for 'controlling all the businesses of the United States and regulating so minutely and in such a short time the delicate interplay between capital and labour'. He attacked 'the extension of the activities of the Executive' and the 'pillorying by irresponsible agitators' of business leaders. As a shrewd American historian puts it:

> Churchill's response to the New Deal was similar to that of the conservative Democrats who, after the passing of the first cooperative planning phase, formed the anti-New Deal Liberty League, and it was somewhat like that of the old American Progressives who were alienated by the President's increasingly collectivist impulse.[60]

In January 1935 Lloyd George outlined a New Deal for Britain in a speech at Bangor. Essentially this was a repeat performance of his 1929 programme of loan-financed public works. Housing, roads, railways, telephones and electricity were all to be included in the Lloyd George plan of national development. Churchill put out a statement to the press announcing that Lloyd George's proposals were 'virile and sober' and deserved 'the closest attention'. Churchill's tactic, like that of the Government, was to humour Lloyd George while keeping him and his proposals at a distance. Instead of following up his press statement with a speech in Lloyd George's favour, he maintained a convenient silence. The Government invited Lloyd George to a series of meetings at which he was invited to discuss his proposals, and there was some talk of his return to office. But when in June 1935 Baldwin stepped into MacDonald's shoes as Prime Minister, there was no place for Lloyd George.[61]

By 1935 the level of unemployment was no longer such a burning issue in British politics. A revival of economic activity had begun in 1933 and was to continue, except for a sharp but temporary relapse in 1937, up until the outbreak of war. The number of registered unemployed fell from 2,955,000 in January 1933 to 1,622,000 by December 1936. This latter figure still represented an unemployment rate of 12 per cent, heavily concentrated in the depressed areas of south Wales, the north of England, and the west of Scotland. The Jarrow March of October 1936, a moral demonstration on behalf of a town where three-quarters of the population were out of work, bore witness to the severity of the slump in certain regions. Yet from the point of view of the National Government, the incoming tide of recovery was of greater importance than the stagnant pools which remained.

When Churchill spoke in the budget debate of April 1936 he listed the disasters which had befallen the economy since 1929. But his tone was optimistic and he was full of praise for the Chancellor, Neville Chamberlain. The budget was balanced, interest rates were low, and protection had compensated for the decline of exports by increasing demand at home. Churchill declared that while he was still attached to the theory of Free Trade, he gave wholehearted support to 'the Protectionist experiment':

> I hope and trust that, now we have embarked on Protection, the Government will try to make a success of it . . . that they will do what they think is right in science, and not just think how far they can carry certain Free Trade members of the Government with them.[62]

As far as Churchill was concerned, the worst of the slump was over and Britain was firmly on the road to recovery.

*

Churchill's commentary on the slump attracted little attention after his resignation as Shadow Chancellor in January 1931. But it is a reminder of the fact that during the 1930s Churchill was by no means a rebel on all fronts. In economic affairs he was in the main a supporter of the National Government. The other interesting feature is the connection between internal and external affairs in his thinking. The slump set him thinking about Anglo-American relations. Similarly, throughout the 1930s, his conceptions of imperial and foreign policy reacted on his position in domestic politics.

Churchill's antagonism to the policies of MacDonald, Baldwin and Chamberlain arose from the conviction that Britain was a great power in decline. This idea first crystallised in his mind during the Labour Government of 1929–1931. The promise of Dominion status for India, the dismissal of his friend Lord Lloyd as High Commissioner in Egypt, and the London Naval Treaty, appeared to him to form a pattern of retreat and surrender. In March 1931, in his rectorial address at Edinburgh University, Churchill warned:

> The evils and dangers of which I speak are of slow growth, and their cure can only be gradual. Unless Great Britain is able by a united and well-instructed effort to grapple with her economic problems, and unless she is worthy to be the heart of her world-wide establishment, you here in this hall today will live long enough to lose

not only your inheritance, but your livelihood. The continuance of our present confusion and disintegration will reduce us within a generation, and perhaps sooner, to the degree of States like Holland and Portugal, which nursed valiant races and held great possessions, but were stripped of them in the crush and competition of the world ... If Great Britain loses her Empire and India and her share in world trade and her sea power, she would be like a vast whale stranded in one of your Scottish bays, which swam in upon the tide and then was left to choke and rot upon the sands.[63]

The title of Churchill's address on this occasion was: 'The Present Decline of Parliamentary Government in Great Britain.' Churchill believed that the decline of Britain as a great power was a direct consequence of the decline of parliamentary democracy from the high standards of debate and leadership which had prevailed in the past. To appreciate his state of mind we have to recall that by 1930 Churchill was separated from most of the leading politicians of the day by a chasm of experience. He had enjoyed a Cabinet career before 1914: they had not. As Churchill aged – he celebrated his 55th birthday in November 1929 – his politics were overlaid by nostalgia for the past.

In the spring and summer of 1930 he completed *My Early Life*, the story of his childhood and youthful adventures as a subaltern and war correspondent. It was a delightful portrait of a Golden Age which had terminated in 1914, and a golden youth which had perished at Gallipoli. By 1930 many of the leading politicians of his youth had also perished, or withdrawn into obscurity. Asquith had died in 1928, Rosebery in 1929, and Balfour in 1930. The heaviest personal blow for Churchill was the death, on 30 September 1930, of Lord Birkenhead, the boon companion of his youth. 'Last night', wrote Clementine, 'Winston wept for his friend. He said several times "I feel so lonely".'[64] Churchill had always believed in the role of Great Men in history. As he looked back to the period before 1914, it seemed to him that parliamentary democracy had given rise to leaders who were great or almost great, and that since 1918 a great deterioration had taken place.

One of the underlying movements of Churchill's lifetime was the decline in the political power of the landed aristocracy. In 1900 they still formed the governing elite. But gradually they withdrew, or were pushed aside, as businessmen, trade unionists and career politicians took their place. In spite of the fact that he was the grandson of a duke, and often stayed at Blenheim, Churchill in his early career displayed little concern for the fate of the landed classes. He threw in his lot with the Liberals, campaigned for the 'People's Budget' and fought the House of Lords. When he was Chancellor of the Exchequer he shocked the Tory back-benches by raising death duties. In his rhetoric he idealised the capitalist class as wealth-creators, but seldom spoke in praise of the aristocracy. But his autobiography, *My Early Life*, expressed for the first time his regret at the passing of the aristocratic ascendancy in politics. And in June 1934 the death of his much-loved cousin, 'Sunny', the 9th Duke of Marlborough, wrung from him the following lament:

> During the forty-two years he was Duke of Marlborough the organism of English society underwent a complete revolution. The three or four hundred families which had for three or four hundred years guided the fortunes of this nation from a small, struggling community to the headship of a vast and still unconquered Empire lost their authority and control. They became merged peacefully, insensibly, without bloodshed or strife, in a much more powerful but less coherent form of national consciousness; and the class to which the late Duke belonged were not only almost entirely relieved of their political responsibilities, but they were to a very large extent stripped of their property and in many cases driven from their homes. This process may well be judged inevitable and by some people salutary. But it cast a depressing shadow upon the Duke of Marlborough's life. He was always conscious that he belonged to a system which had been destroyed, to a society which had passed away, and he foresaw with not ill-founded apprehension that the world tides which were flowing would remorselessly wash away all that was left.[65]

In part, Churchill attributed Britain's decline as a great power to the advance of democracy and the introduction of universal franchise. As he wrote to his son Randolph, in January 1930: 'It may well be that the historians of the future will record that within a generation of the poor silly people all getting the votes they clamoured for they squandered the treasure which five centuries of wisdom and victory had amassed.'[66] Commenting in July 1931 on the qualities of Ramsay MacDonald he wrote:

> It may well be that Mr MacDonald is the type of Prime Minister most in accord with the public mood and wish. The vast, vague, well-meaning electorate of today like the men who never say anything startling, men who cover State action and policy with a glossy surface of well-sounding phrases and platitudes . . . men who know how to drift, placidly and at the same time adroitly, with the movement of the year and the month.[67]

In his Edinburgh address Churchill recalled that when he first entered politics, a Member of Parliament 'could easily address every person who meant to vote and wished to hear him'. But the greater the number of electors, the smaller the proportion who took an interest in public affairs: 'A sort of universal mush and sloppiness has descended on us, and issues are not brought to the clear-cut cleavages of earlier times.' Among the remedies he proposed was his plan for an Economic Sub-Parliament. More surprising was his revival of the case for constitutional reform, with a reformed second chamber representative of the regions, and based on devolved regional assemblies:

Could not the House of Commons be relieved of a mass of controversial business which could far better be fought out within a national framework in extensive local areas? Should we not draw to these new centres fresh streams of public and political capacity to enrich and nourish our attenuated and largely worn out Parliamentary personnel, and might not these bodies form, by the election of their own members, the main part at least of a Senate worthy to sustain the Imperial cause?[68]

After his speech Churchill toured the university and called in at the Women's Union for tea. Asked whether it was true that he had opposed votes for women, he replied that it was. And what, he was asked, did he think of it now? 'I have got to put up with it,' Churchill replied, and went on to explain why he was still apprehensive of the consequences. In the last quarter of the century, Churchill said, the most important event apart from the Great War had been the emancipation of women, and their assumption of full citizenship. According to the report in the *Scotsman*:

Reminding his audience of the present preponderance of women voters, the Rector uttered a solemn warning, calling upon them to think of the shame that would be theirs if, twenty or twenty-five years from now, it were found that things had gone badly, and that Britain was no longer the power she had been, and people were to say: 'No sooner was the franchise extended than they muddled away the great Empire, the inheritance which rugged centuries had gathered together for them!'[69]

Here then, in Churchill's off-the-cuff remarks over the tea-cups, is the key to his mistrust of post-war democracy. Britain had abandoned the masculine democracy of 1914 for a predominantly feminine democracy since 1928. The traditional case against votes for women was that women, by their nature, belonged to the domestic sphere, while the public spheres of government and empire belonged to men. Evidently Churchill feared that women would be too preoccupied with hearth and home to sustain the politics of Empire.

This also helps to explain the proposals he put forward on several occasions between 1931 and 1934 for the reform of the franchise. In the House of Commons in June 1931 he urged that a second vote should be given 'to every householder or breadwinner at the head of a family, the man or woman who pays the rent or the rates'. This, he believed, would restore 'something of the quality of the old electorate' by drawing a distinction between 'those wage-earners who are really bearing the burden and their grown-up children or dependants who live in the same dwelling'. Churchill claimed that his proposal would not in any way discriminate between the sexes. But as the great majority of heads of households were male, the effect would have been to create a large preponderance of male voters.[70]

Churchill kept up his constitutional arguments for some time. Some observers alleged that his views betrayed fascist tendencies, a suspicion aroused perhaps by his praise of Mussolini, whom he described in a speech to the Anti-Socialist Union in February 1933 as 'the greatest law-giver among living men'.[71] In April 1933 Sir Samuel Hoare, the Secretary for India wrote to Lord Willingdon, the Viceroy of India: 'I believe that at the back of his mind he thinks that he will not only smash the Government but that England is going Fascist and that he, or someone like him, will eventually be able to rule India as Mussolini governs north Africa.'[72] It is certainly true that Churchill was impressed – who could fail to be? – by the collapse of parliamentary democracy in many countries. 'The world is losing faith in democracy,' he declared in the House of Commons on 22 February 1933, a few days after the appointment of Hitler as Chancellor of Germany. 'Look at Europe. Much more than half of Europe has degenerated in this century from Parliaments so hopefully erected in the last into arbitrary or military governments, and the movement is steady everywhere.'[73] In May 1933 he wrote to Lord Linlithgow, a supporter of the Government's India proposals: 'The mild and vague Liberalism of the early years of the twentieth century, the surge of fantastic hopes and illusions that followed the armistice of the Great War have already been superseded by a violent reaction against Parliamentary and electioneering procedure and by the establishment of dictatorships real or veiled in almost every country.'[74]

But it would be preposterous to regard Churchill as a British Mussolini in the making. The conclusion Churchill drew from the decline of parliamentary government in other countries was that a renewed period of nationalism had begun in which the great powers were competing for survival. Hence what Britain required was a much more robust imperial and foreign policy. His remedy for the alleged decline in the quality of British parliamentary democracy was the restoration of the more hierarchical political system of his youth. This was old-fashioned but not sinister.

Apart from universal suffrage, Churchill blamed the intelligentsia for undermining national self-confidence. On 9 February 1933, ten days after Hitler became Chancellor of Germany, the Oxford Union Debating Society carried by 275 votes to 153 the motion 'that this House will in no circumstances fight for its King and Country'. Churchill was shocked and condemned the resolution as an 'abject, squalid, shameless avowal'. A fortnight later Churchill was a guest of the University Conservative Association for a question-and-answer session at the Union. Churchill was upset when laughter greeted his view that Britain needed to rearm in order for us to be 'safe in our Island Home'. 'Churchill', writes Martin Gilbert, 'was not to forget this laughter.' Meanwhile Randolph Churchill, a recent undergraduate, prevailed upon the Oxford Union to allow him to return for another debate in which he moved the rejection of the 'King and Country' resolution. So unpopular was Randolph that a record number of students attended the debate and he was defeated by 138 votes to 750.[75]

Churchill did not comprehend the pacific inclinations of the young, or indeed the National Government's faith in disarmament conferences. In a St George's Day speech of 1933, he laid the blame on left-wing political thought:

> The worst difficulties from which we suffer do not come from without. They do not come from the cottages of the wage-earners ... Our difficulties come from the mood of unwarrantable self-abasement into which we have been cast by a powerful section of our intellectuals. They come from the acceptance of defeatist doctrines by a large proportion of our politicians. But what have they to offer but a vague internationalism, a squalid materialism, and the promise of impossible Utopias?[76]

*

In the early 1930s Churchill sounded reactionary about England, but we must recall the company he was keeping. Throughout his campaign over India, from 1931 to 1935, he was acting in alliance with the diehard wing of the Conservative party. He spoke their language and voiced their belief that the National Government represented a surrender of Tory principle and the acceptance of 'socialism' in the person of Ramsay MacDonald. The rise of Hitler's Germany led him towards a new position in British politics. From 1936 onwards Churchill began to explore the politics of national unity. He sought to appeal to all in the three main parties who stood for resistance to Nazi aggression. This change of stance was accompanied by a change of rhetoric. No more was heard from Churchill about the decline of parliamentary democracy or the debilitating influence of the intellectuals. In a transformation scene that no one could have predicted, he reverted to his political past and raised the tattered flag of liberalism. In party politics, the Liberals were down and almost out. But the spirit of liberalism was very much alive in the public life of the 1930s. When Churchill spoke of the defence of civil liberty against tyranny, or the need for all parties and classes to rally to the defence of the League of Nations, he touched a deep chord of moral uplift with well-practised fingers. In so doing he opened up lines of communication with the Liberal and Labour parties and the trade unions, and began to overcome his reputation as a fellow-traveller of continental fascism.

The question of how to respond to Hitler divided itself into two distinct but overlapping areas of debate: defence and diplomacy. Between 1933 and 1936 Churchill was mainly concerned with defence, and his opinions on foreign policy were not always distinguishable from those of the Government. But in the spring of 1936 he began to expound a Churchillian foreign policy which set him apart from Baldwin and Chamberlain.

When Hitler began to rearm Germany in defiance of the Treaty of Versailles, Churchill warned of the possibility that the *Luftwaffe* could be employed to bomb Britain into submission. From 1934 to 1936 he conducted a highly successful campaign for the acceleration of rearmament in order to achieve 'air parity' with Germany. Since defence was a subject on which the Conservative party had strong convictions, Churchill soon found himself marching at the head of a powerful body which included many elder statesmen of the party. In June 1935, when Baldwin succeeded MacDonald as Prime Minister, he appointed Churchill to the Air Defence Research Committee, a sub-committee of the Committee of Imperial Defence.

Rearmament was an economic as well as a military problem. The Treasury, and the Chancellor of the Exchequer, Neville Chamberlain, had good reason to fear that beyond a certain point rearmament would lead to inflation, industrial unrest, and a balance of payments crisis. Time and again the Treasury sought to restrict expenditure on armaments in order

to protect a vulnerable economy. In February 1936 the Cabinet decided
that rearmament must proceed on the basis of 'business as usual' – there
must be no interference with civilian production. It might be thought that
Churchill, as a former Chancellor of the Exchequer, would appreciate
the financial and economic risks. But there is no evidence to suggest
that he did. For him the only risk that mattered was the risk from Nazi
Germany. He urged the Government to disrupt civilian production and
place the economy on a semi-wartime basis. In August 1935 he wrote to
Cunliffe-Lister, the Secretary for Air: 'We ought forthwith to develop our air
force in a wartime atmosphere not hesitating where necessary to interrupt
or deflect normal industry.'[77] As the Government recognised, one of the
major constraints on aircraft production was the shortage of skilled workers
in the engineering and building trades. Although, therefore, a plan for the
expansion of the RAF might be drawn up on paper, delays were inevitable
unless action were taken to expand the labour supply. In the budget debates
of April 1936 Churchill challenged Neville Chamberlain over the Government's adhesion to 'business as usual', and highlighted the problem
of skilled labour: 'I read in a paper to-day that no meeting had yet taken
place between the Government and the trade unions in regard to questions
of apprenticeship and dilution and transference, without settling which you
cannot possibly expand your munitions production.' Churchill urged the
Government to take effective action to prevent profiteering: 'You will not
get the effective co-operation of the working people unless you can make
sure that there are not a lot of greedy fingers having a rake-off.'[78]

Churchill's ideas encountered strong resistance in Whitehall. In July, he
took part in a deputation of eminent Conservatives which lobbied Baldwin
on defence. Churchill urged that the Government ought to impinge by 25
per cent or 30 per cent on ordinary industrial production. When this proposal was circulated for comment in Whitehall, Sir Richard Hopkins of the
Treasury commented: 'In war conditions it is possible to divert and dilute
labour to a high degree without grave political and social consequences:
in peacetime it is not . . . ' There would also be an alarming effect on
the balance of payments: Churchill's proposal would mean banning the
whole of the armaments and allied trades from exporting their goods.[79]

As such discussions show, Churchill's proposals for rearmament were
generally regarded in Whitehall as economically and socially dangerous.
They were not, of course, intended to be. But Churchill did not worry
about the balance of payments. Nor did he fear industrial unrest. In his
view the important thing about the trade unions was that they could be
relied upon to oppose Nazi Germany. In 1935 he contributed a preface to
the autobiography of David Kirkwood, the former Clydeside shop steward.

In 1917, after his release on Churchill's orders from detention, Kirkwood had distinguished himself by his zeal for war production as the manager of Beardmore's Mile End shell factory in London. In his preface Churchill wrote:

> David Kirkwood and the strong type he represents are the natural foes of tyranny. Gripped in the iron regimentation of the Continent, they would resist with an indomitable, or at the worst desperate, tenacity. Many of his readers have disapproved of his views and actions in the past, and will probably do so in the future. But should the life and freedom of our race again be called in question, we shall all find ourselves together heart and hand.[80]

One of the hallmarks of Churchill's response to Nazi Germany was that from the beginning he condemned the regime for its internal character as a tyranny oppressive of minorities. In view of his praise for Mussolini, he is of course open to the charge of hypocrisy – the familiar hypocrisy whereby democratic nations condemn the crimes committed by enemy states against human rights, but pass over the iniquities of their allies in silence. Ever since 1919 Churchill had vilified the Bolshevik regime as the most barbarous of tyrannies. But from 1933 onwards he fell silent on the iniquities of Stalin's regime. Like a bulldog growling in his sleep, he sometimes dreamed of his old enemy. But in his waking hours the new enemy was Nazi Germany, and he recognised the Soviet Union as a potential ally. In the middle of 1934 Churchill made contact with the new Soviet ambassador in London, Ivan Maisky, and from 1936 Churchill was a regular visitor at the Soviet embassy.[81] Churchill was a transparent Machiavelli; this was no time for denunciations of the Stalinist terror.

Having made up his mind that Nazi Germany was the enemy, he condemned the character of Hitler's regime with utter sincerity, and a strong emotional concern for the plight of the Jews. He also appreciated, from the beginning, the profound ideological hostility of the Liberal and Labour parties to Hitler's regime. But if they detested Hitler, they were also strongly opposed to rearmament and regarded Churchill as the most blatant of warmongers. He for his part hoped nevertheless that out of their concern for parliamentary democracy the Opposition parties would rally to the cause of national defence. At the end of a major speech in Parliament on air defence in November 1934 he addressed an appeal to the Liberal and Labour parties:

> We read almost every day – certainly every week – in their great

popular newspapers the most searching and severe criticism of the existing German régime. Nowhere is that criticism put with greater force and ability and from no quarter is it, I believe, more resented by the present rulers of Germany because it is in the main true ... How can hon. Members opposite reconcile that criticism with the other parts of their policy, which is to cover with contumely and mockery and odium every attempt to secure a modest and reasonable defence to maintain the safety of the country?[82]

Between 1934 and 1936 the Opposition parties moved halfway towards an acceptance of rearmament, clothed in the idealism of the League of Nations. Under the Covenant of the League, the League was entitled to impose economic or military sanctions upon an aggressor state. In the 'Peace Ballot' of 1934–5 conducted by the League of Nations Union, eleven and a half million people were canvassed for their opinions on war and peace. Of these, six and three quarter millions favoured military sanctions 'if necessary'. This result, announced in June 1935, conveyed to British politicians the message that faith in the League – the high moral ground of internationalism – was compatible with rearmament and the national interest.

In August 1935, when Mussolini threatened to attack Abyssinia, the Baldwin Government declared that it would enforce collective security by military means if necessary. At the annual conference of the TUC in September a resolution supporting the Government was carried by a large majority. The following month, at the Labour party conference, a similar resolution was moved by Hugh Dalton on behalf of the national executive. This greatly embarrassed the leader of the party, George Lansbury, a lifelong pacifist, who spoke movingly against the resolution, and offered to resign.

At this point the General Secretary of the Transport and General Workers' Union, Ernest Bevin, strode to the rostrum and, addressing Lansbury, rudely denounced him for 'taking your conscience round from body to body asking to be told what you ought to do with it'.[83] Lansbury resigned and was succeeded as acting chairman of the party by Clement Attlee, who led the party into the general election of November 1935.

Although the Labour party was again beaten decisively at the polls, the election showed that it had made a substantial recovery from the disaster of 1931, electing 154 MPs compared with 46. Attlee was then re-elected as leader of the party. At the same time there was a change of leadership in the Liberal party. The Liberals lost ground in the election, returning 17 MPs in place of the 26 elected in 1931. Among the defeated Liberals was Sir Herbert Samuel, who was replaced as party leader by Sir Archibald Sinclair. In the new Parliament, therefore, the Labour and Liberal parties both had leaders more congenial to Churchill than their predecessors. Attlee had fought at Gallipoli and come away with the conviction that the strategic conception behind it was sound. Sinclair, who had served with Churchill as his second-in-command in the trenches, was a personal friend and almost an adopted son. Like Churchill, he was the son of an American mother.

The Hoare-Laval pact of December 1935, an abortive Anglo-French plan to surrender most of Abyssinia before it was conquered, signalled the abandonment of the League by the British and French Governments. This gave Churchill the opportunity of picking up the cause that had slipped through Baldwin's fingers. In his war memoirs he records that in January 1936 he was 'conscious of a new atmosphere' in which the Liberal and Labour parties, and the supporters of the League of Nations, 'were now prepared to contemplate war against Fascist or Nazi tyranny.'[84] On 7 March Hitler marched his troops into the Rhineland in violation of the Treaty of Versailles. On 26 March Churchill called in the House of Commons for a banding together of all the states threatened by Germany to enforce the Covenant of the League.

Prior to this, Churchill had never been a prominent or consistent supporter of the League of Nations. Now Attlee rose to congratulate him on coming over to 'our side'.[85] Churchill had signalled that he was ready to lead a principled resistance to Nazi aggression. During the following weeks he was approached by various groups with offers of support. Lord Robert Cecil invited him to speak on behalf of the League of Nations Union. Two Foreign Office officials, Sir Robert Vansittart and Reginald Leeper, urged him to lead an all-party campaign to 'educate' public opinion in favour of the League and against Germany. The Anti-Nazi Council, a partly Jewish organisation which had won the support of Sir Walter Citrine, the General Secretary of the TUC, and worked behind the scenes to gather support, invited Churchill to attend their meetings. Shortly afterwards the ANC changed its name to the 'Focus'.[86]

The Focus was a secret network of journalists, politicians, business-men, trade unionists and intellectuals, whose existence was not disclosed until 1963 when one of its financial backers, Eugen Spier, published a short account of its history. Churchill made no mention of it in his war memoirs. A list of 36 prominent members, compiled in November 1936, included Liberal, Tory and Labour MPs; the editor of the *Spectator*, Wilson Harris; the proprietor of *The Economist*, Walter Layton; the editor of the *New Statesman*, Kingsley Martin; Robert Waley-Cohen from the City of London;

J. Arthur Rank from the film industry; and two Oxford professors: Arthur Salter and Gilbert Murray.[87]

The Focus was not a conspiracy to make Churchill Prime Minister. It was a conspiracy to change the course of British foreign policy through propaganda, with Churchill as the chief publicist. But Churchill seized the opportunity of casting himself in the role of national leader. He already stood high in the counsels of the Conservative party as the result of his campaign on air defence. With the aid of Focus he was endeavouring to create a Popular Front of Tory patriots, right-wing trade unionists, and liberal publicists.

The British Left of the 1930s were not only afraid of fascism on the Continent. They were afraid of the National Government and convinced that it represented a threat to civil liberty. In 1934, for example, there was a tremendous outcry against the Incitement to Disaffection Act, which strengthened the laws against seditious literature. Since Churchill enjoyed such notoriety on the Left, he was eager to disarm suspicion by stressing the links between collective security abroad, and the maintenance of civil liberty at home. Speaking at Horsham on 23 July he argued that except for a section of the ruling class, the whole of Britain was libertarian and opposed to Nazism:

I can well imagine some circles of smart society, some groups of wealthy financiers, and the elements in this country which are attracted to the idea of a Government strong enough to keep the working classes in order; people who hate democracy and freedom, I can well imagine such people accommodating themselves fairly easily to Nazi domination. But the trade unionists of Britain, the intellectuals of socialism and radicalism, they could no more bear it than the ordinary British Tory . . .[88]

On 24 September Churchill spoke in Paris, where the Popular Front Government of Leon Blum was in power. Churchill pictured the two parliamentary democracies of Britain and France as united in their hostility to authoritarianism:

How could we bear, nursed as we have been in a free atmosphere, to be gagged and muzzled; to have spies, eavesdroppers and dilators at every corner; to have even private conversations caught up and used against us by the secret police and all their agents and creatures, to be arrested and interned without trial . . .

How could we bear to . . . be turned out on parade by tens

of thousands to march and cheer for this slogan or that; to see philosophers, teachers and authors bullied and toiled to death in concentration camps; to be forced every hour to conceal the natural workings of the human intellect and the pulsations of the human heart? Why, I say that rather than submit to such oppression, there is no length we would not go to.[89]

Churchill knew exactly what he was doing. As he wrote to Randolph on 13 November: 'All the left-wing intelligentsia are coming to look to me for protection, and I will give it wholeheartedly in return for their aid in the rearmament of Britain.'[90]

\*

In the short run, Churchill failed in his bid for the leadership of a broad coalition of forces. The activities of Focus were to culminate in a great meeting at the Albert Hall. As Churchill explained in his war memoirs:

Here on December 3 we gathered many of the leading men in all the parties – strong Tories of the Right Wing earnestly convinced of the national peril; the leaders of the League of Nations Peace Ballot, the representatives of many great Trade Unions, including in the Chair my old opponent of the General Strike, Sir Walter Citrine; the Liberal Party and its leader Sir Archibald Sinclair. We had the feeling that we were on the threshold of not only gaining support for our views, but of making them dominant.[91]

But that same day the news broke of the Abdication Crisis. King Edward VIII was determined to marry an American divorcee, Mrs Wallis Simpson. Baldwin was determined that he must either renounce Mrs Simpson or abdicate. Behind the scenes, Churchill and Beaverbrook were urging the King to resist. It was a lost cause, for as Beaverbrook explained to Churchill: 'Our cock won't fight.' It was lost in another sense, too, for the House of Commons was overwhelmingly against the King. From chivalry perhaps, or in the hope of bringing down Baldwin, Churchill rose in the House of Commons on 7 December to plead for more time for the matter to be debated. By so doing he misjudged the moral atmosphere and more importantly gave the impression that he was playing politics with the monarchy. He was howled down and left the Chamber in disgrace. Harold Nicolson described the affair in one of his letters to Vita Sackville-West:

Winston collapsed utterly in the House yesterday. Bob Boothby was so funny about it. 'I knew', he said, 'that Winston was going to do something dreadful. I had been staying the weekend with him. He was silent and restless and glancing into corners. Now when a dog does that, you know he is about to be sick on the carpet. It is the same with Winston. He managed to hold it for three days, and then comes up to the House and is sick right across the floor.' Which is literally true. He has undone in five minutes the patient reconstruction work of two years.[92]

Churchill himself wrote later:

All the forces I had gathered together on "Arms and the Covenant", of which I conceived myself to be the lynchpin, were estranged or dissolved, and I was myself so smitten in public opinion that it was the almost universal view that my political life was finished.[93]

Churchill greatly exaggerated the effects of the Abdication crisis. The principal reason why his campaign faltered after December 1936 was that 1937 witnessed a relaxation of Anglo-German tensions. The year passed without a major threat or act of aggression by Hitler. Tensions did not rise again until 1938, and by that time a second factor, quite separate from the Abdication crisis, was coming into play. Churchill's campaign for air defence had won him substantial support in the Conservative party. But on foreign policy the majority of Conservatives disagreed with him. Throughout 1937 this latent conflict lay concealed. When Chamberlain succeeded Baldwin as Prime Minister, in May 1937, Churchill was hopeful that Chamberlain would adopt a more robust foreign policy. Chamberlain, however, decided to end the drift by adopting a systematic policy of appeasement. This led to the resignation of his Foreign Secretary, Anthony Eden, in February 1938, and subsequently to the partition and sacrifice of Czechoslovakia by the Munich agreement of September.

The overwhelming majority of Conservatives were enthusiastic supporters of Neville Chamberlain. The little band of anti-appeasers looked to Eden as their leader, and were careful not to associate themselves too closely with Churchill. Churchill was too great a rebel, and his policies too unpopular, for the party to stomach. His uncompromising denunciation of the Munich agreement resulted in his almost complete isolation in the party during the winter of 1938–9. On 17 November he voted in the House in favour of a Labour motion to establish a Ministry of Supply. Only two

Conservative MPs, Brendan Bracken and Harold Macmillan, voted with him. This was the true period of exile in the wilderness, when Churchill was almost forced to break with his party. Conservative Central Office fomented a rebellion against him in the Epping constituency with the aim of depriving him of the Conservative nomination at the next general election. Churchill survived a motion of no confidence, at a meeting of his constituency executive, by three votes to two.[94]

What, meanwhile, of Churchill's connections on the Left? In spite of the Abdication crisis Churchill continued to attend Focus meetings in 1937 and 1938, and there can be no doubt that he made some progress in disarming Liberal and Labour suspicions. Focus had excellent Fleet Street connections and Churchill was no mean publicist himself. Kingsley Martin, the editor of the *New Statesman* and a member of Focus, was a weathervane of left-liberal opinion. After the German occupation of Austria in March 1938, he argued in the *New Statesman* for a broadly-based Government to include Churchill, Eden, and the Liberal and Labour leaders.[95] After the Munich crisis, the two leading Liberal newspapers, the *News Chronicle* and the *Manchester Guardian*, both called for Churchill's inclusion in the Cabinet.[96]

In some quarters the old Labour hostility to Churchill persisted. The *Daily Herald*, the organ of the trade unions, refused to join in the Liberal chorus for the appointment of Churchill to the Cabinet. Three weeks after the Munich crisis Robert Fraser, a leader-writer for the *Herald* wrote to Dalton:

There is only one danger of Fascism, of censorship, of the unification of parties, of national "discipline", and that will come if Chamberlain is overthrown by the Jingoes in his own party, led by Winston, who will then settle down, with his lousy and reactionary friends, to organise the nation on Fascist principles for a war to settle scores with Hitler.[97]

The hostility of the *Herald* almost certainly reflected the views of that most formidable figure, Ernest Bevin. In the pages of *The Record*, the journal of the Transport and General Workers, Bevin denounced the idea of an arrangement between Churchill and Labour:

Those who made this suggestion do not understand the Trade Unions, nor do they give us credit for memory.

Winston Churchill restored the gold standard and upset every wage agreement in the country.

He was the chief protagonist in starving the miners into submission when he was Chancellor.

He was the sponsor of the Trade Disputes and the Trade Unions Act of 1927.

He was responsible for breaking the civil servants away from the Trade Union Congress.

He took office in the Baldwin Government on the pledge to reduce Income Tax; to do this he cut down the defences of the country below those fixed by the Labour Government of 1924.

He also raided the reserves of the Approved Societies. Is it any wonder that he makes no appeal to us![98]

Kingsley Martin, meanwhile, was tunnelling away to promote Churchill. In January 1939 he published an interview with him in which Churchill reassured readers of the *New Statesman* that a war would not result in the suppression of democracy on the home front. Choosing his words with care Churchill defined democracy as 'the freedom of the individual, within the framework of laws passed by Parliament, to order his life as he pleases, and the uniform enforcement of tribunals independent of the executive'. This phrasing clearly allowed for the enactment of conscription and a whole range of other emergency powers.[99] Among the Conservatives, the pendulum began to swing back in Churchill's favour in March 1939, when Hitler's troops marched into the rest of Czechoslovakia. Churchill grew in stature as his critique of appeasement was vindicated by events – or at any rate appeared to be. Within a few weeks he succeeded in building up the position in politics which he had aimed for ever since the spring of 1936. At the beginning of July a well-orchestrated press campaign, led by Lord Camrose's *Daily Telegraph* demanded Churchill's inclusion in the Cabinet. With some conspicuous exceptions, including *The Times* and the *Daily Herald*, Conservative, Liberal and Labour newspapers all joined in.[100] Chamberlain refused to budge, but he recognised that in the event of war Churchill's inclusion in the Government was inevitable. On 3 September 1939 war was declared, and Churchill was appointed First Lord of the Admiralty. So at last Chamberlain was forced to admit to the Cabinet a man he had come to regard, for all his great abilities, as a menace: half-American, half-drunk, pro-Soviet, pro-Zionist, pro-Liberal, pro-Labour and – in short – a Trojan horse within the Tory camp.

# 10

# *The War*
# *At Home*

## 1939–45

Political history is full of unexpected conjunctions, but the events of 1940 gave rise to one of the most unexpected of them all. Churchill, on his line of march, met the British people marching in the same direction. A man who up to 1939 had been out of step in politics with everyone, suddenly found himself at the head of a column of millions of men and women drawn from all classes and parties.

The general public, of course, played little part in raising Churchill to the premiership. Signs of his growing popularity may possibly have strengthened his hand when the moment came to choose a successor to Neville Chamberlain. But the public were not consulted: indeed hardly anyone was. The decision to appoint him was taken at a secret conclave of four Conservative politicians of whom Churchill himself was one. His transformation into a democratic hero was a sequel to the premiership and arose from the convergence of his own fighting spirit with a revival of popular patriotism in the summer of 1940.

In spite of all that has been written on the subject, this fusion between the career of a great eccentric aristocrat, and the worlds of industry and suburbia, remains an astonishing phenomenon. It is hardly sufficient to say that Churchill and the people were united by a common determination to win the war. They must surely have been united by something more: a common culture that bridged the social differences and created, for certain purposes, one nation. Churchill had some insight into the people he led, some comprehension of their problems, and a remarkable ability to communicate the confidence and inspiration he felt.

But if Churchill was in harmony with wartime Britain in some respects, he was at odds with it in others. For the purpose of winning the war he was eager to enlist the support of all parties, and formed a Coalition Government in which Labour and the trade unions were strongly represented. But he remained a Conservative with both a large and a small 'c' and succeeded Chamberlain as leader of the party in October 1940. With his strongly traditional outlook on home affairs, he was out of sympathy with left-wing demands for a 'people's war' and resisted, wherever he could, the growing radicalisation of the home front.

In September 1940 the London correspondent of the *New York Herald Tribune* reported: 'Hitler is doing what centuries of English history have not accomplished – he is breaking down the class structure of England.'[1] The belief that some kind of 'social revolution' was taking place in wartime was commonplace and much exaggerated. But it was certainly true that under the impact of war Britain was becoming a more collectivist and egalitarian society than it had been in the 1930s. Contemporaries noted the growing authority of Labour and the trade unions, the creation of a command economy, the expansion of the social services, and the introduction of steeply progressive rates of taxation. Many welcomed them as signposts on the road to a new social order after the war. But Churchill, emphatically, did not.

\* \* \*

Neville Chamberlain was a reluctant war leader. His ambition was to wage a short and limited war, terminating perhaps in a compromise peace with a more 'moderate' German regime. Such a war could be fought and won by a Conservative Government with a minimum of social and economic dislocation. The exclusion of Labour from power would continue, and once the peace terms were settled, Chamberlain would be able to return to the questions of social reform which had drawn him into politics in the first place.

The illusion that the war would somehow peter out, or end in a stalemate, was widespread during the 'phoney war' which followed the German conquest of Poland in September 1939. For six months Hitler made no further move, and it was easy to conjecture that he too shrank from the prospect of an all-out conflict with Britain and France, and a repetition of the trench warfare of 1914–18. On 4 April 1940 Chamberlain foolishly expressed this mood of wishful thinking in a speech to the Central Council of the Conservative party. Was it not extraordinary, he asked his listeners, that in the opening months of the war Hitler had made no effort to overwhelm Britain and France? Hitler, Chamberlain announced, had 'missed the bus'.

Four days later, the Germans invaded Denmark and Norway. The War

Cabinet immediately decided to despatch a British expeditionary force to central Norway. But the expeditionary force was swiftly overwhelmed by German air power and at the end of April the Government was forced to announce an evacuation. The failure in Norway led to a concerted movement for the overthrow of Chamberlain which reached a climax in a two-day parliamentary debate on 7 and 8 May 1940. On 10 May Churchill was appointed Prime Minister and began to form a Coalition Government.

The key to Churchill's behaviour throughout the period from September 1939 to May 1940 was loyalty to Chamberlain and the Conservative party. In the First World War, the struggle for power between Lloyd George and Asquith had split the Liberals and accelerated the downfall of the party. Churchill and Chamberlain were both determined that, whatever the tensions between them, they would present a united front to the world. In this they succeeded, and the alliance between them was to continue right up to Chamberlain's retirement in September 1940. Conservative unity was preserved, but the transition from Chamberlain to Churchill posed a new challenge for the party. Under the Churchill Government the Conservatives were obliged to share power with Labour and the Liberals. Churchill's appointment as Prime Minister therefore marked the beginning of a shift to the left on the home front.

The downfall of Chamberlain was the result of a growing Tory rebellion against him. Ever since the resignation of Anthony Eden, in February 1938, an 'Eden group' of some 20 Tory back-benchers had acted as a focus of opposition to Chamberlain in the party. After the outbreak of war, and the inclusion of Eden in the Government, they continued to meet under the chairmanship of L.S. Amery, and were known as the 'Amery group'.

The Government Whips had no reason to fear the activities of a small group whose names were familiar to them. But the Whips were slow to appreciate the growing disaffection of hitherto loyal Tory back-benchers, dismayed by the Government's lacklustre conduct of the war. The newly discontented gravitated towards one of two new parliamentary groupings created during the early months of the war: the All-Party group, led by Clement Davies and Eleanor Rathbone, and the Watching Committee, a body which included members of both Houses, under Lord Salisbury. After the defeat in Norway, all three groups decided to press for a change of Government, and frantic lobbying began with the aim of mounting a substantial rebellion against Chamberlain in the House of Commons.

The Labour and Liberal parties had been hoping ever since Munich to bring down Chamberlain. But as minority parties they could not act without substantial support from the Tory back-benches. There was no point in putting down a motion of no confidence in the House if the only effect was to rally the Conservative back-benches behind Chamberlain. In the crisis of May 1940, they were galvanised into action by the Tory rebels, who informed them of the rising tide of discontent on the Government benches.

The first day of the debate, 7 May, demonstrated that the Government was in trouble. On the second day Herbert Morrison announced the Labour party's intention to divide the House by putting down a motion to postpone the adjournment – in effect a motion of no confidence. When the division was called the Government's majority, which if all had been well would have been 213, fell to 81. Some Conservative MPs were unavoidably absent. Nevertheless 40 Conservative MPs voted against Chamberlain, and at least another 40 abstained – enough to sink the Government.

Churchill behaved impeccably towards Chamberlain. The two men were natural rivals and opponents, with all the bad blood of Munich between them. They had frequently differed over the conduct of the war. The Opposition parties had tried to drive a wedge between them by praising Churchill and denigrating Chamberlain. In all these circumstances it would not have been surprising had some fatal quarrel arisen. But Churchill was on his best behaviour. Winding up for the Government, on the second day of the debate, he picked a quarrel with Labour which led to rowdy scenes, and pleaded eloquently with the Conservatives not to abandon Chamberlain. After the division, Chamberlain told Churchill that he could no longer continue as Prime Minister and would have to make way for an all-party Coalition. Churchill urged Chamberlain to fight on, ignore Labour, and try to broaden the Government by including some of the Tory rebels, and the Liberals.[2]

Any possibility that this tactic would succeed was blown away when the rebel Conservatives, meeting under Amery's chairmanship on 9 May, put out a statement announcing that they would agree to support any Prime Minister who could form a National Government – that is, bring in the Labour party. Realising that Labour would almost certainly refuse, and that he would therefore have to go, Chamberlain called a meeting at 4.30 that afternoon to determine the succession. It was attended by Halifax, Churchill and the Conservative Chief Whip, David Margesson.

Chamberlain began by saying that he would have to resign and he was prepared to serve under either Churchill or Halifax. He implied that Churchill might not be able to win Labour support. Margesson then spoke, and may have dropped a hint that Conservative MPs would prefer Halifax. It was now for Churchill or Halifax to speak. A brief silence ensued: an invitation, perhaps, for Churchill to say that Halifax would be the candidate most likely to win the confidence of the Labour party, and that he would be proud to serve under him. But Churchill said nothing. He had received a secret pledge of support from a major Tory politician who was closely associated with Chamberlain: Kingsley Wood. At lunch earlier in the day Wood had advised Churchill that he should refuse, if asked, to serve under Halifax. By remaining silent Churchill indicated his reluctance to do so. The silence was broken by Halifax, who said that as a member of the House of Lords he could not hope to conduct a Government when the real source of authority lay in the Commons. 'I could tell', wrote Churchill in 1949, 'that he had thrown in his hand.'

Churchill was to be Prime Minister – if, as predicted, Labour refused to serve under Chamberlain. But Chamberlain insisted on exploring the possibility. At 6.30 Attlee and Greenwood were summoned to meet Chamberlain, Halifax and Churchill. Chamberlain invited them to join a coalition under his leadership, and they were solemnly urged by Halifax and Churchill to do so. Attlee replied that the Labour party would not accept Chamberlain, but agreed to put two questions to the National Executive of the party: (1) Were they prepared to serve under Chamberlain and (2) Were they prepared to serve under anyone else?

The next morning, 10 May, Attlee and Greenwood set off on the train for Bournemouth, where the National Executive was assembling for the annual party conference. Meanwhile the dramatic news had come through of the invasion by Germany of Belgium and Holland. For a moment, Chamberlain believed that he was saved: no changes could be made in the heat of battle. Sinclair, the Liberal leader, weakly put out a statement accepting a postponement of the change of Government. But the Tory rebels stood their ground and so did Labour. At 3.30 on 10 May the Labour Party National Executive resolved that the party would only agree to serve under another Prime Minister. At 5.00 Attlee telephoned 10 Downing Street with Labour's bleak message, and Chamberlain set off for Buckingham Palace to tender his resignation.

Later that evening Churchill was summoned to the Palace and accepted the King's invitation to form a Government. At three in the morning of 11 May he retired to bed in the knowledge that after all he had won, at the age of 65, the supreme prize. 'I was conscious', he wrote in his war memoirs, 'of a profound sense of relief. At last I had the authority to give direction over the whole scene. I felt as if I were walking with destiny and that all my past life had been but a preparation for this hour and this trial.' Chamberlain's friends were appalled, as John Colville recorded in his diary: 'Rab said he thought that the good clean tradition of English politics, that of

Pitt as opposed to Fox, had been sold to the greatest adventurer of modern political history . . . a half-breed American whose main support was that of inefficient but talkative people of a similar type, American dissidents like Lady Astor and Ronald Tree.'[3]

*

The influence of personality on politics can be overstated. If Halifax had been made Prime Minister, he too would have set up a Coalition Government with a small War Cabinet. These were the minimum demands of the anti-Chamberlain forces and had to be met. Nor was Churchill free to compose a Government of individuals congenial to himself. The principal necessity was a Government that would command the support of the most important elements in the House of Commons, and that meant a Government firmly based on party. Churchill's room for manoeuvre was further circumscribed by the fact that although he was Prime Minister, Chamberlain was still the leader of the Conservative party. The majority of Conservative MPs were still loyal to Chamberlain and cheered him when he entered the chamber. When Churchill entered they were silent: at this stage he would have been unacceptable as party leader.

The War Cabinet consisted of Churchill, the leaders of the two main parties, Chamberlain and Attlee, and their unofficial deputies, Halifax and Greenwood. David Margesson, Chief Whip since 1931, remained at his post but set up a joint office with the Labour Chief Whip; Ministerial patronage was divided up between the parties on terms that were broadly satisfactory both to the Conservatives and Labour. The Conservatives obtained the lion's share of appointments and there was no purge of ministers associated with the National Government. At the Foreign Office, Halifax and R.A. Butler carried on as before. Of Chamberlain's 'non-party' appointees, Sir John Anderson remained at the Home Office and Lord Woolton at the Ministry of Food. In the middle ranks there seemed to be no good reason to disturb such obscure figures as Herwald Ramsbotham at the Board of Education, or Walter Womersley at Pensions. Only a handful of insiders realised that the promotion of Kingsley Wood to the Treasury was not quite the tribute to an ally of Chamberlain which it appeared to be. As for the other appeasers, Simon was tactfully elevated to the wool-sack as Lord Chancellor. Only Samuel Hoare, whom Churchill detested, was sent, as ambassador to Madrid, into exile.

The distinctively Churchillian appointments were few. Lloyd George refused the Ministry of Agriculture. Beaverbrook was appointed Minister of Aircraft Production. 'Archie' Sinclair, the leader of the Liberal party, became Secretary for Air. Of the India diehards, Lord Lloyd was rewarded with the Colonial Office, while Sir Henry Page-Croft took up residence as Under-Secretary at the War Office. Curiously, Churchill handed the India Office to a politician who had opposed him over the question: L.S. Amery. Amery, who had hoped for a more important post, believed that his ambitions had been thwarted by Chamberlain and the 'old gang'.[4] Of the anti-appeasement Tories, Eden was promoted to the War Office, Cranborne made Paymaster-General, and Duff Cooper sent to the Ministry of Information. Two rebel back-benchers, Robert Boothby and Harold Macmillan, obtained office for the first time as junior ministers at Food and Supply respectively. Churchill's two most loyal supporters continued to exercise power and influence without ministerial office – Brendan Bracken as his Parliamentary Private Secretary, and Professor F.A. Lindemann – ennobled as Lord Cherwell in 1941 – as chief scientific adviser and head of the Prime Minister's Statistical Section.

The Labour party suffered from the fact that below the top level of leading politicians, it was weak in ministerial talent. Churchill, who was presumably acting on Attlee's advice, stretched the party's resources as far as they would go, and farther. As members of the War Cabinet, Attlee and Greenwood were cast in more important roles than they were capable of sustaining. It is hard to judge whether A.V. Alexander was a great success as First Lord of the Admiralty. The three Labour heavyweights were Herbert Morrison, who came in as Minister of Supply, Hugh Dalton, the Minister of Economic Warfare, and Ernest Bevin, as Minister of Labour and National Service. At the Board of Trade David Grenfell, a former Welsh miner, was appointed as a junior minister in charge of the Mines Department – an attempt, perhaps, to bury the hatchet over Tonypandy. Ellen Wilkinson, MP for Jarrow and organiser of the Jarrow March, obtained a junior post at the Ministry of Pensions.

Since 1936 Churchill had frequently extolled the patriotism of British trade union leaders and their importance in the conversion of the economy to a war footing. One of his first acts as Prime Minister was to invite Ernest Bevin, his antagonist during the General Strike, to become Minister of Labour with the responsibility of organising the supply of manpower. Bevin responded suspiciously. He was determined that he and the official trade union leadership would not be used by the Government as an instrument for the imposition of one-sided controls and sacrifices on labour. He notified Churchill that his acceptance of office was subject to four conditions:

> The first was that his Ministry would not be regarded merely as an institution to supply personnel but would also 'make its contribution to

the actual organisation of production so as to secure the right utilisation of labour'. The second was that in accepting the office it must not be assumed 'that I can accept the status quo in the matter of the social services for which it is responsible'. The third was that the 'present difficulties' in the Trades Disputes Act should 'be dealt with'. And the fourth was 'a complete revision of our attitude to the question of international labour policy.'

Churchill accepted Bevin's conditions.[5] This exchange marked the beginning of a new social contract between the Government and the trade unions. Churchill's readiness to welcome the trade unions into Whitehall, and to treat them as an estate of the realm, was perhaps his most distinctive contribution to the reconstruction of 1940.

Within a few weeks of the formation of the Government, a campaign developed for the removal from office of the 'men of Munich'. At the end of May the bulk of the British Expeditionary Force was evacuated from France via Dunkirk. Although the BEF had escaped, Dunkirk was plainly another defeat, and a clamour arose for scapegoats. The *Daily Mirror* and the *Sunday Pictorial* led a campaign for the removal from office of Chamberlain and his friends: the 'men of Munich'. The *Daily Herald*, the *News Chronicle*, and even the *Daily Mail* took up the cry. In the Commons the agitation was led by Clement Davies, and extended into the Government itself: Amery, Macmillan and Boothby were all disaffected.

Churchill resolved to shield the 'men of Munich' from attack. Although he had disagreed with them in the past, he needed their support. After the War Cabinet on 6 June he spoke to Attlee and Sinclair and urged them to silence the critics. The following day he summoned the chairman of the *Daily Mirror*, Cecil King, and warned him that if his newspapers continued their attacks the Government would fall. On 18 June Churchill met Amery and put an end to the 'under-secretaries plot'. In concert with Lloyd George, Boothby and Macmillan, Amery had written a letter to Churchill calling for a drastic reorganisation of the machinery of government. Churchill, who rightly suspected a plot to purge the Government and promote the malcontents, rebuffed Amery in no uncertain terms: 'If any one of the Government wished to criticise its working or its composition they should resign and criticise from outside. He was going to make no changes of any kind and would sooner resign himself than be pressed to do so . . . '[6] That same day Churchill told the House of Commons that an inquest into the past would be 'a foolish and pernicious process. There are too many in it. Let each man search his conscience and search his speeches. I frequently search mine'.[7]

Discouraged by Churchill, the agitation against the 'men of Munich' subsided in the press and Parliament. But according to the opinion polls, the great majority of the public wanted Chamberlain and his friends to be sacked. The blame for the military disasters of May and June 1940 fell mainly on the pre-war leaders of the Conservative party, while Churchill's reputation floated, like Noah's Ark, above the rising deluge.

At some point between May 1940, and the London blitz of September, the career of Winston Churchill merged with the history of the British people and he was transformed into a popular hero. Churchill himself was puzzled by the turn of events. 'He could not see', recorded John Colville in August, 'why he appeared to be so popular. After all, since he had come to power, everything had gone wrong and he had had nothing but disasters to announce. His platform was only "blood, sweat and tears" '.[8] But it was, of course, the succession of disasters that made Churchill popular. The threat of invasion, and the knowledge that Britain now stood 'alone' against Hitler, produced a wave of tribal feeling that converged with Churchill's own fighting spirit. More remarkable is the fact that his popularity endured beyond the epic moment of 1940, through the long dark tunnel of defeat, deprivation and war-weariness that lay ahead. Month after month, year after year, his approval rating as Prime Minister was never to fall below 78 per cent.

As a democratic politician, Churchill was quite old-fashioned by 1940. He attached little importance to the Ministry of Information and its propaganda activities. His principal means of communication with the public was through speeches to the House of Commons which were then reported by the press and the BBC. His contacts with journalists were few. Beaverbrook, the proprietor of the *Express*, and Camrose, the proprietor of the *Telegraph* were among his friends, and he kept in touch with Barrington-Ward, the editor of *The Times* and Crozier, the editor of the *Manchester Guardian*. But he never met the parliamentary lobby correspondents and rarely gave a press conference.[9]

Although he had broadcast occasionally since 1928 he was slow to appreciate the importance of radio as a medium of mass communication. In the summer and autumn of 1940 he was a reluctant and infrequent broadcaster. His famous promise of 'blood, toil, tears and sweat' was delivered to the House on 13 May but not broadcast. In the House of Commons on 4 June he anticipated the possibility of a German invasion and declared: 'We shall fight on the beaches, we shall fight on the landing grounds . . . ' But Churchill never spoke these words over the radio: they were read out by the announcer in the news bulletin.

On 18 June, following the capitulation of France, Churchill made another great speech in the House ending: 'Let us therefore brace ourselves to our duty and so bear ourselves that if the British Empire and its Commonwealth lasts for a thousand years, men will still say: "This was their finest hour."' This time Churchill reluctantly agreed to deliver the speech over the radio in the evening. But he felt no excitement at the thought of addressing millions of people. He was bored, and spoke with a cigar in his mouth. Harold Nicolson wrote:

He hates the microphone, and when we bullied him into speaking last night, he just sulked and read his House of Commons speech over again. Now, as delivered in the House of Commons, that speech was magnificent, especially the concluding sentences. But it sounded ghastly on the wireless. All the great vigour he put into it seemed to evaporate.

Another disappointed listener was Colville. 'It was too long and he sounded tired,' he noted.[10] On 20 August Churchill spoke in the House on the Battle of Britain, then in progress, and paid his immortal tribute to the fighter pilots of the RAF: 'Never in the field of human conflict was so much owed by so many to so few.' But he did not repeat the speech, or the phrase, over the radio. In recent years it has been alleged that the BBC employed an actor, Norman Shelley, to deceive the public by impersonating Churchill. This seems highly improbable. Between May and December 1940 only five broadcasts to the public at home were ever attributed to Churchill and there is no reason to doubt that he delivered them in person.

In a great national emergency a hero was needed, and Churchill was treated by the press and the BBC as the voice of the nation, above and beyond criticism. This was not the moment for journalists or broadcasters to call into question the record or the judgment of the Prime Minister. That was left to the Nazi propagandist, William Joyce, 'Lord Haw-Haw'. But Churchill was no propaganda creation and his past was in any case largely irrelevant. Everything about him proclaimed a blazingly authentic beligerance. In this he expressed the general will or, as he was to put it himself in later years: 'It was the nation and the race dwelling round the globe that had the lion's heart. I had the luck to be called upon to give the roar.'[11]

\*

Too much can be made of the fact that Churchill was separated from the mass of the British people by an aristocratic mentality and way of life. By profession, Churchill had been a democratic politician for forty years. He had always been a master of the forceful phrase or image that all could comprehend. Besides, he was a showman who borrowed from the music-hall artists of his youth. Like them, he dressed up in a variety of costumes, and rejoiced in theatrical gestures like the big cigar and the V-sign. His accent, like Attlee's, was a manly version of public school English, with barely a trace of the supercilious drawl to be heard in drawing-rooms and common-rooms. But in any case his accent counted for little beside the growling, lisping, individuality of the voice. In Britain, almost everyone over a certain age can do a Churchill impersonation.

What were Churchill's perceptions of the British? He believed profoundly in the patriotism and fighting spirit of the 'common people'. During the retreat from Dunkirk, he had listened in the secrecy of the War Cabinet to the arguments of Lord Halifax, the Foreign Secretary, in favour of a compromise peace with Germany. Fearing that morale was weak at the top, he issued a circular to colleagues and officials instructing them to avoid expressions of defeatism. 'It isn't in the workshop,' he remarked, 'it's all the upper middle class.'[12] Shortly after the fall of France, one of Churchill's private secretaries, John Martin, recorded the receipt of 'a tiresome complaining letter from X. I wish he could see some of the pathetically brave and loyal letters we get from humble people in the P.M.'s mail.'[13]

Churchill expected that if the Germans landed, the British would rise to the occasion. They would go out and fight with scythes and brickbats, and women, too, would enrol as combatants.[14] In the summer of 1940 there were some in Whitehall who feared that civilian morale would crack under attack from the air. Churchill gave no sign of sharing these anxieties, but was eager for the bombing to start in the hope that it would sway opinion in the United States towards entry into the war. He spoke, writes one historian, 'as a leader who possessed a deep faith in the qualities of the led'.[15]

On 7 September the *Luftwaffe* attacked the London docks, the opening of a prolonged assault on the capital which spread, during the winter of 1940-1, to the great industrial centres of the Midlands, the North, and Scotland. Churchill's confidence in popular morale was vindicated. Unlike Hitler, who never visited blitzed areas, Churchill often visited the scene shortly after a raid, and was greeted by cheering crowds. This was the sort of war, he reflected, that would suit the English people once they got used to it: 'They would prefer all to be in the front line taking part in the battle of London than to look on hopelessly at mass slaughters like Passchendaele.' Later the same day he and Attlee swapped electioneering memories and Churchill remarked that he had learned one great lesson from his father: 'never to be afraid of British democracy'.[16]

Yet Churchill was too shrewd a politician to take popular feeling for granted. He acted as his own Minister of Morale, with a special concern for practical measures to maintain the living standards and amenities of everyday life. On a visit to Margate he witnessed the destruction, in an air-raid, of a small restaurant, and the despair of the owner and his family. On the way back to London he dictated a minute to the Chancellor of the Exchequer, Kingsley Wood, laying down that all damage to businesses and property by air-raids must be a charge upon the state. The following day the Chancellor was summoned and meekly complied with Churchill's proposal.[17]

During the blitz of 1940–1 Churchill paid much attention to problems of civilian morale. He wanted to get the London buses running again, so that people could return home from work. He urged that the tube stations should be opened up as deep communal shelters. This measure, which had long been opposed by officials, was rapidly enforced by Londoners who occupied the tubes and slept overnight on the platforms. In Churchill's mind there was little connection between the morale of the general public and promises of better social conditions after the war. Nor did he brood on the need for some spiritual or ethical justification of the conflict. For him, morale was associated with such factors of everyday life as food, rest and transport. It was a matter of sustaining the physical and mental vitality of the working population in order to promote an efficient war effort. Characteristically, Churchill sought to reduce the loss to war production which resulted from air-raids. He modified the system of air-raid warnings so that workers no longer took shelter when a general alert was notified, but waited until a specific alarm was sounded.[18]

Churchill was quick to recognise the political advantage of a change of leadership at the Home Office, the ministry responsible for civil defence. The blitz had revealed that preparations to deal with air-raids had been extremely inadequate. A storm of criticism, partly orchestrated by the Communist party, broke over the head of Sir John Anderson, the Home Secretary. Anderson, a first-class administrator, was quick to appreciate the lessons of the blitz and began to reorganise ARP. But he was a lofty and remote figure without the common touch. In October Churchill moved Anderson out of the firing-line and appointed him Lord President. In his place he appointed Herbert Morrison, the pre-war leader of the London County Council, and expert municipal fixer. At Morrison's request, Churchill appointed Ellen Wilkinson as his Parliamentary Secretary.

Remote as he was from the conditions in which most people lived,

Churchill possessed a certain imaginative sympathy with their lot. One evening during the blitz, when he was driving through one of the poorer parts of London on his way to Chequers, he spotted a long queue of people outside a shop. He stopped the car and sent his detective to find out what the shortage was that had caused the queue. 'It was a queue for birdseed,' recalled his private secretary John Peck. 'Winston wept.'[19] At a meeting of ministers on 31 October he inquired what the smell was like in the tube stations that were being used as shelters. When Malcolm MacDonald, the Minister of Health, explained that it was unpleasant because of the lavatories, and the many unwashed people crowded together, Churchill remarked: 'Oh, I see: *esprit de corps!*'

Such occasional flashes of insight were, however, poor compensation for the lack of prime ministerial grip on the home front. His interventions were too erratic and unpredictable to impress his colleagues. After the meeting on tube shelters, Sir John Anderson confided to Woolton that he was very concerned about 'the sloppy way in which government is now being done – the Prime Minister interfering with everybody's department around the conference table, without any regard to the history of the problems, and suggesting solutions without any intimate knowledge of the difficulties that are below the surface.'[20]

The co-ordination of the home front was gradually accomplished by Anderson himself. In the course of 1941 his Lord President's Committee developed into a domestic War Cabinet which relieved the main War Cabinet of many of its more onerous responsibilities. Churchill, indeed, began to speak of Anderson as the 'home front Prime Minister'.[21] Yet Churchill always kept a watching brief on home affairs and frequently, as ministers put it, 'interfered'.

Running through his interventions was a strong and colourful strand of libertarianism. In Churchill's judgment, morale was best maintained by minimising the sacrifices and restrictions imposed on the general public. He thought it 'absolutely essential', for example, that horse-racing should be allowed to continue in wartime.[22] He disliked rationing and especially the rationing of food. Napoleon had once remarked that an Army marches on its stomach. Churchill extended this maxim to cover the entire population.

Since Britain was heavily dependent on imported food, food supplies made heavy demands on shipping space. But with merchant ships under attack from U-boats, and the competing demands of military supplies, shipping space was limited and had to be rationed. The rationing of imported foods was a logical consequence. But food rationing was opposed by Churchill when it was first introduced, in October 1939. He did so with the assistance of calculations about the available shipping tonnage produced by Lindemann, the head of his 'Statistical Section'. There were signs, he told his colleagues, that 'public opinion was becoming increasingly critical of government control and interference with the liberty of the individual.'[23] To this extent Churchill was the natural ally of the Ministry of Food in its competition with other departments for shipping space. In August 1940, with the support of Lindemann, he encouraged the Ministry to increase its import programme, declaring that 'the country should not inflict upon itself present injury through fear of future delays.'[24]

Unfortunately for Woolton, Churchill also expected the Ministry of Food to minimise the restrictions it imposed. This led to clashes between the two. By the summer of 1940 there was much criticism of the evasion of food rationing by customers in hotels and restaurants, where 'luxury feeding' continued. In July 1940 Woolton instructed hotels and restaurants to shorten their menus and to serve either a fish or a meat course but not both in one meal. Churchill, who believed in menus with a maximum of variety, wrote him an almost contemptuous letter asking him to explain the principles on which his policies were based:

Is it worse for the country for a man to eat a little of three or four courses of food, daintily cooked out of scraps, or a good solid plate of roast beef? Is it more patriotic to avoid luxury by having the food, whatever it is, badly cooked? Is it wrong to eat up the luxury foods which are already in the country, or ought they to be wasted? This is just the sort of criticism that will be raised in Parliament.

I remember in the last war, one of your predecessors, Sir Arthur Yapp leading a campaign against luxury foods at a time when there was a great shortage of basic foods (1917), and being very effectively denounced by the newspapers as "Yapping up the wrong tree".

Secondly, I should like to know whether the beef ration for the public can be increased as a result of the cutting off of our obligations to France, and also, whether now that the Army is at home it can be made to eat a larger proportion of fresh meat so as to liberate more frozen meat for the benefit of the poorer class of manual workers. I mentioned this to you the other day because I think it would be more likely to win more lasting credit for the Food Ministry than the sumptuary laws for restaurants which are already so hardly hit.[25]

The following day, Woolton sent a reasoned reply explaining that some modest restrictions were essential, in his view, for political reasons: 'My mail, which I read every morning, shows that the working-class is concerned that rich and poor should be treated alike, and the reason why I introduced the phrase about luxury feeding into my broadcast was in order to balance the rationing of tea and margarine, which understandably affects the poorer classes the most.'[26]

For Churchill, we may guess, the baiting of Woolton, a dreary businessman of the kind Lord Randolph had made fun of, was a form of light relief from the strains of war. In reply, he resorted to satire:

Almost all the food faddists I have ever known, nut eaters and the like, have died young after a period of senile decay. The British soldier is far more likely to be right than the scientists. All he cares about is beef ... The way to lose the war is to try to force the British public into a diet of milk, oatmeal, potatoes etc., washed down on gala occasions by a little lime juice.[27]

Churchill's antipathy to restrictions on food can be traced back to the late Victorian slogan of the 'free breakfast table', and his own experience of the campaign against 'food taxes' from 1904 to 1906. In February 1941 the luckless Woolton, acting with the support of the whole of the catering trade, issued another order to hotels and restaurants, limiting them to one main course of fish, meat, poultry, eggs or cheese, and enforceable by prosecution if necessary. Churchill had calmed down since July 1940, but he once again took issue with Woolton over the regulations:

When a person has the choice of having a piece of cheese or a slice of roast beef, most will choose the latter. The way not to get fish eaten is to put it in competition with game or meat. When I visited a restaurant on Saturday for the first time for some months, the proprietor told me that your regulations would cause him no inconvenience, as there were many exceptions, e.g. oysters and whitebait. Apparently a lobster is all right, but not a crab.

As Woolton recorded after a meeting to discuss food supplies in March 1941, Churchill was 'benevolently hostile to everything that involved people not being fed like fighting cocks'.[28] The history of Churchill's interventions on the kitchen front could, indeed, be carried further, but it is time to return to the broader context. Churchill regarded wartime restrictions as necessary evils. But he feared that certain departments, especially the Ministry of Food and the Board of Trade, were in the hands of politicians and officials who rejoiced in the extension of bureaucratic powers, and believed in control for control's sake.

Oliver Lyttelton, the President of the Board of Trade, was an aristocrat with City connections, and an old friend of Churchill. He could hardly be suspected of doctrinaire intent in the extension of controls. But Churchill opposed him strongly, in the spring of 1941, when Lyttelton explained that he was about to introduce clothes rationing. Churchill refused his consent and accused Lyttelton of wanting to 'strip the poor people to the buff'. According to Lyttelton, who may have improved the story in the telling, the deadlock was only broken when he arrived at the Admiralty one morning to find Churchill completely absorbed in the hunting of the *Bismarck*. 'Clothes rationing!' exclaimed Churchill. 'Can't you see I'm busy? Do as you wish!'[29]

Despite the assistance of Lindemann and the Statistical Section, Churchill lost most of his battles against rationing and controls. He seems not to have appreciated that broadly speaking the wartime slogan of 'fair shares for all' was extremely popular. Food rationing, for example, was strongly supported by the great majority of the public on the grounds that it was the most equitable arrangement.[30] Nor did Churchill appreciate that hardship and deprivation constituted only one side of the coin. The war tended to standardise the population at about the standard of living of the skilled working man before the war. For many poor people, this represented a gain. They had higher incomes and ate better than before the war. As Herbert Morrison remarked in May 1942, Churchill's concern for the people was sincere but old-fashioned:

> He is full of sympathy, you know, for the ordinary British man and woman, and doesn't like inflicting hardship on them. He's the old benevolent Tory squire who does all he can for the people – provided always that they are good obedient people and loyally recognise his position, and theirs.[31]

\*

Broadly speaking Churchill did follow his father's maxim and 'trust the people' in the Second World War. But he did not trust all of the people all of the time. Like some later Prime Ministers, he feared the influence of subversive minorities, real or imagined. In wartime, of course, the maintenance of civil liberties was no longer guaranteed. The Government possessed draconian emergency powers, conferred by Parliament, for the suppression of the 'enemy within'. But the extent to which civil liberties could or should be restricted was a matter of fine judgment. Whatever the legal powers at the Government's disposal, this was a highly sensitive and controversial area. The first days of the Churchill Government coincided with a growing panic, orchestrated by the press, over the activities of the 'Fifth Column'. The rumour spread that a body of enemy agents and collaborators was preparing to assist a German invasion. According to a joint report by MI5 and the Home Office, the potential Fifth Column consisted of fascists, enemy aliens, communists, and members of the IRA.[32] On the second day of Churchill's premiership the Home Office recommended the detention, under Defence Regulation 18B, of leading members of the British Union of Fascists. Churchill was strongly in favour of action. The leader of the party, Sir Oswald Mosley, was arrested along with 33 other prominent fascists on 22 May, and another 345 officials were detained on 30 May. Though they were held on very understandable suspicion of readiness to assist the enemy, there was in fact no hard evidence against them.

The great majority of 'enemy aliens' were refugees, including of course large numbers of Jews, who had fled from Germany and Austria. By the spring of 1940 the Home Office, the department responsible for aliens, had already filtered out the minority suspected of Nazi sympathies, and placed them in internment camps. But in the panic atmosphere of May and June 1940 the cry went up for the internment of all enemy aliens, on the grounds that some of them might be agents planted by the Nazis. The Home Secretary, Sir John Anderson, resisted the pressure and argued strongly that there was no evidence against the enemy aliens who remained at liberty. But MI5 and the Chiefs of Staff demanded that all enemy aliens be rounded up. They were strongly supported by Churchill who also urged, on 2 June, the mass deportation of enemy aliens.[33] The Home Office finally capitulated on 21 June, when the decision was taken to intern 27,000 enemy aliens. (Owing to the Italian declaration of war on 11 June, some 4,000 of them were Italians.) Among those interned and deported was Eugen Spier, the German Jew who had financed Churchill's pre-war 'Focus'.

Gradually voices were raised in Parliament against the paranoid policy of indiscriminate internment. A further blow was delivered on 2 July, when the liner *Arandora Star*, carrying 1,190 enemy aliens bound for mass deportation, was torpedoed and sunk off the west coast of Ireland with the loss of 559 lives. The Government's claim that all on board were enemy sympathisers failed to conceal a discreditable episode. Policy began to change and Churchill somewhat shamelessly told the House of Commons in August that 'a very great improvement has been effected in the Fifth Column danger. I always thought it exaggerated in these islands.' After this the critics of internment began to gain the upper hand, and as the months passed bona fide refugees were released. On his return to London from Canada in 1941, Eugen Spier found himself gazing at a Ministry of Information poster which seemed to be asking the right question: 'Is Your Journey Really Necessary?'[34]

In accordance with instructions from Moscow, the Communist party of Great Britain had adopted a policy of 'revolutionary defeatism', intended to turn popular opinion against the war. On 18 May Churchill had made it known that he wanted communists, as well as fascists, detained, but nothing came of this. In July MI5 advised that no action should be taken against them, as this would cause resentment among industrial workers, and there was no evidence that communists were prepared to help the enemy.[35] The *Daily Worker* was warned that it was liable to be suppressed under Defence Regulation 2D, for publishing matter intended to foment opposition to the war, but it continued to appear. The suppression of the *Daily Worker*, in January 1941, was a collective War Cabinet decision in which the driving force was Herbert Morrison rather than Churchill.[36]

Churchill appears to have had no desire to lock up the Communists. But after the emergency of May and June had passed he was uneasy about the detainment of fascists. 'The PM said he much disliked locking people up and the suspension of Habeas Corpus', noted Colville in October 1940. 'In any case he thought "those filthy Communists" were really more dangerous than the fascists.'[37] Churchill's unease was compounded by the fact that Sir Oswald Mosley, if not exactly a friend, had once mixed freely in the same social and political circles. In December 1940 he wrote to the new Home Secretary, Herbert Morrison, urging him to improve the conditions in which Mosley was living at Brixton gaol: 'Does a bath a week mean a hot bath, and would it be very wrong to allow a bath every day? What facilities are there for regular outdoor exercise and games and recreation under Rule 8?'[38]

Churchill seems to have thought that a Coalition, representative of all parties, had the right to claim the support of all patriotic citizens. But left-wing writers and publicists continued to criticise and find fault with the conduct of the war. Churchill feared that his own authority, and the authority of the Government, would be undermined. After the failure of the Dakar expedition, in September 1940, he was outraged by criticisms in the *Sunday Pictorial* and the *Daily Mirror*. At the War Cabinet on 7 October, he urged the suppression of both papers:

The immediate purpose of these articles seemed to be to affect the discipline of the Army, to attempt to shake the stability of the

Government, and to make trouble between the Government and organised labour. In his considered judgement there was far more behind the articles than disgruntlement or frayed nerves. They stood for something most dangerous and sinister, namely, an attempt to bring about a situation in which the country would be ready for a surrender peace.[39]

Churchill was dissuaded by his colleagues. The War Cabinet agreed that Attlee should deliver a warning to Cecil King, the editor of the *Pictorial*, and Guy Bartholomew, the editorial director of the *Mirror*. Churchill protested privately that the *Mirror*'s policy was 'just that which it would be most effective for a fifth-column newspaper to pursue'. Later in October he wanted the immediate suppression of the *Sunday Pictorial* for an editorial urging that half the Cabinet should be sacked. But Herbert Morrison managed to deflect him.[40]

Churchill had to contend with the fact that in many ways the war was a war of words. News, information and propaganda were of critical importance in the organisation of a war effort which depended upon continuous communication between Whitehall and the general public. The result was that organisations like the Ministry of Information and the BBC leaned heavily on the skills of writers and publicists. Many of these professional communicators were on the Left, and were indeed employed on the assumption that they were specially qualified to bridge the gulf between the Government and the working-class. Although the Coalition was predominantly Tory in composition, Government propaganda owed more to the Fabians or the Workers' Educational Association than to Conservative Central Office.

Churchill often grumbled about this. At the War Cabinet on 6th November he spoke bitterly of the BBC as an 'enemy within the gate'.[41] In January 1941 he was greatly displeased when the novelist J.B. Priestley broadcast in favour of a declaration of war aims. During the summer of 1940 a series of radio talks had turned Priestley into a famous broadcaster. But he had introduced a note of socialist propaganda, and given offence to Conservative MPs. In January 1941 Churchill wrote to the Minister of Information, Duff Cooper:

I am very sorry you have got Mr J.B. Priestley back, and that his first broadcast should have been an argument utterly contrary to my known views. How many more has he got to do? Have you any control over what he says? He is far from friendly to the Government, and I should not be too sure about him on larger issues.[42]

On 22 June 1941 Hitler invaded the Soviet Union. In a broadcast that evening from Chequers, Churchill declared that while he would not retract any of his criticisms of communism, his policy would be to regard the Soviet Union as an ally and to send all possible help to Russia. An Anglo-Soviet treaty of alliance was concluded the following month. For reasons which had little to do with ideology, popular opinion swung sharply in favour of the Soviet Union. The Russians were fighting the enemy: therefore the Russians were heroes. On 3 February 1942 the weekly Home Intelligence report on public opinion observed: ' "Thank God for Russia" is a frequent expression of the very deep and fervent feeling for that country which permeates wide sections of the public.'[43]

Churchill recognised immediately that the Anglo-Soviet alliance posed a problem at home. The danger was that admiration for the deeds of the Red Army would be translated into a general enthusiasm for communist principles and the Soviet system. Churchill at once instructed the BBC, which played the allied national anthems every Sunday evening before the nine o'clock news, not to play the Soviet national anthem – The Internationale. He also forbad its use on official occasions. Shortly after this the BBC abandoned its attempt to play the allied anthems. At length, in January 1942, Churchill reluctantly accepted that since the Russians were happy to play 'God Save The King', the ban on the playing of the Internationale must be lifted. Churchill also instructed the Minister of Information 'to consider what action is required to counter the present tendency of the British Public to forget the dangers of Communism in their enthusiasm over the resistance of Russia.'[44]

The policy of the Ministry of Information and the Foreign Office was to outflank the British Communist party by creating or assisting pro-Soviet organisations that were under the control of anti-Communists. Clementine Churchill played a part here by raising funds for the Russian Red Cross through her Aid to Russia Fund. But Clementine, a lifelong Liberal, was not entirely sound on the Red Peril. Far more reliable was the official trade union leadership, which again proved itself helpful to Churchill and the authorities. In August 1941 Sir Walter Citrine, the General Secretary of the TUC, approached the Foreign Secretary, Anthony Eden, to propose the formation of an Anglo-Soviet trade union society. As Eden explained to Churchill in August 1941:

You know Citrine's feelings about Communism, which he expressed again with undiminished emphasis, even going so far as to say that, were he given a choice between life under a Nazi or Soviet rule, he would be in doubt which to choose ... Citrine said he would carefully choose

the men to be so employed and that he thought it was wiser to take the
initiative in the matter than to be forced into it, as he almost certainly
would be at the next Trade Union Conference.'[45]

The efforts of Churchill and the government to stem the tide of
pro-communist sentiment were on the whole unsuccessful. Membership
of the Communist party, which had fallen to about 12,000 in June 1941,
began to rise and may have reached 65,000 by September 1942. There
was nothing to stop Communists and fellow-travellers from spreading the
gospel of communism. More significant, perhaps, was the simple absence,
between 1941 and 1945, of any truthful representation of the Soviet
regime. Confirmed anti-Communists were prepared to turn a blind eye
to the nature of Stalinism for the duration, so as not to offend an
ally. Churchill himself contributed to this form of self-censorship, which
lent the Soviet Union a new respectability.

In the autumn of 1941 Churchill was disconcerted to discover that
political discussions were taking place in the Army. Since Dunkirk the
Army Council had recognised that something needed to be done to
counteract boredom among the troops. Churchill's old India ally, Sir
Henry Page-Croft, who was Under-Secretary at the War Office, had
authorised a great expansion in the work of the Army Education Corps.
The Adjutant-General, Sir Ronald Adam, decided to go one step further
by promoting the discussion of current affairs in the Army. This led, in
June 1941, to the setting up of the Army Bureau of Current Affairs with
W.E. Williams as its director. Under ABCA, junior officers were expected to
lead a compulsory weekly discussion, at platoon level, with the troops.
ABCA ran two sets of fortnightly bulletins, which alternated: 'War', on the
military situation, and 'Current Affairs', on civilian topics.

David Margesson, the Secretary for War, had been Conservative Chief
Whip until December 1940. In authorising ABCA he could not be accused of
subversive left-wing tendencies. But he was apprehensive about Churchill's
response and asked Harvie-Watt, the Prime Minister's Parliamentary Private
Secretary, to sound him out on the subject. Churchill, as Harvie-Watt
recalled, 'nearly exploded'. He was 'hopping mad'.[46] On 6 October
Churchill wrote to Margesson: 'Will not such discussions only provide
opportunities for the professional grouser and the agitator with a glib
tongue?' Bracken, who had succeeded Duff Cooper as Minister of Information in July 1941, agreed: 'Out of 10 young officers who essay to lead
their men in these political discussions, 9 are going to get hopelessly tied
up with two or three of the men who really know something about politics
or public affairs ... ' But Adam had received the full backing of the

Army Council, and Margesson was supported by Labour, Liberal and Conservative colleagues. Churchill reluctantly accepted the scheme.[47]

Up until this point Churchill had been apprehensive of radical tendencies on the home front, but they had never taken the form of a personal challenge to his authority. In November 1941 a challenger suddenly announced himself in the person of Sir Stafford Cripps, the British ambassador in Russia. In a series of telegrams, Cripps criticised the British Government for doing too little to assist Russia, and gave notice of his intention to give up his post and return to Britain to campaign on the issue. Churchill warned Cripps that he was ready to oppose and crush him, but Cripps resigned his post and returned home in January 1942.[48]

The Japanese attack on Pearl Harbor in December 1941 brought the United States into the war, and Churchill rejoiced in the knowledge that the war could no longer be lost. But the immediate consequence was a disastrous sequence of events in which the British Empire in the Far East collapsed. Hong Kong fell, Malaya was overrun, and Singapore attacked. In spite of the Anglo-American alliance, and his immense popularity, Churchill began to lose ground in the House of Commons. As yet there was no question of replacing him, but there was much talk of the need to 'reduce the burden' on him, a coded means of calling for a reduction in his powers as a warlord directing the Chiefs of Staff.

It was at this critical juncture, when morale was at a low ebb, that Cripps appeared on the scene. He bore himself, so Churchill was later to write, 'as though he had a message to deliver'. But what was the message? Cripps had once been a fervent socialist and was still widely regarded as a man of the Left. But owing to the fact that he was no longer a member of the Labour party, from which he had been expelled in 1939, he was remarkably acceptable to the Conservatives: the promotion of Cripps would diminish the influence of Labour in the Government. More urgent was the need for new blood at the top. Churchill's style of government left a leadership gap on the home front which Cripps was eager to fill. He presented himself as the embodiment of modernity and efficiency: by contrast with Churchill he stood for expertise, planning, and collective solutions. He was greeted by the press in January 1942 almost as though he were a new saviour of his country.

On 29 January Churchill offered Cripps the Ministry of Supply – a post outside the War Cabinet. But Cripps, who recognised the strength of his position, turned it down. On 11 February he saw Churchill and refused the job a second time: an ominous development from Churchill's point of view. On 15 February military disaster struck with the surrender of Singapore to the Japanese. Churchill, who had realised by this time the importance of broadcasting, went on the radio and tried to rally morale. But he was more vulnerable than ever before and could only escape from his predicament by carrying through a bold reconstruction of his Government. To appease the critics of the 'men of Munich' he dropped Margesson from the War Office and also reshuffled the War Cabinet, excluding Kingsley Wood, the Chancellor of the Exchequer. Beaverbrook, who was locked in conflict with Bevin over war production, was dropped from the War Cabinet, along with Arthur Greenwood but Cripps was invited to join as Lord Privy Seal and Leader of the House – and accepted.

It is often said that Churchill outmanoeuvred Cripps, but the truth is that Cripps outmanoeuvred himself. The War Cabinet was under intense pressure from the United States to negotiate a new constitutional settlement with the Congress party in India. Cripps offered to fly to India to try to negotiate a settlement, and almost contrived a surrender to Congress, but was thwarted by the War Cabinet, Gandhi, and the problem of Muslim resistance. From Churchill's point of view this was the ideal outcome: Cripps was deflated and no longer appeared to be the man of destiny.

In home affairs, Cripps associated himself with austerity and proposed a further cut in rations. Churchill resisted and complained to Cherwell: 'I deprecate the policy of "misery first", which is too often inculcated by people who are glad to see war-weariness spread as a prelude to surrender.'[49] The War Cabinet, however, accepted Cripps's proposals.

In the spring of 1942 Cripps was prepared for a showdown with Churchill over the reorganisation of the coal industry. On 21 April Dalton, the President of the Board of Trade, announced to the House a comprehensive scheme of fuel rationing which had been drawn up by William Beveridge and ratified by the Lord President's Committee: coal, coke, paraffin, gas and electricity were all to be rationed. But the Conservative party, which had digested about as much 'war socialism' as it could take since 1940, broke into revolt, and the alarm bells began to ring at 10 Downing Street. At War Cabinet on 27 April Churchill suggested that the rationing scheme might be held in reserve, while he broadcast an appeal for economy. Beyond the question of rationing lay the more fundamental problem of the wartime organisation of the coal industry. Dalton therefore decided to beat a tactical retreat. At the War Cabinet on 12 May he proposed that fuel rationing be postponed until the Cabinet Committee on the reorganisation of coal had completed its work. Churchill, who had been primed by the chairman of the Conservative party, was inclined to abandon rationing altogether and said so at great length. Dalton recorded:

I have never thought so ill of the PM nor been so vexed by him before. He talks more than half the time and clearly has not concentrated his mind on the details of the subject at all ... He argues at immense length, almost alone, against a substantial majority of his colleagues. He is quite unconvinced of the need for any rationing. He thinks that a broadcast appeal by himself would do the trick, followed up by a press campaign.

Dalton, however, managed to persuade the Cabinet to accept his plan.[50]

The larger question of the reorganisation of the coal industry was under discussion at a War Cabinet Committee chaired by Sir John Anderson. In April Cripps had urged Dalton to stick to his guns on the reorganisation of coal 'since this, he thinks, would make a first-class occasion for a showdown with the PM on wartime Socialism'. On 19 May he told Dalton that coal was an issue on which he was prepared to resign: 'It is essential to requisition the pits. Otherwise our Regional Directors will be thwarted. The question is, who runs the Government? Is it the 1922 Committee?' But with the help of Oliver Lyttelton, the Minister of War Production, Dalton was able to obtain a compromise solution introducing 'dual control' in the mines, and postponing rationing indefinitely. The coal crisis was over, and Cripps thwarted again. Churchill, greatly relieved, praised Dalton and the miners and urged that something should be done to improve the miners' wages: 'The Treasury must not be difficult about this.'[51]

Cripps's final misjudgment was to challenge Churchill on his own ground by demanding a reform of the machinery for the conduct of the war. In the summer of 1942 Churchill was reeling from the after-effects of the fall of Tobruk on 20 June. When Sir John Wardlaw-Milne moved a vote of censure on the conduct of the war in the House, on 1 July 1942, Churchill obtained a massive vote of confidence by 476 votes to 25. But as Cripps appreciated, he might not survive another great military defeat. Early in September he put to Churchill a plan whereby the Chiefs of Staff were to be flanked by an independent War Planning Directorate which would take over the planning of strategy and operations. It was a typical Crippsian exercise: the application of scientific planning to the war effort in place of Churchillian intuition. Cripps offered to resign; but Churchill prudently asked him to withhold his resignation until the outcome of the forthcoming battle in the desert was known. On 3 October Cripps wrote to Churchill placing on record his disagreement over defence policy, and the postponement of his resignation. Churchill would not last out the war, he told his aunt, Beatrice Webb: he was old and had no plan for the future. The following month the Eighth Army under Montgomery won a decisive victory at Alamein, and Churchill ordered the church bells to be rung on a Sunday for the first time since the summer of 1940. As they rang out in celebration, they tolled the knell for Stafford Cripps. Churchill took up his offer to resign and insisted that he go through with it.[52] In a ministerial reshuffle on 22 November Cripps left the War Cabinet and was appointed to the largely administrative post of Minister of Aircraft Production. The Labour party's position was enhanced by the appointment of Herbert Morrison to the War Cabinet in place of Cripps.

*

1942 was the hardest year of the war for Churchill. Apart from his political anxieties, he was fearful about the morale of the Army – as indeed were many others. The surrender of 100,000 British troops to the Japanese at Singapore preyed on his mind. 'In 1915', Churchill told Violet Bonham-Carter, 'our men fought on even when they only had one shell left and were under a fierce barrage. Now they cannot resist dive-bombers. We have so many men in Singapore, so many men – they should have done better.'[53]

Churchill's anxiety about morale in the Army may explain his renewed outburst against the *Daily Mirror* – a paper that was widely read by servicemen, and had a reputation for airing soldiers' grievances. On 6 March 1942 the *Mirror* carried a cartoon by Philip Zec showing a half-dead sailor clinging to a raft in oily seas, with the caption: 'The price of petrol has been increased by one penny – official.' The cartoon appeared to be saying that official blunders were costing the lives of merchant seamen. Bevin and Morrison were no less disturbed than Churchill. On 19 March Bartholomew, and the editor of the *Mirror*, C.E. Thomas, were summoned to the Home Office where Morrison warned that he would suppress the paper under Regulation 2D unless it improved its behaviour. Morrison told the House of Commons of the warning in a speech of 19 March.[54] A few days later Churchill made a speech to the Central Council of the Conservative party in which he referred to 'one limit which I must ask shall be respected. I cannot allow propaganda to disturb the Army.'[55]

In September 1942, when Churchill was tensely awaiting Montgomery's offensive in the western desert, he was alarmed to discover that plans were afoot to make a film entitled *The Life and Death of Colonel Blimp*. This was a production planned by Michael Powell and Emeric Pressburger, with Roger Livesey cast as Blimp. As created by the cartoonist David Low, Colonel Blimp was an upper-class bonehead of invincible stupidity who was opposed to all progress and innovation, including the modernisation of the Army. A film entitled *The Life and Death of Colonel Blimp* was therefore bound to be regarded, whatever its content, as a satire on the traditional type of army officer. The Secretary for War, P.J. Grigg, sent Churchill a careful synopsis of the plot, prefaced by the judgment that he thought it of the utmost importance to get the production of the film stopped. As Grigg wrote:

> The War Office have refused to give their support to the film in any way on the ground that it would give the Blimp conception of the Army officer a new lease of life at a time when it is already dying from inanition. Whatever the film makes of the spirit of the young soldier of today, the fact remains that it focuses attention on an imaginary type of Army officer which has become an object of ridicule to the general public.

Churchill minuted Brendan Bracken, at the Ministry of Information: 'Pray propose to me measures to stop this foolish production before it gets any further. I am not prepared to allow propaganda detrimental to the morale of the Army . . . ' Bracken, however, replied that the Ministry had no power to prevent the production of the film and would need to assume powers amounting to a 'compulsory censorship of opinion' in order to stop it. Bracken suggested, however, that Churchill or the War Office should take the matter up with J. Arthur Rank, who was financing the production. Churchill insisted on taking the matter to the War Cabinet, where it was discussed on 21 September. Grigg, it appeared, had approached Rank and asked that when a rough cut of the film was available, it should be viewed by officials of the War Office and the Ministry of Information. If they took the view that it was undesirable, the film would then be withdrawn.

Fortunately for Powell and Pressburger, the military anxieties of the autumn of 1942 were swept away within a few months by Montgomery's victory at Alamein, the allied landings in north Africa, and Soviet advances on the eastern front. The men from the ministries, viewing the film in May 1943, could see no reason to suppress it, and the War Cabinet endorsed their opinion. Churchill succeeded for a short time in obstructing the export of the film, but finally surrendered in August 1943.[56]

Though Colonel Blimp was a fictional creation, his adventures reflected, like ABCA, the changing character of the British Army in the Second World War. Another manifestation of this was the introduction into selection procedures of psychiatrists and psychologists. This was a development strongly resisted by sections of the officer class, who viewed it as a form of interference by 'trick cyclists' (some of them Jewish) who knew little of the Army. Churchill was firmly on the side of the traditionalists.

The creation of a mass Army between 1939 and 1942 posed on a vast scale the problem of allocating manpower efficiently. The psychologists were introduced for a strictly practical purpose, to prevent the placing of square pegs in round holes. In June 1941 the Army Council accepted the principle of psychological testing for all recruits. But the more sensitive issue politically was the role of the psychologists in officer selection.[57] The officer class were traditionally recruited from the public schools. As the Army expanded it was inevitable that a majority of the candidates for commissions would be drawn from state schools, and a different social background. But the Army's methods of selection failed to keep pace with the change. Selection was in the hands of commanding officers, who nominated candidates they thought suitable for officer training. Candidates had then to appear briefly before a Command Interview Board, after which most of them were sent on to Officer Cadet Training Units or OCTUs.

The system was inefficient. Commanding officers were not always good judges of men, and Interview Boards had to rely on brief social impressions. By January 1941 the Officer Cadet Training Units were rejecting 25 per cent to 30 per cent of the candidates sent to them. Among those who did qualify, and received commissions, a high rate of mental breakdown was reported. When Ronald Adam took over as Adjutant-General he resolved to reform officer selection by adopting a system close to the German model. He instituted War Office Selection Boards which assessed candidates over a three-day period, often spent at a country house. The assessment included a number of intelligence and personality tests administered by psychologists. All candidates were interviewed by a psychiatrist who advised the Board, but the final decision lay with the President of the Board, a high-ranking officer.

The new selection procedure appears to have been a great improvement, since the rate of rejection from OCTUs fell to 8 per cent. 'These Boards are having an extremely good effect throughout the Army,' the Army Council concluded.[58] But Churchill was disturbed. In his view introspection was bad for people, or at any rate for soldiers. When Lord Moran showed him the manuscript of his book, *The Anatomy of Courage*, a study of the ways in which a soldier overcomes fear, Churchill remarked that 'the picture of what goes in a soldier's head, as I had painted it, would discourage the young soldier; it might affect recruiting.'[59]

In the summer of 1942 he prompted the War Cabinet to set up a ministerial committee, under the chairmanship of Cripps, to inquire into criticisms of the work of the psychologists and psychiatrists. But the scientifically-minded Cripps was impressed by what he found. The committee, which included Grigg, the Secretary for War, reported to the War Cabinet on 4 August that there was no substance to the criticisms. But under the supervision of the ministerial committee, an expert committee was set up to co-ordinate the work in all three services.[60]

In December 1942, following Cripps's relegation to the Ministry of Aircraft Production, Churchill returned to the attack. He invited the Lord President, Sir John Anderson, to chair the ministerial committee and stifle the psychologists:

> I am sure it would be sensible to restrict as much as possible the work of these gentlemen who are capable of doing an immense amount of harm with what may very easily degenerate into charlatanry . . . There are no doubt easily recognisable cases which may benefit from treatment of this kind, but it is very wrong to disturb large numbers of healthy, normal men and women by asking the kind of questions in which the psychiatrists specialize.[61]

During the first half of 1943 some important restrictions were placed on the work of the psychiatrists. They were forbidden to ask questions about sex or religion – a major handicap. In March 1943 it was ruled that instead of interviewing all candidates, they must only interview men referred to them by the President of the Board, up to a maximum of 50 per cent of candidates. As the historian of Army psychiatry writes: 'The value to the Board of the psychiatrist as medical examiner was consequently almost entirely stultified.'[62] It is difficult to show that Churchill was directly responsible for these changes: but the circumstantial evidence bears his fingerprints.

Churchill also tried to remove Adam from the post of Adjutant-General. In March 1943, after a talk with Lord Horder, he wrote to Grigg, the Secretary for War:

> 'Lord Horder informed me that when the present Adjutant-General held the Northern Command there were many times more cases of discharge for psychical neurosis than in any other part of the Army. He also stated that the Adjutant-General, I think when holding the Northern Command, desired that each recruit should be asked "with what degree of willingness he had entered the Service". Is it possible that this is true? Considering that we have compulsory service, anything more subversive to morale could hardly be imagined.
>
> Generally speaking, I am informed that the Adjutant-General has an altogether abnormal fad for this questionable process. If the above

facts are true, it would seem it is high time there was a change. I have already drawn your attention to the disadvantage of having an artillery officer, who cannot possibly understand the ordinary feelings of battalion officers, in the position of Adjutant-General. Some other employment could no doubt be found for Sir Ronald Adam.'

In his war memoirs, Churchill published the minute above with the second paragraph omitted. He also left out Grigg's reply, which again shows that his former private secretary at the Treasury was always ready to stand up to him:

I am informed by the Adjutant-General that both of Lord Horder's statements are untrue. One of them he has made before and withdrawn publicly promising never to make it again. General Adam would like your permission to see Horder himself and discuss these questions in order to remove as many misconceptions as possible.

The Adjutant-General has reminded me that the function of psychiatrists is not at all to make it easy for people to get out of the Army but to find in it something useful to do for those who are normally regarded as too unreliable too unintelligent for military service. He points out that since you told him eighteen months ago that Army wastage rates were too high he has, in fact, cut them in half.[63]

Churchill disliked the whole Selection Board procedure and would have preferred to go back to the old system of recommendation by commanding officers.[64] His fear of the psychiatrists was due to the feeling that they were another civilian element undermining the military identity and fighting spirit of the Army. But his interventions brought only limited success. He may have restricted the work of the psychiatrists, but the Selection Boards continued, and so did the psychological tests. Adam remained at his post – and the Army Bureau of Current Affairs soldiered on.

Churchill made another bid to close down ABCA in October 1942. In a minute to Grigg he wrote: 'I hope you will wind up this business as quickly and decently as possible, and set the persons concerned to useful work.' Grigg ignored the instruction.[65] In December a row broke out when one of the ABCA bulletins published a summary of the Beveridge report on social insurance, with an introduction by Beveridge himself. Grigg ordered the offending issue to be withdrawn. Shortly after this the Conservative MP, Maurice Petherick, wrote to Churchill's Parliamentary Private Secretary, Harvie-Watt, urging that something should be done:

I am more and more suspicious of the way this lecturing to and education of the Forces racket is run ... I maintain most strongly that any of these subjects which tend towards politics, even if the lecturers are Tories, are *wrong*! ... for the love of Mike do something about it, unless you want to have the creatures coming back all pansy-pink.[66]

In April 1943 Bevin passed to Churchill an ABCA poster which appeared to contrast the appalling housing conditions of the 1930s with the ideal Britain of the future. Churchill fired off another minute to Grigg: 'The poster is a disgraceful libel on the conditions prevailing in Britain before the war.' There ought, he continued, to be a Cabinet inquiry into ABCA. Grigg, who maintained that Bevin and Churchill had misunderstood the poster, replied with a spirited defence of ABCA, and welcomed a full inquiry. This was conducted by Sir John Anderson, who concluded that allegations against ABCA of political bias were unfounded.[67]

\*

Whether he was dealing with problems of discipline and morale in the Army, or the conditions of the civilian population, Churchill's views were distinctly old-fashioned. He was more of a traditionalist than sound conservatives like Anderson or Grigg, and never understood the incorporation of the liberal intelligentsia in the war effort. Nor, of course, did he see the British people through their eyes, as a people aspiring to a welfare state under the management of enlightened experts and planners.

But in assessing Churchill, however, we must beware of condescension, and indeed of distortion. The radicalism of the Edwardian period was far behind him, and his oratory painted the British people in archaic terms as an 'island race' dwelling in their 'cottage homes'. But perhaps, deep down, the British of the 1940s were an insular people whose ambition was to live in a cottage with a garden. More to the point, Churchill was not oblivious of the welfare and conditions of 'ordinary people'. As his prime ministerial minutes show, he prided himself on the interest he took in the problems of everyday life. 'I am distressed to see the queues for buses lengthening again in a very pronounced manner,' he wrote to the Minister of War Transport in October 1942. 'It seems so easy to make a boast of saving this or that amount of petrol by inflicting hardship and forcing austerity, and yet how heavy is the price when people arrive at their work or homes tired out, and so reduce their output and efficiency.' In November 1943 he wrote to Attlee, the Lord President of the Council: 'I hope that out of the present surplus of grain you will manage to do a little more for the domestic poultry keeper. He can usually provide or collect scrap to balance the grain so that we get more eggs for a given amount than if it were handed to the commercial producer.' To Dalton, the President of the Board of Trade, he wrote in April 1945: 'It is absolutely essential to increase the supply of civilian clothes. The suggestions I have seen that there will be a critical shortage after VE-Day are intolerable and it would be a grave reflection on the Board of Trade if such a thing occurred.'[68]

It was not Churchill's *lack* of interest in the people, their conditions, and their aspirations, which led to his defeat in the general election of 1945. It was the feeling that in his bones he understood all these things much better than his opponents.

# II

## *Post-War*
## *Plans*

### 1940–45

At some point between the retreat from Dunkirk and the start of the blitz, a curtain fell in public life. Conservativism, as it had been preached and practised in the 1930s, began to lose its respectability. The patriotic revival of 1940 led to the repudiation of pre-war foreign policy as weak and shameful. Meanwhile Labour politicians and the publicists of the Left led a powerful assault on the domestic record of the National Government. Never again, it was argued, must the social conditions of the 1930s be allowed to return. There must be, as Harold Laski wrote, 'no more distressed areas, no more vast armies of unemployed, no more slums, no vast denial of equality of opportunity.'[1]

This was a people's war, radicals and socialists declared, and must lead to a people's peace. The working classes, in other words, must be rewarded for their participation in the war effort by the construction of a new social order. The cloudy promises of politicians would not suffice: plans must be ready by the end of the war, and post-war reconstruction treated as an integral part of the war effort. The demand for post-war plans ranged well beyond the Labour party. *The Times* and *The Economist* were consistent advocates of a bold collectivist programme and so was the new Archbishop of Canterbury, William Temple, appointed by Churchill in February 1942. The movement for social reconstruction was, in fact, diverse in character and certainly included some Conservatives. But the response of the Conservative party as a whole was uncertain.

Following the publication of the Beveridge report in December 1942, the Coalition began to draw up a series of blueprints for post-war policy and Churchill himself went to the microphone to declare his support for social reform. Conservative ministers like R.A. Butler at the Board of

Education, and Henry Willink at the Ministry of Health, were key figures in the making of post-war policy. But the Conservative party as a whole lacked a strategy and a programme. The problem was that after 1940 the Conservatives no longer formed a coherent body of opinion. Churchill paid much attention to the politics of the Coalition, and the need to maintain a balance between its Labour and Conservative elements. But he was not much interested in the future of the Conservative party. Neither the state of the party organisation nor the clarification of party thinking were high on his list of priorities, if indeed he was conscious of them at all. When he did reflect on the post-war future, he did so in his personal capacity as a statesman wondering how the country should be run, and who should be invited to serve in a Churchill Government: Bevin, for example, would be a great catch, and Anderson was indispensable. Eden would be Foreign Secretary, of course, and a fair share of jobs would have to go to the Tories. Ought he to invite Labour as well? Perhaps.

Churchill's own conceptions of post-war policy were slowly and reluctantly formed but not as vague as is sometimes thought. It is often said that in his concentration on the war he was oblivious of the future but this is not entirely true. His sentiments were strongly conservative and left to himself he would have continued, with some improvements, the social and economic policies of the 1930s. The course of wartime politics compelled him to commit himself, in principle at least, to a programme of social reform which included employment policy, a comprehensive programme of social insurance, and a National Health Service. But the key to social policy was finance, and Churchill warned that no binding financial commitments could be entered into in wartime. The implementation of post-war reforms would have to depend upon the state of the economy, and the Government's ability to pay for them.

To this extent, the Churchill of 1945 was a social reformer. But he distinguished as sharply as ever between welfare reforms and socialism. The war, indeed, with its apparatus of rationing and controls and restrictions on personal liberty, stimulated his fear of socialism. He was strongly opposed to the doctrine of economic planning and his vision of the future, as the war drew to a close, was libertarian: the restoration of market forces, but tempered by a national minimum standard of welfare. As Butler put it to Woolton in September 1944: 'The Prime Minister's fundamental idea of politics was a mixture of the old Liberal doctrines of cheap food and free trade, combined with the Tory democracy of his father.'[2]

* * *

After the capitulation of France, in June 1940, Ministry of Information officials pressed for a declaration of British war aims to counter Nazi propaganda about Hitler's New Order in Europe. They were supported by Attlee and Bevin. The Minister of Information, Duff Cooper, wrote a paper proposing a federal Europe abroad and the adoption of domestic policies to prevent unemployment and promote educational opportunity. Colville noted in his diary: 'It is noteworthy that this paper has been written by a Conservative, and that the proposed committee will be largely Conservative in composition: as in Disraeli's time perhaps the Tory Party will prove to be the initiators of social revolution.'[3] Churchill was ready to explore the possibilities. On 23 August he took the chair at a meeting of the War Cabinet which agreed to set up a committee under Neville Chamberlain with the following terms of reference:

(1) To make suggestions in regard to a post-war European and world system . . .

(2) To consider means of perpetuating the national unity achieved in this country during the war through a social and economic structure designed to secure equality of opportunity and service among all classes of the community.[4]

Meanwhile Churchill was ruminating privately on the subject. There would have to be, he thought, a United States of Europe. As for domestic affairs, the Tory party was 'the strength of the country: few things needed to be changed quickly and drastically; what conservatism, as envisaged by Disraeli, stood for was the gradual increase of amenities for an ever larger number of people, who should enjoy the benefits previously reserved for the very few.'[5]

At the end of September 1940 Chamberlain was compelled by terminal illness to resign from all his offices, and the leadership of the Conservative party fell vacant. So great was Churchill's stature by now that the leadership was his for the taking – if he wanted it. Clementine, who always wanted him to stand for high principles, warned him that he would alienate much of his working-class support and lose his unique position as 'the voice of the whole nation'. But Churchill decided that he needed the party leadership in order to sustain his authority in the House of Commons. On 9 October he was formally elected, and made a tactful speech maintaining that he had always faithfully served two public causes – 'the maintenance of the enduring greatness of Britain and her Empire and the historical continuity of our island life.' Speaking more as the head of a coalition than as the leader of a party, he attributed the strength of Britain to the interweaving of past and present in the nation: 'In that achievement all living parties – Conservative, Liberal and Labour, and other Parties, like the Whigs who have passed away all have borne a part . . . '[6]

The Cabinet war aims committee had finally convened, under the chairmanship of Attlee, on 4 October 1940. In December Duff Cooper sent to Churchill for his consideration a declaration of war aims, but Churchill turned it down. 'The reason given in Cabinet', wrote Harold Nicolson, 'is that precise aims would be compromising, whereas vague principles would disappoint.'[7] Perhaps Churchill's assumption of the Conservative leadership had changed his mind. When he unburdened himself on the subject to the editor of the *Manchester Guardian*, in March 1941, he struck a Tory note:

> The necessary thing was to win the war, and any statement on peace aims would either be a collection of platitudes or would be dangerous to the present unity. We did not want a statement that dealt with any of the hotly disputed things in domestic affairs, and it was going to be difficult at the end of the war not to have a breach on questions like property and Socialism. We could not expect the Conservatives to swallow the things that would be put forward by the Socialists. Some of the poor wretches were already taxed up to 18s.6d. in the pound. He could not have anything to do with Socialism. What he felt was that Socialism would impair or destroy the individual initiative of millions of small people in the country, which was an immense element in the national strength.'[8]

But Churchill was a subtle politician. While ruling out a declaration of war aims, he recognised that some gesture should be made in the direction of post-war planning. The destruction wrought by the blitz was demonstration enough that a major problem of physical reconstruction lay ahead. On 30 December 1940 Churchill issued an instruction entitled 'Study of Post-War Problems' in which he announced that Arthur Greenwood would assume the responsibility of sifting and co-ordinating reconstruction plans to take effect over a period of about three years after the end of the war. 'The general aim', Churchill explained, 'will be to obtain a body of practical proposals which will command broadly the support of the main elements in all the political parties.' The appointment of Greenwood, a failed minister, to a post with a tiny staff and no executive authority, was not a turning-point in the making of policy. But Churchill was putting down a marker for the future. Shortly afterwards, in a speech to the Central Council of the Conservative party, Churchill conjured up once more the prospect of a post-war Coalition:

I hope also that there will be national unity in certain measures of reconstruction and social advance to enable this country to recover from the war and, as one great family, to get into its stride again. If this hope were not realized, and no common ground could be found on post-war policy between the parties, it would be a misfortune, because we should then have to ask the nation to decide upon the outstanding issues, and a party government would be the result.[9]

Conservatives may have been puzzled by the idea that a party government would be a misfortune. Although Churchill was now the leader of the Conservatives, and often expressed Tory sentiments in the War Cabinet, he failed in practice to lead the party. Professional Tory politicians were well aware that it was necessary, even in wartime, to look ahead. Labour politicians had a clear sense of direction and were quite openly staking out positions for the future. Many Conservatives recognised that they must prepare to meet the Labour challenge. In October 1940 the Chief Whip, David Margesson, was angling for the support of Lord Woolton by telling him 'how important it was that somebody who was a capitalist should be available for the process of reconstruction, so that we don't leave it to the Labour people to do all the thinking and planning.'[10] In May 1941 the General Director of Conservative Central Office, Sir Robert Topping, invited R.A. Butler to chair the Conservative party's Central Committee on Post-War Problems, with David Maxwell-Fyfe as his deputy. Butler sought to create a Conservative 'brains trust' of academics and experts, some of them drawn from outside the party. By September 1941 eight sub-committees were at work.[11]

But in the Conservative party, leadership could only come from the leader, and Butler's attempts to revive the Tory party were thwarted by Churchill's indifference. He neglected the party organisation in the constituencies, and failed to create, within the Coalition, a party high command. The principal members of his 'kitchen Cabinet', Cherwell, Bracken and Beaverbrook, were all indisputably Tory, but like Churchill himself, they were misfits: none of them English, and none of them gentlemen. In March 1942 the right-wing journalist Collin Brooks had lunch with both the outgoing and incoming chairmen of the Conservative party, Sir Douglas Hacking and Sir Thomas Dugdale. As he recorded:

Both agreed that Winston is a difficult leader, and is not a Conservative at all, or even, perhaps, by normal standards a statesman – being a creature of "Palace" favourites, of moods and whims and overriding egotism under his charm and geniality. Dugdale is fearful of what Max Beaverbrook may do. Him he described as a man utterly and completely untrustworthy . . . [12]

In the absence of determined and intelligent leadership, the Conservative party lapsed into a semi-moribund state, and a vacuum was created in party politics. In October 1942 a Conservative MP wrote in despair to the Chief Whip:

> Throughout the country the Conservative Party has become a cheap joke: the press and the BBC treat us with the contempt that we have earned and deserve.
>
> You yourself are aware of what the PM thinks of the Tory Rump: he may not say so himself but R.C. [Randolph Churchill], B.B. [Brendan Bracken] and his other satellites are not so careful of their tongues.
>
> You must agree with the fact that as an effective body of opinion either in the House or the Country, the Conservative Party have ceased to exist. [13]

As Prime Minister, then, Churchill pursued an egocentric path of statesmanship. Though often a Tory in spirit, he paid little attention to the concrete interests of the Conservative party. He appears to have taken no advice at all from his party on post-war policy.

In January 1941 Churchill had vetoed a declaration of war aims. Yet the concept of social security crept into the language of politicians and officials as the principal domestic war aim. In November 1940 Bevin urged 'that at the end of this war, and indeed during the war, we accept social security as the main motive of our national life'. J.M. Keynes included social security in an unpublished draft of war aims composed for the Ministry of Information. In May 1941 the Foreign Secretary, Anthony Eden, spoke of social security as an important allied war aim. [14]

Finally Churchill himself, for all his dislike of cloudy promises, signed his name to a declaration of war aims – the Atlantic Charter. The Charter arose out of the first wartime meeting between Churchill and Roosevelt, at Placentia Bay in Newfoundland in August 1941. With domestic American politics in mind, Roosevelt proposed a joint statement of Anglo-American aims for the post-war world. The most important American aim was the elimination of imperial preference. The War Cabinet, under Attlee's chairmanship, asked for, and obtained, an additional clause calling vaguely for all nations to collaborate with the aim of bringing about 'improved labour standards, economic advancement and social security' after the war. [15]

Churchill almost conceived a war aim of his own: the reform of the public schools. During the Battle of Britain, Beaverbrook produced figures to show that only thirty per cent of the fighter pilots were from public schools. The majority of the 'few' came from elementary or grammar schools. Churchill was deeply impressed by this. At lunch with Herbert Morrison, on 30 October, he 'waxed eloquent on the disappearance of the aristocracy from the stage, and their replacement by these excellent sons of the lower middle class.'[16] A few days before Christmas 1940, Churchill revisited his old school, Harrow, and sketched out his vision of the future in an impromptu speech to the boys:

When this war is won by this nation, as it surely will be, it must be one of our aims to establish a state of society where the advantages and privileges which have hitherto been enjoyed only by the few shall be far more widely shared by the many and the youth of the nation as a whole.[17]

Despite this rhetoric of broadening social opportunity, Churchill did nothing to follow it up and, indeed, attempted to veto educational reform in wartime. In July 1941, on the recommendation of Brendan Bracken, he promoted R.A. Butler to the Board of Education. In picturesque fashion he sketched out for Butler his duties:

'You will move poor children from here to there' – and he lifted up imaginary children from one side of his writing pad to the other – 'and this will be very difficult.' Then he said, 'I am too old now to think that you can improve people's natures.' He looked at me pityingly and said: 'I think everyone has to learn to defend themselves. I should not object if you could introduce a note of patriotism into the schools. Tell the children that Wolfe won Quebec.'[18]

Churchill had no idea that Butler was about to embark on a scheme of educational reform.

Though Churchill was unaware of the fact, officials of the Board of Education had been drawing up plans for post-war educational reform over the previous twelve months. Butler decided to seize the opportunity of promoting a major advance. What he did not realise was that Churchill had vivid memories of the religious controversies and party warfare aroused by the 1902 Education Act, and feared a repetition. On 12 September Butler wrote blithely to Churchill outlining an agenda for educational reform.

Firstly there was the problem of 'industrial and technical training and the linking up of schools closely with employment'. Secondly, there was need of a 'settlement with the Churches about Church schools and religious instruction in schools'. Thirdly, there was the question of the public schools, 'which may easily raise widespread controversy'.

The following day Churchill sent a crushing reply:

It would be the greatest mistake to raise the 1902 controversy during the war, and I certainly cannot contemplate a new Education Bill. I think it would be a mistake to stir up the public schools question at the present time. No one can possibly tell what the financial and economic state of the country will be when the war is over ... We cannot have any party politics in war time, and both your second and third points raise these in a most acute and dangerous form.[19]

Butler decided to pursue negotiations with the churches over a religious settlement without Churchill's permission. At the same time he entered into negotiations with the Governing Bodies Association of the public schools with a view to incorporating the fee-paying sector in the state system. Having at first urged Butler not to raise the public school question, Churchill changed his mind. In February 1942 he offered James Chuter Ede, the Parliamentary Secretary to the Board of Education, a move to the Ministry of War Transport. Chuter Ede said that he would prefer to remain at the Board of Education, where the future of the public schools was under discussion and recorded in his diary:

The PM was glad to know that the public schools were receiving our attention. He wanted 60–70 per cent of the places to be filled by bursaries – not by examination alone but on the recommendation of the counties and the great cities. We must reinforce the ruling class – though he disliked the word 'class'.[20]

*

Arthur Greenwood was dismissed in the Cabinet reshuffle of February 1942, a casualty of his own incompetence and the need to make room for Cripps. A Labour minister outside the War Cabinet, Sir William Jowitt, was put in charge of reconstruction. Since Jowitt carried little more authority than Greenwood, work on post-war policy continued at a low level, in obscure corners of Whitehall.

At the Board of Education, Butler continued his clandestine negotiations with Anglican and Nonconformist leaders, and obtained the support of Bevin, Kingsley Wood, and Anderson. He was about to propose the inclusion in the King's Speech of a bill for 1943 when the Cardinal-Archbishop of Westminster, Dr Hinsley, published a letter in *The Times* threatening the opposition of the Roman Catholic Church. Churchill had the Archbishop's letter cut out, fixed to a card, and sent to Butler with the handwritten message: 'There you are, fixed, old cock.' This, at least, is the story as Butler told it in later years.[21]

It had been clear ever since 1940 that Churchill did not wish the Coalition to evolve into a government of social reconstruction. Although he had spoken romantically of opening up the public schools he had twice vetoed an education bill. But in December 1942 Churchill's policy of procrastination was successfully challenged by Sir William Beveridge – the very man whom Churchill had recruited to the Board of Trade in 1908.

Since May 1941 Beveridge had been the chairman of an inter-departmental committee to inquire into 'social insurance and allied services', which had been appointed in response to pressure from the TUC. The committee was established with the modest aim of rationalising a complicated administrative structure, and filling anomalous gaps in the provision of benefits. By the autumn of 1942 Beveridge had turned this technical inquiry into a vehicle for an ambitious programme of social reform. He proposed a comprehensive system of compulsory social insurance to provide for all classes a minimum standard of living in all eventualities 'from the cradle to the grave'. But if the scheme were to be viable, he argued, three related 'Assumptions' must be brought into play: family allowances, a National Health Service, and policies to prevent mass unemployment. In a verbal flourish the report declared that Want was one of five Giants on the road to reconstruction: the others were Disease, Ignorance, Squalor and Idleness.

The Beveridge Report was due for publication on 2 December. In mid-November Kingsley Wood, the Chancellor of the Exchequer, warned Churchill against it in a scathing critique that was plainly intended to kill the report stone dead. Wood listed nine features which, he predicted, would arouse controversy, but his most telling argument was that Britain would be unable to afford the cost. The overall level of taxation, he predicted, would rise from 3s.5d. in the pound in 1938 to 4s.8d. following the implementation of the report: 'Many in this country have persuaded themselves that the cessation of hostilities will mark the opening of the Golden Age (many were persuaded so last time also). However this may be, the time for declaring a dividend on the profits of the Golden Age is the time when those profits have been realised in fact, not merely in imagination.' Churchill's economic adviser, Lord Cherwell, was also critical of the report, and inclined to think that it would alienate opinion in the United States, where it would be said that Americans were being asked to pay for British social services. But as Cherwell shrewdly observed: 'On the other hand there has unfortunately been so much carefully engineered advanced publicity that the Government's hand may have been forced.'[22] Cherwell had previously held no ministerial post: but on 30 December he was appointed Paymaster-General.

The Beveridge Report was published in a blaze of publicity. It was the lead story in all the national newspapers and the BBC broadcast news of it in 22 languages. Queues to purchase the White Paper formed at stationery offices, and 635,000 copies of this dry, statistical report were sold within a few weeks. Coming shortly after the victory at Alamein, the report represented a psychological release from the war and a pent-up longing for peace – but a peace in which a minimum standard of social security was guaranteed to all, in return for a weekly insurance contribution. It met with overwhelming popular approval. A survey by the British Institute of Public Opinion showed that 86 per cent favoured the adoption of the report while only 6 per cent believed that it should be rejected. Employers, and the upper middle classes, were almost as strongly in favour as manual workers.[23]

Churchill's initial reaction appeared to reflect the views of Kingsley Wood. On 12 January he sent the Cabinet a warning against the uncritical acceptance of the Plan. Firstly, he pointed out, the report would have to be related to other demands on post-war resources, such as defence and the revival of the export trade. Secondly, it was important not to allow too much optimism about the future: 'The broad masses of the people face the hardships of life undaunted, but they are liable to get very angry if they feel they have been gulled or cheated.'[24]

Founded on the principle of compulsory social insurance, the Beveridge Report calls to mind Churchill's long identification with that very principle. Was it not highly inconsistent of him to raise objections? Ought he not to have declared at once that he had always favoured such schemes?

Not necessarily. Firstly, the report would involve a major new financial commitment which, as Churchill rightly pointed out, could not simply be accepted without further consideration. But secondly, the Beveridge plan did not represent a continuation of the schemes of 1908 or 1924. Social insurance as Churchill had known it was a means of providing assistance to the working classes, with the poor law in reserve as the ultimate safety net. As revised by Beveridge, social insurance was to be a means of providing a minimum standard of living for all classes: the middle and upper classes were to be included, and the poor law (in theory at least) was to wither away. In addition the new social service state was to differ radically from the old in the spheres of health and employment policy. It was not inconsistent for Churchill as a pioneer of one type of welfare state to resist the introduction of another. A committee of Conservative MPs, from whom Churchill sought advice, favoured an extension of the old model, with a much less generous system of unemployment insurance than Beveridge proposed, and the exclusion of the middle classes from health insurance.[25] But the Conservatives were divided over the report. At a meeting of Conservative ministers on 30 November, Kingsley Wood gave a hostile briefing. But L.S. Amery, the Secretary for India, said that it would be a great mistake if the party came out against Beveridge: 'Its main features ... were not only sound but essentially Conservative and the cost, when every countervailing factor was taken into account, by no means excessive.' A number of other ministers told Amery afterwards how glad they were that he had given a strong lead.[26]

Churchill, then, had to reckon with cross-currents within his own party. More disturbing was the possibility of a party political rift within the Coalition. With the exception of Bevin, who regarded Beveridge as an enemy of the trade unions, the Labour ministers were eager for the Government to adopt the main principles of the report. Nor was the Beveridge plan the sole issue. It raised the whole question of the readiness of the Coalition Government to enter into the planning of post-war policy in every sphere. The Labour ministers, who believed that Churchill was almost certain to win a post-war general election, wanted to obtain as much as they could in the way of social reform while the Coalition lasted.

In an attempt to resolve the Coalition's identity crisis over Beveridge, the War Cabinet set up, in January 1943, a Reconstruction Priorities Committee under the chairmanship of Anderson, the Lord President. The other members were Bevin, Morrison and Jowitt on the Labour side, and Wood, Lyttelton and Cranborne for the Conservatives. Morrison's enthusiasm for Beveridge was overridden and the committee decided that no post-war social priorities could be determined until claims for defence expenditure and industrial reconstruction had been met.[27]

Churchill was abroad from 12 January to 7 February, attending the Casablanca conference and touring the Middle East. He returned in poor health but managed to issue a further directive to the Cabinet, on 14 February, in which he began to shift his ground on Beveridge. The Government, he wrote, should undertake to prepare the necessary legislation – but only a renewed House of Commons could commit itself to the expenditure involved. At the War Cabinet on 15 February he said that he could not introduce the Beveridge scheme until after an election.[28]

When the report was debated in the House, on 16–18 February 1943, political divisions were much in evidence. On the second day of the debate Sir Kingsley Wood made a speech raising so many doubts and queries as to give the impression that the Government was rejecting the Plan. But Herbert Morrison, winding up for the Government on the third day, skilfully placed a far more positive construction on the Government's response and argued that in principle the Government had already accepted much of the report. At the end of the debate the Parliamentary Labour Party divided the House on a motion calling for legislation as a matter of urgency. Ninety-eight Labour back-benchers voted against the Government, while only two voted in favour. This episode is often said to have created the impression that Beveridge was a party issue, with the Labour party in favour and the Conservatives against. If so, the impression was over-simplified.

Churchill was ill in bed with pneumonia during the debate, which was reported to him by his Parliamentary Private Secretary, Harvie-Watt, who noted: 'He said that the Government had gone farther with Beveridge than he would have gone himself. He said Beveridge was an awful windbag and a dreamer.'[29] But in the weeks following the debate, Churchill adopted a more conciliatory position, and began to reflect more widely on post-war reconstruction. His principal motive, we may guess, was the need to sustain the unity of the Coalition. Perhaps he also noticed, in March 1943, the formation of the Tory Reform Committee, a group of 36 Tory MPs, led by young Conservative MPs, including Quintin Hogg, Peter Thorneycroft, Hugh Molson and Lord Hinchingbrooke, who strongly favoured the Beveridge Report.

Churchill decided to broadcast on the subject of reconstruction and began to solicit advice. Herbert Morrison tackled him on the need for an extension of public enterprise after the war. In support of family allowances, Cherwell pointed to the need to increase the birth-rate 'if this country is to keep its place in the world and survive as a great power'. J.M. Keynes provided a remarkably optimistic assessment of the prospects for the post-war economy. British industry, he claimed, was now far more efficient than it had been before the war. 'Our *economic* future, in the sense of our ability to earn our living, is (to my thinking) the least of our worries ahead.' R.A. Butler, who was summoned to Chequers to discuss the educational passages in the broadcast twice announced: 'I am drafting an Education Bill.' This time Churchill raised no objection, but merely asked that he should be shown the plans when they were ready.[30]

In his reconstruction broadcast Churchill warned against attempts 'to coerce His Majesty's Government to bind themselves, or their unknown successors, in conditions which no one can foresee and which may be years ahead, to impose great new expenditure on the State . . . ' At the same time he announced that the Coalition would draw up a 'Four Years' Plan' for the period of transition following the downfall of Hitler. This would consist of 'five or six large measures of a practical character' to be prepared, but not enacted, in wartime. They would then be presented to the country 'either by a National Government formally representative, as this one is, of the three parties in the State, or by a National Government comprising the best men in all parties who are willing to serve'.[31]

As to the content of policy Churchill was more specific on social insurance than anything else: 'Here is a real opportunity for what I once called "bringing the magic of averages to the rescue of the millions". Therefore, you must rank me and my colleagues as strong partisans of national compulsory insurance for all classes for all purposes from the cradle to the grave.' Churchill also declared himself in favour of educational reform and a National Health Service: 'Here let me say that there is no finer investment for any community than putting milk into babies.' On economic policy Herbert Morrison was pleased to hear him say: 'There is a broadening field for State ownership and enterprise, especially in relation to monopoly of all kinds.'[32]

To the extent that he was unwilling to make binding promises during the war about post-war expenditure, Churchill was following the Treasury line. But in promising that measures would be prepared he was aiming to appease Labour while retaining control of reconstruction, and keeping it up his sleeve for use in the post-war general election. If he went to the country as the leader of a Coalition, post-war plans would be necessary to retain Labour support; if he went to the country as the leader of the Conservative party, he could present himself, as so often in the past, as a social reformer who opposed socialism.

Churchill's speech was an artist's impression of the long-term future. It left unresolved the problem of how far and how fast to proceed with post-war plans in wartime. In the spring and summer of 1943 the Labour ministers on the Reconstruction Priorities Committee experienced growing frustration as Kingsley Wood and the Treasury fought to delay post-war planning on financial grounds. They argued that no decisions could be taken until a realistic estimate of post-war revenue was available, and priorities for post-war expenditure had been agreed. In June 1943, Attlee, Bevin and Morrison protested in a Cabinet paper against the deadlock.[33]

It was much in the interests of Labour ministers to accelerate post-war planning. A substantial body of opinion in the party was hostile to the Coalition and working for a break with the Conservatives. In order to retain their authority, the Labour leaders needed to demonstrate that substantial progress was being made in the field of reconstruction. Looking further ahead, they feared that Churchill would inflict a decisive defeat on the Labour party at the first post-war general election. For men in office who enjoyed power and influence, there was something to be said for prolonging the Coalition – if only the party would consent.

In May 1943 Herbert Morrison, in conversation with the editor of the *Manchester Guardian*, W.P. Crozier, floated the idea of an electorally flexible Coalition. The parties would go to the country pledged to a Coalition Government on an agreed programme. But candidates would compete for seats on the basis of the differences between the parties, and the Coalition, when re-formed, would reflect the changed composition of the House of Commons.[34]

\*

The Labour minister with the greatest influence over Churchill was Bevin. In Churchill's eyes, he was the authentic representative of patriotic trade unionism. He was allowed to build up a trade union empire in Whitehall and to push through, in the teeth of strong Tory opposition, his Catering Wages Bill. In May 1943 Bevin initiated discussions with Churchill over the terms on which a post-war Coalition might be based. Cherwell, the head of the Prime Minister's Statistical Section, acted as intermediary.

Bevin was principally concerned with employment policy and proposed that peacetime responsibility for the co-ordination of a full employment programme should be vested in a reorganised Ministry of Labour. Cherwell, too, was strongly in favour of measures to prevent mass unemployment after the war. Although he enjoyed a well-deserved reputation as a diehard on India, he was turning into a Tory reformer at home, and advised Churchill accordingly. But the negotiations between Churchill and Bevin petered out inconclusively, with the door to a post-war Coalition neither open nor closed.

Meanwhile, on the Reconstruction Committee, progress along the lines of the Beveridge Report was steadily resisted by Kingsley Wood, pending the resolution of a debate over conflicting estimates of the national income after the war. Since educational reform cost relatively little for some years after the war, R.A. Butler was encouraged to go ahead with his plans and published, in July 1943, a White Paper entitled *Educational Reconstruction*. But on other fronts progress was minimal. In June, Attlee, Morrison and Bevin complained of the delay in a Cabinet paper.[35]

The protests of Labour ministers, reinforced by a chorus of criticism in the press and Parliament, finally persuaded Churchill to think again about post-war policy in the autumn of 1943. On 19 October he submitted to the War Cabinet a memorandum entitled 'War–Transition–Peace' in which he mapped out the way ahead. The most important feature was the distinction Churchill drew between two different stages of post-war policy. He recognised the duty of the Coalition to make all necessary preparations for the period of transition from a wartime to a peacetime economy, which he estimated would last about two years after the defeat of Germany. Plans must be ready for demobilisation, the revival of the export trade and the turnover of industry from war to peace. He also flagged two main priorities: 'Any decisions which are needed for the supreme objects of *food* and *employment* in the years immediately after the war must be taken now, whether they involve legislation and whether they are controversial or not.'

Beyond the transition, Churchill continued, lay the true post-war period of 'peace and freedom'. A general election should be held as early as possible during the transition so that electors could express their will upon the shape of post-war society:

We do not know whether this election will be fought on an agreed programme by the parties now composing the Coalition Government or whether the leader of the majority in the present House of Commons will be forced to place his own programme before the electors. In either case it is probable that a Four Year Plan will be announced, which, apart from carrying out the enormous administrative measures required in the transition period, will also comprise a series of large decisions on progress and reform . . .

In the meanwhile there are a number of important policies, such as education, social insurance, the rebuilding of our shattered dwellings and cities, on which there is or may be found a wide measure of general agreement. These steps must be brought to a high degree of preparation now during the war, any necessary preliminary legislation being passed . . .[36]

Churchill may well have borrowed these ideas from Cherwell, who submitted a Cabinet paper arguing along similar lines. Cherwell urged that some progress could and should be made on measures of 'social betterment,' for inclusion in Churchill's 'Four Year Plan':

Whether it will be possible for the parties to agree on such a plan remains to be seen. On a good many points no doubt they will. If the areas of divergence are too great, each party can go to the country on a programme having a certain number of points in common whilst offering different solutions to the other problems.

On employment policy, Cherwell reminded his colleagues that Beveridge was at work on a private report on employment policy. It was 'most desirable' that the Government should produce its own plan before Beveridge brought out his, 'which will no doubt be boosted in the press like his social insurance plan'.[37]

At the War Cabinet on 21 October Churchill delighted Dalton with an enthusiastic exposition of his ideas:

> The Transition has now taken a very firm shape in his mind. We shall not pass direct from War to Peace ... between these two there must be a transition for which it is our duty to make the most careful preparation now, and we should rule out nothing important for the needs of the Transition, merely because it is controversial. He then elaborates, with great dramatic detail, how we should prepare a great book, the Book of the Transition, like the War Book, running perhaps to a thousand closely printed pages or taking the form of a number of Reports and precise plans contained in drawers, one above another, so that, if any amateurish critic says, 'You have no plan for this or that', it would be easy to pull out a drawer, bring out a paper and say, 'Here it all is.'[38]

As Dalton's biographer observes, this marked a turning-point in Churchill's attitude towards post-war planning: 'There were to be many checks and disappointments. But the Prime Minister's declaration – conceived as the basis for a possible peacetime Coalition – became a charter to which hard-pressed ministers could appeal.'[39]

Progress on reconstruction was eased by ministerial changes. The death of Kingsley Wood, in September 1943, removed the most obstructive figure in the War Cabinet. Churchill replaced him at the Treasury by Sir John Anderson, a conservative with a small 'c', who co-operated more easily with Labour ministers. Attlee, who replaced Anderson as Lord President, took over his role as unofficial prime minister on the home front. Churchill also decided to create a Ministry of Reconstruction and, in doing so, to guard against excessive Labour influence in home affairs. To the horror of Labour ministers, he toyed with the idea of appointing Beaverbrook, who had recently returned to the Government as Lord Privy Seal. Dissuaded by Labour protests, Churchill opted instead for another anti-socialist businessman, Woolton, who took up his post which carried with it a seat in the War Cabinet, on 12 November. However, he exercised little authority as Minister of Reconstruction. With no party behind him, and no established Whitehall department, Woolton reigned rather than ruled over the Reconstruction Committee.

Between the autumn of 1943 and the spring of 1944 the Coalition made considerable progress with post-war plans. In October 1943 Churchill vetoed a proposal by the Minister of Fuel and Power, Gwilym Lloyd George, to nationalise the coal industry as a means of increasing wartime output and efficiency. In response to the clamour for nationalisation on the Labour benches, Churchill defined the principle on which the Coalition should operate: 'Everything for the war, whether controversial or not, and nothing controversial that is not needed bona fide for the war.'[40] As the episode demonstrated, Churchill had not lost the will to resist socialism. But neither had he lost all interest in the improvement of capitalism.

In January 1944 he circulated to the War Cabinet two minutes on employment policy which had been prepared at his request by Cherwell. In the first, Cherwell argued that the Government must act to prevent a repetition of events after the First World War, when a short boom was followed by a slump. Central and local authorities, and public utilities, must prepare well in advance a programme of public works to prevent a downswing in the economy. On long-term policy, Cherwell wrote:

> After 6 to 10 years of full employment during the war and the post war boom, the British people will not tolerate a return to the old figures. They will demand that the government produce a programme for achieving comparable results in peace.

Cherwell argued that fluctuations in the trade cycle could be avoided by deficit budgeting and counter-cyclical investment. To prevent the growth of regional unemployment, the state should locate arms factories and public works in the depressed areas, and encourage industries producing consumer goods to move there.[41]

Employment policy was the subject of a complex process of bargaining and compromise in Whitehall. By May 1944 a draft White Paper, which promised that future Governments would maintain a 'high and stable level of employment', was ready for the consideration of the War Cabinet. Churchill, who was full of anxiety about the forthcoming invasion of Europe, enjoyed a few minutes of distraction and mischief. He confessed that he had not read the White Paper, nor a memorandum about it which had been written by Cherwell. But he had read Cherwell's opening sentence, which strongly recommended the White Paper. However, Churchill continued, he would

like before finally committing himself, to hear the views of the Lord Privy
Seal – Lord Beaverbrook. After Beaverbrook had commended the White
Paper as 'magnificent' and 'first-class', Woolton expounded the proposals
for counter-cyclical expenditure in a slump. Churchill, as Dalton observed,
enjoyed himself hugely:

> The PM says he understands that what is proposed for public
> authorities is the exact opposite of what would generally be done by
> private persons, that when things look bad, they should not draw in
> their horns but push them out and launch forth into all sorts of new
> expenditure. Woolton replies that this is exactly so, and that it will be
> necessary to do a good deal of education of the public mind upon it.
> The PM says: 'I suppose that at such times it will be helpful to have
> a series of Cabinet banquets – a sort of Salute the Stomach week?'

Publication of the White Paper was approved.[42]

In February 1944 the Minister of Health, Henry Willink, submitted
to the War Cabinet a draft White Paper on the National Health Service.
In his brief for Churchill, Cherwell observed that the White Paper was
'a courageous attempt to find a *via media* between the conflicting views
and interests that make this problem so difficult'. The aim was to make
available the services of general practitioners, hospitals, and consultants to
the whole population, with a large-scale experiment in the establishment
of health centres. Cherwell warned Churchill to expect opposition from
the doctors, but recommended the White Paper as well-balanced. 'I think it
unlikely', he wrote, 'that anything better would emerge if it were discussed
in detail at the Cabinet, and I hope therefore that it will be accepted.'

Churchill read and initialled Cherwell's minute, but he was not entirely
satisfied. He wrote to Eden: 'It is absolutely impossible for me even to read
the papers let alone pass such a vast scheme of social change through my
mind under present conditions.' He sought the advice of Eden, Bracken
and Beaverbrook and insisted on a second discussion at the War Cabinet.[43]
The White Paper was published unchanged on 17 February. In a speech
to the Royal College of Physicians on 2 March Churchill gave its main
principle his blessing: 'Our policy is to create a national health service in
order to ensure that everyone in the country, irrespective of means, age,
sex, or occupation, shall have equal opportunities to benefit from the best
and most up-to-date medical services available.'[44]

*

At the beginning of 1944 the Government was still under attack in press and Parliament for dragging its heels on post-war plans. In a broadcast in March 1944 Churchill attempted to reply to the critics. He pointed to the Education Bill, the Health Service White Paper, and the forthcoming proposals on social insurance – a revised version of the Beveridge plan – as evidence of the Government's progress in post-war planning. But he had to admit that as yet the Government had made little progress on housing.

Housing was notorious in political memory for the betrayal, after 1918, of Lloyd George's pledge to build 'a fit land for heroes to live in'. Churchill, who had good reason to recall the anger of the Dundee slums, tried to avoid rash promises while putting as bold a construction as he could on the Government's policy. The damage caused by the blitz, he declared, represented 'a magnificent opportunity for rebuilding and replanning' and 'we had better make a clean sweep of all those areas of which our civilisation should be ashamed'. As an emergency measure, Lord Portal, the Minister of Works, had been charged with the responsibility for manufacturing up to half a million prefabricated houses. They were, Churchill claimed, 'far superior to the ordinary cottage as it exists today; not only have they excellent baths, gas or electric kitchenettes, and refrigerators, but their walls carry fitted furniture – chests of drawers, hanging cupboards, and tables – which would cost £80 to buy'. Portal, he claimed, was 'working wonders'. As for permanent homes, the Government proposed to have some 200,000 to 300,000 under construction by the end of the second year after the defeat of Germany. As had been promised in 1941, land for housing would be subject to compulsory purchase at March 1939 values. The state would 'on no account' surrender its powers.[45]

This was a rose-tinted prospectus. Lord Portal was, in fact, sinking into an administrative quagmire. His failure to produce the goods was to lead Churchill to replace him, in November 1944, by his son-in-law, Duncan Sandys. Sandys had to inform the House that owing to labour shortages there was little chance of Portal houses being produced before the end of the war. As for the supply of land, progress was hampered, as we shall see, by acute party political differences.

Churchill was trying, in his broadcast, to demonstrate a constructive interest in home affairs. But only two days later he dissipated the effect by a frivolous intervention in the proceedings on the Education Bill. When the House discussed the remuneration of teachers a member of the Tory Reform Committee, Thelma Cazalet Keir, moved an amendment in favour of equal pay for women teachers. R.A. Butler, for the Government, opposed the amendment. But it was carried by a vote of 117 to 116.

Churchill summoned Butler, who found him 'in a very resolute and jovial mood'. The Lord, said Churchill, had delivered the enemy into his hands:

He was sorry that the issue raised had been on equal pay for women, but the issue in these cases did not much matter and he proposed to rub their noses in it. He had been waiting for this opportunity. The by-elections had been going against him and people seemed to be utterly unaware that there was a war on, or that we had severe struggles ahead. It would be valuable to have a vote of confidence before the Second Front opened.[46]

The following day Churchill told the House of Commons that he proposed to treat the matter as an issue of confidence: the Government, therefore, would resign unless the vote were reversed. This awesome threat crushed the rebellion. On 30 March the amendment was defeated by 425 votes to 23.

As *The Economist* commented, Churchill was entirely within his constitutional rights. But politically he was mistaken. He was behaving, the paper remarked, with a growing petulance and bad temper which was probably due to the influence of Beaverbrook:

The advice the Prime Minister is getting is bad advice. If it goes on it will finish by doing the impossible – that is, alienating him from a large section of the country . . . The leadership of the war is not in question but for every one elector who, two months ago, suspected that the Government was needlessly obstructing reform or who doubted whether Mr Churchill was the man to head the country in peace as well as in war, there must now be three or four . . .[47]

Beaverbrook was indeed close to Churchill. But so was Cherwell, and the two courtiers often gave conflicting advice. The Government was under more or less continuous pressure from the United States over post-war commercial policy, a large theme of which only the briefest note can be taken here. The Roosevelt administration wanted the British to consolidate Article Seven of the Mutual Aid Agreement of 1942 by undertaking to phase out imperial preference after the war. The majority of ministers favoured a liberal commercial policy, but Amery, Beaverbrook, Bracken, and the Minister of Agriculture, Robert Hudson, dug in their heels and fought hard for the perpetuation of a Commonwealth economic bloc. In the spring of 1944 the American proposal for the creation of an International Monetary Fund split the Conservative party and left the Coalition paralysed. Churchill received conflicting advice from Cherwell, who was pro-American, and Beaverbrook, who was anti-, and was unable to resolve the problem. And as he complained to the War Cabinet, in April 1944: 'I really cannot be expected at my age to start to get up all these currency questions which I have thought nothing about for twenty years.'[48]

*

On 15 June 1944, nine days after the D-Day landings in Normandy, the War Cabinet discussed the Town and Country Planning Bill and White Paper, which proposed that local authorities should have the power to acquire at 1939 values the land needed for the rebuilding of the blitzed areas. The Coalition had been deadlocked by party political differences over the compulsory purchase of land and many Conservatives were opposed to the Government's policy of compensation at pre-war prices. Since the outbreak of war the market value of agricultural land had risen, and landowners protested loudly at the prospect of forfeiting wartime capital gains. There were loud complaints against the bill from two landed Tories: Selborne, the Minister for Economic Warfare, and Cranborne, the Secretary for the Dominions. But Churchill, so seldom a friend of the landed order from which he came, was strongly supported by Beaverbrook in the position he had taken up in his broadcast. The War Cabinet ruled in favour of compensation at March 1939 values. 'It is becoming more and more visible, with each succeeding week', observed Dalton, 'that the PM will swallow anything which both the Beaver and Cherwell support.'[49]

When finally unveiled, the Town and Country Planning Bill pleased few MPs on either side of the House. But it was the strength of feeling in the Tory party which most alarmed Churchill, who feared that the Coalition might break up. In a dramatic move he intervened on 6 October to propose that the compensation clauses of the bill be dropped, the rest of the bill passed, and a separate compensation bill introduced later. But his colleagues persuaded him that it was better to patch up a compromise. The Minister of Town and Country Planning, W.S. Morrison, conceded increases of up to 30 per cent in the rate of compensation for agricultural land. Tory anger was sufficiently appeased for the bill to pass into law.[50]

The crisis over the Town and Country Planning Bill reflected the inevitable return to party politics as the allied armies advanced into France and the end of the war came in sight. In October 1944 the National Executive of the Labour party rejected the idea of a 'coupon' election and announced that the party would fight the next election independently on the basis of socialist principles. Later that month, in moving the bill to prolong the life of Parliament once more, Churchill, in partisan mood for once, declared himself in favour of a contest as soon as the war in Europe was over.

Despite the renewal of party political controversy, much common ground was established. The Reconstruction Committee continued its work during the winter of 1944–5 and managed to reach agreement on two important items of legislation: the Family Allowances Bill, and the Distribution of Industry Bill, both of which were passed into law before the general election. Cherwell continued to support the broad thrust of the reconstruction programme. But the deliberations of the committee were often disrupted by the influence of Churchill's two other intimates, Beaverbrook and Bracken, who were spoiling for a showdown with Labour. They were both critical of Dalton's Distribution of Industry Bill, which conferred on the Board of Trade powers to build factories and facilitate employment in the Development Areas. In January 1945 Attlee was prompted to write a stinging complaint against their activities to Churchill:

> The conclusions agreed upon by a Committee on which have sat five or six members of the Cabinet and other experienced ministers are then submitted with great deference to the Lord Privy Seal [Beaverbrook] and the Minister of Information [Bracken], two ministers without Cabinet responsibility neither of whom has given any serious attention to the subject. When they state their views it is obvious that they do not know anything about it. Nevertheless an hour is consumed in listening to their opinions. Time and again important matters are delayed or passed in accordance with the decision of the Lord Privy Seal. The excuse is given that in him you have the mind of the Conservative Party. With some knowledge of opinion in the Conservative Party as expressed to me on the retirement from and re-entry into the Government of Lord Beaverbrook, I suggest that this view would be indignantly repudiated by the vast majority.

Churchill replied: 'You may be sure that I shall always endeavour to profit by your counsels.'[51]

By the autumn of 1944 the conduct of the war was moving out of Churchill's hands and he began to have more time for the consideration of post-war problems, both at home and abroad. But he was physically and mentally exhausted, and no longer able to master his briefs. He was in no fit state to revitalise the Conservative party. Fatigue was exacerbated by indecision. As the end of the war approached, Churchill blew hot and cold at the thought of a return to party politics. In October 1944 Churchill told the House that in his view a general election should take place after the defeat of Germany, even though the war with Japan was expected to continue for another eighteen months after that. Some took this to mean that party government would resume. But others drew the opposite conclusion. 'The assumption is, therefore,' wrote Harold Nicolson, 'that the Coalition will reform after the General Election.'[52]

In the field of post-war plans, Churchill distinguished between social issues (including employment policy) and economic controls. In his view, the parties were broadly in agreement on social legislation. In the King's Speech of November 1944 twelve bills were announced for the coming session of Parliament, including the National Health Service Bill, National Insurance Bill, Industrial Injury Insurance Bill, and Family Allowances Bill. (The Distribution of the bill was added shortly afterwards.) Since no one knew for certain how long the war in Europe would continue, it was impossible to say how long the session would last, and how much legislation would be passed before the dissolution. But Churchill told the House:

> Whatever may be the doubts as to when the election may come, and how it will finish up ... there is one thing which is quite certain: all the leading men in both the principal parties – and in the Liberal Party as well – are pledged and committed to this great mass of social legislation, and I cannot conceive that whatever may be the complexion of the new House, they will personally fail to make good their promises and commitments to the people. There may, therefore, be an interruption in our work, but it will only be an interruption.[53]

Churchill acknowledged the social impact of the war in an address to the boys of Harrow, on 1 December 1944:

> You read in the newspapers a great deal about the future of the public schools. I can assure you that during this war great changes

have taken place in the minds of men, and there is no change which is more marked in our country than the continual and rapid effacement of class differences.[54]

He reiterated his desire to see a broadening of the intake into the public schools. The Fleming Report of July 1944, which proposed that up to twenty-five per cent of places at public schools should be filled by local authorities, went some way towards the realisation of this aim – or appeared to. In fact very little came of it. Post-war experience was to reveal fatal flaws in the scheme.[55] Provided that social reform was politically expedient, and financially under control, Churchill was prepared to embrace it with a paternal warmth that arose quite naturally from his personality. But Government controls over the production and distribution of wealth were a very different matter. And here a new partnership came into its own: 'Beaverbrook and Bracken, long friends and boon companions, had become for the first time inseparable political bedfellows. Both were passionate believers in private enterprise and opponents of nationalization or state controls over business.'[56]

One of the principal differences between the parties towards the end of the war was that their attitude towards the vast apparatus of wartime economic controls. Apart from the rationing of consumer goods, there were controls over imports, raw materials, production, prices, and labour. While there was some bipartisan agreement on the need to retain controls for a transitional period after the war, the issue was too ideological to be dealt with in an atmosphere of rational compromise. In November 1944, when a War Cabinet committee submitted a paper on the future of controls, a row broke out between Attlee and Morrison on one side, and Beaverbrook and Bracken on the other. After the meeting Dalton, the President of the Board of Trade, had a word with Churchill and stressed that some controls would have to be retained. Churchill agreed, but he also inquired: 'Are you sure there aren't a lot of controls which you are keeping on now and which could quite well be taken off?'[57]

It seems very likely that Churchill's suspicion of Labour over the issue of controls was intensified by Beaverbrook and Bracken. Addressing the Conservative party conference in March 1945 he warned:

Control for control's sake is senseless. Controls under the pretext of war or its aftermath which are in fact designed to favour the accomplishment of quasi-totalitarian systems, however innocently designed, whatever guise they assume, whatever liveries they wear, whatever slogans they mouth, are a fraud which should be mercilessly exposed to the British public.

But Churchill's position was less partisan than it sounded. He promised, if the Coalition broke up, to form a Conservative Government broadened by the inclusion of 'men of good will of any party or no party'. And in a little noticed passage he went on to say that if he then won the general election, he would further re-form the Government 'with the sole desire of rallying the strongest forces available'.[58]

Churchill was still playing games with the party system, hankering after a Coalition and hoping, at least, to detach Bevin from the Labour party.[59] He was proud of the position he had established since 1940 as a national leader, and viewed the prospect of a descent to party politics with mixed feelings. 'People who have grown to love me', he confided to Harvie-Watt in March 1945, 'will grow to hate me and that will hurt me.' Sketching out the post-war future he continued:

The social and economic problems are immensely urgent. The action needed is without parallel. Our machinery of government has never had to tackle anything like it before. That is why the parties should continue to work together as they have done since 1940. We have been good colleagues and happy to co-operate. The partnership has been a successful one. Why dissolve it now?

As Harvie-Watt replied, the answer was that Labour was determined to withdraw from the Coalition after the defeat of Germany, and fight the Conservatives at the ensuing general election.[60]

The war in Europe ended on 8 May. Ten days later, after a meeting with Conservative colleagues, Churchill wrote to Attlee and Sinclair inviting the Labour and Liberal parties to remain in the Coalition until the defeat of Japan, which was expected in eighteen months' time. Churchill may have wanted to perpetuate the Coalition in order to enlist right-wing Labour support for a firm stand against the Soviet Union. Other Conservatives believed there was a tactical advantage to be gained by throwing the onus of breaking up the Coalition on the other parties. On 21 May Attlee rang up from the party conference at Blackpool to reject Churchill's proposal, and the Coalition Government resigned two days later.

Churchill now returned at the head of a Conservative or, as the press called it, a 'Caretaker' Government. On the domestic side, Sir John Anderson was Chancellor of the Exchequer, Hore-Belisha Minister

of Social Insurance, and R.A. Butler Minister of Labour. These appointments indicated that Churchill intended to continue the main lines of
Coalition policy. Anderson, who was not a member of the Conservative
party, was thoroughly well versed in the field of reconstruction. He spoke,
during the campaign, of the need for local authorities to prepare public
works in order to prevent unemployment. Hore-Belisha, who had been a
reforming Secretary for War under Neville Chamberlain, was a clever publicist whose task it would be to advertise the Tory commitment to social
insurance. Butler, who had maintained excellent relations with Labour at
the Board of Education, would present the face of social appeasement to
the trade unions. Henry Willink remained at the Ministry of Health, and it
was decided that the National Health Service Bill would be introduced in
the first session of the new Parliament. But Willink had made concessions to
the doctors which Churchill prudently forbad him to make public, on the
grounds that disclosure would lay the Government open to attack during
the election campaign.[61]

The Caretaker Government never had time to settle down to work.
It was immediately overtaken by the general election campaign, which
began with a broadcast by Churchill on 4 June. Polling took place on 5
July but in order to allow time for the ballot boxes to be collected from
servicemen overseas, the count did not begin until 25 July.

The general election of 1945 was the last election in which politicians
on all sides relied mainly on guesswork and placed little reliance on the
allegedly more scientific method of opinion polls in predicting the result.
Since 1942 the Gallup poll had in fact shown a large Labour lead. It
is also clear in retrospect that Labour's victory was foreshadowed in
wartime by-elections. Between 1942 and 1945 eight Conservative candidates, unopposed by Labour under the rules of the wartime electoral
truce, were defeated by independent left-wing candidates. But few could
read the writing on the wall, and by-election upsets were written off as
an expression of war weariness. To Churchill, as to almost everyone else,
it seemed inconceivable that the 'man who won the war' could lose the
election.

The Conservative manifesto, *Mr Churchill's Declaration of Policy to
the Electors*, was a brief and lacklustre document which rehearsed the
principle promises of the Coalition White Papers. But the Conservative
campaign was built around the personality of Churchill on whom there
fell almost the entire responsibility of presenting the Conservative case.
The other Tory leaders – even the glamorous Anthony Eden – were
thrust into the shadows.

The concentration on Churchill was misplaced. Churchill was almost universally acclaimed as a great war leader. But as Woolton wrote to Beaverbrook: 'People wonder whether the great war leader will be a good peace leader. "Is he really interested in reconstruction and social reform" is the question that I find people asking.' Woolton urged that the Government should set out its plans for housing, employment policy and other measures of reform:

> We ought to take – as is our due – the credit for the Health Service and the National Insurance proposals. The Health Service will be very popular, especially now that in its new form the doctors in health centres are not going to be salaried servants under the control of the local authority.[62]

Beaverbrook ignored this advice and so, if it ever reached him, did Churchill. While the Labour party fought a powerful campaign on a programme of social welfare, nationalisation, and economic planning, Churchill decided that it would be a more effective tactic to frighten voters away from Labour than to woo them with social reform. In the belief that after five years of bureaucratic restrictions on their lives, the public wished to be 'free', he played the libertarian card. On 4 June Churchill opened the election campaign with a broadcast delivered from his study at Chequers. He denounced socialism and warned his listener that the introduction of socialism into Britain would require 'some form of Gestapo, no doubt very humanely directed in the first instance.' He could not, of course, allude to the OGPU, or the Communist apparatus of repression: the Soviet Union was still our gallant ally.

Churchill had either read, or somehow obtained the gist of Professor Friedrich von Hayek's book *The Road to Serfdom* (1944), which argued that economic planning resulted inevitably in totalitarian government and the extinction of personal liberty. In a comment some years later Professor Hayek wrote: 'I am afraid there can be little doubt that Winston Churchill's somewhat unfortunately phrased Gestapo speech was written under the influence of *The Road to Serfdom*.' Churchill, it appears, repented of his folly later on. In November 1948 Hayek was introduced to him as the author of *The Road to Serfdom*. Churchill, who had consumed large quantities of brandy over dinner, told him that he was right, but 'it would never happen in England'.[63]

So far-fetched was the Gestapo allegation that many Conservatives were embarrassed. Churchill's daughter, Sarah, who at the time was serving with the RAF, tried to explain to her father where he had gone wrong:

Socialism as practised in the war, did no one any harm, and quite a lot of people good. The children of this country have never been so well fed or healthy, what milk there was, was shared equally, the rich didn't die because their meat ration was no larger than the poor; and there is no doubt that this common sharing and feeling of sacrifice was one of the strongest bonds that united us. So why, they say, cannot this common feeling of sacrifice be made to work as effectively in peace? . . .

Well, then, you say, "What about my Four Year Plan?" It is a wonderful plan, wise and generous, possible, and the most progressive yet produced. But you know they have forgotten about it! It hasn't been plugged enough.[64]

Churchill took heed of his daughter's criticisms. In his second broadcast he strongly emphasised the improvements in health and nutrition brought about in wartime, itemised the measures included in the 'Four-Year Plan', and extolled the Coalition Government's social insurance scheme.[65] But after this he reverted to negative tactics by exploiting the 'Laski affair'. In a statesmanlike gesture, Churchill had invited Attlee to accompany him to the Potsdam conference, to ensure continuity in the event of a change of Government. But the chairman of the Labour party, Harold Laski, put out a statement declaring that Attlee's presence at Potsdam could not bind the party to any decisions reached there, and that Attlee could only be present as an observer. Churchill at once played up this embarrassing rift in the Labour party with a public letter to Attlee saying that he had been invited as 'a friend and counsellor', not as a 'mere observer'. This provoked Laski to further indiscretions, while the *Daily Express* ran a campaign to show that the Labour party was run by a mysterious and sinister body, the National Executive, which pulled the strings behind the scenes. Speaking on 18 June, Beaverbrook said: 'I hereby declare that Laski is aiming at the destruction of the parliamentary system of Great Britain, and that he hopes to set up in its place the dictatorship of something called the National Executive.' Churchill played up the issue in his third election broadcast, on 21 June, and again in his final broadcast of 30 June. The latter contained no reference to social policy except for the expression of a pious hope that the new Parliament would adopt the principle of 'equality of women in industry, in all walks of life, and before the law, and that this will be achieved without any diminution in the chivalry and the protection of the strong right arm of the male warrior or toiler.'[66]

After polling on 5 July, Churchill and Attlee returned to Potsdam while the service vote was collected. On 25 July they returned home to await the results, which began to come in the following morning. By the afternoon it was clear that Labour had won a landslide majority. The final result gave Labour 393 seats to 197 for the Conservatives. At 7 pm Churchill set off for Buckingham Palace in a chauffeur-driven Rolls, to tender his resignation, and at 7.30 pm Attlee arrived at the Palace in a Standard Ten driven by his wife.

## 12

# Set the People Free

## 1945–55

After his defeat at the polls in 1945 Churchill passed through a phase of deep depression. He was old and tired and his colleagues were whispering that it was time for him to retire. Perhaps he thought of doing so: at any rate he tantalised his heir apparent, Anthony Eden, with hints that he was about to depart.[1] But in Churchill's case low spirits were invariably the prelude to a revival of ambition. He resolved to soldier on as Leader of the Opposition in the hope of ultimately returning to power. In February 1950 he fought and lost, by a narrow margin, a second general election. But finally, in the general election of October 1951, the Conservatives obtained an overall majority of 17. Churchill returned to office, survived a stroke which almost killed him, and lived on to celebrate his eightieth birthday at Number 10 in November 1954. He did not retire until April 1955.

As a battle against old age, Churchill's final decade was magnificent in a way, and calls to mind the lines of Dylan Thomas: 'Rage, rage against the dying of the light.' But opinions vary on whether he was right to continue in public life for so long. As a world statesman he grew in stature after the war. His prophecies of the Cold War, his campaign for a United States of Europe, and his quest for *détente* with the Soviet Union, were the work of a powerful intellect addressing the problems of the future. But in party politics and home affairs, it is more difficult to strike the balance.

The remarkable recovery of the Conservative party between 1945 and 1951 has generally been attributed to the efforts of the chairman of the party, Lord Woolton, and the chairman of the Research Department, R.A. Butler. It is less clear what the party owed to the wayward and egocentric behaviour of its leader. Nor is it obvious that he was a great electoral asset to the party. A confidential report on public opinion, commissioned by Woolton in 1949, concluded that his departure would make no difference to the party's standing in the opinion polls.[2]

By the time he returned to Downing Street in 1951 Churchill was 76 and clearly past his best. The diaries of Lord Moran portray him, indeed, as a pathetic old man on the brink of senility, with only the most tenuous grasp of the business of government. But this is misleading. Until the stroke he suffered in June 1953 Churchill was a comparatively effective Prime Minister. His method was to ensure that all politically sensitive questions were submitted to the Cabinet for collective discussion. Whether or not he understood the problems in their technical aspects, this enabled him to reach a political judgment, and thereby keep the main lines of policy in his hands.

Churchill's fitness for office is a less controversial topic than the direction his Government took in home affairs. It was a Government of Tory wets, for whom social harmony was a higher priority than economic efficiency. The Prime Minister himself was soaking wet, and opinions of him vary accordingly. In the course of his impressive study of the Churchill Government, Anthony Seldon depicts Churchill as a leader of great vision who transcended party and ideology, and touched the chords of national unity. But in Keith Middlemas's history of economic management since 1945, Churchill figures as a highly obstructive Prime Minister, who prevented his party from rethinking the relationship between the state and the economy at the critical moment when the Conservatives succeeded Labour.[3]

With Churchill there is always the risk of exaggerating the difference his personality made, and we have to assume that much of what he said or did would have been said or done by any other Conservative leader in his place. But quite apart from the fact that he was a great man and a war hero, certain features of Churchill's leadership marked him out. All Conservatives were opposed to socialism. But Churchill after 1945 adopted a platform of negative anti-socialism which aroused much opposition within the party, and gave the impression that he wanted to put the clock back to the 1930s. As events were to prove, the impression was highly misleading. Churchill's principal aim was to outmanoeuvre the Labour party electorally. Between 1949 and 1953 he led the Conservative party with great vigour and flair towards the middle ground of politics. As he did so he played upon his past, but in two different ways. He wooed the Liberals with greater persistence than other Tory leaders, and much nostalgic harking back to the great days of 1906. At the same time he was determined to lay the ghost of the General Strike by entering into a harmonious relationship with the leaders of the TUC.

\* \* \*

Churchill's intimates knew that he was deeply wounded by his defeat at the polls in 1945. But in public the mask of resolution and humour never slipped. When he spoke at the opening of the new Parliament, on 16 August 1946 Hugh Gaitskell described the speech in his diary as 'a real masterpiece ... the phraseology, the vigour with which it was expressed, and the brilliant repartee to a number of interruptions from our own side were first class. The old boy was really enjoying himself.' A few days later Churchill steadied morale at a meeting of Conservative back-benchers in Committee Room 14. 'He made a sensible speech,' noted Cuthbert Headlam, 'telling us how much wiser and better informed we were than the other side and adjuring us to keep ourselves *au courant* with everything and never give the enemy any respite.'[4] On a good day, Churchill was still a great parliamentarian. But it soon became obvious that he had no intention of applying himself to the daily grind of Opposition. In order to recuperate physically he sought long periods of rest, preferably in sunlit spots by the Italian lakes, or the shores of the Mediterranean. In the House of Commons he found himself addressing a new generation of middle-class Labour MPs who regarded him as *passé*. But he could be sure of a rapturous reception throughout the United States and western Europe. Last but not least, he was distracted from politics by the composition of his war memoirs. In the long years of opposition he relived the past and replenished the fortunes of the Churchill family.

Churchill's leadership conferred one great advantage on the Conservatives. As long as he wished to continue, his personal authority was beyond dispute, and there was no likelihood of major splits or revolts in the party. This was important at a time when the Tory party was troubled by latent conflicts which might have got out of control under the leadership of a less commanding personality. If Churchill had retired, the succession would certainly have devolved on Anthony Eden. But Eden had many enemies in the party and carried little of Churchill's weight.

Churchill's authority was undisputed but his detachment posed problems for party managers. In the aftermath of defeat the Conservatives were demoralised, and divided over tactics and policy. In the House, there was disarray on the Opposition front-bench, where Churchill was seldom to be seen. The situation drifted on until November 1945, when an explosion of anger and frustration at the 1922 Committee forced Churchill into action. He summoned the Shadow Cabinet and put down a motion of censure

17  *Right:* VE Day: Churchill on the balcony of Buckingham Palace with King George VI, 8 May 1945.

18  *Below:* Coalition Comrades: as Chancellor of Bristol University, Churchill in April 1945 confers the honorary degree of Doctor of Law on two of his Labour colleagues, Ernest Bevin (left) and A. V. Alexander.

19  *Overleaf:* The Campaign Trail: from the balcony of the Red Lion Hotel, High Wycombe, where Disraeli made his first speech as a parliamentary candidate, Churchill addresses a crowd of 15,000 people in June 1945.

20 The Frustrations of Anthony: Churchill and Eden return to Britain after a visit to Washington in July 1954, with Churchill still refusing to set a firm date for the handing over of the premiership.

which the House debated on 5–6 December. Churchill spoke well and attacked the Government for the slow pace of demobilisation. But the motion of censure was transparently contrived. When Attlee rose to reply, he 'delighted his supporters and demoralized the Opposition with a sober yet extremely forceful counter-attack'.[5]

Worse was to follow. The abrupt cancellation of Lend-Lease by President Truman in August 1945 had forced the Government to open negotiations in Washington for a loan to bridge the chasm of Britain's balance of payments deficit. Since the only alternative to the loan was a drastic cut in the British standard of living, the United States Government was able to drive a hard bargain which the Cabinet reluctantly accepted on 5 December. Under the terms of the loan, Britain was to receive $3.75 million at 2 per cent, to be repaid over 50 years as from 31 December 1951. The British in return promised to liberalise their trade policy through reductions in imperial preference and the introduction of convertibility for sterling twelve months after the approval of the loan by Congress.

The loan agreement was submitted to Parliament for approval on 13 December. Churchill was in an awkward position. Within the party the loan was opposed by two groups: supporters of imperial preference, and others who criticised the financial terms as too severe. In one of the feeblest speeches he ever delivered on a great occasion, Churchill called for his party to abstain in the vote. While seeking to dissociate the party from the loan agreement, on the grounds that it was being rushed through with too little time for discussion, he strongly urged Conservatives not to vote against the agreement, since this would be 'injurious to our interests in America'. Although the Conservatives could not accept responsibility for the agreement, 'the financial obligations once entered into by His Majesty's Government are binding upon all parties . . . ' On the divisive issue of imperial preference, Churchill tried to reassure the party's economic imperialists. The agreement, he argued, did not commit Britain to eliminate imperial preference except as part of a sweeping liberalisation of world trade, a prospect that was unlikely to be realised. In the division, 118 Conservative MPs followed Churchill's advice and abstained. But eight voted in favour and 71 against. Happily for Churchill, the loan agreement was in no danger of rejection. The House of Commons approved it by 345 votes to 18. But the fact remained that under his leadership, or lack of it, the Conservative party in the House had been reduced to a shambles.[6]

Fortunately Churchill was about to depart for a prolonged holiday in the United States. This enabled him to hand over the daily conduct of the Opposition in the House to Anthony Eden. By the time he returned, at the end of March 1946, Eden had played himself in as the unofficial

Leader of the Opposition in the House, and Churchill was content for the arrangement to continue. He was a semi-detached leader who attended the House at irregular intervals. He did, indeed, make a practice of inviting members of the Shadow Cabinet to a fortnightly lunch at the Savoy, but this was often a social rather than a political gathering. There was little co-ordination of policy, and Churchill exercised the right to intervene in a debate at the last minute, and without consulting his colleagues about the line he was going to take.[7]

Between 1945 and 1947 Churchill took part in none of the debates over nationalisation, social insurance, or the National Health Service. The politics of legislation interested him far less than headlines in the right-wing press about the hardships inflicted on the people in their everyday lives by 'socialist mismanagement' and 'bureaucratic controls'. In the spring of 1946 he began to attack the Government over food shortages, a theme the Conservatives were to exploit to the full as rations were reduced to below the wartime level. In July he moved the annulment of the Government's order for the rationing of bread, which had never been rationed in wartime. As he told Moran, his blood was up: 'A short time ago I was ready to retire and die gracefully. Now I'm going to stay and have them out . . . I'll tear their bleeding entrails out of them.'[8]

Apart from the performance of the parliamentary party, Conservatives were fearful that two other factors would prevent a recovery. They had fought the general election with a party machine that was rusting away: both the central organisation and the constituency associations were in urgent need of an overhaul. The work of reorganisation began in the autumn of 1945 under the chairmanship of Ralph Assheton. But Churchill decided that a more dynamic personality was needed. He chose Lord Woolton, his wartime minister of Food and Reconstruction, who had joined the Conservative party the day after the 1945 general election. Woolton demanded and received from Churchill a completely free hand in the reorganisation of the party machine, and his appointment was announced on 1 July 1946.[9] True to his word, Churchill trusted Woolton to get on with the job. The importance of his reforms, and still more of his achievements in the raising of funds and the recruitment of members, is a familiar story.

The second problem which most Conservatives regarded as urgent was the lack of a party policy. The Labour Government was carrying through a colossal programme of economic and social reform. The nationalisation of the Bank of England in February 1946 was followed by the nationalisation of coal in July and civil aviation in August. Bills for the nationalisation of the railways, electricity and gas were foreshadowed. The National Insurance

Bill and the National Health Bill, two major instalments of the Beveridge plan, reached the statute-book in 1946. Britain, it seemed, was marching steadily towards socialism. The illusion was sustained by the perpetuation of the vast apparatus of wartime economic controls. Rationing, food subsidies, import and price controls, were still part and parcel of everyday life.

The Labour party had a doctrine, a programme, and a mandate. But the Conservatives had none of these, and were uncertain which way to go. On the Right of the party were economic libertarians who condemned the works of the Attlee Government root-and-branch, and wished to restore a full-blooded policy of 'free enterprise'. But they lacked a plausible leader. Bracken and Beaverbrook, the most likely candidates, were mavericks on the fringes of the party. On the Left, Eden, Butler, Macmillan, and the Tory Reformers argued strongly for a commitment to a mixed economy and the welfare state. The rest of the party occupied an ill-defined no man's land of platitude and pragmatism. Churchill repeatedly argued that it would be a mistake for the Conservatives to make policy, or to draw up a detailed programme, in Opposition. This was wholly characteristic of his approach to politics. He believed that policies flowed from the exercise of power in circumstances which could not be predicted in advance. He did not wish to bind a future Cabinet to specific legislation, or levels of public expenditure. To do so, he believed, was irresponsible, and also unwise, since it provided the Government with a means of attacking the Opposition. Conjecture suggests that he may also have had a second consideration in mind: the unity of the party. By keeping policy as vague as possible he prevented the airing of contentious issues.

Churchill's concept of Opposition was to attack ministers individually for their mistakes, and the Government as a whole for imposing socialism on the British people: socialist controls, socialist taxes, socialist bureaucracy, and socialist industries. In the censure debate of December 1945 he appealed to Sir Stafford Cripps, now President of the Board of Trade, to clear his conscience of Socialism:

> I assert that the revival of this country is at the moment being stopped, stifled, even strangled, by the resolve of the Board of Trade, followed by other cognate Departments of the Government, to regulate everything. Why can they not realise that the impulse and volume of national productive ingenuity and progress is overwhelmingly greater and far more fertile than anything that can be produced by Government officials or party planners? If the right. hon. Gentleman would only realize the limitations of beneficial Government functions ... and would set the

people free, half his problems at least would end themselves.[10]

Churchill's speeches often fell flat. His oratory was too opulent and studied for the workmanlike age of Attlee, and his ideas were out of fashion. Between 1945 and 1947 the rhetoric of the hour was planning. To a great extent it was the doctrine of enlightened opinion in all parties. When ministers spoke of the necessity of social and economic planning they were applauded by *The Times* and *The Economist*.

\*

Churchill paid some attention to the clamour for the intellectual reinforcement of Conservatism. At the end of 1945 he decided to revive the Conservative Research Department and put R.A. Butler in charge of it. At the same time a parliamentary secretariat was created, under the direction of David Clarke, to brief the Shadow Cabinet on day-to-day issues. Early recruits to the Secretariat included Iain Macleod, Reginald Maudling, and Enoch Powell. But the task of the secretariat was the relatively humble one of supplying the front-bench with facts and figures for speeches. The Research Department had more ambitious terms of reference and was charged with re-examining party policy. But it was only an advisory body.[11]

Churchill's one specific proposal for the future was to change the party's name from 'Conservative' to 'Unionist'. The term 'Unionist' dated back to the Home Rule crisis of 1886, and the secession of the Liberal Unionists from the party led by Gladstone. In Churchill's youth it had been customary to bracket the Conservatives and their Liberal Unionist allies together as 'Unionist', a term which had persisted after 1918 in Scotland and Northern Ireland. As he explained to Woolton in August 1946, Churchill believed the change of name would broaden the party's appeal:

I am of the opinion that we should go forward with the proposal to make "The Union Party", whose members would be called Unionists, but who might be Conservative Unionists, Liberal Unionists, Trade Unionists, or Labour Unionists. I should like to discuss this when the Shadows meet on September 23, and if there were general agreement I would myself open the matter at Blackpool on October 5.

Among those who agreed with Churchill were Woolton and Macmillan.[12] But when the question was aired at the first post-war conference of the party in October 1946, no conclusion was reached. 'Whatever name we use,' Churchill told the delegates, 'this party is in fact and has been for sixty years "the Union Party", standing for the Union of the Kingdom and the Empire and the union of men of good will of all classes against tyrannical and subversive elements.'[13] His words were in vain. In England and Wales Conservatives continued to call themselves Conservatives.

On the second day of the Blackpool conference the demand for a statement of party policy came to a head. A resolution calling for a declaration of policy, principles and programme was carried by a large majority. Late that night Anthony Eden and Oliver Stanley sat up with Churchill and tried to convince him that he should make a policy statement. Churchill responded by spelling out the party's aims in terms so vacuous as to invite the suspicion that he was pulling somebody's leg. It was the objective of the party, he declared, 'to uphold the Christian religion ... to defend our Monarchical and Parliamentary Constitution; to provide adequate security against external aggression ... to uphold law and order ... to regain a sound finance ... to defend and develop our Empire ... to promote all measures to improve the health and social conditions of the people; to support as a general rule free enterprise and private initiative ... '[14]

Churchill also spoke of the need to create a new partnership in industry between worker and employer. Shortly after the conference he announced the setting up, under the chairmanship of R.A. Butler, of the Industrial Policy Committee. Apart from Butler the committee included four other members of the Shadow Cabinet: Oliver Stanley, Oliver Lyttelton, Harold Macmillan and David Maxwell-Fyfe. Churchill, as R.A. Butler tells us, 'gave strict injunctions that no detailed policy was to be published'.[15]

In an effort to give a broad idea of the party's philosophy Churchill reverted to the principles of Edwardian Liberalism. As he explained to a meeting of the Conservative Central Council on 14 March:

> Our policy can be stated in a nutshell. We accept and affirm the principles of minimum standards of life and labour and the building up of those standards continually as our resources allow. But above these minimum standards the British people must not be fettered or trammelled. There must be competition upwards – not downwards.[16]

This was not enough to satisfy the demand for a constructive alternative. At a conference of young Conservatives a fortnight later Miss Margaret

Roberts of Oxford, better known later as Margaret Thatcher, declared that 'at the moment Conservatism meant nothing more than anti-Socialism. We must have a clear and unified statement of policy'.[17]

In the spring of 1947 the Industrial Policy Committee produced a draft of the 'Industrial Charter'. According to Harold Macmillan, Churchill received a copy of the Charter in draft and paid a surprising amount of attention to both the wording and the substance.[18] While avoiding detail, as Churchill had instructed, the Committee did sketch out a map of post-war policy.

The Industrial Charter had been framed after extensive consultation with businessmen and contained much to please the free enterprise lobby. It pledged the Conservatives to cut back the 'swollen ranks' of the civil service and reduce direct taxation. A Conservative Government, the Charter promised, would do away as soon as possible with rationing and controls. But decontrol was subject to an overriding social pledge: 'We will not remove the control from any necessity of life until we are certain that it is within the reach of every family.' The Labour Government had repealed the Trade Disputes Act of 1927. The Charter promised that a Conservative Government would restore three important features of the Act: the ban on the affiliation of civil service unions to the Labour Party, the prohibition of the closed shop in the public sector, and the principle of contracting-in to the political levy.[19]

The Charter was intended to show that the party now stood for a reformed capitalism in which the state played a far more positive role than it had in the 1930s. Much of the Labour Government's nationalisation programme was accepted as irreversible, though the line was drawn at steel and long-distance road haulage: these were to be returned to private ownership. As an alternative to further nationalisation, a 'Workers' Charter' was proposed to humanise industrial relations. The status of the worker was to be improved through schemes of profit-sharing, joint consultation, and advances in education and training. The 'Workers' Charter' was not, however, to be enforced by legislation: a code of industrial conduct, analogous to the Highway Code, was to be submitted to Parliament for approval. Most important of all was the acceptance of a leading role for the state in the management of the economy and the maintenance of full employment. 'The Conservative Party', the Charter declared, 'stands by the Coalition White Paper and would in some respects go further to ensure that the demand for goods and services is always maintained at a level which will offer jobs to all who are willing to work.'[20]

In the week of the Charter's publication, in May 1947, Churchill made a speech at Ayr in which he gave it a very general blessing while blurring the policy outlines:

> Britain, like any other country is always changing but like nature never draws a line without smudging it. We have not the sharp logic of Continental countries. We seek to benefit private enterprise with the knowledge and guiding power of modern governments, without sacrificing the initiative and drive of individual effort under free, competitive conditions.

He continued in this vein, without endorsing any of the specific Charter pledges.[21]

It was prudent of Churchill to prevaricate. The response of the Conservative party had yet to be gauged and over the following months a somewhat muffled debate took place between rival tendencies. Critics on the Right attacked the Charter as crypto-socialist, while Tory Reformers spoke out strongly in favour. But when the annual party conference assembled at Brighton in October 1947 the Charter received the overwhelming approval of the delegates. Churchill realised that he would have to include a passage on the subject in his conference speech but, according to Reginald Maudling, he was not enthusiastic:

> 'I was working for Winston on his concluding speech to the Conference and we came to the topic of the Industrial Charter. "Give me five lines, Maudling", he said, "explaining what the Industrial Charter says." This I did. He read it with care, and then said: "But I do not agree with a word of this." "Well, sir," I said, "that is what the conference adopted." "Oh well," he said, "leave it in", and he duly read it out in the course of his speech, with the calculated coolness which he always accorded to paragraphs in speeches, rare as they were, which had been drafted by other people . . . '[22]

This story may have improved in the telling. Churchill said very little in his conference speech that he had not said before. While reiterating the party's commitment to a minimum standard of life and labour he again avoided specific pledges on social, industrial or employment policy. As he explained to the conference: 'I am sure it would not be wise for us to bind ourselves to a rigid programme of exactly what we should do . . . We cannot tell what misfortunes are going to befall our country. We cannot tell when a new House of Commons will be chosen or what its composition will be.' He was a little more specific in defining the national minimum in terms of food, the prices of basic necessities, and housing, and he also promised an attack on 'monopolistic abuses'. But otherwise he placed the rhetorical emphasis firmly upon the decontrol of the economy: 'We propose to sweep away with sturdy strokes the vast encumbrance of regulations and penalties which are today preventing our people from making a good living in their island home.'[23]

After the Brighton conference the word went forth in the press that the right of the party had been routed by the reformers. But it had yet to be shown that the reformers had captured the party leader. Churchill continued along his chosen path of negative opposition, with sporadic attacks on the Government over housing, controls, and the perils of socialism.

*

In 1947 the Government suffered two major economic disasters which dented its popularity and seemed to vindicate Churchill's tactics. In February a shortage of coal stocks at the power stations, coupled with heavy snow and freezing temperatures, plunged the Government into a fuel crisis. It had no alternative but to cut off electricity supplies to private consumers for long periods of the day. Major industries were shut down entirely and the unemployment total rose, in March, above 2,000,000.

The Opposition exploited the situation to the full. Churchill pointed to the fact that under the Coalition a winter coal crisis had been regularly avoided. The Government, he argued, ought to have been prepared. 'The brute fact is,' he told the House of Commons, 'that Socialism means mismanagement.'[24] On 12 March, in a debate in the House on the economic crisis, he mounted a full-scale attack on the Government for inflicting unnecessary hardships on the people in the form of bread rationing, the coal shortage, the slow progress of the housing programme, excessive public expenditure, and nationalisation. 'In most cases', said Churchill, 'management by private enterprise is not only more efficient, but far less costly to the wage earners than management by the huge official staffs now quartered upon the producers.' On Conservative policy Churchill was brief and extremely vague: the 'native energies, genius and contrivance of our race' had to be 'liberated', after which the state would 'guide and aid all the forces that these negative energies generate into the right channels.'[25] Churchill gave no indication of how the Conservatives would deal with the balance of payments crisis, inflation, food subsidies, public expenditure or fiscal policy.

In July 1947 the Government experienced a second crisis. In fulfilment of the Anglo-American loan agreement the Chancellor of the Exchequer,

Hugh Dalton, made the pound freely convertible into dollars. A run on the pound followed, and rumours began to circulate of a Coalition Government under Bevin. At the same time Churchill's colleagues attempted to persuade him to retire and invited the Chief Whip, James Stuart, to deliver the message on their behalf. These colleagues presumably included such professed admirers and friends of Churchill as Anthony Eden, Harold Macmillan, and Oliver Lyttelton. Stuart bravely delivered the message and was firmly informed by Churchill that he intended to continue.[26]

The fact was that senior Tories were impotent. Whatever Churchill's failings as leader of the Opposition, they were transcended by his fame as the 'saviour of his country'. Besides, he was idolised by the constituency parties. On 4 August 1947 he addressed a vast open air rally in the grounds of Blenheim Palace. Triumphantly evading the dilemmas posed by the financial crisis, he delighted his audience with familiar sallies against the Government, and a pleasing vision of a future in which the sunlight shone on both sides of the Iron Curtain. On 16 August he broadcast on the crisis and addressed the question of the hour with sublime effrontery:

I am asked: "What would you do Mr Churchill, if you had the responsibility and the power which you had in the days of Dunkirk?" If I had that power, with a Cabinet of the best ability and experience in the country, which I certainly would gather, I would give you promptly and in good time the decisions which are necessary, and I have no doubt Britain would survive.[27]

Ten days later Oliver Lyttelton wrote to Churchill with radical advice. A future Conservative Government, he wrote, would have to reverse Labour policy through deflation, devaluation, and decontrol. 'As a general part of a decontrol policy', wrote Lyttelton, 'it would be necessary to unpeg the pound in relation to the dollar ... at one sweep of the pen it would be necessary to abolish most of the controls and allow price rises to take place.'[28]

The idea of a floating pound was financial and political dynamite and could only be discussed in the strictest secrecy. Whether Churchill did entertain the idea is not known, but it seems unlikely. When he returned to office in 1951 he did so without any plan or intent to float the pound, and he passed over Lyttelton's claims to be Chancellor of the Exchequer. Churchill was more interested in politics than policy. After the First World War he had argued in favour of a united front of Liberal and Conservative resistance to socialism. Now he was hopeful that Labour's plans to nationalise the iron and steel industry would bring about an alliance of anti-socialist forces. 'In my opinion', he wrote to Woolton, 'all this will come to an issue in 1948, and it is my belief that we shall all be together in one line against this vile faction.'[29]

Churchill was genuinely distressed by the economic plight of Britain, which merged in his thoughts with the melancholy of old age, and the frustrations of exclusion from office. At a dinner party on his seventy-fourth birthday he confessed his worries to his former private secretary, John Colville:

> He says that the anxiety he suffered during the Battle of the Atlantic was "a mere pup" in comparison. We could only get through if we had the power of the spirit, the unity and the absence of envy, malice and hatred which are now so conspicuously lacking. Never in his life had he felt such despair and he blamed it on the Government whose "insatiable lust for power is only equalled by their incurable incompetence in exercising it". The phrases and epigrams rolled out in the old way, but I missed that indomitable hope and conviction which characterised the Prime Minister of 1940–41.[30]

A week later Churchill prophesied at a Conservative rally in Manchester that under Labour policies Britain would be unable to support its current population of 48 million. At least a quarter of the population 'will have to disappear in one way or another', and many would die of poverty and malnutrition: 'Emigration, even if practised on a scale never before dreamed of, could not operate in time to prevent this melancholy decline.' The Conservatives, Churchill declared, would have to cut public expenditure by £500 million when they returned to office – but of where the cuts would fall he said nothing. It was left to *The Economist*, which criticised Churchill for 'inspissated Malthusian gloom' to point out that a cut of that order implied the complete abolition of food subsidies.[31]

After the economic disasters of the spring and summer the Tory party's electoral hopes were high. In November the Conservatives made sweeping gains in the local elections and a Gallup poll showed them 11 points ahead of Labour. By varying margins they continued to lead Labour in the polls throughout the following year. But discontent with Churchill's leadership was always present. In January 1948 Harold Macmillan wrote a confidential memorandum on Opposition strategy for Woolton and Churchill. The organisation of the party, he wrote, had been immensely improved over the past eighteen months. But the party still had no mechanism for co-ordinating policy. The Shadow Cabinet had neither secretary, agenda, papers or minutes, and was ill-adapted to the task. Macmillan therefore proposed that 'a small or managing committee' be set up to take over the task of policy-making. The membership would consist of Churchill, Eden, Salisbury, the leader in the Lords, and James Stuart, the Chief Whip.

Woolton told Macmillan that he entirely agreed with his memorandum. But Churchill wrote:

I do not agree with what you propose, and I do not think our colleagues would either. It would be a great mistake to formalise the loose and unsubstantial association which governs the work of an Opposition. I propose to continue with the present system as long as I am in charge.

Macmillan returned to the attack, listing various questions of foreign and domestic policy on which decisions were needed. What, he inquired, was the party's real view of the immediate economic crisis? 'We seem sometimes to ask for less austerity, sometimes for more. Have we a "deflationary" plan? Are we to remain silent about "food subsidies" or be more precise (risking temporary unpopularity)?'[32] Churchill was unmoved.

Conservatives feared that while the Labour Government was vulnerable on economic policy its welfare policies were popular. By the spring of 1948 this was beginning to pose a problem, since two major aspects of welfare reform, comprehensive social insurance and the National Health Service, were due to come into operation on 5 July. As the date approached, Churchill took the lead in seeking to claim the credit for the Conservative party and, indeed, for himself. Addressing an audience of Conservative women in April 1948 he declared:

The Socialists dilate upon the National Insurance Scheme, Family Allowances, improved education, welfare foods, food subsidies, and so forth. They point to the benefits flowing to the people from these schemes and particularly to the housewives and children ... All these schemes were devised and set in motion in days before the Socialists came to office. They all date from the National Coalition Government of which I was the head. I have worked at national insurance schemes almost all my life and am responsible for several of the largest measures ever passed. The main principles of the new Health Schemes were hammered out in the days of the Coalition Government, before the party and personal malignancy of Mr Bevan plunged health policy into its present confusion.

The Family Allowance Act was passed by the Conservative Care-taker Government. School milk was started in 1934 by a Conservative

Parliament. The idea of welfare foods was largely developed by Lord Woolton. The Education Act was the work of Mr Butler ... These facts should be repeated on every occasion by those who wish the truth to be known.

A few days before the health and social insurance schemes were due to come into operation, Churchill repeated these claims to an open air rally at Luton Hoo, attended by 60,000 people.[33]

It was indeed true that in social policy there was a measure of consensus between the parties. Yet the inauguration of the health service was followed by one of the most bitter expressions of mutual hatred during the Attlee years. Aneurin Bevan, the Minister of Health, spoke of the Conservatives as 'lower than vermin'. On 10 July Churchill retaliated: 'We speak of the Minister of Health, but ought we not rather to say the Minister of Disease, for is not morbid hatred a form of mental disease, moral disease, and indeed a highly infectious form? Indeed, I can think of no better step to signalize the inauguration of the National Health Service than that a person who so obviously needs psychiatrical attention should be among the first of its patients.' In case his assault on Bevan should be taken to imply hostility to the NHS Churchill added: 'I trust however that no one will in any way relax his or her efforts to make a success of the new health scheme.'[34]

*

By the summer of 1948 the Conservatives were well ahead in the polls and, at a deeper level, the intellectual current was moving in their favour. Sir Stafford Cripps, who succeeded Dalton as Chancellor in November 1947, was an impressive figure who gave the economic policy of the Labour Government a new moral authority. But the persistence of rationing, shortages and controls was generating a reaction in favour of deregulation. In 1945 the intellectual advantage rested with socialists and planners. After 1947 it passed into the hands of businessmen and liberal economists. In a controversial pamphlet the economist Roy Harrod asked: *Are These Hardships Really Necessary?* Another prominent economist, John Jewkes, supplied theoretical chapter and verse for Churchill's attacks on socialism in his book *Ordeal by Planning.*

Churchill's Edwardian economics no longer appeared absurd. And as the temperature in the Cold War fell to freezing point, his emphasis on the liberty of the individual acquired a sharper cutting edge. George Orwell had been a stern critic of Churchill in the past. But the hero of *1984* was called Winston Smith. Meanwhile the body of earnest opinion represented by *The Times*, the *Manchester Guardian* and *The Economist*, was turning away from the Government.

Another sign of the times was the growth of opposition to the Labour Government's programme of nationalisation. The Conservatives had accepted the nationalisation of gas, electricity, coal and the railways as irreversible. But in November 1948 the Government introduced its bill for the nationalisation of iron and steel. The bill was hotly opposed by the iron and steel companies and, of course, by the Conservative party. For Churchill the most stimulating factor was the vehement opposition of the Liberals. When he led the attack on the bill in the House he seemed for a moment to forget that he was a Conservative, and quoted from one of his Edwardian speeches: 'Socialism attacks capital, Liberalism attacks monopoly.'[35]

For the Conservatives the danger was that Labour, sensing the change in the political weather, would take the lead in the retreat from collectivism. By the late 1940s they appeared to be moving towards decontrol of the economy and the abolition of rationing. In the early months of 1949 the Conservatives began to fear that after all they would lose the next general election. A wave of disappointment swept through the party when their hopes of capturing a seat from Labour at a by-election were dashed by the result at Hammersmith on 5 March. 'The demand for a policy', wrote *The Economist*, 'is no longer confined to the moderate wing who advocate a form of welfare state, but has spread to the right wing Conservatives who demand a clear-cut anti-socialist policy.'[36]

The party now rebelled against the Churchill line. Central Office surveys showed that many voters still associated the party with the mass unemployment of the 1930s, and that much more needed to be done to impress on the electorate the sincerity of the party's commitment to the Industrial Charter. On 1 April 1949 the shadow Cabinet agreed that a full statement of Conservative policy should be issued and the first draft of a manifesto, *The Right Road for Britain*, was drafted by Quintin Hogg.

Churchill realised that he must give ground. Abandoning his lordly indifference to policy-making, he threw himself into the drafting of the programme. As John Ramsden writes, he asked to be consulted at all stages, and 'contributed in substance and detail to the successive drafts.'[37]

Published in July 1949 the new policy statement was the most substantial Tory declaration to date. To a great extent the domestic section was a reworking of the Industrial and Agricultural Charters, but with more detail. The detail, however, did not extend to specific pledges on taxation or public expenditure. The Conservatives promised policies to create employment but a commitment to 'full employment' was carefully avoided. 'Under present conditions', the document warned, 'we cannot spend ourselves into prosperity. The one policy for Britain to-day is lower costs to prevent mass unemployment and reduce the cost of living.'[38]

The Labour Government was now on the brink of a third economic crisis. In September 1949 the Chancellor of the Exchequer, Sir Stafford Cripps, resolved to devalue the pound. Cripps called in Churchill for a confidential briefing in advance of the announcement. Churchill seemed greatly moved by the gravity of the decision and complimented Cripps on his wisdom and bravery. But, he added: 'I shall have to make the utmost political capital out of it.' Following the announcement, Churchill launched a withering personal attack on Cripps alleging that his reputation for honesty had been destroyed.[39]

Devaluation led to a round of cuts in public expenditure. Churchill again repeated his warning that a Conservative Government could not commit itself in advance to public spending plans which might be impossible to fulfil. In October 1949 he told the annual party conference in London:

> We are not going to try to get into office by offering bribes and promises of immediate material benefit to our people ... It would be far better for us to lose the election than to win it on false pretences.[40]

In *The Right Road for Britain* the party had committed itself, on the basis of equal pay for equal work, to equal pay for women. But when challenged in the House about the cost of this commitment, Churchill replied:

> I and my colleagues have made it absolutely clear that in present developments we shall not go an inch further than the financial resources of the country warrant and, in view of all that has occurred and is occurring, we shall hold ourselves entirely free to take a new view of the position should we be granted the opportunity.[41]

A gleeful Brendan Bracken reported to Beaverbrook: 'Churchill in a very firm and polite way has washed away all Butler Charters and now rightly declares that devaluation has created a situation that does not allow us to commit ourselves to policies that involve large expenditures of public money.'[42]

On 11 January 1950 it was announced that a general election would take place on 23 February. Churchill at once returned from a holiday in Madeira and the Research Department under R.A. Butler drew up a manifesto entitled *This Is The Road*. Churchill spent so much time redrafting the manifesto for literary style that Butler had to wrest it from his grasp before it was too late.[43] But he had not changed the substance. The manifesto was a more concise version of *The Right Road for Britain*, with a sharper cutting edge. On employment policy the manifesto stated: 'We regard the maintenance of full employment as the first aim of a Conservative Government'.[44]

The Conservatives also tried to exploit the recent revival of Scottish nationalism. Scotland was promised a Minister of State with Cabinet rank, to act as deputy to the Secretary of State for Scotland, and a Royal Commission to inquire into 'the whole situation as between Scotland and England'. During the election campaign Churchill took care to repeat these pledges in Edinburgh, and flirted outrageously with nationalist sentiment. Scotland, he claimed, would be justified in rejecting the sovereignty of the Westminster Parliament if England became a socialist state: 'I would never adopt the view that Scotland should be forced into the serfdom of Socialism as the result of a vote in the House of Commons.'[45]

By contrast with 1945, Churchill played a less dominant role in the Conservative campaign, and avoided the sensationalism of 1945. He also recognised the need to live down his reputation as a class warrior and warmonger. For decades he had been dogged by the accusation, revived during the election campaign, that he had sent troops to shoot down miners at Tonypandy. Speaking at Cardiff on 8 February, he tried to set the record straight: 'This is the true story of Tonypandy, and I hope it may replace in Welsh villages the cruel lie with which they have been fed all these years.'[46] Speaking in Edinburgh on 14 February, he followed up his tartan tease by adopting the mantle of a peacemaker. Urging a 'parley at the summit' with the Soviet Union he declared: 'The idea appeals to me of a supreme effort to bridge the gulf between the two worlds, so that each can live their life, if not in friendship, at least without the hatreds of the cold war.'[47] Bevin, the Foreign Secretary, dismissed this as 'a stunt' – unfairly, as events were to prove.

The national swing of 3.3 per cent from Labour to Conservative produced a House of Commons in which Labour had an overall majority of only six seats. For the time being neither party wanted another general election and the Government did its best to carry on as though nothing unusual had happened. Churchill's thoughts now turned to parliamentary arithmetic and the tactical significance of the Liberal vote. The leader of the Liberal party, Clement Davies, had played a leading role in the manoeuvres which had brought Churchill to power in 1940. Was he now to play the role of kingmaker for a second time?

In the spring Churchill set up a Consultative Committee under R.A.

Butler to explore the possibility of co-operation with the Liberals. By the summer, Churchill was in contact with them via Lady Violet Bonham-Carter, and three possible lines of advance were under discussion: a joint statement of the overlap between Liberal and Conservative policies, electoral pacts in the constituencies, and proportional representation in the cities – where, it was calculated, Liberal intervention damaged the Conservatives at the expense of Labour.[48]

With his Liberal past, and cavalier outlook on party, Churchill was happy to contemplate a substantial sacrifice of Tory interests. It is hardly surprising that other leading Tories, including Butler, Woolton, and Cranborne, were reluctant to follow his lead. In July Woolton wrote to Churchill urging that it would be 'quite useless' to pursue the possibility of electoral pacts with the Liberal leader, Clement Davies, who was 'of the opinion that his Party will be returned to power at the next election'. Churchill replied:

> I am sorry you have formed so adverse an opinion about Mr Davies. I do not think he imagines his Party will be returned to power at the next Election. He and his followers in the House have been most helpful lately and you have no doubt noticed the natural drawing together of the actions and opinions of Liberals and Conservatives. I understood from you that you would see Mr Davies and have a talk to him, and I mentioned this to him and he told me he had heard nothing from you. I am sorry for this.[49]

Churchill continued secret negotiations with Clement Davies during the autumn, and it was rumoured that he was offering to stand down Conservative candidates in 39 constituencies. If so he had not consulted the shadow cabinet, nor the chairman of the party. Both Woolton and Cranborne were deeply alarmed.[50] The negotiations appear to have failed because Clement Davies ruled out a national agreement between the party leaders. Local constituency parties, he explained, had complete freedom of action. But even so, there was a body of Liberals in every constituency who regarded the Conservatives as the traditional enemy.[51] In the event, the Conservatives were to benefit electorally from the Liberal vote, but without having to enter a pact.

The Labour Government might well have gone on to win the next general election but for the outbreak, in June 1950, of the Korean war. With the full support of the Opposition, the Government sent British troops to Korea and embarked, at the request of the United States Government, on a massive rearmament programme. This in turn produced rapidly rising prices and gave the Conservatives a substantial lead in the Gallup poll by the beginning of 1951. As the months passed the Conservatives turned up the heat in the House of Commons and Churchill, enjoying himself hugely, sat up through all-night sessions. Harold Macmillan detected the motive behind the mischief:

> Conscious that many people feel he is too old to form a Government and that this will probably be used as a cry against him at election, he has used these days to give a demonstration of energy and vitality. He has voted in every division; made a series of brilliant little speeches; shown all his qualities of humour and sarcasm; and crowned all by a remarkable breakfast (at 7.30 p.m.) of eggs, bacon, sausages and coffee, followed by a large whisky and soda and a huge cigar.[52]

The Labour Government was in poor shape, enfeebled by the death of Ernest Bevin and the retirement through ill health of Stafford Cripps. In April 1951 Aneurin Bevan resigned in protest against the excessive burden of the rearmament programme, and the imposition of charges for teeth and spectacles by the Chancellor of the Exchequer, Hugh Gaitskell. In September King George VI, who was due to depart on a royal tour of Australia and New Zealand in the New Year, urged Attlee to hold a general election before he left Britain. Attlee agreed and an election was called for 25 October. Shortly afterwards the King was forced to cancel his tour: he was fatally ill.

Churchill hoped to win the election with broad statements of principle and a bare minimum of detailed policy. As he said in his only election broadcast: 'We are seeking to build a lighthouse rather than dress a shop-window.' In home affairs he emphasised the common ground between the Conservatives and the Liberals, and the gulf between socialism and free enterprise: 'The difference between our outlook and the Socialist outlook in life is the difference between the ladder and the queue.'[53]

Ever since 1945 he had harried Aneurin Bevan over the Government's housing record, and argued that with the help of private enterprise the Conservatives would be able to build at a faster rate. With some four million families still forced to share accommodation because of the housing shortage, the issue was electorally damaging to Labour. But the old warhorse had taken great care not to commit himself to a numerical target. Then, at the party conference in October 1950 he was outflanked by a motion from the floor which pledged a Conservative Government to build a minimum of 300,000 houses a year. Churchill was compelled to accept the motion but accepted the target of 300,000 as 'our first priority in time of peace'.

Since the Korean war was in progress, this was obviously an important qualification. In October 1951 the war was still on, and Churchill stopped well short of a definite promise of 300,000 houses a year.[54]

Churchill was more specific about his desire for good relations with the trade unions. Since the days of the Industrial Charter the party had retreated from a confrontation with the unions and promised that no trade union legislation would be introduced. But during the election campaign there was a brief wobble when David Maxwell-Fyfe, one of the authors of the Industrial Charter, declared in an election broadcast that the party would take no legislative action *without prior union agreement*. Labour spokesmen were quick to exploit the implication that the Conservatives had legislative plans up their sleeve. Churchill intervened and reaffirmed that no legislation affecting trade unions would be introduced in the next Parliament.[55]

It may have been for the purpose of conciliating the trade unions that Churchill introduced into the manifesto an Excess Profits Levy to prevent profiteering in defence contracts. In 1937 Churchill had denounced a very similar proposal, Neville Chamberlain's National Defence Contribution. But he and Eden had been impressed by the success of more recent legislation in the United States. The printing presses had to be stopped for the pledge to be incorporated.[56]

Churchill did not forget the Liberal vote. He took the extraordinary step of delivering a speech on behalf of his old friend Lady Violet Bonham-Carter, the Liberal candidate for Colne Valley. Even though the local Conservative party had agreed not to contest the seat, the appearance of a Tory Prime Minister on a Liberal platform was a strange sight. Naturally Churchill discoursed on the common ground between Liberalism and Conservatism. The following week the *Manchester Guardian*, which had refused to endorse the Conservatives in the previous general election, declared in favour of a Churchill Government.[57]

The Labour party meanwhile attempted to portray Churchill as a warmonger and the *Daily Mirror* put the loaded question: 'Whose finger do you want on the trigger, Attlee's or Churchill's?' In view of the fact that a Labour Government had already sent British troops to fight in Korea, and almost blundered into a war with Persia, this was a dubious card to play, and perhaps a desperate one. All in all Churchill's campaign signalled a Government of extreme moderation:

What we need is a period of steady, stable administration by a broadly-based Government, wielding the national power and content to serve the nation's interests rather than give party satisfaction . . .

There will be no vindictive triumph for Tories over Socialists, no dull exclusion of Liberal and independent forces, but rather a period of healing and revival.[58]

*

At the general election the Conservatives won 321 seats, Labour 295, the Liberals 6, and others 3. More people voted Labour (13,948,605) than Conservative (13,717,538). But the Conservatives obtained an overall majority of 17: large enough for security in the division lobby, but small enough to remind the party that it was on probation with the electorate. The improvement on the 1950 result was mainly due to a reduction in the number of Liberal candidates from 475 to 109. The Liberal share of the national vote fell from 9.1 per cent to 2.5 per cent and it was estimated that in constituencies where there was no Liberal candidate, the Liberal vote divided 3:2 in favour of the Conservatives. But for this, Churchill would not have won.[59]

His first task was to compose a Cabinet. In some respects it was a deliberate revival of his wartime administration. Churchill himself resumed the post of Minister of Defence and insisted – a curious footnote this – on the recreation of the Home Guard. The Red Army, had it stormed the beaches, would have found Dad's Army lying in wait. Eden, meanwhile, returned to the Foreign Office. In home affairs Churchill had in mind the wartime success of Sir John Anderson as the co-ordinator of domestic policy and appointed a number of 'overlords' to supervise the departments. Churchill hoped that Anderson himself would return, with a peerage, as overlord of the Treasury and economic policy in general, but Anderson refused.[60] In lieu of an Overlord in economic affairs Churchill placed on either side of the Treasury two ministers to act as watchdogs: Cherwell, the Paymaster General, and the quintessential non-party grey eminence Sir Arthur Salter, who was appointed Minister of State.

Churchill had to be content with three overlords instead of four. Woolton, now Lord President of the Council, was to supervise and co-ordinate the policies of the Ministers of Food (Gwilym Lloyd George) and Agriculture (Sir Thomas Dugdale). Lord Leathers, who had been Minister of War Transport, was to be Secretary of State for the Co-ordination of Transport (John Maclay) and Fuel and Power (Geoffrey Lloyd). Cherwell was to co-ordinate scientific research and development, and act once more as the head of the Prime Minister's Statistical Section. The main flaw in the 'Overlord' experiment was that it blurred the bounds of ministerial responsibility, and the accountability of departmental ministers to the House of Commons. The Overlords became increasingly shadowy figures, and Churchill brought the experiment to an end in September 1953.

Churchill hoped at first to avoid a Party Government and form a coalition with the Liberals. The Liberal leader, Clement Davies, was offered the Ministry of Education – a portfolio, it must be said, of no great importance in Churchill's eyes. Davies consulted other senior Liberals – including Lady Violet Bonham-Carter – but they were strongly opposed and the plan fell through.[61] Churchill still hoped to add a flavour of Edwardian Liberalism by including in his Government both a Lloyd George and an Asquith. Gwilym Lloyd George was appointed once more to the Ministry of Food, an office he had previously held in the wartime Coalition. But Cyril Asquith, the judge and younger son of the former Prime Minister, refused the Lord Chancellorship.

Churchill's wooing of the Liberals was a sign of his desire to form a moderate and broadly-based Government. He evidently had no wish to recreate the Beaverbrook-Bracken axis which had cost him so dear in 1945. No invitation was extended to Beaverbrook, who set sail for Jamaica. Bracken was offered the Colonial Office – a job that would have kept him out of mischief at home – but declined on grounds of ill-health. Two very different advisers enjoyed Churchill's confidence in 1951: his son-in-law Christopher Soames, and the Cabinet Secretary, Sir Norman Brook. Soames was a Tory wet and Brook a statesman in disguise, gently steering Churchill towards workable decisions in social and economic policy.

Political observers were quick to remark on the appointment of R.A. Butler to the Treasury in preference to Oliver Lyttelton, who was associated with the more right-wing views of the City. Similarly Maxwell-Fyfe, who had offended the trade unions during the election campaign, was passed over in favour of Walter Monckton as Minister of Labour. Harold Macmillan, a strong protagonist of progressive Toryism, was the new Minister of Housing and Local Government. Allowing also for the fact that Eden, the Foreign Secretary, was a progressive in home affairs, it is clear that moderates dominated the Cabinet. Some notable right-wing figures, like Ralph Assheton and Charles Waterhouse, were excluded from office.[62]

The signals were read on the Labour benches. Richard Crossman wrote in his diary:

> ... the real free enterprisers and deflationists seem to have been kept out and there is a good deal in the view that the general make-up of the Churchill Cabinet means that it will only be very slightly to the

right of the most recent Attlee Cabinet. Just as Attlee was running what was virtually a coalition policy on a Party basis so Churchill may well do the same.[63]

On the Opposition front-bench Hugh Gaitskell observed:

'What the intelligent Tories will, of course, want to do is to be able to say to the electorate when the election comes: "No war: no unemployment: not cuts in the social services. Just good government." '[64]

Though Churchill aimed for tranquillity in home affairs, the new Government inherited an economic crisis which threatened to drive it to extremes. At the first meeting of the Cabinet, on 30 October, ministers were presented with a Treasury memorandum revealing that the balance of payments deficit had increased to an annual rate of £700 million, with another deficit of £550 million forecast for 1952. The Treasury concluded that with a probable reserve of £1000 million at the end of 1951, it would be impossible to fund the deficit in 1952.

Churchill had no pretensions to economic expertise and looked to his colleagues for guidance. But he kept an eye on the Government's public relations. At the first meeting of the Cabinet he announced that senior ministers earning £5,000 a year would have their salaries cut to £4,000: he himself proposed to accept a cut of £3,000 a year, to £7,000. The reductions were to last for three years, or the period of rearmament, whichever was the shorter.[65]

In the debate on the address on 6 November, Churchill stressed the gravity of the economic situation, and urged the House to avoid class and party strife. Plainly the objective of setting the people free had to be postponed for the time being: Churchill announced that the meat ration would be reduced at once to 1s.5d. per week – a lower level, after allowing for inflation than in wartime. On 7 December the Chancellor, R.A. Butler, raised the Bank Rate from 2 per cent to 2½ per cent, and announced a new round of austerity. The tourist allowance was cut from £100 to £50 per year, and a three month ban imposed on all building except for houses. Churchill readily accepted that economies must also be made in defence. The Labour Government had planned to devote £4,700 million to rearmament over the next three years. To the delight of Aneurin Bevan, who had condemned Labour's rearmament programme as too great for the economy to bear, Churchill announced on 6 December that the Government would be unable to meet the first year's total – a clear indication that the programme would have to be scaled down.[66]

In January Churchill set sail on the *Queen Mary* for the United States and discussions with President Truman. During his absence an Economy Committee under R.A. Butler laboured over another package of cuts. When Churchill read their conclusions he tried to tinker with them from afar. On 23 January he wrote to Butler and Eden to say that while he appreciated the work of his colleagues their proposals fell short of what was necessary. The defence estimates, he pointed out, were to be cut by nearly £200 million, but the civil estimates by only £40 million. The reduction of the civil estimates by another £50 million would provide, he thought, such convincing evidence of financial probity that the Government would be able to carry forward the whole of the budget surplus for 1951/2 instead of putting it into the new Sinking Fund. Butler and Eden merely replied that Churchill was wrong about the civil estimates: the figures included cuts which had already been made.[67] On 29 January Butler announced a second round of cuts including further import restrictions and a reduction in the tourist allowance to £25. Local education authorities were to be asked to reduce expenditure by 5 per cent. A prescription charge of one shilling was imposed on the National Health Service and a basic dental charge of £1 for all treatment except dentures.

In February an attempt was made by Treasury officials and the Bank of England to bounce the Cabinet into more drastic action. This was 'Operation Robot', a plan to make sterling convertible and float the pound. The name of the plan, supposedly, derived from its originators, Leslie ROwan, the Second Secretary at the Treasury, George BOlton, the Governor of the Bank of England, and OTto Clarke, another Treasury official. They argued that by floating the pound, the Government could take the pressure off the external balance, and place it on the internal economy. The falling pound would bring imports and exports back into equilibrium. But this was by no means an exercise in free market economics. 90 per cent of the sterling balances held by Commonwealth countries in London were to be blocked, leaving only 10 per cent freely convertible. The Chancellor, R.A. Butler, was captivated by the plan. On 19 February he dined with Churchill and the Governor of the Bank and it was decided that if the plan were adopted it should be announced on budget day, 4 March.

'The controversy that ensued', Sir Alec Cairncross writes, 'was perhaps the most bitter of the post-war years in Whitehall.'[68] The opponents of Robot began to mobilise, and Sir Robert Hall, the head of the Economic Section of the Cabinet, persuaded Butler to postpone the budget by a week. When the Robot plan was put to a small group of ministers including Churchill, Lyttelton and Cherwell on 20 February, strong opposition was expressed by Cherwell. He and Lyttelton began to bombard Churchill with conflicting advice. But Cherwell was now joined in his opposition by Sir Arthur Salter, the Minister of Economic Affairs.

Both supporters and opponents of the plan acknowledged that it would mark a clean break in the development of domestic policy. As Butler explained to Churchill:

It will be seen that this new course in our external policy requires a complete rethinking of the whole of the economic policies which have been in operation, fundamentally with the support of all parties, during the last few years ... the basic idea of internal stability of prices and employment, which has dominated policy for so long, will not be maintainable.[69]

The issue was then debated at great length in Cabinet meetings on 28 and 29 February. This was the point at which the momentum in favour of Robot was halted. The discussions revealed that the Cabinet was deeply divided. Churchill summed up by declaring that the division of opinion made it too hazardous for Butler to go ahead with the plan. The Cabinet approved, as an alternative, a more orthodox package of measures including a major reduction in food subsidies, further restrictions on imports, and a rise in the Bank Rate to 4 per cent. Butler duly announced these measures in his budget on 11 March.

'Robot' had been postponed, but its supporters continued to urge that it be put into operation soon. Cherwell was dismayed to hear Churchill musing on the attractions of 'setting the pound free', and sent him a lively warning of the political consequences:

I hope you will be under no misapprehension as to what this all means. It means that whenever our exports fail to pay for our imports, the value of the pound will fall until imports diminish ...

If this fails to close the gap the Bank Rate will have to be raised until more firms close down and dismiss their workers, leading to a further fall in demand for imported food and materials. If a 6 per cent Bank Rate, 1 million unemployed and a 2s. loaf are not enough, then there will have to be an 8 per cent Bank Rate, 2 million unemployed and a 3s. loaf ...

To rely frankly on high prices and unemployment to reduce imports would certainly put the Conservative party out for a generation.

Forwarding this to Butler, Churchill minuted: 'This is a formidable statement and arises I am sure from a purely objective view. No decision is called for at the present time but all should be borne in mind.'[70]

If Churchill had thrown his weight behind Robot the plan would, of course, have been put into action, and the framework of post-war consensus smashed to pieces. But he hesitated. This, perhaps, was the point at which his enthusiasm for market forces (which Robot allegedly represented) was overridden by his desire to maintain, for electoral reasons, the politics of the Centre. As he confided to Soames and Colville, the programme of the Tory party must be: 'Houses and meat and not getting scuppered'.[71]

The Whitehall debate rumbled on in great secrecy until June, with the opponents of Robot gradually gaining the upper hand. In May R.A. Butler remarked to Harold Nicolson (who cannot have realised the full significance of his words): 'Winston is so brave in war and so cowardly in peace.'[72] Finally Robot was pigeonholed. Convertibility was eventually reintroduced, at a fixed exchange rate, in February 1955.

The early measures taken by the Churchill Government were unpopular. In his budget on 11 March Butler announced an increase in the Bank Rate to 4 per cent and a reduction of food subsidies from £410 million to £250 million per annum. In order to cushion the impact of higher food prices, pensions and family allowances were raised. Nor was this the only conciliatory gesture towards Labour. In fulfilment of Churchill's promise, Butler announced an Excess Profits Levy of 30 per cent on all net profits above the average level for the years 1947–9. But voters were disappointed by the failure of the Conservatives to raise the standard of living. From December 1951 to February 1953 the Labour party held a clear lead in the opinion polls. Churchill, however, ran consistently ahead of his party. In May 1952, for example, Gallup recorded 42.5 per cent in support of the Conservatives, while 51 per cent were satisfied with Churchill as Prime Minister.[73]

\*

With his mind concentrated by the imminent prospect of economic disaster, Churchill set out from the start of his premiership to woo the trade unions. He was fearful, of course, of the damage that industrial unrest would inflict on the economy and hence on the Government. But to a greater extent than previous Conservative leaders he also trusted the dominant elements in the TUC. They had supported rearmament, collaborated in the war effort, and championed the Cold War. In Churchill's view they formed a patriotic estate of the realm.

To conciliate the unions Churchill chose as Minister of Labour

Walter Monckton, a barrister with long experience of labour questions but no party political record. 'Winston's riding orders to me', wrote Monckton, 'were that the Labour Party had foretold great industrial troubles if the Conservatives were elected, and he looked to me to do my best to preserve industrial peace. I said that I should seek to do that by trying to do justice . . . without caring about party politics.'[74]

The consequence of the Churchill/Monckton axis was a series of inflationary wage settlements in the nationalised industries, as public sector unions campaigned for comparability with the private sector. Monckton's technique was to refer disputes to independent courts of inquiry which arbitrated between the state and its employees. Anthony Seldon writes: 'In order not to prejudice the government's posture of impartiality, the Ministers and other government spokesmen refrained from comment on the substance of the dispute, even if it was widely held that the union's claim was unrealistic.'[75]

The Conservative Government's policy of industrial appeasement has been strongly criticised as one more example of the failure to develop a strategy for the modernisation of British industry after the war. But it was almost impossible for British politicians to create a new industrial consensus when the party system was based on rival combinations of unions and employers, and the parties were approximately equal in electoral strength. The Churchill/Monckton line was generally supported by other ministers on the grounds of political realism. A major strike leading to a run on the pound and savage deflationary measures might well have resulted in a Labour Government.

The Government's sense of insecurity was particularly acute in the first few months. In November 1951, when the Cabinet were considering the latest pay claim from the miners, Cherwell wrote to Churchill on the imperative need for higher coal production:

> Deliberately to make the miners a privileged class, perhaps with a guaranteed wages differential, would of course be a very big decision requiring most careful consideration. But I am inclined to believe it is a decision we should take, and take quickly. A "New Deal for the Miners" would have to be put across to the country as a major part of Government policy . . .
>
> We must always remember that a coal strike lasting even a week would be disastrous; a fortnight would compel us to surrender.[76]

Churchill disagreed with Cherwell's second paragraph. But so vital was it for Britain to increase exports of coal that he favoured special treatment for the miners. As he wrote to Lord Leathers, the 'overlord' of fuel and power: 'The recent increase in the number of miners is encouraging and we must try to get even more. If necessary, we shall have to give them still greater privileges and wages.'[77] Shortly after this the Government announced a special housing programme for selected mining areas.

Churchill himself had memories of industrial conciliation at the Board of Trade. By 1951 the system of wage councils, which he had introduced in 1909, had been extended to cover some two million workers. In 1952 Monckton decided to exercise his right as Minister of Labour to call for the reconsideration of Wages Councils' awards affecting a million workers in the distributive and allied trades. At the urgent request of the General Council of the TUC, Churchill received a delegation of trade union leaders at 10 Downing Street. The report in *The Times* captures the flavour of the event:

Mr Churchill listened attentively to all that the TUC representatives had to say. In promising to give full consideration to their arguments he recalled that when he was President of the Board of Trade, over forty years ago, he was responsible for the legislation which established trade boards to protect conditions of employment of the lowest paid workers, and added that he had always taken a close personal interest in the subject.

Churchill assured the trade union leaders that there was no intention of interfering with the machinery of negotiation.[78]

As this episode shows, Churchill practised the art of diplomacy on the trade unions. He wanted to demonstrate that the Government was ready not only to listen to the unions, but to heed their advice. In February 1952 the Minister of Education, Florence Horsbrugh, announced a minor economy of £25,000 in Government support for adult education classes run by the WEA, and the extra-mural departments of Universities. Among the protests the Government received was a letter from the General Secretary of the TUC, which Churchill circulated to the Cabinet. He then composed and published a reply which pulled the rug from under Miss Horsbrugh's feet. The Minister, he declared, had only put forward 'proposals': consultations were still in progress and no decision had yet been reached.

Churchill rounded off the letter with a grandiloquent conclusion:

There is perhaps no branch of our vast educational system which should more attract within its particular sphere the aid and encouragement of the State than adult education. How many must there be in Britain, after the disturbance of two destructive wars, who thirst in later life to learn about the humanities, the history of their country, the philosophies of the human race, and the arts and letters which sustain and are borne forward by the ever-conquering English language? This ranks in my opinion far above science and technical instruction, which are well sustained and not without their rewards in our present system. The mental and moral outlook of free men studying the past with free minds in order to discern the future demands the highest measures which our hard-pressed finances can sustain. I have no doubt myself that a man or woman earnestly seeking in grown-up life to be guided to wide and suggestive knowledge in its largest and most uplifted sphere will make the best of all the pupils in this age of clatter and buzz, of gape and gloat. The appetite of adults to be shown the foundation and processes of thought will never be denied by a British Administration cherishing the continuity of our Island life.

Here was a text for every lecturer in adult education to frame and hang on the wall. What golden possibilities the Great Man's words opened up! What price the 'continuity of our island life'? A cool million at least! But it was not to be. The Cabinet decided to reduce the cut from £25,000 to £15,000.[79]

In June Churchill was greatly alarmed when the unemployment figures threatened to exceed 500,000. Measures were already afoot to reduce unemployment in the Lancashire textile trades. Churchill now argued that 'the Government should make plans well ahead against the possibility of more widespread unemployment as a result of trade recession. Early consideration should be given to the measures which might be taken ... including such public works projects as the reclamation of marginal land, highway development and the construction of a Severn Barrage.' A Cabinet committee was appointed to recommend appropriate action.[80] As things turned out the committee proved to be unnecessary, since unemployment fell again, but the very fact that it was set up in the first place shows how seriously Churchill took the pledge he had given to maintain 'full employment'.

Over and above his desire for a gentleman's agreement with organised labour, Churchill was on the alert for rumbles of popular discontent. On 6 March he told the Cabinet that he was greatly disturbed by the sudden announcement of increased bus and rail fares in the London area. The decision was the work of the Transport Tribunal, an independent statutory body. At Churchill's suggestion, a statement was put out claiming that the Government had no responsibility for the increases.[81] In April he raised the issue again, when a draft White Paper on transport policy proposed to confirm the powers of the Tribunal. Churchill argued that the Government of the day should have the power to intervene in the fixing of railway fares. He did not believe, he told the Cabinet, 'that the railways should be obliged to recover all their costs, including a return on the capital invested in them'. The phrasing of the White Paper was modified to accommodate Churchill's wishes.[82]

In the course of his usual careful reading of the press Churchill noticed, towards the end of 1952, a number of stories about white hostility to Commonwealth immigrants. The total black population of the United Kingdom was only about 40,000 at this period, but the steady flow of immigrants from the West Indies was already the subject of much press comment. Churchill's racial attitudes were old-fashioned and mildly intolerant. When someone asked him whether he had seen the film *Carmen Jones* he replied that he had walked out early because he did not like 'blackamoors'.[83] Churchill feared that continued immigration would give rise to growing popular discontent, and raised the matter at the Cabinet. After a discussion on 18 December the Cabinet invited the Home Secretary to 'examine the possibilities of preventing any further increase in the number of coloured people seeking employment in this country'. The Chancellor of the Exchequer was requested 'to arrange for concurrent examination of the possibility of restricting the number of coloured people obtaining admission to the Civil Service'. It soon became apparent that the only way to restrict the size of the immigrant population was by introducing legislation, a policy certain to arouse so much Commonwealth and parliamentary opposition that ministers preferred to postpone the issue. According to the Cabinet minutes of February 1954:

> The Prime Minister said that the rapid improvement in communications was likely to lead to a continuing increase in the number of coloured people coming into the country, and their presence here would sooner or later come to be resented by large sections of the British people. It might well be true, however, that the problem had not yet assumed sufficient proportions to enable the Government to take adequate counter-measures.[84]

In social policy Churchill's broad objective was to show that the Conservatives were as committed as Labour to the welfare state. But the balance of payments crisis, and the consequent pressure for reductions in public expenditure, placed a question mark over Labour's welfare reforms. Privately Churchill himself favoured a reduction in the school-leaving age from 15 to 14, a measure that would have been fiercely attacked by Labour and the trade unions. On another front, the Treasury pressed, in the opening weeks of the Government, for swingeing cuts in cost to the Exchequer of the National Health Service.

Churchill had appointed as Minister of Health Harry Crookshank, a Tory of the old school who was eager to assist the Treasury. He proposed a variety of charges including a fee of a guinea a week for residence in hospital, and graduated charges for hospital appliances. If they had ever been announced, these proposals would have branded the Conservatives as opponents of the NHS and undermined Churchill's attempt to manoeuvre into the middle ground of politics. But they were gradually whittled away in ministerial discussions and in the event Crookshank had only minor economies to announce.[85] But even these aroused the opposition of Conservative back-benchers, and Crookshank was plainly losing the confidence of the House.

On 27 March 1952 the House was debating the second reading of the National Health Service Bill, which introduced dental and prescription charges. They were vigorously denounced by Aneurin Bevan, who claimed that the Treasury was seeking to dismantle the National Health Service. Churchill, who had come into the chamber to hear Bevan, was rising to leave the House when Iain Macleod stood up and began to reply to Bevan from the Conservative back-benches. 'I want to deal closely and with relish', said Macleod, 'with the vulgar, crude and intemperate speech to which the House of Commons has just listened.' Impressed by this opening gambit, Churchill stayed to listen as Macleod pressed home the attack in a first-class debating speech. A nearby Conservative MP overheard the whispered conversation between Churchill and the Conservative Chief Whip, Patrick Buchan-Hepburn:

> 'Who is this?' enquired Churchill. 'Macleod, sir.' There was a pause, then: 'Ministerial material?' suggested the Prime Minister. Buchan-Hepburn had learnt to be watchful of Winston's enthusiasms and replied cautiously: 'He's still quite young' – to which Churchill, who had himself been Home Secretary at the age of thirty-three, snapped back: 'What's that got to do with it?'[86]

After further soundings Churchill appointed Macleod Minister of Health in May 1952. Bevan naturally alleged that Churchill had appointed Macleod with the intention of destroying the NHS. But unlike Crookshank, Macleod believed in the health service and maintained it with very little change. Whether Churchill intended this to be the outcome is hard to say.

In Churchill's view the paramount theme in home affairs was housing. He was determined that the party should fulfil its pledge to increase the annual rate of houses built to 300,000 a year. At the Ministry of Housing and Local Government, Harold Macmillan applied great drive and ingenuity to the task. He proposed to increase the building programme in stages, with 260,000 as the target for 1953, and 300,000 for 1954. Where the outgoing Labour Government had allowed local authorities to license the building of one private house in five, Macmillan increased the ratio to one in three. To alleviate shortages of building materials, he also encouraged local authorities to build smaller houses. In the summer of 1952 there was a prolonged dispute between Macmillan and the Treasury over the scale of capital investment in the housing programme. The Treasury argued, with much justice, that capital investment in housing diverted resources from industrial investment and the export trade. At a critical Cabinet meeting on 24 July Churchill ruled that it would be wrong to accept a reduction in the programme for 1953: 'The target of 260,000 houses should be retained, but within that target every effort should be made to reduce the use of building labour and imported materials.'[87] In the event, the target for 1953 was met and the target for 1954 exceeded.

Under rent controls which dated back to the First World War more than nine million homes were occupied at rents well below an economic rate of return, and gradually falling into disrepair. Macmillan proposed that some of these houses should be demolished under a scheme of subsidised slum clearance, while others were restored to good condition by an upward revision of the controlled rents. Churchill was enthusiastic but as always eager to prevent the Opposition from obtaining an advantage. According to the Cabinet minutes, Churchill ruled 'that any legislation amending the Rent Restrictions Act must be so designed as to bring no financial benefit to the landlords: it must be made evident that the Government had no other purpose than to increase the number of habitable homes.'[88]

In housing policy the Conservatives diverged from Labour by allowing greater scope to the private sector. But there was continuity in the field of social security. In April 1952 a Cabinet chaired by Churchill rejected a proposal by the Minister of National Insurance, Osbert Peake, to raise the retirement age for men and women, and mount a general inquiry into the future growth of superannuation payments. According to the Cabinet minutes, ministers were determined to bury the idea: 'It would in any event be undesirable to aim at increasing the minimum age of eligibility for national insurance pensions or to allow it to be thought that this possibility was being contemplated. Even if such an increase were to prove acceptable to the trade unions, it would be widely misunderstood and would involve

By comparison with later Prime Ministers, Churchill took little interest in television. But on one occasion he did pass on Conservative complaints of left-wing bias to the Director-General Sir Ian Jacob – formerly a member of his wartime inner circle. 'In the current television series "Our Concern is the Future" ', he wrote, 'two prospective Labour candidates are being used – Mr Peter Parker, candidate for Bedford, and Miss Shirley Catlin, candidate for Harwich. I understand that Mr Aidan Crawley, the prospective Labour candidate for Buckingham, is at present in India preparing a programme which will be put out to the public in August.' Keeping a straight bat, Sir Ian replied that there was no lack of balance. Broadcasting, he commented, was closely monitored by supporters of both sides, neither of whom were quick to remark on favourable items. There the matter rested.[98]

It was for commercial, and not for political reasons, that the Churchill Government took the decisive step of ending the BBC's monopoly in television. There had been no mention of this in the manifesto, but following the party's return to power a commercial lobby with vocal allies on the back-benches began to put pressure on the Government. In the past Churchill had greatly resented the power of the BBC and he did indeed say to Moran: 'I am against the monopoly enjoyed by the BBC. For eleven years they kept me off the air.' But when it came to the point he was lukewarm to the point of boredom about the introduction of commercial television. It was a tiresome issue which gave rise to divisions within the party – and he was deeply uninterested in television. Beyond the fact that he allowed it to happen, the ending of the BBC's monopoly by the Television Act of 1954 owed nothing to Churchill.[99]

The introduction of commercial television reflected the wider Conservative objective of liberalising the economy or 'setting the people free'. Between 1951 and 1954 the Churchill Government swept away almost all of the economic controls which had been introduced in wartime and retained by the Attlee Governments. As R.A. Butler wrote, 1954 was the year when the war finally ended for the British trader and consumer:

Nearly all State trade had been given back to private enterprise. Competition had been restored in the steel and road haulage industries. Most price controls were abolished. Thousands of controls on the allocation of materials and the manufacture and sale of goods were removed. Import controls had been greatly relaxed. The great commodity markets had been re-opened. Above all, food rationing and other restrictions on consumption had been brought to an end.[100]

The deregulation of the economy was largely the work of Peter
Thorneycroft at the Board of Trade and Swinton at the Ministry of
Materials. Churchill's main contribution was to harry his ministers on
the subject of food rationing, which offended his conception of a Tory
Democracy of cottage-homes with well-stocked larders. When he returned
to power in October 1951 some basic foods were still rationed and the
weekly ration per person was as follows:

| Bacon and ham | 3 oz |
| Cheese | 1.5 oz |
| Butter and margarine | 7 oz |
| Cooking fats | 2 oz |
| Meat | 1s.7d. |
| Sugar | 10 oz |
| Tea | 2 oz |
| Chocolate and sweets | 26 oz |

Churchill monitored the food situation with very great care. He called
for information on levels of food consumption by comparison with the
pre-war and wartime periods, and instructed the Ministry of Food to
notify the Cabinet of all changes in the price controls.[101] When he came
to examine the size of the food ration he was puzzled by the figures and
asked the Minister of Food, Gwilym Lloyd George, to arrange for a scale
model to be made showing the individual ration. The rest of the story has
been told by Harold Macmillan:

> This exhibit duly appeared on a large tin dish – a painted piece of
> meat, a little heap of sugar and the rest. The Prime Minister looked
> at it with some satisfaction.
> 'Not a bad meal', he said. 'Not a bad meal.'
> 'But these', cried the Minister, 'are not rations for a meal or
> for a day. They are for a week.'
> 'A week!' was the outraged reply. 'Then the people are starving.
> It must be remedied.'[102]

What most exercised Churchill was the minuscule size of the meat ration. In
March 1952 he pressed hard for the restoration of meat imports to private
traders, but was told by the Minister of Food that they were reluctant to
re-enter the market. His response was to fire off a minute to Woolton and
Lloyd George: 'Would it be possible to make a plan to de-ration pork and
let it rip? . . . The great mass of the people should be taught to eat pork,

which Lord Cherwell declares contains many more calories than beef or mutton ... ' Churchill discoursed at several Cabinets on the virtues and productivity of the pig, and the need for a pig drive to fill the gap until plentiful supplies of beef and mutton were restored. But Woolton advised against on the grounds that pork would be diverted from bacon and endanger the bacon ration.[103]

Food supplies were also restricted by import controls. Brooding over the Ministry of Food's monopoly over the import of bananas, Churchill addressed a minute on the subject to the Minister of Food and the Colonial Secretary:

When Mr Joseph Chamberlain was Colonial Secretary, he introduced a striking feature into our life, the banana on the street barrow. I suggest to you that you try to make a plan for this. There was a Liverpool merchant called Jones, long since dead, who ran a line of ships especially for the banana trade during the particular season of the year. The banana is a valuable food for the people, as well as being a variation. I am sorry that it seems to have vanished from the scene.[104]

In January 1953 the Ministry of Food abandoned its monopoly and licensed private imports from countries in the sterling area.

Of course Churchill did not personally put an end to food shortages. All he could do was goad his ministers to act as soon as it was prudent to do so. He was fortunate in the fact that in 1952 the terms of trade began to shift in Britain's favour, and world food supplies increase. Nevertheless he took great pleasure in the progressive abolition of food rationing. Proceeding in stages, the Government first increased the rations and then abolished them as follows:

| | |
|---|---|
| 5 October 1952 | Tea |
| | Gammon and Ham |
| 5 February 1953 | Chocolate and sweets |
| 26 September 1953 | Sugar |
| 8 May 1954 | Cheese |
| | Butter and Margarine |
| | Cooking fats |
| 3 July 1954 | Bacon |
| | Meat |

While rationing continued, so did the Ministry of Food with its panoply of regulations enforceable in the courts. Churchill was eager to temper the powers of officials. Following a case in May 1952, in which a magistrate criticised a Ministry of Food enforcement officer, he wrote to the Minister of Food: 'How many of these so-called "snoopers" did you inherit from the last administration and how many are you now employing?' The answer was not at all to his taste and inspired another prime ministerial minute:

> I was shocked by your reply ... It seems that between April 1950 and October 1951 when you took over an immense reduction was made by the Socialist Government, namely from 1,112 to 671; and that all you have been able to achieve in the following eleven months is a reduction of six. These are figures which could not be defended in Parliament should they become public.[105]

When rationing ended, so did the necessity of a separate Ministry of Food. In October 1954 it was merged with the Ministry of Agriculture and Fisheries.

*

The Churchill Government dismantled economic controls at a much faster rate than Labour would have done. But much of Labour's nationalisation programme was accepted as irreversible. The exceptions were iron and steel, and long distance road haulage. Churchill was eager at first to press ahead with the denationalisation of steel or, as we would now say, its 'privatisation'. He appointed his son-in-law, Duncan Sandys, to the Ministry of Supply, the department responsible for the steel industry. At the first meeting of the Cabinet, in October 1951, Churchill expressed the hope that a bill for the denationalisation of steel could be passed by Christmas.

Ministers quickly discovered that the return of the steel companies to private ownership was a complex problem. Who, for example, would buy them when Labour were threatening to renationalise them with no compensation for capital gains? By March 1952, when a draft bill was discussed by the Cabinet, Churchill wanted to give priority to the denationalisation of long-distance road haulage.[106] He was determined, as he saw it, to protect the public from the monopoly powers of nationalised transport. A recent case of a widow who had inherited three lorries from her husband, and been forbidden by the local council to operate them outside a certain radius, had kindled his anger and concern.[107] In April the Cabinet agreed that road haulage should come first, with steel postponed to the next session of Parliament.

Further discussion revealed a split in the Cabinet between two schools of thought over steel. In July 1952 a number of ministers, including Butler, Salisbury and Macmillan, urged a compromise with Labour. The foreign exchange position, they argued, was so menacing that the Government should do everything it could to create a spirit of national unity. The export drive, they pointed out, would require the full co-operation of the trade unions in the form of wage restraint and the avoidance of industrial disputes. An agreement with Labour would also ensure continuity of policy. But other ministers argued that the party must carry through its pledge, and that confidence in sterling would be strengthened by the bill. Churchill summed up in favour of going ahead, stating that he thought an agreement with the Labour party on this issue was out of the question.[108] But Churchill displayed no great confidence in the measure. At lunch with Beaverbrook in September he remarked that the sale of the companies was impossible. The best solution would be to leave control to private enterprise and ownership to the Government.[109]

The bill for the denationalisation of steel was finally introduced into the House on 5 November 1952, and after proceeding through all the necessary stages received the royal assent on 14 May 1953. It was not a laissez-faire measure. The owners of the steel industry had enjoyed a close corporate relationship with the Government since the 1930s, and wanted it to continue. Duncan Sandys, likewise, favoured a measure of state intervention. While therefore the bill provided for the restoration of private ownership, it also set up an Iron and Steel Board to supervise the industry. The sale of the assets took ten years, and was completed just in time for Labour to return to power and renationalise the industry.[110]

The Conservatives had promised a radical reorganisation of the industries which remained in public ownership. This did not materialise. In April 1953 a demand by the 1922 Committee for a root-and-branch inquiry into the National Coal Board was stifled by Geoffrey Lloyd, the Minister of Fuel and Power.[111] From his detached position outside the Government, Brendan Bracken was convinced that the boards in charge of nationalised industries were incompetent, and tried in vain to rally Churchill on the subject. 'Churchill doesn't want to change anything in his Government', he wrote, 'and one cannot blame him for taking this line which is one that has been taken by most of his predecessors.'[112]

As the balance of payments deficit turned into a surplus, the fortunes of the party improved. In his second budget, on 19 April 1953, R.A. Butler took sixpence off the standard rate of income tax, bringing it down to 9s., and a multiplicity of other tax reliefs included the abolition, from 1 January 1954, of Churchill's Excess Profits Levy. Churchill was over-joyed. In a speech to Scottish Conservatives a few days after the budget he savoured his success in outmanoeuvring the Opposition. The Gov-ernment, he pointed out, was growing in popularity. It had confounded all Labour predictions of an era of Tory reaction. Unemployment was falling. Relations with the trade unions were excellent. The claim that the Conservatives would 'slash the social services and ruin the welfare state' had been disproved: the Conservatives were spending more on edu-cation, health and housing than Labour had. (This appears to have been the first occasion on which Churchill used the expression 'welfare state', which had only entered into general use in the late 1940s.) The balance of payments crisis had been resolved and taxation reduced. The 'cruel and wicked falsehood' of depicting the Conservatives as warmongers had been disproved: 'Is there a new breeze blowing on the tormented world? Certainly sudden hopes have sprung up in the hearts of peoples under every sky.'[113]

Until the spring of 1953, Churchill was active in shaping or inspiring the domestic agenda. He paid close attention to the details of the Coronation of Elizabeth II, the last great imperial pageant in British history, which took place on 2 June. But on 23 June he suffered a stroke and for some days his life was in the balance. The facts were suppressed and an announcement put out stating that his doctors had ordered him to rest. For nearly three months Churchill lived in the shadows of convalescence. Since Anthony Eden was also out of action, recovering from an operation, the chair-manship of the Cabinet devolved on R.A. Butler, who could perhaps, by revealing Churchill's condition, have seized the premiership.[114] But the conspiracy of silence prevailed. Churchill staged a partial recovery and returned to make a successful fighting speech at the annual party conference in October.

After his return to work, Churchill devoted his ebbing life and strength to the pursuit of *détente* between East and West. Both Russia and the United States now possessed the hydrogen bomb, and Churchill feared that Eisenhower's administration would force a showdown at the risk of a global Armageddon. Dogged for most of his life by the accusation that he was a warmonger, Churchill wanted to go down in history as a peacemaker. To the dismay of Eden and others, who believed that he was physically and mentally unfit to remain in office, the quest for *détente* also supplied Churchill with a heroic pretext for staying on.[115]

Against this background, Churchill's only remaining interest in home affairs was to keep things quiet. When a railway strike threatened in December 1953, he was even more anxious than Monckton to settle the dispute on the railwaymen's terms. As the Cabinet minutes record, he proposed, in effect, to cook the books:

> The Prime Minister said that he had been wondering whether the Government might not help in this by relieving the Commission of some of the interest charges with which they had been saddled on nationalisation. If a part of the capital sum were transferred to the National Debt, the Railway Staff National Tribunal could then be invited to review railwaymen's wages in the light of this improvement in the financial position of the railways.

Churchill was, in fact, mistaken in his assumption and the Cabinet turned his proposal down. But owing to the pressure he brought to bear on the Transport Commission, the dispute was resolved on terms favourable to the railwaymen.[116]

On the right wing of the party, there were rumblings of discontent over the Government's tendency towards social appeasement. In the Cabinet both Woolton, the party chairman, and Thorneycroft, the President of the Board of Trade, were sharpening the knives for cuts in social welfare. *The Economist*, in February 1954, mischievously coined the phrase 'Butskellism' to describe the convergence of policies between R.A. Butler and his Labour predecessor, Hugh Gaitskell. The following month the Cabinet Secretary, Norman Brook, sent Churchill a memorandum in which he drew his attention to the persistence, under a Conservative Government, of high levels of income and surtax.

Here we must colour in a little of the background. Although the Conservatives had been restored to office in 1951, there had been no return for the middle classes to the palmy days of the 1930s. Under R.A. Butler the standard rate of income tax was down to 9s.; under Baldwin it had never risen above 4s.6d. The wealthy, meanwhile, were subject in principle to a penal regime. In 1933 a bachelor with an earned income of £10,000 p.a. retained after tax £6,103; in 1953 he retained £3,411. Owing to steeply progressive rates of surtax, the marginal rate of tax on incomes over £5,000 was 90 per cent.

In his memorandum to the Prime Minister Brook noted that Churchill had privately mentioned the possibility of reducing the top rate of tax to 15s. in the pound – 75 per cent. The Cabinet Secretary, who was no more passive politically than most of the civil servants with whom Churchill had dealt in the past, argued that current tax rates had produced tax avoidance on a large scale and tax evasion 'on a scale large enough to endanger business morality'. At the same time they had removed 'much of the normal incentive to hard work – and all reason for taking commercial risks.' Then came a party political sting in the tail:

> If, therefore, Ministers conclude – as Mr Butler does – that we have got to go on 'for year and years in a long, slow grind' with income tax at 9s.6d. [sic] in the pound and surtax at its present levels, they will, in fact, be deciding that a Conservative government must perpetuate, or is at least powerless to alter, the pattern of society which the Socialists set out deliberately to create. It may be that this is inevitable. But Ministers should look this prospect squarely in the face before deciding that it is so.

Meeting the following day the Cabinet resolved that in the course of 1954 means must be found of securing 'a drastic reduction in public expenditure'.[117]

In the event some reduction was achieved. Total expenditure fell from £6,102,000 in 1953–4 to £6,037,000 in 1954–5. By Conservative standards the Government's record was indeed a virtuous one, or so it appears in retrospect. As a proportion of GDP, public expenditure fell from 39.4 per cent to 35 per cent in 1955. But Conservatives at the time were more conscious of the fact that taxes and public expenditure were so much higher than they had been in the 1930s. The only way of bringing about a major reduction would have been to lay the axe to the defence estimates or the welfare state. But as long as Churchill was Prime Minister, both were protected areas, and the radical tax-cutters were defeated.

By the spring of 1954 thoughts were turning towards the next general election and the timing of Churchill's retirement had become a topic of great urgency. The Grand Old Man's patent desire to cling on as long as possible was a source of anguish and embarrassment to his colleagues, who wanted him to step down in time for Eden to play himself in before the election. At a meeting of senior Conservatives on 13 April Woolton, the party chairman, was horrified when Churchill said that he himself might lead the Conservatives into another general election. At Cabinet the following day Woolton spoke up for an election in October but Churchill said that he was most anxious for the Government to have another year in office. When Woolton remarked that six months' preparation would be necessary before the campaign, Churchill replied that this was quite unnecessary: he had never had six months. 'I looked at him very hard', Woolton recorded in his diary, 'and hoped he knew what I was thinking – that he had lost more elections than any other living politician.'[118]

During the summer of 1954 Churchill was under strong pressure to retire before the annual party conference, but kept changing his mind and finally announced that he would stay on. His conference speech at Blackpool on 9 October gave no hint of his impending departure, and he followed it up with a Cabinet reshuffle in which Macmillan was appointed Minister of Defence, and Duncan Sandys succeeded him at Housing and Local Government.[119]

Stubborn and resourceful to the end, Churchill hoped that some last minute triumph in foreign policy would reprieve him from the death sentence of resignation. Insofar as home affairs entered his calculations, his aim was popularity, and if this meant spending money so be it. On 29 November 1954 – the eve of his eightieth birthday – the Cabinet discussed a paper by the Minister of Health, Iain Macleod, which drew attention to the state of the hospitals. According to the Cabinet minutes, Churchill said that he had been 'impressed by the extent to which this country was falling behind others in the provision of up-to-date hospitals, and by the urgent need to improve the hospital services in London and elsewhere. He considered that a great campaign should be undertaken to improve this part of our social services as soon as the Government's programme for pensions was completed.'[120]

Churchill's eightieth birthday, on 30 November, was marked by official celebrations and a deluge of presents and tributes. Three weeks later Churchill took Woolton aside after the Cabinet and said he thought that 'if there was going to be an early election he might lead it and he thought the large present he had received on his 80th birthday showed that he had great electoral value'. Woolton replied that although the public were affectionate this did not mean they would vote for him.[121]

By this time another wage dispute had arisen on the railways. The two main railway unions, ASLEF and the NUR, demanded a larger increase in pay than the Transport Commission was prepared to concede, and a national strike was threatened as from 20 December. The Transport Commission argued that as the railways were already running at a deficit they could not afford an increase and were, in any case, under a statutory obligation to balance the books. The unions replied that since railwaymen's wages were falling behind the wages of comparable workers in the private sector, a substantial increase was necessary and ought to be paid for by a Government subsidy if necessary.

The Minister of Labour, Walter Monckton, and the Chairman of the Transport Commission, Sir Brian Robertson, were determined to avoid a second surrender to the rail unions. Monckton put in a Cabinet paper urging the Government not to weaken the Commission's bargaining position by intervening. When the Cabinet discussed the situation on 8 December there was strong opposition to a wage subsidy. But already a crack was appearing in the Government's resolve. There was less objection to the idea of allowing the railways to run at deficit during a programme of modernisation in which the Government assisted with capital expenditure.[122]

When the Cabinet resumed its discussion two days later, Woolton and other ministers spoke strongly in favour of resisting the pay claim and Monckton warned against the consequences of giving way: 'He said it would start off another series of demands from the miners, postmen, engineers etc.'[123] But as the Cabinet minutes record, Churchill gave a clear and decisive ruling in favour of the railway unions:

> The Prime Minister said that for political and economic reasons every effort must be made to avert a railway strike. It was generally recognised that railwaymen's wages were low in relation to the level of wages generally; and the Transport Commission ought to be ready to pay reasonable wages, even if this meant increasing the deficit on their current operations. He doubted whether it was necessary to link this, as proposed, with a promise of Government support for the Commission's modernisation plans. These should certainly be considered with care, when they were submitted; but he was not himself convinced that it would be possible to bring back prosperity to British Railways by elaborate schemes of modernisation. The importance of the railways was shrinking, with the development of more modern forms of transport, and it might well be found that they would have to play in future a smaller part in the national economy. He would himself be in favour of making it plain to the Chairman of the Transport Commission that, in the Government's view, it was his duty to pay reasonable rates of wages and that, if he thought this was in conflict with his statutory duty to make the railways pay, the Minister would be ready to cover this point by a formal direction.[124]

Other members of the Cabinet expressed strong opposition to the idea of a formal direction by the Minister of Labour. But Churchill got his way. Monckton announced the appointment of a Court of Inquiry and the strike was called off. In January the Court of Inquiry duly declared that the railwaymen should receive a fair wage irrespective of the cost of running the railways, and the strike was settled on the men's terms.

This was Churchill's last significant intervention in British politics. The failure of his attempts to achieve a spectacular breakthrough in East-West relations led him to accept, at long last, that his retirement was inevitable. On 5 April 1955 he took the chair for the last time at Cabinet and announced his resignation. His final words, according to the Cabinet minutes, were as follows:

> The Prime Minister said that it remained for him to wish his colleagues all good fortune in the difficult, but hopeful situation which they had to face. He trusted that they would be enabled to further the progress already made in rebuilding the domestic stability and economic strength of the United Kingdom and in weaving still more closely the threads which bound together the countries of the Commonwealth or, as he preferred to call it, the Empire.[125]

# Conclusion

Churchill in his time was overestimated as a military leader and under-estimated in civilian affairs. In the Second World War patriotism and propaganda combined to create the legend of a statesman of almost superhuman qualities: the prophet in the wilderness, genius of grand strategy, and saviour of his country. But party political tradition was generally speaking hostile to his domestic record. Both Labour and the Tories had unflattering recollections of him while the Liberals, among whom he still had some admirers, were in a minority. Churchill's record at home was pictured, if at all, as a picaresque tale in which eccentricity and failure predominated. The conception of Churchill as a uniquely inspired war leader was not only compatible with the idea that he was inadequate in peacetime but reinforced it: war, it could be argued, was his true *métier*, but as the British people perceived in 1945 he was irrelevant to the social and economic future. He looked, wrote Aneurin Bevan, 'like a dinosaur at a light engineering exhibition'.[1]

Since Churchill's death in 1965 the main effect of historical research has been to narrow the gap between these two perceptions. No one would dispute the fact that of all the roles Churchill played his leadership in war was the most important. But we have come to see that he was exactly the same man between 1940 and 1945 as he always had been. His war-time and peacetime careers were all of a piece, a mixture of insight and error, triumph and tribulation.

Consciously or unconsciously it was Churchill's aim in life to evade classification. He was not so much a character in British politics, as a number of different characters all played by the same actor. By turns he was a romantic and a realist, a political opportunist and a statesman of conviction. Though often described as a gambler, he could be the most cautious and calculating of politicians. His reputation as an extremist, pushing every conflict to the brink, overlooks the occasions when he was all for conciliation and compromise. His judgment was equally variable. His ideas, the offspring of a restless mind working intuitively over the surface of events, were sometimes brilliant and sometimes at odds with reality.

Churchill, then, is a man of whom almost everything that can be said is true in part. From such complexity there is no escape: to simplify is to falsify. But if his wartime record now appears more variegated, so too does his career at home, and the revision works in his favour. In the long and eventful transition from a liberal to a social democracy, which coincided with his lifetime, he was no paragon of statesmanship: but he was more central, more perceptive, and more consistent than his detractors allow.

His domestic politics were a characteristic mixture of failure and success. His cavalier attitude towards party, the consequence of a profoundly egocentric personality, was a primary source of the widespread mistrust he inspired up to 1940. Paradoxically he could sometimes be very effective in a partisan role. At 35 he was more Liberal than the Liberals. At 55 he was on his best behaviour as a Tory. But over the long run he was a freelance who resented the restraints imposed by party on the liberties of Cabinet ministers. He would have liked to govern the country with an inner circle of friends and non-party administrators, at the apex of some broadly-based government. Hence his preference for peacetime coalitions. If matters had been arranged as Churchill wished, there would never have been an exclusively Liberal Government in 1906, or an exclusively Conservative Government at any time after 1918. Several of his early attempts to create a cross-party administration were thwarted. But in 1940, and again in 1951, he managed to create something very close to the type of government he desired.

In home affairs the opening and closing phases of Churchill's career – before 1914 and after 1940 – were the most successful. The more we learn of his youthful phase of radicalism and reform, the more his activities stand out as a firework display of experiment against a background of bourgeois Liberal prudence. But the nature of the achievement is debatable. In the shaping of the state his welfare reforms were of great long-term significance. But in party politics the revival of Liberalism was short-lived and the future for which Churchill and Lloyd George were working failed to materialise.

Churchill's career was seldom free of blunders. But in the long and stormy middle passage of his life, between Gallipoli and 1940, they seemed to be more frequent. At the Ministry of Munitions he bungled the affair of the skilled workers' bonus and set off a spiral of wage inflation. The wisest heads in the Conservative party deplored the stridency of his attacks on Labour, and the return to Gold – the most respectable of all his decisions – turned out badly. Yet here again there is a risk of condescension and caricature. In the Lloyd George Coalition of 1918–22 Churchill took a far more intelligent interest in social and industrial policy than his rhetoric suggested. On the Gold Standard, derating, and employment policy, he rates highly as a politician who mastered the arguments and subjected the doctrines of his officials to rigorous and intelligent scrutiny. Unlike Montagu Norman, the Governor of the Bank of England, Churchill had a vision of the factories and shipyards as the real economy, beyond the ivory towers of the City. But although he was an expansionist at heart, he could not find the right levers to pull.

His metamorphosis into a war hero in 1940 did little or nothing for his reputation in home affairs. His obstructive attitude towards social reconstruction, and the foolish 'Gestapo' speech in the General Election of 1945, conveyed the impression that he was an antediluvian figure. It is certainly true that Churchill's inability to think in party terms helped to erode the identity of Conservatism at a critical period, and contributed to the party's defeat in 1945. But here again there is scope for revision. Churchill was right, for example, to fear that the state of the economy in the aftermath of war would make it difficult to afford social reform: the experience of the Attlee Governments bore him out. In the long run he was also correct in the belief, premature in 1945, that the tide would turn against rationing, controls, and economic planning.

This brings us to a second dimension of his record: the character and consistency of his beliefs. Parties change their policies over time, but in doing so they retain, supposedly, certain underlying values. Party allegiance, therefore, is the most reliable measure of what a politician stands for in public life. In the case of a major politician the analysis can usually be taken a step further, and a career identified with a particular group or tendency within a party. But Churchill was a politician without a permanent address. He changed parties twice and seldom occupied for long the same position within a party. The conclusion, inevitably, was drawn that Churchill had no convictions at all. He was a naked adventurer whose course was determined by rootless ambition and the love of conflict.

Here again Churchill was underestimated. He was a politician whose actions arose from the interplay of ambition and belief. The workings of his ambition were undisguised, but coloured by conviction at every stage. It may, for example, seem obvious that in abandoning the Conservatives for the Liberals in 1904 he was merely a young man on the make. But in many ways his sympathies were Liberal and had been for some time. In 1897, while still a subaltern at Bangalore, he wrote to Lady Randolph:

> I am a Liberal in all but name. My views excite the pious horror of the mess. Were it not for Home Rule – to which I would never consent – I would enter Parliament as a Liberal. As it is – Tory Democracy will have to be the standard under which I range myself.[2]

The young Churchill saw himself as a progressive with liberal and popular sympathies. In this, he imagined, he was following his father's footsteps. The hero of his novel *Savrola* was a democrat and reformer pitted against a military autocrat. When he entered the House of Commons, Churchill soon found himself in harmony with the Liberals on a number of issues, including the South African war, the Army estimates and, of course, free trade.

His change of parties was the result of a natural progression in which his ambitions and opinions reinforced one another. And having joined the Liberals he was swept along for a time by a radical undercurrent and a spirit of adventure. At this juncture Churchill was a genuine radical in two senses. In his platform oratory he spoke the language of Victorian class conflict, with its picture of an industrious people struggling against a parasitical upper class of landlords, militarists and monopolists. At the same time he preached, and practised, the New Liberalism of collective social reform. At the Board of Trade and the Home Office he extended the boundaries of the state with a fervent and almost Fabian belief in the power of 'scientific organisation' to solve social problems. Yet Churchill's radicalism co-existed with more conservative features of his politics. The sheet anchor of his Liberalism was not social policy but the defence of free trade. And if Liberalism entailed, on the one hand, a steady opposition to the introduction of tariffs, it also implied resistance to socialism. Churchill spelt out the implication in no uncertain terms. Liberalism and socialism, he declared in May 1908, were antithetical: 'Socialism would kill enterprise; Liberalism would rescue enterprise from the trammels of privilege and preference.' Socialism, he continued, was 'a monstrous and imbecile conception which can find no real foothold in the brains and hearts of sensible people'.[3]

Hostility to socialism was often an alibi for indifference to poverty. But

Churchill had a strong sense of pity for the underdog. When he was First Lord of the Admiralty, shortly before the First World War, he was driving in the wilds of Sutherland in the north of Scotland when he saw an old woman bent double under the weight of two pails of water which she was struggling to carry back to her cottage. He stopped the car, spoke to the old woman, and carried the water back for her.[4] She reminded him, no doubt, of his devoted nurse Mrs Elizabeth Everest. Churchill was a patrician with a sense of *noblesse oblige* towards loyal social inferiors. Charles Masterman wrote of him: 'He desired in England a state of things where a benign upper class dispensed benefits to an industrious, *bien pensant*, and grateful working class.'[5]

Paternalism is more than a matter of kindness. It is a means of sustaining authority. Churchill believed that social reform would strengthen the authority of the state both at home and abroad. 'The Government of a State is like a pyramid', he said in April 1908, 'and I have told you before that the function of Liberalism is to broaden the base of the pyramid and so increase the stability of the whole.'[6] Churchill at this period stood on the left wing of the party. But the strong emphasis he placed on the authority of the state marked the point at which he was to diverge from the New Liberalism.

Churchill took the constitution seriously. He believed that the authority of the state was vested in Parliament, an institution of which he was deeply in awe. If, therefore, attempts were made to subvert the authority of Parliament, the Government was entitled to crack down on them. The consequence was that during the period of industrial unrest between 1910 and 1914 Churchill began to turn against the Labour movement. With workers who went on strike in the course of a dispute with an employer he had no quarrel. But the widespread talk of 'direct action', and a general strike to coerce the Government, convinced him that subversive forces were at work, and he was determined to suppress the challenge.

This perception of a potential enemy within coincided, in the summer of 1911, with his discovery of a potential enemy abroad. The Agadir crisis, and his own translation to the Admiralty, led to a phasing out of his radicalism in foreign policy and defence, and aligned him more closely with the Conservatives. A third consideration in his mind was the need to free the two main parties at Westminster from the machinations of Irish politics. From 1911 Churchill no longer saw the future in terms of the alliance between the Liberals and Labour. He wanted the Liberals to develop an alliance, or at any rate an understanding, with the Conservatives. Whether such an alliance would be directed mainly against Labour, mainly against Germany, or mainly against the Irish, is not entirely clear.

In spite of the humiliation inflicted on him by the Conservatives in 1915, Churchill's politics continued to evolve towards the Right. By the end of the war he was firmly allied with the dominant Conservative wing of the Lloyd George Coalition. But to say that Churchill was changing is to over-simplify. The political world was changing around him, and bringing to the fore the more conservative aspects of his outlook. The disintegration of the Liberal party, the rise of Labour, and the Bolshevik revolution of 1917, were creating a new political order. As Churchill explained to Sinclair in 1918, the trend of development was 'to consolidate the Tories and Radicals in one great bourgeois party – democratic and progressive but based on the existing social order – and to leave the Labour Party to fight for the New Social Order.'[7]

Churchill in the 1920s was no longer the radical of Edwardian times. His critique of Toryism had, of course, to be scrapped and replaced by the case in favour. The rhetoric of anti-socialism was enlarged to several times its pre-war size, and the theme of social progress diminished. Arguments in favour of increasing the legal rights of trade unions had to be abandoned in favour of arguments for reducing them. But in spite of all this there were marked continuities between the post-war and the pre-war Churchill: he continued, for example, to put the case for devolution.

Churchill after 1918 never gave to social reform the priority he had attached to it before 1911. But the contrast was partly accidental. If Baldwin had sent him to the Ministry of Health in 1924, as Churchill hoped, continuity would be the dominant impression. As it was, a strong thread of paternalism, interwoven at times with calculations about the enfranchisement of women, ran all through his politics in the 1920s.

Churchill also carried over from Liberalism to Toryism his commitment to free trade. Although he was prepared to make some minor concessions, he fought hard on the main issue and routed the protectionists. The most plausible explanation of his attachment to free trade is that it was so ingrained in him. It was an essential part of the economic doctrines in which he had been schooled long ago, and an essential part of his political identity as the embodiment of a union between Liberalism and Toryism.

The Slump produced an identity crisis. Churchill was disorientated for a time by the collapse of free trade and announced his conversion to protectionism – though he soon relapsed. At the same time he wandered off into the wilderness in the company of the India diehards and slipped for a while into the role of a Colonel Blimp, full of grumbles about the decline of Britain. He was only saved from irrelevance and restored to the mainstream of British politics by the impact of Hitler.

Churchill believed at first that resistance to Nazi Germany could be organised without any change in domestic policy. When he sought allies on the Left in the late 1930s he did not, for example, propose that in return for the participation of the trade unions in the rearmament campaign, they should be rewarded by concessions over the 1927 Trade Disputes Act. Nor, when he formed the Coalition Government in 1940, did Churchill imagine that far-reaching changes in social and economic policy would follow. But the point can be put more strongly. Military victory was by far the most important of Churchill's objectives: but he was also fighting for the status quo at home. Though he accepted the necessity of 'war socialism' for the duration of the conflict, he believed that social and economic policy at home should continue along the lines marked out by the National Government since 1931. He did not believe in social engineering and was entirely out of sympathy with left-wing conceptions of a planned economy or an egalitarian social order.

Churchill was by no means an absentee Prime Minister on the home front. He fought hard to hold the line against proposals for change, but in the end his hand was forced by the crisis over the Beveridge Report. In order to keep the Coalition together he was obliged to adopt a compromise position, skilfully constructed, in which he promised that the Government would make the necessary preparations for the transition to the peace, but leave the final decisions to the electorate and the first post-war Parliament.

There was a great contrast here with earlier times. At the Board of Trade, the Home Office and the Treasury, Churchill dealt with domestic policy as a subject in its own right. But in World War Two social reform was thrust upon him by the imperatives of war leadership. Having made the change, and announced his 'Four Years Plan', Churchill was sincere enough in his commitment to social reform. If a Churchill Government had been elected in 1945 some form of National Health Service would have been introduced, along with comprehensive social insurance and policies to maintain full employment. But it was no accident that he sounded unconvincing in 1945. Such policies were perfectly compatible with his long-established view that social reform was the best alternative to socialism. But they were not his: left to himself he would have played things differently. Churchill's primary emotion in 1945 was anti-socialism.

In the course of his odyssey through British politics Churchill journeyed from Right to Left in his youth, and from Left to Right in middle age. Finally, in old age, he gravitated towards the Centre. Since he never allowed himself to be hampered by a fixed programme or a rigid ideology, his ideas evolved as he adapted himself to the times. But it was a two-way process. Churchill always tried to adapt the times to himself and in doing so he drew on simple convictions and a vision of Britain acquired early on in life.

To Churchill the past was alive and Whig history was true. Magna Carta, Habeas Corpus, and the Glorious Revolution of 1688 were stepping stones in the making of a nation whose destinies both at home and abroad were guided by Providence. The achievements of nineteenth century liberalism in extending the franchise and removing the barriers to social advancement were another stage in the creation of Anglo-Saxon liberties. For Churchill, it was a story interwoven with the deeds of his own family. If the first Duke of Marlborough took his place in the pageant in the era of the Glorious Revolution, so too did Lord Randolph with his banner of Tory Democracy. It was an aristocratic vision of British history, which Churchill carried into the twentieth century by investing his Liberal welfare reforms with a magic aura of historical continuity.

If Churchill's sense of history was aristocratic, so too was his vision of society. It is often said that he did not understand the working classes and therefore lacked sympathy with them. But Churchill always had a vivid conception of the working-class and a lively sense of the potential power of the masses in a parliamentary democracy. In Churchill's view, moreover, this mass electorate was fundamentally conservative. Socialists were unrepresentative of the working-class and their doctrines antagonistic to basic working-class liberties such as the right to strike. Trade unionists, on the other hand, were authentic spokesmen of the world of labour. Although Churchill clashed with the unions in the General Strike, his experience of the trade union leaders he met in Whitehall taught him that many were pillars of society. In the Edwardian period, and again in the Second World War, he invited the trade union moderates into the corridors of power.

Churchill had a clear conception of the relationship between a paternal state and all those for whom life was a material struggle for existence. His sympathies extended to the struggles of the 'small man' – the shop-keeper, the tradesman and the clerk. It was the upper middle classes, secure in the leafy suburbs, who puzzled him: the business leaders, professionals and Hampstead intellectuals. Though recognising the value of their expertise, he could not enter into the spirit of respectable ambition which moved them. In politics he acknowledged the abilities of Bonar Law, Neville Chamberlain, Woolton, Cripps and Attlee. But for Churchill's taste there was too little risk and romance in their view of things. He much preferred the company of buccaneers like Birkenhead and Beaverbrook, or the more raffish members of his own class.

Churchill was used to a world of high stakes and glittering prizes.

Though always the aristocrat, he was also an adventurer who stood out-side the old order of the landed élite. The world of the landed estate, the fate of the rural community, the problems of agriculture, the pastoral image of England with its rolling countryside and cricket on the village green, were all too slow and static to capture his imagination. Churchill was a restless figure who needed a restless world. He belonged in spirit to the metropolis, the ever changing democracy of the towns and cities, and the world of capitalism and commerce. The society in which he grew up was plutocratic: aristocrats rubbed shoulders with financiers, press magnates, and the occasional business tycoon.

As we all know, Churchill's mind was captivated by war. But it was no less captivated by the idea of competition as the mainspring of social progress. 'The existing organisation of society', declared Churchill in 1906, 'is driven by one mainspring – competitive selection. It may be a very imperfect organisation of society, but it is all we have got between us and barbarism.'[8] When H.G. Wells claimed to discover in the Bolshevik revolution some seeds of social progress Churchill retorted:

> 'The scientific apparatus which has rendered possible the great expan-sion of the populations of the world in modern times is the result of capitalist production by individual effort. And from much earlier times the power of men to form themselves into civilised communities depended upon the observance of laws which secured personal pos-session of the fruits of work, or enterprise, or thrift, which procured respect for contracts entered into between man and man, which gave even greater prizes for greater efforts or greater aptitudes. These con-ceptions were based on the primary desire of man to seek his own benefit and that of his family. By harnessing this desire into laws, capable, no doubt, of infinite improvement, the motive power of material progress was obtained.'[9]

It was a characteristic of Churchill that he exhibited all his ideas in public. He seemed to feel a compulsion to define and explain his position. Alongside his Whig vision of history the most consistent strand in his rhetoric was his exposition of the virtues of capitalism. It was always a form of capitalism in which the state maintained a balance between the classes, and sought to shield the poor and the working-class through fiscal or social policy. Churchill, in Kenneth Morgan's phrase, stood for 'free enterprise with a human face'.[10] Beyond this he detested all peacetime plans for the regulation and control of the economy. They smacked to him of regimentation and dictatorship. Churchill was often dismissed as an adventurer but it was, of course, this quality of individualism for which, above all else, he stood. It was in his nature to believe in a land fit for adventurers to live in, and he imagined that his own conceptions of liberty and progress were shared by the mass of the people.

# Notes

The following abbreviations are used frequently in the Notes:

WSC, *MEL*           Winston S. Churchill, *My Early Life*, 1944 edition.

RSC, *WSC I–II*      Randolph S. Churchill, *Winston S. Churchill, Vols I–II*, 1966–7.

MG, *WSC III–V*     Martin Gilbert, *Winston S. Churchill, Vols III–V*, 1971–76.

RSC, *WSC CV I–II*   Randolph S. Churchill, *Winston S. Churchill: Companion Vols I–II, Parts 1, 2*, and *3*, 1967–69.

MG, *WSC CV III–V*  Martin Gilbert, *Winston S. Churchill: Companion Vols III–V, Parts 1–3*, 1972–79.

RRJ, *CS I–VIII*     Robert Rhodes James, *Winston S. Churchill: His Complete Speeches Vols I–VIII*, New York, 1974.

For all works cited below, the place of publication is London, except where otherwise stated.

## Introduction

1   John Vincent (ed), *The Crawford Papers: The journals of David Lindsay twenty-seventh Earl of Crawford and tenth Earl of Balcarres 1871–1940 during the years 1892–1940*, Manchester, 1984, p.153, diary for 9 May 1910.
2   Victor Wallace Germains, *The Tragedy of Winston Churchill*, 1931, p.278.
3   Winston S. Churchill, *Thoughts and Adventures*, 1932, p.40.
4   Quoted in David Irving, *Churchill's War: The Struggle for Power*, 1989, p.9.
5   Michael Foot, *Loyalists and Loners*, 1986, p.171.
6   Martin Gilbert, *Churchill: A Life*, 1991, p.xix.
7   Anthony Seldon, *Churchill's Indian Summer: The Conservative Government 1951–1955*, 1981, p.438.

## Prologue 1874–1900

1  WSC, *MEL*, p.47.
2  Ibid., p.60.
3  RSC, *WSC CV I Part 2*, p.856, Churchill to Lady Randolph, 10 January 1898.
4  RRJ, *CSI*, p.35, speech of 26 June 1899.
5  Churchill to Balfour 8 July 1899, Balfour Papers, British Museum Add MSS 49,694.
6  WSC, *MEL*, p.313.
7  Frederick Woods, *Young Winston's Wars*, 1972, pp.347–8, despatch of 9 March 1900; Thomas Pakenham, *The Boer War*, 1982, pp.365–6.
8  Peter de Mendelssohn, *The Age of Churchill*, 1961, p.172; *Oldham Chronicle Supplement*, 18 August 1900, p.6.
9  Churchill to Milner, 8 September 1900, Bodleian Library, Milner MSS, Dep 213, folios 128, 132–4; Churchill to Rosebery, 4 October 1900, National Library of Scotland, MSS Rosebery 1009.

I

## Peace, Retrenchment and Reform 1900–6

1  A.J.P. Taylor, 'The Statesman', in *Churchill: Four Faces and the Man*, Harmondsworth, 1973, p.14.
2  Lady Victoria Hicks Beach, *The Life of Sir Michael Hicks Beach Vol II*, 1932, pp.117–20.
3  *Parl. Deb., 4th series Vol 92*, cols 624–6, 18 April 1901.
4  Churchill to Milner, 17 March 1901, Milner MSS, Dep 214, folios 24–6.
5  WSC, *MEL*, p.381.
6  Churchill to Harcourt, 14 March 1901. Bodleian Library, MS Harcourt dep 243.
7  RRJ, *CSI*, p.78, speech of 13 May 1901.
8  Ibid.
9  RSC, *WSC CV II Part I*, p.72.
10  Alfred Havighurst, *Radical Journalist: H. W. Massingham, 1860–1924*, 1974, p.124.
11  Hicks Beach, *Hicks Beach II*, p.151.
12  RSC, *WSC CV II Pt I*, p.79; Hicks Beach, *Hicks Beach II*, p.158.
13  Winston S. Churchill, *Thoughts and Adventures*, 1932, pp.54–5.
14  Robert Rhodes James, *Rosebery*, 1963, pp.431–3.
15  Churchill to Rosebery, 17 December 1901, Rosebery MSS 1009.
16  RRJ, *CS I*, Speech of 10 January 1902 at Oldham.
17  Martin Pugh, *The Making of Modern British Politics 1867–1939*, 1982, p.103.
18  Churchill to Vincent, 17 December 1901 and 29 December 1901, D'Abernon Papers, BM Add MS 48922B.
19  RRJ, *CS I*, p.160, speech of 20 January 1903 at Hyde, Cheshire.
20  RSC, *WSC CV II, Part I*, p.122, Hamilton to Churchill 20 April 1902.
21  RRJ, *CS I*, pp.146–7, speech of 14 April 1902.
22  WSC, *MEL*, p.385. Churchill dates the dinner to the evening of the debate on the affair of Major Cartwright. This took place on 24 April.
23  RRJ, *CS I*, pp.152–3, speech of 12 May 1902.
24  RSC *WSC CV II Part I*, pp.126–134; RSC, *WSCII*, 1967, p.40.
25  Hicks Beach, *Hicks Beach II*, p.174.
26  RSC, *WSC CV II Part I*, p.168, Churchill to Rosebery 10 October 1902.
27  *Liberal Magazine*, Vol X 1902, p.609.
28  On the mythologising of Lord Randolph by Winston, see the superb analysis in Roy Foster, *Lord Randolph Churchill: A Political Life*, Oxford, 1981, pp.382–403. RSC, *WSC*

*CV II Part I*, pp.170–1: Tipper to Churchill, 3 November 1902; Churchill to Tipper 4 November 1902.

29  Ibid., p.175; Churchill to Lady Randolph, 19 December 1902.
30  *Liberal Magazine*, Vol XI 1903, pp.245–6, Churchill to the Chairman of the Oldham Unionist Association, 24 April 1903.
31  Churchill's letter to Strachey of 21 May is quoted in Richard A. Rempel, *Unionists Divided*, 1972, p.38; RRJ, *CS I*, p.191, speech at Hoxton, 21 May 1903; RSC, *WSC II*, pp.58–9, Churchill to Balfour 25 May 1903; *Liberal Magazine 1903*, p.303.
32  RRJ, *CS I p.192*, speech of 28 May.
33  Churchill to Harmsworth 26 August 1903, Northcliffe Papers BM Add MSS 62156.
34  RSC *WSC CV II Part I*, p.230, Churchill to J. T. Travis-Clegg, 9 October 1903.
35  Ibid., p.227.
36  Churchill to Morley, 16 October 1903, BM Add MS 60391AA; RSC, *CV II Part I*, p.243, Churchill to Cecil 24 October 1903.
37  A. MacCallum Scott, *Winston Spencer Churchill*, 1905, pp.200–202.
38  *Liberal Magazine*, Vol XI, 1903, p.745, letter of 19 December 1903.
39  Churchill to Gladstone 13 January and 16 January 1904, Gladstone Papers, BM Add MSS 45,986.
40  RSC, *WSC CV II Part I*, pp.279–85, Trevelyan to Churchill 31 December 1903 and Churchill to Cecil, 1 January 1904; Churchill to Trevelyan, 31 December 1904, Newcastle University Library, Trevelyan MSS, CPT 13.
41  Churchill to Morley 26 March 1904, British Museum Add MSS 60391AA.
42  RRJ *CS I*, p.277, speech of 29 April 1904.
43  *Liberal Magazine*, 1903, p.312.
44  J. B. Atkins, *Incidents and Reflections*, 1947, p.134.
45  Michael Wolff (ed), *The Collected Essays of Sir Winston Churchill Vol III: Churchill and People*, 1976, p.168; from 'My Entry into Politics,' *News of the World*, 17 February 1935.
46  Churchill, *Thoughts and Adventures*, p.55.
47  Beatrice Webb, *Our Partnership*, 1948, p.288, entry for 8 July 1903.
48  John Vincent, (ed), *The Crawford Papers*, 1984, p.57.
49  D. A. Hamer, *John Morley: Liberal Intellectual in Politics*, Oxford, 1966, p.57. I have followed Hamer in my description of Morley's life and personality.
50  RSC, *WSC CV II Part I*, p.102, Churchill to Lady Randolph 13 December 1901.
51  Ibid., p.366.
52  RRJ, *CS I*, p.369, speech of 18 October 1904.
53  RSC, *WSC CV II Part I*, p.372, Churchill to Hugh Cecil 14 November 1904.
54  RRJ, *CS I*, p.293, speech of 13 May 1904.
55  RSC *WSC II*, p.90, quoting from the Glasgow speech of 10 November 1904.
56  John Grigg, *Lloyd George: the People's Champion*, 1978.
57  Vincent, *Crawford Papers*, p.73, diary entry for 29 March 1904.
58  RRJ, *CS I*, p.499, speech of 6 October 1905.
59  RSC, *WSC II*, p.118, quoting from Bailey to Churchill 16 January 1905.
60  F. Bealey and H. Pelling, *Labour and Politics 1900–1906*, 1958, p.204.
61  RSC, *WSC CV II Part I*, p.335, T.W. Tillick to Churchill, 13 April 1904.
62  RSC, *WSC II*, p.79.
63  Michael J. Cohen, *Churchill and the Jews*, 1985, p.18.
64  Ibid., pp.21–2.
65  Churchill to Royle 11 June 1904, William Royle MSS, Manchester Central Library.
66  Vincent, *Crawford Papers*, p.75, diary for 23 June 1904.
67  RRJ, *CS I*, p.539, speech of 8 January 1906.
68  Churchill to C. P. Trevelyan, 31 December 1903, Trevelyan MSS, CPT 13, Newcastle University Library.
69  RRJ, *CS I*, p.293, speech at Newcastle, 13 May 1904.

70　Webb, *Our Partnership*, p.327, diary for 10 June 1904; RRJ, *CS I*, p.318, speech at Streatham, 16 June 1904.
71　RRJ, *CS I*, p.517, speech of 19 December 1905.
72　Ibid., p.384, speech of 11 November 1904.
73　Churchill to Royle, 21 December 1904, Royle MSS.
74　Roger Fulford, *Votes for Women*, 1957, pp.127–8; Churchill to Royle, 16 October 1905, Royle MSS.
75　Churchill to Royle, 28 November 1905, Royle MSS.
76　RRJ, *CS I*, p.529, speech of 5 January 1906.
77　RSC, *WSC II*, p.106.
78　RSC, *WSC II*, p.427, Churchill to Cecil, 17 January 1906.

## 2

## The Cause of the Left-Out Millions 1905–9

1　A. G. Gardiner, *Prophets, Priests and Kings*, 1914, p.228.
2　RRJ, *CS I*, p.676, speech of 11 October 1906.
3　Ronald Hyam, *Elgin and Churchill at the Colonial Office 1905–1908*, 1968, p.357.
4　Lucy Masterman, *C.F.G. Masterman: A Biography*, 1939, p.97.
5　Ibid., p.97.
6　Violet Bonham-Carter, *Winston Churchill As I Knew Him*, 1965, p.161.
7　Hyam, *Elgin and Churchill*, pp.503–4.
8　G.H. Mungeam, *British Rule in Kenya 1895–1912*, 1966, p.173.
9　RRJ, *CS I*, p.647, speech at Cockermouth of 25 July 1906.
10　Ibid., speech of 6 August 1906 at Wimborne.
11　Churchill to Murray 28 September 1906, Elibank MS 8801, National Library of Scotland.
12　For the speech as a whole see RRJ, *CS I*, pp.671–6, speech of 11 October 1906 at Glasgow.
13　Bentley B. Gilbert, *David Lloyd George, A Political Life: The Architect of Change 1863–1912*, 1987, p.290.
14　Roy Jenkins, *Asquith*, 1964, p.170.
15　Henry Phelps Brown, *The Origins of Trade Union Power*, Oxford, 1986, chapter 3; Rhodes James (ed), *CSI*, p.683, speech of 18 October 1906 in Manchester.
16　P. F. Clarke, *Lancashire and the New Liberalism*, Cambridge, 1971, p.190.
17　Sir Henry Lucy, *The Diary of a Journalist*, 1920, p.256.
18　Christopher Hassall, *Edward Marsh: Patron of the Arts*, 1959, p.129; Rhodes James (ed), *CSI*, p.779, speech of 20 April 1907.
19　RRJ, *CSI*, p.795, speech of 18 May 1907; Rhodes James, *Rosebery*, p.461.
20　Churchill to Spender, 22 December 1907, Spender Papers, BM Add MSS 46,388.
21　RRJ, *CSI*, p.873, speech of 22 January 1908 at Manchester.
22　Kenneth O. Morgan (ed), *The Age of Lloyd George*, 1971, pp.144–8.
23　Beatrice Webb, *Our Partnership*, 1948, p.404, diary entry for 11 March 1908.
24　For Churchill's relationship with the New Liberals see Michael Freeden, *The New Liberalism: An Ideology of Social Reform*, Oxford, 1978, pp.160–2; Peter Clarke, *Liberals and Social Democrats*, Cambridge, 1978, pp.113–17.
25　RSC, *WSC CV II Part 2*, pp.755–6, Churchill to Asquith 14 March 1908.
26　Hassall, *Edward Marsh*, p.140.
27　RSC, *WSC CV II Part 2*, p.927, Churchill to Morley 23 December 1909.
28　For Churchill's election speeches between 12 April and 23 April, see RRJ, *CSI*, pp.939–1012.
29　Ibid., pp.953–4, speech of 14 April 1908.
30　Michael J. Cohen, *Churchill and the Jews*, 1985, pp.35–8.

31  RRJ, *CS I*, pp.981–3, speech of 20 April 1908.

32  RSC, *WSC CV II Part 2* p.788, Churchill to Sir Edward Donner, 29 April 1908.

33  RSC, *WSC II*, p.261.

34  Tony Paterson, *Churchill: A Seat for Life*, Dundee, 1980, p.47.

35  William M. Walker, *Juteopolis: Dundee and its Textile Workers* 1885–1923, Edinburgh, 1979, p.379.

36  RRJ, *CS I*, p.1021, speech of 1 May 1908.

37  Ibid., pp.1028–30, speech of 4 May 1908.

38  Walker, *Juteopolis*, p.380.

39  Paterson *Churchill*, p.74.

40  CAB 37/93/83, Memorandum for the Cabinet Committee on Estimates, 17 June 1908.

41  CAB 37/94/89, 'A Note Upon British Military Needs', 27 June 1908.

42  M. V. Brett (ed), *Journals and Letters of Reginald Viscount Esher*, 1934, p.327, diary entry for 8 July 1908.

43  Edward David (ed), *Inside Asquith's Cabinet: From the Diaries of Charles Hobhouse*, 1977, p.73; Stephen Koss, *Asquith*, 1985, p.108.

44  RSC, *WSC II*, p.282.

45  Bentley B. Gilbert, *Lloyd George*, p.354.

46  Pat Jalland, *Women, Marriage and Politics 1860–1914*, 1988, p.74, quoting Lady Selborne to her husband 27 August 1908.

47  Lord Riddell, *More Pages From My Diary 1908–1914*, 1934, p.1, entry for October 1908.

48  RSC, *WSC CV II Part 2*, p.864, Gladstone to Churchill 18 December 1908.

49  RRJ, *CS II*, p.1066, speech of 6 July 1908; R. Page Arnot, *The Miners: A History of the Miners' Federation of Great Britain 1889–1910*, 1949, p.197.

50  Roger Davidson 'Llewellyn Smith the Labour Department and Government Growth 1866–1909' in Gillian Sutherland (ed), *Studies in the Growth of Nineteenth Century Government*, 1972, p.255; 'Sir Hubert Llewellyn Smith and Labour Policy 1886–1916', Cambridge Ph D, 1971, p.248. I have followed Dr Davidson closely in my account of Llewellyn Smith.

51  José Harris, *William Beveridge: A Biography*, Oxford, 1977, p.145.

52  Ibid., pp.100–1, 135, 138.

53  Ibid., p.139.

54  Ibid., pp.139–40.

55  RSC, *WSC CV II Part 2*, pp.827–31, 'Memorandum by WSC', pp.834–5, Llewellyn Smith to Churchill 11 August 1908.

56  Beveridge Papers III/26, Typescript address by Beveridge on the 50th anniversary of labour exchanges, London School of Economics.

57  Harris, *Beveridge*, p.169.

58  CAB 37/96/159 'Unemployment', 30 November 1908; RSC, *CV II Part 2*, p.853, Memorandum by WSC 11 December 1908.

59  RSC, *WSC CV II Part 2*, p.863, Churchill to Asquith 29 December 1908.

60  Harris, *Beveridge*, pp.154–5; José Harris, *Unemployment and Politics: A Study in English Social Policy 1886–1914*, Oxford, 1972, p.291.

61  RSC, *WSC CV II Part 2* pp.883–4. Memorandum by WSC, 17 April 1909

62  Ibid., pp.886–7, Churchill to Clementine, 27 April 1909.

63  Harris, *Beveridge*, p.176.

64  Quoted in Bentley B. Gilbert, *The Evolution of National Insurance in Great Britain*, 1966, p.272.

65  Bentley B. Gilbert, p.273.

66  *Parl. Deb.* 5th series, vol V, cols 512–521, 19 May 1909.

67  Elie Halévy, *The Rule of Democracy 1905–1914*, 1961 edition, p.252. I have followed Halévy in my description of the emergence of the issue.

68  RSC, *WSC CV II Part 2*, p.887, Churchill to Clementine 28 April 1909.

69  Ibid., p.880, Cabinet Memorandum of 12 March 1909.
70  CAB 37/94/107, Memorandum on the State of Employment and Trade during the first six months of 1908. Circulated on 17 August with a note by Churchill dated 8 August.
71  RSC, *WSC CV II Part 2*, pp.934–7, Churchill to McKenna September 1908 and McKenna to Churchill, 24 September 1908; Asquith to King Edward VII 20 October 1908, MS Asquith 5.
72  RRJ, *CS II*, pp.1095–6, speech of 9 October 1909.
73  BT 13/134, Churchill to Llewellyn Smith 8 April 1909 and minute by Llewellyn Smith of the same date.
74  RSC, *WSC CV II Part 2*, pp.895–8, Churchill to Lloyd George 20 June 1909.

## 3

## The Peers Versus the People 1909–11

1   RRJ, *CS II*, p.1289, speech of 17 July 1909 in Edinburgh.
2   Winston S. Churchill, *The World Crisis 1911–1914*, 1923, pp.39–40, quoting his minute to the Cabinet of 3 November 1909; pp.50–2.
3   Quoted in Grigg *Lloyd George*, p.173.
4   RSC *WSC CV II Part 2*, p.860, Churchill to Asquith 26 December 1909.
5   David (ed), *Inside Asquith's Cabinet*, p.77, diary entry for 12 April 1909.
6   Churchill to Lloyd George 8 April 1909, National Library of Wales, Lloyd George MS 20462C.
7   RSC, *WSC CV II Part 2*, pp.887–8, 904–5, Guest to Churchill 4 May 1909; Churchill to Lloyd George 13 August 1909.
8   Masterman, *C. F. G. Masterman*, p.137, note for 14 August 1909.
9   RSC, *WSC CV II Part 2*, p.909, Churchill to Clementine 14 September 1909.
10  RRJ, *CS II*, pp.1329–30, speech of 16 October at Ballo Mill, Abernathy.
11  Ibid., p.1307, speech of 7 August 1909 at Saltburn.
12  Bruce K. Murray, *The People's Budget 1909–10: Lloyd George and Liberal Politics*, Oxford 1980, p.5.
13  RRJ, *CS II*, p.1332, speech of 16 October 1909 at Ballo Mill, Abernathy.
14  Ibid., p.1318, speech of 4 September 1909.
15  Ibid., pp.1322–3; Clarke, *Liberals and Social Democrats*, pp.116–17.
16  Ibid., p.1320.
17  RRJ, *CS II*, p.1285, speech at Edinburgh of 17 July 1909.
18  Asquith to Edward VII, 21 July 1909, MS Asquith 5.
19  Grigg, *Lloyd George: The People's Champion*, pp.210–11, quoting Edward VII to Lloyd George, 7 August 1910.
20  RSC, *WSC CV II Part 2*, pp.919–20, Memo by Churchill of 8 November 1909; RRJ, *CS II*, pp.1385–6, speech of 6 December 1909 at the Manchester Free Trade Hall.
21  Quoted in the introduction by Cameron Hazlehurst to Winston S. Churchill, *The People's Rights*, 1970, pp.6–7.
22  RRJ, *CS II*, pp.1424–5, speech of 19 December 1909.
23  Quoted in Winter, *A Seat for Life*, p.83. These words do not appear in the text of the speech in Rhodes James edition.
24  Bentley B. Gilbert, *David Lloyd George: A Political Life: The Architect of Change 1863–1912*, 1987, p.404.
25  Halévy, *The Rule of Democracy p.322*.
26  RSC, *WSC CV II Part 2* pp.965–6, Cabinet Memorandum of January 1910.

27 Ibid., pp. 968–71, Cabinet Memorandum of 14 February 1910.

28 Gilbert, *Lloyd George*, pp.405–6.

29 RSC, *WSC CV II Part 2*, pp.977–8, Scott to Churchill, Royle to Churchill, 24 February 1910.

30 RRJ, *CS II* pp.1515–6 speech of 19 March 1910.

31 Ibid., p.1530, speech of 30 March 1910 in the House of Commons.

32 David Ayerst, *Garvin Of The Observer*, 1985, pp.94–6. Ayerst misses the point about imperial preference, but the scheme would have been unintelligible without it.

33 Diary of Wilfred Scawen Blunt, 31 July 1910, Blunt MSS, Fitzwilliam Museum, Cambridge.

34 RSC, *WSC CV II Part 2*, pp.1023–4, Lloyd George to Churchill 25 September 1910.

35 J. M. McEwen (ed), *The Riddell Diaries 1908–1923*, 1986, pp.46–7, diary entry for 2 July 1912.

36 Masterman, *C.F.G. Masterman*, p.165.

37 RSC, *WSC CV II Part 2*, p.1024, Churchill to Lloyd George, 6 October 1910.

38 Gilbert, *Lloyd George*, p.417.

39 Robert Blake, *The Unknown Prime Minister: The Life and Times of Andrew Bonar Law 1858–1923*, 1955, p.67.

40 John Ramsden, *A History of the Conservative Party: The Age of Balfour and Baldwin 1902–1940*, 1978, p.36.

41 RRJ, *CS II* p.1627, speech of 26 November 1910 at Bradford; p. 1650, speech at Chester, 3 December 1910.

42 Ibid., p.1635, speech of 30 November 1910 at the Drill Hall, Sheffield.

43 RSC, *WSC CV II Part 2*, p.1032, Churchill to Asquith 3 January 1911.

44 Pat Jalland, *The Liberals and Ireland*, 1980, pp.37–8.

45 RSC, *WSC CV II Part 3*, p.1375, paper of 24 February 1911; p.1377, paper of 1 March 1911.

46 Jalland, *Liberals and Ireland*, p.39.

47 RSC, *WSC CV II Part 2*, Churchill to King George V 23 February 1911; RRJ, *CSII* p.1699, speech of 22 February 1911.

48 John Campbell, *F. E. Smith: First Earl of Birkenhead*, 1983, p.235.

49 RRJ, *CS II* p.1808, speech of 15 May 1911.

50 Bentley B. Gilbert, *David Lloyd George*, pp.433–4.

51 Campbell, *F. E. Smith*, pp.267–70.

52 Vincent (ed), *Crawford Papers*, p.198, diary entry for 24 July 1911.

53 Ramsden, *Age of Balfour and Baldwin*, 1978, p.67; Koss, *Asquith*, p.134; Robert Blake, *The Unknown Prime Minister*, p.56.

# 4

## Two Faces of a Home Secretary 1910–11

1 RRJ, *CS II*, p.1464, speech of 13 January 1910.

2 RSC, *WSC II*, p.364, Churchill to Asquith 5 February 1910.

3 W. S. Blunt, *My Diaries: Being a Personal Narrative of Events 1888–1914 Part Two 1900–1924* (1921 impression), p.281, diary entry for 5 September 1909; Violet Bonham Carter, *Winston Churchill As I Knew Him* 1965, p.220.

4 RSC, *WSC CV II Part 2*, p.1151, Galsworthy to Churchill 8 March 1910; Leon Radzinowicz and Roger Hood, *The Emergence of Penal Policy in Victorian and Edwardian England*, Oxford 1990, pp.594–5.

5 Radzinowicz and Hood, *Penal Policy*, p.699.

6 Ibid., p.745.

7 *Parl. Deb.*, 5th series, vol 19, col 1347, 20 July 1910.

8 Minute by Churchill of 8 July 1910, HO 45/10631/200605.

9 Chief Constable of Birmingham to the Home Office, 10 October 1910, HO 45/10631/200605.

10 'The Abatement of Imprisonment', Cabinet memorandum of 25 October 1910, Runciman Papers, WR40 Newcastle University Library.

11 Undated note by Runciman, Runciman Papers, WR40.

12 Churchill to Asquith, 'December 1910', MSS Asquith 12.

13 Radzinowicz and Hood, *Penal Policy*, p.651.

14 RSC *WSC CV II Part 2*, p.1186, Churchill to Charles Hobhouse 25 June 1910; RRJ, *CS II*, p.1597, speech of 12 July 1910.

15 Ibid., p.1141, Gladstone to Churchill 19 February 1910.

16 See the correspondence and press cuttings in HO 144/1072/19134.

17 Radzinowicz and Hood, *Penal Policy*, p.283.

18 RSC, *WSC II*, pp.391–2; Radzinowicz and Hood, *Penal Policy*, pp.284–7.

19 Radzinowicz and Hood, *Penal Policy*, p.770.

20 RRJ, *CS II*, pp.1595, 1598, speech to the House of Commons of 20 July 1910; Masterman, *Masterman*, pp.168–9.

21 RSC, *WSC II*, pp.411, 418; Radzinowicz and Hood, *Penal Policy*, p.677.

22 Gladstone to Churchill 19 Feb 1910, Gladstone Papers, BM Add MSS 45,986.

23 RSC, *WSC CV II Part 2*, p.1015, Churchill to George V, 4 June 1910.

24 *Parl. Deb.*, 5th series, vol 18, col 1342, 4 July 1910.

25 Michael Winstanley, *The Shopkeeper's World 1880–1914*, Manchester, 1983, pp.98–9.

26 Churchill to Asquith, December 1910, MSS Asquith 12, Bodleian Library.

27 *Parl. Deb.*, 5th Series, vol 23, cols 1750–1, 31 March 1911.

28 Correspondence between Churchill and Nathan Laski 29 June to 19 July 1911, HO 45/10584.

29 RRJ, *CS II*, p.1896, speech to the House of Commons of 30 November 1911.

30 RSC, *WSC CV II Part 2*, p.1037, Churchill to George V 10 February 1911.

31 See the excellent book by G. R. Searle, *Eugenics and Politics in Britain 1900–1914*, Leyden, 1976. I have followed Searle in my account of the eugenics movement.

32 Minutes of Churchill to Troup, 27 May 1910; Donkin to Troup, 31 May 1910. The pamphlet was sent to Churchill by Walter Hely-Hutchinson, the Conservative politician and sixth earl of Donoughmore H.O. 144/1098/197900.

33 RRJ, *CS II*, p.1588, reply to deputation at 10 Downing Street, 15 July 1910.

34 Minute by Churchill of 9 September 1910 H.O. 144/1098/197900.

35 Churchill to Asquith, December 1910, MSS Asquith 12.

36 Michael J. Cohen, *Churchill and the Jews*, 1985, p. 38.

37 W. S. Blunt, *My Diaries*, p.336, diary entry for 14 October 1910.

38 Christopher Andrew, *Secret Service*, 1986 edition, pp.103–4.

39 Mendelssohn, *Age of Churchill*, p.503; Hassall, *Edward Marsh*, p.171

40 RSC, *WSC CV II Part 2*, pp.1244–5, Cabinet memorandum of 19 January 1911; Colin Rogers, *The Battle of Stepney: the Sidney Street Siege: Its Causes and Consequences*, 1981, pp.145–8.

41 Jill Pellew, *The Home Office 1848–1914: From Clerks to Bureaucrats*, 1982, p.89; Bonham Carter, *Churchill As I Knew Him*, pp.220–1.

42 RRJ *CS II*, p.1336, speech of 18 October 1909; Mendelssohn, *Age of Churchill*, p.437.

43 Antonia Raeburn, *Militant Suffragettes*, New English Library, 1974 edition, pp.150–155; Memorandum of 11 February 1910, HO 1054/187986.

44 Memorandum of 28 February 1910, HO 1054/187986.

45 Copies of Churchill to Troup, 28 February 1910 and Troup to Churchill, 4 March 1910, in Viscount Gladstone Papers, BM Add MSS 45,986.

46 *Parl. Deb.*, 5th series, vol 15, col 178, 15 March 1910; Gladstone to Churchill 16 March 1910, Churchill to Gladstone 17 March 1910, Viscount Gladstone Papers, BM Add MSS 45,986.

47  RSC, *WSC CV II Part 3*, pp.1427–34, 1443–4 Brailsford to Churchill 13 April and 15 April 1910; Churchill to Brailsford 19 April; Lytton to Churchill 15 July and memorandum by Churchill of 19 July.

48  Masterman, *Masterman*, p.166.

49  *Parl. Deb.*, 5th series, vol 19, cols 220–28, 12 July 1910.

50  RSC, *WSC CVII Part 3*, pp.1436, 1442, Brailsford to Churchill 12 July 1910, Lytton to Churchill 15 July.

51  Hassall, *Edward Marsh*, p.164, quoting Churchill to Marsh 26 September 1910.

52  Churchill to Troup 18 October 1910, minute by Churchill of 18 October, Henry to Troup 21 October, minutes by Churchill and Troup of 21 October, HO 144/1102/199183.

53  Andrew Rosen, *Rise Up Women!*, 1974, p.138.

54  Ibid., pp.138–9.

55  Copy of the Memorandum forwarded by Brailsford on 17 February 1911, HO 144/1043/183461.

56  Churchill to Henry and Henry to Churchill, 22 November 1910. Churchill initialled Henry's reply three days later. HO 144/1106/200455.

57  RSC, *WSC CV II Part 3*, p.1470. In her letter to *The Times* of 3 March 1911, Mrs Solomon was quoting from her letter to the Home Office.

58  Minute by Troup of 23 November 1911, along with a copy of the Mansell-Moulin letter and related correspondence, HO 144/1106/200455.

59  *Parl. Deb.*, 5th series, vol 20, 10 March 1911, col 1834; Emmeline Pankhurst, *My Own Story*, 1979, p.179.

60  RSC, *WSC CV II Part 2*, pp.1465–6, reply to a deputation from the Women's Freedom League reported in the *Dundee Advertiser* of 2 December 1910.

61  Rosen, *Women!*, p.150, quoting Lloyd George to Elibank 5 September 1911.

62  Beatrice Webb, *Our Partnership*, pp.465–6, diary entry for 30 November 1910.

63  Halévy, *The Rule of Democracy 1905–1914*, 1961, p.446.

64  In my account of Churchill's handling of the industrial troubles of 1910–11 I have plagiarised myself by drawing heavily on some passages of Paul Addison, 'Churchill and the Working Class 1900–1914' in Jay Winter (ed), *The Working Class in Modern British History*, Cambridge 1983, pp.43–64. My account of Tonypandy is greatly indebted to D. Smith, 'Tonypandy 1910: Definitions of Community', *Past and Present*, no. 87, May 1980, pp.158–84, and *Colliery Strike Disturbances in South Wales*, Parliamentary Papers 1911, lxiv, Cd 5568.

65  R. Page Arnot, *South Wales Miners*, 1967, pp.187–8.

66  *Colliery Disturbances*, p.5.

67  RSC, *WSC II*, pp.373–8.

68  *Colliery Disturbances*, p.48.

69  Smith, *Tonypandy*, p.160.

70  *Parl. Deb.*, 5th series, 20, 20 November 1910; 21, 7 February 1911; 22, 6 March 1911.

71  Diary of J. A. Pease, entry for 15 November 1910, Gainford MSS, Nuffield College, Oxford.

72  RSC, *WSC CV II Part 2*, p.1247, Churchill to Lloyd George 3 March 1911.

73  Jane Morgan, *Conflict and Order: the Police and Labour Disputes in England and Wales 1900–1939*, Oxford, 1987, pp.46, 48–9.

74  Diary of J. A. Pease, entries for 13 October and 22 November 1910.

75  Asquith to George V 24 November 1910. MS Asquith 5.

76  *Parl. Deb.*, 5th series, vol 26, cols 1015, 1017, 30 May 1911.

77  *Parl Deb.*, 5th series, vol 26, cols 508, 509, 25 May 1911.

78  For troop movements in south Wales see HO 45/10649/210615.

79  Troup to Henry 4 August 1911, HO 144/1157/212342.

80  RRJ, *CS II*, pp.1860–1, 1865, speeches of 15 August and 16 August 1911.

81  RSC *WSC CV II Part 2* p.1264, memorandum by Churchill of late July 1911.

82  Ibid., p.1113, Churchill to George V 11 August 1911.
83  B. Tillett, *Memories and Reflections*, 1931, pp.243–4.
84  RSC, *WSC CV II Part 2*, p.1114, Churchill to George V 12 August 1911.
85  *The Times*, 23 August 1911, p.8.
86  RSC, *WSC II*, pp.383–4.
87  *The Times*, 21 August 1911, p.6.
88  C. J. Wrigley, *David Lloyd George and the British Labour Movement*, 1976, pp.62–5.
89  *The Times*, 16 August 1911, p.7.
90  RSC, *WSC CVII Part 2*, pp.1271–2; Sir A. Fitzroy, *Memoirs Vol II* (n.d.), p.462, diary for 18 August 1911.
91  For criticisms of Churchill by Ramsay MacDonald and Keir Hardie, see *Parl. Deb.*, 5th series, vol 29, cols 2296–8, 2335–7 22 August 1911.
92  Masterman, *Masterman*, p.208.
93  Churchill to Royle 5 September 1911, Royle MSS.

# 5

# 'Undertones of War' 1911–18

1   Kenneth Grahame, *The Wind in the Willows*, 1926, (first published October 1908), p.41.
2   David French, 'Business as Usual', in Kathleen Burk (ed) *War and the State*, 1982, p.14.
3   RSC, *WSC CV II Part 2*, p.1123, Churchill to McKenna, 13 September 1911; Churchill to Asquith 23 October 1911.
4   David French, *British Economic and Strategic Planning 1905–1915*, 1982, pp.65–6.
5   Ibid., pp.66–8; French, 'Business as Usual', p.17.
6   Arthur J. Marder, *From the Dreadnought to Scapa Flow*, Oxford, 1961, pp.254–5.
7   'Pay of Men of the Royal Navy', Cabinet Paper by Churchill of 17 October 1912. Seeley Papers, Mottistone 14, Nuffield College, Oxford.
8   Marder, *From the Dreadnought to Scapa Flow*, p.267.
9   Cabinet memorandum by Churchill of 11 November 1912, Seeley Papers, Mottistone 14; Diary of J. A. Pease, 1 November 1912, Gainford MSS 39, Nuffield College, Oxford; Edward David (ed), *Inside Asquith's Cabinet: From the Diaries of Charles Hobhouse*, p.124, diary for 27 November 1912.
10  Marian Jack, 'The Purchase of the British Government's Shares in the British Petroleum Company', *Past and Present*, No. 39, April 1968, pp.139–68.
11  Jack, 'The Purchase of the British Government's Shares', pp.164–5; Marder, *From the Dreadnought to Scapa Flow*, p.270; RRJ, *CS II*, p.2131, speech to the House of Commons of 17 July 1913.
12  This paragraph reiterates the main conclusions of Marian Jack.
13  RSC, *WSC CV II Part 3*, pp.1497–8, 1500, Roberts to Churchill 21 January 1912; Churchill to Roberts 23 January 1912.
14  J. M. McEwen (ed), *The Riddell Diaries*, p.58. Diary entry for 21 March 1913.
15  David (ed), *Inside Asquith's Cabinet*, p.134, diary entry for 10 April 1913, describing the previous day's Cabinet.
16  RSC, *WSC CV II Part 3*, p.1473, Churchill to Elibank, 18 December 1911.
17  Trevor Wilson (ed), *The Political Diaries of C.P. Scott 1911–1928*, 1970, p.59, diary entry for 23 January 1912; RSC, *WSC CV II Part 3*, pp.1454–5, Memorandum by Troup of 17 July 1910.
18  Riddell, *More Pages From My Diary*, p.51: diary entry for 31 March 1912
19  David (ed), *Inside Asquith's Cabinet* pp.129–30, diary entry for 8 January 1913.
20  Cabinet memorandum of 8 January 1913, Runciman MSS WR32.
21  Walker, *Juteopolis*, pp.304–7.

22  McEwen (ed), *The Riddell Diaries*, p.32, diary entry for 15 February 1912.
23  Churchill to McKenna, 3 September 1911, McKenna Papers 3/21, Churchill College, Cambridge.
24  RRJ, *CS II*, p.1917, speech to the Eighty Club Dinner, Cecil Hotel, 1 March 1912.
25  Diary of J. A. Pease, 16 March 1912, Gainsford MSS 39; for an excellent analysis of the political reaction to the strike, see C. J. Wrigley, *David Lloyd George*, 1976, pp.67–72.
26  Diary of J.A. Pease, 21 March 1912.
27  McEwen (ed), *The Riddell Diaries*, p.41, diary for 27 April 1912.
28  Ibid., p.48, diary entry for 27 July 1912.
29  RRJ, *CS II*, p.1886, speech at Dundee, 4 October 1911.
30  Ibid., p.2014, speech at Dundee, 11 September 1912.
31  Riddell, *More Pages From My Diary*, p.85, diary entry for 27 July 1912; Don M. Cregier, *Bounder from Wales: Lloyd George's Career Before The First World War*, Missouri, 1976, p.199.
32  RSC, *WSC II*, pp.554–5; Cregier, *Bounder From Wales*, p.205.
33  McEwen (ed), *The Riddell Diaries*, pp.61, 64, diary entries for 4 April and 1 May 1913.
34  RRJ, *CS II*, p.2180, speech at the Manchester Free Trade Hall, 18 October 1913.
35  McEwen (ed), *The Riddell Diaries*, p.71, diary entry for 31 October and 1 November 1913.
36  Winston S. Churchill, *The World Crisis*, p.185.
37  Pat Jalland, *The Liberals and Ireland*, 1980, p.146.
38  RRJ, *CSII*, p.2022, speech of 12 September 1912. Churchill reiterated his support for a federal system in another speech at Dundee on 9 October 1913. See RRJ, *CSII*, pp.2167–8.
39  Jalland, *The Liberals and Ireland*, p.250.
40  RSC, *WSC II*, p.718, undated Cabinet notes.
41  Lord Beaverbrook, *Politicians and the War*, 1928, pp.22–5; Blake, *The Unknown Prime Minister* pp.220–1.
42  There are many estimates of the total British war dead between 1914 and 1918. I have taken the figure of 772,000 from J. M. Winter, *The Great War and the British People*, 1985, p.68.
43  Philip Magnus, *Kitchener: Portrait of an Imperialist*, 1958, pp.283–4; French, *British Economic and Strategic Planning*, p.170.
44  David (ed), *Inside Asquith's Cabinet*, p.184, diary entry for 25 August 1914; Cameron Hazlehurst, *Politicians and the War*, 1971, p.301.
45  RSC, *WSC II*, p.719, undated note from Churchill to Lloyd George.
46  Michael and Eleanor Brock (ed), *H.H. Asquith: Letters to Venetia Stanley*, Oxford, 1982, p.448, Asquith to Venetia Stanley, 25 February 1915.
47  MG, *CV III Part 1*, pp.619–22, Cabinet memorandum of 3 March 1915.
48  Wrigley, *David Lloyd George*, p.97; MG, *WSC III*, p.330.
49  Churchill to Lloyd George, 7 April 1915, Lloyd George Papers C3/16.
50  Riddell, *More Pages From My Diary*, p.139, diary entry for 13 April 1913.
51  Wrigley, *David Lloyd George* pp.110–15; MG *WSC CVIII Part 2*, p.999, Memo of 9 June 1915.
52  Quoted in Middlemas, *The Politics of Industrial Society*, 1979, p.82.
53  Wrigley, *David Lloyd George* pp.118–21; Middlemas, *Politics of Industrial Society*, p.75.
54  MG, *WSC III*, pp.527–9.
55  A.J.P. Taylor (ed), *Lloyd George: A Diary by Frances Stevenson*, pp.68–9, diary entry for 19 October 1915.
56  MG, *WSC CV III Part 2*, p.1485, Churchill to Lloyd George 10 April 1916.
57  Alexander MacCallum Scott MSS, Glasgow University Library MS Gen 1465/7, diary entry for 18 August 1916.
58  RRJ, *CS III*, p.2489, speech of 22 August 1916.
59  MG, *WSC III* p.33.
60  MacCallum Scott diary, entries for 23 June, 18 July and 6 August 1917, MS Gen 1465/8.

61  Tony Paterson, *Churchill*, pp.147–60.
62  Christopher Wrigley, 'The Ministry of Munitions' in Kathleen Burk (ed), *War and the State: The Transformation of British Government, 1914–1919*, 1982, p.44.
63  Winston S. Churchill, *The World Crisis 1916–1918 Part 2*, 1927, pp.298–301.
64  Wrigley, 'The Ministry of Munitions', pp.42, 44.
65  Wrigley, *David Lloyd George*, p.198, and see chapter 12 throughout.
66  Margaret Cole (ed), *The Diaries of Beatrice Webb vol 1*, 1952, p.ix, quoting from Beatrice Webb's diary of 3 June 1917.
67  Wrigley, *David Lloyd George*, pp.203–4; *History of the Ministry of Munitions vol 5: Wages and Welfare*, 1923, pp.55–6, cited below as *HMM V*, 1923, pp.55–6.
68  MG, *WSC IV*, pp.35–7.
69  *HMM V*, p.60.
70  Ibid., pp.172–80.
71  CAB 23/4, War Cabinet 248, 12 October 1917.
72  MG, *WSC IV*, p.51.
73  CAB 23/4, War Cabinet 305, 24 December 1917.
74  McCallum Scott diary, 30 January 1918, MS Gen 1465–9.
75  MG, *WSC CV IV Part 1*, p.361. Draft statement of 26 July 1918.
76  *HMM V*, p.234, interview with the Management Committee of the Engineering Employers Confederation, 4 October 1918.
77  Ibid., p.2, no specific date given.
78  Paul Barton Johnson, *Land Fit For Heroes*, Chicago, 1968, pp.103–5. Churchill's directive to the Reconstruction Committee was dated 15 November 1917.
79  CAB 23/8, War Cabinet 282, 3 October 1918.
80  MG, *WSC CV IV Part 1*, pp.402–3, extract from War Cabinet minutes of 16 October 1918.
81  Middlemas, *The Politics of Industrial Society p.142*; CAB 23/8, War Cabinet 491, 24 October 1918; War Cabinet 499, 7 November 1918.
82  B. A. Waites, 'The Effect of the First World War on Class and Status in England' in *Journal of Contemporary History*, January 1976, p.37.
83  Kenneth O. Morgan, *Consensus and Disunity The Lloyd George Coalition Government, 1918–1922*, Oxford, 1979. My account of the origins and history of the Lloyd George coalition is deeply indebted to this excellent book.
84  I am grateful to Dr Gerard De Groot for permission to see his unpublished biography of Sir Archibald Sinclair, and to quote from Sinclair's letter to his wife Marigold.
85  Henry Pelling, *Winston Churchill*, 1974, p.244.
86  MG, *WSC CV IV Part 1*, p.422, Churchill to Lloyd George 21 November 1918.
87  Walker, *Juteopolis*, p.448.
88  MG, *WSC CV IV Part 1*, p.447, Churchill to Lloyd George, 26 December 1918.

# 6

## The Impact of Labour

1  CAB 23/10 WC 575, 3 June 1919. Churchill was opposing the removal of wartime powers of censorship.
2  Lord Beaverbrook, *The Decline and Fall of Lloyd George*, 1963, pp.30–2.
3  Maurice Cowling, *The Impact of Labour*, Cambridge, 1975.
4  MG, *WSC IV*, p.181.
5  Ibid., p.192.
6  MG, *WSC CV IV, Part 1*, p.502, Churchill to Haig 31 January 1919; Robert Blake (ed), *The Private Papers of Douglas Haig 1914–1919*, 1952, p.353, diary entry for 1 February 1919.

7   MG, *WSC CVIV, Part 2*, p.881, Churchill to Lloyd George 25 September 1919.
8   Jane Morgan *Conflict and Order p.*78.
9   *Daily Herald*, 13 May 1919, p.1.
10  CAB 23/9, WC 522, 30 January 1919.
11  Iain McLean, *The Legend of Red Clydeside*, Edinburgh, 1983, pp.125–7.
12  CAB 23/9, WC 525, 4 February 1919.
13  CAB 23/10, WC 556, 14 April 1919.
14  RRJ, *WSC CS IV*, p.2788, speech of 29 May 1919.
15  CAB 23/9, WC 525, 4 February 1919.
16  *Lord Riddell's Intimate Diary of the Peace Conference and After 1918–23 1933*, p.15, diary entry for 26 January 1919; for the second half of the quotation see John M. McEwen (ed), *The Riddell Diaries*, 1986, p.255.
17  CAB 23/10, WC 557, 16 April 1919.
18  Churchill to Bonar Law, 5 July 1910, Bonar Law MSS 97/5/4, House of Lords Record Office, Morgan, *Consensus and Disunity* p.59.
19  McEwen, *Riddell Diaries*, p.285, diary entry for 22 July 1919.
20  CAB 23/15, WC 607A, 7 August 1919.
21  Morgan, *Consensus and Disunity* p.65.
22  Mary Elizabeth Short, 'The Politics of Personal Taxation: Budget-Making in Britain 1917–31', Cambridge D Phil. 1985, pp.62–8. I am greatly indebted to this excellent thesis for its lucid and authoritative treatment of the politics of postwar taxation.
23  Ibid., pp.14–16.
24  MG, *CV IV Part 2*, pp.782–5, Cabinet memorandum of 1 August 1919.
25  Ibid., p.791, Churchill to Lloyd George 4 August 1919.
26  Short, 'The Politics of Personal Taxation', p.83.
27  MG, *CV IV Part 3*, p.1642, Churchill to Lloyd George 8 October 1921.
28  R.H. Ullman, *Anglo-Soviet Relations 1917–21 Vol II*, 1961, pp.89, 96–7.
29  See Winston S. Churchill, 'Mr Wells and Bolshevism: A Reply', *Sunday Express*, 5 December 1920.
30  H.G. Wells was to develop this conception of Churchill into a sparkling satirical novel, *Men Like Gods*, 1923.
31  MG, *WSC CV IV Part 1*, p.587, Massingham to Churchill 16 March 1919.
32  For an excellent summary of the line taken by the *Herald* see Cowling, *Impact of Labour*, pp.36–8.
33  *Daily Herald*, 2 May 1919 p.4.
34  RRJ, *CS III*, p.2792, speech of 29 May 1919.
35  Morgan, *Consensus and Disunity*, pp.177–8.
36  RRJ, *CS III*, p.2818, speech of 15 July 1919.
37  John Campbell, *F.E. Smith: First Earl of Birkenhead*, 1983, p.528.
38  Morgan, *Consensus and Disunity*, p.180; RRJ, *CS III*, p.2921, speech of 3 January 1920 at Sunderland.
39  *The Nation*, 10 January 1920, p.496.
40  Morgan, *Consensus and Disunity*, p.182.
41  RRJ, *CS III*, pp.2940–2, speech of 14 February 1920 at Dundee.
42  Morgan, *Consensus and Disunity*, p.185.
43  Keith Middlemas (ed), *Thomas Jones: Whitehall Diary Vol III Ireland 1918–1925*, Oxford, 1971, p.22.
44  Christopher Andrew, *Secret Service: The Making of the British Intelligence Community*, 1985, pp.378–9.
45  MG, *CV IV Part 2*, pp.1174, 1182–3, Churchill to Lloyd George 18 August 1920; Churchill to Lloyd George 25 August 1920.
46  Andrew, *Secret Service*, pp.386–8; MG, *CVIV Part 2*, pp.1213–4, memorandum of 21 September 1920.

47  MG, *CV IV Part 2*, p.1241, Birkenhead to Churchill 17 November 1920.
48  RRJ, *CS III*, pp.3024–6, speech at Cannon Street Hotel London, 4 November 1920.
49  Beaverbrook, *Decline and Fall of Lloyd George*, pp.30–4. 'Lloyd George and Churchill', wrote Beaverbrook, 'looked out on one another like two distant snow-clad mountain peaks.'
50  Keith Middlemas (ed), *Thomas Jones: Whitehall Diary Vol I 1916–1925*, Oxford, 1969, pp.160–1, diary entry for 24 May 1921.
51  Campbell, *F. E. Smith*, pp.541–2; Cowling, *Impact of Labour*, pp.120–1.
52  W. M. Walker, *Juteopolis*, p.3.
53  Morgan, *Consensus and Disunity*, pp.102–3.
54  *Lord Riddell's Intimate Diary*, p.325, diary entry for 15 September 1921.
55  Walker, *Juteopolis*, pp.426–7; RRJ, *CS III*, pp.3128–30, 3137, speeches of 23 and 24 September at Dundee.
56  MG, *CV IV Part 3*, pp.1631–3, Churchill to Lloyd George 28 September 1921.
57  Ibid., pp.1637–9, 1642–3, Lloyd George to Churchill 1 October 1921, Churchill to Lloyd George 8 October 1921.
58  Walker, *Juteopolis*, pp.469–70.
59  Beaverbrook, *Decline and Fall of Lloyd George*, pp.120–1.
60  RRJ, *CS III*, p.3162, speech of 20 January 1922 at the Central Hall, Westminster.
61  CAB 23/20, Committee on Home Affairs 29 May 1922.
62  RRJ, *CS III*, p.3281, speech of 25 March 1922 at Northampton; MG, *WSC CVIV Part 3*, p.1861, Churchill to Lloyd George 12 April 1922.
63  Short, 'Politics of Personal Taxation' p.176, quoting Churchill to Horne 30 March 1922; MG, *WSC CV IV Part 3*, p.1864, Churchill to Lloyd George 12 April 1922.
64  Short, 'Politics of Personal Taxation' pp.172–5; MG, *CV IV Part 3*, p.1878.
65  Kenneth Morgan, 'Lloyd George's Stage Army: The Coalition Liberals 1918–1922', in A.J.P. Taylor (ed), *Lloyd George: Twelve Essays*, 1971, pp.243–5; MG, *WSC CV IV Part 3*, p.1917, Churchill to Lloyd George 15 June 1922.
66  Cowling, *Impact of Labour*, p.189.
67  RRJ, *CS IV*, p.3375, election address of 11 November 1922.
68  MG, *WSC CV IV Part 3*, p.2126, Churchill to Wolfe 20 November 1922.
69  RRJ, *CS IV*, p.3386, speech of 4 May 1923.
70  McEwen (ed), *Riddell Diaries*, p.388, diary entry for 30 May 1924.
71  John Barnes and David Nicholson (ed), *The Leo Amery Diaries Vol I, 1896–1929*, 1980, p.347, diary entry for 29 September 1923.
72  MG, *WSC CV Part 1*, pp.15–19.
73  RRJ, *CS IV*, p.3415, speech of 24 November 1923 at Leicester.
74  MG, *WSC CV Part 1*, p.70, Churchill to Barstow 30 November 1923.
75  Ibid., pp.92–4, Churchill to Violet Bonham-Carter 8 January 1924.
76  Ibid., pp.100–1.
77  Ibid., p.113, Churchill to Clementine 24 February 1924; MG, *WSCV*, p.29.
78  RRJ, *CS IV*, p.3443, speech at Caxton Hall 12 March 1924.
79  Cowling, *Impact of Labour*, p.428, quoting Chamberlain diary for 21 March 1924.
80  RRJ, *CS IV*, p.3454, speech of 7 May 1924 at Liverpool.
81  W. J. Reader, *Architect of Air Power: The Life of the First Viscount Weir of Eastwood 1877–1959*, 1968, pp.117–20; see also Churchill to Weir 6 June 1924; Weir to Churchill 10 June 1924 and Churchill to Weir 7 July 1924 in Weir of Eastwood MSS, DC 96/1/91 Glasgow University Library; and Winston S. Churchill, 'How to Get the Houses', *The Weekly Dispatch* 13 July 1924, reprinted in Michael Wolff (ed), *The Collected Essays of Sir Winston Churchill Vol II: Churchill and Politics* pp.141–2.
82  Andrew, *Secret Service*, p.431.
83  MG, *WSC CV V Part 1*, p.244, Churchill to Austen Chamberlain 14 November 1924.
84  MG *WSC V*, p.59.

# 7

## The Return to Gold 1924–5

1  MG, *WSC CV V Part 1*, p.533, Chamberlain to Baldwin 30 Aug 1925.
2  P. J. Grigg, *Prejudice and Judgment*, 1948, p.195.
3  Ibid., p.175.
4  *Parl. Deb.*, 5th series vol 311, col 327, 23 April 1936. My account of Churchill's economic ideas is greatly indebted to Dr Peter Clarke's essay, 'Churchill's Economic Ideas 1900–1930'. I am grateful to Dr Clarke for permission to refer to his essay in advance of publication.
5  Grigg, *Prejudice and Judgment*, p.174.
6  MG, *WSC CVV Part 1*, p.271, Churchill to Baldwin 28 Nov 24.
7  For Churchill's retrospective claim to have considered the question at the Board of Trade see MG, *WSC CV V Part 1*, p.465, Churchill to King George V, 23 April 1925; Gilbert, *Lloyd George*, pp.431–2.
8  MG, *WSC CV V Part 1*, pp.263–4, Neville Chamberlain diary, 26 November 1924.
9  Middlemas (ed), *Whitehall Diary I*, p.307, diary for 28 November 1924.
10  Bentley B. Gilbert, *British Social Policy 1914–1939*, 1970, p.243.
11  MG, *WSC CV V Part 1*, p.261, Cabinet minutes 26 November 1924.
12  Keith Middlemas and John Barnes, *Baldwin: A Biography*, 1969, p.328, pp.329–34.
13  MG, *WSC CV V Part 1*, p.268, Churchill to Hopkins 28 November 1924; pp.300–1, Churchill to Hopkins 14 December 1924.
14  *The Economist*, 2 May 1925, p.843.
15  T 171/247 Churchill to Warren Fisher and Colonel Guinness, 21 November 1924; Memo by Sir Richard Hopkins, n.d.
16  Ibid., Churchill to Chamberlain 30 December 1924.
17  Ibid., Deputation from National Confederation of Employers Organisations to the Chancellor of the Exchequer on the Social Services, House of Commons 4 March 1925.
18  Ibid., Niemeyer to Churchill 28 March 1925.
19  Neville to Hilda Chamberlain 5 April 1926, Neville Chamberlain Papers, Birmingham University Library, NC18/1/376–488.
20  *Parl. Deb.*, 5th series, Vol 183, 28 April 1925, cols 72, 95.
21  Keith Feiling, *Neville Chamberlain*, 1946, p.131, quoting Chamberlain's diary for 1 May 1925.
22  RRJ, *CS IV*, pp.3511–7, speech of 17 December 1924.
23  Ibid., p.3570, speech of 28 April 1925.
24  Neville to Hilda Chamberlain 2 May 1925, Chamberlain Papers NC 18/1/376–488.
25  T. J. Hatton, 'The Outlines of a Keynesian Solution', in Sean Glynn and Alan Booth, *The Road to Full Employment*, 1987, p.86; D. E. Moggridge, *The Return to Gold 1925*, Cambridge, 1969, p.95.
26  Lord Moran, *Winston Churchill: The Struggle for Survival*, 1966, pp.303–4, diary for 10 September 1945.
27  RRJ, *CS II*, p.872, speech of 14 April 1908 at Manchester. I owe this reference to Peter Clarke, 'Churchill's Economic Ideas'.
28  D. E. Moggridge, *British Monetary Policy 1924–1931*, Cambridge, 1972, pp.16–26.
29  Ibid., pp.18–21.
30  Ibid., p.58.
31  T171/246, undated memo by Churchill headed: 'Secret'; Moggridge, *Monetary Policy*, p.261. T171/246 is the principal Treasury file on the Gold Standard. But as the key documents have been published in the works of Martin Gilbert and Donald Moggridge

I have preferred to cite one of the published sources.

32  Moggridge *Monetary Policy*, pp.271, 276, Norman's reply of 2 February, and Bradbury's reply of 5 February.

33  Ibid., pp.75–6 Churchill to Niemeyer, 22 February 1926.

34  Ibid., p.77, Niemeyer to Churchill undated.

35  Sir Frederick Leith-Ross, *Money Talks*, 1968, p.92.

36  Grigg, *Prejudice and Judgment*, pp.182–4.

37  Moggridge, *British Monetary Policy*, pp.78–9.

38  *Parl. Deb.*, 5th series vol 183, 4 May 1925, cols 669–70.

39  Ibid., cols 671–2.

40  Ibid., cols 672–3.

41  MG, *WSC CV V Part 1*, pp.490–1, Churchill to Baldwin 12 June 1925; pp.494–6, Churchill to Baldwin 19 June 1925.

42  Barnes and Nicholson (ed), *Amery Diaries I*, pp.414–5, entry for 26 June 1925.

43  MG, *WSC CV V Part 1*, pp.593–5, Minutes of the Cabinet Committee on Civil Research for 19 November 1925; John Ramsden, *The Age of Balfour and Baldwin*, 1978, p.270.

44  Gordon Phillips, *The General Strike*, 1976, pp.51–2.

45  Quoted in D. E. Moggridge, *Keynes*, 1976, p.72.

46  RRJ, *CS IV*, p.3734, speech of 11 July 1925 at Epping; p.3744, speech to House of Commons 5 August 1925.

47  Phillips, *The General Strike*, pp.52–61.

48  Ibid., pp.62–5.

49  RRJ, *CS IV*, pp.3750–2, speech to House of Commons of 6 August 1925.

50  Ibid., p.3775, speech to the Engineers' Club Annual Dinner, 23 October 1925; MG, *WSC CV V Part 1*, p.591, Minutes of Cabinet Standing Committee on Expenditure 18 November 1925.

51  Ibid., p.3765, speech at Birmingham, 16 September 1925; p.3778, speech at Sheffield, 3 November 1925.

52  MG, *WSC CV V Part 1*, p.547, Churchill to Steel-Maitland, 19 September 1925.

53  Weir to Stonehaven 21 October 1925, Weir of Eastwood MSS, DC 1/251.

54  MG, *WSC CV V Part 1*, p.419, Churchill to Chamberlain 25 February 1925; David Dilks, *Neville Chamberlain: Volume I Pioneering and Reform 1869–1929*, 1985, p.424; Reader, *Architect of Air Power*, p.124; T172/1489.

55  Printed diary of Thomas Jones at the National Library of Wales, Aberystwyth. Only the first sentence of the above passage is reproduced in the published edition of the diaries.

56  Diary of Neville Chamberlain 1 November 1925, Chamberlain Papers 2/21.

57  Mary Short, 'The Politics of Personal Taxation', pp.207–8.

58  *The Economist* 20 March 1926, p.554; *Annual Register 1926*, pp.26, 40–1; Dilks, *Neville Chamberlain*, pp.453–5.

59  T 172/1494, Deputation to the Chancellor of the Exchequer 22 December 1925.

60  Ibid., with cutting from the *Sporting Life*, 11 June 1926.

61  *The Economist*, 1 May 1926, p.875.

# 8

## The General Strike and After 1926–9

1  MG, *WSC CV V Part 1*, p.521; Margaret Morris, *The General Strike*, 1976, p.187.

2  Ibid., p.685, Churchill to Grigg, 11 April 1926.

3  Keith Middlemas (ed), *Thomas Jones: Whitehall Diary Vol II 1926–30*, p.18, diary entry for 23 April 1926.

4 Ibid., pp.25–34.
5 MG, *WSC V*, p.173; G.G. Eastwood, *George Isaacs* (n.d.), pp.79–80; Henry Pelling, *A History of British Trade Unionism*, 1963, p.177. The sentence was dropped from later editions.
6 Barnes and Nicholson (ed), *Amery Diaries I*, pp.451–2, diary entry for 26 May 1926; Robert Rhodes James, *Memoirs of a Conservative: J.C.C. Davidson's Memoirs and Papers 1910–1937*, 1969, p.232.
7 Rhodes James, *Memoirs*, p.232.
8 Middlemas (ed), *Whitehall Diary II*, p.41 diary entry for 7 May 1926.
9 Rhodes James, *Memoirs*, pp.238–9.
10 Ibid., pp.242–3, 249; Thomas Jones diary, 9 May 1926, National Library of Wales.
11 Ibid., p.243.
12 CAB 23/52 CAB 25(26), Cab 26(26), 7 May 1926.
13 Charles Stuart (ed), *The Reith Diaries*, 1975, p.96, entry for 11 May 1926; and see pp.93–6.
14 PREM 11/239, Norman Brook to Churchill 29 September 1952, D. B. Pitblado to Brook 13 October 1952.
15 H. G. Wells, *Meanwhile*, 1933 edition, p.106.
16 Middlemas, *Whitehall Diary II*, p.36.
17 Phillips, *General Strike*, pp.252–3.
18 MG, *WSC CV V Part I*, pp.728–9, Churchill to Baldwin 9 June 1926.
19 Ibid., pp.773–4, Baldwin to Churchill 5 September 1926.
20 Ibid., pp.782, 805, Notes of a Meeting between Cabinet Ministers and the Mining Association, 6 September 1926.
21 MG, *WSC CV V Part I*, pp.824–6, Londonderry to Churchill 11 September 1926; p.826, Birkenhead to Churchill 12 September 1926; Middlemas, *Politics in Industrial Society*, p.201.
22 MG, *WSC CV V, Part I*, pp.831–2, Minutes of the Cabinet Coal Committee of 16 September 1926; Barnes and Nicholson, *Amery Diaries I*, p.459, entry for 24 September 1926; Middlemas, *Whitehall Diary II*, p.88, entry for 27 September 1926.
23 MG *WSC CV V, Part I*, p.863, Cabinet memorandum of 2 November 1926; and see T172/1558.
24 PRO CAB 23/53, Cab 55(26), 3 November 1926.
25 MG, *WSC CV V Part I*, pp.876–7, Notes by Churchill on the Coal Situation 11 November 1926.
26 RRJ, *CS II*, p.1826, speech to the House of Commons of 30 May 1911.
27 Middlemas, *Whitehall Diary I*, pp.311–2, Churchill to Baldwin 22 February 1925.
28 MG, *WSC CV V Part I*, p.424, Winston to Clementine 8 March 1925.
29 Phillips, *General Strike*, pp.165–6.
30 Ibid., pp.276–7.
31 Ibid., pp.276–8; MG, *WSC CVV Part I*, pp.857–8, Memo of 27 October 1926.
32 D. F. MacDonald, *The State and the Trade Unions*, 1976, pp.108–9.
33 MG, *WSC CV V Part I*, p.1000, Churchill to Spears 27 May 1927.
34 Alan Bullock, *The Life and Times of Ernest Bevin Vol I*, 1960, p.378.
35 MG, *WSC CV V Part I*, pp.577–85, Cabinet Memorandum of 17 November 1925; John Campbell, *F. E. Smith: First Earl of Birkenhead*, 1983, pp.795–6.
36 MG *WSC CV V, Part I*, pp.585–7, Cabinet memo of 17 November 1925.
37 CAB 27/336 E.F.(26), 3rd meeting, 21 February 1927.
38 CAB 27/336 E.F.(26), 2nd meeting, 14 February 1927; MG, *WSC CV V Part I*, pp.958–966, Cabinet memo of 8 March 1927.
39 Stuart (ed), *The Reith Diaries*, pp.99–100, entries for 13 April and 15 April 1928.
40 MG, *WSC CV IV Part 3*, p.1458, Cabinet memorandum of 6 May 1921.
41 MG, *WSC V*, p.226; T 172/1598, 'Mr Churchill's Visit to Italy'.
42 Mary Short, 'The Politics of Personal Taxation', pp.209–10 and see T172/1690 for

the subsequent argument between Snowdon and Churchill on the subject.

43   *The Economist* 16 April 1927, p.791; for Churchill's 1927 budget proposals see RRJ, *CS IV*, pp.4160–4188, speech of 11 April 1927.

44   Grigg, *Prejudice and Judgment*, p.193.

45   MG, *WSC CV V Part 1*, pp.998–9, Churchill to Niemeyer, 20 May 1927; Churchill to Hopkins 22 July 1928.

46   Feiling, *Chamberlain*, pp.132–3, 143; Barnes and Middlemas, *Baldwin*, pp.454–5.

47   Barnes and Nicholson (ed), *Amery Diaries I*, p.486, entry for 16 December 1926.

48   MG, *WSC V*, pp.215–6, 229.

49   MG, *WSC CV V Part 1*, p.1172, Churchill to Macmillan 5 January 1928; Harold Macmillan, *Winds of Change 1914–1939*, New York, 1966, p.176.

50   MG, *WSC CV V Part 1*, pp.1006–11, Churchill to Baldwin 6 June 1927; Churchill to Chamberlain, 7 June 1927.

51   MG, *WSC V*, p.246, quoting Churchill to Sir Richard Hopkins and Alfred Hurst, 27 September 1927.

52   Neville to Hilda Chamberlain 30 October 1927, Chamberlain Papers NC 18/1/489–601.

53   Neville to Hilda Chamberlain 11 December 1927, Chamberlain Papers NC 18/1/489–601.

54   MG, *WSC CV V Part 1*, pp.1128–1137, Cabinet memorandum of 12 December 1927.

55   CAB 24/192, CP 8(28), Memorandum by the Chancellor of the Exchequer, 20 January 1928.

56   CAB 23/57 Cab 2(28), 20 January 1928.

57   For the story in more detail see MG, *WSC V*, chapter 14.

58   Diary of Neville Chamberlain, 19 April 1928, Chamberlain Papers 2/21; CAB 23/57 Cab 23(28), 20 April 1928.

59   RRJ, *CS IV*, p.4338, speech of 24 April 1928.

60   Barnes and Nicholson (ed), *Amery Diaries I*, p.547, diary for 24 April 1928; *The Economist*, 21 April 1928, p.852.

61   Philip Williamson, 'Safety First: Baldwin, The Conservative Party and the 1929 General Election' in *Historical Journal*, vol 25, 1982, pp.395–7.

62   RRJ, *CS V*, p.4548, speech of 6 February 1929.

63   Peter Clarke, *The Keynesian Revolution in the Making 1924–1936*, 1988, pp.48–9, 53.

64   Ibid., p.58.

65   Ibid., p.61, and see CAB 24/202 CP53(29) memorandum by the Chancellor of the Exchequer, 25 February 1929.

66   John Campbell, *Lloyd George: The Goat in the Wilderness*, pp.224–5.

67   Middlemas, *Whitehall Diary II*, pp.175–6, diary entry for 6 March 1929.

68   Clarke, *The Keynesian Revolution*, pp.65–7.

69   RRJ, *CS V*, p.4593, House of Commons 15 April 1929.

70   Ibid., p.4577, speech of 15 April 1929.

71   Ibid., pp.4596, 4600, 4590, speech of 15 April 1929.

72   T 172/1495, Deputation from the Jockey Club, the National Hunt Committee and the National Coursing Committee; CAB 24/189, CP 265(27), 7 November 1927; CP 308(27), 6 December 1927; CAB 24/193, CP 90(28), 'The Totalisator from all angles', 24 March 1928; CAB 23/57 Cab 13(28), 7 March 1928.

73   RRJ, *CS V*, p.4630, speech at Wanstead 25 May 1929.

74   Ibid., p.4613, speech of 27 April 1929 at Thanet; p.4615, broadcast of 30 April 1929.

75   RRJ, *CS V*, p.4627, speech at Wanstead of 21 May 1929.

76   Pelling, *Churchill*, p.321.

77   Middlemas (ed), *Whitehall Diary II*, p.186, Thomas to Eirene Jones, 1 June 1929.

# 9

## Right Turn, Left Turn 1929–1939

1 MG, *WSC V*, p.350; Winston S. Churchill, *The Second World WAr Vol I: The Gathering Storm*, 1948, pp.27–8.

2 Ibid., p.335; John Barnes and David Nicholson (ed), *The Empire at Bay: The Leo Amery Diaries 1929–1945*, 1988, pp.40–1, diary entry for 27 June 1929.

3 RRJ, *CS V*, p.4644, speech of 3 July 1929; MG, *WSC V*, p.336; Barnes and Nicholson (ed), *Empire at Bay*, p.42, diary entry for 9 July 1929.

4 Barnes and Nicholson, *Empire at Bay*, pp.43–4, diary for 11 July 1929.

5 RRJ, *CS V*, pp.4891–3.

6 Robert Skidelsky, *Politicians and the Slump*, 1967, p.137.

7 Ibid., pp.80–2.

8 RRJ, *CS V*, p.4640, speech of 3 July 1929; pp.4647, 4653, speech of 16 July 1929.

9 Barnes and Nicholson (ed), *Empire at Bay*, p.49, diary entry for 5 August 1929.

10 MG, *WSC V*, p.343, *MG WSC CV V Part 2*, 1981, pp.61–2, Churchill to Clementine, 27 August 1929.

11 Feiling, *Neville Chamberlain*, p.172.

12 Jones, *Whitehall Diary II*, p.229, Jones to Burgon Bickersteth, 23 December 1929.

13 Feiling, *Chamberlain*, p.173, quoting Chamberlain's diary for 8 December 1929.

14 Nicolson (ed), *Harold Nicolson: Diaries and Letters* p.41, entry for 23 January 1930.

15 Michael Freeden, *Liberalism Divided: A Study in British Political Thought 1914–1939*, 1986, pp.121–4.

16 Skidelsky, *Politicians and the Slump*, pp.113, 124–5, 130.

17 Ibid., pp.145–6.

18 RRJ, *CS V*, p.4738, speech of 28 March 1930.

19 Ibid., p.4758, speech of 15 April 1930.

20 Ibid., p.4811, speech of 28 May 1930.

21 MG, *WSC CV V Part 2*, p.142, Churchill to Frank Morrish, 3 March 1930.

22 RRJ, *CS V*, pp.4731–3, speeches of 18 March, 26 March and 27 March 1930.

23 Ibid., p.4728, speech of 18 March 1930.

24 Winston Churchill, *Thoughts and Adventures*, 1932, pp.234–5.

25 Ibid., p.239.

26 MG, *WSC CV V Part 2*, p.163, Fisher to Irwin, 20 June 1930.

27 Churchill, *Thoughts and Adventures*, p.236.

28 Nigel Nicolson (ed), *Harold Nicolson: Diaries and Letters 1930–1939*, p.51, entry for 6 July 1930.

29 Barnes and Middlemas, *Baldwin*, pp.576–7.

30 MG, *WSC CV V Part 2*, pp.193–4, 204, 207, Baldwin to Churchill 14 October 1930; Churchill to Baldwin 16 October 1930; Baldwin to Churchill 21 October and footnote; Baldwin to Davidson 23 October 1930.

31 Ibid., p.111, Hoare to Irwin 13 November 1929.

32 Ibid., p.186, Churchill to Baldwin 24 September 1930.

33 Ibid., pp.250–1, Churchill to Baldwin 27 January 1931.

34 RRJ, *CS V*, p.5023, speech of 29 April 1931.

35 Tom Clarke, *My Lloyd George Diary*, 1939, p.95.

36 MG, *WSC V*, p.835, footnote 1; p.436 footnote 1; MG, *WSC CV V Part 2*, p.438, footnote 2; p.460, Churchill to Vickers 21 June 1932.

37 RRJ, *CS V*, p.4980, speech of 18 February 1931.

38 MG, *WSC CV V Part 2*, pp.275, 282–3, Churchill to Robert Boothby, 21 February 1931; Churchill to Clementine 26 February 1931.

39 Barnes and Nicholson (ed), *The Empire at Bay*, p.146, diary entry for 30 January 1931.

40 Charles Loch Mowat, *Britain between the Wars*, 1955, p.371.

41 Barnes and Nicholson (ed), *The Empire at Bay*, p.160, diary for 27 April 1931.

42 *Parl. Deb.*, 5th series, vol 254, cols 845, 847–8, 26 June 1931.

43 *Parl. Deb.*, 5th series, vol 256, cols 47–9, 8 September 1931. RRJ, *CS V*, p.5072, speech of 8 September 1931.

44 RRJ, *CS V*, p.5074, speech of 11 September 1931.

45 Kenneth Young (ed), *The Diaries of Sir Robert Bruce Lockhart 1915–1938*, 1973, p.186, entry for 20 September 1931.

46 RRJ, *CS V*, p.5083, speech of 29 September 1931.

47 *Parl. Deb.*, 5th series, vol 259, cols 131, 141, 11 November 1931.

48 *Parl. Deb.*, 5th series, vol 265, col 1181, 4 May 1932.

49 Barnes and Nicholson (ed), *The Empire at Bay*, p.384, diary entry for 19 July 1934; RRJ, *CSV*, p.5198, speech of 23 November 1932.

50 *Parl. Deb.*, 5th series, vol 274, cols 1231–3, 16 February 1933.

51 *Parl. Deb.*, 5th series, vol 256, cols 700–4, 15 September 1931.

52 Ibid., p.5134, speech of 21 April 1932, p.5285, speech of 10 July 1933; Ian M. Drummond, *The Gold Standard and the International Monetary System 1900–1939*, 1987, p.46. Few economic historians now accept Cassel's theory.

53 RRJ, *CS V*, p.5130, speech of 3 February 1932; MG, *WSC CV V Part 2*, p.399, Churchill to Boothby 6 February 1932.

54 21 April 1932, 8 May 1932, 10 May 1932, see RRJ, *CSV*, pp.5142–4, 5160–1, 5163–70.

55 Douglas Jay, *Sterling*, 1986, p.104.

56 *Parl. Deb.*, 5th series, vol 280, col 785, 10 July 1933.

57 Ibid., p.5283, speech of 10 July 1933, p.5293, speech of 12 August 1933.

58 Fraser J. Harbutt, *The Iron Curtain: Churchill, America and the Origins of the Cold War*, New York 1986, p.18, quoting from an article by Churchill in *Collier's* 22 August 1935.

59 I am grateful to Professor Warren Kimball of Rutgers University, the editor of the Churchill-Roosevelt correspondence, for this information.

60 Harbutt, *The Iron Curtain*, p.18.

61 MG, *WSC CV V Part 2*, p.989, Churchill's statement to the press of 18 January 1935.

62 *Parl. Deb.*, 5th series, vol 311, col 332, 23 April 1936.

63 RRJ, *CS V*, p.4990, speech of 5 March 1931.

64 John Campbell, *F. E. Smith*, p.834.

65 MG, *WSC CV V Part 2*, p.820, Churchill to *The Times* 1 July 1934.

66 MG, *WSC V*, p.379, quoting Churchill to Randolph, 8 January 1931.

67 *Sunday Pictorial*, 26 July 1931, p.8.

68 RRJ, *CS V*, p.4990, speech of 5 March 1931.

69 *The Scotsman*, 6 March 1931, p.6.

70 RRJ, *CS V*, pp.5039–40, speech of 2 June 1931.

71 MG, *WSC V*, p.457.

72 Ibid., p.477.

73 RRJ, *CS V*, p.5222, speech of 22 February 1933.

74 MG, *WSC CV V Part 2*, p.595.

75 *Oxford Magazine* 16 February 1933, pp.440–1; Gilbert, *WSC V*, pp.455, 504–5; Barnes and Nicolson (ed), *Empire at Bay*, p.289, diary entry for 19 February 1933.

76 RRJ, *CS V*, p.5268, speech of 24 April 1934.

77 G. C. Peden, *British Rearmament and the Treasury 1932–1939*, 1979; R. A. C. Parker, 'British Rearmament 1936–9: Treasury, trade unions and skilled labour', in *English Historical Review*, 1981, Vol 96, pp.306–7; Gilbert, *WSC V*, p.660, Churchill to Cunliffe-Lister 16 August 1935.

78 MG, *WSC V*, pp.726–7, quoting Churchill in the House of Commons 23 April 1936.

79 Parker, 'British Rearmament', p.310.

80  David Kirkwood, *My Life of Revolt*, 1935, p.vi.
81  Ivan Maisky, *Spanish Notebooks*, 1966, p.72.
82  RRJ, *CS V*, p.5499, speech of 28 November 1934.
83  Mowat, *Britain between the Wars*, pp.551–3.
84  Churchill, *Gathering Storm*, p.147.
85  *Parl. Deb.*, 5th series, vol 331, col 1531, 26 March 1936.
86  MG, *WSC V*, pp.721–6; Irving, *Churchill's War*, 1987, pp.54–7.
87  Eugen Spier, *Focus: A Footnote to the History of the Thirties*, 1963, pp.53–4.
88  RRJ, *CS V*, p.768, speech of 23 July 1936 at Horsham.
89  RRJ, *CS V*, p.788, speech of 24 September 1936.
90  MG, *WSC V*, p.800, Winston Churchill to Randolph 13 November 1936.
91  Churchill, *Gathering Storm*, p.170.
92  N. Nicolson (ed), *Letters and Diaries 1930–1939*, p.284, Nicolson to Vita Sackville-West, 9 December 1936.
93  Churchill, *Gathering Storm*, p.171.
94  Ibid., p.259.
95  Pelling, *Churchill*, p.387, quoting *New Statesman* 19 March 1938.
96  Stephen Koss, *The Rise and Fall of the Political Press in Britain Vol II*, 1984, pp.581–2.
97  Ibid., p.583, quoting Robert Fraser to Hugh Dalton, 20 October 1938.
98  *The Record*, December 1938, p.128.
99  MG, *WSC CV V Part 3*, p.1312, quoting *New Statesman*, 7 January 1939.
100  MG, *WSC V*, pp.1080–2.

## 10

# The War At Home 1939–45

1   *New York Herald Tribune*, 21 September 1940, quoted in Arthur Marwick (ed), *Britain in the Century of Total War*, 1969, p.298.
2   My description of the events leading to the fall of Chamberlain is based on my own previous account: Paul Addison, *Road to 1945*, 1975, pp.94–102.
3   Churchill, *The Gathering Storm*, p.526; John Colville, *The Fringes of Power: Downing Street Diaries 1939–1955*, 1985, p.122, diary for 10 May 1940.
4   Barnes and Nicholson, *The Empire at Bay*, p.617 diary entry for 13 May 1940.
5   Gilbert, *Finest Hour*, p.331 and see Bevin to Churchill 13 May 1940, Bevin Papers 8/1, Churchill College, Cambridge. Churchill subsequently rejected all wartime representations by the TUC in favour of a revision of the Trade Disputes Act of 1927.
6   Addison, *Road to 1945*, pp.108–10; Barnes and Nicholson, *The Empire at Bay*, pp.625–6, diary for 18 June 1940.
7   *Parl. Deb.*, 5th series, vol 362, col 52, 18 June 1940.
8   Colville, *The Fringes of Power*, p.217, diary for 10 August 1940.
9   James Margach, *The Abuse of Power: The War Between Downing Street and the Media from Lloyd George to James Callaghan*, 1978, p.66.
10  Nigel Nicolson (ed), *Harold Nicolson: Diaries and Letters 1939–1945*, 1970, p.97 Nicolson to Sackville-West 19 June 1940; Colville, *Fringes of Power*, p.165, diary for 18 June 1940.
11  Gilbert, *Never Despair*, p.318, quoting a speech by Churchill at Westminster Hall, 30 November 1954.
12  Winston S. Churchill, *The Second World War Vol II: Their Finest Hour*, 1951, p.81; Ben Pimlott (ed), *The Second World War Diary of Hugh Dalton 1940–1945*, 1986, p.35, entry for 3 June 1940.
13  Sir John Martin, *Downing Street: The War Years*, 1991, p.13.
14  Colville, *The Fringes of Power*, pp.192–3, diary for 12 July 1940.

15    Iain McLaine, *Ministry of Morale: Home Front Morale and the Ministry of Information in World War II*, 1979, p.99.

16    Colville, *The Fringes of Power*, pp.262, 264, diary for 12 October 1940.

17    Churchill, *Finest Hour*, p.307; Colville, *The Fringes of Power*, pp.231–2, diary for 28–29 August 1940.

18    Colville, *The Fringes of Power*, p.244, diary for 22 September 1940; Churchill, *Finest Hour*, pp.310–13.

19    Pelling, *Churchill*, p.644.

20    Diary of Lord Woolton, Bodleian Library, Woolton MS2, diary for 31 October 1940.

21    J.W. Wheeler-Bennett, *John Anderson, Viscount Waverley*, 1962, p.271.

22    A.J.P. Taylor (ed), *W. P. Crozier: Off The Record: Political Interviews 1933–1943*, 1973, p.213, conversation with Churchill of 20 March 1941.

23    Gilbert, *Finest Hour*, p.162, and see CAB 65/1, War Cabinet of 28 October 1939.

24    R.J. Hammond, *Food Vol I: The Growth of Policy*, 1951, p.76.

25    Churchill to Woolton 12 July 1940, MS Woolton 11.

26    Ibid., Woolton to Churchill 12 July 1940.

27    Gilbert, *Finest Hour*, p.663, quoting Churchill to Woolton 14 July 1940.

28    Churchill to Woolton 2 March 1941, MS Woolton 12; Woolton Diary 12 March 1941, MS Woolton 2.

29    *Memoirs of Lord Chandos*, 1962, p.205.

30    Addison, *Road to 1945*, pp.161–2.

31    A.J.P. Taylor (ed), *W. P. Crozier: Off The Record: Political Interviews 1933–1943*, 1973, p.323, interview with Herbert Morrison of 28 May 1942.

32    F.H. Hinsley and C.A.G. Simkins, *British Intelligence in the Second World War*, 1990, p.48.

33    Churchill, *The Second World War Vol III: The Grand Alliance*, 1950 p.561, Churchill to Cabinet Secretary, 3 June 1940.

34    Hinsley and Simkins, *British Intelligence*, pp.50–59; Bernard Wasserstein, *Britain and the Jews of Europe*, 1988, pp.97–8.

35    Hinsley and Simkins, *British Intelligence*, p.57.

36    Bernard Donoughue and G.W.Jones, *Herbert Morrison: Portrait of a Politician*, 1973, p.298.

37    Colville, *The Fringes of Power*, p.263, diary for 12 October 1940.

38    Churchill, *Finest Hour*, p.627, Churchill to Morrison 22 December 1940.

39    CAB 65/9 War Cab 267(40) 7 Oct 1940.

40    Stephen Koss, *The Rise and Fall of the Political Press in Britain Vol II*, 1984, p.606.

41    Stuart (ed), *The Reith Diaries*, p.270, diary for 6 November 1940.

42    Prime Minister's Personal Minute M96/1, Churchill to Duff Cooper 29 January 1941, PREM 4/57/7.

43    Addison, *Road to 1945*, p.134.

44    Ibid., pp.134–5.

45    Eden to Churchill 22 August 1941, PREM 4 21/3.

46    G. S. Harvie-Watt, *Most of My Life*, 1980, p.177.

47    Harvie-Watt, *Most of My Life*, p.177; Addison, *Road to 1945*, pp.147–8.

48    Gilbert, *Finest Hour*, p.1236.

49    Winston S. Churchill, *The Second World War Vol IV: The Hinge of Fate*, 1951, p.756, Churchill to Cherwell 10 March 1942.

50    Pimlott (ed), *Diary of Hugh Dalton*, pp.432–4, diary for 12 May 1942.

51    Pimlott (ed), *Diary of Hugh Dalton*, pp.416, 439, 447, 449, entries for 24 April, 19 May, 27–8 May 1942, p.449, 29 May 1942.

52    Addison, *Road to 1945*, p.210.

53    Nicolson (ed), *Diaries and Letters 1939–1945* p.211, diary for 12 February 1942.

54    Koss, *The Rise and Fall of the Political Press*, pp.606–7.

55    RRJ, *CS VI*, p.6606, speech of 26 March 1942.

56    For a complete transcript of the relevant file on the film, PREM 4 14/15, see

Ian Christie, *The Colonel Blimp File* in *Sight and Sound*, Vol 48 No 1, Winter 1978–9, pp.13–14.

57 In my discussion of the role of psychiatrists and psychologists in the Army I am greatly indebted to the as yet unpublished research of Mr Jeremy Crang.

58 W.O. 163/89, E.C.A.C./P(42) 132. I am grateful to Mr Crang for this reference.

59 Moran, *Winston Churchill*, p.127, diary for 16 November 1943.

60 Grigg to Churchill 30 March 1943, W.O. 259/77.

61 Churchill, *History of the Second World War Vol IV The Hinge of Fate*, 1951, pp.814–5, Minute of 19 December 1942.

62 Robert H. Ahrenfeldt, *Psychiatry in the British Army in the Second World War*, 1958, p.64.

63 Churchill to Grigg 13 March 1943; Grigg to Churchill 30 March 1943, WO 259/77.

64 Churchill to Grigg, 14 December 1942; Grigg to Churchill 23 December 1942, WO 259/75.

65 Addison, *Road to 1945*, p.151.

66 Petherick to Watt 23 December 1942, PREM 4/14/13.

67 Addison, *Road to 1945*, p.151.

68 Cherwell papers, F 245, Prime Minister's Personal Minute M 473/2, 21 October 1942; F 247, Prime Minister's Personal Minute M 792/3, 11 November 1943; F 251, Prime Minister's Personal Minute M 332/5, 14 April 1945.

## 11

## Post-War Plans 1940–45

1 Quoted in Harold Perkin, *The Rise of Professional Society: England since 1880*, 1989, p.414.

2 Note by R.A. Butler of 8 September 1944, Butler Papers G16, Trinity College, Cambridge.

3 Colville, *Fringes of Power*, pp.228–9, diary for 21 August 1940.

4 CAB 65/8, Cabinet of 23 August 1940.

5 Colville, *Fringes of Power*, p.216, diary for 10 August 1940.

6 Gilbert, *Finest Hour*, pp.829, 835–6, quoting Churchill's speech of 9 October 1940.

7 Nicolson (ed), *Diaries and Letters 1939–1945*, p.139, diary for 22 January 1941.

8 Taylor (ed), *Off The Record*, p.212, interview of 20 March 1941.

9 Memorandum by Churchill of 30 December 1940, PREM 4 88/1; RRJ, *CS VI 1935–42*, p.6364, speech of 27 March 1941.

10 Diary for 22 October 1940, MS Woolton 2.

11 Anthony Howard, *RAB: The Life of R.A. Butler*, 1987, pp.142–4.

12 Diary of Collin Brooks, 12 March 1942.

13 Philip Goodhart, *The 1922: The Story of the Conservative Backbenchers Parliamentary Committee*, 1973, p.124.

14 Memorandum by J.M. Keynes of January 1941, PREM 4/100/5; Anthony Eden, *Freedom and Order*, 1941, p.154.

15 Churchill, *The Grand Alliance*, p.392.

16 Colville, *The Fringes of Power*, p.278, entry for 30 October 1940.

17 Gilbert, *Finest Hour*, pp.949–50, speech of 18 December 1940.

18 Howard, *RAB*, pp.107–10.

19 Butler to Churchill 12 September 1941; Churchill to Butler 13 September 1941, PREM 4/11/6.

20 Chuter Ede diary, 4 February 1942, quoted in Anthony Howard, *RAB: The Life of R.A. Butler*, 1987, p.119; Churchill made the same point three days later to L.S. Amery: see Barnes and Nicholson, *The Empire at Bay*, p.770, entry for 7 February 1942.

21 Howard, *RAB*, pp.128–9.

22 Memo by Kingsley Wood of 17 November 1942; Memo by Cherwell, 25 November 1942, PREM 4/89/2.

23 Angus Calder, *The People's War: Britain 1939–1945*, 1969, pp.527–8; BIPO, *The Beveridge Report and the Public*, 1943.

24 Note by Churchill for the Cabinet, 12 January 1943, in Winston S. Churchill, *Hinge of Fate*, pp.861–2.

25 Addison, *Road to 1945*, p.221.

26 Barnes and Nicholson, *Empire at Bay*, p.848, diary for 30 November 1942.

27 CAB 87/13, Interim Report of the Committee on Reconstruction Priorities P.R.(43), 13, 11 February 1943.

28 Churchill, *Hinge of Fate*, p.862; Pimlott, *Diary of Hugh Dalton*, p.553, 16 February 1943.

29 Harvie-Watt, *Most of My Life*, p.117.

30 Pimlott, *Dalton Diaries*, p.569, diary for 22 March 1943; Cherwell Papers F 173, Cherwell to Churchill 8 March 1943 and H 223, Keynes to Cherwell 11 March 1943; Howard, *RAB* p.134.

31 RRJ, *CS VII*, pp.6756, 6759, broadcast of 21 March 1943.

32 Ibid., p.6760, 6764, broadcast of 21 March 1943.

33 Addison, *Road to 1945*, pp.233–4.

34 Taylor (ed), *Off The Record*, p.360, conversation of 28 May 1943.

35 On Bevin's negotiations with Churchill see Rory Macleod, 'The Promise of Full Employment' in Harold Smith (ed), *War and Social Change: British Society in the Second World War*, Manchester, 1986, pp.85–6; Addison, *Road to 1945*, pp.233–4.

36 Churchill, *History of the Second World War Vol V Closing The Ring*, 1952, pp.151–2, Memorandum of 19 October 1943.

37 Memorandum on Reconstruction Plans W.P.(43) 465, 20 October 1943, Cherwell Papers F255.

38 Pimlott *Diary of Hugh Dalton*, p.656, entry for 21 October 1943.

39 Ibid., p.xxxii.

40 W.H.B. Court, *Coal*, 1951, pp.242–8; RRJ (ed), *Collected Speeches VII*, p.6859, speech of 13 October 1943.

41 Memoranda by Cherwell of 26 October 1943 and 6 January 1944, PREM 4/96/9.

42 Pimlott, *Dalton Diaries*, diary for 19 May 1944.

43 Minute by Cherwell initialled 'W.S.C. 9.2', Churchill to Eden 10 February 1944, PREM 4/36/3.

44 RRJ, *CS VII*, p.6896, speech of 2 March 1944.

45 Ibid. pp.6911–4, broadcast of 26 March 1944.

46 Note by Butler of April 1944, R. A. Butler Papers G 16.

47 *The Economist*, 8 April 1944, p.458.

48 Pimlott (ed), *Diary of Hugh Dalton*, p.736, diary for 14 April 1944.

49 Ibid., p.758, diary for 15 June 1944.

50 Kevin Jefferys, *The Churchill Coalition and Wartime Politics*, 1991, pp.178–9.

51 Pimlott (ed), *Diary of Hugh Dalton*, pp.807, 828, diary for 16 November 1944, 7 February 1945; Addison, *Road to 1945*, p.237.

52 Nicolson, (ed), *Diaries and Letters 1939*–1945, p.409, diary for 31 October 1944.

53 RRJ, *CS VII*, pp.7041–2, speech of 29 November 1944.

54 Ibid., p.7048, speech of 1 December 1944.

55 Howard, *RAB*, pp.120–1.

56 Charles Lysaght, *Brendan Bracken*, 1979, p.247.

57 Pimlott, *Diary of Hugh Dalton*, p.804, diary for 2 November 1944.

58 RRJ, *CS VII*, pp.7131, 7133, 15 March 1945.

59 Lysaght, *Bracken*, p.248. On 28 May 1945, Churchill wrote to Bevin: 'We must hope for reunion when party passions are less strong.' Bevin Papers 8/1.

60 Harvie-Watt, *Most of My Life*, pp.185–6.

61 Unpublished autobiography of Henry Willink, 1968, pp.81–2, Willink Papers Box 2 Churchill College, Cambridge.

62 Woolton to Beaverbrook 31 May 1945, MS Woolton 20.

63 Friedrich von Hayek to the author, 13 April 1980.

64 Gilbert, *Never Despair*, pp.35–6, Sarah to Winston Churchill, 5 June 1945.
65 RRJ, *CS VII*, pp.7183–88, broadcast of 13 June 1945.
66 Ibid., pp.7194, 7199, broadcasts of 21 June and 30 June 1945.

## 12

## Set The People Free 1945–55

1 Kenneth Young (ed), *The Diaries of Sir Robert Bruce Lockhart 1939–1955*, 1980, pp.510, 537.
2 Chairman's Confidential Report No 8: 'Public Opinion on Mr Churchill', MS Woolton 21.
3 Anthony Seldon, *Churchill's Indian Summer: The Conservative Government 1951–1955*, 1981, pp.436–439: Keith Middlemas, *Power, Competition and the State: Volume I: Britain in Search of Balance 1940–1961*, 1986, pp.221–2.
4 Philip Williams (ed), *The Diary of Hugh Gaitskell 1945–1955*, 1983, pp.18–19, diary entry for 13–24 August 1945; Diary of Sir Cuthbert Headlam, 21 August 1945, Durham County Record Office.
5 J.D. Hoffman, *The Conservative Party in Opposition 1945–1951*, 1964, p.230.
6 RRJ, *CS VII*, pp.7274–80, speech of 13 Dec 1945.
7 Harold Macmillan, *Tides of Fortune 1945–1955*, 1969, p.44; Anthony Howard, *RAB: The Life of R. A. Butler*, 1987, p.150.
8 Moran, *Winston Churchill*, 1966, p.313, diary for 27 June 1946.
9 Hoffman, *Conservative Party*, p.81.
10 RRJ, *CS VII*, p.7270, speech of 6 December 1945.
11 Hoffman, *Conservative Party*, p.72.
12 Churchill to Woolton 9 August 1946, Conservative Party Papers CCO 20/2/1, Bodleian Library, Oxford; Macmillan, *Tides of Fortune*, pp.292–3.
13 RRJ, *CS VII*, p.7388, speech of 5 October 1946.
14 Hoffman, *The Conservative Party*, pp.141–2; RRJ, *CS VII*, pp.7388–9, speech of 5 October 1946.
15 R.A. Butler, *The Art of the Possible: The Memoirs of Lord Butler*, 1979, p.150.
16 RRJ, *CS VII*, p.7463, speech of 14 March 1947.
17 *Daily Herald*, 2 April 1947.
18 Macmillan, *Tides of Fortune*, pp.302–3.
19 Conservative Political Centre, *Conservatism 1945–1950*, 1950, pp.56–8.
20 Ibid, p.59.
21 RRJ, *CS VII*, p.7498, speech of 16 May 1947.
22 John Ramsden, *The Making of Conservative Party Policy*, 1980, p.114.
23 RRJ, *CS VII*, pp.7532–3 speech of 4 October 1947.
24 *Parl. Deb.*, 5th series vol 434, col 122, 10 February 1947.
25 *Parl. Deb.*, 5th series vol 434, cols 1352–3, 12 March 1947.
26 Martin Gilbert, *Never Despair: Winston S. Churchill 1945–1965*, 1988, p.341.
27 RRJ, *CS VII*, p.7520, broadcast of 16 August 1947.
28 Lyttelton to Churchill 26 August 1947, Chandos Papers 4/5, Chandos II, Churchill College, Cambridge.
29 Gilbert, *Never Despair*, p.346.
30 Colville, *The Fringes of Power*, pp.620–1, diary for 30 November 1947.
31 RRJ, *CS VII*, pp.7572–9, speech of 6 December 1947; *Economist*, 13 December 1947, p.947.
32 Macmillan to Woolton 7 January 1948; Woolton to Macmillan 23 January; Churchill to Macmillan 9 February; Macmillan to Churchill 12 February, Conservative Party Papers CCO 20/1/3.
33 RRJ, *CS VII*, pp.7628, 7674, speeches of 21 April and 26 June 1948.
34 Ibid., p.7679, speech of 10 July 1948.

35  *Parl. Deb.*, 5th series, vol 458, col 223, 16 November 1948.
36  Macmillan, *Tides of Fortune*, p.91.
37  Ramsden, *Conservative Party Policy*, pp.133–40.
38  Conservative Political Centre, *Conservatism*, p.180.
39  Philip Williams, *Hugh Gaitskell: A Political Biography*, 1979, p.203.
40  RRJ, *CS VII*, p.7863, speech of 14 October 1949.
41  Ibid., p.7877, speech of 27 October 1947.
42  Bracken to Beaverbrook 8 December 1949, Beaverbrook Papers B17, House of Lords Record Office.
43  Butler, *Art of the Possible*, pp.152–3.
44  Conservative Political Centre, *Conservatism*, p.232.
45  RRJ, *CS VIII*, p.7937, speech of 14 February 1950.
46  Ibid., p.7922, 8 February 1950.
47  Ibid., p.7944, speech of 14 February 1950.
48  Churchill to Chief Whip, 29 March 1950; Memo by S.H. Pierssené of 15 March 1950, Conservative Party Papers CCO 20/2/1; Notes by R.A. Butler dated 12 June 1950, R. A. Butler Papers, Trinity College, Cambridge.
49  Woolton to Churchill 31 July 1950; Churchill to Woolton 2 August 1950, Conservative Party Papers CCO 20/2/1.
50  Cranborne to Woolton 24 September 1950; Woolton to Cranborne 28 September, MS Woolton 21.
51  Note by Clement Davies: 'Liberal position as put by me to Mr Winston Churchill and Lord Woolton 1950', Clement Davies Papers C/1/54, National Library of Wales, Aberystwyth.
52  Macmillan, *Tides of Fortune*, p.322.
53  RRJ, *CS VIII*, pp.8256, 8258, broadcast of 8 October 1951.
54  Ibid., p.8276, speech of 17 October 1951.
55  Seldon, *Churchill's Indian Summer*, pp.18–19.
56  Robert Rhodes James, *Anthony Eden*, 1986, pp.338–9.
57  RRJ, *CS VIII*, pp.8247–8, speech at Liverpool of 2 October 1951.
58  David Ayerst, *Guardian: Biography of a Newspaper*, 1971, p.607.
59  Kenneth O. Morgan, *Labour in Power 1945–1951*, Oxford 1984, p.486.
60  Seldon, *Churchill's Indian Summer*, p.102.
61  Roy Douglas, *The History of the Liberal Party 1895–1970*, 1971, p.265.
62  Seldon, *Churchill's Indian Summer*, p.81.
63  Janet Morgan (ed), *The Backbench Diaries of Richard Crossman*, 1981, p.30, entry for 31 October 1951.
64  Philip M. Williams (ed), *The Diary of Hugh Gaitskell*, p.307, entry for 23 November 1951.
65  CAB 128/23, 30 October 1951.
66  RRJ, *CS VIII*, p.8309, speech of 6 December 1951.
67  Churchill to Butler and Eden, 23 January 1952; Eden and Butler to Churchill 25 January, PREM 11/132.
68  Alec Cairncross, *Years of Recovery: British Economic Policy 1945–1951*, 1985, p.244. I have drawn freely on the definitive account of the Robot affair in chapter 9 of Professor Cairncross's book.
69  Memorandum on 'External Action' by the Chancellor of the Exchequer accompanying Butler to Churchill, 21 February 1952, PREM 11/140.
70  Cherwell to Churchill 18 March 1952, Churchill to Butler 20 March, PREM 11/137.
71  Colville, *Fringes of Power*, diary for 22–3 March 1952.
72  Nigel Nicolson (ed), *Harold Nicolson: Diaries and Letters 1945–1962*, 1971, p.207, diary entry for 22 May 1952.
73  For the opinion poll ratings see Seldon, *Churchill's Indian Summer*, pp.442–3.
74  Middlemas, *Power, Competition and the State*, p.257.
75  Seldon, *Churchill's Indian Summer*, p.203.

76 Cherwell to Churchill 15 November 1951, Cherwell Papers J 110.
77 Churchill to Leathers 2 February 1952, PREM 11/346.
78 D. F. MacDonald, *The State and the Trade Unions*, 1976 edition, pp.152–3; *The Times* 25 July 1952.
79 Churchill to Horsbrugh 9 February 1953; Churchill to Sir Vincent Tewson 11 March, PREM 11/385.
80 CAB 128/25, 10 June 1952.
81 CAB 128/24, 6-7 March 1952.
82 CAB 128/24 22 April 1952.
83 Moran, *Winston Churchill*, pp.651–2, diary for 8 April 1955.
84 See the correspondence and minutes contained in PREM 11/824 and CAB 128/24, 18 Dec 1952.
85 Charles Webster, *The Health Service since the War Vol I: Problems of Health Care: The National Health Service before 1957*, 1988, pp.185–94.
86 Nigel Fisher, *Iain Macleod*, 1973, p.82.
87 CAB 128/25, 24 July 1953.
88 CAB 128/25, 1 October 1953.
89 CAB 128/24, 4 April 1952.
90 Seldon, *Churchill's Indian Summer*, p.500.
91 Butler to Churchill 8 October 1952, Churchill to Butler 13 October, PREM 11/129.
92 Diary of Collin Brooks, 17 December 1952.
93 James Margach, *The Abuse of Power: The War Between Downing Street and the Media from Lloyd George to James Callaghan*, 1978, p.69.
94 David Gammans to Lord Swinton 27 May 1952; note by 'A.R.' of 30 June, Fife Clark Papers 2/2/1, Churchill College, Cambridge.
95 Grace Wyndham Goldie, *Facing The Nation: Television and Politics 1936–1976*, 1977, pp.169–72.
96 Michael Cockerell, *Live From Number 10: The Inside Story of the Prime Ministers and Television*, 1988, pp.15–16, 21–2.
97 *Parl. Deb.*, 5th series, vol 537, col 1277, 23 February 1955.
98 Churchill to Jacob 30 May 1953, PREM 11/336.
99 Seldon, *Churchill's Indian Summer*, pp.143–6.
100 Butler, *Art of the Possible*, p.172.
101 See the correspondence and papers in PREM 11/662.
102 Macmillan, *Tides of Fortune*, p.491.
103 Prime Minister's Personal Minutes to the Lord President of the Council and the Minister of Food, 24 and 25 March 1952; Woolton to Churchill 4 April 1952, MS Woolton 25; Macmillan, *Tides of Fortune*, p.491.
104 Prime Minister's Personal Minute to Secretary of State for Colonies and Minister of Food, n.d. but arising out of a report in the *Manchester Guardian* of 20 June 1952, PREM 11/44.
105 Churchill to Minister of Food 11 May 1952 and 26 May 1952, PREM 11/99.
106 Kathleen Burk, *The First Privatisation: The Politicians, the City and the Denationalisation of Steel*, 1991, pp.41–62.
107 Moran, *Winston Churchill*, p.383, diary for 23 March 1952.
108 CAB 128/25, 14–15 July 1952.
109 Seldon, *Churchill's Indian Summer*, p.190.
110 Ibid., p.191: see also Kathleen Burk, *The First Privatisation*.
111 Goodhart, *The 1922*, p.165.
112 Bracken to Beaverbrook 7 January 1953, Beaverbrook Papers C/57.
113 RRJ, *CS VIII*, pp.8466–70, speech of 17 April 1953.
114 Howard, *RAB*, 1987, pp.199–200.
115 John W. Young, 'Cold War and Detente with Moscow' in John W. Young (ed), *The Foreign Policy of the Churchill Administration 1951–1955*, Leicester, 1988, p.66.

116 CAB 128/26 Part 2, Cabinet of 15 December 1953.

117 Norman Brook to Churchill 2 March 1954 and Cabinet Minute of 3 March 1954, PREM 11/653.

118 Woolton Diary 14 April 1954, MSS Woolton 3.

119 On Churchill's masterly procrastination see Gilbert, *Never Despair*, chapters 50 and 53.

120 CAB 128/27 24 November 1954.

121 Woolton Diary 22 December 1954, MS Woolton 3.

122 CC(54) 382, Memo by the Minister of Labour and Minister of Transport and Civil Aviation, 7 December 1954; Cabinet of 8 December 1954, PREM 11/1026.

123 Woolton Diary 13 December 1954, MS Woolton 3.

124 Cabinet of 10 December 1954, PREM 11/1026.

125 CAB 128/28 5 April 1955.

# Epilogue

1 Aneurin Bevan, 'History's Impresario' in *Churchill by his Contemporaries: An 'Observer' Appreciation*, 1965, p.57. For Labour scepticism see the obituary of Churchill in *Tribune* reprinted in Michael Foot, *Loyalists and Loners*, 1986, pp.168–72. A more favourable portrait, from a Liberal point of view, was offered in Violet Bonham Carter, *Winston Churchill As I Knew Him*, 1965. The tradition of Conservative scepticism was revived in Robert Rhodes James, *Churchill: A Study in Failure 1900–1939*, 1970.

2 RSC, *WSC CV I Part 2*, p.751, Churchill to Lady Randolph 6 April 1897.

3 RRJ, *WSC CS II*, 1974, pp.1028–30, speech of 4 May 1908.

4 I owe this story to Mr Barrigail Keith, who was present. Mr Keith served for many years as manager of the Highland estate of Churchill's friend Sir Archibald Sinclair.

5 Rhodes James, *Churchill: A Study in Failure*, p.45.

6 RRJ, *CS II*, p.954, 14 April 1908.

7 Ibid., p.196.

8 RRJ, *CS I*, p.676, speech of 11 October 1906.

9 Winston Churchill, 'Mr Wells and Bolshevism: A Reply', *Sunday Express*, 5 December 1920.

10 Kenneth O. Morgan, *Consensus and Disunity* p.182.

# Bibliography

## A Note on the Sources

Since the death of Winston Churchill in 1965 our knowledge of him has been transformed in two respects. Firstly his life has been documented and chronicled in almost encyclopaedic detail. The official biography, begun by Randolph Churchill and continued by Martin Gilbert, consists of eight volumes of narrative and thirteen companion volumes of documents. The narrative is complete but the companion volumes currently stop at 1939. A dazzling scholarly achievement, the official life has made available the cream of the Churchill papers up to 1939, together with a wealth of documents from the Public Record Office and other archives. The store of primary printed sources has been further enriched by the work of Mr Frederick Woods, and the late Michael Wolff, in collecting and republishing Churchill's journalism. In another major contribution, Mr Robert Rhodes James has compiled in eight large volumes an edition of Churchill's complete speeches from 1897 to 1963 – though even at this length the edition is not in fact entirely complete.

Meanwhile our picture of Churchill has been affected by a second development. If the life has come into focus, so has the relationship between the life and the times. This is especially true of the domestic theme discussed in this book. A generation of political historians has been mapping out the contours of British history in Churchill's lifetime. As a consequence there now exists a wide range of monographs on party politics and public policy which enable us to see many of the roles Churchill played in the contexts to which they belonged. The works of Peter Clarke, José Harris, Maurice Cowling and Keith Middlemas spring to mind, though several other names can and should be added.

The materials in print are, therefore, abundant and almost overwhelming: so much so that at one stage in the writing of this book I planned to confine myself to the evidence already published, and concentrate on problems of analysis and interpretation. But curiosity overcame me and when I began to look into the archives I discovered hitherto unpublished material of great fascination. After this I abandoned my original plan and read as widely as I could in collections of private papers and the files of the Public Record Office. But I have not attempted to found the book on unpublished sources. The effect of the archives has been to sharpen or deepen the story at certain points.

The Churchill papers, unfortunately, were closed throughout the writing of this book to all except a handful of researchers working on specialised aspects of his life. But I still recall with pleasure the experience, more than twenty years ago, of working on them myself. I was a research assistant to Randolph Churchill, in the congenial company of Tom Hartman, Andrew Kerr, and Michael Wolff. My brief was to revise and complete the companion volumes for 1910–1914, which were already set up in galley proof. The Churchill papers were stored in a metal hut in Randolph's garden at East Bergholt, and I used to work there checking the original text of documents, or searching the files to see if anything significant had been overlooked. It was Randolph's aim to ensure that all important documents were published, and Martin Gilbert has no doubt followed in his footsteps. But the importance of a document lies partly in the eye of the beholder and I feel sure that when at last the papers are thrown open, historians will make some interesting discoveries.

One final point. In addition to sources directly cited in the text, I have included in the bibliography a small number of books which have been important indirectly in clarifying the contexts and the problems.

# UNPUBLISHED SOURCES

## 1 Public Record Office

Board of Trade: BT 13/134

Cabinet papers: CAB 23/4; 23/8; 23/9; 23/10; 23/15; 23/20; 23/52; 23/53; 23/57; 24/189; 24/192; 24/193; 24/202; 27/336; 37/93/89; 37/94/89; 37/96/159; 37/94/107; 65/1; 65/8; 65/9; 87/1; 87/13; 128/23; 128/24; 128/25; 128/26; 128/27; 128/28

Home Office: HO 45/10631/200605; 45/10584; 45/10649/210615; 144/1072/19134; 144/1098/197900;144/1102/199183;144/1043/183461;144/1106/200455;144/1157/212342; 1054/187986

Prime Minister's papers: PREM 4/11/6; 4/14/13; 4/14/15; 4/21/3; 4/36/3; 4/57/7; 4/88/1; 4/89/2; 4/96/9; 4/100/5; 11/44; 11/99; 11/129; 11/132; 11/137; 11/140; 11/239; 11/336; 11/346; 11/385; 11/653; 11/662; 11/824; 11/1026

Treasury: T171/246; T 171/247; T 172/1489; T 172/1494; T 172/1558; T 172/1598; T 172/1494 172/1495 T 172/1690

War Office: WO 259/75; 259/77

## 2 Personal Papers

D'Abernon (Sir Edgar Vincent) Papers, British Library
Asquith Papers, Bodleian Library
Balfour Papers, British Library
Beaverbrook Papers, House of Lords Record Office
Beveridge Papers, London School of Economics
Bevin Papers, Churchill College, Cambridge
W.S. Blunt Diary, Fitzwilliam Museum, Cambridge
Collin Brooks Diary, in the possession of Miss Vivian Brooks
Butler Papers, Trinity College, Cambridge
Campbell-Bannerman Papers, British Library
Neville Chamberlain Papers, Birmingham University Library
Chandos (Oliver Lyttelton) Papers, Churchill College, Cambridge
Cherwell (F.A. Lindemann) Papers, Nuffield College
Fife Clark Papers, Churchill College, Cambridge
Conservative Party Papers, Bodleian Library
Clement Davies Papers, National Library of Wales
Elibank (Alexander Murray) Papers, National Library of Scotland
Gainford (J.A. Pease) Papers, Nuffield College, Oxford
Lloyd George Papers, House of Lords Record Office; National Library of Wales
Herbert Gladstone Papers, British Library
Sir William Harcourt Papers, Bodleian Library
Sir Cuthbert Headlam Diary, Durham County Record Office
Thomas Jones Diary, National Library of Wales

Bonar Law Papers, House of Lords Record Office
McKenna Papers, Churchill College, Cambridge
Milner Papers, Bodleian Library
Morley-Churchill correspondence, British Library
Mottistone (J.E. Seeley) Papers, Nuffield College, Oxford
Northcliffe (Alfred Harmsworth) Papers, British Library
Rosebery Papers, National Library of Scotland
William Royle Papers, Manchester Central Library
Walter Runciman Papers, University of Newcastle
Alexander McCallum Scott Diary, Glasgow University Library
J.A. Spender Papers, British Museum
C.P. Trevelyan Papers, Newcastle University Library
Weir of Eastwood Papers, Glasgow University Library
Henry Willink Papers, Churchill College, Cambridge
Woolton Papers, Bodleian Library

## PUBLISHED SOURCES

Note: Place of publication is London except where otherwise stated.

### 1 The official biography

Randolph S. Churchill, *Winston S. Churchill Vol I: Youth 1874–1900* (1966)
Randolph S. Churchill (ed), *Companion Volume I Parts 1 and 2* (1967)
—*Winston S. Churchill Vol II: Young Statesman 1901–1914* (1967)
—(ed) *Companion Volume II Parts 1, 2 and 3* (1969)
Martin Gilbert, *Winston S. Churchill Vol III 1914–1916* (1971)
Martin Gilbert (ed) *Companion Vol III, Parts 1 and 2* (1972)
—*Winston S. Churchill Vol IV 1916–1922* (1975)
—(ed) *Companion Vol IV Parts 1, 2 and 3* (1977)
—*Winston S. Churchill Vol V 1922–1939* (1976)
—(ed) *Companion Vol V Parts 1, 2 and 3* (1979)
—*Finest Hour: Winston S. Churchill 1939–1941* (1983)
—*Road to Victory: Winston S. Churchill 1941–1945* (1986)
—*Never Despair: Winston S. Churchill 1945–1965* (1988)

### 2 Diaries, memoirs, biographies, and contemporary publications

J.B. Atkins, *Incidents and Reflections* (1947)
David Ayerst, *Guardian: Biography of a Newspaper* (1971)
—*Garvin Of The Observer* (1985)
John Barnes and David Nicholson (ed), *The Leo Amery Diaries Vol I 1896–1929* (1980);
    *Vol II: The Empire at Bay: The Leo Amery Diaries 1929–1945* (1988)
Lord Beaverbrook, *Politicians and the War* (1928)
—*The Decline and Fall of Lloyd George* (1963)
Robert Blake (ed), *The Private Papers of Douglas Haig 1914–1919* (1952)
—*The Unknown Prime Minister: The Life and Times of Andrew Bonar Law 1858–1923* (1955)
W.S. Blunt, *My Diaries: Being a Personal Narrative of Events 1888–1914* Part Two *1900–1924*
    (1921 impression)
Piers Brendon, *Winston Churchill: A Brief Life* (1984)
M.V. Brett (ed), *Journals and Letters of Reginald Viscount Esher* (1934)
Michael and Eleanor Brock (ed), *H.H. Asquith: Letters to Venetia Stanley*, Oxford (1982)
Alan Bullock, *The Life and Times of Ernest Bevin Vol I* (1960)
British Institute of Public Opinion, *The Beveridge Report and the Public* (1943)
R.A. Butler, *The Art of the Possible: The Memoirs of Lord Butler* (1979)

John Campbell, *Lloyd George: The Goat in the Wilderness* (1977)
—*F.E. Smith: First Earl of Birkenhead* (1983)
Violet Bonham Carter, *Winston Churchill As I Knew Him* (1965)
*Churchill by His Contemporaries: An 'Observer' Appreciation* (1965)
Winston S. Churchill, *The People's Rights*, Cape (1970 edition)
—'Mr Wells and Bolshevism: A Reply', *Sunday Express*, 5 December 1920
—*The World Crisis 1911–1914* (1923)
—*The World Crisis 1916–1918* Part 2 (1927)
—*My Early Life* (1944 edition)
—*Thoughts and Adventures* (1932)
—*Great Contemporaries* (1937)
—*The Second World War Vol I: The Gathering Storm* (1948)
—*The Second World War Vol II: Their Finest Hour* (1949)
—*The Second World War Vol III: The Grand Alliance* (1950)
—*The Second World War Vol IV: The Hinge of Fate* (1951)
—*The Second World War Vol V: Closing The Ring* (1952)
Tom Clarke, *My Lloyd George Diary* (1939)
Margaret Cole (ed), *The Diaries of Beatrice Webb vol I* (1952)
*Colliery Strike Disturbances in South Wales*, Parliamentary Papers 1911, lxiv, Cd 5568
John Colville, *The Fringes of Power: Downing Street Diaries 1939–1955* (1985)
Conservative Political Centre, *Conservatism 1945–1950* (1950)
Don M. Cregier, *Bounder from Wales: Lloyd George's Career Before The First World War*, Missouri (1976)
Edward David (ed), *Inside Asquith's Cabinet: From the Diaries of Charles Hobhouse* (1977)
David Dilks, *Neville Chamberlain: Volume I Pioneering and Reform 1869–1929* (1984)
Bernard Donoughue and G.W. Jones, *Herbert Morrison: Portrait of a Politician* (1973)
G.G. Eastwood, *George Isaacs* (n.d.)
Keith Feiling, *Neville Chamberlain* (1946)
Nigel Fisher, *Iain Macleod* (1973)
Sir A. Fitzroy, *Memoirs Vol II* (n.d.)
Michael Foot, *Loyalists and Loners* (1986)
Roy Foster, *Lord Randolph Churchill*, Oxford (1981)
A.G. Gardiner, *Prophets, Priests and Kings* (1914)
Victor Wallace Germains, *The Tragedy of Winston Churchill* (1931)
Bentley B. Gilbert, *David Lloyd George, A Political Life: The Architect of Change 1863–1912* (1987)
Martin Gilbert, *Churchill's Political Philosophy* (1981)
Martin Gilbert, *Churchill: A Life* (1991)
Grace Wyndham Goldie, *Facing the Nation: Television and Politics 1936–1976* (1977)
Philip Goodhart, *The 1922* (1973)
Kenneth Grahame, *The Wind in the Willows* (1926 edition)
John Grigg, *Lloyd George: the People's Champion* (1978)
—*Lloyd George: from Peace to War 1912–1916* (1985)
P.J. Grigg, *Prejudice and Judgment* (1948)
D.A. Hamer, *John Morley: Liberal Intellectual in Politics*, Oxford (1966)
José Harris, *William Beveridge: A Biography*, Oxford (1977)
G.S. Harvie-Watt, *Most of My Life* (1980)
Christopher Hassall, *Edward Marsh: Patron of the Arts* (1959)
Alfred Havighurst, *Radical Journalist: H.W. Massingham* (1974)
Lady Victoria Hicks Beach, *The Life of Sir Michael Hicks Beach Vol II* (1932)
*History of the Ministry of Munitions Vol V: Wages and Welfare* (1923)
Anthony Howard, *RAB: The Life of R.A. Butler* (1987)
Roy Jenkins, *Asquith* (1964)
David Kirkwood, *My Life of Revolt* (1935)

Stephen Koss, *Fleet Street Radical: A.G. Gardiner and the Daily News* (1973)
—*Asquith* (1985 edition)
*Liberal Magazine*, Vols X–XI, 1902–3
Sir Frederick Leith-Ross, *Money Talks* (1968)
Charles Lysaght, *Brendan Bracken* (1979)
Oliver Lyttelton, *Memoirs of Lord Chandos* (1962)
Sir Henry Lucy, *The Diary of a Journalist* (1920)
J.M. McEwen (ed), *The Riddell Diaries 1908–1923* (1986)
Harold Macmillan, *Tides of Fortune 1945–1955* (1969)
Philip Magnus, *Kitchener: Portrait of an Imperialist* (1958)
—*King Edward VII*, Harmondsworth (1967 edition)
Sir John Martin, *Downing Street: The War Years* (1991)
Ivan Maisky, *Spanish Notebooks* (1966)
Lucy Masterman, *C.F.G. Masterman: A Biography* (1939)
Peter de Mendelssohn, *The Age of Churchill* (1961)
Keith Middlemas (ed), *Thomas Jones: Whitehall Diary Vol I 1916–1925; Vol II 1926–1930; Vol III: Ireland 1918–1925*, Oxford (1971)
Keith Middlemas and John Barnes, *Baldwin: A Biography* (1969)
Lord Moran, *Winston Churchill: The Struggle for Survival* (1966)
Janet Morgan (ed), *The Backbench Diaries of Richard Crossman* (1981)
Nigel Nicolson (ed), *Harold Nicolson: Diaries and Letters 1930–1939* (1966)
—*Harold Nicolson, Diaries and Letters 1939–1945* (1970 edition)
—*Harold Nicolson: Diaries and Letters 1945–1962* (1971 edition)
*Oldham Chronicle* 1899–1900
Emmeline Pankhurst, *My Own Story* (1979 edition)
Tony Paterson, *Churchill: A Seat for Life*, Dundee (1980)
Henry Pelling, *Winston Churchill* (1974)
Ben Pimlott (ed), *The Second World War Diary of Hugh Dalton 1940–1945* (1986)
W.J. Reader, *Architect of Air Power: The Life of the First Viscount Weir of Eastwood 1877–1959* (1968)
Robert Rhodes James, *Rosebery*, Weidenfeld and Nicolson (1963)
—*Memoirs of a Conservative* (1969)
—*Churchill: A Study in Failure 1900–1939* (1970)
Robert Rhodes James (ed), *Winston S. Churchill: His Complete Speeches Vols I–VIII 1897–1963*, New York (1974)
Robert Rhodes James, *Anthony Eden* (1986)
*Lord Riddell's Intimate Diary of the Peace Conference and After 1918–23* (1933)
Lord Riddell, *More Pages From My Diary 1908–1914* (1934)
Alexander MacCallum Scott, *Winston Spencer Churchill* (1905)
Janet Adam Smith, *John Buchan*, Oxford (1985 edition)
Eugen Spier, *Focus: A Footnote to the History of the Thirties* (1963)
Charles Stuart (ed), *The Reith Diaries* (1975)
A.J.P. Taylor (ed), *Lloyd George: A Diary by Frances Stevenson* (1971)
A.J.P. Taylor (ed), *W.P. Crozier: Off The Record: Political Interviews 1933–1943* (1973)
A.J.P. Taylor and others: *Churchill: Four Faces and the Man*, Harmondsworth (1973 edition)
Ben Tillett, *Memories and Reflections* (1931)
John Vincent (ed), *The Crawford Papers: The journals of David Lindsay twenty-seventh Earl of Crawford and tenth Earl of Balcarres 1871–1940 during the years 1892–1940* (1984)
Beatrice Webb, *Our Partnership* (1948)
H.G. Wells, *Men Like Gods* (1923)
—*Meanwhile* (1923 edition)
J.W. Wheeler-Bennett, *John Anderson, Viscount Waverley* (1962)
Philip Williams, *Hugh Gaitskell: A Political Biography* (1979)
Philip Williams (ed), *The Diary of Hugh Gaitskell 1945–1955* (1983)

Trevor Wilson (ed), *The Political Diaries of C.P. Scott 1911–1928* (1970)
Michael Wolff (ed), *The Collected Essays of Sir Winston Churchill Vol II: Churchill and Politics* (n.d.)
—*The Collected Essays of Sir Winston Churchill Vol III: Churchill and People* (n.d.)
Frederick Woods (ed), *A Bibliography of the Works of Sir Winston Churchill*, Toronto (1969 edition)
Frederick Woods (ed), *Young Winston's Wars* (1972)
Kenneth Young (ed), *The Diaries of Sir Robert Bruce Lockhart 1939–1955* (1980)

## 3   Secondary works on themes and problems

Paul Addison, *The Road to 1945: British Politics in the Second World War* (1975)
—'The Political Beliefs of Winston Churchill', in *Transactions of the Royal Historical Society* 5th series Vol 30 (1980)
—'Churchill and the Working Class 1900–1914' in Jay Winter (ed), *The Working Class in Modern British History*, Cambridge (1983)
—'Churchill in British Politics 1940–1955' in J.M.W. Bean (ed), *The Political Culture of Modern Britain: Studies in Memory of Stephen Koss* (1987)
Robert H. Ahrenfeldt, *Psychiatry in the British Army in the Second World War* (1958)
Christopher Andrew, *Secret Service* (1986 edition)
F. Bealey and H. Pelling, *Labour and Politics 1900–1906* (1958)
Kathleen Burk, *The First Privatisation: The Politicians, the City and the Denationalisation of Steel* (1991)
Alec Cairncross, *Years of Recovery: British Economic Policy 1945–1951* (1985)
Angus Calder, *The People's War: Britain 1939–1945* (1969)
David Cannadine, *The Decline and Fall of the British Aristocracy* (1990)
Ian Christie, *The Colonel Blimp File* in *Sight and Sound*, Vol 48 No 1, Winter 1978–9
P.F. Clarke, *Lancashire and the New Liberalism*, Cambridge (1971)
—*Liberals and Social Democrats*, Cambridge (1978)
—*The Keynesian Revolution in the Making 1924–1936* (1988)
—'Churchill's Economic Ideas 1900–1930' (unpublished article). I am grateful to Dr Clarke for permission to refer to this paper in advance of publication.
Michael Cockerell, *Live From Number 10: The Inside Story of the Prime Ministers and Television* (1988)
Michael J. Cohen, *Churchill and the Jews* (1985)
W.H.B. Court, *Coal* (1951)
Maurice Cowling, *The Impact of Labour 1920–1924*, Cambridge (1971)
—*The Impact of Hitler: British Politics and British Policy 1933–1940*, Cambridge (1975)
Roger Davidson, 'Llewellyn Smith, the Labour Department and Government Growth 1886–1909' in Gillian Sutherland (ed), *Studies in the Growth of Nineteenth Century Government* (1972)
—'Sir Hubert Llewellyn Smith and Labour Policy 1886–1916', Cambridge Ph D (1971)
Roy Douglas, *The History of the Liberal Party 1895–1970* (1971)
Ian M. Drummond, *The Gold Standard and the International Monetary System 1900–1939* (1987)
Michael Freeden, *The New Liberalism: An Ideology of Social Reform*, Oxford (1978)
David French, 'Business as Usual', in Kathleen Burk (ed), *War and the State* (1982)
—*British Economic and Strategic Planning 1905–1915* (1982)
Roger Fulford, *Votes for Women* (1957)
Bentley B. Gilbert, *British Social Policy 1914–1939* (1970)
Elie Halévy, *The Rule of Democracy 1905–1914*, (1961 edition)
R.J. Hammond, *Food Vol I: The Growth of Policy* (1951)
Fraser J. Harbutt, *The Iron Curtain: Churchill, America and the Origins of the Cold War*, New York (1986)
José Harris, *Unemployment and Politics: A Study in English Social Policy 1886–1914*, Oxford (1972)
T.J. Hatton, 'The Outlines of a Keynesian Solution', in Sean Glynn and Alan Booth, *The Road to Full Employment* (1987)

Cameron Hazlehurst, *Politicians and the War* (1971)

F.H. Hinsley and C.A.G. Simkins, *British Intelligence in the Second World War* (1990)

J.D. Hoffman, *The Conservative Party in Opposition 1945–1951* (1964)

Ronald Hyam, *Elgin and Churchill at the Colonial Office 1905–1908* (1968)

David Irving, *Churchill's War: The Struggle for Power* (1989)

Marian Jack, 'The Purchase of the British Government's Shares in the British Petroleum Company', *Past and Present*, No. 39, April 1968

Pat Jalland, *The Liberals and Ireland* (1980)

—*Women, Marriage and Politics 1860–1914*, Oxford (1986)

Kevin Jefferys, *The Churchill Coalition and Wartime Politics* (1991)

Paul Barton Johnson, *Land Fit For Heroes*, Chicago (1968)

Stephen Koss, *The Rise and Fall of the Political Press in Britain Vol II* (1984)

D.F. MacDonald, *The State and the Trade Unions* (1976)

Iain McLaine, *Ministry of Morale: Home Front Morale and the Ministry of Information in World War II* (1979)

Iain McLean, *The Legend of Red Clydeside*, Edinburgh (1983)

Arthur J. Marder, *From the Dreadnought to Scapa Flow*, Oxford (1961)

James Margach, *The Abuse of Power: The War Between Downing Street and the Media from Lloyd George to James Callaghan* (1978)

Arthur Marwick, *Britain in the Century of Total War*, (1969 edition)

Keith Middlemas, *The Politics of Industrial Society* (1979)

—*Power, Competition and the State: Volume I: Britain in Search of Balance 1940–1961* (1986)

D.E. Moggridge, *The Return to Gold 1925*, Cambridge (1969)

—*British Monetary Policy 1924–1931*, Cambridge (1972)

Jane Morgan, *Conflict and Order: the Police and Labour Disputes in England and Wales 1900–1939*, Oxford (1987)

Kenneth O. Morgan (ed), *The Age of Lloyd George* (1971)

—'Lloyd George's Stage Army: The Coalition Liberals 1918–1922', in A.J.P. Taylor (ed), *Lloyd George: Twelve Essays* (1971)

—*Consensus and Disunity: The Lloyd George Coalition Government 1918–1922* (1979)

—*Labour in Power 1945–1951*, Oxford (1984)

Margaret Morris, *The General Strike* (1976)

C. L. Mowat, *Britain Between The Wars* (1955)

G.H. Mungeam, *British Rule in Kenya 1895–1912* (1966)

Bruce K. Murray, *The People's Budget 1909–10: Lloyd George and Liberal Politics*, Oxford (1980)

Thomas Pakenham, *The Boer War* (1982)

R.A.C. Parker, 'British Rearmament 1936–9: Treasury, trade unions and skilled labour' in *English Historical Review* Vol 96 (1981)

G.C. Peden, *British Rearmament and the Treasury* (1979)

Jill Pellew, *The Home Office 1848–1914: From Clerks to Bureaucrats* (1982)

Henry Pelling, *A History of British Trade Unionism* (1963)

Harold Perkin, *The Rise of Professional Society: England since 1880* (1989)

Henry Phelps Brown, *The Origins of Trade Union Power*, Oxford (1986 edition)

Gordon Phillips, *The General Strike* (1976)

Martin Pugh, *The Making of Modern British Politics 1867–1939* (1982)

Leon Radzinowicz and Roger Hood, *The Emergence of Penal Policy in Victorian and Edwardian England*, Oxford (1990)

Antonia Raeburn, *Militant Suffragettes* (1974 edition)

John Ramsden, *A History of the Conservative Party: The Age of Balfour and Baldwin 1902–1940* (1978)

—*The Making of Conservative Party Policy* (1980)

Richard A Rempel, *Unionists Divided* (1972)

Colin Rogers, *The Battle of Stepney: the Sidney Street Siege: Its Causes and Consequences* (1981)

Andrew Rosen, *Rise up Women!* (1974)

G.R. Searle, *Eugenics and Politics in Britain 1900–1914*, Leyden (1976)

Anthony Seldon, *Churchill's Indian Summer: The Conservative Government 1951–1955* (1981)

Mary Elizabeth Short, 'The Politics of Personal Taxation: Budget-Making in Britain 1917–31', Cambridge D Phil. (1985)

Robert Skidelsky, *Politicians and the Slump* (1967)

David Smith, 'Tonypandy 1910: Definitions of Community' in *Past and Present* No 87 (May 1980)

Harold Smith (ed), *War and Social Change: British Society in the Second World War*. Manchester (1986)

R.H. Ullman, *Anglo-Soviet Relations 1917–21 Vol II* (1961)

William M. Walker, *Juteopolis: Dundee and its Textile Workers 1885–1923*, Edinburgh (1979)

Bernard Wasserstein, *Britain and the Jews of Europe* (1988)

Charles Webster, *The Health Service since the War Vol I: Problems of Health Care: The National Health Service before 1957* (1988)

Philip Williamson, 'Safety First: Baldwin, the Conservative Party and the 1929 General Election' in *Historical Journal* Vol 25 (1982)

Michael J. Winstanley, *The Shopkeeper's World 1830–1914*, Manchester (1983)

C.J. Wrigley, *David Lloyd George and the British Labour Movement* (1976)

—'The Ministry of Munitions' in Kathleen Burk (ed), *War and the State: The Transformation of British Government 1914–1919* (1982)

John W. Young, 'Cold War and Detente with Moscow' in John W. Young (ed), *The Foreign Policy of the Churchill Administration 1951–1955*, Leicester (1988)

# Acknowledgments

In writing this book I have incurred many debts. Firstly I would like to thank my publishers, Jonathan Cape, for continuing to support a project which has changed so much in character since it was first commissioned, long ago, as a biography. My thanks in particular are due, in the final stages of revising and editing the manuscript, to Tony Colwell and Marion Steel. I am grateful to them for all their assistance, including much helpful and constructive criticism of the text. My thanks, also, to Cathie Arrington for excellent picture research.

To the University of Edinburgh I am grateful for granting me, in the course of the 1980s, two terms of sabbatical leave during which I wrote the first part of this book. I am also grateful to the Warden and Fellows of All Souls College, Oxford, for their generosity in appointing me to a year's Visiting Fellowship, which enabled me to write most of the rest.

Though history is mainly written by individuals it is partly a collective effort. I am greatly indebted, therefore, to the historians whose work I have drawn upon, and have tried to indicate the extent of the debt in both the notes and the text. Above all I am conscious of how much the book owes to the official biographers of Churchill: Randolph Churchill and Martin Gilbert.

I used to wonder whether interest in Churchill was waning, and my own curiosity about him somewhat eccentric. But in recent years I have given many talks and papers on Churchill to a variety of audiences. Time and again I have been delighted to discover the extent to which the subject generates the most animated historical debate. To all those who took part in such discussions I am grateful for the stimulus, encouragement and criticism I received. Best of all were the questions that completely stumped me: I have tried to answer some of them in this book.

For comments, questions and advice on these and other occasions I particularly wish to thank the following: Asa Briggs, Gordon Brown, John Brown, David Butler, David Cannadine, Peter Clarke, Harry Dickinson, Ian Donnachie, Owen Dudley Edwards, Roy Foster, Martin Gilbert, Peter Ghosh, Sir John Habbakuk, José Harris, Brian Harrison, Peter Hennessy, Roger Hood, Lord Jenkins of Hillhead, Victor Kiernan, Colin Matthew, Jane Morgan, Kenneth Morgan, Henry Pelling, Ben Pimlott, Sir David Pitblado, Nicholas Phillipson, Roland Quinault, Victor Rothwell, Anthony Seldon, George Shepperson, Robert Taylor, Jay Winter and Chris Wrigley. I also benefited greatly from the comments of the late Charles Wenden, and can only record with sorrow that it is too late to thank him in person. To Iain Campbell I am grateful for research conducted on my behalf at the Public Record Office, and to Jeremy Crang and Gerard De Groot for allowing me to quote from unpublished drafts of their work. Alan Bell, the Librarian of Rhodes House, Oxford, is a friend to whom I owe much helpful advice.

My work in the archives was made all the more enjoyable by the helpfulness and efficiency of the keepers of manuscripts and staff of the Libraries in which I worked. In particular I wish to thank the staff of the Public Record Office at Kew, the British Library, the House of Lords Record Office, the London School of Economics, the Bodleian Library, the Library of Nuffield College, Oxford, the Library of Trinity College, Cambridge, the Churchill College Archive, Cambridge, the Fitzwilliam Museum, Cambridge, the National Library of Wales, and the Libraries of the Universities of Birmingham, Glasgow and Newcastle.

Bruce Hunter has been the most generous, patient and appreciative of literary agents. To John Campbell, who very kindly read a draft of the manuscript for me, I owe many years of conversation, inspiration, and friendship. Angus Calder, an expert on the history of morale, has done more than anyone else to sustain my own and I am grateful to him for the question he would so often put to me over a refreshment at the end of the day: 'How's Churchill?' Finally I recall with gratitude the delightful company and sparkling observations of A.J.P. Taylor.

For permission to quote from documents by Sir Winston Churchill of which they hold the copyright I am grateful to C and T Publications. I am also grateful to the Controller of Her Majesty's Stationery Office for permission to reproduce Crown Copyright material. The author also wishes to thank the owners of other copyright material who have given their permission for it to be used, and apologises to any whom he has failed to approach.

I am grateful to the following sources for permission to reproduce illustrations: Hulton Deutsch Collection (plates 6, 7, 8, 9, 11, 14, 18); S & G Press Agency (plates 1, 4, 5, 10, 16); Syndication International (plates 2, 3, 12, 20); Times Newspapers Ltd. (plates 15, 17, 19); Topham Picture Source (plate 13).

Finally, in expressing my thanks to all those mentioned, I would like to emphasise that the responsibility for any remaining errors and flaws in this book is entirely my own.

P.A.

# *Index*